D.C. THIELMANN

YOU SAY SO:

The Trial of Jesus of Nazareth

Writers'

BRANDING

BRANDING
Writers' Branding
1800-608-6550
www.writersbranding.com
orders@writersbranding.com

Contents

Preface.. v

Chapter 1 1
*"They watched him to see whether he would cure him on the Sabbath,
so that they might accuse him."*
(Mark 3:2)

Chapter 2 17
*"He entered into the House of God and took and ate the Bread of
Presence, which is not lawful for any but the priests to eat...."*
(Luke 6:4)

Chapter 3 51
"It is not the thing entering into the mouth which defiles a person...."
(Matthew 15:11)

Chapter 4 93
*"The Pharisees went out and immediately conspired with the
Herodians...."*
(Mark 3:6)
*"In the same hour approached some Pharisees saying, 'Get away from
here, for Herod wants to kill you'." (Luke 13:31)*

Chapter 5 177
"Jesus no longer walked openly among the Jews...." (John 11:54)

Chapter 6 217
"Do quickly what you are going to do."
(John 13:27)

Chapter 7 237
"And the High Priest tore his garment and said, 'He has blasphemed'!"
(Matthew 26:65).

Chapter 8 273
"... They bound Jesus, led him away, and handed him over to Pilate."
(Mark 15:1)

"... Having learned he was under Herod's jurisdiction, he sent him off to Herod...."
(Luke 23:7)

Chapter 9 309
"But you have made it a den of thieves"
(Matthew 21:13).

Chapter 10 357
"Release unto us Barabbas!" (Luke 23:18)

Epilogue 371

Bibliography 383

Preface

After completing the writing of my two-volume book, *On Earth As It Is In Heaven*, I knew that there were far too many details surrounding the betrayal, arrest, and trial of Jesus of Nazareth that I had only briefly touched upon in that book, and therefore, I believed that it was necessary to write a book that further expounded upon these matters that I had only briefly touched upon. My hope is that this book will sufficiently cover all of the matters that were only briefly touched upon in my two-volume book, *On Earth As It Is In Heaven*. For truth be told, the fact is that correctly interpreting and understanding all of *these* particular matters are the *key* to correctly interpreting and understanding the "historical" Jesus as opposed to the Jesus of "faith."

Virtually every modern New Testament scholar has noted that the Gospels contain many discrepancies in the accounts of the betrayal, arrest, and trial of Jesus. These discrepancies can even be found being described by the Church historian, Eusebius, *Ecclesiastical History* 5:28, where Eusebius refers to "heresy hunters" who were all claiming that many "heretics" were altering the texts to make them say what *they* wanted the Gospels to say, (as well as even Paul's letters and the other Epistles), in order to promote a certain desired doctrinal interpretation of Jesus and the events surrounding his life and teachings. Eusebius even makes a list of quite a few examples of these "heresy hunters,"[1] and as Barrie Wilson writes,[2] "During this period, no one tradition was 'right' and the others 'heretical.' They all attracted members, promoted themselves as the authentic expression of the faith, and considered others to be disseminators of falsehoods." Also, as C. Leslie Mitton writes,[3] "It must be conceded, therefore, that later writers did alter the tradition as they received it, to make it express more clearly the faith as they had come to hold it and understand it." Mitton goes on though, to erroneously state,[4] "We find it difficult to believe, however, that the story as a whole was so distorted to a degree that totally obscures the basic facts. The time between the death of Jesus and the writing of the Gospels was not long enough for such total distortion to have taken place." Now, there is a *new* "theory" proposed by Bart Ehrman that claims that the Gospel stories *were not* deliberately altered, but simply "misremembered," or what psychologists' term, "confabulation," (a matter that will be discussed further below as well as in many other chapters, but primarily discussed in Chapter 3). But for the moment we will just focus on Mitton's quote above, for the greatest problem with Mitton's claim here lies in the fact that no *original* complete copy of *any* of the four canonical Gospels can be found, which can be dated to the time from which the majority of these scholars try to *claim* that the Gospels were written, and *especially* written in a form as *we* have them today! In essence, no *proof* exists for what *was actually written down in the original first copies of any of the four canonical Gospels*![5] As Roger P. Booth rightly states,[6] "In short, we do not presume authenticity of Gospel statements, but consider them as evidence before judgment on historicity

1   See the comments for example in, *The Lost Gospel of Judas Iscariot*, Bart D. Ehrman, p 148; *Jesus Interrupted*, Bart D. Ehrman, pp. 212-223; *How Jesus Became God*, Bart D. Ehrman, p. 294; *The New Testament*, Bart D. Ehrman, pp. 445-460; *Jesus and Israel*, Jules Isaac, pp. 290-296; *Jews, Greeks and Christians*, (Edited by Robert Hammerton-Kelly and Robin Scroggs), C. K. Barrett commenting, pp. 220-244; *Gnosis*, Kurt Rudolph, pp. 9-25; and see the entire book *Orthodoxy and Heresy in Earliest Christianity*, Walter Bauer.

2   *How Jesus Became Christian*, Barrie Wilson, p. 168.

3   *Jesus*, C. Leslie Mitton, p. 48.

4   *Jesus*, C. Leslie Mitton, p. 70.

5   See the comments in *The New Testament*, Bart D. Ehrman, pp. 479-489; and see the comments in *The Search for the Real Jesus*, Chester Charlton McCown, p. 116.

6   *Jesus and the Laws of Purity*, Roger P. Booth, p. 18.

is reached." Walter Bauer points out that Papias in his *Explanations of the Sayings of the Lord*, disapproves of the three Synoptic Gospels, (Matthew, Mark, but especially Luke), because of the *falsities* (as Papias saw them), that were contained in these Gospels, which Eusebius fails to mention when referring to Papias' opinions.[7] Furthermore, as Thomas Kazen rightly states,[8] "In the case of Mark particularly, there is no safe way of judging what is original and what is added. In addition, it is reasonable to suppose that the material has gone through various stages of redaction, and the chain of transmission is at best conjectural." Yet, despite these *facts* there are still some scholars who will try to claim that the Gospel discrepancies regarding the trial of Jesus *can be* reconciled.[9]

But a further error in such scholarly claims, as those of Mitton's noted just above, derives from the *fact*, which *every* scholar knows to be truth, namely, that the accounts were *all* originally transmitted orally, (with the exception of the scholarly claim that there was a "written" Q source, but which likewise, must have been originally an "oral" source as well). This *fact* concerning an "oral" transmission of the stories about Jesus is even noted in 1 Corinthians 15:3.[10] In regards to this *theoretical* Q source though, (which virtually every New Testament scholar holds to a belief that such *did* originally exist), Samuel Sandmel makes an excellent point regarding this matter when he states that,[11] "It needs to be noted, however, that a somewhat different but not unreasonable alternative explanation is at hand, that is, either that Luke used Matthew, or that Matthew used Luke; in either case, no written form of Q needs to be assumed. Those who would deny that Q existed in an independent, written form argue that had it been available, the author of Mark would hardly have ignored

---

7   See the comments on this in *Orthodoxy and Heresy in Earliest Christianity*, Walter Bauer, pp. 184-189, and 214-215.

8   *Jesus and Purity Halakah*, Thomas Kazen, pp. 30-31.

9   See for example *The Trial of Jesus of Nazareth*, Max Radin, p. 156.

10 See the comments on this in *The Crucifixion of Jesus*, Gerard S. Sloyan, p. 70, but Sloyan's conclusions he offers are erroneous since Paul was a "heretic" as will be pointed out in Chapter 4.

11 *A Jewish Understanding of the New Testament*, Samuel Sandmel, p. 137, but see also his comments on p. 169; see also the blog of Richard Carrier, "Why Do We Still Believe in Q?"; *The Case Against Q*, Mark Goodacre.

it so completely… Most scholars hold to the existence of Q. I do not share this view." Thus, there are several *reasonable* questions that should be asked in regards to this *theoretical* Q source, and the first question being, is it then possible that the *actual* Q source is what is known now as the *Didache*?[12] Now, when the *Gospel of Thomas* was first discovered in 1945 many scholars thought that *this* particular writing might in fact *be* the Q source. Yet, eventually the majority of scholars have concluded that the *supposed* Q source was only something similar to the *Gospel of Thomas*.[13] Therefore, the *far better* question to ask is this: could it be that the *true* Q source can be found within the Dead Sea Scrolls?[14]

Virtually everyone remembers playing the game, (either as a child in school, or as an adult at parties at someone's home), where a group sits down, (usually in a circle), and one person starts off by whispering something into the next person's ear, who in turn whispers what they *believe* that they heard into the person's ear sitting next to them, and so on, until it finally comes back around to the first person, who then announces, not only what they had first transmitted to the person sitting next to them, but also, announces what the *altered* message had become, which had come back around to them, (i.e. "confabulation" in other words). Such an alteration from the original statement in this game only took minutes to occur.[15] But in regards to the *oral accounts of Jesus' life, we are speaking of decades for which an orally transmitted message went through such similar alterations before finally being written down!*[16] As Dale C. Allison writes,[17] "Ancient and fragmentary traditions from contradictory sources that were written down only after a period of oral tradition cannot be taken at face value; and as soon as one begins the inevitable task of composing hypothetical

---

12   See the comments concerning this of James D. Tabor, "Discovering a Lost and Forgotten Early Christian 'Gospel'," *Huffington Post*, September 4, 2014, updated December 6, 2014.

13   See the comments in *Jesus Before the Gospels*, Bart Ehrman, p. 280.

14   See the comments of James D. Tabor, "The Signs of the Messiah: 4Q521," *Archaeology and the Dead Sea Scrolls*; James D. Tabor and Michael Wise, "4Q521 'On Resurrection and the Synoptic Gospel Tradition: A Preliminary Study," *Qumran Questions*, edited by James Charlesworth, pp. 161-163.

15   See the comments in *The New Testament*, Bart D. Ehrman, pp. 48-60, and 210.

16   See the excellent comments in *The Crucifixion of Jesus*, Gerard S. Sloyan, p. 212.

17   *Jesus of Nazareth*, Dale C. Allison, p. 96.

tradition histories, the possibilities multiply." Likewise, as Chester Charlton McCown writes,[18] "That there are elements in the Gospel narratives which are unhistorical and that those elements are among the weaknesses and handicaps of modern Christianity should not be denied."

Now, N. T. Wright discusses the fact that repetitively telling the same story brings about clear memory, which was a very ancient Jewish traditional way of remembering stories.[19] Yet, while this is quite true in regards to ancient *Jewish* story telling (i.e. that which resulted in becoming the Mishnah and Talmud for example), the *fact* is though, that what we are discussing in regards to the New Testament are primarily *gentile* orally transmitted accounts, which are most often distortions brought about by one individual (i.e. Paul) who was *never* an actual eye witness to the teachings of Jesus, and adding this to the *historical fact* of the split that came about between the Jewish followers of Jesus and the gentile followers of Jesus, which by the way, resulted from the "heretical" teachings of Paul (as will be further discussed in Chapter 4), and which became the predominant church traditions, then *if*, (as N. T. Wright maintains), this *were* the case regarding the orally transmitted stories about Jesus then we would find *zero discrepancies* in the Gospel accounts! A further fact that will be discussed in Chapter 3, as well as being mentioned in other chapters, is the fact that the Greeks and Romans, as well as many other gentile cultures, were infamous for being able to completely fabricate fantastic sounding stories about godmen, and this fact plays a major role in regards to *how*, and *why* the Gospel accounts of Jesus came into being the stories as we know them today.

Jacob Neusner writes in regards to Jesus and his teachings, and in particular, Jesus' "Sermon on the Mount" that, "So the sage sets for himself a worthy challenge, one that every sage in every generation does well to meet: receive a tradition whole and perfect, hand it on never intact but always unimpaired, so taking a rightful place in the chain of tradition from Sinai."[20] But it is *essential* for one to remember that Paul *was never an original follower of Jesus*, nor did Paul hear Jesus' direct teachings such

---

18   *The Search for the Real Jesus*, Chester Charlton McCown, p. 86.

19   See the comments on this in *The New Testament and the People of God*, N. T. Wright, pp. 423-424.

20   *A Rabbi Talks with Jesus*, Jacob Neusner, pp. 21-22.

as the Sermon on the Mount, and thus, the "tradition" that was "passed on" by Paul, (again, as will be discussed further in Chapter 4), that came to be the foundation for the later Church "traditions," *was not* the same "traditions" that were "taught" by Jesus and then "passed on" by his *genuine* disciples, and thus, we find *not* "confabulation" but a *deliberate* "alteration" of Jesus' "teachings"!

Going further into this matter though, Joel Carmichael rightly points out in regards to the fact that Jesus predicted, and his earliest followers believed that the coming of the "Kingdom of Heaven" would happen within *their generation*, and therefore,[21] "Indeed it is obvious that the event did not in fact justify these words, and so the early generation of Christians was bound to extend their significance at least to make them refer to the Second Coming of Jesus: when that was also postponed, or adjourned *sine die*, the Church was forced to alter the entire conception that lay behind the words, so simple in themselves, and content itself with an altogether spiritualized interpretation of Jesus' message." Even as early as Paul, (as can be found in 2 Thessalonians 2:2), Paul was clearly aware of *false* writings that were purported to be from the genuine Apostles of Jesus.[22] But, it is essential to point out the all-important *fact* though, that the "practice of giving authority to a new writing by attributing it to some earlier person of eminence was a literary custom of the New Testament age, and was commonly used both among the Jews and among the Greeks."[23]

Thus, these discrepancies, alterations, and spiritualized interpretations have led scholars to propose many wild and bizarre theories about what actually happened to not only bring about Jesus' arrest, but also, what happened *during* Jesus' arrest, and trial, which thus, ultimately led to what happened after he was crucified. There is a very eloquent statement that has been made that should be noted here, and this being that,[24] "Comparison is often an extremely subjective judgment: where one scholar finds a connection, another finds disjunction.... Did he (Jesus) in fact issue all

---

21   *The Death of Jesus*, Joel Carmichael, p. 94.

22   See the comments on this in *Orthodoxy and Heresy in Earliest Christianity*, Walter Bauer, p. 182.

23   See *A Jewish Understanding of the New Testament*, Samuel Sandmel, p. 213.

24   See the Introduction, pp. 1-2 of, *The Historical Jesus in Context*, Levine, Allison Jr. and Crossan.

the statements attributed to him, or were some added by his followers and attributed to him, just as both gentile and Jewish writers attributed material to prominent teachers?" Going further though, as Larry Hurtado states,[25] "The details of the religious innovation represented by earliest Christianity are only imperfectly preserved in the historical sources, and any attempt to organize into an orderly picture what scattered details survive runs the risk of being charged with being more clever than persuasive or, almost certainly, of suffering eventual correction or even refutation." And, as N. T. Wright states,[26] "All accounts 'distort,' but some do so considerably more than others. All accounts involve 'interpretation'; the question is whether this interpretation discloses the totality of the event, opening it up in all its actuality and meaning, or whether it squashes it out of shape, closing down its actuality and meaning."

The discrepancies in the Gospel accounts can get further compounded by what is found being stated in regards to certain parts of these matters in the Book of Acts, as well as the other New Testament Epistles. As Hugo mantel writes regarding this matter,[27] "The Gospel narratives of the trial not only fail to accord with what we know of Roman and Jewish law, but also fail to accord with one another." Also, as David B. Gowler points out,[28] "The Gospels give decisive evidence that they were created using the basic rhetorical exercises of the *Progymnasmata*, such as the techniques for expounding or condensing *chreiai*. The issue is not whether some sort of 'corporate memory' was there to impose standards of accuracy on oral traditions that varied from the very beginning. The critical issue is that changes in the tradition by the Gospel authors were *deliberate*, and that such changes were standard rhetorical exercises used to teach students how to read/write/speak Greek. This standard rhetorical practice meant that changes could be slight or substantial. The type and amount of expansion, elaboration, or other changes in the *chreiai* found in the Synoptics are generated by the author's rhetorical interests and perspective." But as Hyam Maccoby believes, he sees these discrepancies as a benefit in regards to determining the *genuine* "historical" Jesus. As

---

25   *One God One Lord*, Larry W. Hurtado, p. vii.

26   *The New Testament and the People of God*, N. T. Wright, p. 92.

27   See *Studies in the History of the Sanhedrin*, Hugo Mantel, p. 254.

28   See *The Historical Jesus in Context*, Levine, Allison Jr., and Crossan, p 135.

Maccoby writes, "Fortunately, however, we have four Gospels, not just one, and by comparing them and noting their inconsistencies many facts can be gleaned, especially when their order of composition is taken into account. Often a revealing and significant fact is retained in one of the Gospels though it has been censored in the other three. If such an incident *contradicts* the prevailing pro-Roman tenor of the narratives one can assume it is authentic, since such an incident would not have been added at a later stage in the development of the Gospels and must be a survival from the earliest versions." Maccoby's statement noted here brings into question one of the most essential criteria that modern New Testament scholars like to use, namely, the criteria of "multiple attestation," of which will be mentioned, and utilized further in several chapters. Also, though, as Nils Dahl writes,[29] "The passion narratives contain features that are to be characterized as legendary not only in a form-critical but also negatively in a historical sense. But they also contain historical facts. The dispute arises over the degree to which one and the other element are present."

There is also a further problem that sometimes occurs when some scholars seemingly become confused over what is an obvious discrepancy in the Gospel accounts, and one which in actuality is not easily explained nor is it easily understood.[30] I must offer a demonstration of my point on this matter, but at the same time I must state clearly that this is pertaining to a matter that will not even be covered in this book, namely, the actual crucifixion of Jesus, yet it serves as a perfect demonstration of my point. Bart D. Ehrman,[31] referencing Mark 15:42 writes, "... Mark also indicates that Jesus died on a day that is called 'The Day of Preparation' (Mark 15:42). That is absolutely true – but what these readers fail to notice is that Mark tells us what he means by this phrase: it is the Day of Preparation 'for the Sabbath' (*not* the Day of Preparation for the Passover). In other words, in Mark, this is not the day before the Passover meal was eaten but the day before the Sabbath: it is called the day of 'Preparation' because one had to prepare the meals for Saturday on Friday afternoon." Now, while Ehrman is correct to a certain degree here, and while he seems to remember that in Leviticus 23 there are *seven* "special festival" days that are *also* referred

---

29   *The Crucified Messiah and other Essays*, Nils Dahl, p. 18.

30   See for example the comments in *Jesus Interrupted*, Bart D. Ehrman, pp. 23-29.

31   *Jesus Interrupted*, Bart D. Ehrman, p. 27.

to as, "Sabbath days," his overall assessment on this passage from Mark's Gospel falls short of fully explaining this matter. For the day of Passover *was* one of those "special festival" days that were referred to *as* a "Sabbath day," and as such, the Torah assigned many duties that one was to perform on the eve of Passover, and therefore, the eve of Passover was rightly referred to *as*, "the *Day of Preparation*," and, when Passover fell the day before Shabbat, which also had special Torah based matters that one was required to perform, then this too was thus considered to be a "*Day of Preparation*," or in simplest terms, this *could* result in either *two consecutive* "*Days of Preparation*," (one for Passover and one for Shabbat), or at times, *the very same day* was actually a "Day of Preparation" for *both* Passover and Shabbat, as noted in the Mishnah and Talmud Babli *Bezah* 2, 15b, and also by Josephus in *Antiquities* 16.6.2, and which is confirmed by what is stated in Matthew 27:62; Luke 23:54; John 19:14, 31, and 42, (more will be explained about this very matter in Chapter 9 as it relates to what is termed, the "Last Supper"). Also, though, Josephus in *Jewish Wars* 6.9.3 clearly indicates that the Passover sacrifices occurred between the ninth and eleventh hours *on* the "*Day of Preparation*" for Passover, (i.e. 13 Nissan since Passover *always* fell on 14 Nissan), precisely in accordance with when they were commanded to be performed in Exodus 12:21-28, which puts the error to Ehrman's statement that, "this was not the day before the Passover meal was eaten." For in actuality, according to the Gospel accounts this *was* in fact "the day before the Passover meal was eaten." For the Passover Seder was to be eaten at sunset on 14 Nissan as commanded in Exodus 12:6; Leviticus 23:5; Numbers 9:1. What confuses so many scholars, in regards to these matters, is what the Gospels state in regards to what is called, the "Last Supper." For according to the Gospel accounts, Jesus *would have* eaten the "Last Supper," (or in other words, what has generally been interpreted as being a Passover Seder), *on* 13 Nissan instead of when it is supposed to be eaten on 14 Nissan, (and again, this is a matter that will be discussed further in Chapter 9). Furthermore, at the time of Jesus there was an "extra day" celebrated at all major festivals that *is not* Torah based, but which was put in place because of two major factors, and these being, the fact that the Jews had been scattered into the Diaspora, and because the Jewish calendar was lunar based. Thus, since it was the Great Sanhedrin based in Jerusalem who declared *when* a "new moon" started a "new month," it took time for the messengers to get sent out to the scattered

Jews in these distant lands to announce when the "new month" started, and therefore, the scattered Jews did not always know the exact "correct day" to start a festival. Therefore, an "extra day" was added for every major festival.[32] Now it is true though, that there was debate over whether or not the Jewish calendar should be lunar based or solar based, and this debate derived from the writings of *Jubilees* and *1 Enoch* and the fact that these writings were of such importance to certain Jews such as the Essens.[33] It is also quite true that there has been a great deal of debate amongst scholars in regards to the precise year in which Jesus was actually crucified based on the Gospel accounts. Yet, *all* scholars *know* and agree that this historical event took place sometime between 26 CE and 36 CE, or in other words, during the years in which Pilate was Procurator of Judea and in which Caiaphas was the High Priest, both of which ended, or were removed from their seats in 36 CE. Thus, the *only* years during this ten year period in which both Passover and Shabbat occurred at such a time to correspond with not only scholarly opinion, but also with the four Gospel accounts combined, (but one must also include Church tradition in this as well), are the years 27 CE, (a year in which Passover fell on Friday, April 11 of the Gregorian Calendar); 30 CE, (with Passover falling on Friday, April 7); 33 CE, (with Passover falling on Saturday, April 4); and 34 CE, (with Passover falling on Thursday, April 22).[34] Now, the majority of scholarly opinions believe that Friday, April 7, 30 CE was the day and year in which Jesus was crucified. Yet, many other scholars hold to the opinion that Jesus was crucified on Friday, April 3, 33 CE, or in other words, *on* the "Day of Preparation" for *both* Passover and Shabbat. Even though there is this debate in the scholarly world over the precise year in which Jesus was crucified, the fact remains that this debate does show though, that the overwhelming majority of scholars believe that Jesus was crucified on a

---

32 See the comments on this matter by Tracey R. Rich, *Judaism 101*, (1995-2011); Joseph Jacobs and Cyrus Adler, "Calendar, History of," *Jewish Encyclopedia*; Kaufmann Kohler and Wolf Willner, "Second Day of Festivals," *Jewish Encyclopedia*; Marcus Jastrow and Michael Friedlander, "Bezah ('Egg')," *Jewish Encyclopedia*.

33 See the comments on this matter in *Jewish Literature Between the Bible and the Mishnah*, George W. E. Nickelsburg, pp. 47-48, 74-75; *The Apocalyptic Imagination*, John J. Collins, pp. 46-47, 58, 64-67, 116; *On Earth As It Is In Heaven*, D. C. Thielmann, pp. 583-584.

34 See Pastor G. Reckart, "Passover Crucifixion Dates (26-34AD)."

Friday, which happened to be either the day *of* Passover, *or*, the "Day of Preparation" *for* Passover, and which would then *also be* the "Day of Preparation" for the Sabbath. This apparently is what seems to be confusing Ehrman, as well as so many other scholars. For John's Gospel seemingly has Jesus being placed onto the cross on the "Day of Preparation" for the Passover, (John 19:14). Yet, John also places Jesus' actual death on the cross as being on the "Day of Preparation" for the Sabbath, (John 19:31), and since Church tradition has always held that Jesus died on the cross on the same day that he was placed *onto* the cross, then John's Gospel, to some scholars, seemingly makes it appear to be indicating events that occurred on two separate days. So in essence, and in all reality if one then follows Church tradition on this matter, then it must be assumed that John's Gospel is clearly indicating that both Passover and Shabbat fell upon the same day, which *only* occurred during the ten year period just noted above on Saturday, April 4, 33 CE. So, for a moment, let us consider *all* of the highly complex factors in this matter: first in Matthew's Gospel ((Matthew 27:62), it states that guards were placed around Jesus' tomb on the "next day" *after* "the Day of Preparation," but Matthew *does not* specify whether this is the "Day of Preparation" for Passover, *or* the "Day of Preparation" for Shabbat, *or* whether it is the "Day of Preparation" for *both* Passover *and* Shabbat. Now, going back to Mark's Gospel noted above, (Mark 15:42), Mark says *absolutely nothing* about the "Day of Preparation" for Passover. Luke's Gospel (Luke 23:54), similarly to Mark's Gospel, seemingly refers to Jesus' body being taken down from the cross on the "Day of Preparation" for Shabbat and similarly to Mark, Luke states *absolutely nothing* about the "Day of Preparation" for Passover. Thus, there *is* the possibility that all four Gospels *are in fact* referring to the exact same day! Now, let us consider *one more all-important factor* in all of this matter and this being what is stated in 1 Corinthians 5:7. As early in church tradition as the writing of this Epistle of 1 Corinthians by Paul, Jesus was considered to be the *expiation* or "substitution" for the sacrificing of the Paschal lamb, and since as Josephus states, (noted just above), in accordance with Exodus 12:21-28, the Passover sacrifices occurred *upon* the "Day of Preparation" *for* Passover, therefore, in order to fulfill this church tradition as early as the time of Paul in conjunction with what each of the four Gospels state, then, the *only* possible date that fulfills all of these variable factors just discussed would be that Jesus was placed onto the cross and died on the cross on

Friday, April 3, 33 CE contrary to the majority scholarly opinion that holds to that of 30 CE as the year in which Jesus was crucified! All of these highly complex variable factors are precisely what brings about the scholarly confusion, such as that of Bart Ehrman, over the Gospel of John's timetable in accordance with what is stated in Mark 15:42 and the debate in the scholarly world over which year Jesus was actually crucified. Yet, if one considers *all* of these highly complex variable factors just noted in conjunction with the fact that we *do not know* who actually wrote each Gospel, or *when* each Gospel was actually written, or even *where* each Gospel was written, then *if* John's Gospel, (as well as each of the other three Gospels), were written by someone in a non-Palestinian community who *did not* fully understand all of these highly complex variable factors, then it is easy to answer why John's Gospel has this seeming discrepancy over the *actual* "Day of Preparation" that Jesus was taken before Pilate and crucified, which again, this was a matter that had been passed along orally for decades before being written down by the Gospel authors. But the ultimate point being made here is Ehrman's, (as well as so many other highly acclaimed scholars), seeming confusion over all of these highly complex variable factors, and especially the fact that there *were* two distinctly separate days referred to as the "*Day of Preparation*" that *could in fact* end up occurring *upon the same day*, which not only *could*, but obviously *would* account for at least this one particular seemingly obvious discrepancy in the four Gospel accounts. Thus, if even such highly acclaimed scholars as Ehrman can become confused over all of these highly complex variable factors, then how much more would the simple authors of the Gospels, (who were quite possibly *gentiles*), be confused over these highly complex variables that were "orally" transmitted before being written down?

Now, Marcus Borg makes an excellent point when he writes,[35] "But seeing the Gospels as a developing tradition means that they are not primarily concerned with historical reporting… Within this framework, the authors of the Gospels are seen as 'evangelists' as they have long been called, and not primarily as writers whose primary purpose was historical reporting of the past." Therefore, *my hope* in writing this book is to try and present an "historically" accurate examination of what actually *did* occur

---

35 *Jesus: Uncovering the Life, Teachings, and Relevance of a Religious Revolutionary*, Marcus Borg, p. 42. But see also the comments in, *How Jesus Became God*, Bart Ehrman, p. 88.

in regards to the betrayal, arrest, and trial of Jesus in order to put an end to the many wild and bizarre theories, which even some of the world's most well respected and renowned scholars have put forth trying to explain what ultimately happened in regards to all of these matters. But, despite this attempt on my part, Bart D. Ehrman is quite correct though, when he states,[36] "Disagreement is simply something that scholars do…. It may seem strange that the more information you have, the less you realize you know, or the more you disagree with others about what you think you know. But that's how scholarship works sometimes." Yet, while Ehrman is correct in this statement, according to the interpretation of Deuteronomy 11:16 at the time of Jesus, "if we hear that someone did or said something improper, we should not accept it as absolute truth."[37]

There have been suggestions made by many scholars over the past centuries, (and primarily these suggestions have come from Jewish scholars I might add), who believe that the Gospel accounts of Jesus having some sort of a trial before the Great Sanhedrin are grossly misunderstood. The suggestions made by these scholars is that because there is an account in the Talmud of a trial before the Sanhedrin of an individual named Jesus, and this individual was condemned to death by the Sanhedrin, the Gospel evangelists took this account, (which many believe was still just an "oral account" at the time that the Gospels were written), and misinterpreted it as being a reference to Jesus of Nazareth, and thereby, fabricated their Gospel accounts to reflect a trial of Jesus of Nazareth before the Sanhedrin. Since it *is quite possible* that this is exactly what occurred in writing the Gospel accounts, there are, therefore, several matters that need to be pointed out in regards to this matter of a trial before the Sanhedrin of an individual named Jesus spoken of in the Talmud and these are matters, which virtually *all* scholars today, both Christian and Jewish, agree upon. First, the name "Jesus" (*Yeshua*) was a very common Jewish male name, so there were many individuals named *Yeshua* throughout all of Jewish history. Second, the *Yeshua* spoken of in the Talmud as having a trial before the Sanhedrin only had five disciples, whereas we know that Jesus of Nazareth had twelve disciples. Third, and finally, the *Yeshua* spoken of in the Talmud

---

36   Bart D. Ehrman is correct though in *The Lost Gospel of Judas Iscariot*, Bart D. Ehrman, p. 100.

37   *Love Your Neighbor*, Rabbi Zelig Pliskin, pp. 382-383.

as having a trial before the Sanhedrin lived almost a century *before* Jesus of Nazareth was even born. It is true though, as some scholars are quick to point out, that even Jewish later additions to the Talmud mistook *Yeshua ben Notzri* for Jesus of Nazareth in their Talmudic writings. This will be further expounded upon in Chapter 5.

It is also essential to point out that Jesus of Nazareth was *not* the only "would be Messiah" during that last century BCE and the first century CE in Palestine. Richard A. Horsley and John S. Hanson rightly point out that the English word "Christ," which derives from the Greek word, *Christos*, is really a translation of the Hebrew word, *moshiah*, which simply means, "anointed." As Horsley and Hanson write concerning this, "What later became the Orthodox Early Christian understanding of 'Christ' was a creative synthesis of several different strands of Jewish expectation and Greek philosophical concepts."[38]

Therefore, since Jesus *was not* the *only* "would be" messiah, these different messianic movements were really divided between two distinctly different types – the "oracular prophet" movement, and the "action prophetic" movement.[39] As Richard A. Horsley and John S. Hanson write, "Judging from several reports by Josephus, there were a number of prophetic figures that appeared among the people around the time of Jesus. Indeed, Jesus was understood as a prophet (see Mark 6:15-16).[40] Although our sources are fragmentary, and in the case of Josephus, hostile, careful analysis indicates that these popular prophets were of two fairly distinct types. The principle function of the one, the oracular prophet, was to pronounce the impending judgment or redemption by God. The characteristic feature of the other, the action prophet, was to inspire and lead a popular movement to vigorous participation in an anticipated redemptive action by God. The peasantry, from whose ranks the popular prophets and their followers came, was probably acquainted with the expectations of an eschatological prophet, especially those of the fiery Elijah. However, none of the popular prophets

---

38 *Bandits, Prophets, and Messiahs*, Richard A. Horsley and John S. Hanson, p. 89.

39 See the comments in *Bandits, Prophets, and Messiahs*, Richard A. Horsley and John S. Hanson, p. 135; for an excellent explanation of the differences between the two, see the comments in *The Way of God*, Moshe Chaim Luzzatto, pp. 221-237.

40 See the comments on Mark 6:15-16 in *Prophecy in Early Christianity*, David E. Aune, pp. 153-169.

appear in any distinctive way to be a fulfillment of this expectation of Elijah as the eschatological prophet." Yet, this is though, precisely how the Gospels portray John the Baptist, as being the "oracular prophet," followed then by the "action prophet" of Jesus. Therefore, the essential question becomes, which sort of prophet actually *was* Jesus of Nazareth – an "oracular prophet," or an "action prophet," or can Jesus even be interpreted or portrayed as being *any* type of "prophet"? This question is important to ask when one considers what Walter Brueggemann states,[41] and this being that, "Clearly Jesus cannot be understood simply as prophet, for that designation, like every other, is inadequate for the historical reality of Jesus. Nonetheless, among his other functions it is clear that Jesus functioned as a prophet."

Going further into this matter of whether or not Jesus was an "oracular prophet" as opposed to an "action prophet," we are faced with another all important question, and this being, if Jesus *was* in fact just an "oracular prophet," (as so many scholars attempt to portray Jesus), then why did he not *be* precisely as the "oracular prophets" of centuries past in the history of the Jewish people, such as Isaiah (see for example Isaiah 8:16-18 and 30:8-11)? Jesus most assuredly was quite familiar with the style that characterized an "oracular prophet," so then, why do we not find anywhere in the Gospels that he acted as an "oracular prophet" by instructing his disciples to "write down and seal up," or "inscribe in a book ... for the time to come" all of his own "oracular prophecies"? Instead we find Jesus appointing seventy individuals and sending them forth in pairs, (Luke 10:1-24 and a matter that will be further discussed in Chapter 5). We also find Jesus sending out his own disciples to perform "actions" at his behest in Luke 9:1-6; Mark 6:6-13; Matthew 9:35: Matthew 10:1-42; Luke 24:44-49; Luke 22:35; Matthew 28:19-20; Mark 16:15 (which is a verse questioned as to its validity, by the way); Matthew 24:14; Matthew 22:21; Mark 12:17. This *fact* that Jesus dispatched others to do and perform "actions" at his behest *proves* that Jesus *was not* an "oracular prophet," but instead he was an "action prophet"![42] For as Gerhard von Rad rightly points out concerning this,[43] the "action prophet" was expected to "deliver oracles

---

41   *The Prophetic Imagination*, Walter Brueggemann, p. 80.

42   See the comments on this in *The Crucifixion of Jesus*, Gerard S. Sloyan, p. 50; *How Jesus Became Christian*, Barrie Wilson, pp. 88-91.

43   *The Message of the Prophets*, Gerhard von Rad, pp. 31-32.

against foreign nations" (i.e. Matthew 7:6; 15:26-27; Mark 7:27-28 all of which will be mentioned further in later chapters). But we also know from 1 Kings 20:13-28; 22:6-15; 2 Kings 3:16-19; 6:9 that the "action prophet" also "gave the command to attack" foreign enemies (Matthew 5:5 for example[44]). As Walter Brueggemann rightly states,[45] "We will not understand the meaning of prophetic imagination unless we see the connection between the *religion of static triumphalism* and the *politics of oppression and exploitation.*" Thus, regardless of whether or not any scholar chooses to perceive, or label Jesus as a "prophet" – i.e., either "oracular" or "action" – a *prophet always* combined *religion* with *politics*. Brueggemann further states,[46] "No prophet ever sees things under the aspect of eternity. It is always partisan theology, always for the moment, always for the concrete community, satisfied to see only a piece of it all and to speak out of that at the risk of contradicting the rest of it."

Trying to utilize the Gospels and Epistles alone, or incorrectly, to determine the *genuine historical nature* of Jesus' movement creates several problems. As Hyam Maccoby rightly states concerning this,[47] "Re-Judaizing tendencies are seen in certain passages of the Gospels, especially that of Matthew, where Jesus is portrayed as a Jewish rabbi: this, the argument goes, is not because he was one, but because the author of the Gospel or the section of the Church to which he belonged was affected by a re-Judaizing tendency, and therefore rabbinized Jesus and tempered the extent of his rebellion against Judaism." Maccoby goes on to state that, "All the evidence of the Jewishness of Jesus in the Gospels, on this view, is due to late tampering with the text, which originally portrayed Jesus as rejecting Judaism."[48] It is essential to point out here that according to Jewish law at the time of Jesus, as noted in *Baba Metzia* 59b, to criticize one who has converted to Judaism was a clear *violation* of Jewish law! Thus, Paul's

---

44   See the comments concerning Matthew 5:5 in *On Earth As It Is In Heaven*, D. C. Thielmann, pp. 691-693 and the corresponding scholars notations to these pages.

45   *The Prophetic Imagination*, Walter Brueggemann, p. 17.

46   *The Prophetic Imagination*, Walter Brueggemann, p. 24.

47   *The Mythmaker*, Hyam Maccoby, p. 128.

48   See Maccoby's further comments on this matter in, *The Mythmaker*, Hyam Maccoby, p. 206; but see also the comments on this matter in *Jews, Greeks and Christians*, (Edited by Robert Hammerton-Kelly and Robin Scroggs), Eduard Schweizer commenting, pp. 245-260.

repeated criticisms in his Epistles of those who converted, (i.e. became "circumcised"), was a clear *violation* of his very claims of *being* a "Jew," and especially a "Pharisaic Jew," (a matter that will be further discussed in a Chapter 4).[49] The fact that it was a clear *violation* of Jewish law to criticize one who converted is based primarily on what is stated in Deuteronomy 10:19.[50] Moshe Chaim Luzzatto points out concerning Genesis 12:3,[51] that "Abraham was thus made the father of all converts," (*Yevamoth* 63a; Yerushalmi, *Bikkurim* 1:4[3b]; *Bikkurim* 4:3; *Shabbat* 105a; *Genesis Rabbah* 49:6; and as can be found also in the later *Zohar* 1:105a, all of which refer to Genesis 17:5 for the basis of this interpretation).[52]

But another real problem that we encounter derives from the *fact* that we do not really know *who* wrote the Gospels in the form that we have them today with the attached names, Matthew, Mark, Luke, and John.[53] As Amy-Jill Levine writes concerning this,[54] "Any argument based on the identity of the Gospel writer or on the composition of the original audience must remain speculative since both who wrote the Gospels and where the Gospels were written remain unknown. We have no original manuscripts from the hands of the Evangelists, and the names 'Matthew,' 'Mark,' 'Luke,' and 'John were appended to the originally anonymous texts we do have." As Matt Jackson-McCabe writes,[55] "The early Christians display a clear penchant for creating pseudonymous works of literature: texts that effectively identify the beliefs and concerns of some later group with those of the apostles by means of fictive claims of apostolic authorship." Now, regarding this matter of not knowing *where* the Gospels were written, this

---

49   See the comments on this in *Love Your Neighbor*, Rabbi Zelig Pliskin, pp 176-177.

50   See the comments in *Love Your Neighbor*, Rabbi Zelig Pliskin, pp. 380-382.

51   *The Way of God*, Moshe Chaim Luzzatto, p. 139.

52   *The Way of God*, Moshe Chaim Luzzatto, n. 54, p. 416.

53   See the comments in *Jesus Interrupted*, Bart D. Ehrman, pp. 101-112, 144-145, and 183-189; *The New Testament*, Bart D. Ehrman, pp. 8-9, 49, 215-216 and on p. 12 Ehrman freely admits that we *do not* have any of the "originals"; *Judas Iscariot and the Myth of Jewish Evil*, Hyam Maccoby, pp. 38, 50, 61, 72; *Studies of the Historical Jesus*, Ernst Fuchs, p. 14; *How Jesus Became Christian*, Barrie Wilson, pp. 64-65; *The Son of Man in Myth and History*, Frederick Borsch, pp. 257-258.

54   *The Misunderstood Jew*, Amy-Jill Levine, p. 104.

55   *Jewish Christianity Reconsidered*, Matt Jackson-McCabe, p. 11.

fact contributes to another matter that will be discussed further below, and this being, the matter of certain "Aramaic" sayings being left untranslated in the Gospels. If the Gospels were written in an area where Aramaic was the dominant language then it is easy to account for these untranslated Aramaic sayings that are found in the Gospels.[56] As Joseph A. Fitzmyer rightly states concerning this,[57] "But this question of the diversity of the New Testament books and the varied approach to a possible Aramaic substratum is compounded by the problem of just how many of the Greek New Testament writings were actually composed in Palestine itself."

The next problem that we encounter is that we do not even know exactly *when* the Gospels were written into the form they appear in the canon today.[58] N. T. Wright, while admitting that,[59] "we simply do not know" by whom or when the Gospels were written still tries to attempt to hold onto the long standing scholarly opinion that Mark's Gospel was first written sometime around 70 CE, followed by Matthew, Luke, and John sometime between 80-90 CE,[60] and Wright does so with an apologetically biased statement that, "the old scholarly 'consensus' for a relatively late date has been whittled away from most angles over the last generation…." Likewise, many other scholars as well hold to similar opinions as this opinion of N. T. Wright.[61] Donald Juel for example, writes concerning Mark 14:58 that,[62] "The interpretation of the charge in Mark is not dependent upon the dating of the work, but the author's concern makes most sense if he is writing at a time soon after the destruction of the Temple." Now, as Gerard S. Sloyan writes,[63] "Mark is all but universally acknowledged to have been written the first of the four Gospels." But Sloyan then goes on to write in

---

56 See the comments on this in *A Jewish Understanding of the New Testament*, Samuel Sandmel, p. 13; *The Story of Hebrew*, Lewis Glinert, p. 30.

57 *A Wandering Aramean*, Joseph A. Fitzmyer, pp. 4-5.

58 See the comments on this from Gert J. Malan, "Is Rewritten Bible/Scripture the Solution to the Synoptic Problem?" *HTS Theological Studies*, Volume 70, n. 1, Pretoria, January 2014.

59 N. T. Wright in *Judas and the Gospel of Jesus*, p. 76.

60 See the comments, for example, on the for the dating of the writing of the Gospels in *The Search for the Real Jesus*, Chester Charlton McCown, p. 85.

61 See for example *The Historical Jesus in Context*, Levine, Allison Jr. and Crossan, p. 5.

62 *Messiah and Temple*, Donald Juel, pp. 212-213.

63 *Jesus On Trial*, Gerard S. Sloyan, p. 29.

a notation,[64] "Even if one should opt for the priority of Matthew, rather than Mark, as a few do, it makes little difference in the Passion section, since Mark and Matthew follow basically the same lines of development, compared with the rather different accounts in Luke and John." But as will be shown, this opinion simply cannot be substantiated in any way, shape, or form.

There is an important matter to make note of here though, that relates specifically to *when* John's Gospel was written and which is discussed at some length by Joseph Ratzinger and Pope Benedict XVI.[65] They discuss a certain papyrus fragment of John's Gospel that was found in Egypt written in Greek, and based on the finding of this fragment they write,[66] "The radically late dating's of John's Gospel to which this view gave rise have had to be abandoned because papyrus from Egypt dating back to the beginning of the second century have been discovered; this made it clear that the Gospel must have been written in the first century, if only during the closing years." But such a claim on their part is really quite rash and without merit, for the simple fact is that this fragment of papyrus that they are referring to is actually a very *small* "fragment," and as far as to the claim of the dating of this fragment the fact is that this is a very hotly debated matter amongst scholars. The debate over the dating of this fragment, (the *Rylands Library Papyrus* P52), range from around 100 CE (as Ratzinger and Pope Benedict XVI have done) to as late as more than the year 200 CE! The fact of this debate alone puts the error to the claims of Ratzinger and Pope Benedict XVI! But going further, even Ratzinger

---

64 *Jesus On Trial*, Gerard S. Sloyan, n. 1, p. 121citing, R. H. Lightfoot, *The Gospel Message of St. Mark*, [Oxford: Clarendon 1968]; Rudolf Bultmann, *The History of the Synoptic Tradition*, [German 1921], English translation by John Marsh, 2nd Edition [New York: Harper & Row, Oxford: Basil Blackwell 1968]; Willi Marxsen, *Mark the Evangelist: Studies on the Redaction History of the Gospel*; Eduard Schweizer, *The Good News According to Mark: A Commentary On the Gospel.*For more recent scholarship on the Passion see John R. Donahue and Daniel J. Harrington, *The Gospel of Mark*, Sacra Pagina Series [Collegeville, Minnesota: Liturgical Press 2006], 401-453; Francis J. Moloney, *The Gospel of Mark: A Commentary*, [Peabody, Ma: Hendrickson, 2004], 297-316).

65 See *Jesus of Nazareth: Part One*, Ratzinger and Pope Benedict, pp. 222-226; but see also the comments in *The Jews and the Gospel*, Gregory Baum, pp 104, and 108-111.

66 See *Jesus of Nazareth: Part One*, Ratzinger and Pope Benedict, p. 218.

and Pope Benedict XVI point out themselves that the Church historian Eusebius (*Ecclesiastical History* III, 39) writes about Papias, the Bishop of Hierapolis, (who died around 220 CE), stating that he had never known *any* of the Apostles of Jesus, but that he *did know* of a "Presbyter John," whom he clearly distinguished as someone different than the "Apostle John." The significance of this historically recorded *fact* then begs the question to be asked: could this individual known as "Presbyter John" then in fact be the *actual* author of not only the Gospel of John, but also all of the other New Testament works supposedly written by someone called "John"?[67] This question is essential for the simple fact, (which even Joseph Ratzinger and Pope Benedict XVI point out),[68] that in the Second and Third Epistles of John it is found being *clearly* stated (2 John 1:1; 3 John 1) that they were written *by* an individual who was known as a "presbyter," (the Greek word *presbuteros*, which is sometimes translated as "elder"). Thus, not only are the conclusions of Joseph Ratzinger and Pope Benedict rash and without merit as I stated above, *any* scholar trying to make such claims about *when* the Gospel of John was written, (in the form as we have it today), and even *who* exactly the author was, are *clearly unsubstantiated!* Furthermore, Bart Ehrman points out that there are certain "signs and faith in the fourth Gospel," which in all actuality helps, (seemingly without Ehrman's knowledge of this help), to identify the author of John's Gospel *as not* being the Apostle John.[69] For Ehrman stresses here the "signs" or "miracles," and in particular what is stated about the necessity of these "signs" in John 2:23-25; 3:2-10; 4:48; 6:26; 11:45-48; 20:28; 20:30-31 in regards to people coming to "believe" in Jesus. In simplest terms, it is a discussion regarding the need of some people to have "proof" by way of "signs" and/or "miracles" as opposed to those who believe "without seeing" such "signs!" In essence, this then can, and should be used as a manner to

---

67 See the comments on this matter in *The Search for the Real Jesus*, Chester Charlton McCown, pp. 161-162; *A Jewish Understanding of the New Testament*, Samuel Sandmel, pp. 236-237.

68 See *Jesus of Nazareth: Part One*, Ratzinger and Pope Benedict, p. 226.

69 See *The New Testament*, Bart D. Ehrman, Box 10.3 specifically, but see his full comments, pp. 161-175; see also the comments in *Jewish Christianity Reconsidered*, Matt Jackson-McCabe, p. 233, (John W. Marshall commenting on the Book of Revelations being written by, "an otherwise unknown figure named John").

identify the author of John's Gospel as one who *never actually witnessed* any of these "signs" for himself, but simply became an individual of "faith without seeing" any "miraculous signs." As it is *clearly* written in John 20:30, (italics mine, but see also John 19:35), "Now Jesus did many other signs *in the presence of his disciples* ...." Now, *if* the author of John's Gospel *was*, in fact, the "Disciple John," would he not then have *clearly* written this down as, "*in the presence of me and the other disciples*"? Ehrman suggests though,[70] that John's Gospel may even have had "multiple authors" because of seeming differences in writing style in certain places in the Gospel, as well as "multiple sources" for his narrative accounts, and Ehrman offers excellent examples as proof for his contention.

There have been some scholars though, who have claimed that Matthew's Gospel was the first to be written, (as noted already above), but such opinions are in the minority. As C. Leslie Mitton writes concerning this,[71] "The age-old tradition of the Church had taught that Matthew was the earliest of the Gospels, written by an actual disciple, and so full of firsthand information." But Mitton then goes on to rightly state,[72] "Now that Mark had been proved to be the earliest of the Gospels this old tradition assumed a new possibility," to which he further points out,[73] "But this research into literary antecedents could not be traced back beyond the years A.D. 60-65, and this was thirty years after the death of Jesus." Yet, the simple fact is that other than the finding of a mere fragment here or there, including amongst the Dead Sea Scrolls, *none of the Gospels exist in the forms which we have them today prior to the second century CE*, and only then *from* that period of history do we really have any confirmation of *any* individuals even quoting *any* sayings attributed to Jesus, which are found in the Gospels as we have them today.[74] As Bart Ehrman writes concerning this matter,[75]

---

70 *The New Testament*, Bart D. Ehrman, pp. 164-165.

71 *Jesus*, C. Leslie Mitton, p. 16.

72 *Jesus*, C. Leslie Mitton, p. 17.

73 *Jesus*, C. Leslie Mitton, p. 25.

74 See the comments in *Judas and the Gospel of Jesus*, N. T. Wright, pp. 38, and 77; *The Trial of Jesus*, Josef Blinzler, p. 46; *Revolution in Judaea*, Hyam Maccoby, Appendix 2, pp. 200-201; *Matthew and Empire*, Warren Carter, pp. 36-37; *The Trial of Jesus of Nazareth*, Max Radin, pp. 22-23; *Jesus Before the Gospels*, Bart Ehrman, pp. 118-125.

75 *Jesus Before the Gospels*, Bart Ehrman, p. 115.

"When Papias talks about a Gospel written by Mark and another written by Matthew, is he actually talking about the Gospels that *we* know about by these names? At first this seems to be a weird question, but in fact what Papias says about the two books he references (Matthew and Mark) suggests he is referring to books different from the ones we have."

Even more alarming though, is the fact that *no two copies* of *any* of the oldest complete New Testament books that we have in existence are exactly alike.[76] There are in fact more than 70,000 variations of the New Testament.[77] Acts 20:35, John 21:25 clearly note that many sayings of Jesus were never recorded, and Luke 1:1-4 clearly indicates that "many Gospels" were written.[78] Furthermore, 2 Timothy 4:13 speaks of "scrolls and parchments," to which many scholars and theologians have claimed is referring to the Torah and the prophetic writings. But this simply is not the truth because 2 Timothy 3:15-16 *does* specifically refer to the Torah. These "scrolls and parchments" referred to in 2 Timothy 4:13 are something else entirely![79] Now, it is true that many modern scholars do not believe that Paul actually wrote 2 Timothy and that it was written sometime after Paul's death, but this does not change the fact that it is completely unknown as to what these "scrolls and parchments" that are referred to consisted of, thus, as N. T. Wright so rightly points out,[80] "I have no problem with saying that some of the non-canonical Gospels may well preserve, here and there, genuine memories of Jesus that have not survived elsewhere."

76　See the comments concerning this matter in *A Jewish Understanding of the New Testament*, Samuel Sandmel, pp. 13-17; *The Trial of Jesus of Nazareth*, Max Radin, pp. 21-22.

77　See *On Earth As It Is In Heaven*, D. C. Thielmann, n. 3, p. 148; *Honest To Jesus*, Robert W. Funk, p. 94; *Jesus Interrupted*, Bart D. Ehrman, pp. 112-137.

78　See the comments in *The Lost Gospel of Judas Iscariot*, Bart Ehrman, p. 54; *A Jewish Understanding of the New Testament*, Samuel Sandmel, p. 169; and see also the comments in *The Jews and the Gospel*, Gregory Baum, p. 74 who believes that Luke was just an "editor" and "compiler" who utilized the many sources that he references in these verses to create and write *his* Gospel version.

79　See the comments on this in *Essays on the Semitic Background of the New Testament*, Joseph A. Fitzmyer, p. 61.

80　*Judas and the Gospel of Jesus*, N. T. Wright, p. 78.

An even more important statement to understand though comes from Hyam Maccoby, who writes,[81] "We should remember that the New Testament, as we have it, is much more dominated by Paul than appears at first sight. As we read it, we come across the Four Gospels, of which Jesus is the hero, and do not encounter Paul as a character until we embark on the post-Jesus narrative of Acts. Then we finally come into contact with Paul himself, in his letters. But this impression is misleading, for the earliest writings in the New Testament are actually Paul's letters, which were written about AD 50-60, while the Gospels were not written until the period AD 70-110. This means that the theories of Paul were already before the writers of the Gospels and colored their interpretations of Jesus' activities. Paul is, in a sense, present from the very first word of the New Testament. This is, of course, not the whole story, for the Gospels are based on traditions and even written sources which go back to a time before the impact of Paul, and these early traditions and sources are not entirely obliterated in the final version and gave valuable indications of what the story was like before Paulinist editors pulled it into final shape. However, the dominant outlook and shaping perspective of the Gospels is that of Paul, for the simple reason that it was the Paulinist view of what Jesus' sojourn on earth had been about that was triumphant in the Church as it developed in history. Rival interpretations, which at one time had been orthodox, opposed to Paul's very individual views, now became heretical and were crowded out of the final version of the writings adopted by the Pauline Church as the inspired canon of the New Testament."

Paul's Epistles, (which *all* scholars agree were written *before* any of the Gospels were written), focus completely on the notion of a "crucified and glorified" Jesus. These Epistles give very, very scant information about Jesus *the historical individual*, or any of Jesus' specific activities and/or teachings.[82] As Joel Carmichael writes concerning this,[83] "Paul, in fact, seems to take it for granted that the details of the man Jesus and his life are of no consequence at all except insofar as they serve as necessary but sufficient points of departure for his real interest, namely, Christological

---

81   *The Mythmaker*, Hyam Maccoby, p. 4; but see also the similar comments in *Paul Was Not a Christian*, Pamela Eisenbaum, pp. 34-35.

82   See the comments in *Jesus Before the Gospels*, Bart Ehrman, pp. 103-106.

83   *The Death of Jesus*, Joel Carmichael, pp. 48-49.

doctrine." Thus, the real point to be made here is that a desired portrait of Jesus was *already in place*, thanks to Paul, *long before* any of the Gospels were ever written, and therefore, the Gospels were written in a particular *biased* manner in order to *substantiate that very portrait that had already been put into place by Paul*. Also, as Joel Carmichael further points out,[84] "Indeed, estimates have been made of the time it would actually have taken Jesus to utter all of the discourses attributed to him and to perform all the actions reported: they amount to a few weeks all told." Therefore, for *any* scholar to attempt to refer to the Gospels as "biographies" of the life of Jesus is in all reality quite inaccurate.[85] Bart Ehrman can be given as a prime example of the point being made here, for Ehrman wrote an entire book titled, *Jesus Before the Gospels*, in which Ehrman bases his entire theories and conclusions regarding the Gospel accounts on the psychological term, *confabulation*. Yet, we then find Ehrman stating,[86] "He (Jesus), spent almost his entire life in Galilee before making a trip to Jerusalem in the last week of his life." We *do not know* this to be true at all, and a scholar the caliber of Bart Ehrman, (especially after taking such great pains to study and then write about *confabulation* in regard to the stories about Jesus recorded in both the canonical and non-canonical Gospels), *should not* be making such an unsubstantiated statement and claim as this! For there are in fact ancient documented stories that claim that Jesus spent many of his early adult years in India studying Buddhism![87] This is *precisely* why the Gospels *cannot* be considered as "biographies" of the life of Jesus!

Matthew 1:1, (by way of the Greek word *biblos*, "book," or "scroll"), Mark 1:1, (by way of the Greek word *evagellion*, "message," or more often,

---

84   *The Death of Jesus*, Joel Carmichael, p. 2.

85   See as an example of this inaccuracy *The New Testament*, Bart D. Ehrman, pp. 64-66; *The New Testament and the People of God*, N. T. Wright, p. 402; *What are the Gospels*, Richard A. Burridge, the entire book; *The Writings of the New Testament*, Luke Timothy Johnson, p. 145; W. Vorster, "Gospel Genre," *Anchor Bible Dictionary* 3, pp. 1077-1079; *Mark the Evangelist*, Willi Marxsen, p. 16.

86   *Jesus Before the Gospels*, Bart Ehrman, p. 101.

87   See for example James M. Hanson, "Was Jesus a Buddhist?" *Buddhist-Christian Studies*, Annual, 2005, v25, pp. 75-89; Marcel Theroux, "Did Jesus Spend His Missing Years Studying Buddhism in India? Marcel Theroux Visits Ladakh to Find Out," October 9, 2017; "Jesus was a Buddhist Monk BBC Documentary," *DiscloseTV*.

"gospel"), and Luke 1:1, (by way of the Greek word *diegesin*, "narrative"), all *clearly* denote that their writings and accounts *are not bios*! As Chester Charlton McCown accurately states,[88] "This is the crucial problem. Are the first three Gospels biographies? Do they even furnish materials for a biography?" Also, as Samuel Sandmel states,[89] "A Gospel, it must be understood, is not a full-length biography, nor is it a product of the kind of painstaking research which modern historians' practice in what they call the science of history. A Gospel is an interpretation of Jesus." Furthermore, as Rabbi Joseph Telushkin points out, the writing of "biographies" about individuals was *never* an ancient Jewish form of writing![90] Likewise, as William Klassen states,[91] "In the Jewish world, apart from Josephus, who wrote his autobiography, no one wrote biographies in the modern sense." Now, this is not to say that the Gospels do not, in any way, "contain some biographical material or features,"[92] but simply that the overall content in the Gospels *cannot* be considered as "biographies" regarding the life of Jesus even under the ancient *genre* that constituted a *bio*!

It is necessary though, to discuss this matter of whether or not the Gospels are actually "biographies" further, simply because there are so many New Testament scholars who desire to claim that the Gospels *are* indeed "biographies" by way of referencing the ancient "genre" of what constituted a "biography." For example, Richard A. Burridge writes that,[93] "Some dictionary definitions of 'genre' do not even include literary types or kinds."[94] So let us examine, for a moment, a couple of the definitions as found in a couple of dictionaries: first, "biography" as defined by *The American Heritage Dictionary of the English Language*,[95] "1) an account of a person's life written, composed, or produced by another (derives from the

---

88 *The Search for the Real Jesus*, Chester Charlton McCown, p. 170.

89 *A Jewish Understanding of the New Testament*, Samuel Sandmel, p. 113.

90 See the comments on this in *Hillel*, Rabbi Joseph Telushkin, p. 59.

91 *Judas*, William Klassen, p. 12, and n. 3, p. 25.

92 See the comments in *What are the Gospels*, Richard A. Burridge, p. 23.

93 *What are the Gospels*, Richard A. Burridge, p. 39.

94 *What are the Gospels*, Richard A. Burridge, n. 53, p. 39 notes, "Absent in the *Shorter Oxford English*, but defined by *Chambers Twentieth Century Dictionary* as 'a literary species'."

95 *The American Heritage Dictionary of the English Language*, p. 183.

Greek words *bio* and *graphia*),"[96] and then as defined by the *New Oxford American Dictionary*,[97] "1) an account of someone's life written by someone else. Writing of such type as a branch of literature. A human life in its course, from French (17ᵗʰ century), *biographie*, or Latin *biographia*, from Medieval Greek, *bios* (life), + *graphia* (writing)." And then, "biography" as defined by *Webster's Third New International Dictionary of the English Language Unabridged*,[98] "1) a usual written history of a person's life, 2) Biographical writings in general: such writings considered as a genre, 3) An account in biographical form of the life of something."[99]

Now, the word, "genre" as defined by *The American Heritage Dictionary of the English Language*,[100] "1a) a category of artistic composition, as in music or literature, marked by a distinctive style, form, or content, b) a realistic style of painting that depicts scenes from everyday life. 2) a type or class." Then, "genre," as defined by the *Oxford American Dictionary*,[101] "a category of artistic composition as in music or literature, characterized by similarities in form, style, or subject matter," and finally "genre" as defined by *Webster's Third New International Dictionary of the English Language Unabridged*,[102] "1) kind, sort, style, species, category, 2) a category of artistic composition characterized by a particular style, form, or content... a distinctive type or category of literary composition."[103] Thus, the *fact* is that the Gospels, in all reality, fall more under the ancient *genre* of either brief "essays" or brief "memoirs," or even more so an "epic" more than

---

96   In *What are the Gospels*, Richard A. Burridge, p. 62, Burridge mentions this very matter concerning the Greek words *bio* and *graphia*.

97   *New Oxford American Dictionary*, Edited by Angus Stevenson and Christine A. Lindberg, p. 169.

98   *Webster's Third New International Dictionary of the English Language Unabridged*, Encyclopedia Britannica, Inc. Volume I, p. 218.

99   See also *The World Book Encyclopedia*, Volume B, pp. 312-314; *Encyclopedia Britannica*, Volume 3, pp. 636-641.

100   *The American Heritage Dictionary of the English Language*, p. 733.

101   *New Oxford American Dictionary*, Edited by Angus Stevenson and Christine A. Lindberg, p. 724.

102   *Webster's Third New International Dictionary of the English Language Unabridged*, Encyclopedia Brittanica, Inc., Volume I, p. 947.

103   *The World Book Encyclopedia*, Volume G has no article on "genre."

---

they do under the ancient *genre* of a "biography." Again, Luke 1:1 *clearly* uses the Greek word, *diegesin*, which means, "narrative,"[104] and under the ancient Graeco-Roman *genres*, a "narrative" falls under the ancient *genre* of an "epic," (i.e., an "essay," or "memoire" but *not* a "bio").[105]

Thus, it is necessary to examine these ancient *genres* more closely and accurately so as to demonstrate this *fact* that the Gospels *cannot* be considered as "biographies" of the life of Jesus. Now, concerning these ancient *genre*, Richard A. Burridge writes that,[106] "The period of the last centuries BC and the first century AD is a time of flexible genres... The Gospels are written, therefore, during this period of flexibility and innovation." The first problem with this statement is what has already been noted in that we *do not know* exactly *when* the Gospels were written except for the *fact* that we *know* that they *could not* have been written during "the last centuries BC." Now, since Burridge chooses to focus only on the ancient *genres* and ignore any modern definition of *genre*, then the *only* ancient *genre* that the Gospels could even remotely fall under would be the ancient *genre* of an "*epic*," which is in essence, an "essay," or "memoire," but certainly *not* a "biography," or simply the ancient term, "bio." Burridge though, seemingly desires to place the Gospels as a "bio" by claiming that they are the combined *genres* of "history, encomium and moral philosophy" using Plutarch as his example.[107] Burridge even admits[108] that *genuine* ancient *bios* all contained certain *topoi*, ("topic," or "line of argument"). As Burridge states, "There are various *topoi* basic to them all, such as nationality, parentage, early pursuits, education, death and burial, as well as specific areas related to each individual, morals, virtues, deeds and so on." While the Gospels in general *do* contain *some* of these *topoi* briefly, the Gospels certainly *do not* contain *all* of these *topoi* in complete detail, which as just noted that Burridge states are "basic" to writings that are considered to be under the *genre* of a "biography." For instance, the Gospels certainly *do not*

---

104   See the *BDAG Greek-English Lexicon*, p. 245; *Liddell and Scott's Greek-English Lexicon*, p. 201.

105   See *Epic: The Genre, Its Characteristics*, Peter Toohey; *Reading Epic: An Introduction to the Ancient Narratives*, Peter Toohey.

106   *What are the Gospels*, Richard A. Burridge, p. 58.

107   *What are the Gospels*, Richard A. Burridge, pp. 68-69.

108   *What are the Gospels*, Richard A. Burridge, pp. 74, 145-147, and 178-180.

tell us anything about Jesus' "education," or "early pursuits," nor do each of the Gospels give us details about his parentage, (such as is found only in Matthew and Luke, which give a detailed genealogy full of discrepancies between them), and there certainly is not enough of *any* of the *topoi* that can give us an accurate assessment about Jesus' "morals" and "virtues," which is why there is so much scholarly debate over the "historical" Jesus! Thus, the very "basic" *topoi* that Burridge lists that are necessary to classify ancient writings under the ancient *genre* of a "bio" are missing from the Gospels and adding this *fact* with the *fact* that there are discrepancies in the Gospels regarding certain other parts of the "basic" *topoi* that Burridge states are necessary to classify a writing as a *bio*, it is, therefore, *impossible* for *any* scholar to refer to the Gospels as "biographies" of the life of Jesus! Burridge even admits[109] that Luke's Gospel *does not* meet all of the necessary *topoi*, yet he still attempts to claim that Luke's Gospel falls under the ancient *genre* of a "bio." Burridge further admits[110] that 79.1% of Luke's Gospel surrounds only three years of Jesus' life; 98% of Mark's Gospel surrounds only three years of Jesus' life; 91.6% of Matthew's Gospel surrounds only three years of Jesus' life; and 98% of John's Gospel surrounds only three years of Jesus' life, and Burridge further admits[111] that some of the most *necessary topoi*, ("birth, boyhood, and education"), are all completely missing from John's Gospel, (and other than the "birth" narratives in Matthew and Luke), the *necessary* "boyhood and education" *topoi* are missing in all four Gospels, and the *necessary* "birth" *topoi* is missing in Mark's Gospel! So once again, it is *impossible* for *any* scholar to refer to the Gospels as "biographies" of the life of Jesus! As Nils Dahl rightly states,[112] "The Gospels are not sources for the biography of Jesus, but rather are 'Sermons on the Messiahship of the Crucified,' 'passion stories with a lengthy introduction'." Dahl then rightly states further,[113] "That a biography of Jesus cannot be written is a truism today. We cannot even write the history of Jesus' development within the period of his public ministry."

---

109   *What are the Gospels*, Richard A. Burridge, pp. 207-209, and 224.

110   *What are the Gospels*, Richard A. Burridge, pp. 197-198.

111   *What are the Gospels*, Richard A. Burridge, p. 231.

112   *The Crucified Messiah and other Essays*, Nils Dahl, p. 60.

113   *The Crucified Messiah and other Essays*, Nils Dahl, pp. 71-72.

So the question begs to be asked, from which account then should we begin to search for the *historical truth* as to the betrayal, arrest, and trial of Jesus of Nazareth?[114] For each Gospel was written specifically for an individual community of followers,[115] and thus, the very reason for the many discrepancies in the Gospel accounts surrounding the matters of Jesus' betrayal, arrest, and trial.[116] Therefore, scholars have come to the point of perceiving the Gospels as "developing tradition" and not so much as being "concerned with historical reporting."[117] But, it must also be further pointed out, that these "developing traditions" also demonstrate the gap that kept getting wider and wider between the Jewish followers of Jesus, and the gentile followers of Jesus,[118] but especially a widening gap between Jews who were *not* followers of Jesus and Jews and gentiles who *were* followers of Jesus! As Ernst Fuchs writes,[119] "In a certain sense the New Testament owes its existence to theology. For this reason, we cannot merely say that it is just the product of the early Christian mission; that it had to proclaim or interpret Jesus in a way that gentiles could understand him. There is more weight to the argument that the events at Jesus' death raised the person of Jesus to a level above his historical word." The problem with this claim by Fuchs is that the "historical" truth *is* in fact that the Gospels were written *specifically* in such a way so that gentiles could be able to interpret Jesus based upon their own *pagan* backgrounds. This is precisely how and why the accounts became altered. Now, in regards to the usage of this word "pagan," or even the word "gentile," Bart Ehrman

---

114   See the comments in *Creation Continues*, Fritz Kunkel, p. 3.

115   See the comments in *Jesus: Uncovering the Life, Teachings, and Relevance of a Religious Revolutionary*, Marcus Borg, pp. 28-29.

116   See the comments in *The Mythmaker*, Hyam Maccoby, p. 118 and n. 3, p. 217; *The Death of Jesus*, Joel Carmichael, pp. 44-45.

117   See the comments in *Jesus: Uncovering the Life, Teachings, and Relevance of a Religious Revolutionary*, Marcus Borg, p. 42; *Pontius Pilate*, Ann Wroe, pp. 228-229; *The Lost Gospel of Judas Iscariot*, Bart Ehrman, p. 173.

118   See the comments in *Jesus On Trial*, Gerard S. Sloyan, pp. 104-107; *The Trial of Jesus: Cambridge Studies in Honour of C. F. D. Moule*, pp. 1-2; *Judas Iscariot and the Myth of Jewish Evil*, Hyam Maccoby, p. 40.

119   *Studies of the Historical Jesus*, Ernst Fuchs, p. 66.

makes an excellent point to note here when he writes,[120] "When historians use the term 'pagan,' they do not assign negative connotations to it (as you may do when using it in reference, say, to your roommate or next-door neighbor)... The term 'gentile' designates someone who is not a Jew, whether the person is pagan or Christian."

The Gospel of John has, in all reality, virtually been deemed the most unreliable of all of the Gospels in regards to reporting *any* historical truth about Jesus' life and ministry by virtually *all* critical scholars.[121] But despite this fact, the Gospel of John contains, *at the least*, one of the most profoundly important matters concerning the betrayal, arrest, and trial of Jesus, and in essence, it might even be *the* most *historically accurate fact* surrounding the betrayal, arrest, and trial of Jesus, which will be looked at in detail in a later chapter. Ultimately though, as Joel Carmichael so rightly states,[122] "As indicated, there is actually no source material for a full biography of a living, breathing Jesus. Even his specific actions are hidden from us by the dearth of information, in which random fragments are disclosed to us only through the distorting mirror of the earliest Christian tradition."

The majority of critical scholars though, are missing the most fundamental aspect when studying and searching for the *historical Jesus*, and all of the matters surrounding not only his life and ministry, but also surrounding his betrayal, arrest, and trial, and this aspect being – Jesus

---

120 *The New Testament*, Bart D. Ehrman, p. 20.

121 *Christianity: A Jewish Response*, Rabbi Moshe Reiss, Chapter 7 where he refers to John's Gospel as the "odd man out" because of the 386 statements attributed to Jesus in this Gospel, the consensus scholarly opinion holds that 383 of these statements are historically un-attributable to actually having been said by Jesus. (See for example, the comments in *The Changing Faces of Jesus*, Geza Vermes, Penguin, New York, [2002], pp. 11, 22; *The Five Gospels*, Robert W. Funk and R. W. Hoover, Macmillan, NY, [1993]). Of the 3 remaining sayings attributed to Jesus in John's Gospel, 2 are believed to be highly unlikely, John 12:24; 12:30. The only remaining statement attributed to Jesus that is believed to be without question by any scholar is the one in John 4:44, because it has parallels in Matthew 13:57; Mark 6:4; Luke 4:24. See further on this in *From Jewish Prophet to Gentile God*, P. M. Casey, pp. 23, 27-28, 178; *On Earth As It Is In Heaven*, D. C. Thielmann, Chapter 12A).

122 *The Death of Jesus*, Joel Carmichael, p. 163.

of Nazareth was *wholly Jewish*! As Hyam Maccoby puts it,[123] "There are certain advantages in being Jewish when attempting to understand the Gospels, especially if one has been brought up in close contact with the Jewish liturgy, the ceremonials of the Jewish religious year, the Rabbinic literature and the general Jewish moral and cultural outlook. Many aspects of the Gospels which, for the non-Jew, are matters for scholarly enquiry are for the Jew as familiar as the air he breathes."

Therefore, it becomes an essential necessity to sift out the totally Hellenized depictions of Jesus that far too many scholars portray him as being[124] and search back into the understandings of the *original Hebrew* out of the Greek translations.[125] For Galilee, (the primary location for Jesus' ministry), was *hardly* as "Hellenized" as far too many Christian New Testament scholars have believed and claimed![126] In regards to my statement here, "far too many scholars," (or as I will also state elsewhere throughout this book), "far too many scholars for far too long now," it is essential and quite appropriate to quote here Max Radin, and for readers of this book to constantly remember these words of Max Radin, (even in regards to *my own* scholarly opinions put forth in this book), and this essential to remember statement of Radin being,[127] "Consequently, we are not required to accept even the unanimous agreement of scholars without question, and if we feel ourselves competent to judge their materials, we may insist on knowing how such scholars arrived at the conclusions they set forth." To further demonstrate that Radin is not alone in making such a statement, the late renowned scholar Robert W. Funk once stated,[128] "No matter how many illusions we dispel, no matter how firm the conclusion

---

123 *Revolution in Judaea*, Hyam Maccoby, p. 11.

124 See as an example the comments in *The Partings of the Ways*, James Dunn, pp. 9-10; *How Jesus Became Christian*, Barrie Wilson, pp. 7-30, 92-94, 101-102; *Jews, Greeks and Christians*, (Edited by Robert Hammerton-Kelly and Robin Scroggs), E. P. Sanders commenting, pp. 11-44.

125 See the comments in *Understanding the Difficult Words of Jesus*, David Bivin and Roy Blizzard, pp. 1-2.

126 See the comments in *Roman Society and Roman Law in the New Testament*, A. N. Sherwin-White, pp. 125-143; *Galilee*, Sean Freyne, pp. 22-56.

127 *The Trial of Jesus of Nazareth*, Max Radin, p. 9.

128 *Honest to Jesus*, Robert W. Funk, p. 26.

we reach this time around, we will turn out to be wrong in some way, perhaps many ways, down the road. Someone, somewhere, sometime will come along and correct our mistakes while adding their own. This brings us back to Rule One: human knowledge is finite." Also, we have the similar comments from the renowned Jewish scholar, J. J. Petuchowski, who states,[129] "It would be quite out of keeping with their professed dedication to objective scholarship for any Bible scholars to claim absolute truth and finality for their particular conclusions." And finally, to quote from the New Testament, and specifically, James 3:1-2: "Not many of you should become teachers, my brothers, for you know that we who teach will be judged with greater strictness. For all of us make many mistakes. Anyone who makes no mistakes in speaking is perfect, able to keep the whole body in check with a bridle."

Now, many scholars try to use Acts 6:1 to claim that Palestinian Jews, as well as Diaspora Jews were highly "Hellenized."[130] But the simple *fact* is that the Greek word used in Acts 6:1, *helleniston* ("Hellenists"), derives from the base word, *hellen*, meaning, "Greek," or "gentile," and thus, scholars *should not* be jumping to such rash claims that the word *helleniston* is referring to "Hellenized Jews."[131] For the simple fact is that Acts 6:1 makes a *clear* distinction between "Hellenists" and "Hebrews" in the same way as when Paul argues with these "Hellenists" in Acts 9:29. Now, in Acts 11:19-20, (a verse that will be further referenced in Chapter 2), it states that, "They spoke the word to no one except Jews," yet again, we find here a *clear* distinction being made between "Jews" and "Hellenists" when these verses further state, "But among them were some men ..." who *"spoke to the Hellenists also...."* This is, in all reality, no different than Paul's *clear*

---

129   *Ever Since Sinai*, J. J. Petuchowski, pp. 22-23.

130   See as an example *The Partings of the Ways*, James Dunn, pp. 61-74; *How Jesus Became Christian*, Barrie Wilson, p. 139; *Jewish Christianity Reconsidered*, Matt Jackson-McCabe, p. 205, (Patrick J. Hartin commenting); *Prophecy in Early Christianity*, David E. Aune, pp. 16-17.

131   See the correct comments on this in *Jesus and the Laws of Purity*, pp. 72-73, but yet Booth goes on to erroneously refer to these "Hellenists" as "Diaspora Jews" and even "Palestinian Jews" on pp. 78 and 95; but see also a similar erroneous reference in *Essays on the Semitic Background of the New Testament*, Joseph A. Fitzmyer, pp. 277-279; *A Wandering Aramean*, Joseph A. Fitzmyer, p. 4 and n. 15, p. 21.

distinction of "the Jew first, and also to the Greek" (or "gentile") found in Romans 1:16; 2:9-10; 10:12; Colossians 3:11. Scholars should be very wary of trying to claim that these *clear* distinctions are somehow referring to "Hellenized Jews."[132] James Dunn even recognizes the fact that what is meant in Galatians 2:15 is a *clear* reference to "gentiles!"[133] Also, another matter related to this, (that will be elaborated upon in the Epilogue), surrounds three synonymous words – *ekklesia, sunagoge,* and *synedrion* – which these three words *do not* place any *clear* distinctions between them in regards to any sort of "buildings," or "classes of people" as many today would by referring to each as "Church," "Synagogue," and "Sanhedrin." These three synonymous Greek words simply referred to a "gathering of people." There are some scholars who are greatly in error when they claim that simply because these Greek terms are found being used in the Talmud that this offers *proof* to justify their claims that Palestine was extremely "Hellenized."[134]

Going further though into this matter of whether or not there was an extreme "Hellenization" of first century Palestine, Hyam Maccoby writes,[135] "From the standpoint of Greco-Roman society the Jews were 'barbarians.' That is to say, the Jews of Palestine did not form part of the general culture nowadays called 'Hellenistic' which dates from the conquests of Alexander the Great and derives ultimately from the great cultural advances of Athens." Also, as Samuel Sandmel rightly states,[136] "The Maccabean warfare was directed against both the Seleucidian Greeks and against Hellenizing. As a byproduct Palestinian Judaism thereafter deliberately shunned Greek ways and practices and enhanced all the more the significance of its own religion and of its group solidarity." Likewise, M. Rostovtzeff writes,[137]

---

132   For more on this see the comments of Carl Siegfried and Richard Gottheil, "Hellenism: 'To Speak Greek,' or 'To Make Greek'," *Jewish Encyclopedia.*

133   See the comments in *The Partings of the Ways*, James Dunn, p. 131.

134   See for example *Paul and Rabbinic Judaism*, W. D. Davies, pp. 5-8. But to counter these erroneous claims see the comments of Henry Albert Fischel, "Rabbinical Knowledge of Greek and Latin Language," *Encyclopedia Judaica*; Richard Gottheil and Samuel Krauss, "Greek Language and the Jews," *Jewish Encyclopedia.*

135   *Revolution in Judaea*, Hyam Maccoby, p. 47.

136   *A Jewish Understanding of the New Testament*, Samuel Sandmel, p. 19.

137   *Social and Economic History of the Hellenistic World*, M. Rostovtzeff, Volume II, p. 1106.

"The mass of the natives was never absorbed by Greek culture and never Hellenized. They held fast to their traditional life-style, to their religious, social, economic, legal and cultural peculiarities. They never felt themselves part of a greater unit whose upper class was formed by the Greek and Hellenized *bourgeoisie*."[138] Also, as Richard A. Horsley states,[139] "In contrast to what was done in other areas, neither the Ptolemies nor the Seleucids imposed Hellenistic political forms directly on traditional Judean Society." Sean Freyne rightly points out that the *only* real "Hellenized" influence pushed onto Galilee, or Palestine as a whole was in regards to economic and commercial matters.[140] Now, Hyam Maccoby goes on further to state,[141] "Yet as the representatives of Hellenism the Romans felt themselves entitled to feel superior to the Jews, a 'barbarian' nation who had actually refused to conform to the Hellenistic mold. Not that the Jews were not untouched by Hellenism; but they had the audacity to approach it in a critical spirit, to assess it in the light of their own cultural tradition, to approve part of it and reject part of it."[142] Also, Maccoby notes that,[143] "It was no accident that Jesus gave rise to a new-world religion. Though Christianity was a falsification of everything that Jesus stood for, yet every detail of this falsification was built on something that existed in his temperament and outlook. It was only a step for the Hellenistic gentiles to transform Jesus' soaring conviction of his universal mission into a dogma of his divinity; or to transform his confidence of victory by the hand of God, rather than by guerrilla methods, into a pacifist other-worldly doctrine which transferred the concept of victory on to a 'spiritual' plane." Also, as Craig

---

138   See further on this the comments in *Gnosis*, Kurt Rudolph, pp. 288-290; *Jewish Literature Between the Bible and the Mishnah*, George W. E. Nickelsburg, pp. 71-73; *Conflict, Holiness & Politics*, Marcus Borg, p. 55; *Maccabees, Zealots, and Josephus*, W. R. Farmer, pp. 56-60.

139   *Jesus and the Spiral of Violence*, Richard A. Horsley, p. 7.

140   See the comments in *Galilee*, Sean Freyne, pp. 155-200.

141   *Revolution in Judaea*, Hyam Maccoby, p. 49.

142   See also the similar comments in *One God One Lord*, Larry W. Hurtado, p. 5 even though Hurtado then erroneously claims that Hellenism had a much broader influence on Palestinian Judaism than is actually historically true on pp. 7-9, 12.

143   *Revolution in Judaea*, Hyam Maccoby, p. 145.

C. Hill writes,[144] "Christianity instead is the product of the Hellenistic Church (ironically, those who did not have the benefit – or, apparently, the distraction – of having known Jesus), especially the Apostle Paul… In my judgment, the recovery of the Jewishness of early Christianity on the part of a number of major scholars is the greatest accomplishment of modern New Testament scholarship, albeit one that has yet to win the field. Ant-Jewish bias is still much in evidence, not least in the continued depreciation of the Jerusalem Church." Now, Robin Scroggs does an excellent job to help elaborate further upon this when she writes concerning Paul being a "Hellenistic" Jew that,[145] "In fact, what is striking is that the integration (or eclecticism) of the cultures is so deep in the Apostle's mentality that he was probably unaware, most of the time, in what respect he was 'Jewish' and in what respect 'Greek'." This is essential to understand as more will be said in Chapter 4 concerning Paul's "*Hellenistic*" influence that altered not only the teachings of Jesus, but also the manner in which the Pharisees, and for that matter, *all* Jews came to be viewed by the Church in regards to the trial of Jesus.

Far too many scholars for centuries have tried to claim that the primary language of first century Palestinian Jews was Aramaic,[146] and in fact, some scholars even mistake certain *Hebrew* words as actually being Aramaic words.[147] As examples of what is meant here, the *Hebrew* words shalaḥ, "send,"[148] (a word which will be discussed further in Chapter 4), which can be found being used for example in Genesis 24:21; 24:40; 24:54; 24:56; 27:45; 30:25; 37:13; 38:17; 38:23; 39:2; 42:16 and the list can go on and on thru Exodus, Leviticus, Numbers, Deuteronomy, Joshua, Judges, etc.,

144 *Jewish Christianity Reconsidered*, Matt Jackson-McCabe, pp. 41-42 (Craig C. Hill commenting).

145 *Jews, Greeks and Christians*, (Edited by Robert Hammerton-Kelly and Robin Scroggs), Robin Scroggs commenting, p. 271.

146 See for example, as just a few of the many, many possible examples of such erroneous conclusions, *The Historical Jesus in Context*, Levine, Allison Jr., and Crossan, pp. 7 and 15; *Who is Jesus*, Darrell L. Bock, pp. 22-23; *Jesus*, C. Leslie Mitton, p. 76; *Jesus and Israel*, Jules Isaac, pp. 27-28; *The New Testament*, Bart D. Ehrman, p. 219; the entire book *A Wandering Aramean*, Joseph A. Fitzmyer.

147 See for example *A Wandering Aramean*, Joseph A. Fitzmyer, pp. 188 and 205-215.

148 See *Etymological Dictionary of Biblical Hebrew*, p. 263.

or the *Hebrew* word *kal*, "all," which is the shortened form of the *Hebrew* root word *kalal*,[149] which likewise has far too many Scriptural references that could be offered here, are proof that there are many Hebrew words which some scholars claim to be *Aramaic* words instead of the truth that they are *Hebrew* words! It is essential here though, to point out a prime example of the scholarly claims that Aramaic was the dominant language in Palestine and the errors that accompany such claims. Bruce Chilton,[150] for example, writes, "By the time of Jesus, Aramaic had become the common language of Judea, Samaria, and Galilee (although distinctive dialects were spoken); Hebrew was understood by an educated (and/or nationalistic) stratum of the population,[151] and some familiarity with Greek was a cultural necessity, especially in commercial and bureaucratic contexts." Chilton then goes on further[152] to speak about the *meturgeman*, or "translator," of the Synagogues who, after the liturgist would read from Scripture in Hebrew this *meturgeman* would "translate" the reading into Aramaic. But Chilton's implications in regards to these *meturgeman*, and even more so to the matter of Aramaic being the dominant language used are simply erroneous.[153] Chilton then claims[154] that in Mark 4:11-12 Jesus is using the Palestinian Aramaic Targum of Isaiah 6:9-10, for Chilton "interprets" Mark 4:12 as reading, "… lest they repent and it be forgiven them." It must be first pointed out here that the word *Targum* simply means, "translation," or "interpretation," which in essence are actually *synonyms*.[155] Furthermore,

---

149 See *Etymological Dictionary of Biblical Hebrew*, p. 119; *A Comprehensive Etymological Dictionary of the Hebrew Language*, p. 276.

150 See *The Historical Jesus in Context*, Levine, Allison Jr. and Crossan, p. 238.

151 Other scholars claim that "Hebrew" was *only* "used widely as the religious language," see for example *Caiaphas*, Helen K. Bond, p. 25.

152 *The Historical Jesus in Context*, Levine, Allison Jr., and Crossan, p. 239.

153 See the articles "Meturgemen," *Jewish Encyclopedia*, Solomon Schechter and Casper Levias; "Targum," *Jewish Encyclopedia*, William Bacher; and see also the very correct comments in *The Parable of the Wicked Tenants*, Klyne Snodgrass who points out that "Aramaic" was simply one of the languages used occasionally at the time of Jesus, he *does not* state that it was the *dominant* language of first century Palestinian Jews.

154 *The Historical Jesus in Context*, Levine, Allison Jr., Crossan, pp. 245-246.

155 See the comments on this fact in *On Earth As It Is In Heaven*, D. C. Thielmann, n. 52, pp. 158-159.

since Chilton's rendering of Mark 4:12 is derived from the Greek in which the Gospel was written, and since *neither* Hebrew, or Aramaic readily translate into either Greek or English, (nor for that matter does Hebrew always readily translate into Aramaic, nor does Greek readily translate into English), then one *must* be very careful in trying to make such a claimed assumption as Chilton has done. For in reality, given the *context* of the Greek of Mark 4:12, this verse is actually *better* rendered as, "... never repenting and having it forgiven them," which in essence, is a *completely opposite* "interpretation" than the one Chilton is claiming, and which, by the way, this *better* "interpretation," is then *totally* in tune with the *best* understanding of what the *Hebrew* of Isaiah 6:9-10 actually states! But the clearest indication that a scholar is in error by what they are claiming is when one finds this scholar inadvertently contradicting themselves. This is precisely what we find Chilton doing in his conclusions to his opinions when he states,[156] "Evidently, the Targumim represent traditions that were a formative influence on the tradition of the Gospels at an early stage. Once the Gospels emerged in their Greek form, however, Targumic influence all but disappeared." Chilton's stated opinion here thus begs for this question to be asked then: were the Gospel authors and redactors the ones who were actually influenced by the Targums in writing *their* accounts *about* Jesus' teachings instead of Jesus actually being the one influenced by the Targums in how he taught? For as Chilton himself states, (and thus, this being the very contradiction that I mentioned),[157] "On the evidence of the Gospels, Jesus seems never to have cited Targumic wording exactly." Bingo!

Also, another scholar, namely Jules Isaac, who while claiming that Aramaic was the predominate language makes the mistake of pointing out his own error[158] when Isaac cites Eusebius, *Ecclesiastical History* 3:39:16, which *clearly* talks about the *fact* that matters were "in a Hebraic language," but which seems to be a statement by a Church Historian that is either ignored by scholars, or which they try to claim that Eusebius was simply utilizing Papias' testimony, and thereby, Eusebius actually meant to say "Aramaic." Still another scholar, for example, Chester Charlton McCown,

---

156   *The Historical Jesus in Context*, Levine, Allison Jr., Crossan, p. 251.

157   *The Historical Jesus in Context*, Levine, Allison Jr., Crossan, p. 252.

158   *Jesus and Israel*, Jules Isaac, n. 2, p. 28.

refers to *Aramaic* as being the "commercial language"[159] at the time of Jesus, and McCown refers to Greek as being the language used by "common people" throughout the Roman empire.[160] But then later McCown claims that *Aramaic* was actually the dominant language in Palestine.[161]

Yet, the fact of the matter is that after the Hasmonean-Seleucid war *Hebrew* once again was called upon to become the predominate language in Palestine. In fact, many of the scholars who claim that Aramaic was the dominant language in Palestine at the time of Jesus will contradict themselves by admitting this fact that after the Hasmonean-Seleucid war *Hebrew* once again began to be put back into place as the dominant language of Palestine![162] Now, Sean Freyne believes that Hebrew and Aramaic were a *digglosia* in first century Palestine,[163] and Joseph Fitzmyer refers to the debates by scholars[164] regarding the statement made by Josephus in *Antiquities* 20.12.1(263-265) concerning the "native tongue" of Josephus.[165] But, the *fact* is that the "native tongue" of Josephus *was Hebrew*, as Josephus *clearly* denotes in *Antiquities* 10.10.6 when Josephus states that he once translated *Hebrew* books into Greek, (but see also *Antiquities* Preface 2; *Jewish Wars* Preface 1; *Jewish Wars* 5.6.3; *Jewish Wars* 5.9.2; *Jewish Wars* 6.2.1 where Josephus further *clearly* denotes that not only *his* "native tongue" was *Hebrew*, but that the "native tongue" of *all of Palestine was Hebrew*)! In Nehemiah 12:24-26 we find that Nehemiah scolds the Jews who were no longer using Hebrew and it was this very matter of Nehemiah's scolding the Jews for no longer using Hebrew that weighed heavy upon the Maccabees' reasoning to reinstate Hebrew as the "native tongue" of Palestine! The sages at the time of Jesus referred to the "native tongue" of *Hebrew* as, "the Holy Tongue," (*leshon ha Kodesh*), or even as, "the language of the sages," (*leshon Hakhamim*).[166] As Lewis Glinert writes concerning this,[167] "The number of Hebrew speakers

---

159   See also the comments on this in *The Story of Hebrew*, Lewis Glinert, p. 23.

160   See the comments in *The Search for the Real Jesus*, Chester Charlton McCown, p. 115.

161   *The Search for the Real Jesus*, Chester Charlton McCown, pp. 135-137.

162   See for example *A Wandering Aramean*, Joseph A. Fitzmyer, pp. 29-30, 38-39.

163   See the comments on this in *Galilee*, Sean Freyne, p. 144.

164   *A Wandering Aramean*, Joseph A. Fitzmyer, pp. 33-34.

165   *A Wandering Aramean*, Joseph A. Fitzmyer, n. 36, p. 51.

166   See the comments in *The Story of Hebrew*, Lewis Glinert, pp. 36-37.

167   *The Story of Hebrew*, Lewis Glinert, p. 39.

is unknown, but probably in the tens of thousands," and in regards to the discovered letters written during the 132-135 CE revolt, written by none other than Bar Kochba himself, Glinert writes, "They suggest that the writers still used Hebrew as a spoken language, since languages that exist only in writing don't have vernacular forms."[168] It was only *after* this unsuccessful revolt of 132-135 CE when the Jews were basically kicked out of Judea by the Romans, (into areas where other dialects were the dominant languages), that other dialects, (including Aramaic), began to take over as being a dominant language among Jews while Hebrew was only used in the synagogues.

Now, the inscription placed on Jesus' cross noted in Luke 23:38 for example, is further *clear proof* of this *fact* that *Hebrew* was the dominant language of Palestinian Jews! For it *clearly* states in this verse, "Greek, Latin, and *Hebrew*," and *not Aramaic*![169] But despite this *fact*, there are still some scholars who try to claim that this meant *Aramaic* and *not Hebrew*![170] Furthermore, in Acts 21:40-22:2 it very *clearly* refers to the fact that Paul addressed a crowd in *Hebrew* and *not Aramaic*! 85% of the Dead Sea Scrolls were written in *Hebrew*[171] as opposed to only 13% in *Aramaic*, and only 2% in *Greek*.[172] Also, even though *1 Maccabees* only survives now in Greek, it was *originally* written in Hebrew,[173] as too was *Jubilees*, which is cited in the Dead Sea Scroll the *Damascus Document*, and also *Ecclesiasticus* or the *Wisdom of Ben Sirah*,[174] (which is referenced in the Mishnah and the

---

168 See the further comments on this in *The Story of Hebrew*, Lewis Glinert, p. 41.

169 See *Understanding the Difficult Words of Jesus*, David Bivin and Roy Blizzard, p. 8.

170 See for example *Pontius Pilate in History and Interpretation*, Helen K. Bond, p. 192.

171 As Lewis Glinert comments on this in *The Story of Hebrew*, pp. 37-39, this demonstrates just how strict the sect of the Essens were in holding on to Hebrew as the "sacred native tongue" of Israel.

172 See the comments by Gary A. Rendsburg in a chapter titled, "Qumran Hebrew (With a Trial Cut [1QS])," *The Dead Sea Scrolls at 60*, Lawrence A. Schiffman and Shani Tzoref, p. 217.

173 See the comments on this in *Hillel*, Rabbi Joseph Telushkin, p. 209; Crawford Howell Toy, George A. Barton, Joseph Jacobs, Israel Abrahams, "Maccabees, Books of," *Jewish Encyclopedia*.

174 See the comments in *"Caught in the Act,"* Roger David Aus, p. 15.

Yerushalmi Talmud and Babli Talmud).[175] Also, the *Psalms of Solomon*[176] was originally written in Hebrew, and some scholars even believe that *4 Ezra* was originally written in *Hebrew*[177] as well as *2 Baruch*.[178] Now, concerning the *Titulus* placed on Jesus' cross, Joseph Ratzinger and Pope Benedict XVI very rightly state,[179] "It is true, of course, that the title Messiah, 'King of the Jews,' is placed over the cross – publicly displayed before the whole world. And it is permissible to place it there – *in the three languages of the world at that time* (cf. John 19:19f) – because now there is no longer any chance of its being misunderstood." In Acts 2:1-13 it speaks of "devout Jews from every nation," and "each one heard speaking in the native language." The *key words* here in these verses are, "devout Jews," and "native language." For the "native language" of "devout Jews" was *Hebrew* with only a small spattering of Aramaic mixed in occasionally, exactly the same as in the Hebrew Scriptures, which consist of *less than* 10% being written in Aramaic.[180] In *Baba Kamma* 82b; *Sotah* 49b it clearly states that learning the Greek language was perfectly okay, but *usage* of Greek in Palestine as opposed to the "*sacred tongue*" of Hebrew, or even the usage of Aramaic should *not* be done. R. Judah I, or as he was also known, Judah ha-Nasi ("The Prince"), who lived roughly one hundred years *after* the time of Jesus absolutely despised Aramaic as known from the Talmud, *Sotah* 49b.[181] Thus, as virtually every scholar agrees, even though the Gospels and the New Testament as a whole as we have them today, were written in Greek, we know that they originated from a *Hebrew original oral transmission* and possibly even an *original Hebrew text*.[182] Now, what *did occur*, (beginning with the time of Ezra), was that the main script style for writing Hebrew

---

175   See Solomon Schechter, "The Quotations from Ecclesiasticus in Rabbinic Literature," *Jewish Quarterly Review*, Volume 3, No. 4, (July 1891), pp. 682-706.

176   *"Caught in the Act,"* Roger David Aus, p. 22.

177   *The Apocalyptic Imagination*, John J. Collins, p. 156.

178   *The Apocalyptic Imagination*, John J. Collins, p. 170.

179   *Jesus of Nazareth: Part One*, Ratzinger and Pope Benedict, p. 321, (italics mine).

180   See the comments on this in *Understanding the Difficult Words of Jesus*, David Bivin and Roy Blizzard, pp. 4-5.

181   See the comments on this in *Studies in the History of the Sanhedrin*, Hugo Mantel, n. 125, p. 21.

182   See *Understanding the Difficult Words of Jesus*, David Bivin and Roy Blizzard, p. 15.

changed to an Aramaic style, although it is quite true that at times the more ancient Paleo-Hebrew, (as it is termed today), script style *was* still occasionally used especially on ossuaries.[183] Modern archaeology has uncovered coins dating from after the time of the Maccabees that were *all* inscribed in *Hebrew*, some of which bore the inscription, "*Shekel Yisrael/ Yerushalayim Hakedosha*," ("Shekel of Israel/Holy Jerusalem")![184]

But there is one *very* essential point to make here in regards to this matter of these verses from Acts 2 (mentioned just above) and the referring to "devout Jews," and this point being what Jules Isaac so rightly states regarding the rise of Christianity. Isaac writes,[185] "…For there is another incontestable fact: the spread of Christianity took place at first because of the Dispersion of the Jews. The Apostles, the first Christian missionaries and themselves Jews, went from Synagogue to Synagogue across the ancient world. 'Without the Synagogue and … without the Dispersion of Israel, the establishment of the universal Church would have been impossible, humanly speaking, and the conversion of pagans would have required a thousand years of miracles'."[186] Jules Isaac is referring here to the long held "Christian claim" that "the Jews" rejected Jesus, (i.e. the old standard of blaming *all* Jews for the arrest, trial, and crucifixion of Jesus).

Now, Marcus Borg is partially correct when he states,[187] "… Much of the language of the Gospels is metaphorical…." In order for one to correctly understand the *historical Jesus* and the things that happened to him historically in regards to his betrayal, his arrest, and ultimately his trial, one *must have* a thorough knowledge and understanding of Judaism, and specifically, *first century Palestinian Judaism*.[188] Christianity as a whole and primarily Fundamentalist Christians, have failed to study and gain a

---

183   See the comments in *The Story of Hebrew*, Lewis Glinert, pp. 25-27.

184   See the comments on this in *The Story of Hebrew*, Lewis Glinert, p. 35.

185   *Jesus and Israel*, Jules Isaac, p. 90.

186   *Jesus and Israel*, Jules Isaac, n. 8, pp. 90-91, *The Life and Times of Jesus the Messiah*, Alfred Edersheim, Volume I, p. 119.

187   *Jesus: Uncovering the Life, Teachings, and Relevance of a Religious Revolutionary*, Marcus Borg, p. 51.

188   *The Trial of Jesus from Jewish Sources*, Rabbi A. P. Drucker, p. 5 writes, "without a thorough knowledge of Jewish history, the New Testament cannot be correctly and truthfully understood."

thorough knowledge of Judaism in order to correctly understand the very founder of their faith. But what is even more astounding is the fact that so many *non-Jewish* New Testament critical scholars have failed to do a thorough job in regard to the study of Judaism. N. T. Wright is quite correct when he points out that Fundamentalist Christianity "in America, has done its best to keep these two figures, the Jesus of history, and the Jesus of faith, from ever meeting."[189] This was precisely why I wrote my book *On Earth As It Is In Heaven,* and this is precisely why I have written this book specifically regarding the betrayal, arrest, and trial of Jesus in order to try and put an end to this trend of keeping the "Jesus of faith" from meeting the "Jesus of history." Although this is a very lengthy Preface to this book it was necessary in order to briefly summarize everything that will be discussed in detail throughout this book. But the most appropriate way to close this Preface is by quoting Bart D. Ehrman:[190] "The reason we need books like these is that the Gospels cannot simply be taken at face value as giving us historically reliable accounts of the things Jesus said and did. If the Gospels were those sorts of trustworthy biographies that recorded Jesus's life 'as it really was,' there would be little need for historical scholarship that stresses the need to learn the ancient Biblical languages (Hebrew and Greek), that emphasizes the importance of Jesus's historical context in this first-century Palestinian world, and that maintains that a full understanding of the true character of the Gospels as historical sources is fundamental for any attempt to establish what Jesus really said and did. All we would need to do would be to read the Bible and accept what it says as what really happened. That, of course, is the approach to the Bible that Fundamentalists take. And that is one reason why you will never find Fundamentalists at the forefront of critical scholarship."

---

189 *Simply Jesus,* N. T. Wright, Preface, p. x.

190 *How Jesus Became God,* Bart Ehrman, p. 88.

Chapter 1

"They watched him to see whether he would cure him
on the Sabbath, so that they might accuse him."
(Mark 3:2)

For any serious scholar attempting to make an accurate historical
assessment of what actually brought about the arrest, and trial of
Jesus such scholars must first look to see whether or not Jesus did in
fact violate, alter, or in some way attempt to abrogate the Torah and/or the
Jewish "oral" Torah. Now, there have already been several thorough scholarly
examinations that have *proved* that Jesus *did not* violate, alter, or attempt
to abrogate *any* Jewish laws whatsoever.[1] Yet, despite this fact there is still
the tendency amongst the majority of Christian New Testament scholars
to assert that Jesus *did* indeed teach contrary to the Torah, (whether that
be the written Torah, or the "oral Torah), and therefore, it is necessary to
prove, once again, that such assertions are totally without merit, and the
most logical place to begin such an examination is in regards to the Sabbath
and what precisely *was* Jesus' attitude towards observance of the Sabbath,
as well as what precisely were the Jewish laws at the time of Jesus in regards
to proper Sabbath observance. The reason for starting our examination

---

1   See for example the comments in *Studies in the History of the Sanhedrin*, Hugo Mantel, pp.
268-290 and all of his corresponding scholar's notations to these pages.

here is because it is here in these matters surrounding the observance of the Sabbath that so many apologetic,[2] and even the moderate scholars,[3] (such as those who either were, or still are a part of the *Jesus Seminar*), and even some Jewish scholars,[4] who either have very badly misunderstood the Gospel accounts concerning the Sabbath, or these scholars, (and by this I am referring to primarily the Christian scholars), will claim to have found such a violation of Jewish laws concerning the Sabbath that somehow so angered some sort of "Jewish authorities" to such a point so as to have them desire that Jesus be put to death.

We therefore must first take a look at what the Hebrew word *Shabbat* actually means in order to determine whether or not Jesus did in fact violate any of the legal precepts regarding *Shabbat*.[5] Now, since the Hebrew word *Shabbat* has no equivalent in *any* other language,[6] (including even Aramaic as stated in the Preface that Hebrew does not always readily translate into Aramaic), it is therefore, quite often misrepresented, misunderstood, and mistranslated by apologetically biased Christian scholars.[7] For the Hebrew word *Shabbat* is far too often rendered out by a word meaning, "rest." But the fact is that this is in all reality a very erroneous interpretation of the Hebrew word *Shabbat*.[8] Isaiah 40:28 clearly indicates that God does not "weary," and therefore, He does not "rest." This is precisely what is stated as well in John 5:17, "My Father is still working...." Thus, the *better* English interpretation of the Hebrew word *Shabbat* is, "cessation," or "a temporary stop." But, even offering such an interpretation as this for the Hebrew word *Shabbat* the *fact* still remains that *this* interpretation simply *does not* properly give the word *Shabbat* its full and appropriate meaning. For even this interpreted meaning tends to give one the impression that

---

2   See for example *Jesus of Nazareth: Part One*, Ratzinger and Pope Benedict, pp. 106-112.

3   See for example *Jesus and the Laws of Purity*, Roger P. Booth, pp. 111-112; *How Jesus Became Christian*, Barrie Wilson, pp. 77-81; *Conflict, Holiness & Politics*, Marcus Borg, pp. 145-162.

4   *A Rabbi Talks with Jesus*, Jacob Neusner, pp. 58-74.

5   See the comments in *On Earth As It Is In Heaven*, D. C. Thielmann, pp. 477-479.

6   See the comments in *God In Search of Man*, Abraham Joshua Heschel, pp. 416-417.

7   See for example, *Simply Jesus*, N. T. Wright, pp. 136-139.

8   See the comments in *The Rabbinic Mind*, Max Kadushin, p. 274; *Creation Continues*, Fritz Kunkel, p. 181.

there were times when *necessary* "work[s]" *could not* and/or *should not* be done at all on *Shabbat*. Therefore, the overall *best* English interpretation of the word *Shabbat* indicates that one is "to finish an action," or situation that *should not* "be left undone." This is clearly indicated by the Hebrew wording of Genesis 2:1-2.[9] *Shabbat* is a reminder to us that there is no distinction between "master and slave," "rich or poor," or even between one's own "successes and failures" as noted in Job 31:13-15. *Shabbat* is thus, merely "Holiness in Time."[10] *Shabbat*, in essence then, is a weekly "day of freedom" for one to be and to do what is "holy."[11]

The first matter to now examine in regards to whether or not Jesus actually violated any Sabbath laws involves the accounts of Jesus and his disciples supposedly "plucking corn" on the Sabbath, (Matthew 12:1-2; Mark 2:23-26; Luke 6:1-5).[12] But we find that there are discrepancies between the accounts in Matthew's and Luke's Gospels as well as those in Mark's Gospel regarding this matter. Therefore, it becomes essential to take a closer examination of each of these accounts separately in order to ascertain the correct *historical* actions taken by Jesus and his disciples as to whether or not they did in fact violate any Sabbath laws in *any* of these accounts. Yet, before doing so it is essential to point out that Edgar Goodspeed believes that the Greek word used in this incident *does not* actually mean "corn," but instead, Goodspeed interprets this to be a "wheat field," and that Jesus and his disciples were thus, pulling the tops of the "wheat" off.[13]

So, let us look at the accounts in Matthew 12 and Luke 6 first, for in both of these accounts it clearly states that Jesus' disciples "were hungry." If

---

9 See *Exploring Exodus*, Nahum N. Sarna, p. 215; *The Star of Redemption*, Franz Rosenzweig, p. 311.

10 See *The Rabbinic Mind*, Max Kadushin, p. 274; *The Sabbath*, Abraham Joshua Heschel, p. 9 and n. 7, p. 120; *The Book of Words*, Rabbi Lawrence Kushner, p. 23; *The Way of God*, Moshe Chaim Luzzatto, pp. 331-339.

11 See *The Thirteen Petalled Rose*, Adin Steinsaltz, pp. 180-181; *The Star of Redemption*, Franz Rosenzweig, pp. 358-359.

12 See the comments in *On Earth As It Is In Heaven*, D. C. Thielmann, p. 480, and n. 93, pp. 500-501; also for a brief discussion, but one that covers a wide variety of the varying opinions on this matter see *Who is Jesus*, Darrell L. Bock, pp. 65-76.

13 See the comments on this in *Problems of New Testament Translation*, Edgar J. Goodspeed, pp. 55-56.

so, then as it is stated in the Mishnah *Pe'ah* 8:7 and *Pe'ah* 4:8 the "plucking of corn" by a "poor" and/or "hungry" individual to be used as a source of food by individuals who were "poor," (which Jesus and his disciples clearly were), *even on the Sabbath*, was wholly allowed under Jewish law. Now, there are some scholars who attempt to reference Mishnah *Pesaḥim* 4:8 as a reference to a prohibition of the "picking up of fruit" to eat on the Sabbath.[14] But the *truth* of the matter of understanding Mishnah *Pesaḥim* 4:8 is that it makes reference to Mishnah *Pe'ah* 4:8 and 8:7 just mentioned above, and *Pesaḥim* 4:8 specifically discusses the leaving of fruit that has fallen to the ground for the "poor" and "hungry," and thus, such references by these scholars are simply erroneous understandings of what is *actually* stated in the Mishnah. Therefore, what would *not have been* allowed to occur on the Sabbath would have been if Jesus and his disciples had actually "harvested" the corn, such as by way of the use of a sickle for example.[15] But according to both Matthew's and Luke's accounts of this matter, the disciples only picked the ears of corn off and left the stalk intact, which therefore, such action *did not* constitute "reaping," or "harvesting" under Jewish law.[16] The factor in these accounts, which makes this even more important to clearly understand is the fact that Jesus had declared that particular year to be a "Sabbatical year," (Luke 4:17-19; Luke 13:10-16), although some scholars claim that it is impossible to "prove or disprove" whether or not this is what Jesus actually meant,[17] nor is it possible to determine for certain whether or not this event actually *did* occur during a "Sabbatical year." Now, in regards to this matter of it *possibly* being a "Sabbatical year," after the exile of the ten northern tribes of Israel, the practice of the *eved ivri*, ("Hebrew servant"), had ended, as noted in the

---

14   See for example *Jesus and Purity Halakha*, Thomas Kazen, p. 58.

15   See *The trial and Death of Jesus*, Haim Cohn, pp. 43-44, and n. 11, p. 352 in which he cites Talmud Babli, *Shabbat* 21a; Yerushalmi Talmud, *Shabbat* 5.1; but see also, "The Rabbinic Law Presupposed By Matthew 12:1 and Luke 6:1," *Harvard Theological Review*, Volume 23, (1930), pp. 91-92; Mishnah *Pe'ah* 4.4, 4.10; Mishnah, *Menahot* 10.3; and see the comments in *The New Testament and Jewish Law*, James G. Crossley, pp. 34-41 who points out that at the time of Jesus this was a matter of great debate.

16   See *The Trial and Death of Jesus*, Haim Cohn, n's 12-13, p. 352.

17   See the comments in *Jesus and the Spiral of Violence*, Richard A. Horsley, pp. 251-255 as an example of a scholarly opinion that one cannot "prove or disprove" that this is what Jesus meant.

Talmud, *Erchin* 29a and 32b. Yet, one could still "voluntarily" become an *eved ivri* because they were impoverished, but the master was still required to give them "release" and treat them with "kindness and compassion" and a master was to *never* "over-burden" the *eved ivri* (*Kidushin* 20a).[18] Thus, as stated in Mishnah, *Shabbat* 7:2 regarding Exodus 34:21, "plucking of corn" by a "poor" and "hungry" individual during a "Sabbatical year" was wholly permissible, for the law *only* applied to actual "field workers" as noted in Deuteronomy 23:25-26; Mishnah, *Bava Metzia* 7:2. Furthermore, when one's life might be in danger, as say for example, because one was "hungry," then even "*stealing*" from someone else's field in order to eat was wholly permissible, as stated in the Yerushalmi Talmud, *Sheviit* 4:2 [35a]; Talmud Babli, *Sanhedrin* 74a.[19] Thus, *absolutely nothing* in either Matthew's or Luke's accounts of this matter violated or abrogated *any* Sabbath laws, and therefore, there are now many scholars who believe that what is found being stated in at least Matthew's account is fabricated.[20]

Regarding the account that we have in Mark's Gospel though, we find again the mention of Jesus and his disciples being "hungry." But, the problem that we first encounter with this account resides in the fact that just prior to this incident of "plucking corn" one finds in Mark 2:15-16[21] that it appears to indicate that this incident occurred right after Jesus and his disciples had just come from what was basically a "banquet" in which they had been "reclining" and eating with "tax collectors and sinners." So, why has Matthew and Luke omitted this all-important detail out of *their* accounts? But the better question to ask is, how, or even better still, *why* would Jesus and his disciples still be "hungry" right after having just come from a banquet? Therefore, it has been suggested by some scholars that in all reality Mark's account is simply stating that Jesus and his disciples were just walking across this field, sort of like taking a shortcut to get to their next destination, and therefore, they *were not* actually "plucking corn" but

---

18   See *Love Your Neighbor*, Rabbi Zelig Pliskin, pp. 334-335.

19   See *The Mythmaker*, Hyam Maccoby, p. 42, and p. 181 where he refers to this as *Piqquah Nefesh*, "the saving of a soul."

20   See for example the comments in, *The New Testament and Rabbinic Judaism*, David Daube, pp. 67-71

21   For a somewhat erroneous commentary on these verses from Mark see *Mark*, Robert H. Gundry, pp. 139-149.

simply making a "pathway through the grain field."[22] Now, the matter that causes Mark's account to become suspect as to its legitimacy, and thus in turn, what ends up causing the accounts in Matthew's and Luke's Gospels to also be suspect in regards to *their* legitimacy, (for one must remember what was discussed in the Preface that according to the consensus scholarly opinion, Mark's Gospel was first written and then Matthew and Luke borrowed from and expanded upon Mark's Gospel), is found by what is stated in Mark 2:26. In this verse from Mark's Gospel it is reported that Jesus referred to Abiathar as being the High Priest at the time when David took the shewbread. But the fact is that the High Priest at that time was actually Ahimelek as clearly stated in 1 Samuel 21:2-3.[23] More will be said on this matter concerning Abiathar in Chapter 2, but for now, in regards to the matter at hand, all three Gospels therefore, appear to be, in all reality, a pure fabrication simply to try and deliberately incriminate the Jews in general when no real cause can actually be found that is in any way a violation or abrogation of *any* Jewish law regarding the Sabbath.[24]

It is quite true though, that at the time of Jesus rabbinic debate concerning the proper observance of the Sabbath was still an ongoing matter. This debate began, and derived from the post Maccabean period and what had transpired during that period as known from *1 Maccabees* 2:29-41 and from Josephus, *Antiquities* 12.274-276 where the Maccabees had allowed their enemies to attack and slay them on the Sabbath simply because they were trying to *strictly* observe what the Sabbath requirements were at that time in history.[25] Thus, starting around the time of the Maccabees, which predates Jesus by more than a century, a relaxing of strict adherence to

22 See for example the comments in *Sunday: The History of the Day of Rest and Worship in the Earliest Centuries of the Christian Church*, W. Rordorf, p. 61; *Lord's Day*, P. K. Jewett, p. 37.

23 See *Studies in Pharisaism and the Gospels* 1, Israel Abrahams, pp. 133-134.

24 See the comments in *Sabbath: Restoring the Sacred Rhythm of Rest*, Wayne Muller, p. 30; *Historical Jesus*, Gaalyah Cornfield, p. 69.

25 See *On Earth As It Is In Heaven*, D. C. Thielmann, pp. 496-501; *A Tree of Life: Diversity, Flexibility, and Creativity in Jewish Law*, Louis Jacobs, p. 45; *A Guide to Jewish Religious Practice*, Isaac Klein, pp. 85, 88; *The Trial and Death of Jesus*, Haim Cohn, pp. 42-43; *Ora<u>h</u> <u>H</u>ayyim*, 306.1; *Jewish Law from Jesus to the Mishnah*, E. P. Sanders, pp. 7-8.

the Sabbath had already begun,[26] and as Josephus *clearly* states in *Jewish Wars* 2.19.2(517-518) this relaxing of strict adherence to the Sabbath still held true as well during the 66-73 Jewish revolt against the Romans.[27] The relaxing in the strict observance of the laws concerning Shabbat was derived from Psalm 119:126, which in its *best* English rendition states, "There comes a time when you may set aside the Torah in order to do the work of the Lord." This is precisely why the Talmud, *Yoma* 84b-85b states, "A man may profane one Sabbath in order that he may observe many Sabbaths."[28] *Yoma* 85b further states that, "The Sabbath is committed to your hands, not you to its hands," which is basically the same thing that Jesus is reported to have stated in Mark 2:27 for example.[29] In *Yoma* 35b one can find it reported that there is a story concerning Hillel, (who died at least twenty years before Jesus even began his ministry), which states in regards to a particular matter involving the Sabbath, that, "This man deserves to have the Sabbath laws violated on his behalf,"[30] and if Passover fell on the Sabbath, which occurred every fourteen years, (a matter discussed previously in the Preface), then the Passover activities superseded the Sabbath laws.[31] Also, one can find an account in *Pesaḥim* 6:1; *Pesaḥim* 66a regarding certain matters of Temple sacrifices overriding Sabbath laws and this decision on this matter, once again involved Hillel![32] Therefore, the relaxing of strict Sabbath observance in such matters as, for example, the "plucking of corn" just discussed above, was in fact, and in all reality, *a Pharisaic interpretation that predates Jesus by quite some time.*

In Matthew 12:11 Jesus is reported to have said, "What man shall there be among you that shall have one sheep, and if it falls into a pit on

---

26   See the comments on this in *Conflict, Holiness & Politics*, Marcus Borg, pp. 75-76; *Jewish Literacy*, Rabbi Joseph Telushkin, p. 111.

27   See the comments on this in *Maccabees, Zealots, and Josephus*, W. R. Farmer, pp. 78-81.

28   See the comments in *Kosher Jesus*, Rabbi Shmuley Boteach, pp. 30-31; *Jewish Literacy*, Rabbi Joseph Telushkin, pp. 583-584.

29   See *Studies in Judaism*, Solomon Schecter, p. 244; *The New Testament and Jewish Law*, James G. Crossley, pp. 29-30.

30   See the comments on this in *Hillel*, Rabbi Joseph Telushkin, pp. 4-8; *The Life and Teachings of Hillel*, Yitzhak Buxbaum, pp. 16-17.

31   *The Life and Teachings of Hillel*, Yitzhak Buxbaum, pp. 22-23.

32   See the comments on this in *Hillel*, Rabbi Joseph Telushkin, pp. 13-17, and 57.

the Sabbath day, will not lay hold on it and lift it out?" On the surface this seems to be a criticism of the Essens, (a matter that will be further discussed in Chapter 4), and a direct reference to one of the Dead Sea Scrolls, namely, the *Damascus Document* 10:14-11:18 and one of the strict Sabbath restrictions found in this particular writing. For there is a clause in this writing about an animal giving birth on the Sabbath, and if the offspring were to somehow fall into a pit, or cistern, that it should not be lifted up on the Sabbath. But here again though, what Jesus is teaching is actually a Pharisaic teaching that predates Jesus as it is recorded in *Shabbat* 128b; *Baba Metzia* 32b, which were derived directly from what is stated in Deuteronomy 22:4.[33] Yet, we find that even Jesus himself is reported in Mark 11:16 to have refused to carry anything on Shabbat even though small items *were* permitted to be carried on Shabbat as recorded in Mishnah *Eruvin* 1:2; *Eruvin* 6:1-10; *Shabbat* 128a. So there *were* times when the Pharisees were far more relaxed in *their* interpretations of what could or could not be done on the Shabbat than even Jesus was, and so far as noted, nothing that Jesus taught or did on the Sabbath violated or abrogated *any* "oral" interpretations of the Biblical laws regarding what could or could not be done on Shabbat.[34] As E. P. Sanders rightly states,[35] "… But there is no indication that the Pharisees tried to impose their own rules on others – especially since there were serious internal disputes about numerous important issues …. One of the points being an Essene or a Pharisee, however, was to have one's own set of interpretations." In essence, as Sanders is saying, there were varying interpretations amongst first century Jews regarding correct observance of the Sabbath, yet *none of the different first century Palestinian Jewish philosophies imposed its own interpretations onto the other philosophies.* Sanders, (referencing the *Damascus Document* 12:3-6), goes on to state,[36] "The two main pietist parties – which in many ways made the Sabbath law more difficult to fulfill – seem to have been intent on reducing the penalty for transgression." My only objection to Sanders' comment here is in regards to his usage of the term "party" as

---

33   See *Love Your Neighbor*, Rabbi Zelig Pliskin, pp. 412-414.

34   See the comments in *The New Testament and Jewish Law*, James G. Crossley, pp. 29-32.

35   *Jewish Law from Jesus to the Mishnah*, E. P. Sanders, p. 12.

36   *Jewish Law from Jesus to the Mishnah*, E. P. Sanders, p. 18.

opposed to the word "philosophy," a matter that will be further discussed in Chapter 9.

The next matter to examine is whether or not it was permissible to heal an individual on Shabbat.[37] The fact is that under Jewish law at the time of Jesus "all medical treatment" on the Sabbath was permissible.[38] Again, *Yoma* 85b clearly states, "If circumcision, which concerns *one* of the 248 members of the body, overrides the Sabbath, shall not a man's whole body override the Sabbath?" This is precisely what is found being stated in John 7:23.[39] Even bathing a newly circumcised child was permissible on the Sabbath as stated in Mishnah, *Shabbat* 9:3; 19:3 based on what is stated in Genesis 34:25.[40]

There are many apologetic scholars though, who still attempt to claim that the Pharisees held very staunch restrictions *against* one doing *any* healing on the Sabbath.[41] But, as *Genesis Rabbah* 19, 3 clearly states, "There is nothing more important, according to the Torah, than to preserve human life … even when there is the slightest possibility that a life may be at stake one may disregard every prohibition of the law."[42] Leviticus 19:16, at the time of Jesus was interpreted to indicate that, "we are obligated to save people whose lives are endangered,"[43] and based on the interpretation of Deuteronomy 11:22 at the time of Jesus, "someone who has reached the highest levels of closeness with God is obligated to think about the welfare of his fellow man."[44] Another important matter to mention here is the manner of healing someone that involved the "laying on of hands."

---

37 In regards to this matter and in particular the verse used as the Title to this chapter, see the somewhat erroneous commentary conclusions in *Mark*, Robert H. Gundry, pp. 149-156.

38 See the comments in *A Guide to Jewish Religious Practice*, Isaac Klein, pp. 85, 88.

39 See *Christianity a Jewish Perspective*, Rabbi Moshe Reiss, Introduction; *Kosher Jesus*, Rabbi Shmuley Boteach, pp. 30-31.

40 See *The New Testament and Rabbinic Judaism*, David Daube, p. 70.

41 See for example, *From Sabbath to Sunday*, Samuel Bacchiochi, p. 34; *Who is Jesus*, Darrell L. Bock, pp. 76-78.

42 See the comments in *The Sabbath*, Abraham Joshua Heschel, p. 17, and n. 8, p. 121; *What is Judaism*, Emil L. Fackenheim, p. 68; *Worship and Ethics*, Max Kadushin, p. 215; *Love Your Neighbor*, Rabbi Zelig Pliskin, pp. 52-58; *Ritual and Morality*, Hyam Maccoby, pp. 162-164.

43 See the comments on this in *Love Your Neighbor*, Rabbi Zelig Pliskin, pp. 271-275.

44 *Love Your Neighbor*, Rabbi Zelig Pliskin, pp. 383-384.

Although this practice is never actually mentioned, or prescribed in the Torah or elsewhere in Scripture, it is a matter that is mentioned in certain Dead Sea Scrolls as a practice used by the Essens.[45] Therefore, we must now examine a few of the specific Gospel accounts of Jesus' healing on the Sabbath. First, from Mark 1:29-30; Luke 4:38-39 we find in this example Jesus healing Simon's mother-in-law on the Sabbath because her health was in grave danger. But, if one then takes a very careful reading of Mark 1:32; Luke 4:40 one will find it being stated that there were *other* individuals who were in need of healing as well, but whom were held off from receiving Jesus' healing abilities until *after* "the sun had set" and the Sabbath had ended.[46] Thus, Jesus had properly followed and observed the Sabbath (Mark 1:35) as wholly prescribed in the "oral" interpretations of the Torah.[47] Now it is quite true though, that some of the Gospel accounts of supposed "healings" being performed by Jesus were in *fact* simply *metaphorical* "healings" and *not literal* "healings" as even noted by the very explanations of these metaphors in John 9:39-41 and John 12:39-40 for example.

It is essential here to now look at the account in Luke 13:10-16, for it has been claimed by some apologetic scholars that this account is simply a clarifying of "the meaning of the Sabbath."[48] But at that time in history it was believed that an individual became "imprisoned" in their "transgressions" until they "repented" and were thus, "loosed from their imprisonment" in their "transgression."[49] This is precisely what we find being stated, and meant by what is stated in John 8:34. Therefore, the entire basis for the claims of a "clarifying" of "the meaning of the Sabbath" revolve around a complete misunderstanding of this historical fact.[50] For there is no such known Jewish law that prohibited one from "loosing," or "untying" an

---

45   See the comments on this in *Judaism and the Origins of Christianity*, David Flusser, pp. 21-22.

46   See also what is stated in John 9:4-6, and see the comments on this matter in *The New Testament and Jewish Law*, James G. Crossley, p. 26.

47   See the comments in *Jesus the Jew*, Geza Vermes, n. 69, p. 231; *Jesus*, D. Flusser, p. 49; *Jewish Law from Jesus to the Mishnah*, E. P. Sanders, p. 13.

48   See for example *From Sabbath to Sunday*, Samuel Bacchiochi, p. 36.

49   See the comments in *On Earth As It Is In Heaven*, D. C. Thielmann, Chapters 2 and 14 for more on this matter.

50   See the comments in *On Earth As It Is In Heaven*, D. C. Thielmann, pp. 484-489.

animal on the Sabbath. There are two more very similar such accounts in Luke 14:1-6; Matthew 12:10-13, but neither of these again violated *any* Jewish law.[51] The *only* Jewish law that can be claimed that even remotely comes close to what is being claimed in these accounts though, *did allow*, and in fact, *required* that one loose an animal to be able to eat and drink on the Sabbath, and this can be found in Mishnah, *Yoma* 8.6; *Mekhilta* 109b; *Shabbat* 15:3; *Berakhot* 40a; *Gittin* 62a, but see also *Jubilees* 50:10-13; *Judith* 8:6.[52] The final important aspect to point out about this account in Luke 13:10-16 comes from the fact that the Greek words that are generally translated as "having a spirit of illness," actually are *better* understood as indicating that the individual was, "exhausted" or "out of breath" from being "overworked." Thus again, since Jesus had declared it to be a "year of release," as already noted above, (again Luke 4:17-19), then Jesus was simply telling this woman that she was "loosed" from her responsibilities as being someone's "servant." As just noted in the paragraph above, certain Gospel accounts of supposed "healings" are in actuality *metaphorical* in nature and are therefore, *not* actual "healings" on the Sabbath.

Now, there are some scholars who perceive the Gospel stories about Jesus "healing on the Sabbath," or even the story of the "plucking of the corn on the Sabbath," as simply being a literary form referred to as "tripartite":[53] "revolutionary action – protest – silencing of the remonstrators." But in reality there was nothing "revolutionary" about *any* of the "words" or "actions" of Jesus, or any other rabbi at the time of Jesus, who engaged in debate over "interpretations" of the Torah.[54] Such debates at times became heated exchanges, (as will be further discussed in Chapter 4), but in the end one side or the other was *always* "silenced" by the "majority opinion." The very Gospel accounts of these encounters and debates are in essence no different than the debates found in the Talmud, which were sometimes

---

51   See the comments in *On Earth As It Is In Heaven*, D. C. Thielmann, n. 108, pp. 503-504.

52   For more on this matter see the comments in *Worship and Ethics*, Max Kadushin, pp. 29, 56, and n. 44, p. 242.

53   See for example the comments in *The New Testament and Rabbinic Judaism*, David Daube, pp. 170-195.

54   See the comments in *Christianity: A Jewish Perspective*, Rabbi Moshe Reiss, 3, "Hillel and Jesus"; *Everyman's Talmud*, Abraham Cohen, Introduction, p. xxii.

won by the sages from the school of Shammai,[55] but more often than not they were won by the sages of the School of Hillel. Therefore, for these scholars who are making such claims about Jesus' actions, such as, for example, the claim that, "at the time, those actions, far from irrelevant, were striking, unheard of, a new way of life,"[56] are hardly true or accurate statements *historically*. Some of these scholars even refute their own claims when they reference these very rabbinic debates from the Talmud. There was no "new way of life" in *any* of Jesus' actions or teachings. Jesus was simply teaching with "authority,"[57] even though the very same scholars who are making these absurd claims are also trying to assert and claim that Jesus was never given any "official authority" to teach as a "learned rabbi" based on what is found being stated in Matthew 21:23; Mark 11:27; Luke 20:1 for example. But the fact that Jesus simply refused to give any answer in these Gospel examples *does not* in any way indicate that Jesus *had not* been given "authority" as a "learned rabbi" by someone. Each of the different first century Palestinian Jewish philosophies had their own "ordaining authorities," a *fact* that is found being attested to, for example, in *Ecclesiasticus* 30:11; 45:17; *1 Maccabees* 1:13; 10:35; 11:58; *1 Ezra* 8:22, and even in the New Testament, such as is found, for example, in Acts 9:14; 26:10-12; John 19:10, and since the Essens are nowhere mentioned in the New Testament it is quite possible that Jesus was an "ordained learned rabbi" from the philosophy of the Essens,[58] and the references to the Teacher of Righteousness mentioned in the Dead Sea Scrolls is a *clear*, and *best* example of this *fact!*[59] John J. Collins points out an important

---

55   See the comments in *Christianity: A Jewish Response*, Rabbi Moshe Reiss, 6, "The Torah and the Gospel of Matthew," who points out that since the School of Hillel was not opposed to "healing on the Sabbath," then all such Gospel stories that refer to opposition to Jesus' "healings on the Sabbath" must involve members of the school of Shammai who *did* oppose "healings" being performed "on the Sabbath."

56   See for example the comments in *The New Testament and Rabbinic Judaism*, David Daube, p. 182.

57   See the comments in *The New Testament and Rabbinic Judaism*, David Daube, pp. 205-223.

58   See for example *The New Testament and Rabbinic Judaism*, David Daube, pp. 224-246; *Collaboration with Tyranny*, David Daube, pp. 10-11, and 13-14 and which he points out that *Genesis Rabbah* 94 may allude to the "law books" of the Essens.

59   See the comments on this in *The Partings of the Ways*, James Dunn, p. 175.

matter to note here when he writes concerning the Essens and the Dead Sea Scrolls,[60] "The paucity of pro-Hasmonean literature among the scrolls remains striking. The omission of whole categories of writings cannot be dismissed as fortuitous. It is more plausible that the people who collected the scrolls had a quarrel with both the Hasmoneans and the Pharisees." It must be remembered that the individuals referred to as the "Sadducees" in the New Testament are the remnants of the individuals who were previously in history referred to as the "Hasmoneans." Thus, as even Collins rightly points out, *nowhere* in the New Testament are the Essens *ever* mentioned and this *fact* in conjunction with the *fact* that Jesus is reported to have disputes with both the Sadducees and Pharisees, (a matter that will be further mentioned and discussed in later chapters), makes this *fact* that the Essens are never referenced by Jesus an *historical fact* that is far too *coincidental* to just be *ignored* by scholars! Nevertheless though, the bottom line is that Jesus *never* violated or abrogated *any* Sabbath laws that would have somehow drawn the ire of either the Pharisees, or any other first century Palestinian Jewish philosophy or "authority," to the point of having them desire that he be arrested, tried, and executed![61] Nor did Jesus violate *any other* Jewish law as will be proven in the remaining chapters of this book. As James G. Crossley writes,[62] "In terms of historical Jesus studies, the idea of Jesus and the law continues to be full of arguments whereby Jesus still has to override at least one commandment in some way. This may be the case historically, but given the range of legal views in early Judaism it should at least be done after an exhaustive study of parallels in Jewish legal texts. That said, some recent work is now showing that Jesus' views on the law were all paralleled in early Judaism." Furthermore, it is essential to point out that Josephus, *Contra Apion* 2.39 talks about how there were even many gentiles, of their own volition, who chose to follow the Jews in regards to not only observing *all* of the Sabbath regulations, but also in regards to the Jewish laws pertaining to the abstaining from eating certain foods, (a matter that will be discussed further in Chapter 3).[63]

---

60   *The Scepter and the Star*, John J. Collins, pp. 6-7.

61   See the comments in *Revolution in Judaea*, Hyam Maccoby, pp. 63-64, and Appendix 4, pp. 206-210; *Jesus and Israel*, Jules Isaac, pp. 56-60.

62   *The New Testament and Jewish Law*, James G. Crossley, p. 116.

63   See the comments on this in *Hillel*, Rabbi Joseph Telushkin, n. 3, p. 222.

The final important aspect to understand clearly here is in regards to the Sabbath commandment itself. The first thing for one to clearly understand is that when the Sabbath commandment was given at Sinai, it was nothing *new*. For as it says, "*remember*," it *does not* say, "thou shall," or "thou shall not," as with certain other commandments.[64] There are in fact two different versions of the Sabbath commandment being given in the Torah, and there was a specific reason as to *why* these two different versions were given. The first version is found in Exodus 20:8, which says, "remember," and as noted earlier in this chapter concerning the meaning of the word *Shabbat*, we are to *keep* this "holiness in time," "holy," meaning that upon this day we are to "remember to be holy" – to do "righteously" in other words. The second version, found in Deuteronomy 5:12, says, "Observe," the Sabbath day, which again indicates that we are to *do* what is "righteous" upon this day.[65] But "observance" of Shabbat was *not* something newly introduced at Sinai as most scholars should already know. For not only do we have written records from Babylon predating the giving of the Torah by Moses at Sinai that refer to a day named *Shabattu*,[66] but in Exodus 16:5; 16:23; 16:25; 16:29 the Israelites were told that the following day would be a *Shabbat* and these events pre-date the actual giving of the commandments. Thus, one doing "righteous" acts upon the Sabbath such as the "healing" of others as Jesus did was *not* a violation of *any* Jewish law, and such would certainly *not* have angered *any* Jew at the time of Jesus in any way.[67] In fact, the Pharisees/rabbinic Judaism referred to the Sabbath as the "pearl of creation," (*Midrash Tehillim* 92.1).[68] Therefore, *no scholar*[69] should consider the *supposed* "Conflict Stories," (a term that will be further discussed in Chapter 4), of Jesus' healing on the Sabbath,

---

64 See the comments in *Judaism: An Analysis and Interpretation*, Israel Herbert Levinthal, pp. 107-108.

65 See the comments in Matthew Henry's *Commentary On the Whole Bible*, p. 124.

66 See the comments in *Exploring Exodus: The Heritage of Biblical Israel*, Nahum M. Sarna, p. 147.

67 See the comments in *How Jesus Became God*, Bart D. Ehrman, p. 98; *The Misunderstood Jew*, Amy-Jill Levine, pp. 30-33; *Revolution in Judaea*, Hyam Maccoby, p. 11; *Jesus the Pharisee*, Harvey Falk, pp. 148-149, 153-154.

68 See the comments in *The Misunderstood Jew*, Amy-Jill Levine, p. 27.

69 See for example the comments in *Jesus and His Adversaries*, Arland J. Hultgren, pp. 82-84.

even when that healing of someone did not involve someone with a "life threatening illness," (such as the story in Mark 3:1-5; Matthew 12:9-13; Luke 6:6-10), to be something contrary to Pharisaic teaching or belief!

Chapter 2

"He entered into the House of God and took and ate the
Bread of Presence, which is not lawful for any but the
priests to eat...."
(Luke 6:4)

In this chapter we are going to examine whether or not Jesus and his
movement were in reality similar to other first century Palestinian
messianic movements, as well as many other Palestinian Jews in regards
to their disillusionment with the Sadducees in general, and in particular,
the legitimacy of the High Priest as a political appointee and collaborator
with the Romans. *If* this matter *is* in *fact* the *historical* truth then one can
very easily pinpoint the real factors that culminated in Jesus' arrest, trial,
and crucifixion.

Opposition towards the Sadducees, and in particular, the High Priest
was rampant at the time of Jesus.[1] Caiaphas was especially disliked for his
being one of the most extreme collaborators with the Romans as clearly
stated even in the Talmud, *Yoma* 9a, and 35b; *Pesaḥim* 57a.[2] The High

---

1   See the comments in *The Trial of Jesus from Jewish Sources*, Rabbi A. P. Drucker, pp. 36-
40; *No Stone on Another*, Lloyd Gaston, pp. 112-128; *Jesus*, David Flusser, pp. 105-111.

2   See for example the comments in *The Last Week*, Marcus Borg and John Dominic Crossan,
pp. 39-40; *Caiaphas*, Helen K. Bond, pp. 48-49; *The Life and Teachings of Hillel*, Yitzhak

Priest, in Jewish history, was always expected to be sort of the "model" of righteousness and purity for the entire Jewish people, and as such, the High Priest should never bring about the ire of the Jewish people as a whole, nor should he ever be the cause of animosity amongst all other Jews, or it would be considered a "distortion and mockery of the concept of the High Priest!"[3] But by the time of Jesus the historical fact was, as Josephus writes in *Antiquities* 20.180, "Hostility and violent factionalism flared between High Priests on one side, and the priests and leaders of the Jerusalem masses on the other."[4] *Tosephta Zebaḥ* 11:16-17; Babli *Yevamoth* 86ab; Babli *Ketuboth* 26a; Yerushalmi *Ma'asrot* 5:15 all likewise speak of this "violent factionalism" from the High Priestly families,[5] and one can further find mention of such "violence" on the part of the High Priestly families in several of the Dead Sea Scrolls. Yet, despite these "multiply attested" references to this "violent factionalism from the High Priestly families," which includes the confirming statement by Josephus in regards to this "violent factionalism," there are still some scholars who will try to claim that this is an exaggeration of the *historical* truth.[6] But Josephus also writes in *Antiquities* 20.251, in regards to the High Priests at the time of Jesus that, "The High Priests were entrusted with the leadership of the Nation." This statement by Josephus is referring to the fact that the High Priests were being appointed and/or removed by the Romans in total disregard of the Torah's prescribed method of an individual becoming the High Priest through their lineage from Aaron, and thus, if a High Priest *did not* cater himself to the will of the Romans then he could, and would get himself removed by the Romans at a moment's notice for not being capable of keeping control of the populace. Prior to the Romans taking control of Palestine though, the High Priesthood was being offered to the "highest bidder," or in essence, one could "buy" the right to become the

---

Buxbaum, pp. 71, 76, and n. 8, p. 317.

3   See the comments in *Love Your Neighbor*, Rabbi Zelig Pliskin, p. 227.

4   See the comments in *Bandits, Prophets, and Messiahs*, Richard A. Horsley and John S. Hanson, p. 61.

5   See the comments of Craig Evans, "Jesus' Action in the Temple: Cleansing or Portent of Destruction?" *Catholic Bible Quarterly* 51, pp. 259-260.

6   See for example the comments of D. Seeley, "Jesus' Temple Act," *Catholic Bible Quarterly* 55, pp. 255-256.

High Priest! Now, Josephus also makes reference to the fact that many of the Temple priests were Pharisees, and the Pharisees were loyal patriots of Israel as were the majority of the Jewish populace, not only in Palestine, but also in the Diaspora communities as well. The majority of the Jewish people listened to and respected the Pharisees more than they did the High Priest (a matter that will be further discussed in Chapter 4). This is therefore, the precise reason why we find it being stated in Acts 6:7 that even some priests became followers of Jesus, for they were, in reality, Pharisees.[7] Now, a matter that will be discussed in more detail in Chapter 6 surrounds the fact that there are some scholars who believe that John's Gospel (John 18:15-16) indicates that at least one of Jesus' disciples had direct connections with the Jewish aristocracy and High Priestly collaborators with the Romans.[8] But this matter raises some serious questions as will be noted in Chapter 6. For it was this very opposition to the Sadducean family of High Priests (as well as to the Herodians, who were associated with the Sadducees[9]) that led to the execution of Stephen (Acts 6-7), James the brother of John (Acts 12), and James the brother of Jesus (Josephus, *Antiquities*, 20.197-203).

This opposition to the Sadducees and High Priests had been an ongoing matter for quite some time since the Hasmonean-Seleucid war as reflected in *The Psalms of Solomon*, which is believed to have been written by someone from the Pharisees simply because of certain characteristics in these Psalms that reflect Pharisaic interpretations as opposed to either Sadducean or Essen interpretations.[10] This opposition began at the end of the Hasmonean war with the Seleucids when the Hasmoneans[11] reneged upon their promises to establish a legitimate Zadokite priesthood and a legitimate Davidic King,[12] but instead, granted and appointed themselves to the roles of both

7   See the comments in *The Jews and the Gospel*, Gregory Baum, p. 137.

8   See the comments on this in *Jesus of Nazareth: Part One*, Ratzinger and Pope Benedict, pp. 220-222.

9   See the comments on this of Kaufmann Kohler, "Herodians," *Jewish Encyclopedia*.

10   See the comments on this in *Jewish Literature Between the Bible and the Mishnah*, George W. E. Nickelsburg, pp. 203-212.

11   See the comments in *Bandits, Prophets, and Messiahs*, Richard A. Horsley and John S. Hanson, pp. 24-25; *Who is Jesus*, Darrell L. Bock, p. 132.

12   See the comments in *The Apocalyptic Imagination*, John J. Collins, p. 114.

king and High Priest,[13] claiming and attempting to portray themselves as the successors "after the order of *Melkhizedek*."[14] This, as we know from the New Testament Epistle to the Hebrews, was precisely what the Early Church believed about their own "Jesus movement." As Joseph Ratzinger and Pope Benedict XVI point out about the Book of Hebrews and the Jesus movement,[15] "If the Letter to the Hebrews treats the entire Passion as a prayer in which Jesus wrestles with God the Father and at the same time with human nature, it also sheds new light on the theological depth of the Mount of Olives prayer. For these cries and pleas are seen as Jesus' way of exercising his High Priesthood. It is though his cries, his tears, and his prayers that Jesus does what the High Priest is meant to do: he holds up to God the anguish of human existence. He brings man before God." Ratzinger and Pope Benedict XVI then go on to reference what Albert Vanhoye points out in, *Let us Confidently Welcome Christ Our High Priest*, that the Greek word *teleioun*, "made perfect," used in Hebrews 5:9, goes back to the Pentateuch in which this expression 'to make perfect," or 'made perfect" is used exclusively to mean, "consecrate as priest."

But, we also know from the Dead Sea Scrolls that the Qumran community of the Essens likewise believed that *they* were the "legitimate" priests "after the order of *Melkhizedek*"[16] as even noted in *Kidushin* 71a. Rabbi Moshe Reiss notes that *1 Enoch* 104:10 even speaks of this illegitimate Hasmonean priesthood stating,[17] "For the sinners shall alter the word of truth and many sinners will take it to heart: they will speak evil words and lie and they will invent fictitious stories and write out my Scriptures on the basis of their words." He then goes on to note the *Psalms of Solomon* 4:1-2;

---

13   See the comments in *On Earth As It Is In Heaven*, D. C. Thielmann, n. 83, pp. 663-664; *The Concise Guide to Judaism: History, Practice, Faith*, Rabbi Roy A. Rosenberg, p. 56; *The Jews and the Gospel*, Gregory Baum, pp. 24-25.

14   See the comments in *The Four Witnesses*, Robin Griffith-Jones, p. 254.

15   *Jesus of Nazareth: Part Two*, Ratzinger and Pope Benedict, pp. 163-164.

16   See the comments in *On Earth As It Is In Heaven*, D. C. Thielmann, p. 633; *The Dead Sea Scriptures: In English Translation*, Theodor H. Gaster, pp. 433-434; *Jewish Law from Jesus to the Mishnah*, E. P. Sanders, p. 38; *Jesus the Pharisee*, Harvey Falk, p. 40; *Paul Was Not a Christian*, Pamela Eisenbaum, pp. 71-72.

17   See *Christianity: A Jewish Perspective*, Rabbi Moshe Reiss, 6 "The Torah and the Gospel of Matthew."

4:8, 22; 8:9; 14:1-2; and 14:10,[18] which speaks about the corrupt Temple priests and how they "break the law," and are "hypocrites," and "only the faithful remain true to God's Law," and these "devout will inherit life."[19] Even in the Talmud, *Yoma* 71b there is a story regarding the two teachers of Hillel, namely Shmaya and Avtalion, in which this story states that these two teachers of Hillel tell the High Priest, "May the descendants of gentiles who do the work of Aaron go in peace, but may the descendants of Aaron who do not do the work of Aaron not go in peace."[20] Therefore, it is essential to ask the important questions, who *were* the "legitimate line of High Priests," and what precisely constituted the "legitimate High Priesthood"?[21] There is a very interesting interpretation that needs to be noted in regards to this matter before going on to identify who constituted the "legitimate High Priesthood." Joseph Ratzinger and Pope Benedict[22] utilize John 17:1-26 (which is seemingly a long prayer) to claim that Jesus is the *legitimate* "High Priest" and that the Church followers of Jesus are the *legitimate* "Priesthood." While this is a "unique" interpretation, the fact is that claiming that *all* of Jesus' "Church followers" are the "legitimate priesthood" is simply *untrue*, but it is an interesting interpretation on their part nonetheless.[23] Furthermore, 1 Peter 2:9 is quite often erroneously used as a reference to the "Christian Church,"[24] but the very fact that this verse from 1 Peter says, "You are a chosen race…" eliminates such claims from actually being true! For we *know* that the "Church" was/is comprised of many different "races" of peoples. Thus, this reference in 1 Peter 2:9 can

---

18 For more on this see the comments of Joseph L. Trafton in *The Historical Jesus in Context*, Levine, Allison Jr., and Crossan, pp. 265-266 who does an excellent job outlining and demonstrating, from the *Psalms of Solomon*, that at the time of Jesus it was a widely held belief amongst the people that the High Priest and many other Temple priests were illegitimate.

19 In regards to such individuals who abuse their "secular powers" of "office," see the excellent comments on this matter in *Purity and Danger*, Mary Douglas, pp. 132-133.

20 See the comments on this in *The Life and Teachings of Hillel*, Yitzhak Buxbaum, pp. 69-77.

21 See the comments in *On Earth As It Is In Heaven*, D. C. Thielmann, pp. 831-833 and the corresponding scholars notes to these pages.

22 *Jesus of Nazareth: Part Two*, Ratzinger and Pope Benedict, pp. 76-102.

23 See also the similar comments in *The Partings of the Ways*, James Dunn, pp. 91-93.

24 See for example the comments in *The Partings of the Ways*, James Dunn, p. 92.

only be a reference to *Israel* as the "chosen people" amongst *all* of God's children!

Now, in order to determine this line of legitimate High Priests it is necessary to mention again the reference in Mark 2:26 to Abiathar and how this verse speaks of David having taken the shewbread. This reference in Mark 2:26 is referring to the story found in 1 Samuel 21:1-9. But in this story in 1 Samuel 21, David was *given* this shewbread by the High Priest Ahimelek while David was on the run for his life fleeing from the wrath of Saul. Therefore, the question that must be asked is; what about this priest named Abiathar? Now, Abiathar is not even first mentioned in 1 Samuel until *after* this incident involving David being *given* the shewbread (1 Samuel 22:20), and Abiathar is mentioned only because he had escaped Saul's slaying of many of the priests because they had "conspired against" Saul by *giving* David this bread and a sword (1 Samuel 22:12-13). Abiathar is next mentioned in 1 Samuel 23:6-9 as the "*son* of Ahimelek," and again, it was *Ahimelek* who *actually* gave David the shewbread, and thus, the actual author of the account in Mark 2:26 either has made a very gross error by not fully understanding the accounts in 1 Samuel, or this account in Mark's Gospel is a pure fabrication! For Ahimelek was the actual High Priest at the time that David was *given* the shewbread.

In 1 Kings 1:7 we learn that Abiathar turned against David and followed after, and helped Adoniyah. As a result, we find in 1 Kings 1:32-34 that David called upon his *loyal* priest Zadok to go with the prophet Nathan and anoint Solomon. This matter had actually been foretold would occur in 1 Samuel 2:27-36 and that the House of Eli, or Abiathar's family in other words, would fall and a *new* High Priestly family would be raised up and "walk before God *forever*." As a result of Abiathar's betrayal of David, in 1 Kings 2:22, 26 Solomon deposes Abiathar and banishes him to Anathoth. This is the first and *only* time in the entirety of Scripture of a legitimate deposing of a High Priest. Thus, Zadok and *his* descendants became the "*legitimate*" line of High Priests of God "*forever*."[25]

So, a question now begs to be asked, and this question being, at the time of Jesus was there any one philosophy amongst first century

---

25 See the comments in *Jesus: A Revolutionary Biography*, John Dominic Crossan, pp. 72-73; *The Religion of Israel*, Yehezkel Kaufman, pp. 193-195; *On Earth As It Is In Heaven*, D. C. Thielmann, n. 28, p. 652.

Palestinian Jews who believed that *they were indeed* the "legitimate" Zadokite descendants? Indeed, we now know from the Dead Sea Scrolls that the residents of the Judean community referred to as Qumran did in fact refer to themselves, (as just one of many references made about the inhabitants of their community), as the "sons of Zadok."[26] But as noted above, hostility towards the Sadducees, and the High Priest in particular, was not limited to just those of this one philosophy of Jews who considered themselves to be the "legitimate" descendants of the Zadokite priesthood. Josephus, *Antiquities* 20.180, (noted already above), again *clearly* points out that hostility flared against the illegitimate priests from *all sides*.[27] But this hostility towards the illegitimate priesthood *did not* in any way indicate that the first century Palestinian Jewish people were angry about the Temple in general. It simply indicates that they wanted and desired a "legitimate" High Priest in the Temple and *not* "political appointees" from the will of Rome.[28] As Marcus Borg and John Dominic Crossan write concerning this fact,[29] "It was, in other words, quite possible of first century Judea to deny the validity of the ruling High Priesthood or to be against High Priestly competition and collaboration without that involving any negation of the Jewish priesthood in general or even of the High Priesthood in particular. It was possible to be against a particular High Priest and the manner in which he was fulfilling his role without being against the office of High Priest itself. There was a terrible ambiguity in that the priest who represented the Jews before God on the Day of Atonement also represented them before Rome the rest of the year." Borg and Crossan also note that during the 66-73 revolt the Roman appointed High Priestly families, (as well as many of the other priests) in Jerusalem were killed by the Zealots and replaced by a "legitimate" lineal Zadokite

---

26 See the comments in *On Earth As It Is In Heaven*, D. C. Thielmann, pp. 622-623, and pp. 831-833; *Maccabees, Zadokites, Christians and Qumran*, Robert Eisenman, pp. 44-45 *The Jews and the Gospels*, Gregory Baum, pp. 111-112; *The New Testament and the People of God*, N. T. Wright, p. 170.

27 See the comments in *Bandits, Prophets, and Messiahs*, Richard A. Horsley and John S. Hanson, p. 61.

28 See the comments in *The Parable of the Wicked Tenants*, Klyne Snodgrass, pp. 73-80, and 107-108.

29 *The Last Week*, Marcus Borg and John Dominic Crossan, p. 41.

High Priest. Also though, Richard A. Horsley and John S. Hanson point out a very important matter, (which will be discussed further in Chapter 9), and this being the fact that the Temple was beloved by all of the Jewish people,[30] a fact which far too many scholars try to claim was not true, but as will be discussed in Chapter 4, the Pharisees, even though they beloved the Temple, they simply considered its significance as being only secondary to other matters. So, as Horsley and Hanson write,[31] "Yet precisely because of the importance of the Temple as a religiopolitical symbol, the High Priests of the late Second Temple period and the Temple administration generally seemed of questionable legitimacy. The Hasmoneans, originally leaders of the popular revolt against Hellenizing elite, were non-Zadokite usurpers of the High Priestly office. The High Priestly families which Herod brought in and which monopolized the chief priestly offices right up to the Jewish revolt were, some of them, not even from Palestinian Jewish families, but powerful families from the diaspora."

Now, there are some scholars who try to claim that Caiaphas and his family *were* in fact of Zadokite lineage.[32] But the very fact that there were twenty four divisions (or "courses") of priests, plus the fact that priestly families kept very detailed records of their lineage, one finds that *we do not have* such detailed lineage records in regards to Caiaphas, which creates a serious problem for such scholarly claims. Helen K. Bond even notes[33] that *Tosephta Yevamoth* 1.10 records that Caiaphas' family came about via a Levirite marriage, (see also Yerushalmi *Yevamoth* 1:6; 3:1), which *does not* necessarily offer one a *direct* Zadokite lineage and adding this to the fact, (which will be discussed further in Chapter 4), that since we really *do not* have any surviving Sadducean writings, this then places any claims that Caiaphas *was* a "legitimate Zadokite Priest" into extreme doubt! The greatest problem though, is derived from what Hyam Maccoby rightly points out when he writes,[34] "More important was the fact that the Romans now actually appointed and dismissed High Priests at will. Valerius Gratus, the Procurator immediately before Pontius Pilate, deposed and appointed

---

30   See the comments in *The New Testament and the People of God*, N. T. Wright, pp. 224-226.

31   *Bandits, Prophets, and Messiahs*, Richard A. Horsley and John S. Hanson, P. 62.

32   See for example *Caiaphas*, Helen K. Bond, pp. 24, 149-153.

33   *Caiaphas*, Helen K. Bond, n. 3, p. 164.

34   See *Revolution in Judaea*, Hyam Maccoby, pp. 44-45.

four High Priests. His last appointment was Caiaphas, the High Priest who was concerned in the arrest of Jesus. Again, the Romans did not achieve what they expected by these tactics; the result was not a deeper submission to Roman rule but an increased contempt for the occupant of the High Priest." Now it is true though, that there is a legend concerning the origin of the Sadducees, which in its own way pertains to Caiaphas *not* being a "legitimate Zadokite priest." In Mishnah *Abot* 1:3 is a story, which speaks of Antigonus of Soko who had two highly notable students – *Zadok* and *Boethus* – who broke away from their teacher and formed two branches[35] of the Jewish philosophy, which came to be known as the "Sadducees," and which one of the prime beliefs of this philosophy was that there was no afterlife, i.e. "resurrection of the dead." This particular *Zadok*, the disciple of Antigonus of Soko, *was not*, in any way from the lineage of the *Zadok* who was made High Priest by David, and thus, *if* this account in *Abot* 1:3 is in *fact* the *true* "origin" of the philosophy known as the "Sadducees," then any claims by scholars that the Sadducean High Priests, such as Caiaphas, were the "legitimate Zadokites" are unfounded! Now, it is true that the name "Sadducee" *does* derive from the word/name *Zadok*. But, as was just shown from the story recorded in *Abot* 1:3, the particular *Zadok* who formed this philosophy that was named after him known as the "Sadducees," *was not* from the lineage of the "*legitimate*" *Zadok* who was appointed to be High Priest by David!

After the death of Herod, the Great, the people were hungry for a restoration of both a "legitimate" High Priest *and* a "legitimate" Davidic King, or in essence, *two* "anointed ones" or "Messiahs." This fact is written about by multiply attested sources,[36] such as the historian Josephus, *Jewish Wars* 6.312, but also by Tacitus, *Histories* 5.13, who speaks of how the majority of Jews, (at that time immediately after the Death of Herod the Great), firmly believed that they were living in the very time in which both of the legitimate rulers, (the High Priest and rightful king from the lineage

---

35   See the comments by Kaufmann Kohler, "Sadducees," *Jewish Encyclopedia*; Kaufmann Kohler and Louis Ginzberg, "Boethusians," *Jewish Encyclopedia*.

36   See *The Apocalyptic Imagination*, John J. Collins, pp. 11-112, 122-126; *Judaism and the Origins of Christianity*, David Flusser, pp. 423-425 and n. 124, p. 424.

of David), the two "anointed ones" would arise.[37] We also find this being spoken of as well in Babli *Sukkah* 52a,[38] for example, as well as in the Dead Sea Scrolls.[39] But this matter is in *fact* a very ancient Jewish understanding that was deeply imbedded in the message of the prophets of Israel.[40] Thus, the fact that this desire is found amongst the vast majority of the Jewish people of first century Palestine should not be surprising to *anyone* in the least. Once again, "multiple attestation" is an important factor in scholarly research, which cannot and should not just be ignored,[41] and all of these sources attest to the fact that the majority of first century Palestinian Jewish people desired and wanted a "charismatic judge" who was of "humble origins" such as noted in Judges 6:12; 8:22 as their "legitimate" High Priest and they wanted the prototypical "mighty man of valor," modeled after what is stated in 1 Samuel 16:18 for example, as their "legitimate" king.[42] There have been though, far too many Christian scholars who surprisingly make quite a few errors in their attempts to assess the Jewish interpretations and understandings at the time of Jesus regarding these "anointed ones," or "Messiahs," (plural), and far too many, in fact, to try and list all of these scholars, or even to try and explain all of their various

---

37 See the comments on this in *Bandits, Prophets, and Messiahs*, Richard A. Horsley and John S. Hanson, p. 110. But see also the comments in *The Rule of Qumran and its Meaning*, A. R. C. Leaney, p. 95; *How Jesus Became Christian*, Barrie Wilson, p. 260; *Prophecy in Early Christianity*, David E. Aune, p. 123; *Paul and Rabbinic Judaism*, W. D. Davies, pp. 276-277; *On Earth As It Is In Heaven*, D. C. Thielmann, p. 583.

38 See the comments of Kaufmann Kohler and Ludwig Blau, "Preexistence," *Jewish Encyclopedia*.

39 See the comments on this in *The Crucified Messiah and other* Essays, Nils Dahl, pp. 133-141. Now, in *Who Did Jesus Think He Was*, J. C. O'Neill, pp. 64-68, O'Neill seems to doubt, for some reason, that the Dead Sea Scrolls actually are referring to *two* "anointed ones."

40 See the comments on this in *The Message of the Prophets*, Gerhard von Rad, p. 253; *Messiah in Context*, Jacob Neusner, pp. 25-29, 123, 187-191; *Essays on the Semitic Background of the New Testament*, Joseph A. Fitzmyer, pp. 127-160.

41 See the comments on the importance of "multiple attestation" in *Who Is Jesus*, Darrell L. Bock, pp. 16-19.

42 See the comments in *Bandits, Prophets, and Messiahs*, Richard A. Horsley and John S. Hanson, pp. 115-116.

errors here.[43] But a matter of great importance to point out here comes from what is stated in Mishnah *Sanhedrin* 4:10, and this being that, "A king cannot be appointed outside the land of Israel, nor can one be appointed unless he be eligible for marriage into the priestly families," (meaning that the "appointed king" *must be* a full Israelite from the lineage of David, and the Herodians *were most certainly not* considered to be "full Israelites" from the lineage of David).[44]

The majority of what so many scholars refer to as "peasant uprisings," (a debatable term that will be discussed further in Chapters 3 and 4), that occurred before, during, and after the time of Jesus all surrounded such "charismatic judges" and "mighty men of valor," and that the majority of these uprisings were concentrated around the cities of Bethlehem, Sepphoris, and Emmaus (the city noted in Luke 24:13-32 as one of the places of Jesus' resurrection appearances).[45] As John J. Collins writes concerning this matter,[46] "Jewish expectations around the turn of the era were not for a generic 'messiah,' but for a royal messiah who would be the Branch of David, or a priestly messiah of Aaron, or a prophet like Moses... These were different messianic paradigms, not one composite concept of Messiah." Collins goes on further to point out though,[47] "Josephus, who is virtually our only source for popular movements in Judaism in this period, preserves no stories of priestly messianic pretenders. The idea of a messiah of Aaron, who would take precedence over the Messiah of Israel, was not a common Jewish concern, and appears to have been distinctive to sectarian circles." But Jacob Neusner demonstrates though, that this comment by Collins is not quite *historically* accurate,[48] but it is a matter which will not be elaborated upon here.

Thus, for all of the mainline modern New Testament scholars, (such as those of the past *Jesus Seminar* era for example), who attempt to try and separate the "Jesus movement" from all of these other such "movements" surrounding "charismatic" leaders is tantamount to the old cliché of trying

---

43   See for example *Jesus Interrupted*, Bart D. Ehrman, pp. 225-236.

44   See the comments in *Conflict, Holiness & Politics*, Marcus Borg, p. 37.

45   See *Bandits, Prophets, and Messiahs*, Richard A. Horsley and John S. Hanson, p, 117.

46   *The Scepter and the Star*, John J. Collins, pp. 195-196.

47   *The Scepter and the Star*, John J. Collins, p. 199.

48   See the entire book *Messiah in Context*, Jacob Neusner.

to "separate a needle from a haystack." As Richard A. Horsley and John S. Hanson write concerning all of these movements, "The memory of these popular messianic movements would no doubt have been fresh in the minds of most of the Jewish peasants who witnessed Jesus' activities."[49] Hyam Maccoby rightly points out,[50] "The title 'Messiah' (Greek – 'Christos') was not a divine title among the Jews. It simply means 'anointed.' It was given to two Jewish officials, the King and the High Priest, who were both anointed with oil at their inauguration ceremony… Every Jewish king of the House of David was known as Messiah, or Christ, and a regular way of referring to the High Priest was 'the Priest Messiah,' i.e. the Priest Christ; even the corrupt Roman appointees of Jesus' day had this title. It is necessary to labor this point because the word 'Christ' has become so imbued with the idea of deity that it is very hard for a non-Jew to appreciate what these words meant to the average Jew in the time of Jesus." This is an important statement to clearly understand and remember not only in regards to what will be discussed later in Chapter 7 concerning "blasphemy," and specifically in regards to how claiming to *be* "Messiah" *was not* "blasphemous,"[51] but also in regards to a matter that will be discussed below in this chapter regarding Jesus' reference to Daniel 7:13.[52] For as Maccoby clearly and very rightly states, "It is very hard for a non-Jew," (and this is also quite true, it seems, even in the scholarly world of today), "to appreciate what these words meant to the average Jew." Maccoby, though, goes on further to state that, "This is not to deny that the word 'Messiah' had acquired a strong aura of romance and glamour. It had come to mean not just 'king' but the deliverer who would rescue Jews from their subjection to the cruel

---

49 See *Bandits, Prophets, and Messiahs*, Richard A. Horsley and John S. Hanson, p, 117. For more on this subject of these uprisings surrounding these "charismatic mighty men of valor," see the comments in *The Messianic Idea in Judaism*, Gershom Scholem, p. 5; *On Earth As It Is In Heaven*, D. C. Thielmann, pp. 819-822 and the corresponding scholars notations to these pages; *Maccabees, Zadokites, Christians, and Qumran*, Robert Eisenman, p. 35; *The Dead Sea Scrolls in English Translation*, Theodor H. Gaster, p. 35.

50 *Revolution in Judaea*, Hyam Maccoby, pp. 75-82.

51 See for example the comments in *Who is Jesus*, Darrell L. Bock, pp. 152-173 in which his pure poppycock opinion claims that this matter by Jesus was somehow "blasphemous."

52 See also the erroneous comments in *Jesus of Nazareth: Part Two*, Ratzinger and Pope Benedict, pp. 178-180.

and humiliating power of Rome." Likewise, as Jacob Neusner writes,[53] "There can be no doubt that the Messiah was expected to fulfill a political task, specifically, to replace the pagan rulers of Israel and to institute his own just government. Indeed, to Samuel was attributed the opinion that the sole point of difference between the present age and the Messiah's time was that the Israelites would no longer live in Exile and be subject to pagan rule (Babli *Sanhedrin* 91b; Babli *Shabbat* 63a; Babli *Shabbat* 151b; Babli *Pesaḥim* 68a)."

It is quite true though, that at the time of Jesus there was no single consensus opinion regarding the "Messiah."[54] As John J. Collins writes concerning this,[55] "James Charlesworth reports that, 'no member of the Princeton Symposium on the Messiah holds that a critical historian can refer to a common Jewish messianic hope during the time of Jesus'...."[56] This is quite true in the same sense as other matters that will be noted in later chapters such as the fact that there was *no single* Pharisaism, or even an overall *single Judaism* at the time of Jesus. All of these matters went hand-in-hand. But the basic point to remember is that the Christian concept of the Messiah is far different from what the Jewish concept of the Messiah actually was, because the Christian concept contains many *pagan* influences that came from *outside of Judaism!* As Rabbi Joseph Telushkin rightly states,[57] "Did he (Jesus) see himself as the 'Messiah'? Probably, although one must remember that in the first century of the Common Era the word 'Messiah' had a different meaning than it has today. Contemporary believers usually think of the Messiah as a wholly spiritual figure. Then, it meant a military

---

53 *Messiah in Context*, Jacob Neusner, p. 181.

54 See the comments on this in *Who Did Jesus Think He Was*, J. C. O'Neill, pp. 24-41; David J. Zucker and Moshe Reiss, "Downplaying the Davidic Dynasty," *Jewish Bible Quarterly* Vol. 40, No.3, 2014, pp. 185-192.

55 See *The Scepter and the Star*, John J. Collins, pp. 4, 12-13; *Jesus and Israel*, Jules Isaac, pp. 134-138, and 394.

56 See *The Scepter and the Star*, John J. Collins, n. 17, p. 15, J. H. Charlesworth, "From Messianology to Christology: Problems and Prospects," in *The Messiah*, p. 5; and see also "The Heavenly Representative: The 'Son of Man' in the Similitudes of Enoch," *Ideal Figures in Ancient Judaism: Profiles and Paradigms*, John J. Collins, pp. 111-134; *One God One Lord*, Larry W. Hurtado, p. 66.

57 *Jewish Literacy*, Rabbi Joseph Telushkin, p. 122.

leader who would free the Jews from foreign (i.e. Roman) rule, bring them back from the four corners of the earth, and usher in an age of universal peace." Telushkin goes on to point out that despite the fact that there was no one consensus opinion regarding the "Messiah" at the time of Jesus, *all* of the varying opinions though, *did* contain five common elements, and as Telushkin writes concerning these five common elements,[58] "… Jewish tradition affirms at least five things about the Messiah. He will: be a descendant of King David, gain sovereignty over the land of Israel, gather the Jews there from the four corners of the earth, restore them to full observance of Torah law, and, as a grand finale, bring peace to the whole world."

This then brings about a very interesting matter to bring up and ask questions about, and this being in regards to the individual in the New Testament named "Simon the Zealot." For there are conflicting Church historical accounts as to what ultimately happened to this Apostle of Jesus known in the Gospels as "Simon the Zealot," as well as conflicting scholarly opinions as to his ultimate demise. These facts do make for a very interesting scholarly discussion and debate in that "Simon the Zealot," and an individual named "Simon ben Giora," (whose name meant, "son of the proselyte"), who was the very leader of a large portion of the "Zealot revolt" of 66-73 CE, are both *presumed* to have been arrested and martyred at *approximately* the exact same time in history. So, my suggestion to the scholarly world is that much more *unbiased* scholarly research needs to be examined in regards to whether or not these supposedly two different individuals *were not in fact*, and *in all historical reality*, one in the same individual. *If* in *fact unbiased scholarly research into this matter* were to uncover that these two supposedly separate individuals *were in fact* one in the same individual, then this would shed a whole new light onto the entire *Jesus movement* as a whole![59] Now it is true though, that the name "Simon" was *the* most widely used and popular name given to male Jewish children around the time of these individuals,[60] but there is simply too much *coincidental evidence*, (and I must add in here the fact that I do not personally believe that there

---

58   *Jewish Literacy*, Rabbi Joseph Telushkin, p. 614.

59   See the comments on this in *Revolution in Judaea*, Hyam Maccoby, p. 175.

60   See the comments on this in *Essays on the Semitic Background of the New Testament*, Joseph A. Fitzmyer, pp. 105-112.

is any such thing as "coincidence"), concerning the time of martyrdom of these *supposedly* two separate individuals, as well as the *fact* that one of these individuals held the nickname, "the Zealot," while the *presumed* other individual just happened to be one of the very *Zealot leaders* of the 66-73 revolt. There is simply just too much *coincidental evidence* surrounding these supposedly two separate individuals to just *ignore* the possibility that instead of two different individuals they *were in fact one in the same individual* despite this fact of the popularity of the name "Simon"!

Going further though, back into the discussion of this matter of "two Messiahs," all such first century Palestinian "movements" surrounding these "charismatic leaders" desired a "legitimate High Priest," *and* a "legitimate Davidic King" – *two "Messiahs,"*[61] i.e. "anointed ones" in other words. The High Priest of Israel was *always* likewise referred to by the Hebrew word *moshiah*, (or it can be pronounced, *mashiah*, or even *meshiah*), "Messiah," (see Numbers 3:3 for example),[62] as just pointed out above. Jesus and all of his followers as well desired and promoted a return to the *two* "legitimate *anointed ones*," despite the fact that Christianity as a whole, and even many *modern* Christian scholars of today as well, have tried to make out that Jesus was in fact a combination of both High Priest and King. Gerard Sloyan makes a very gross error when he refers to Psalm 110:4, (a verse that will be discussed further below), and writes,[63] "It was a song in praise of a princely (110:3), hence a messianic, figure to which Israel's God had given power at his enthronement. In doing so, the Lord

---

61 See the comments in *Born of a Woman*, John Shelby Spong, p. 119; *The Messianic Idea in Judaism*, Joseph Klausner, p. 494; *The Jewish Messiah*, James Drummond, pp. 356-359; *Sabbatai Zevi: The Mystical Messiah*, Gershom Scholem, pp. 9-10; *He That Cometh*, S. Mowinckel, p. 290; *The Lost Tribes: A Myth*, Allan H. Godbey, p. 431; *The First Coming*, Thomas Sheehan, p. 46; *The Concise Guide to Judaism: History, Practice, Faith*, Rabbi Roy A. Rosenberg, p. 232; *An Aramaic Approach*, Matthew Black, p. 77; *Aramaic Origin*, C. F. Burney, p. 75; *The Scepter and the Star*, John J. Collins, pp. 11, and 74-135; *No Stone on Another*, Lloyd Gaston, pp. 164-167.

62 See further on this the comments by Jeff A. Benner, "Biblical Word of the Month – Savior," *Ancient Hebrew Research Center Biblical Hebrew E-Magazine*, Issue #020, October, 2005.

63 *Jesus on Trial*, Gerard S. Sloyan, p. 38; for a similar but more lengthy misunderstanding, and misrepresentation of ancient Jewish metaphoric interpretations regarding "Melchizedek" see *Essays on the Semitic Background of the New Testament*, Joseph A. Fitzmyer, pp. 221-267.

(YHWH) had designated him his son from the dawning (v. 3). This royal figure possessed priestly power as well, not by way of Levitical descent but after the manner of the king-priest of ancient Salem, Melchizedek (v. 4). It is relatively easy to see how the early church would use the Psalm in its preaching about Jesus, whom it thought to be king, priest, Son of God, and one who had been set over God's enemies by his resurrection; and indeed, the church did so use it." Likewise, as Lloyd Gaston writes,[64] "Jesus lays claim to Psalm 110 as a passage referring to the eschatological priest rather than to the king, in agreement with Qumran." The problem though, lies in the interpretation/translation of Psalm 110:4. Now, going back to Sloyan's comment, Sloyan is speaking of this in regards to Mark 14:62 as coming from Jesus at his trial. The problem arises from a poor understanding of the actual *best* English reading of Psalm 110:4, which again will be discussed below, and the other matter concerns the reference to the Book of Daniel, which also will be discussed below.

Mark 14:62 and the referencing of the Book of Daniel, as well as what is stated in Mark 13:24-27, are questioned by some scholars as to whether or not this really is a legitimate saying of Jesus.[65] As an example, Marcus Borg and John Dominic Crossan write,[66] "Whether this kind of eschatology goes back to Jesus himself is a separate question." But the very fact that in Acts 7:55-56 we find Stephen likewise using this combination of Daniel 7:13 and Psalm 110:1 causes many questions to arise, such as did Stephen get this from Jesus, or was Stephen's statement then placed onto the lips of Jesus? For as Robin Scroggs writes,[67] "Scholars have, of course, long recognized that this is not an actual speech of Stephen; but I think it can be claimed, as I have argued elsewhere, to be a sermon, perhaps stemming out of the Christian mission to Samaria, which Luke has used. Acts 7 is thus evidence for a sermonic form within (Hellenistic) Jewish Christianity." Yet, the *real* question that needs to be asked is this: *if*, as the consensus New Testament scholarly opinion holds that the Gospel of

---

64 *No Stone on Another*, Lloyd Gaston, p. 90 and n. 2, p. 90.

65 See for example *No Stone on Another*, Lloyd Gaston, p. 389; *The Partings of the Ways*, James Dunn, pp. 171-175.

66 *The Last Week*, Marcus Borg and John Dominic Crossan, pp. 82-83.

67 *Jews, Greeks and Christians*, (Edited by Robert Hammerton-Kelly and Robin Scroggs), Robin Scroggs commenting, pp. 291-292.

Mark was the first Gospel written, *and*, as the claim goes, it was written sometime around 70 CE, then why, or better still, what would motivate the author of this Gospel to use imagery from this part of the Book of Daniel in Jesus' teachings when this part of the Book of Daniel *had not yet even become a part of a Jewish canon at the time of Jesus or even by the time of this supposed writing of Mark's Gospel?* The Book of Daniel at the time of Jesus, for the most part, was a highly debated matter and was still primarily considered to be a "sectarian writing,"[68] even though a portion of Daniel *is now* a recognized part of the Septuagint. But the fact is that Daniel was a later addition to the *original* Septuagint! In addition to *this* fact, this portion of Daniel referenced by Mark was even a *later* addition to the Septuagint than the scholarly claimed time of *when* Mark's Gospel was written, and thus, the Book of Daniel at the supposed time that Mark's Gospel was written *was not* the same Book of Daniel that is part of the Biblical canon of today and no fragments or copies of the *original* Septuagint that contains that *original* form of Daniel exist any longer for anyone to examine in regards to what the Book of Daniel was actually like when it was *originally* made an addition to the Greek Septuagint. The unknown author of *Ecclesiasticus*, or the *Wisdom of Ben Sirah*, *does not* even mention the now canonical Books of Ecclesiastes, Esther, (a Jewish writing that will be discussed in greater detail in Chapter 10), or Daniel as having any part in any accepted Jewish canon, (if one were even able to say that there was such a thing as a "Jewish canon" at the time that *Ecclesiasticus* was written), and neither does *2 Maccabees* 2:13-15 make mention of Esther or Daniel as having any part in any accepted "Jewish canon." Likewise, Philo *does not* list the Book of Daniel as being any part of an accepted "Jewish canon" that he knows.[69] Now, it is true that Josephus, *Antiquities* 10.266-268 talks about how much the Book of Daniel was one of the favorite writings amongst first century Jews,[70] and especially amongst the

---

68   See the comments in *A Wandering Aramean*, Joseph A. Fitzmyer, p. 162 concerning how much the Jewish sect of the Essens were so devoted to the Book of Daniel.

69   See the comments on this from Emil G. Hirsch, Ludwig Blau, Kaufmann Kohler, and Nathaniel Schmidt, "Bible Canon," *Jewish Encyclopedia*.

70   See the comments on this in *The New Testament and the People of God*, N. T. Wright, p. 266, and as a consequence of this Wright repeatedly references the Book of Daniel

Essens[71] where copies of a *form* of the Septuagint were found at Qumran.[72] But the *fact* remains though, that there are no known copies of the *original* form of the Septuagint, and the Septuagint was no longer accepted as having any authoritative use by the time of Jesus by the Pharisaic/rabbinic schools because of the many additions and alterations that were made to the Septuagint, (as even noted by Josephus, *Antiquities* 12.2.1-13), with even some of these additions and alterations to the Septuagint having been made by *non-Jews!*[73] In Mishnah *Soferim* 1:7 it states that the *original* Septuagint contained *only* the Torah, (i.e. the first five books of Moses), and in *Megillah* 9a it clearly states that it was *only* permissible to translate the Torah into any language other than Hebrew while all of the other books *must be* written *only in Hebrew*. It is true though, that in Mishnah *Megillah* 1:8; Yerushalmi *Megillah* 71c; Babli *Megillah* 9a there can be found conflicting opinions concerning the Torah portions of the Septuagint *as being acceptable*.[74] But as Jules Isaac writes,[75] "Since Daniel did not even figure in the Biblical canon at that time and was known only to a small number of 'the most learned,' what chance was there for the Jewish people 'as a whole' to associate this term with Daniel's vision?" Also, as John J. Collins points out,[76] "Ancient Judaism did not have a creed that defined Orthodoxy, in the manner of later Christianity. The reason that some notions, such as the expectation of a Davidic Messiah, were widely shared was that by this time (approximately 150 BCE to 70 CE) a corpus of Scriptures had come to be accepted as authoritative in Judaism. Eventually, these Scriptures took the form of the canonical Hebrew Bible that we know today. Whether

---

failing, it seems, to realize that despite what Josephus states this was a highly debated writing at the time of Jesus.

71   See the comments in *The Apocalyptic Imagination*, John J. Collins, p. 141.

72   See the comments on this in *Mark*, Robert H. Gundry, p. 351.

73   See the comments of Crawford Howell Toy and Richard Gottheil, "Bible Translations: Septuagint," *Jewish Encyclopedia*; *The Apocalyptic Imagination*, John J. Collins, pp. 70 and 85.

74   See the comments on this by Aryeh Reich, "The Greek Bible – Light or Darkness?", *Bar-Ilan University's Parashat Hashavua Study Center*, Parashat Va-Yigash 5765/December 16, 2004.

75   *Jesus and Israel*, Jules Isaac, p. 170.

76   *The Scepter and the Star*, John J. Collins, p. 20.

one may properly speak of a canon in the period before 70 CE, however, is a matter of dispute." There are some scholars though, who attempt to claim that there *was* a "Jewish canon" prior to the council of Jamnia, such as, for example, the erroneous statement of David E. Aune, who writes,[77] "The formation of the OT canon, a process which was completed by the first century B.C.,[78] appears to have had no connection with the view that prophecy had ended in Jerusalem… The canon, it must be insisted was not created by rabbinical fiat at the legendary 'council' of Jabneh, ca. A.D. 90."[79] While this statement might be true to a certain extent, the errors in his opinion will be shown below, because not only was Daniel not yet fully accepted by everyone, there were also debates over several of the Psalms, portions of the Book of Ezekiel, Song of Songs, and even over the Books of Ecclesiastes and Esther, plus several of the Pseudepigraphic writings, such as *Ecclesiasticus* at Jamnia, even though these writings were known, and were frequently read by many common Jews *prior to* Jamnia. But the only books that *anyone* can *really* claim to be a part of a set "Jewish canon" prior to Jamnia is the Torah and the Prophets, and Daniel *was not*, and still *is not* considered by Jews to be part of the Prophets – it is recognized as being a part of the *Ketuvim*, "Writings." Going further though into the matter of just the Book of Daniel, even the fragments of the Book of Daniel that were found amongst the Dead Sea Scrolls date from around 40-60 CE, or in other words, *after* the time of Jesus. Even Joseph Ratzinger and Pope Benedict XVI rightly state concerning the Book of Daniel,[80] "The Book of Daniel – written in the second century before Christ – does speak of God's Lordship in the present, but it mainly proclaims to us a hope for the future, for which the figure of the 'son of man' now becomes important, as it is he who is charged with ushering in God's Lordship." The important point to be observed in this quote is in regards to their stating, "Written in the second century before Christ." There is also a further point to be made,

---

77 *Prophecy in Early Christianity*, David E. Aune, p. 106.

78 *Prophecy in Early Christianity*, David E. Aune, n. 26, p. 375 citing *The Canonization of Hebrew Scripture: The Talmudic and Midrashic Evidence*, S. Z. Leiman.

79 *Prophecy in Early Christianity*, David E. Aune, n. 28, p. 375 citing several sources for his erroneous opinion.

80 *Jesus of Nazareth: Part One*, Ratzinger and Pope Benedict, p. 56. But see also the comments on this same point in *On Earth As It Is In Heaven*, D. C. Thielmann, p. 814.

which John J. Collins states very well when he writes,[81] "In the same way, the 'son of man' passage in Mark 13:26 alludes to Daniel, but the figure in Mark does not have the same reference as it had in Daniel, and the full narrative of Daniel 7 is not implied."

Now, in regards to this debate over the Book of Daniel at the time of Jesus, the debate revolved around several factors, the first of these being whether or not *only six chapters* were legitimate, (which would thus, possibly eliminate the very chapter 7 Jesus supposedly quoted from as being considered by many Jews to be a legitimate chapter of the Book of Daniel *at* the time of Jesus), while others accepted portions of Daniel beyond just 6 chapters, but they debated whether the *legitimate* portions beyond these 6 chapters ended with what is now chapter 12, or whether it ended with an additional unknown chapters 13 and 14.[82] It is true though, that the division into verse and chapter did not actually occur until the Middle Ages,[83] but what is being discussed here are the additions to the Book of Daniel that were *known* to be additions at that time in Jewish history, but which are no longer known *at this time* in history as to exactly what was contained in those additions. Now, as John J. Collins rightly states,[84] "It is noteworthy that the tales in Daniel 1-6 are set in Babylon. There again a Diaspora origin is possible, although the visions in Daniel 7-12 were certainly composed in Judea." Another problem with the Book of Daniel resides in the fact that certain portions were written exclusively in Hebrew while other portions were written exclusively in Aramaic and there is no consistency to this fact either. For instance, Daniel 1:1-2:4a and Chapters 8-12 were written in Hebrew while Daniel 2:4b-7:28 were written in Aramaic.[85] It is only logical for one to assume then, that the portion of Daniel that was written in Hebrew was written at one point and time in history and in one location by one individual while the portion that was written in Aramaic was written at another point in time in history and in another location by some other individual. Thus, this fact then begs the

---

81   *The Apocalyptic Imagination*, John J. Collins, p. 16.

82   For a brief breakdown of the Book of Daniel see *Jewish Literature Between the Bible and the Mishnah*, George W. E. Nickelsburg, pp. 19-30, 83-90.

83   See the comments on this in *On Earth As It Is In Heaven*, D. C. Thielmann, p. 132.

84   *The Apocalyptic Imagination*, John J. Collins, p. 21.

85   See the comments on this in *The Apocalyptic Imagination*, John J. Collins, pp. 70-72, 85.

question to be asked, which portion of Daniel was written first, and then which portions were added much later? This not only goes back to the very point discussed in the Preface about Hebrew once again becoming the dominant language in Palestine after the time of the Maccabees, but it also demonstrates clearly one of the very reasons *why* there was so much debate over whether or not the Book of Daniel should even be recognized as a legitimate part of the Jewish canon. An additional matter to make note of here, (and one which goes back to what was discussed in the Preface in regards to *when* the Gospels were written), is this: in the *exact same manner* that the majority scholarly opinion utilizes to recognize that the Books of Daniel, Esther, (again as will be discussed in Chapter 10), and even Isaiah had additions made to them, which therefore, culminates in the scholarly claim that Daniel, (as just the example being used here), was *not* written, in the form that we know it today, prior to the second century BCE, then, *by their own standards* used in this regard with the Old Testament writings, scholars *cannot claim* that the Gospels were written *prior to* the second century CE *because of the known additions made to the Gospels that were made in the second and third centuries CE! Two completely different set of standards for dating when specific Biblical books were written* – one for the Old Testament writings, and one for the New Testament writings – *cannot be legitimately utilized by genuine competent scholars!*

In essence, and in *historical* truth then, the Book of Daniel as we have it today, and even more specifically, the portion of the Book of Daniel that Jesus supposedly quoted from, *did not* become an accepted part of the Jewish canon *until after* the Council of Jamnia in 90 CE![86] Furthermore, the Book of Daniel, (as just noted above), *was not* considered to be a part

---

86   There is much debate about not only the matter of whether or not Jamnia was in fact an actual "Council" but also as to when this "Council" actually gathered. See the comments on this matter in *The Jews and the Gospel*, Gregory Baum, pp. 106-107; *The Scepter and the Star*, John J. Collins, pp. 20-21, and n. 2, p. 41; J. P. Lewis, "What do we mean by Jabneh?" *Journal of Bible and Religion* 32 (1964), pp. 125-132; *The Canonization of Hebrew Scripture*, S. Z. Leiman, pp. 120-124; G. Stemberger, "Die sogenannte 'Synod von Jabne' und das Fruhe Christentum," *Kairos* 19, (1977), pp. 14-21; *The Old Testament Canon of the New Testament Church and its Background in Early Judaism*, R. Beckwith, pp. 276-277; *Oracles of God*, J. Barton, p. 24; William Bacher, "Academies in Palestine," *Jewish Encyclopedia*; *The Story of Hebrew*, Lewis Glinert, pp. 17 and 25; *The New*

of the *prophetic* books or *Nevi'im*, but instead it was relegated to being just among the writings or *Ketuvim*. Now, Darrell L. Bock makes a comment about the fact that R. Akiba offers a comment upon Daniel 7:9 in the Talmud Babli, *Sanhedrin* 38b.[87] But Bock's mentioning of this fact is actually a moot point because R. Akiba *did not* even begin his studies to become a Rabbi until roughly 75-80 CE, and therefore, this referencing of the Book of Daniel by R. Akiba occurred *after* Jamnia, (more will be said about this in a later chapter), but it is essential to point out here what John J. Collins writes about this,[88] "Rabbi Akiba is said to have explained the plural 'thrones' in Daniel 7:9 as 'One for Him, and one for David.'[89] The Messianic interpretation remained standard in both Jewish and Christian traditions down to the Enlightenment but is rarely defended in recent times."[90] The fact is though, that there is really nothing written about a precise Jewish canon until Josephus discusses it in *Contra Apion* 1.7, which speaks of 22 accepted books while 4 *Ezra* 14:45 speaks of 24 books. Now, there is also a reference in 2 *Maccabees* 2:14-15, but this reference is *only* in regards to books that were collected, which had been previously thought to have been "lost," because of the war, but there is nothing stated in 2 *Maccabees* about which books, or even about how many books etc. The clearest evidence though, that there was no set Jewish canon at the time of Jesus comes from what is stated in the Epistle of Jude, which references the Book of Enoch, which has *never* been accepted into the Jewish canon![91] Once again though, as noted already above, it is true that Josephus writes in *Antiquities* 10.268; 10.276 that the Book of Daniel was quite popular amongst many Jews at the time of Jesus, but Josephus refers to this popularity of Daniel being in regards to *specifically* Daniel 2, which the majority of Jews interpreted the fourth kingdom that is mentioned as referring to the

---

Testament, Bart D. Ehrman, pp. 4-5 who erroneously places the dating for a fixed Jewish canon "about a century after Jesus," but which it was actually more like only 60-70 years.

87 See *Blasphemy and Exaltation in Judaism*, Darrell L. Bock on p. 19

88 *The Scepter and the Star*, John J. Collins, p. 36.

89 *The Scepter and the Star*, John J. Collins, n. 89, p. 46, Babli, *Hagigah* 13a; Babli, *Sanhedrin* 38b.

90 *The Scepter and the Star*, John J. Collins, n. 90, p. 46, for a recent defender, G. R. Beasley-Murray, "The Interpretation of Daniel 7," *Catholic Bible Quarterly* 45, (1983), pp. 44-58.

91 See the comments on all of this in *The Scepter and the Star*, John J. Collins, p. 21.

Romans, and again, this portion now known as Daniel Chapter 2 was part of the six readily accepted portions of the Book of Daniel and it *was not* one of the hotly debated portions of Daniel – i.e. what is now known as Daniel Chapters 7 thru 12 or 14. But again, the Book of Daniel that was added to the *original* Septuagint *was not* the same Book of Daniel that was accepted at Jamnia, and thus, one must ask the question, to which version of Daniel was Josephus referring to since he likewise wrote *after* Jamnia?[92]

Going further into this matter, Bart D. Ehrman does rightly state though,[93] that at the time of Jesus, "most scholars now think that a hard and fast canon of Jewish Scripture did not yet exist," only that "most Jews did subscribe to the special authority of the Torah," and that, "many Jews accepted the authority of the prophets as well." But, Ehrman then erroneously goes on to state that by the end of the first century people were considering Jesus' words as "Scripture," which he bases on the Greek word *graphe* used in 1 Timothy 5:18. But this Greek word *graphe* is *best* understood to simply mean "writing," or "to write down a law to be proposed."[94] Thus, the *best* understanding of what is stated in 1 Timothy 5:18 is *not* "Scripture," but simply, "for says the written proposed law." This holds true as well for 2 Peter 3:16. For the English word "Scripture" indicates a "sacred writing" which is why trying to use this English term in regards to the Greek word *graphe* being used in these verses, at the time that they were written, is quite erroneous. Now, it *can be* assumed that similar to the Essens and their writings, (i.e. the Dead Sea Scrolls), the early Church *may have* considered their various writings as being what the English word "Scripture" implies, but considered as such *only* for the particular set of followers of the Jesus Movement. Therefore, *if* this is what Ehrman is suggesting regarding his use of the word, "people," then one *could* inadvertently interpret his statement as being accurate. For as Pamela Eisenbaum states in regards to this matter,[95] "The modern reader must remember that there was no such thing as the New Testament in the first century. For that matter, there are

---

92   See the further comments on this matter in *The Parable of the Wicked Tenants*, Klyne Snodgrass, p. 69 who refers to the Theodotian version of the Book of Daniel.

93   *The New Testament*, Bart D. Ehrman, p. 11.

94   See *Liddel and Scott's Greek-English Lexicon*, p. 169; *BDAG Greek-English Lexicon*, pp. 206-207.

95   *Paul Was Not a Christian*, Pamela Eisenbaum, p. 169.

no distinctively Christian writings that have the status of Scripture in the first century. When Paul refers to Scripture – whatever term he uses – he is referring exclusively to Jewish sacred writings, roughly the equivalent of what Christians would later come to call the Old Testament."

Therefore, to place a date for the writing of the Gospel of Mark, at least in the form that we have it today, any earlier than sometime *after* the Council of Jamnia, or even more so, earlier than sometime at the beginning of the second century CE is foolish on the part of New Testament scholars, and since the consensus opinion also believes that Matthew and Luke utilize the Gospel of Mark in the writing of their Gospels, then these two Gospels, in the form that we have them today, can likewise be placed no earlier than the second century CE.[96] But the matter of even greater importance is the fact that this supposed usage of this "sectarian portion" of the Book of Daniel is what supposedly brings about the charge of "blasphemy" against Jesus, which again, will be discussed in Chapter 7.[97] Thus, it is essential that we examine closely this verse of Mark 14:62, which is in fact, a verbal "slap in the face" to the Sadducee High Priest Caiaphas. For as noted above, the Sadducees did not believe in the resurrection of the dead, and therefore, this supposed response by Caiaphas of, "blasphemy,"[98] (which is a matter entirely separate from the discussion at hand, and again, this will be discussed in detail, and proven to be nonsense, in Chapter 7), would therefore not be surprising as a result of Caiaphas' "Sadducean" beliefs.

Mark 14:62, as already stated above, is actually a combination of two different verses from what the majority of people refer to as the Old Testament, (Psalm 110:1 and Daniel 7:13 specifically), which actually was not unusual for rabbis of the time of Jesus to do in regards to offering a particular interpretation or teaching lesson. Donald Juel is quite in error when he writes,[99] "The difficulty is that the verse seems to contain two distinct images, two separate Scriptural allusions that do not fit together coherently."

---

96   But see again what has already been noted in the Preface regarding the comments in *Judas and the Gospel of Jesus*, N. T. Wright, pp. 76-77.

97   See the comments in *The Last Week*, Marcus Borg and John Dominic Crossan, pp. 130-131.

98   See for example *Blasphemy and Exaltation in Judaism*, Darrell L. Bock, pp. 28-29 who joins many other scholars in believing that Jesus' remark to Caiaphas does indeed constitute "blasphemy."

99   *Messiah and Temple*, Donald Juel, p. 94.

Juel seems to be totally unfamiliar with the Pharisaic/Rabbinic practice of combining two or more separate verses of Scripture together, which at times "contained two distinct images," or "two separate Scriptural allusions," which on the surface only seemingly "do not fit together coherently," in order to make a certain desired point, or to give a certain desired teaching lesson.[100] Therefore, the two verses combined in Mark 14:62 fit together perfectly *if* one is interpreting them in the appropriate manner, and thus, it is also essential to understand though, that any interpretation of Mark 14:62 that one desires to offer *must* come not only from the *Hebrew* of Psalm 110:1 (even though the portion from Daniel 7:13 was written in Aramaic), but also the Hebrew of which Jesus himself spoke, *if* in fact this is an actual legitimate saying by Jesus. Therefore, it is necessary to first separate these two combined verses out and examine each of the idioms of these verses independently of each other in order to fully understand the interpretation that Jesus was making to Caiaphas. For there have been some scholars, and even some theologians as well who have taken Jesus' reference to Psalm 110:1 as actually indicating a reference to Psalm 110:1-4,[101] (as noted already above), but which in reality these scholars have all very badly misunderstood and misinterpreted these verses because they have used either the Greek Septuagint or Aramaic Targums as the basis for their interpretations.[102] As an example, Darrell L. Bock references Mark 12:35-37 in relation to Psalm 110:1.[103] Bock writes concerning this,[104] "In considering authenticity issues tied to the use of Psalm 110:1, the key text is Mark 12:35-37, where Jesus raised the question why David calls

---

100   See the comments concerning the Pharisaic/Rabbinic common practice of combining two or more verses to arrive at a desired interpretation in *Essays on the Semitic Background of the New Testament*, Joseph A. Fitzmyer, pp. 71-72.

101   See for example, *Jesus on Trial*, Gerard Sloyan, p. 38; *The Scepter and the Star*, John J. Collins, p. 142.

102   See for example *A Wandering Aramean*, Joseph A. Fitzmyer, p. 90.

103   See *Blasphemy and Exaltation in Judaism*, Darrell L. Bock, pp. 220-224; but see also the comments in *Essays on the Semitic Background of the New Testament*, Joseph A. Fitzmyer, pp. 113-126.

104   *Blasphemy and Exaltation in Judaism*, Darrell L. Bock, p. 220.

the Christ Lord, if he is supposed to be David's son."[105] But such opinions as Bock's have been thoroughly refuted.[106] Thus, we need to also examine what Psalm 110:4 states as well.

It would seem that far too many scholars are simply unaware that *Melchizedek* was none other than Shem, the son of Noah, and therefore the references to this individual *are not a name, but simply a title!* So, let us then first take a look at what is stated in Psalm 110:4 in regards to its *best* English interpretation: "Submit (*nisheve*)[107] yourself to God (YHWH) and He will not change His mind. Come to (`*ethah*)[108] the priests forever on account of the reason (`*el-diberathiy*)[109] you are the King of Righteousness (*melkhi zedek* – two separate words)." Thus, such a reference being spoken by Jesus *to* Caiaphas would, in essence, have been a very mocking gesture on Jesus' part, for on the one hand Jesus is referring to himself as the rightful and legitimate King of Righteousness, while on the other hand he is referring to his coming before an illegitimate High Priest who had instead of *submitting to the authority of God*, had *submitted to the authority of Rome!*[110]

In regards to the second part of Mark 14:62, as well as what is found in Mark 13:24-27, and the referencing of Daniel 7:13-14,[111] all that really needs to be pointed out surrounds the reference to the "coming in the clouds." For as noted, the Sadducees, of which the High Priest Caiaphas was associated, did not believe in the resurrection of the dead. Now, James Drummond

---

105   *Blasphemy and Exaltation in Judaism*, Darrell L. Bock, n. 87, p. 220, for a full treatment of Psalm 110:1 and its suitability to this setting, see Darrell Bock, "Luke 9:51-24:53," *Baker Exegetical Commentary On the New Testament*, pp. 1630-1641.

106   See for example *On Earth As It Is In Heaven*, D. C. Thielmann, pp. 194-195 and all of the scholar's notations to these pages.

107   See *Etymological Dictionary of Biblical Hebrew*, p. 254: *A Comprehensive Etymological Dictionary of the Hebrew Language*, p. 637.

108   See *Etymological Dictionary of Biblical Hebrew*, p. 19.

109   See *A Comprehensive Etymological Dictionary of the Hebrew Language*, pp. 114, 472.

110   See the comments on this in *Judaism and the Origins of Christianity*, David Flusser, pp. 186-192.

111   See again the comments in *The Last Week*, Marcus Borg and John Dominic Crossan, pp. 82-83 and 130-131.

notes concerning *Sanhedrin* 98a,[112] that Rabbi Yehoshua ben Levi interprets this vision from Daniel by combining this verse with a different verse of Scripture. Rabbi Levi's interpretation is thus: "If they deserve, he will come on the clouds of heaven; if they do not deserve, poor, and sitting on an ass." Drummond goes on to interpret "clouds" as meaning,[113] "forgiveness of sin," based on Isaiah 44:22, along with "refreshing," or "cooling," (Isaiah 4:5), and a "separation" of "God from man," (Lamentations 3:44), and "judge," or "judgment" (Psalms 83 and 84). But the actual *best* contextual understanding of the very *idiomatic* and *metaphoric* Hebrew word, (which gets so often translated out in Scripture as, "cloud"), as well as the *idiomatic metaphors* of the Aramaic word *anan*, has in reality the *better* meanings of, "soothsayer,"[114] or even, "to fructify,"[115] and this meaning "fructify" needs to be clarified further, for "clouds" represented God's Protective "Essence," or "Illumination," and was related to *Sukkot*, or the "Feast of Tabernacles," which has a partial significance related to the "harvest time."[116] These are far different meanings than that of the Greek words *nephele*, or *nephos*, (a word, which gets used only once in Hebrews 12:1).[117] But this word *nephele* was quite often used as a *metaphor* for a "martyr," such as it is used in Acts 1:9 in order to *metaphorically* symbolize one's death.[118] There are some scholars though, who argue the point that Jesus *did*, in fact, make some sort of statement about "coming in the clouds," and these scholars reference 1 Thessalonians 4:13-18 as there basis for their contentions[119] claiming these verses give clear indication of an early tradition regarding such a statement being made by Jesus. But if one looks very carefully at these verses in 1 Thessalonians 4:13-18, one will notice that these verses likewise, fall into the category of such Jewish *metaphoric* terminology symbolizing the deaths of individuals. Going further though into the

---

112   *The Jewish Messiah*, James Drummond, pp. 234-235.

113   *The Jewish* Messiah, James Drummond, p. 237.

114   See *A Comprehensive Etymological Dictionary of the Hebrew Language*, p. 477.

115   See *Etymological Dictionary of Biblical Hebrew*, p. 188.

116   See the comments on this in *The Way of God*, Moshe Chaim Luzzatto, p. 343.

117   See the comments on this by Al Maxey, "A Cloud of Witnesses: An Analysis of Hebrews 12:1," *Reflections*, Issue #241, March 25, 2006.

118   See further, *Liddell and Scott's Greek-English Lexicon*, p. 530.

119   See for example the comments in *Jesus of Nazareth*, Dale C. Allison, p. 119.

demonstration of the differences between these two Greek words (*nephele*, and/or *nephos*) and the Hebrew word (*anan*), *Nephele* was also a "cloud nymph" in Greek mythology playing an essential part in the stories about Phrixus and Helle.[120]

So again, this statement by Jesus would have been a very mocking gesture on his part towards Caiaphas. Furthermore, as noted already above, the Book of Daniel at the time of Jesus was a highly debated matter and for the most part it was considered a "sectarian writing" and not yet a part of the accepted Jewish canon in the form we know today. So, for Jesus to have referenced a portion of what was considered a non-canonical sectarian writing before the High Priest as being an authoritative writing of God's Word would only identify Jesus' Jewish philosophical stance on matters of interpretation. For at the time of Jesus, the only Jewish philosophies even remotely devoted to the *full* acceptance of every portion of the Book of Daniel, as we know it today, were a few of the more *zealous* Pharisees, but most of all, the Essens (the very ones noted above who believed that *they* were the "legitimate *sons of Zadok*"). Therefore, once again, Jesus statement in Mark 14:62 is nothing more than a direct verbal "slap in the face" to Caiaphas. It must be noted here though, that some scholars look at what is stated in Matthew 24:27-28 as a reflection of an "apocalyptic battle scene" similar to such scenes as depicted in "*The War Scroll* from Qumran, *4 Ezra* 11-13; *2 Baruch* 39-40." These scholars therefore conclude that this later reference to the "coming in the clouds" is as a "victorious Messiah" precisely as was hoped for by so many in first century Palestinian Jewry.[121] Although it is quite true that such a statement *does* reflect the concept of a "victorious Messiah," the error of such scholars is in their misunderstanding of Jewish *metaphoric* terminology.[122] As Rabbi Joseph Telushkin rightly points out,[123] "We sometimes need to read even the words of the Torah with an eye to the metaphorical."

But it must be pointed out that some scholars take this matter concerning Jesus' supposed reference to Daniel 7:13 even further by claiming that the use of such imagery by *any* individual was claiming a right that only "deities"

---

120   See "Nephele," *Greek Mythology.com*, May 26, 2017.

121   See for example *Matthew and Empire*, Warren Carter, pp. 86-88.

122   See Kaufmann Kohler and Ludwig Blau, 'Preexistence," *Jewish Encyclopedia*.

123   *Hillel*, Rabbi Joseph Telushkin, p. 89.

possessed referencing Exodus 14:20; Numbers 10:34; Psalm 104:3; Isaiah 19:1.[124] As an example, Darrell L. Bock makes the interesting comment that Jesus in effect was saying,[125] "if you judge me now, I will judge you later," which is in reality almost an illusion to Matthew 7:1-2; Luke 6:37, and thus, the question begs to be asked, is this account not then something which was invented as a result of what is stated in these verses? Yet, according to Jewish interpretations at the time of Jesus, it was believed that individuals would be judged, "measure for measure," and therefore, such a statement, if made, would fall under standard Jewish teachings of the time.[126] Thus, according to so many *Christian* New Testament scholarly interpretations of this matter, Jesus *was* then, committing a form of "blasphemy" because, as they are claiming, this was an authority only God possessed, (a matter which once again will be discussed in greater detail in Chapter 7). But as will be proven in later chapters such scholarly claims are simply untrue and quite erroneous. As Hyam Maccoby writes,[127] "In the last chapter the view was put forward that Jesus was a rebel against Rome, not against Judaism; that the Kingdom *was* of this world; that his aim was to be an earthly king on the throne of David and Solomon, not an angel sitting on a cloud. One of the implications we can now draw is that Jesus *did not go to his death voluntarily.* The whole idea of a god-man who sacrifices himself in order to atone for the sins of mankind is alien to the Jewish tradition." This is quite true, and as will be pointed out in Chapter 7 it is a matter regarding the Jewish understanding that the Messiah would "bear the sins" of the people.

It is long past the time for scholars to admit, and for theologians, and the general church laity to accept and understand the truth of what Jesus was really all about. For Jesus was all about shedding the "yoke" of Roman, Herodian, and Sadducean oppression. As Rabbi Shmuley Boteach

---

124   See for example the comments in *Blasphemy and Exaltation in Judaism*, Darrell L. Bock, p. 201 and his reference in, n. 44, p. 201 to J. A. Emerton, "The Origin of the Son of Man Imagery," *Journal of Theological Studies* n. s. 9 (1958), pp. 225-242.

125   *Blasphemy and Exaltation in Judaism*, Darrell L. Bock, pp. 202-203.

126   See the comments on this matter in *The Way of God*, Moshe Chaim Luzzatto, p. 117, n. 29, p. 413, p. 347, and pp. 373-377.

127   *Revolution in Judaea*, Hyam Maccoby, p. 103.

rightly states,[128] "The stage has been set for us to see Jesus for who he truly was: a wise and learned rabbi who despised the Romans for their cruelty to his Israelite brethren, who fought the Romans courageously and was ultimately murdered for trying to throw off the yoke of oppression. He was a man who worked to rekindle Jewish ritual observance of every aspect of the Torah and to counter the brutal Roman occupation of his people's land. He never wavered in this mission even when he realized the consequences would be fatal. So greatly did Jesus love his people, so deeply did he believe in his messianic mission to grant the Jews independence from Rome, that he was willing to suffer and die to end Roman dominion and renew Jewish sovereignty in Ancient Israel." This is precisely what is actually meant by Jesus' statement in Matthew 11:28-30. The term "yoke," such as is found in Matthew 11:28-30 is far too often believed by scholars and theologians to be a reference to Jewish law, and they will likewise, make similar claims regarding what is stated in Galatians 5:1.[129] James Drummond for example,[130] uses *The Apocalypse of Baruch* Chapter 41 as his example of the term "yoke" being a reference to Jewish law. But the fact is that in Jewish imagery and *metaphoric* terminology, a reference to "yoke" *always* referred to "political control," and most often it was used specifically as a reference to the imposition of harsh imperial power," (see as just a few examples, Genesis 27:40; Leviticus 26:13; Deuteronomy 28:48),[131] and also as it is found in *1 Maccabees* 13:41, which states, "The yoke of the gentiles was removed from Israel," (but see also *1 Maccabees* 13:39). Therefore, Matthew 11:28-30 *is not* a reference to Jewish law; it is a reference to "the Roman political system."[132] For far too long now, far too many scholars have misrepresented and misinterpreted Matthew 11:28-30

---

128   See *Kosher Jesus*, Rabbi Shmuley Boteach, Introduction p. xvii.

129   See for example *Paul and Rabbinic Judaism*, W. D. Davies, pp. 69, 150, and 261-263.

130   *The Jewish Messiah*, James Drummond, p. 125.

131   See the comments in *The Misunderstood Jew*, Amy-Jill Levine, p. 126; *Matthew and Empire*, Warren Carter, p. 122; *The Way of God*, Moshe Chaim Luzzatto, pp. 279, 291-293, 313-315; *Jesus*, David Flusser, pp. 84-92; *On Earth As It Is In Heaven*, D. C. Thielmann, p. 530.

132   See *Matthew and Empire*, Warren Carter, pp. 109, 112-129, and n. 12, p. 203; Blaine Charette, "'To Proclaim Liberty to the Captives': Matthew 11:28-30 in the Light of OT Prophetic Expectation," *New Testament Studies* 38, pp. 290-297.

by offering what amounts to Anti-Semitic biased interpretations instead of using the more *historically accurate* interpretations of the term "yoke."[133] Jesus' *real* adversaries were the Romans, the Herodians, and their Sadducee collaborators with these two entities. One can even find this *metaphoric* meaning of the term "yoke" being used in the *Didache* 6:1-3 when it states, "For if you can bear the entire yoke of the Lord, you will be perfect; but if you cannot, do as much as you can,"[134] as well as the example that can be found in *Song of Songs Rabbah* 2:7:1. Now again, far too often scholars desire to interpret even these two references as indicating "Jewish law." But one must *clearly* understand that the Torah was/is *not* just a "set of laws," as it has far too often been interpreted. The Torah is a "teaching" of a "Way of life" including the "political governance" of an entire people – i.e. Israel – as it is clearly stated in Mishnah *Berakhot* 2:2! As Jonathan Draper comments on this,[135] "… it depends on the interpretation of 'perfection' as an ethical category rather than a code word for living according to the Torah… 'Taking on oneself the yoke of the Lord' is a technical term for obedient observance of the Torah in both the *Didache* and Matthew," to which Draper then references Mishnah *Abot* 3:5; 6:2; Talmud Babli *Baba Metzia* 85b; *Sotah* 14:4; and *2 Baruch* 41:3. "Taking on oneself the yoke of the Lord" meant shedding the "yoke" of *any* "foreign political governance."

Jesus was so closely aligned to Pharisaic thinking and teaching that it is remarkable that it has taken this long for modern Christian scholarship to recognize this fact. As Rabbi Shmuley Boteach rightly points out citing *Tosefta Pesaḥim* 9:2,[136] which states, "Silence becomes a scholar; how much more so a fool?" The meaning of this statement is that if even a great scholar ought to know when to remain silent, how much more so an ignoramus, who has much less to offer. Thus, as Rabbi Boteach writes

---

133   See the comments on this in *On Earth As It Is In Heaven*, D. C. Thielmann, n. 42, p. 899; *Matthew and Empire*, Warren Carter, pp. 130-144 where he points out that this also involves the matter of Jesus' saying, "render unto Caesar…" etc., which will be discussed in Chapter 8.

134   See the comments in *On Earth As It Is In Heaven*, D. C. Thielmann, pp. 938, and n.187, pp. 979-980; *The Sermon on the Mount*, Dale C. Allison Jr., pp. 2-3.

135   *Jewish Christianity Reconsidered*, Matt Jackson-McCabe, pp. 261-263 and 277-280, (Jonathan A. Draper commenting).

136   *Kosher Jesus*, Rabbi Shmuley Boteach, p. 27.

concerning this,[137] "Indeed, when we see Jesus' teaching any variation of those words, 'how much more so,' it seems as a sign he is using a classic rabbinic reasoning...." This mode of teaching was one of the seven modes of teaching proposed by Rabbi Hillel, and in this instance, this mode is referred to as *kal ve-ḥomer*, or "light and heavy," (see as examples, Matthew 7:11; Luke 12:24).[138] As Pamela Eisenbaum rightly states,[139] "Yet, contrary to long-standing stereotypes, ancient Jews did not have a peculiarly excessive interest in law; they did not preoccupy themselves with picayune legal details while neglecting more serious ethical matters. Thus, the idea that Judaism is a religion in which one is 'saved by works' is not an accurate characterization." Jesus' teachings, actions and everything else that he was all about *must be* understood from the standpoint of first century Palestinian Judaism,[140] and *not* from the standpoint of the later gentile Church's misinterpretations which they wrote about in regards to his life, teachings, and actions.[141] Acts Chapter 4 gives clear indication that the *real* "enemies" of Jesus were the Romans, the Herodians, and the High Priest and other Sadducees.[142] Also, Acts 11:19 is essential to understand in regards to this *fact*, for as this verse clearly states (italics mine), "Now those who were scattered because of the persecution that took place over Stephen travelled as far as Phoenicia, Cyprus, and Antioch, and *they spoke the word to no one except Jews.*" This statement, according to one of the most important criteria used by modern scholars, namely, that which is an "embarrassment to the gentile Church," *must be* clearly recognized in this verse. In essence, this verse *clearly indicates* that the followers of the teachings of Jesus avoided gentiles, which would then likewise, give

---

137   *Kosher Jesus*, Rabbi Shmuley Boteach, p. 27.

138   See the further comments on this in *The New Testament and Rabbinic Judaism*, David Daube, pp. 68 and 119-120; *The Misunderstood Jew*, Amy-Jill Levine, p. 32; *Hillel*, Rabbi Joseph Telushkin, pp. 197-198; *Jews, Greeks and Christians*, (Edited by Robert Hammerton-Kelly and Robin Scroggs), Birger Gerhardsson commenting, p. 137; *Judaism and the Origins of Christianity*, David Flusser, p. 496.

139   *Paul Was Not a Christian*, Pamela Eisenbaum, p. 91.

140   See the comments in *Simply Jesus*, N. T. Wright, Preface, p. xii.

141   See the comments in *The Lost Gospel of Judas Iscariot*, Bart D. Ehrman, pp. 56-58.

142   See the comments in *Pontius Pilate*, Ann Wroe, p. 119; *No Stone on Another*, Lloyd Gaston, p. 303.

clear indication that they also avoided anyone else who most likely was a "collaborator" with the gentiles, (i.e. the Romans), such as the Herodians, Sadducees, and High Priestly families.

Chapter 3

"It is not the thing entering into the mouth which
defiles a person...."
(Matthew 15:11)

I n this chapter we will examine a few of Jesus' teachings that many
Christian New Testament scholars claim is the proof that Jesus deviated,
in some way, from standard Jewish teachings of that time in history
to such an extent that caused Jesus to be arrested, tried, and crucified
under Jewish law. First, and primarily, we are going to look at the Jewish
kosher dietary laws to see if Jesus' teachings in regards to these laws were
in fact some sort of a drastic deviation of these laws. But also, we will
examine several other matters regarding Jesus' life, and teachings, which
many other Christian New Testament scholars have likewise, attempted
to utilize in regards to *their* particular claims that Jesus deviated from
standard Jewish teachings, and thus, got Jesus into trouble with some sort
of Jewish authorities.

The verse used as the title to this chapter, as well as the variation version
found in Mark 7:15, have oft been cited by so many scholars as an example
that Jesus somehow deviated from standard Jewish teachings.[1] But these

---

1   See for example *The Five Gospels*, Robert W. Funk, p. 69; Hans-Werner Bartsh, "Brethren,
    Life, and Thoughts," *New Theology* 6, (1969), pp. 185-198; W. Horbury, "The Trial of

scholars who attempt to utilize these verses for such claims have, in reality, very badly distorted what Jesus was intending for his listeners to learn and understand from what he was actually teaching.[2] For the common interpretation of these verses offered by so many scholars is that Jesus was somehow declaring that *all foods* taken into the mouth are "clean," and thus, creating a violation of not only the Torah prohibitions, but also the "oral" Torah prohibitions regarding eating only what constituted "kosher foods" under Jewish law.[3] But in all reality, the more accurate interpretation of Jesus' teaching here is actually more closely aligned with what is found in *Midrash Psalms* 2,[4] which states, "As the sea throws up its debris upon the shores, so the wicked have filthiness upon their mouths," and Rabbi Boteach points out that this is referred to as *lashon nekiah*, "clean language," which goes alongside the term *lashon ha-ra*, "evil language."[5]

In *Leviticus Rabbah* 33:1 there is a story of a rabbi telling one of his students to go to the market and buy some "good food." The student returned with "tongue." The rabbi then tells the student to go to the market and buy some food that is "bad." Again the student returned with "tongue," to which the rabbi said to his student, "When I told you to buy food that is good, you bought tongue, and when I told you to buy food that is bad, you also bought tongue." The student then replied to his teacher, "From a tongue can come good and from a tongue can come bad. When a tongue is good, there is nothing better. But when a tongue is bad, there is nothing worse,"[6] and from this story it should then become very easy

---

Jesus in Jewish Tradition," in *The Trial of Jesus: Cambridge Studies in Honour of C. F. D. Moule*, pp. 103-121; *Victory Over Violence*, Martin Hengel, p. 56; *The Jews and the Gospel*, Gregory Baum, pp. 27-28; *Mark*, Robert H. Gundry, pp. 347-371.

2   See the comments in *On Earth As It Is In Heaven*, D. C. Thielmann, pp. 697-698, and pp. 701-704; *Jewish Law from Jesus to the Mishnah*, E. P. Sanders, p. 28.

3   For a brief commentary on Jewish abstinence from certain "foods," see the comments in *The New Testament and Jewish Law*, James G. Crossley, pp. 103-109.

4   See the comments on this in *Kosher Jesus*, Rabbi Shmuley Boteach, pp. 32-33, and see his further comments in *Kosher Jesus*, Rabbi Shmuley Boteach, pp. 106-108.

5   See the comments on this term in *Love Your Neighbor*, Rabbi Zelig Pliskin, pp. 24, 98-106, 134-135, 231-239, 261-270, 417-419; *Jewish Literacy*, Rabbi Joseph Telushkin, pp. 585-587, 612-613.

6   *Love Your Neighbor*, Rabbi Zelig Pliskin, pp. 325-331.

for *anyone* to recognize exactly what Jesus was actually teaching in these verses noted above!

Lloyd Gaston points out another matter concerning this when he writes,[7] "It is twice emphasized (Luke 10:7-8) that the messengers are to eat whatever is put before them, without questioning whether or not it is clean or whether or not tithes have been paid. As we shall see (Luke 11:39, 42) these two points are ones the Church disputed with the Pharisees, as well as among themselves (Acts 11:3)."[8] Thus, Gaston's comments give clear indication that these matters from Luke/Acts are in *fact* only a reflection of a much later interpolation that arose from the separation of Church from Synagogue noted several times already in the two previous chapters, and which will be noted even further in later chapters.[9] Therefore, it is hardly the accurate interpretation of this parable teaching of Jesus to believe that he declared *all foods* "clean." In fact, there is an excellent article regarding the fact that it is a totally erroneous interpretation to believe that Jesus had somehow "declared all foods clean."[10] This article rightly points out that it was *never permitted* to eat *any* foods offered to idols (see for example, Revelation 2:20). Mary Douglas as well,[11] rightly points out that even in *The Penitential of Theodore*, (Archbishop of Canterbury, CE 668-690), it is found being written, "If without knowing it one eats what is polluted by blood or any unclean thing, it is nothing; but if he knows, he shall do penance according to the degree of pollution...." Josephus in *Jewish Wars* 2.8.10(152) *clearly* writes about the Jewish attitude regarding Torah forbidden foods, and thus, if one were to attempt to negate, or abrogate the Torah regulations regarding such forbidden foods they most certainly *would not* have gained any followers the likes of which Jesus is reported to have gained. It is true though, that it seems that more and more

---

7   *No Stone on Another*, Lloyd Gaston, p. 318.

8   See also the comments on this in *Jewish Christianity Reconsidered*, Matt Jackson-McCabe, p. 146, (William Arnal commenting).

9   While I admit that James Dunn does an excellent overall job in detailing this separation in *The Partings of the Ways*, I also desire to state that I *do not* agree with all of his assertions, and therefore I recommend that readers read his book with an "open and critical mind."

10 See "Does Romans 14 Abolish Laws on Unclean Meats," January 31, 2011, by *United Church of God*.

11 *Purity and Danger*, Mary Douglas, p. 75.

Christian scholars are beginning to change their opinions and somewhat admit that this "common interpretation" that so many scholars for far too long now have offered is "possibly biased."[12] The fact is though, that such interpretations are more than just *possibly* biased," there should be no doubt in the mind of *any* scholar that such interpretations *are* "biased."[13] For the real truth to the matter is that the *best* interpretation of the Greek words used actually refer to the *natural bodily gastrointestinal function of* "purging" everything "we eat,*" and thus, this then *does not* distinguish nor does it give any indication whatsoever as to whether this is in regards to *kosher foods* consumed by Jews, or *non-kosher foods* that *may be* consumed by gentiles. *Period!*

Going further into this matter though, let us take for example, pigs, which were considered to be an "unclean" animal to Jews, and therefore, not to be consumed as food,[14] and to which even Jesus in Matthew 7:6 considered pigs to be "unclean." Modern archaeologists have found very few skeletal remains of pigs anywhere in Galilee and those skeletal remains that *have been* discovered were found *only* in areas of Galilee that were dominated by a gentile population.[15] The breeding of pigs was forbidden as stated in *Menahot* 64b, and it was also further forbidden to even keep any flocks of pigs as stated in *Baba Kamma* 7:7; *Baba Kamma* 82b; *Yerushalmi Shekalim* 47c; *Sotah* 49b, and thus, pigs came to be referred to as the "emblem of filthiness," *Berakhot* 43b.[16] Thus, this is the very reason why we find the accounts in Mark 5:1-20; Luke 8:26-39 of Jesus casting out demons into a herd of *unclean swine*. Jesus' parables have been very badly misunderstood and misinterpreted by so many scholars for far too

---

12   See the comments in *The Historical Jesus in Context*, Levine, Allison Jr., and Crossan, pp. 5-6 and 32; *Jesus and the Laws of Purity*, Roger P. Booth, pp. 68-74.

13   See the proof to this in *Revolution in Judaea*, Hyam Maccoby, p. 107; *On Earth As It Is In Heaven*, D. C. Thielmann, scholars notations n. 114-116, p. 771.

14   See the comments on this in *Purity and Danger*, Mary Douglas, pp. 36-40, 51-71.

15   See the comments in *The Misunderstood Jew*, Amy-Jill Levine, p. 25; *The Historical Jesus in Context*, Levine, Allison Jr., Crossan, p. 53.

16   See the comments of Emil G. Hirsch and I. M. Casanowicz, "Swine," *Jewish Encyclopedia*.

long now.[17] But Hyam Maccoby points out though, that,[18] "A live pig, for example is totally 'clean' in the ritual purity sense. To touch one does not produce impurity. In the case of dead animals, however, the two senses of 'unclean' already impinge on one another: for the carcass of an 'unclean' animal (in the sense of 'forbidden for food') produces 'uncleanness' (in the sense of 'ritual impurity') more readily than the carcass of a 'clean' (permitted for food) animal, the later causing impurity only if it dies of natural causes." This matter that Maccoby is referring to here is derived directly from what is stated in Leviticus 11:8; 11:24-40.

Now, Warren Carter makes an interesting interpretation worth noting here in regards to this matter when he asserts that Jesus' casting out of the demons into the herd of swine was actually a direct reflection of Jesus' disdain for Roman Imperial power. As Carter writes,[19] "One example is especially compelling. Jesus throws out demons into pigs who charge over a cliff to their watery doom (Matthew 8:28-34). The pig was the mascot of Rome's Tenth Fretensis Legion that was stationed at Antioch and that played a prominent part in the destruction of Jerusalem in 70 CE."[20] Each Roman legion had some sort of animal on its flag standard to distinguish one legion from another, and it was the very placement of such a flag standard by Pilate in Jerusalem, (which was a *clear* violation of Jewish law as found in Exodus 20:4; Deuteronomy 4:16; 5:8), that sparked a Jewish uprising in protest.[21] The importance of understanding this matter regarding the Tenth Fretensis Legion lies in the fact that the Roman governor of Judea, (i.e. Pontius Pilate at the time of Jesus), could call upon the Roman

---

17   See the comments in *On Earth As It Is In Heaven*, D. C. Thielmann, pp. 694-697 for a good
       explanation of these misunderstandings. But as examples of these various misunderstandings
       see *Jesus: Uncovering the Life, Teachings, and Relevance of a Religious Revolutionary*,
       Marcus Borg, pp. 52-54, and an excellent refutation to Borg's claims in *The Misunderstood
       Jew*, Amy-Jill Levine, pp. 34-36; and see further, *Understanding the Difficult Words of
       Jesus*, David Bivin and Roy Blizzard, p. 47; *The Mythmaker*, Hyam Maccoby, p. 44.

18   *Ritual an Morality*, Hyam Maccoby, p. 67.

19   *Matthew and Empire*, Warren Carter, p. 71.

20   *Matthew and Empire*, Warren Carter, n. 43, p. 191, *Matthew and the Margins: A Socio
       Political and Religious Reading*, Warren Carter, pp. 211-214.

21   See the comments on this in *Jesus and the Spiral of Violence*, Richard A. Horsley, pp.
       100-105.

legion stationed at Antioch to assist the Judean governor in any matter that Pilate, (or any other Roman governor/procurator of Judea), deemed necessary for such use of these Roman troops. Thus, as will be pointed out in later chapters, quite often if the Romans were searching for even just *one* individual who was "wanted" for a violation of a *Roman law*, they would use the threat of calling upon these troops stationed in Antioch to come and utterly destroy Jerusalem, the Temple, and all of the Judean population if there was any refusal to assist the Romans in the capture, and/or the "turning over" of this "wanted" individual to the Romans.[22] To go one step further into this though, the fact that Mark 5:9, 15; Luke 8:30 use the name "Legion" for this demonic spirit that Jesus cast out adds further weight to the implication that this Greek word used, (*legion*),[23] is an actual reference to this Roman Tenth Fretensis Legion consisting of 6000 soldiers,[24] and in *Leviticus Rabbah* 13:5 the "pig" was referred to as the representation of Rome in its entirety. But Carter goes on further to state that, "The exorcism represents, among other things, Jesus' victory over the demonic forces, the throwing out of Rome." While this interpretation may possibly be true, one needs to also look at Matthew 7:6, for the real point to be made here is in the *fact* that Jesus casts demons into an *unclean* animal, which *directly contradicts* any claims that Jesus "declared all foods clean." Once again it must be stated for emphasis that it is true though, that many modern scholars have now begun to realize, accept, and admit that they have very badly misunderstood the teachings that Jesus was putting forth in his parables[25] as well as his other actions.

One of the main causes for the misinterpretations of Matthew 15:11; Mark 7:15 derives from the fact that Paul, in 1 Corinthians 8:1-13 allows gentiles to continue to eat foods that were offered to idols, and this despite the fact that this was in direct contradiction to the decision that had been made by James and the Jerusalem Church that is found in Acts 15:19. This fact, according to some scholars,[26] is precisely what led to the later

---

22   *Pontius Pilate in History and Interpretation*, Helen K. Bond, pp. 5, 13-14.

23   See the *Strong's Concordance*, Greek Dictionary, #3003; *BDAG Greek-English Lexicon*, pp. 587-588.

24   See the comments on this in *Mark*, Robert H. Gundry, pp. 262-263.

25   See for example *The Last Week*, Marcus Borg and John Dominic Crossan, p. 193.

26   See for example the comments in *The Mythmaker*, Hyam Maccoby, p. 149.

Gospel authors' interpolation that seemingly has Jesus declaring that "all foods are clean." While this may be true to some degree, this does not explain the reason why so many scholars still misunderstand what Jesus really meant by what he stated in this parable. Therefore, it is essential to present a completely different interpretation of what Jesus actually said in Matthew 15:20,[27] for as Matthew's Gospel has it, Jesus only meant that, "to eat with unwashed hands does not defile a man," which then *would not* contradict any Jewish understanding of the law at the time of Jesus! It was from Paul's teachings where the concept was then placed onto Jesus' lips that Jesus had declared "all foods clean" as can be found derived from 1 Corinthians 10:25-26 for example, and thus, it is from Paul's teachings that the Christian concept of Jesus' negating the "purity" laws arose.[28] Yet, Paul, in 1 Timothy 5:22 *clearly* instructs one to "keep yourself pure," and the historical fact is that even the majority of Diaspora Jews held to the Torah regulations regarding forbidden foods,[29] a matter that can be found mentioned in Romans 14:1-4, 14, 17-21 in which Paul distinguishes between those who hold to the Torah in regards to food restrictions and those who do not hold to the Torah food restrictions, and Paul does so without distinguishing whether or not he was referring to Jews or gentiles. But one can assume that such a distinction is being implied based on Romans 1:16; 2:9-10; 10:12. Furthermore, as will be discussed in Chapter 4, Paul's teachings were "heretical" in that they deviated from the very teachings of Jesus!

Now, James Dunn contradicts himself on this matter,[30] for while Dunn at first claims that Jesus tried to negate the "purity" laws, especially in regards to the supposed matter of declaring "all foods clean," Dunn then goes on to rightly point out concerning Acts 10:14; 11:8 that, "Such testimony as to the earliest community's continuing faithfulness on the matter of food laws and table-fellowship provides one of the strongest reasons for questioning

---

27   See the comments on this in *No Stone on Another*, Lloyd Gaston, p. 93.

28   See the comments on this in *The Partings of the Ways*, James Dunn, pp. 81-85; *Jesus*, David Flusser, p. 44.

29   See the comments on this in *Jewish Law from Jesus to the Mishnah*, E. P. Sanders, pp. 272-284.

30   See *The Partings of the Ways*, James Dunn, p. 118 contradicting what is noted above from pp. 81-85.

whether Jesus was so clearly as radical on the subject of food laws as Mark 7:15 and 19 indicate." Other scholars, such as Roger P. Booth for example, also erroneously attempt to reference Leviticus 17:15 in regards to this matter. For as Booth writes,[31] "The most likely cultic purification for a man defiled by food eaten would be immersion in a miqvah followed by waiting until sunset (cf. Lev. 17:15)." But Mark 7 refers *specifically* to the eating of bread, whereas Leviticus 17:15 speaks of the eating of an animal that has died on its own, whether in the wild, or a domesticated animal in the field, or also to an animal that had died in a trap or snare, and there is a *vast* difference between these very matters! Also, as Barrie Wilson points out concerning the *Epistle of Barnabas*,[32] it came to be believed by many that the Torah's "dietary" laws were *not* to be understood "literally." Now, while it is true that the Hebrew Scriptures, including the Torah, *should not* be interpretedwith "literal-mindedness,"[33] because Hebrew is a very "idiomatic" language, at the same time one *should not* over "spiritualize" the Hebrew, which will cause far too many misrepresentations of meaning as the *Epistle of Barnabas* proves! Wilson then writes about what is stated on this matter in the *Epistle of Barnabas*, saying, "No one would consider advancing such a wild argument today." Yet, the *Epistle of Barnabas* was a fairly widely distributed writing that influenced the thinking of many, and it seems that it even still influences the opinions of many modern scholars today!

In regards to the matter of Mark 7, discussed above, many scholars[34] refer to the Greek word *koinas* that is used in Mark 7:5, (which is more often than not, translated out as either, "unclean," or "defiled"), coupled with the Greek word *chersin*, (which is generally translated as "hands"), and thus, based on these usual translations/interpretations of these two Greek words the conclusion arrived at is that this verse is talking about Jesus violating

---

31 *Jesus and the Laws of Purity*, Roger P. Booth, p. 72.

32 *How Jesus Became Christian*, Barrie Wilson, pp. 202-204.

33 See the comments on this in *On Earth As It Is In Heaven*, D. C. Thielmann, pp. 129-139 and the corresponding scholars notations to these pages.

34 See for example, *Jesus and the Laws of Purity*, Roger P. Booth, pp. 32-33; but see also the erroneous comments in *Conflict, Holiness & Politics*, Marcus Borg, pp. 96-99.

some "tradition of the elders."[35] Yet, it seems that no scholar has bothered to even consider that what is *actually* being referred to, by way of the other possible meanings of these two Greek words used in Mark 7:5, is what is now referred to as the *Eucharist* – the "communal breaking of bread"![36] For these two Greek words, as they are found in their contextual usage in this verse, offer the meaning of, "communicating by way of handing over to eat, bread," just as is done in the Last Supper, and the Communal Meal described in 1 Corinthians 11:17-34, the *Didache* 9:1-5,[37] and also in the Dead Sea Scrolls. Roger Booth does rightly make mention though,[38] of the fact that "of the feedings of the thousands, and of the Last Supper, Jesus blessed, broke and gave the food," exactly as prescribed in *Berakhot* 6:1-8! So again, is the truth of this matter then, in all reality, that Mark 7 has been very badly misunderstood and taken completely out of context simply because of the later teachings of Paul? (Once again, more will be said about Paul's teachings in Chapter 4).

Going further though, into the interpretation of the Greek word *koinas* that is used in Mark 7:5, this word has been interpreted by some scholars as "shared,"[39] such as it gets used, for example, in Acts 2:44; 4:32. Such an interpretation would then lend further *proof* to the fact that this matter in Mark 7 has been very badly misinterpreted for far too long. For this then demonstrates that the meaning in these verses from Mark's Gospel indicate the "breaking and sharing of the bread." But as with most scholars who choose to interpret this word *koinas*, Roger Booth chooses to interpret this word as meaning "ceremonially impure." Booth then

---

35   For more on this matter see the comments in *On Earth As It Is In Heaven*, D. C. Thielmann, n. 157, p. 784.

36   For more on this matter see the comments in *On Earth As It Is In Heaven*, D. C. Thielmann, pp. 619-620 and the corresponding scholars notations to these pages. The matter of the "washing of hands before eating bread," is referred to as *netilat yadayim*, as found in the Talmud Babli *Hullin* 106a, and Talmud Babli *Hagigah* 18b, and for more on this see *Jesus of Nazareth*, Joseph Klausner, p. 122; *Jesus and Judaism*, E. P. Sanders, p. 265.

37   In *How Jesus Became Christian*, Barrie Wilson, pp. 156-162, Wilson points out that the *Didache* differs "markedly from Paul's account of the Eucharist and from later Christian tradition, which built on Paul's version."

38   *Jesus and the Laws of Purity*, Roger P. Booth, p. 109.

39   See *Jesus and the Laws of Purity*, Roger P. Booth, pp. 120-124.

chooses to interpret the Greek word *artous*, (which generally is translated as "loaves," or "bread"), as having a meaning of "food" in general, as in "*any kind of food*"! Now, although it is true that while there are some Greek Dictionaries and Lexicons that start off the definition of this Greek word as "baked goods," they *do* tend to then provide such an interpretation for the Greek word *artous*,[40] with a definition of, for example, "any kind of food or nourishment, *food*." Yet, these same Lexicons will *immediately* follow this definition up by stating, "since bread is the most important food," and these Lexicons often cite Isaiah 65:25; Amos 8:11 as proof texts from the Septuagint as their reasoning for giving it a meaning that attempts to indicate, "*all foods*." But other Greek Dictionaries and Lexicons will *only* offer the definition of, "bread"[41] for the Greek word *artous*. Thus, for whatever reason Booth *chooses* to interpret the meaning of *artous* in the context of its usage in Mark 7 is totally without merit! For Booth then utilizes examples of things considered as "defilements" from Leviticus 15, and the Dead Sea Scroll the *Damascus Document* 12:15-17 as proof for his desired interpretation even though the things listed in Leviticus 15 and *The Damascus Document* 12:15-17 have absolutely nothing whatsoever to do with "food." At this point it is essential to point out what is written in the *Didache* 6:1-3, which states, "And concerning food, bear what you can. But especially keep from food sacrificed to idols; for this is a ministry to dead gods."[42] The importance of understanding this lies in the fact that this is *precisely* what is commanded in the Noahide covenant, which was *exactly* what was reiterated by James and the Jerusalem Church found in the dispute between Paul, James and Peter in Acts 15!

But going a step further into this matter, there is a question that begs to be asked, and this being, if Mark's Gospel had intended that the interpretation be indicating "*all* foods," then why did the author of Mark's Gospel not use the Greek word *trophe*? For the use of this particular Greek word, in conjunction with the Greek word *bromata* in Mark 7:19, (a word which generally gets translated out as "foods," but is *best* understood as only indicating "meats," just as it is found being used in 1 Corinthians

---

40   See for example the *BDAG Greek-English Lexicon*, p. 136 under definition #2.

41   See for example *Liddell and Scott's Greek-English Lexicon*, p. 121.

42   See the comments on this in *Jewish Christianity Reconsidered*, Matt Jackson-McCabe, pp. 260-263, (Jonathan A. Draper commenting).

6:13 for example), would then bring about another question, (which as just pointed out above will be discussed further in Chapter 4), and this question being, did Mark derive what is written in 7:1-23 from an actual historical Jesus event, or did he simply derive this story from the teachings of Paul in 1 Corinthians 6:13? Going a step further into this matter of "meats," Rabbi Joseph Telushkin rightly points out[43] that in Deuteronomy 12:21 Moses instructs the Israelites that they, "may slaughter any kind of cattle or sheep that the Lord gives you," yet Telushkin notes that, "but we look in vain for any verses in the Torah with instructions about how to carry out the kosher slaughter of animals." Therefore, this is just one example of the very debates over the "oral" interpretations of what constituted something being "ritually clean" or "ritually unclean" in such matters as the consuming of "food," which goes all the way back to the time that the Torah was written, (this matter regarding the "oral" Torah will be expounded upon in Chapters 4 and 5, especially in regards to the scholars who claim that no such "oral" Torah even existed until the Mishnah was written). Thus, Booth does rightly state then,[44] that there *were* very divergent views amongst the different factions of the Pharisees over the matters of "defilement" by things considered to be "unclean." Booth then states that,[45] "The possibility that many or even the large majority of, Pharisees did *not* feel legally obliged to wash their hands is not then important to our enquiry, for if *some* did, it is reasonable to assume that it was they who asked the question." Indeed, this could be quite true, but the main focus by scholars then should be on the words, "tradition of the elders." For *if*, as Booth rightly admits, that only *some* of the Pharisees *did* hold to such a standard, but *not* the "large majority of Pharisees," then the entire matter *would not*, nor *could it be* termed a "tradition of the elders!" Booth is quite correct when he writes,[46] "If it was neither legally required, nor customary, for Jews or a group of Jews to wash their hands before eating, then the previously posited authenticity of the earliest form of the

---

43   *Hillel*, Rabbi Joseph Telushkin, p. 31.

44   *Jesus and the Laws of Purity*, Roger P. Booth, pp. 125-126.

45   *Jesus and the Laws of Purity*, Roger P. Booth, p. 127, but see also his additional comments on p. 153.

46   *Jesus and the Laws of Purity*, Roger P. Booth, p. 151; but see also the comments in *Jesus and Purity Halakah*, pp. 60-78.

dispute is seriously prejudiced."[47] But now it is true, (as was pointed out in Chapter 2 and will be again noted in Chapter 4), that many Pharisees *were* in fact Temple Priests,[48] who were thus, required to then follow the Levitical laws of purity even in their own homes, and thus, this incident recorded in Mark's Gospel might have involved a Pharisaic Priest, which then provides the possibility that it *could* be historically true.[49] As Thomas Kazen states,[50] "As for officiating priests, the washing of hands *and* feet were part of their purification, but for ordinary people, we have to admit that evidence is uncertain, both with regard to meals and visits to the Temple." Yet nonetheless, Jesus *would not have*, nor should it be interpreted by any scholar as indicating that Jesus declared "*all* foods clean," for it *must be* reiterated that Mark 7:1-5 *specifically* refers to *only* the eating of "bread" and *not* to the eating of *all foods*!

Now, Booth goes on and relates this matter to *Shabbat* 14b, (as well as to several other Talmudic Tractates),[51] but once again, *Shabbat* 14b *only* specifically discusses matters as they relate to *terumah*, which means, "heave offering,"[52] (a matter that deals *only specifically* with "Priests" in other words, and *not* to *all* Jews at the time of Jesus).[53] For *terumah* was a "present made to the Tabernacle or Temple for the use by the Priests" *only* and which even applied to Priests eating in their own homes, and which Booth clearly states that the "laymen Jew" at the time of Jesus did not partake in the matters concerning *terumah*.[54] As Hyam Maccoby states

---

47   See further the comments in *Jesus and the Laws of Purity*, Roger P. Booth, pp. 199-200.

48   See the comments on this in *Jesus the Pharisee*, Harvey Falk, pp. 151-152.

49   See the comments on this in *Jesus and the Laws of Purity*, Roger P. Booth, pp. 202-203.

50   *Jesus and Purity Halakah*, Thomas Kazen, p. 254; but see also the comments in *Ritual and Morality*, Hyam Maccoby, pp. 155-161.

51   *Jesus and the Laws of Purity*, Roger P. Booth, pp. 169-187.

52   See the comments on the word *terumah* in *Jesus and the Laws of Purity*, Roger P. Booth, p. 151; Emil G. Hirsch, "Heave Offering," *Jewish Encyclopedia*; *Galilee*, Sean Freyne, p. 278.

53   See the comments in *A Rabbi Talks with Jesus*, Jacob Neusner, pp. 116-132; *Jewish Law from Jesus to the Mishnah*, E. P. Sanders, pp. 39-40.

54   *Jesus and the Laws of Purity* Roger P. Booth, p. 194; *Paul Was Not a Christian*, Pamela Eisenbaum, p. 130; but see also the comments on this entire matter in *Jews, Greeks and Christians*, (Edited by Roger Hammerton-Kelly and Robin Scroggs), Jacob Neusner commenting, pp. 96-111.

---

concerning this,[55] "Only a tiny minority of Jews, known as *haberim*, or Associates, made a special undertaking to keep themselves in a state of ritual purity, as an exercise in piety and in order to perform the service to the community of separating the priestly dues (*terumah*) from the crop without causing them defilement."[56]

It is true though, that one can find an account in *Numbers Rabbah* 20.21 of an inn-keeper who mistook a Jew for an "idolater" because the individual did not wash or give the prescribed blessing[57] before eating, but it is also known that this *particular* story derives from some time well *after* the time of Jesus. So while this story could be used by some scholars to try and establish that there *was* such a "tradition of the elders" at the time of Jesus, the fact is that this *does not* place any sort of "tradition of the elders" as this at the time of Jesus as *Avodah Zarah* 3:10; *Eruvin* 21b give *clear* evidence as *proof* of this *fact!*[58] Josephus in *Antiquities* 3.320 talks about a year in which a severe drought was occurring at Passover time and the priests refused to eat leavened bread even though it was the only bread available at the time during this drought whereas others *were* eating leavened bread at that particular Passover despite the prohibition found in Exodus 12:8. Josephus also writes in *Antiquities* 20.181, 206-207 about priests allowing themselves to starve to death rather than violate the dietary laws, a matter which occurred because someone had stolen the tithes that the priests depended upon. Thus, there were times when the priests were far stricter in regards to observing dietary matters, but placed such a strict

---

55 *Ritual and Morality*, Hyam Maccoby, p. 149, but see also his further comments on pp. 209-213.

56 See further on this in *Ritual and Morality*, Hyam Maccoby, n. 1, p. 149 who references Solomon J. Spiro, "Who was the *Haber*? A New Approach to an Ancient Institution," *Journal for the Study of Judaism*, 2, (1980), pp. 186-216. But see also on this matter Solomon Schecter and S. Mendelsohn, "Haber, ('associate'; 'colleague'; 'fellow')," *Jewish Encyclopedia*.

57 There were even many debates between the Schools of Hillel and Shammai over this matter of whether or not a "blessing" was required before, or even after the eating of even just "bread" much less the debates over the "washing of hands" before the eating of even "bread" as can be found noted in the comments in *On Jewish Law and Lore*, Louis Ginzberg, p. 104.

58 See the comments on this in *Jesus and His Adversaries*, Arland J. Hultgren, p. 115.

observance *only* upon themselves, to which some scholars equate this strict observance of dietary matters to what is stated in portions of Daniel,[59] (a writing already discussed previously in Chapter 2).

Now, some scholars are quite in error when they claim that,[60] "Interpretations in terms of hygiene belong almost exclusively to the modern era, and were in the past often coupled with attempts to find rationale explanations for otherwise incomprehensible rules." But the Mishnah tractate *Berurah* and specifically, *Berurah* 2:7; 27:15, 260; and 551 are simply loaded with examples of halakha related to "personal hygiene." Rabbi Joseph Telushkin even discusses the specific matters at the time of Hillel, (or in other words, some twenty to thirty years or more prior to the ministry of Jesus), surrounding "personal hygiene," stating that, "standards of personal hygiene were low."[61] Now, simply because the "standards of hygiene" amongst the everyday Jew were "low," *does not* mean that there were no "halakhic interpretations" regarding "personal hygiene" at or before the time of Jesus. For Telushkin goes on to then relate a story in *Leviticus Rabbah* 34:3 of how Hillel gave a teaching lesson to his students about going to the *miqvah* after his class lesson in order to teach the importance of "personal hygiene." Thus, one finds that this is a perfect example of how there *was not* any *one standard* that could be called a "tradition of the elders" at the time of Jesus in regards to the "washing of hands" before the eating of "bread!"[62] As examples of this diversity of opinions, in *Yoma* 83b; *Hulin* 106a it is stated that the "washing of hands" before saying the blessing for a meal was superior to the "washing of hands" before actually eating a meal, and in *Hulin* 106b it is found being stated that "washing" first thing in the morning would cause one to be "ritually clean" to eat meals for the entire day. Yet, in *Eduyot* 5:6 Eleazar ben Ḥanok was excommunicated[63]

---

59   See for example *Paul Was Not a Christian*, Pamela Eisenbaum, pp. 86-88.

60   See *Jesus and Purity Halakah*, Thomas Kazen, pp. 2-3.

61   See the comments on this in *Hillel*, Rabbi Joseph Telushkin, pp. 65-66, and 165.

62   In *How Jesus Became Christian*, Barrie Wilson, pp. 190-191, Wilson is in error in his overall conclusions about this matter, but he is quite correct in stating that this matter was highly debated at the time of Jesus; see also the correct comments on this in *Jesus the Pharisee*, Harvey Falk, pp. 149-150.

63   See the comments of Solomon Schechter and Julius H. Greenstone, "Excommunication (Hebrew, 'niddui,' 'ḥerem')," *Jewish Encyclopedia*; Morris Jastrow, Jr., Kaufmann Kohler,

for "undermining the authority of the elders"[64] by not "ritually washing" before meals, and then we further have the account in *Baba Kamma* 1:6 of Simeon the Essen who refused to even "wash his hands or his feet" before even entering the Temple, much less before eating meals because he believed that his ascetic life that he lived already made him "ritually clean" enough to both enter the Temple and to eat meals.[65] Another example can be found in *Tosephta Berakhot* 5:13, which states that, "Washing hands before a meal is a matter of choice, ablution after a meal is obligatory."[66] Yet, *none* of these individuals who gave these opinions that are recorded in the Mishnah and Talmud was *ever* condemned to a "death sentence" by the Great Sanhedrin for their varying opinions on this matter, which only serves to *prove* that *any* scholar attempting to claim that it was this very matter that got Jesus into trouble with some sort of Jewish authorities to the point that they desired his death is grossly in error!

In *Yoma* 77b and *Tosefta Yoma* 5:2 is related an account about one *not* "washing" even their "hands" on Yom Kippur even to feed their children, which then talks about this practice being suspended so that for the child's health *only*, one *should* "wash" both "hands" before feeding their child, but *not* in regards to feeding themselves, or anyone else![67] Rabbi Telushkin further points out[68] that out of the many debates between the different Pharisaic Schools before, during, and even long *after* the time of Jesus a vast majority of these debates were in regards to the matters of "ritual purity." *Sanhedrin* 88b records that the differences of opinions on these matters virtually amounted to "two Torahs!"[69] As Telushkin writes in regards to *Eruvin* 13b,[70] "There isn't necessarily *only* one way to perform a ritual act that's

---

and Marcus Jastrow, "Banishment," *Jewish Encyclopedia.*

64 See further on this the comments of Jacob Voorsanger and Kaufmann Kohler, "Anathema," *Jewish Encyclopedia.*

65 See the comments on all of this by Bernard Drachman and Kaufmann Kohler, "Ablution," *Jewish Encyclopedia.*

66 See the comments on this in *Jesus*, David Flusser, pp. 46-48.

67 See the comments on this in *Hillel*, Rabbi Joseph Telushkin, p. 84 and n. 1, p. 226.

68 *Hillel*, Rabbi Joseph Telushkin, pp. 112-113.

69 For more on this matter see the comments in *The Literature of the Sages*, Shmuel Safrai, p. 186.

70 *Hillel*, Rabbi Joseph Telushkin, p. 119.

acceptable to God. The disputes of Hillel and Shammai were largely about issues such as purity and impurity, and matters concerning blessings, issues for which you would think that there is only one right way. Nonetheless, the Heavenly Voice teaches: 'The teachings of both are the words of the Living God'." Furthermore, as E. P. Sanders rightly states,[71] "We now ask the meaning of *purity* in Biblical law. This much-abased word deserves to be used with some respect. Scholars, especially New Testament scholars, often use 'ritual purity' pejoratively to describe the requirements of any group to which they are hostile." The Jewish literature from the period just prior to the time of Jesus to just after the time of Jesus demonstrates and proves this divergence of opinions regarding "purity" and "impurity," and this divergence of opinions derived from the different interpretations of the Torah that pertained to the matters of "purity" and "impurity."[72]

Edgar Goodspeed comments on the Greek word *pugme* used in Mark 7:3, a word that in English is often rendered out as either "oft," or sometimes as "with a fist," or even as "in a particular way."[73] But the *best* and more accurate meaning of this Greek word is, "to fist fight," such as in "boxing," and thus, what is most likely to be the truth behind what is being stated in this account in Mark 7 is that there was "disagreement" and "fighting" not only amongst the different factions of Pharisees, but also amongst the different Jewish philosophies at the time of Jesus, (and more will be said on this matter in Chapter 4), in regards to interpretations surrounding the matter of "washing of hands," (each faction of each Jewish philosophy interpreted the matter according to their own "traditions"), which would then make this *best* understanding of the words to be a more accurate understanding of the *historical* truth of this matter in Mark 7. It is true though, that this matter *was* in fact a matter that was much more prominent amongst Diaspora Jews and pagan gentiles than it was with Palestinian Jews as noted by Josephus *Antiquities* 12.206; *Letter of Aristeas* 304-306; *Iliad* 24.302-306.[74] This fact then, once again proves that the

---

71 *Jewish Law from Jesus to the Mishnah*, E. P. Sanders, p. 137.

72 See the comments on this in *The Idea of Purity in Ancient Judaism*, Jacob Neusner, pp. 32-71.

73 See the comments in *Problems with New Testament Translation*, Edgar J. Goodspeed, pp. 59-60.

74 See the comments on this in *Jewish Law from Jesus to the Mishnah*, E. P. Sanders, pp. 260-262.

statement in Mark's Gospel about a "tradition of the elders" could only have come about from a period *long after* the time of Jesus when the Church had become dominated by gentiles as well as by a few Diaspora Jews![75] Now, these matters of debating over what was and was not "ritually pure," were in regards to one's own home and private affairs. But, when it came to the Temple this then was a different matter entirely, for *no one* was to enter the Temple unless they were *tahor*, (meaning "ritually pure" at the time), and we know from the Gospel accounts that Jesus went to the Temple on more than one occasion, and thus, if Jesus had been *tamei*, (meaning "ritually impure" at the time), he would have been forbidden to enter the Temple before first immersing in a *miqvah*, and possibly even having to bring an offering to the Temple, depending on the severity of the *tamei*.[76] Now of course, this would be true *unless* Jesus believed, (just as Simeon the Essen noted above), that the "ascetic" life that Jesus lived already made him "ritually pure"!

Roger Booth, in connection with Mark 7:1-7, (but primarily in regards to Mark 7:6-7), also discusses Isaiah 29:13,[77] since these particular verses in Mark's Gospel reference Isaiah 29:13. Although Booth rightly points out that the Septuagint version of Isaiah 29:13[78] is quite different from what is actually stated in the Hebrew version of Isaiah 29:13, and Booth further points out that Mark is utilizing the erroneous Septuagint version in Mark 7:6-7, yet Booth quite erroneously interprets Isaiah 29:13 as referring to "the commandments of men." But the fact is that the more accurate and *best* understanding of the Hebrew words used in the overall *context* of Isaiah 29:13 – *yir'atham ethiy mitzvoth anashiym melumadah* – means, "giving more reverence to the *mitzvoth* of the learned men." In essence, and in simplest terms, Isaiah 29:13 *does not* state that the people were "following the commandments of men," it states that the people were, "*giving more reverence to the mitzvoth of the learned men*" than they were "giving reverence"

---

75   See the comments on this from Rabbi Steven Bernstein, "Traditions of the Elders." *Aydat HaDerekh.*

76   See the comments in *Hillel*, Rabbi Joseph Telushkin, pp. 215-216.

77   *Jesus and the Laws of Purity*, Roger P. Booth, pp. 38-40.

78   See also the comments in *Jesus and Purity Halakah*, Thomas Kazen, pp. 62-72, yet Kazen's conclusions, which are based on the comments of Roger P. Booth are just as erroneous as those of Booth and other scholars, (see further Kazen's erroneous comments on pp. 86-88).

to God! Christian scholars have for far too long now, badly misunderstood the Hebrew word, *mitzvah*, (one of the few Hebrew words that simply *cannot* be accurately translated into any other language),[79] and it is this very misunderstanding that is showing forth in Booth's erroneous assertions. For there is a *vast* difference in understanding between "revering the *mitzvoth* of men," and "following the commandments of men!" Now, Booth *does* in fact point out later this more accurate interpretation of Isaiah 29:13,[80] but he does so only in reference to its possible usage by the later Church against the Synagogue. Booth also references Philo, *The Special Laws* III.208-209,[81] which comments upon Numbers 19:22 and which seemingly parallels Jesus' remarks found in Mark 7:15. But from this reference to Philo, the question begs to be asked; if Philo speaks similarly to Jesus on this matter, then would the Pharisees not also then have likewise been aware of this interpretation of Philo? Also, another question that begs to be asked, which even Booth seems to ask,[82] is this; is it not then possible that Mark actually just created this story by deriving it from Philo's comments?

A further point to make though, derives from the fact that so many modern Christian New Testament scholars have erroneously misunderstood Jesus' teachings regarding "families," and especially in regards to what they refer to as, "peasant families." I am specifically referring here to Matthew 10:34-36; Mark 3:31-35; 10:29; and Luke 12:51-53, which speak of setting "a man at variance against his father," etc. (which, by the way, is simply a reflection of a statement found in *Sotah* 49a). The claim most often offered by such scholars is that Jesus was trying to repair and replace families who were "not viable."[83] But this is hardly an accurate interpretation of

---

79 See the comments on this Hebrew word *mitzvah* in *On Earth As It Is In Heaven*, D. C. Thielmann, pp. 64-72 and the corresponding scholars notations to these pages.

80 *Jesus and the Laws of Purity*, Roger P. Booth, pp. 91-94.

81 *Jesus and the Laws of Purity*, Roger P. Booth, pp. 83-90.

82 *Jesus and the Laws of Purity*, Roger P. Booth, p. 105.

83 See as an example, *The New Testament*, Bart D. Ehrman, Box 16.9, p. 269, but on p. 428 Ehrman points out that this interpretation actually came about at a much later time from the early followers of Jesus, so it is confusing as to why scholars would still claim such when they know that this interpretation derived from a much later time.

what Jesus was actually teaching here.[84] Leviticus 19:17 *clearly* states that one should *not* "hate your brother," and Leviticus 19:18 states that one should, "not take revenge or bear a grudge against members of your own people," which can be found noted in the Talmud, *Erchin* 16b,[85] and this is precisely what Jesus is reported to have stated as well in Matthew 5:22-24.[86] But one should also not forget that Exodus 20:12 states that one should, "Honor your father and mother that your days may be long in the land which the Lord your God gives you."[87] As David Bivin and Roy Blizzard point out[88] the Hebrew idioms for the word, "house," offers a wide array of meanings from, "a dwelling," "home," "household," "family," "tribe," "dynasty," "a rabbinic school," and even the "Temple" itself. Now, "Torah teachers," (such as Jesus was), "should consider his students" (or in the case of Jesus, his "disciples," in other words), "as his children" based on Deuteronomy 6:7.[89] Hyam Maccoby goes a step further[90] by pointing out that Jesus' own "brothers," James and Judas, and even his mother became prominent figures in the Jerusalem church, with his "brothers" even writing their own Epistles! Thus, in Maccoby's opinion, (which he very clearly states, and one to which, I might add, that I am in total agreement with), Maccoby believes that this entire notion put forth by scholars about this being about families who were "not viable" is sheer nonsense. The very ending of Malachi (3:22-24), states that, God would "turn the heart of fathers to their children, and the heart of children to their fathers" and that this would occur *after* God had first "sent Elijah," and since the Church, (even in the very Early Church), interpreted John the Baptist to be Elijah sent by God, then this should *clearly* demonstrate that this interpreted notion about Jesus replacing families who were "not viable" is inaccurate, and one which makes absolutely no sense whatsoever! The scholars who

---

84   See the comments in *On Earth As It Is In Heaven*, D. C. Thielmann, pp. 678-680 and the corresponding scholars notations to these pages.

85   See the comments on this in *Love Your Neighbor*, Rabbi Zelig Pliskin, pp. 275-278.

86   See the comments on this in *Problems of New Testament Translation*, Edgar J. Goodspeed, pp. 20-23.

87   See the comments on this in *A Rabbi Talks with Jesus*, Jacob Neusner, pp. 40-57.

88   *Understanding the Difficult Words of Jesus*, David Bivin and Roy Blizzard, p 55.

89   *Love Your Neighbor*, Rabbi Zelig Pliskin, p. 377.

90   *Judas Iscariot and the Myth of Jewish Evil*, Hyam Maccoby, pp. 31-32.

put forth these "nonsensical" interpretations love to refer to Jesus and his movement as a "voice of peasant religious voices," which in all reality is simply a reflection of what is found being stated in *Abot* 1:5; "The poor shall be members of your family."[91] Furthermore, in *Baba Metzia* 58b it clearly indicates that to distress someone with words was worse than cheating them financially.[92] This then, is actually the *best* understanding of Jesus' actions and teachings on this matter.

But another fact though, is that *very few*, if even *any one* of Jesus' closest followers *were* from, so-called, *"peasant"* families. Mark 1:20 *clearly* points out that the "Thunder Brothers" were *hardly* peasants! For they left to follow Jesus leaving behind their father with only "the hired servants," and *peasants did not have* "hired servants." Likewise, neither were Peter and Andrew peasants, (Matthew 4:18-19; Mark 1:16-17)! For "fisherman" and fishing in Galilee was a highly lucrative occupation in first century Palestine![93] Galilee as a whole, in fact, because of how fertile the land was in Galilee, resulted in many highly lucrative occupations,[94] such as vineyards (*Megillah* 6a; *Berakhot* 44a), olive oil (to which it is written in *Genesis Rabbah* 20.6, "It is easier to raise a legion of olive trees in Galilee than one child in Palestine"), plus the manufacturing of special jars to store the olive oil (*Kelim* 2:2), and fine spun home linens were specially woven in Galilee (*Baba Kamma* 119).[95] Although it is true that the *individual* land owners of Galilee struggled to compete with the major *aristocratic* land farmers in regards to the matter of *financial coinage* earned, these small individual family land owners, despite the heavy taxation placed upon them, were still able to make a nice living for their families, and thus, Galilee can hardly be considered as the homeland to a great many, so-called, "peasants"! Eusebius, in *Ecclesiastical History* 3:20 even *clearly* states that the grandchildren of Jude, the brother of Jesus, owned 39 acres of land, which could *hardly* be

---

91   See the comments on this in *Love Your Neighbor*, Rabbi Zelig Pliskin, pp. 153-162.

92   See the comments on this in *Love Your Neighbor*, Rabbi Zelig Pliskin, p. 154.

93   See the comments in *Herod Antipas: A Contemporary of Jesus Christ*, Harold W. Hoehner, pp. 67-70; *The Jews and the Gospel*, Gregory Baum, p. 77; *Jesus and Purity Halakah*, Thomas Kazen, p. 287; *Galilee*, Sean Freyne, pp. 173-176.

94   See the comments in *Galilee*, Sean Freyne, pp. 15-16.

95   See the comments of Emil G. Hirsch, Frants Buhl, and Solomon Schechter, "Galilee," *Jewish Encyclopedia*.

considered as something belonging to a "peasant"! Josephus, in *Life* 66-71 clearly indicates that only the lower-class citizens of the cities of Tiberias and Sepphoris (and the closely surrounding small villages to these two cities) were the *only* Galileans to which one could truly consider as being "suffering peasants"! As Sean Freyne states concerning the individual family land owners of Galilee,[96] "What was readily distinctive about their class was their non-involvement in the larger commercial life of the area. Their farming of the land was not a business but a duty to ancestral loyalties that were deeply embedded and thus resistant to change. Not that they were to be thought of as a ghetto, since life in the country does not give rise to the kind of social isolationism which could be regarded as typical of the city ghetto. Rather their lifestyle and occupation did not bring them into any kind of meaningful contact with the real agents for social change."

The greatest problem with the portrait of the historical Jesus that is most often put forth by modern Christian scholar's lies in the fact that first century Palestinian Jewish people were eager, hungry, and begging for a return to Jewish life to be as it was so clearly laid out in the Torah. Therefore, any and all attempts by these modern Christian New Testament scholars to portray Jesus as somehow teaching a "relaxed attitude towards the Torah" while at the same time claiming that Jesus was somehow gaining a mostly so-called "peasant" following simply *does not* fit the *historical facts*.[97] Moshe Chaim Luzzatto[98] points out that it had long been taught before the time of Jesus that one should not involve themselves with the Torah "scornfully or frivolously," (*Abot* 3:11; *Yoma* 85b; *Shavuot* 13a; *Berakhot* 17a). Thus, trying to offer a "relaxed attitude towards the Torah" to people hungry for things to return to the way matters were laid out in the Torah would *never* have been accepted by *any* first century Palestinian Jewish individual, regardless of whether they were Galilean or Judean! Also, as Joseph Ratzinger and Pope Benedict XVI write,[99] "Jesus lived by the whole of the Law and the Prophets, as he constantly told his

96   *Galilee*, Sean Freyne, p. 195.

97   The Dead Sea Scrolls, the *Psalms of Solomon* 17 and in particular, the entire book *Bandits, Prophets, and Messiahs*, Richard A. Horsley and John S. Hanson, and primarily p. 145 of this book, clearly demonstrate this fact.

98   *The Way of God*, Moshe Chaim Luzzatto, p. 263, and n. 14, p. 426.

99   *Jesus of Nazareth: Part One*, Ratzinger and Pope Benedict, p. 333.

disciples."[100] Likewise, as Joel Carmichael states,[101] "…Hence ultimately of Jesus' Judaism too, it was the Jewish Torah alone that guided the way." Carmichael goes on further to state,[102] "Now, if these instances were really to be interpreted as a systemic form of opposition to Jewish ceremonial, it would be inconceivable why the tradition in the early Church, which eventually swept away the entire Jewish ritual, did not refer this back to Jesus. For the contrary is the case: in Paul's struggle against the 'Judaizers' in the early Church he could not base his relaxation of the Jewish ritual, including the cardinal Jewish rite of circumcision, on anything Jesus was reported to have said."[103]

A further additional problem derives from the claim by so many Christian scholars that the majority of first century Palestinian Jews, (or even Jews in general regardless of where they lived), were "illiterate," even in regards to reading the Torah.[104] Yet, so many of these very scholars who claim that Jesus, as well as most other first century Palestinian Jews were "illiterate," will then reference a writing known as the *Infancy Gospel of Thomas*, and specifically to verses 6:1-7:4 as well as 14:1-15:4, which contains several stories talking about the young Jesus being sent "to school to learn to read."[105] So while on the one hand these scholars have in their hands

---

100　See also the comments in *Jewish Christianity Reconsidered*, Matt Jackson-McCabe, pp. 203-231, (Patrick J. Hartin commenting).

101　*The Death of Jesus*, Joel Carmichael, p. 103.

102　*The Death of Jesus*, Joel Carmichael, pp. 108-109.

103　For more on this very matter see *On Earth As It Is In Heaven*, D. C. Thielmann, Chapter 7.

104　See *Bandits, Prophets, and Messiahs*, Richard A. Horsley and John S. Hanson, p. 160; *Matthew and Empire*, Warren Carter, p. 17; *Jesus and His Contemporaries*, Etienne Trocme, p. 53; *The New Testament*, Bart D. Ehrman, p. 19; *Jesus and the Laws of Purity*, Roger P. Booth, p. 56; *Jesus and the Spiral of Violence*, Richard A. Horsley, p. 155; and the entire book, *Jewish Literacy in Roman Palestine*, Catherine Hezser for examples of the claims that the majority of first century Palestinian Jews were "illiterate." But see also the brief critique that refutes Catherine Hezser's (as well as these other scholars' conclusions) by Meir Bar-Ilan, "Literacy among the Jews in Antiquity: A Review of *Jewish Literacy in Roman Palestine: Texts and Studies in Ancient Judaism 81*, by Catherine Hezser," *Hebrew Studies* 44, (2003), pp. 217-222.

105　See the comments on this in *The New Testament*, Bart D. Ehrman, p. 207; *Jesus Before the Gospels*, Bart D. Ehrman, pp. 35-37.

direct references from ancient documents from a faction of Christians that attest to the existence of elementary schools for Jewish children, they will still, on the other hand, erroneously claim that first century Palestinian Jews were "illiterate"! This makes absolutely no sense whatsoever! Now, even though these examples given in the *Infancy Gospel of Thomas* are just "stories" not to be taken seriously,[106] the greatest problem with these stories lies in the fact that these stories have the teachers of Jesus desiring to teach Jesus the *Greek* alphabet as opposed to the *Hebrew* alphabet, which *no first century Palestinian scribe* would have even *considered* doing! Yet, the fact remains, why would anyone just fabricate such "stories" involving children going to school if in fact there were no elementary schools for Jewish children at the time of Jesus, even supposed "peasant" children? But the fact is that long before the time of Jesus schools for even young children had been established in every town and village, even in very small villages to educate children from very early on in their lives how to read no less than the Torah[107] in accordance with what is stated in Deuteronomy 6:7! As Mishnah *Megillah* 4:6 states, "A child may read in the Torah and translate" at the local synagogue, and this reading by a child was done *in Hebrew*.[108] But also, one was also taught to read the prophets as noted in *Megillah* 2a, and furthermore, one was obliged to be able to read the Book of Esther, even though at the time of Jesus Esther was not yet considered to be part of any Jewish "canon" (a matter that will be discussed further in Chapters 9 and 10), as noted in Mishnah *Megillah* 2:7.[109] It was considered a "duty" of parents to teach their children every aspect of religious practice

---

106   See the comments in *The New Testament*, Bart D. Ehrman, p. 220.

107   See *On Earth As It Is In Heaven*, D. C. Thielmann, pp. 1001-1002, and n. 61, P. 1047, n. 62, pp. 1047-1050; *The Trial of Jesus*, Josef Blinzler, p. 84; *The Mythmaker*, Hyam Maccoby, p. 24; *Simply Jesus*, N. T. Wright, p. 6; *Herod Antipas*, Harold W. Hoehner, pp. 54 and 58; *The New Testament and Rabbinic Judaism*, David Daube, pp. 88 and 96; Ray Vander Laan, "Rabbi and Talmidim," *That the World May Know*; *Jewish Law from Jesus to the Mishnah*, E. P. Sanders, pp. 78-81; *The Story of Hebrew*, Lewis Glinert, pp. 28-29; Josephus, *Contra Apion* 2.25; Mishnah *Shabbat* 1:3.

108   See the comments on this in *Ritual and Morality*, Hyam Maccoby, p. 41.

109   See the comments on this by Meir Bar-Ilan, "Literacy among the Jews in Antiquity: A Review of *Jewish Literacy in Roman Palestine: Texts and Studies in Ancient Judaism 81*, by Catherine Hezser," *Hebrew Studies* 44, (2003), pp. 217-222.

including the ability to read, and *write* no less than the Torah, (but also the prophets as well), and they were taught to read and write *in Hebrew* in accordance with Deuteronomy 11:18-20, as noted in *Yoma* 82a; *Nazir* 29b; *4 Maccabees* 18:9-19; Josephus *Contra Apion* 2.204, and as a further part of this teaching children to learn to read and write, children were given "honey-cakes" inscribed with *Hebrew* letters, and even complete *Hebrew* sentences in accordance with Ezekiel 3:3![110] As Samuel Sandmel writes,[111] "The Bible was read to Jews in their local assembly, for which the Greek word is *synagogue*. The distinction between the Synagogue and the Temple, and the unique importance of each in the Jewish history and religion of New Testament times, are basic necessities to an understanding of the New Testament. The origin of the Synagogue is obscure, but in all probability, it arose as a center where Jews gathered during the Babylonian exile (586-520 BCE). At first the Synagogue was primarily a place of study, a school, as witnessed by the fact that European and some American Jews still today use the Germanic word Shul (*Schule*),[112] or school, to name it." Sandmel goes on further to refer to the Synagogue at the time of Jesus as, "the common man's house of prayer and study," to which even Josephus, *Antiquities* 16:164, refers to the synagogue as a "public school." Now, there are some scholars who question how many synagogues actually existed at the time of Jesus simply because modern archaeology has not uncovered very many actual structures that can be easily identified as being a synagogue.[113] But quite often one's own home was being used as a synagogue, which goes way back in ancient Jewish history as noted, (for just a few examples), in 2 Samuel 15:25; Isaiah 33:20; Jeremiah 50:7. Now, a great many inscriptions *have been* discovered that refer to a synagogue being located near where the inscription was discovered even though no actual structure that could be readily identified as being a synagogue was discovered, and Mishnah *Megillah* 3:1, states that there were 480 such

---

110   See the comments on this by Emil G. Hirsch and Kaufmann Kohler, "Consecration or Dedication," *Jewish Encyclopedia*.

111   *A Jewish Understanding of the New Testament*, Samuel Sandmel, pp. 21-22.

112   See also the comments on this in *The Story of Hebrew*, Lewis Glinert, p. 29.

113   See for example *Jewish Law from Jesus to the Mishnah*, E. P. Sanders, pp. 77-78.

synagogues located in Jerusalem alone![114] Therefore, as Yitzhak Buxbaum writes concerning this matter,[115] "But at the end of the day Hillel would offer teaching directed at the common working people in the House of Study… and perhaps there would even be some who would be inspired enough to seek to become fully learned in the Torah and, like Hillel himself once, do what is necessary to that end." Furthermore, one finds it being stated in the Mishnah *Abot* 4:20 that, "He who learns as a child, to what may he be compared? To ink written down on new paper. And he who learns while old, to what may he be compared? To ink written on used paper." Likewise, *Nedarim 81a* states, "Be careful not to neglect the children of the poor, for from them Torah will go forth."[116] Roger David Aus points out that the two leaders of the insurrection against Herod the Great before his death, (namely, Judas and Matthias), were well known, (as even noted by Josephus in *Antiquities* 6.2.149), for being "educators of the youth," which made them very popular with the masses of Palestinian Jews,[117] and the very teachers of Hillel, namely Shemaya and Avtalion (who were the sons of gentile converts), were likewise known as "teachers" of no less than the ability to read the Torah to not only children, but to the masses as well, as is noted in *Gittin* 57b; *Sanhedrin* 96b.[118] This is *precisely* who, and what the individuals known in the New Testament as "scribes" were – they were "teachers" for the common individual and they *were not* just individuals who knew how to write – and this was true ever since the time of the Babylonian exile.[119] Thus, the entire claim being made by far too many scholars, for far too long now that the majority of

---

114   See the comments on this of Steve Rudd, "Schools, Education and Literacy of Jews In Synagogues," (2017).

115   *The Life and Teachings of Hillel*, Yitzhak Buxbaum, p. 116.

116   See the comments on this in *Hillel*, Rabbi Joseph Telushkin, pp. 147-148, and on pp. 151-155 Telushkin speaks much further on the matter of elementary schools even amongst peasant villages at the time of Jesus; see also *Talmudic Images*, Adin Steinsaltz, p. 11.

117   See *"Caught in the Act,"* Roger David Aus, pp. 155.

118   See the comments on this in *The Life and Teachings of Hillel*, Yitzhak Buxbaum, p. 72, and n. 8, p. 317.

119   See the comments on this of Isadore Singer, M. Seligsohn, Wilhelm Bacher, and Judah David Eisenstein, "Scribes," *Jewish Encyclopedia*; Yitzhak Dov Gilat, "Soferim," *Jewish Virtual Library*.

first century Palestinian Jews were "illiterate" is nothing but a claim out of *ignorance* and as a result of a failure on their part to do complete and thorough studies on this matter *before* making such absurd claims! The Jewish people as a whole have been the most *literate* of peoples out of all ancient societies and peoples because they were *commanded* to be such in the Torah – Deuteronomy 11:18-21 (bold, underlined italics mine), "And you shall lay up these words in your heart and in your soul, *and bind them for a sign upon your hand, and they will be as frontlets between your eyes. And you shall teach them to your children,* speaking of them when you do sit in your house, and when you do walk by the way, and when you lie down, and when you rise up. *And you shall **write them*** upon your door posts of your house, and upon your gates that your days may be multiplied, and the days of your children in the land which the Lord swore to your fathers to give them, as the days of heaven upon earth"!

It is high time that *genuine* New Testament scholars finally come to the realization that such stories as these examples from *The Infancy Gospel of Thomas*, noted just above, were written in the manner in which they were for the sole purpose of trying to distance Jesus from his true Jewish roots and turn him into another paganized, or Hellenized gentile godman, (i.e. a "Christian" of the gentile Church and not a "*Jew*" of the synagogue). The pagan Greek gentiles were infamous for being able to *fabricate* fantastically true sounding stories. For more than a thousand years before the time of Jesus the pagan Greek gentiles had an "oral tradition" passed along, before finally being first written down by the poet Hesiod around 700 BCE, of godmen such as Zeus, and Apollo, for example. The proficiency of the Greek gentiles to fabricate stories of godmen to which great temples and statues were erected to not only honor, but also to worship these godmen is well known from history, and these stories had nothing whatsoever to do with "memory," (or "confabulation," a term mentioned previously in the Preface), as scholars such as Bart Ehrman claim in regards to such stories regarding Jesus! The stories about these pagan godmen even included stories of dying and rising godmen who performed miraculous deeds, and even a few of these godmen were born of virgins who would one day be the saviors of the world.[120] Josephus in *Contra Apion* 2.242-254 even writes about

---

120   See the comments on all of this in *On Earth As It Is In Heaven*, D. C. Thielmann, Chapters 4-6.

all of these godmen stories! Now certainly scholars such as Bart Ehrman are not going to try and claim that these Greek mythological stories were actually based on "real human beings" in which, over time, the people began to "misremember" the *true* stories about these supposed "real human beings" that had been passed along "orally" before Hesiod began to write these stories down? Most assuredly the answer is a resounding, "NO"! The pagan gentiles, and especially the Greeks, were *infamous* in regard to their ability to completely fabricate and invent fantastic sounding stories about godmen, and thus, in order for individuals such as Paul to "win over" these pagan gentiles who worshipped these godmen to a belief in the concept of the Jewish Messiah, then stories needed to be created about Jesus that rivaled these pagan gentile godmen stories! Now, Bart Ehrman *does* in fact briefly mention these ancient Greek "oral" stories that were finally placed into written form, as well as other examples from other ancient cultures.[121] Yet, despite Ehrman's brief mentioning of these "oral" ancient stories, Ehrman seemingly fails to comprehend the significance of these ancient Greek mythologies becoming a belief system, or religion that was founded upon these ancient "oral" stories as they relate to the stories that turned Jesus into a "godman"! As N. T. Wright so rightly states,[122] "The pagan pantheon cannot simply be dismissed as metaphysically nonexistent and therefore morally irrelevant. It signals an ancient phenomenon within the surrounding culture that must be faced and dealt with, not simply sidestepped." While this matter does stray far afield from the overall matter of this chapter, and even more so this entire book, nevertheless, this is a necessary matter to address in regards to understanding *how* and *why* the Gospel accounts of the trial of Jesus became so distorted, full of errors and discrepancies.

Getting back to the essential matter of whether or not first century Palestinian Jews were "illiterate" or not though, Ben Witherington III rightly points out,[123] "Most scholars are convinced that Jesus both knew, and used the Hebrew Scriptures, as we find evidence of this in all our

---

121   *Jesus Before the Gospels*, Bart Ehrman, pp. 179-193.

122   *The Climax of the Covenant*, N. T. Wright, p. 128; but see also "Greek Mythology," *History.com Editors*, December 2, 2009.

123   See *The Historical Jesus in Context*, Levine, Allison Jr., and Crossan, p. 402; see also the comments on this matter in *Revolution in Judaea*, Hyam Maccoby, p. 50.

primary source material – in Mark, Q, Special M, Special L, and John. We also find it in the editorial work of all four Evangelists. There are then multiple confirmations that Jesus drew on the Hebrew Scriptures." This statement by Witherington does one other thing, and this being that it adds further proof to what was pointed out in the Preface that *Hebrew* as opposed to *Aramaic* had in fact once again become the dominant language in Palestinian Jewry. But Hyam Maccoby takes this matter a step further, (and a very important step to understand, I might add), when Maccoby writes,[124] "What about Jesus' education? There can be no doubt that he was educated as a Pharisee, for this was the only kind of education available to the poor, and Jesus' style of teaching and preaching is stamped with Pharisaic characteristics (e.g. his use of parables, and his use of actual Pharisaic maxims). The contention of John (the last Gospel writer) that Jesus was an uneducated man was probably invented to enhance the miracle of his alleged theological victories over learned Pharisee opponents, and to stress the primacy of faith over reason, an emphasis characteristic of ecstatic sects. Jesus' own sayings, his detailed knowledge of Scripture, and the fact that he was addressed as 'rabbi,' all show him to have been highly educated." One further piece of evidence that proves that the Jews had long been taught to read and to write as well comes from the archaeological discovery in 1935 of Lachish letters dating from the sixth century BCE, and these letters that were discovered were written, not by trained scribes, but by common soldiers of Israel![125] In Jewish history, referring to one by way of the English term "illiterate," simply indicated that whoever was being referred to as such only designated that individual as being "willfully ignorant of the Torah," (a term that will be mentioned again in Chapter 4). Therefore, in no way did this designation indicate that the individual was unable to either read or write, but rather it indicated that one was either unfamiliar with certain aspects of "Jewish customs," or unfamiliar with certain parts of "Jewish history." In essence, we arrive at the very misunderstood, misused, and abused terms, *am ha-eretz* and *minim*, (two terms that will be discussed further in Chapter 4).

Now, it is true that many scholars use John 7:15; Mark 6:2 and Acts 4:13 as an indication that Jesus was accused of having "never gone through the

---

124   *Revolution in Judaea*, Hyam Maccoby, pp. 105-106.

125   See the comments on this in *The Story of Hebrew*, Lewis Glinert, p. 20.

prescribed course of studies, or been authorized to teach by any governing body,"[126] such as, for example, thru either one of the Pharisaic schools of Hillel or Shammai. As a result many scholars and/or "interpreters" of particularly the verse from John's Gospel (7:15), have concluded that this verse indicates "one who is illiterate," (a matter just discussed above).[127] But this verse, (as well as the other verses mentioned), are actually referring to the matter of Jesus never having gone to one of the schools of "higher education" such as either the Pharisaic "schools" of Hillel or Shammai. Yet, the fact is that neither had the majority of the Essens, nor had *any* of the Sadducees gone thru such so-called "prescribed" or "authorized" Pharisaic schools! For the simple fact is that there was no such thing as a "governing body" that determined whether one was competent to teach as a "learned rabbi." Each Jewish philosophy at the time of Jesus had *their own* individual "schools of higher learning," and therefore, any and all modern scholarly claims that such accusations levelled against Jesus, if in fact such accounts are actually *historically true*, are in essence meaningless in regards to trying to utilize them as a claim that Jesus was both "illiterate," and to claim that this is what got Jesus into trouble with some sort of "Jewish authorities."

Jesus' main area for spreading his teachings was Galilee and it is from this very *fact* that so many modern Christian scholars are in error in their attempts to portray the historical Jesus as someone who was teaching "a relaxed attitude towards the Torah," or teaching something contrary to some sort of "standard Jewish law." As Sean Freyne rightly states,[128] "On the other hand Christian writing on Galilee has often been influenced, either consciously or sub-consciously by the quest for the historical Jesus, and as a result has for the most part adopted a too narrow approach." For the fact is that Galileans were very strict in their observance of the Torah and in their teaching the Torah,[129] a *fact* that is even noted in Mishnah

---

126 See for example the comments in *The Trial of Jesus*, Josef Blinzler, p. 84.

127 See for example *Problems of New Testament Translation*, Edgar J. Goodspeed, pp. 102-104.

128 *Galilee*, Sean Freyne, Introduction, p. x.

129 See the comments in *Herod Antipas*, Harold W. Hoehner, pp. 58-59; *The New Testament and the People of God*, N. T. Wright, pp. 168 and 239; Ray Vander Laan, "Rabbi and Talmidim," *That the World May Know*.

Yadayim 4:8. The New Testament itself even attests to this very fact.[130] But it is true though, that Galileans did lack a good, clear understanding of the Torah even though they were desperately trying to grasp the best understanding of the Torah.[131] This is precisely one of the main reasons *why* Jesus concentrated on Galilee as his main area of teaching in order to assist Galileans in coming to a better and clearer understanding of the Torah. So while Judeans were "more traditionally minded" in their observance of the Torah, Galileans "were stricter to the letter of the law."[132] The very *fact* that the Jewish philosophy, which came to be referred to as the "Zealots," (or in other words, one who was "zealous for the Torah"), arose from Galilee as Josephus, *Antiquities* 18.4-9 rightly comments about,[133] attests to this *historical fact* that Galileans were very strict in their adherence to the Torah! Joel Carmichael also rightly states that,[134] "The crux of the matter was that the Kingdom of God concept entailed a total transformation of the universe in which the pagan powers – primarily Rome – were to be destroyed and the fortunes of the Jews restored. This idea was the source of the religious ardor that imbued the Zealots – their 'zeal' for God." Carmichael goes on to state,[135] "Thus, even though both Josephus and the Gospels disregard the content of the Kingdom of God agitation – Josephus through bias, the Gospels through silence – it is possible, by fusing the Gospels, the Acts of the Apostles (both with many nuggets of camouflaged fact), Paul of Tarsus's Letters, and Josephus's histories, to perceive the true fate of Jesus – radically different from the traditional account."

It is essential now to mention several more of the claims made by so many modern Christian scholars regarding the teachings of Jesus that

---

130   For much more on this see the entire book *Akiba: Scholar, Saint and Martyr*, L. Finkelstein, Philadelphia, (1936).

131   See the Yerushalmi Talmud, *Shabbat* 16.8; Mishnah *Nedarim* 2:4; *Nedarim* 5:5; Babli *Nedarim* 48a.

132   See the comments in *Herod Antipas*, Harold W. Hoehner, p. 61; Emil G. Hirsch, Frants Buhl, and Solomon Schechter, "Galilee," *Jewish Encyclopedia*.

133   For more on this see the comments in *Bandits, Prophets, and Messiahs*, Richard A. Horsley and John S. Hanson, pp. 194-199, and n. 3, p. 241; *Christianity: A Jewish Perspective*, Rabbi Moshe Reiss, 3 "Hillel and Jesus" and all of his corresponding scholars notions.

134   *The Death of Jesus*, Joel Carmichael, p. vi.

135   *The Death of Jesus*, Joel Carmichael, p. x.

these scholars attempt to use as examples that Jesus somehow deviated from "standard first century Palestinian Jewish teachings and thinking," and thus, got Jesus into trouble with some sort of "Jewish authorities." These claims surround and involve the fact that Jesus associated with "tax collectors and sinners," (a matter that will be discussed further in Chapter 4), and that Jesus was also accused of being a "glutton and a drunkard." But all such claims by these modern scholars have in fact been thoroughly refuted as being nothing but nonsense![136] For in all reality Jesus' actions were no different than the very teachings of Hillel. As Yitzhak Buxbaum writes concerning the teaching of Hillel,[137] "The *hasid* enjoys life; he eats and drinks, like a normal person, showing *hesed* to his own self."

The next aspect of Jesus' activities and teachings that so many scholars try to utilize as a claim that Jesus got into trouble with some sort of Jewish authorities arises from Jesus' associating with women.[138] Yet, there are so many of these very scholars making such claims who will contradict themselves by pointing out the number of women who were influential, not only in the Church, but also amongst the Jewish rabbis, and in the Synagogues as well.[139] Bart Ehrman, for example, states that,[140] "Women were generally viewed as inferior by men in the ancient world, but there were exceptions." Now, this may have been true in the *gentile* "ancient world," but *not* in the *Jewish* "ancient world," and the only "exceptions" he refers to are the Epicureans and Cynics in the *gentile* "ancient world," who "advocated equality for women." But all such claims in actuality derive from gentile misunderstandings of Paul's teachings, which seemingly give a very Anti-Semitic portrait of Jewish attitudes towards women.[141] But at the time of

---

136   See for example the comments in *The Secrets of Hebrew Words*, Rabbi Benjamin Blech, p. 13; *On Earth As It Is In Heaven*, D. C. Thielmann, pp. 719-724 and the corresponding scholars notes to these pages; *The Misunderstood Jew*, Amy-Jill Levine, pp. 37-38; *Jesus Before Christianity*, Albert Nolan, p. 127; *Understanding the Difficult Words of Jesus*, David Bivin and Roy Blizzard, pp. 59-60.

137   *The Life and Teachings of Hillel*, Yitzhak Buxbaum, p.189.

138   See as an example, *The New Testament*, Bart D. Ehrman, p. 262.

139   See for example, *The New Testament*, Bart D. Ehrman, pp. 395-407.

140   *The New Testament*, Bart D. Ehrman, p. 397.

141   See the comments in *On Earth As It Is In Heaven*, D. C. Thielmann, pp. 405-407 and the corresponding scholars notations to these pages; *Jesus: Uncovering the Life, Teachings,*

Jesus women even wore *tefillin*, (or what the New Testament refers to as "phylacteries," the very things required of Jews as just noted above from Deuteronomy 11:18-21), as noted in the Talmud Babli, *Eruvin* 96a, and the Talmud Yerushalmi, *Nedarim* 9:4 as well as noted in pseudepigraphic writings such as the *Testament of Dan* 5:3; *Testament of Issachar* 5:2.[142] Such stories as that of Jesus' meeting with the Samaritan woman at the well are merely reflections of stories that can be found in Genesis 24, and 29; Exodus 2; and 1 Samuel 9:11. Song of Songs 4:12-15 even refers to a woman, or bride, as a "well of living waters."[143] Hyam Maccoby actually points out the real truth to this matter when he writes,[144] "For example, all the safeguards for the position of women which had been developed in Pharisee law were jettisoned by the new Pauline law…[145] For example, the right of women to divorce, and the right of married women to own their own property."[146] David Daube cites from Mishnah, *Niddah* 4:1,[147] which speaks of Samaritan women being referred to as "menstruants from the cradle." But Daube points out that this opinion was the one held by only those of the school of Shammai who consistently demonstrated a more chauvinistic attitude (Talmud Babli, *Shabbat*, 16b). But the moderates from the school of Hillel eventually won the day in this regard (Talmud Yerushalmi, *Shabbat* 3c). Daube then cites Mishnah *Kelim* 1:1 because it

---

and Relevance of a Religious Revolutionary, Marcus Borg, n. 11, p. 326; *Paul Was Not a Christian*, Pamela Eisenbaum, pp. 36-39.

142   See the comments in *The Misunderstood Jew*, Amy-Jill Levine, pp. 16-18; "Obligation of Women in Commandments," *Legal-Religious Status of the Jewish Female*, Tirzah Meacham.

143   See the comments in *The Misunderstood Jew*, Amy-Jill Levine, pp. 136-138. *Bandits, Prophets, and Messiahs*, Richard A. Horsley and John S. Hanson, p. 163 who note an incident recorded in Josephus, *Antiquities*, 18.85-87 who refers to a matter involving Samaritans being subdued by Pilate, which is an interesting account in regards to how it relates to the story of Jesus and the Samaritan woman at the well.

144   *The Mythmaker*, Hyam Maccoby, p. 194.

145   *The Mythmaker*, Hyam Maccoby, n. 5, p. 220.

146   See D. W. Amram, *The Jewish Law of Divorce*, London, [1897]; K. Kahana, *The Theory of Marriage in Jewish Law*, London, [1966]; Z. W. Falk, *The Divorce Action By the Wife in Jewish Law*, Jerusalem, [1973])" and see further Hyam Maccoby's comments in *The Mythmaker*, pp. 199-203; *Hillel*, Rabbi Joseph Telushkin, pp. 97-100.

147   *The New Testament and Rabbinic Judaism*, David Daube, p. 373.

refers to not drinking from a vessel used by a menstruating woman, and he refers to *Tosephta Niddah* 5.3; Babli, *Niddah* 33b, which states that Jews do not use vessels used by Samaritans.[148] Daube goes on to point out though,[149] that the terminology simply meant to "not become familiar," or "to become friendly" in the sense of association through "sexuality." He then questions whether the Gospel account of Jesus' meeting the Samaritan woman at the well is indeed historical truth or whether it was something added in simply based on a misunderstanding of rabbinic sources. Thus again, all such claims about Jesus getting into trouble with some sort of Jewish authorities because he had associations with women have likewise been thoroughly refuted.[150]

Example after example could be offered here as *proof* that Jesus' teachings *never* deviated from any "standard Palestinian Jewish teachings" that would have, or could have gotten Jesus into trouble with some sort of "Jewish authorities."[151] Even Jesus' teaching about divorce in Matthew 5:31-32 is merely a reflection of the Jewish teaching found in Malachi 2:14-16. But more will be said on this particular topic in Chapter 4.

Another matter to be mentioned here is in regards to "celibacy" in first century Palestinian Judaism. Dale C. Allison is quite in error when he claims that,[152] "In first-century Judaism, sex was largely thought of as serving the purpose of procreation, not pleasure...."[153] Allison seems to either completely ignore, or completely misunderstand that 1 Corinthians 7:25-40 *does not* encourage "non-marriage," or "celibacy."[154] The sole point that Paul is making in these verses surrounds "being free from anxieties"

---

148   See *The New Testament and Rabbinic Judaism*, David Daube, p. 374.

149   *The New Testament and Rabbinic Judaism*, David Daube, pp. 375-382.

150   See further on this the comments in *The Misunderstood Jew*, Amy-Jill Levine, pp. 193-204.

151   For more on this see the comments in *On Earth As It Is In Heaven*, D. C. Thielmann, pp. 731-732 and the corresponding scholars notes to these pages; *The Misunderstood Jew*, Amy-Jill Levine, pp. 41-51.

152   *Jesus of Nazareth*, Dale C. Allison, pp. 175-216.

153   *Jesus of Nazareth*, Dale C. Allison, n. 33, p. 177 referencing, Dale C. Allison, Jr., "Divorce, Celibacy, and Joseph," *Journal for the Study of the New Testament* 49, (1993), pp. 3-10.

154   See the comments in *A Jewish Understanding of the New Testament*, Samuel Sandmel, p. 73.

about whatever one's status in life may be (1 Corinthians 7:32),[155] and most of Jesus' disciples were married as noted in Matthew 8:14 and 1 Corinthians 9:5.[156] Both 1 Timothy 3:1-5 and Titus 1:5-8[157] speak of Bishops *not* being "celibate," and in regards to what is stated in 1 Timothy 4:1-4 Samuel Sandmel writes,[158] "The allusion here is probably to early teachers of celibacy and asceticism, the holders of a 'heresy' known from the church fathers as 'encratism.' Such heretics might have pointed, for the justification of their actions to Paul's reluctance to endorse marriages, in First Corinthians 7; if so, the Epistle is trying to correct those who took literally or with over-persuasion what Paul had taught." Sandmel goes on further to rightly state,[159] "For example, rabbinic Judaism offers almost nothing comparable to Paul's advice to shun marriage. On such a basis, some analysts attribute to all the New Testament, or to all Christianity, the attribute of Paul. The neutralizing factor about which I have spoken above escapes the notice of these scholars." Marriage, as well as sexual relations at the time of Jesus, is extensively discussed in the Mishnah and Talmud, as well as by Philo, *Life of Moses* 2:68. The *only* verses in the Hebrew Scriptures that discuss "abstinence" from having sexual relations, other than for just procreation reasons, can be found in Exodus 19:10-15, and this was ordered *only* to "prepare the people for the Sinai experience" with God. We also find that Jeremiah (Jeremiah 16:2) was "celibate,"[160] but only because Jeremiah felt that it was wrong to bring a child into the coming destruction being brought on by the Babylonians. It is from these very verses in Exodus 19 though, that Pharisaic interpretations of these verses at the time of Jesus determined that it was *only* Moses who "should abstain permanently,

---

155   For more on this see the comments of Samuel Belkin, "The Problem of Paul's Background," *Journal of Biblical Literature* 54.1, (1935), pp. 49-52.

156   See the comments on this in *How Jesus Became Christian*, Barrie Wilson, n. 9, p. 289.

157   It must be noted here, regardless of the point being made, that the majority of New Testament scholars no longer believe that the Epistles of 1 Timothy or Titus were actually written by Paul. As an example of this opinion see the comments in *Paul Was Not a Christian*, Paula Eisenbaum, pp. 16-22.

158   *A Jewish Understanding of the New Testament*, Samuel Sandmel, p. 291.

159   *A Jewish Understanding of the New Testament*, Samuel Sandmel, p. 312.

160   See the comments of Kaufmann Kohler and Max L. Margolis, "Celibacy," *Jewish Encyclopedia*.

since God spoke to him on numerous occasions." Thus, Jewish "oral" law, as well as the Torah itself, taught that "celibacy" was wrong, and that "abstaining from sexual relations" for any length of time went contrary to God's command to "be fruitful and multiply," which on the surface may appear to mean *only* for "procreation" as Allison claims, but *not* according to Jewish interpretations at, and long before the time of Jesus.[161] As Rabbi Joseph Telushkin points out[162] in Mishnah *Gittin* 4:5, Shammai discusses this very matter of "celibacy" and uses Isaiah 45:18 as his proof text for his opinion, which states, "He did not create the world to be desolate. He formed it to be inhabited." Now it is true, that *if* Jesus believed that he, (just like Moses), had God speaking "to him on numerous occasions," then thus, it could be true that Jesus *did* "abstain" from "sexual relations" just as Moses did. Yet, there is absolutely no evidence anywhere in the New Testament that Jesus was either "celibate," or that he "abstained from sexual relations."[163] In fact, all evidence points to the contrary![164] Now, Allison does rightly note the Essens, and the Qumran community,[165] but as Allison himself rightly notes,[166] the Essens and the Qumran community did so in order to prepare for the "forty year eschatological war" that they believed was in their near future.[167] But the fact is that some of the Essens *did* in fact marry and have children as even Allison rightly admits.[168] Therefore, if in fact Allison's conjectures are indeed correct, then the *only logical conclusion*

---

161   See, for example, the comments of Wendy Nelson, "Sexuality in Judaism," 1999.

162   *Hillel*, Rabbi Joseph Telushkin, pp. 109-110.

163   See the very excellent article on this entire matter by Harvey McArthur, "Celibacy in Judaism at the Time of Christian Beginnings," *Andrews University Seminary Studies*, Summer 1987, Volume 25, No. 2, pp. 163-181; and see also the comments in *On Earth As It Is In Heaven*, D. C. Thielmann, p. 395 and the corresponding scholars notations to this page.

164   See the comments on this matter in *On Earth As It Is In Heaven*, D. C. Thielmann, pp. 587-588 and the corresponding scholars notations to these pages.

165   *Jesus of Nazareth*, Dale C. Allison, pp. 192-193.

166   *Jesus of Nazareth*, Dale C. Allison, n. 94, p. 192.

167   See the comments on this matter in *On Earth As It Is In Heaven*, D. C. Thielmann, pp. 812-838 and the corresponding scholars notations to these pages.

168   *Jesus of Nazareth*, Dale C. Allison, pp. 213-214; but see also the comments in *The Apocalyptic Imagination*, John J. Collins, p. 117.

that one can draw is that Jesus, (in the exact same manner as the Essens were "abstaining from sexual relations"), was likewise "preparing for a forty year" time period for an "eschatological war!" The simple fact is though, (as will be stated again below for emphasis), Allison's interpretations of Jewish attitudes towards "celibacy" and "abstinence of sexual relations" at the time of Jesus is just another example of scholars demonstrating a genuine lack of understanding of Pharisaic/rabbinic Jewish teachings at the time of Jesus!

Far too many scholars misunderstand Jesus for the simple fact that they perceive him, and attempt to portray him from a gentile perspective as a "Hellenized Jew,"[169] (noted already previously in the Preface). As N. T. Wright states,[170] "But in a world of many gods, many religious movements, many philosophies (many of them varieties of Platonism, with its inherent dualism of spirit and matter), and many teachings combining ideas in ever new ways, it is not surprising that we find groups and writers seeking to use the name of Jesus to propagate and legitimize teachings very different from his own. It is not the last time in history that such a thing has happened." But possibly the most important point is made by David Bivin and Roy Blizzard when they write,[171] "It is most unfortunate that our Bible colleges and seminaries focus their attention on Greek and Hellenistic theology, and fail, by large, to equip their students with the proper tools that would allow them to do serious Biblical exegesis, a strong statement, to be sure, but sadly, all too true. *It cannot be overemphasized*, that the key to an understanding of the New Testament is a fluent knowledge of Hebrew and an intimate acquaintance with Jewish history, culture, and rabbinic literature." Unfortunately, there are so many, and in fact, far too many New Testament scholars who are lacking in the needed training to understand the Talmud and first century Palestinian Judaism. As Amy-Jill Levine rightly states,[172] "The comparison only gets worse, for, as noted, New Testament experts tend to lack training in rabbinic sources; specialized training is needed, for these documents are often opaque to the uninitiated. Like legal documents today, they presuppose knowledge of

---

169 See for example, the entire Chapter 2 of *How Jesus Became God*, Bart D. Ehrman.

170 *Judas and the Gospel of Jesus*, N. T. Wright, pp. 40-41.

171 *Understanding the Difficult Words of Jesus*, David Bivin and Roy Blizzard, pp. 15-16.

172 See *The Misunderstood Jew*, Amy-Jill Levine, p. 133.

the history of interpretation and they adopt an in-house jargon frequently incomprehensible to outsiders."[173] Likewise, as Chester Charlton McCown writes,[174] "The Talmud is a vast sea of materials which have hardly been touched by careful criticism, a great treasure cave whose forbidding aspect has frightened Christian scholars away" (again, more will be said on this matter of the Mishnah and Talmud in Chapters 4 and 5). But to go further along these lines though, is to offer here the quote of Roger David Aus, who states,[175] "Christian New Testament scholars with very few exceptions are not able to deal adequately with Judaic, especially rabbinic sources, as part of the background of the New Testament accounts. Many remain dependent on collections of background materials such as those of P. Billerbeck, J. Lightfoot, C. Montefiore and M. Smith. Although more and more Judaic sources are becoming available in English translation, thanks in great part to Jacob Neusner and his students, Christian students of the New Testament must become more knowledgeable in Hebrew, including Rabbinic Hebrew, in order to appreciate and properly evaluate the original sources." Although Aus, for the most part, is correct in what he states, his statement regarding Jacob Neusner is not entirely accurate as will be addressed in Chapter 5.

Also, as already pointed out in the Preface, far too many New Testament scholars attempt to interpret Jesus' teachings from the standpoint of Aramaic instead of the actual Hebrew used by Jesus in his teachings. Once again though for emphasis, (since this matter was already discussed in the Preface), Hebrew had once again become the dominant language used by first century Palestinian Judaism.[176] As David Bivin and Roy Blizzard write,[177] "Are there any passages that have been misinterpreted to such an

---

173   See also another further important statement relating to this in *The Way of God*, Moshe Chaim Luzzatto, p. 21.

174   *The Search for the Real Jesus*, Chester Charlton McCown, p. 206.

175   *Barabbas and Esther*, Roger David Aus, p. 25.

176   See the comments in the *Jewish Encyclopedia*, "Aramaic Language Among the Jews," Richard Gottheil and William Bacher, and the entire book, *Understanding the Difficult Words of Jesus*, David Bivin and Roy Blizzard.

177   See *Understanding the Difficult Words of Jesus*, David Bivin and Roy Blizzard, pp. 67-68; but see also the similar comments in *Judaism and the Origins of Christianity*, David Flusser, Introduction p. xii.

extent that they are potentially damaging to us spiritually? Unfortunately, the answer is 'yes.' In fact, had the church been provided with a proper Hebraic understanding of the words of Jesus, most theological controversies would never have arisen in the first place."

Matthew 5:23-47 is a perfect example of how Jesus' teachings were simply a matter that had been long referred to by the Jewish sages as, "building a fence around the Torah,"[178] exactly the same as is found stated in *Abot* 1:1. As Amy-Jill Levine writes,[179] "The term 'antithesis' itself is an unfortunate label that gives the impression of separating Jesus from Jewish tradition, for it suggests that Jesus is antithetical to the Torah. Jesus does not 'oppose' the law; he extends it. Moreover, his attitude toward it is not liberal, but highly conservative." Likewise, Matthew 7:5 is a direct reflection of the rabbinic teaching found in the Talmud, *Arachin* 16b, which states, "If someone urges you to remove the speck from your eye, he must first be given the answer, 'take the plank out of your own!'"[180] Also, the teachings found in Matthew 5:43 are mirrored in the Talmud, *Rosh Hashanah* 17a. As Rabbi Shmuley Boteach rightly states,[181] "Virtually everything Jesus taught was based on classical Biblical, Pharisaic, and Talmudic teaching. Not only did he *not* break from the Torah, he sought to reestablish Torah observance over the course of his campaign for spiritual renewal and political liberation." First century Palestinian Judaism and the observance of the Torah has been very badly misunderstood and misrepresented for far too long by gentile New Testament scholars and theologians. As Marcus Borg rightly points out,[182] "We should also not think of observing the Torah, of practice, as 'works' or Judaism as a 'religion of law,' as Christians (especially Protestants) have commonly done."

In Matthew 16:19 when Jesus tells his disciples that whatever they "bind" or "loose" on earth will be "bound" or "loosed" in heaven, Jesus was

---

178   See the comments in *The Way of God*, Moshe Chaim Luzzatto, pp. 401-403; *Jewish Christianity Reconsidered*, Matt Jackson-McCabe, pp. 266-267, (Jonathan A. Draper commenting); *A Rabbi Talks with Jesus*, Jacob Neusner, pp. 23-36.

179   *The Misunderstood Jew*, Amy-Jill Levine, p. 47.

180   See the comments in *Kosher Jesus*, Rabbi Shmuley Boteach, p. 24.

181   See *Kosher Jesus*, Rabbi Shmuley Boteach, p. 108.

182   *Jesus: Uncovering the life, Teachings, and Relevance of a Religious Revolutionary*, Marcus J. Borg, p. 95.

simply reflecting a very common first century Palestinian Jewish Pharisaic/ rabbinic teaching regarding debate over the interpretation of the Torah. As it is clearly found being stated in the Yerushalmi Talmud, *Shabbat* 1.4a, at times while the Pharisaic school of Shammai would "bind" a certain matter of interpreting the Torah, the Pharisaic school of Hillel would "loose" the very same matter.[183]

Jesus was wholly Jewish loyal to his Judaism[184] and dedicated to the Torah and this *fact* is clearly reflected in his teachings, and in his actions. As David Flusser states,[185] "The Synoptic Gospels, however, if read through the eyes of their own time, still portray a picture of Jesus as a Jew who was faithful to the law." Jesus even celebrated Hanukkah, or the victory of the Maccabees in the Hasmonean-Seleucid war that restored the Temple to "purity" as noted in John 10:22,[186] (and this matter of "purity" in regards to Jesus' teachings and actions will be further discussed in Chapter 4). Matthew 5:19 is a prime example of this clear indication that Jesus was wholly dedicated to his Judaism and modern New Testament scholars, and seminarians need to stop putting forth all of these nonsensical notions and opinions that Jesus somehow deviated from the Torah, which thus, resulted in Jesus getting into some sort of trouble with some sort of Jewish authorities.[187] Now it is true though, that there have been some modern

---

183   See also *Sotah* 9:14; *Nedarim* 6:5-7; *Berakhot* 2:6; *Demai* 6:11 and the comments in *The New Testament and Rabbinic Judaism*, David Daube, pp. 55-89; *Understanding the Difficult Words of Jesus*, David Bivin and Roy Blizzard, pp. 105-109; *The Mythmaker*, Hyam Maccoby, p. 122; *Judas Iscariot and the Myth of Jewish Evil*, Hyam Maccoby, n. 8, p. 188; Kaufmann Kohler, "Binding and Loosing (Hebrew, 'asar we-hittir'; Aramean, 'asar we-shera')," *Jewish Encyclopedia*.

184   See the comments on this in *Jesus and Israel*, Jules Isaac, pp. 11-29, and his summary conclusions pp. 401-405; *Jesus of Nazareth*, Dale C. Allison, pp. 68-69; *Conflict, Holiness & Politics*, Marcus Borg, p. 71; *Jewish Law from Jesus to the Mishnah*, E. P. Sanders, pp. 90-96; and see the entire book *Hillel*, Rabbi Joseph Telushkin where one will find example after example of how the teachings of Jesus directly parallel the teachings of Hillel.

185   *Jesus*, David Flusser, p. 46.

186   See the comments on this in *Maccabees, Zealots, and Josephus*, W. R. Farmer, pp. 141-145; Kaufmann Kohler, "Hanukkah," *Jewish Encyclopedia*.

187   See the comments in *The Mythmaker*, Hyam Maccoby, pp. 172-173; *Judas and the Gospel of Jesus*, N. T. Wright, p. 65; *Judas Iscariot and the Myth of Jewish Evil*, Hyam

New Testament scholars who have in fact come to realize this fact and have changed their opinions to reflect this recognition of the historical Jesus as an individual who was wholly dedicated to first century Palestinian Judaism and the Torah.[188] As Roger David Aus puts it,[189] "The more I have worked with Judaic materials, the more I have come to appreciate the great debt early Jewish Christians owed to their mother faith. Their thought patterns, and the way they dealt with specific passages from the Hebrew or Greek Bible, betrayed their Jewish heritage. I now find it absolutely necessary, for example, when analyzing the Gospels, to understand and appreciate the nature of *Haggadah*. Without such an understanding, often the wrong questions are asked of a text. In addition, the hotly debated issue of the historicity of a specific passage, provoked by Fundamentalists or some Evangelicals, unfortunately at times defers attention from the religious meaning(s) of the text." Likewise, Barrie Wilson very accurately writes,[190] "All Jewish groups agreed upon keeping the law," and this included even the "Jesus movement." The problems were in regards to the differences of opinions regarding exactly *how* one should "keep the law" as will be further discussed in Chapter 4. Wilson goes on to state that,[191] "For most groups, everything depended on keeping the law," to which he further very rightly states concerning Jesus that,[192] "He challenged his followers to observe Torah, strictly." Jacob Neusner very rightly points out concerning the

---

Maccoby, p. 99; *Kosher Jesus*, Rabbi Shmuley Boteach, p. 138.

188 See for example the comments in *The Last Week*, Marcus Borg and John Dominic Crossan, p. 30; *The New Testament*, Bart D. Ehrman, pp. 35-36; *Jesus: Apocalyptic Prophet of the New Millennium*, Bart D. Ehrman, p. 164 cited in *On Earth As It Is In Heaven*, D. C. Thielmann, pp. 704-705; *The Mythmaker*, Hyam Maccoby, n. 1, p. 19 citing *The Origins of Anti-Semitism*, John G. Gager, pp. 129 and 141; *Christianity: A Jewish Perspective*, Rabbi Moshe Reiss, 6 "The Torah and the Gospel of Matthew" who cites Anthony Saldarini, *Matthew's Christian-Jewish Community*, and J. A. Overman, *Matthew's Gospel and Formative Judaism*.

189 *Barabbas and Esther*, Roger David Aus, p. ix.

190 *How Jesus Became Christian*, Barrie Wilson, p. 45.

191 *How Jesus Became Christian*, Barrie Wilson, p. 58.

192 *How Jesus Became Christian*, Barrie Wilson, p. 63, and see his further comments on pp. 73-74, 95, and 103.

Hebrew word *Torah* that,[193] "It bears two meanings, one with a capital T, the other with a small t. Torah with a capital T stands for God's revelation to Moses at Mount Sinai. When we write 'torah' with a small t, we mean, 'the instruction of a master – in the context of the teaching of the Torah'."[194]

Luke 3:8, and even more so, Romans 9:6-7 seem to give a very clear indication of a distinct separation between Jews who were collaborators with the enemies of Israel, (i.e. the Romans), and Jews who were loyal patriots of Israel. Lloyd Gaston, in fact, points out concerning Luke 3:8,[195] that the word "eagle" at the time of Jesus was a reference to the Romans as found in a great many sources from the period, such as in the Dead Sea Scroll *1QpHab* 111:11; *The Assumption of Moses* 10:8; *4 Esdras* 11; *Sibylline Oracles* 3:611; Josephus *Antiquities* 17.151-155; *Jewish Wars* 1.650-653. Gaston also points out in regards to Luke 17:37 that the Greek word used in this verse that far too often gets translated out as "vultures," is actually the Greek word for, "eagle," which also then has this verse making a direct reference to the Romans! Thus, the *only* "authorities" that Jesus got into trouble with were the Romans and those who were collaborators with the Romans, namely, the Herodians, and the High Priestly families of the Sadducean philosophy who were political appointees of the Romans, as will be proven in later chapters.[196]

---

193   *A Rabbi Talks with Jesus*, Jacob Neusner, p. 4.

194   See further the comments on this in *Jewish Law from Jesus to the Mishnah*, E. P. Sanders, pp. 97-130.

195   *No Stone on Another*, Lloyd Gaston, p. 353.

196   See the comments in *On Earth As It Is In Heaven*, D. C. Thielmann, pp. 869-890 and the corresponding scholars notations to these pages: *Jesus On Trial*, Gerard Sloyan, p. 34; *Barabbas and Esther*, Roger David Aus, pp. 26-27; *Jesus and Purity Halakah*, Thomas Kazen, p. 45; *Judaism and the Origins of Christianity*, David Flusser, pp. 575-587.

Chapter 4

"The Pharisees went out and immediately conspired
with the Herodians...."
(Mark 3:6)

—

"In the same hour approached some Pharisees saying,
'Get away from here, for Herod wants to kill you'."
(Luke 13:31)

O ne can very easily recognize from the two Gospel verses used as
the title to this chapter that there is a very clear contradiction
not only in the Gospels' depiction of the Pharisees, but also in
regards to the Pharisees having any possible connection or involvement
in the arrest and trial of Jesus.[1] As Lloyd Gaston points out in regards
to this,[2] "It is extraordinary that the Herodians should be mentioned in

---

1 See the comments in *On Earth As It Is In Heaven*, D. C. Thielmann, pp. 864-867 and the
   corresponding scholar's notes to these pages; *Bandits, Prophets, and Messiahs*, Richard
   A. Horsley and John S. Hanson, pp. 178-179; on p. 220 of *Herod Antipas*, Harold W.
   Hoehner, after going back and forth on the preceding pages in regards to his claims about
   the Pharisees, he finally puts forth a claim that the Pharisees were both hated and were
   friendly with Jesus, which simply does not make any sense at all.
2 *No Stone on Another*, Lloyd Gaston, pp. 77 and 298.

both Mark 3:6 and Mark 12:13 as being in alliance with the Pharisees, a confederation which would have been historically possible only during the reign of Herod Agrippa."[3] Now, some scholars though, are of the belief that a group referred to as the "Herodians" did not even exist at the time of Jesus.[4] But as will be shown later in this chapter regarding Paul and his writings, such a claim is not true and is totally without merit.[5]

Yet, despite this very obvious contradiction just noted in the first paragraph of this chapter, one will still find very prominent New Testament scholars, (such as Bart Ehrman, for example), putting forth quite erroneous depictions of the Pharisees! As Ehrman, for example, so erroneously writes,[6] "The Pharisees may have been a relatively closed society in Jesus' day, to the extent that they stayed together as a group, eating meals and having fellowship only with one another, that is, with those who were like-minded in seeing the need to maintain a high level of obedience before God. They did not have close ties with those who were less stringent in maintaining purity before God, and avoided, therefore, eating meals with common people." The greatest error in Ehrman's comment derives from the fact that the Pharisees themselves were primarily members of the "common people" as will be proven in this chapter. Furthermore, it seems that Ehrman has missed the fact that on three different occasions in the Gospel of Luke,

3   *No Stone on Another*, Lloyd Gaston, n. 1, p. 77, cf. B. W. Bacon, "Pharisees and Herodians in Mark," *Journal of Biblical Literature* 39, (1920), pp. 102-112; *Das Evangelium des Markus*, E. Lohmeyer, n. 2, p. 67; *The Sources of the Synoptic Gospels*, W. L. Knox, p. 8; *On the Trial of Jesus*, P. Winter, p. 128. "Matthew and Luke could not understand these Herodians and so in all but one case omitted them. It is extraordinary how Bultmann too ignores them in *Die Geschichte der synoptischen Tradition*, Gottingen, (1958), p. 54." But see also the comments in *Jesus and His Adversaries*, Arland J. Hultgren, pp. 156-157 regarding the fact that this could only have occurred during the reign of Agrippa.

4   See for example the comments in *Jesus and His Adversaries*, Arland J. Hultgren, pp. 154-155, and n. 14-15, p. 169.

5   See the comments of Kaufmann Kohler, "Herodians," *Jewish Encyclopedia*.

6   *The New Testament*, Bart D. Ehrman, p. 236; but see also the similar erroneous comments in *Conflict, Holiness & Politics*, Marcus Borg, pp. 80-96; *The Theological Significance of Jesus' Temple Action in Mark's Gospel*, Emilio G. Chavez, pp. 40-43.

(Luke 7:36; 11:37; 14:1), Jesus is found dining with a Pharisee.[7] But the historical truth of this matter is that at the time of Jesus, and even long before the time of Jesus, it was customary for Pharisees to hang a white cloth on the outside of the door of their house to let "strangers," (especially the poor), know that they were welcome to come into their home and partake of a meal. Also, at other times, members of the philosophy of the Pharisees would set a complete meal outside on a table for the poor to come and partake as noted in *Baba Batra* 93b; *Abot* 3:6; *Berakhot* 55a; *Ta'anit* 20b,[8] but as noted in *Kidushin* 40b, this meal that was set outside for the poor was required to be taken to one's own residence and was not to be eaten in the street.[9] The depictions of the Pharisees that are far too often put forth by such prominent Christian, (or in some instances, "agnostic"), New Testament scholars, such as Bart Ehrman, are in actuality rather confusing, especially since these very same scholars go to such great lengths to demonstrate how and where the New Testament has been "distorted," or "altered" in regards to the depictions of the "historical Jesus." Yet, despite the obvious fact that these scholars recognize that there are contradictions, and thus, "distortions" and "alterations" in the overall New Testament, for some unknown reason these same New Testament scholars' will ignore the contradictory "distortions" regarding the depiction of the "historical Pharisees," and it seems to appear that these scholars do so, with very tainted biases I might add, simply to put forth conclusions that the Pharisees were somehow hostile towards Jesus in order to fit their "desired interpretations" that Jesus somehow violated some sort of Jewish law! As Samuel Sandmel so rightly states,[10] "No group in history has had a greater injustice done to its fine qualities than have the Pharisees through parts of the Gospels."

---

7   See the comments on how guests were to act in someone's home at the time of Jesus in
    Love Your Neighbor, Rabbi Zelig Pliskin, pp. 71-72.

8   *Love Your Neighbor*, Rabbi Zelig Pliskin, pp. 89-90; Kaufmann Kohler, "Agape," *Jewish
    Encyclopedia*.

9   See the comments on this by Solomon Schecter and Judah David Eisenstein, "Etiquette,"
    Jewish Encyclopedia.

10 *A Jewish Understanding of the New Testament*, Samuel Sandmel, p. 24; but see also the
    comments in *Jewish Literacy*, Rabbi Joseph Telushkin, pp. 127-128.

The fact is though, that there were in actuality seven different factions, or types[11] of the philosophy known as the *Pharisees* at the time of Jesus, as noted in the Talmud, *Berakhot* 14b, *and Sotah* 22b. Yet, only two of these seven different factions of Pharisees were well respected and held in high regard by all, which is also noted in the Talmud, *Eruvin* 13b, and these two well respected factions being those from the school of Hillel, and those from the school of Shammai.[12] It is also quite true though, and this fact is even spoken of in the Talmud, that amongst the five other factions of Pharisees, there were Pharisees that at times were referred to as, "hypocrites."[13] But *no one*, whether scholar, theologian, or general laity should think, or claim that this term "hypocrite" should be applied to *all*, or even to the *majority* of the Pharisees![14] Thus, the very fact that the Gospels do not in any way distinguish between any of these differing factions and schools of Pharisees[15] leads not only those of the general church laity, but also many scholars as well, to erroneous conclusions and misrepresentations of not only the Pharisees in general, but also to first century Palestinian Judaism as a whole. N. T. Wright correctly states,[16] "We constantly need to be on guard against this danger. A decade or two ago there was a fashion for declaring that we could no longer talk about 'first century Judaism,' only

---

11 See the comments on this by Reverend Jack Barr, "There were seven types of Pharisees; Claim: Pharisees and Sadducees were not Priest and Levites and Scribes," and see also the comments in *Jesus and the Laws of Purity*, Roger P. Booth, pp. 190-194.

12 See the comments in *Jesus*, D. Flusser, p. 53.

13 See the comments on this in *Jesus and Israel*, Jules Isaac, pp. 39 and 270; *Jesus and the Laws of Purity*, Roger P. Booth, p. 191.

14 See the comments on this in the excellent article by the Yashanet Staff, "Not Subject to the Law of God: Part 7. Historical Reality Concerning What Yeshua and His Followers Believed"; *A Rabbi Talks with Jesus*, Jacob Neusner, pp. 100-115; *A Jewish Understanding of the New Testament*, Samuel Sandmel, pp. 24-25.

15 See the comments in *The Jews and the Gospel*, Gregory Baum, pp. 25-26

16 See *Judas and the Gospel of Jesus*, N. T. Wright, p. 30; but see also the comments in *The New Testament and the People of God*, N. T. Wright, pp. 148 and 244, yet despite Wright's correct statement in *Judas and the Gospel of Jesus* and his similar comments on the pages referenced in *The New Testament and the People of God*, Wright does not actually give an accurate depiction of this diverse sect known as the "Pharisees" on pp. 181-203 of *The New Testament and the People of God*.

'first century Judaisms,'[17] with the plural reminding us, somewhat sniffly, that there were of course many different varieties of Judaism, some of them bitterly opposed to one another, and that to lump them all together risked that kind of gross oversimplification. Some have made the same point about types of early Christianity: perhaps, they say, we should talk about Christianities,[18] plural, fair enough – up to a point."[19]

Going further into this matter though, of labeling *all* Pharisees as "hypocrites," Marcus Borg, for example,[20] equates Matthew 23:27-28; Luke 11:44 with Pharisaic hypocrisy. Likewise, Hyam Maccoby as well, interprets these verses to be indicating a matter solely about "hypocrisy,"[21] while at the same time we have other scholars, such as Jacob Neusner, who interpret these verses as having to do with matters of "purity."[22] But such interpretations, regardless of whether or not they are interpreted as being about "hypocrisy," or about "purity," attempting to apply to *both* what is stated in Matthew's Gospel, as well as to what is being stated in Luke's Gospel, is quite difficult for *any* scholar to actually justify! For in all reality it appears that we have a duality of meanings being offered, or in essence, each evangelist, (the author of Matthew's Gospel and the author of Luke's Gospel), is implying a "uniquely" different meaning for *their* community in which their Gospels were written. Thus, it would be far more accurate to interpret what is stated in each Gospel separately with Luke's Gospel appearing to be more in line with the matters of "purity," (a matter that will be discussed further below), while Matthew's Gospel would appear to be more in line with a matter concerning "hypocrisy," simply because of the fact that the word "hypocrites" gets used in Matthew's Gospel. Reason being for such a duality of interpretation is that the "whitewashing" of

---

17 See also the comments on this matter in *Jewish Law from Jesus to the Mishnah*, E. P. Sanders, pp. 255-256.

18 See as an example for this term in *The Partings of the Ways*, James Dunn, pp. 4-5.

19 See also the lengthy comments on this matter in *The New Testament*, Bart D. Ehrman, pp. 362-371; *Jewish Christianity Reconsidered*, Matt Jackson-McCabe, p. 204, (Patrick J. Hartin commenting); *Jesus and Purity Halakah*, Thomas Kazen, pp. 263-264.

20 *Conflict, Holiness & Politics*, Marcus Borg, pp. 113-115.

21 See *Ritual and Morality*, Hyam Maccoby, pp. 151-155.

22 See for example Jacob Neusner, "First Cleanse the Inside," *New Testament Studies* 22, (1976), pp. 486-495.

"graves" before Passover was a very ancient Jewish practice, and thus, to apply Borg's, as well as Maccoby's, entire interpretation to both versions in that the "Pharisees appear righteous ('beautiful'), but inside they are full of hypocrisy and iniquity," (Matthew's version), and/or "the Pharisees, like a grave, are a source of defilement, but people are not aware of that, for the Pharisees are like unmarked graves," (Luke's version), does not make sense, and therefore, it is quite erroneous to attempt to apply the same interpretation to both versions. Now, while it is true that the Pharisees did use "metaphoric" terminology when referring to "hypocrites," as can be found, for example, in Babli *Berakhot* 28a, which refers to the fact that a person's "inside should be like his outside," but the "hypocrites" are like "white pitchers full of ashes," (but see also Babli *Yoma* 72b). Another example is found in Babli *Yoma* 28a, which refers to "hypocrites" as being "one who has no court, but makes a gateway for his court," yet, this is not the type of "metaphoric" terminology being applied in these verses from either Matthew's Gospel or Luke's Gospel, and therefore, the *truth* of the matter is that the dead, the burial of the dead, and graves were treated with great respect not only by the Pharisees, but by the Jewish people in general. The "whitewashing" of "graves," or, since quite often many prominent Jews were placed into stone sepulchers, such as the one the body of Jesus was placed into after his crucifixion, then the "walls" of these sepulchers were likewise "whitewashed," (such as can be found being referred to in the account in Acts 23:3). This practice was done just prior to the pilgrimage festivals not only out of this *respect* for the dead and buried, but also so that no one travelling to Jerusalem from a distant land who was unfamiliar with the locations of gravesites would inadvertently come in contact with, or come too close to the grave/sepulcher and become "ritually impure" before going to the Temple, as taught by the Pharisees long before the time of Jesus, as found in Mishnah *Shekalim* 1:1,[23] and which was derived

---

23　See Joseph Jacobs and Samuel Krauss, "Tombs," *Jewish Encyclopedia*; Kaufmann Kohler, "Burial, *Jewish Encyclopedia*; Sefton D. Temkin, "Cemetery," *Jewish Virtual Library*; Professor Ya'akov S. Spiegel, Department of Talmud, translated by Mark Elliot Shapiro, "Rachel's Tombstone: The Reasons for Erecting a Tombstone," *Bar Ilan University*; Cyrus Adler and Gotthard Deutsch, "H̲ebra K̲addisha (more correctly H̲abura" *Jewish Encyclopedia*; Emil G. Hirsch and Samuel Krauss, "Corpse," *Jewish Encyclopedia*.

from Ezekiel 39:15 and Numbers 19:16, and therefore, the very reason *why* one *cannot* apply an interpretation of "hypocrisy" to both versions.

The simplest way to demonstrate Jewish respect for gravesites and their adherence to avoiding coming into contact with graves can be derived from the fact that Herod Antipas built his capital city of Galilee, (Tiberias), right on top of a graveyard, and as a result, Antipas had a very difficult time trying to get people to come and live in this city because anyone either entering this city or living in this city was immediately rendered "impure" as noted by Josephus, *Antiquities* 18.36-38.[24] As E. P. Sanders rightly states,[25] "In assessing the possible affront which Jesus might have given the pious because he was not sufficiently strict with regard to purity, we might note what is not in the Gospels: there is no reference to Jesus' going to Tiberias. From the point of view of social history, the absence of the three Galilean cities (Sepphoris, Tiberias and Scythopolis) from the Gospels is striking and important. With regard to purity, however, Tiberias is especially significant... One must always hesitate before making too much of what someone did not do: perhaps Jesus just did not think of going to Tiberias but naturally went to his own kind – villagers. Nevertheless, this observation, coupled with the fact that handwashing was to most Jews a relatively unimportant matter, leads to the conclusion that Jesus was not in serious dispute with his contemporaries over laws of purity," (the matter of "handwashing" mentioned by Sanders here was previously discussed in Chapter 3). Maccoby himself even points out that there is doubt that any such "purity halakha" regarding the "inside and outside" (Mark 7:1-5 discussed in Chapter 3) even existed at the time of Jesus.[26] This applies also to the matter found in Matthew 23:24 regarding the "straining out a gnat," which is seen by some scholars as a corruption in the transmission of the story,[27] while other scholars see this as being a matter derived from the "oral" Torah of Mishnah *Parah* 9:2;[28] *Tosefta Horayot* 1:5. Now, while

---

24 See the comments on this in *Jewish Law from Jesus to the Mishnah*, E. P. Sanders, pp. 17 and 34; *Crime before Calvary*, Guy Schofield, pp. 64-65; *Galilee*, Sean Freyne, p. 129.

25 *Jewish Law from Jesus to the Mishnah*, E. P. Sanders, pp. 40-41.

26 See the comments on this in *Ritual and Morality*, Hyam Maccoby, p. 152.

27 See for example the comments in *On Earth As It Is In Heaven*, D. C. Thielmann, pp. 711-712 and the corresponding scholars notations to these pages.

28 See for example *Ritual and Morality*, Hyam Maccoby, p. 71.

it is true, (as will be discussed further in Chapter 5), that many scholars desire to disregard everything in the Mishnah and Talmud simply because it was compiled long after the time of Jesus, and while it is also true that many matters discussed in the Talmud *did* only come about *after* the destruction of the Temple during the 66-73 revolt, the fact is though, that matters dealing with, for example, the Temple, and the Sanhedrin, (as well as many other matters), *did* derive from long before the time of Jesus. Thus, for anyone to interpret this matter from Matthew's Gospel and Luke's Gospel as simply being so that these graves/sepulchers (i.e. "Pharisees") could "appear righteous ('beautiful') outside" while "inside they are full of hypocrisy and iniquity," and/or "defilement," such as Borg and Maccoby do is in all reality simply a "maligning" of the true character of the Pharisees, as noted above from Samuel Sandmel's statement! Luke's version of this supposed account and Matthew's version of this supposed account are quite different as anyone can clearly see, which even Borg comments upon, and if one then adds into this the matter noted just above from Acts 23:3 then all of these differences thus, turn out to have, in fact, quite different interpretations from many different perspectives! For the matter in Acts 23:3 tends to indicate that this account is a reference *solely directed at the High Priest*, a matter discussed in Chapter 2, which tends to suggest that it is quite possible that the Gospel accounts have substituted a reference to the Sadducees, and in particular the High Priesthood, for a reference to the Pharisees, (a matter that will be discussed further below). As an example of this, it is found in the Dead Sea Scroll referred to as the *Damascus Document* 8:12; 19:25 a reference to individuals as being "whitewashed," which many scholars have interpreted to be a reference to the Pharisees. But as will be discussed throughout this chapter, and elsewhere in this book, the Pharisees and Essens shared much in common and indeed for the most part had a close relationship with each other, and therefore, it is more probable that this reference in the *Damascus Document*, just as with the reference in Acts 23, is actually a reference to the High Priesthood, and/or the Sadducees.

Thus, in all reality then, each of these accounts regarding "whitewashing graves/walls" tends to indicate that *all* of these stories, (Luke's, Matthew's, and Acts), in reality appear to be nothing but an alteration of an actual *true* account regarding a matter of criticism of the High Priest and Sadducees, *or*, (if scholars tend to ignore the inclusion of the matter in Acts), this is more probably simply a matter of possible debate with the Pharisees over either "ritual purity," or a matter of critical debate regarding giving the Palestinian Jewish people of the time a "false sense of security" while being under the oppression of the Romans and Herodians, (derived from Ezekiel 13:10-15, and a matter which will be discussed further in Chapter 9), *or*, there is even the more probable fact that this could even be a matter of debate that involves a combination of *all* of these factors. Nonetheless though, it should be obvious to *any* scholar that this matter of referring to individuals as "whitewashed graves/walls" involves an alteration made by the later Church, which thus, is simply a reflection of the split that came about between the Jewish followers of Jesus and the gentile followers of Jesus. Going further though, Borg eventually contradicts himself when he makes reference to a particular Pharisaic/rabbinic teaching that was "most centrally in Jesus' teaching concerning the heart."[29] Thus, as Harvey Falk rightly asks,[30] "A reading of his (Jesus') great attack on the Pharisees (Matthew 23) virtually leaves one in a state of shock. Is this the same person who wandered off as a boy to discuss the Torah with the Doctors of the Law at the Temple (Luke 2:46)?" As Falk rightly points out further, this is one of the most common problems with Christian New Testament scholars in regards to their portraits of both the Pharisees and Jesus – contradiction! Either Jesus *did* teach and practice a faith according to strict Torah observance similarly to the Pharisees and Essens, or Jesus *did not* teach and practice a faith according to strict Torah observance – which is it? And in answering this question, scholars *must offer indisputable, undeniable "historical fact"*!

Also, of importance to note here, are the comments of Amy-Jill Levine, who states,[31] "The appropriate focus in New Testament studies on Jesus, Paul, James, and the other great figures makes another unfortunate contribution to Anti-Jewish thinking. The professor and the textbook do not have the time or the inclination to emphasize, repeatedly, the diversity of Jewish beliefs in the first century. In churches, such historical details concerning diverse Jewish views, regardless of how accurate they are, have no place in the sermon already packed with comments about Jesus and justice… Moreover,

---

29 See *Conflict, Holiness & Politics*, Marcus Borg, pp. 239-240.

30 *Jesus the Pharisee*, Harvey Falk, p. 111; Roy Blizzard, "Mishnah and the Words of Jesus," *Bible Scholars: Question and the Answers*.

31 *The Misunderstood Jew*, Amy-Jill Levine, pp. 123-124.

even if the sermon does indicate that the opponents are a few members of one particular Jewish school of thought, the Christian congregation will still hear 'the Jews'." Amy-Jill Levine goes on to state,[32] "But knowledge of Judaism on its own terms, and not (simply if at all) as a means to the evangelistic end, should have a special place in any serious study of Jesus and the New Testament, not only because Jesus and all his immediate followers were Jews, but also because the New Testament has been read and taught in a manner that perpetrates hatred of Jews." Furthermore, as Hyam Maccoby rightly states,[33] "This statement will come as a surprise to those whose knowledge of the Pharisees depends on New Testament accounts. The Pharisees there are represented as being concerned only to safeguard their own official positions. The idea that such people could take part in subversive activities, that they could risk their lives for freedom, that they could die, as so many of them did, heroically and in agony on the cross, seems quite remote from the New Testament portrayal... Fortunately, there exists a wealth of source-material from which it is possible to obtain a more truthful picture of the Pharisees."

Debate over the interpretations of the Torah was commonplace at the time of Jesus between not only the different Jewish philosophies, but also within the different factions of each of these philosophies, and at times, these debates even became heated arguments.[34] Now, it is essential to note at this point, regarding these matters of "debate" over interpretations of the Torah, that Marcus Borg is quite in error, as well as so many other New Testament scholars who claim that Jesus put forth some sort of "new" or "unique" teaching when Jesus teaches one to, "love your neighbor."[35] Borg, as well as so many other New Testament scholars,[36] claim that according to the *Pharisaic teaching* of "love your neighbor," this Pharisaic teaching *only* applied to "fellow Jews" or "proselytes to Judaism." But this is far from the truth of this matter as noted in the Mishnah *Terumoth* 1:1; *Berakhot* 5:21;

---

32   *The Misunderstood Jew*, Amy-Jill Levine, pp. 123-124.

33   *Revolution in Judaea*, Hyam Maccoby, pp. 56-57.

34   See the comments in *Jewish Law from Jesus to the Mishnah*, E. P. Sanders, pp. 84-89.

35   *Conflict, Holiness & Politics*, Marcus Borg, pp. 127-134.

36   See for example *Paul and Rabbinic Judaism*, W. D. Davies, pp. 58-66.

Shabbat 16:6; *Peah* 2:9.[37] Borg does admit though, that the image of the Pharisees portrayed in the Gospels and the overall New Testament is tainted,[38] yet Borg seemingly fails to grasp the *fact* that debate over interpretations of the Torah was commonplace at the time of Jesus and *long before* the time of Jesus and these debates *did not* indicate that there was any "animosity" towards those who held an opposing interpretation as a result![39] Thus, as Hyam Maccoby rightly points out,[40] "It should be remembered that Jesus would have been a most unusual Pharisee if he had never disagreed with other Pharisees. As explained earlier, amicable disagreement was an essential ingredient in Pharisaism, and the Pharisee literature is full of disagreements between the various sages of the movement." In *Abot* 5:20 it states that, "Every debate that is for the sake of Heaven will make a lasting contribution. Every debate that is not for the sake of Heaven will not make a lasting contribution."[41] Rabbi Barry Schwartz writes concerning this,[42] "The first of two crucial points that emerge from this critical teaching is the deep respect for differing opinions," and Exodus 23:2 specifically refers to the matter of the importance of debating interpretations of the Torah, but in the end this verse points out that everyone must "follow the majority ruling." Schwartz goes on to point out[43] that the very first such debate that is recorded in Scripture is found in Genesis 18:22-32 when Abraham debates with none other than God Himself, and in *Abot* 5:7 it is

---

37 See Joan Poulin, "Loving Kindness towards Gentiles According to the Early Sages," *Theologiques* 11(1-2), (Autumn, 2003), pp. 89-112; *Judaism and the Origins of Christianity*, David Flusser, pp. 494-508.

38 *Conflict, Holiness & Politics*, Marcus Borg, pp. 139-143.

39 See the comments on this in *Paul and Rabbinic Judaism*, W. D. Davies, n. 2, p. 144 who references David Daube, "Mark 1:22 and 27," *Journal of Theological Studies* 39, no. 153, (January 1938), pp. 45-59; Babli *Sotah* 47b; Babli *Megillah* 3a, which all refer to the disputes between the schools of Hillel and Shammai essentially becoming "two oral Torahs"!

40 *The Mythmaker*, Hyam Maccoby, p. 43; but see also the similar comments in *Jewish Literacy*, Rabbi Joseph Telushkin, p. 124; Aidan Kelley, "Jesus was a Rabbi on Hillel Side," *The Teachings of Jesus*, September 19, 2006.

41 See the comments on this in *Judaisms Great Debates*, Rabbi Barry L. Schwartz, p. xi; *The Life and Teachings of Hillel*, Yitzhak Buxbaum, p. 107.

42 *Judaisms Great Debates*, Barry L. Schwartz, p. xii.

43 *Judaisms Great Debates*, Barry L. Schwartz, pp. 3-10 and 16.

pointed out that Scripture also records a debate that *was not* "for the sake of Heaven," (Numbers 16:1-16).

Arland Hultgren though,[44] believes that he can identify four distinct differences between the Gospel accounts involving "debates," (or what the majority of scholars term, "Conflict Stories"), and the "debates" that are found in the rabbinic writings such as the Mishnah and Talmud.[45] Hultgren likewise believes[46] that he can identify three distinct differences between the Gospel "Conflict Stories" and the writings concerning "Hellenistic debates," or "conflict stories."[47] As Hultgren writes in regards to his opinion,[48] "The conflict stories in the synoptic Gospels have no formal dependence on other literary or popular forms of the period. They are as new in form as they are in content. They are presented in a form composed by early Christian storytellers specifically for the needs of the newly developing Christian movement." Yet, the fact is that the "Conflict Stories" in the Gospels *can be* seen as a somewhat shorter version of say, for example, Justin Martyr's *Dialogue with Trypho*. Simply because the "*written form*" of the "debates" found in say, for example, the Mishnah are not of the same "*written form*" as the "Conflict Stories" in the Gospels *does not* mean that the actual "debates" in say, the Mishnah, did not actually occur *historically* in the exact same manner as the "Conflict Stories" found in the Gospels, and this, I believe, is precisely what Hultgren is indicating by his statement just quoted above. For Hultgren even references *Abot* 5:20,[49] noted in the paragraph above, as part and parcel of his opinion! Hultgren, therefore, is quite correct in stating that the "Conflict Stories" in the Gospels were written in the "different form" that they were solely for the purpose of "the needs of the newly developing Christian movement," and these "needs" of this "newly developing movement" were to separate themselves from their roots in Pharisaic/Essen Judaism. In order to illustrate what is meant here, let us use as an analogy the rulings of the United States Supreme Court, which, (just the same as with the Mishnah and Talmud), records both

---

44 *Jesus and His Adversaries*, Arland J. Hultgren, p. 33.

45 *Jesus and His Adversaries*, Arland J. Hultgren, pp. 206-212.

46 *Jesus and His Adversaries*, Arland J. Hultgren, p. 35.

47 *Jesus and His Adversaries*, Arland J. Hultgren, pp. 213-214.

48 *Jesus and His Adversaries*, Arland J. Hultgren, p. 39.

49 *Jesus and His Adversaries*, Arland J. Hultgren, pp. 40-41.

the "minority" and the "majority" judicial opinions. Yet, these judicial opinions presented publicly *do not* give us the full extent of the "debate" that occurred "privately" behind closed doors between the different Supreme Court Justices. We are given "publicly" only a "summary" of the "majority" and "minority" opinions. The newspapers, which then report on the "majority" rulings of the Supreme Court, will then write their articles, and at times an individual news reporter writes his/her article about those Supreme Court rulings with a taint of bias in regards to each ruling without providing the full details of the summarized ruling, and thus, we have two different literary forms of writing about the same matter, exactly as we have differences in literary form regarding the "debates" found in the Mishnah/ Talmud and the "Conflict Stories" found in the Gospels. Hultgren thus, divides the "Conflict Stories" in the Gospels into two categories – those that originated in Palestine, (i.e. with Jesus), and those that originated in the Hellenistic Church, (i.e. post-Jesus' time) – and therefore, Hultgren rightly states that,[50] "What is most characteristic of the Palestinian conflict stories, however, is that they are all, with one exception, *apologetic.*" In regards to the "Conflict Stories" that Hultgren believes were derived from the "Hellenistic Church" though, he believes that these stories were,[51] "less apologetic than the Palestinian stories, they are essentially *catechetical.*"

The two highly respected Pharisaic schools of Hillel and Shammai were very bitter rivals whose schools at times even engaged in knock-down-drag-out fights over their differing interpretations of the Torah, as well as other matters.[52] Yet, despite these heated disagreements between Hillel and Shammai they were still very close friends and allies as noted in *Yevamoth* 13b; *Yevamoth* 14b; *Abot* 5:17; *Eduyot* 1:4,[53] and in Mishnah *Yevamoth* 1:4 it even clearly states that despite the disagreements between

---

50 *Jesus and His Adversaries*, Arland J. Hultgren, pp. 175-176.

51 *Jesus and His Adversaries*, Arland J. Hultgren, p. 179.

52 See the Mishnah *Shabbat* 1:4; Talmud Babli, *Sukkah*, 28a; *Baba Batra* 134a; *Shabbat* 17a, and see also the comments in *Christianity: A Jewish Perspective*, Rabbi Moshe Reiss, 2 "Jesus Comes From the Jewish Tradition"; *The Jewish Messiah*, James Drummond, p. 164; *Studies in the History of the Sanhedrin*, Hugo Mantel, p. 15; *Hillel*, Rabbi Joseph Telushkin, pp. 83 and 118; *Jesus the Pharisee*, Harvey Falk, pp. 154-156.

53 See *Love Your Neighbor*, Rabbi Zelig Pliskin, pp. 348-351; *Hillel*, Rabbi Joseph Telushkin, pp. 116-117.

these two schools there was still intermarriage between members of these two divergent schools of interpretation and opinion. As Rabbi Joseph Telushkin writes concerning this,[54] "Both sages play for the same team; the battles between Hillel and Shammai should be seen as signs of health within the religion, for they are fights about alternate interpretive pathways to the same God." Jesus' disagreements with the Pharisees were in no way any different than these debates between the differing philosophies, and factions within each of these philosophes, and in fact, at times Jesus' teachings were in full agreement with those from the school of Hillel, while at other times his teachings were in full agreement with those from the school of Shammai.[55] For example, Jesus' statement in Matthew 7:21-23, is more of a reflection of the opinions of Shammai than that of Hillel as noted in *Rosh Ha-Shanah* 16a-17b.[56] It is virtually the exact same still today where it is an *undeniable fact* that modern scholars engage in debate over interpretations of Scripture and the "historical Jesus" just exactly the same as the Pharisees had debated amongst their own philosophy over interpretations of the Torah, as well as the debates that Jesus had with the Pharisees over interpretations of the Torah![57]

Now, Robert Gundry is quite in error when he contends that the "debate" recorded in Mark 11:27-12:33 was between Jesus and the Sanhedrin.[58] For there is absolutely no evidence whatsoever for such a contention as this! As Gerard S. Sloyan rightly states concerning the matter of Jesus' debates over interpretations of the Torah,[59] "It is quite clear that his religious opinions fell

---

54   *Hillel*, Rabbi Joseph Telushkin, p. 97.

55   See the comments in *The Misunderstood Jew*, Amy-Jill Levine, pp. 28-29; *Revolution in Judaea*, Hyam Maccoby, Appendix 4, pp. 203-206; *Jesus and Purity Halakah*, Thomas Kazen, p. 265. Far too many scholars have tried to distance Jesus from being similar to the Pharisees in this regard, but in each instance they fail in their understanding of these rivalries amongst first century Palestinian Jewish sects, (see for example, *The Trial of Jesus: Cambridge Studies in Honour of C. F. D. Moule*, pp. 48-54; and see also the erroneous comments in *The Partings of the Ways*, James Dunn, pp. 110-111 who asserts that Jesus was "threatening" the very "identity" of the Pharisees with his disagreements with them).

56   See the comments on this in *The Life and Teachings of Hillel*, Yitzhak Buxbaum, pp. 109-113.

57   See the comments in *A Jewish Understanding of the New Testament*, Samuel Sandmel, p. xvii.

58   See *Mark*, Robert H. Gundry, pp. 656-691.

59   *The Crucifixion of Jesus*, Gerard S. Sloyan, p. 27.

within the allowable limits of dispute in the Israel of his day." Furthermore, as Rabbi Joseph Telushkin writes concerning these disagreements between Hillel and Shammai, (which one could even include Jesus' disagreements with the Pharisees on matters of interpretation of the Torah as well, and which puts the error to Ehrman's statement mentioned above),[60] that, "Associating only with like-minded people, reinforcing one another's views without ever hearing a credible exposition of opposing views, might have caused them to think that those who thought differently from them were not only wrong, but evil. A contemporary upshot of this text is that we should not read only books and publications that agree with and reinforce what we already believe." Telushkin goes on further to write in regards to Jesus most likely being influenced by the teachings of Hillel,[61] "The two men, both of whom lived in the first century – though Hillel is two generations older – are frequently compared, and it is worth considering them briefly side by side. Just as Shammai is at times cast unfairly in the role of inflexible literalist when compared with Hillel, so has Hillel often been cast, very unfairly, in a similar role when compared by some Christian scholars with Jesus." But taking this matter one step further, even *after* a majority ruling had arisen from these debates over interpretations of the Torah, nothing was ever "etched in stone," so to speak, in such a manner that the matter could not still be further debated and possibly changed in regards to the majority opinion at some other later date in time. As Hyam Maccoby states concerning this,[62] "To give any greater authority to rabbinic legislation (in the form of a doctrine analogous to that of 'Papal infallibility') would have been to infringe against the Biblical injunction, 'Thou shalt not add to it, nor shalt thou take away' (Deuteronomy 12:32)."

In Jesus' Sermon on the Mount, and specifically the Beatitudes portion in Matthew's Gospel, there is one particular Beatitude that in all reality has Jesus praising the Pharisees, especially the Pharisees from the school of Hillel. For when Jesus states in Matthew 5:9, "Blessed are the peacemakers ..." Jesus is reflecting the very teaching of Hillel, and Hillel's teachers Shemaya and Avtalion who taught, (as is noted in Mishnah *Abot* 2:8; *Berakhot* 64a; *Gittin* 5:8, 59b, 61a; and *Abot de Rabbi Nathan* 12),

---

60   *Hillel*, Rabbi Joseph Telushkin, p. 120.

61   *Hillel*, Rabbi Joseph Telushkin, p. 129.

62   *Ritual and Morality*, Hyam Maccoby, pp. 7-8.

that "Sages increase peace throughout the world," and that one should "increase peace," and to "'seek' peace in your own place and 'pursue' it in another place," which was based on Malachi 2:6; Psalm 34:15.[63] Also, in Mishnah *Abot* 4:20 it states, "Always be first in greeting all men with the blessing of peace," and it must be noted that this is virtually the way so many of the New Testament Epistles begin – with a "blessing of peace." Thus, we find another example of Pharisaic teachings being reflected in the teachings of Jesus! But did such a teaching indicate that one was to be a "pacifist"? The answer is a resounding, "NO"! For as Yitzhak Buxbaum rightly states,[64] "Hillel understood that the relations between people are dynamic; a person cannot have peace simply by avoiding harming others or by not arguing or by being passive." This too, as will be demonstrated in later chapters, was Jesus' attitude regarding obtaining "peace" as well! Another matter though, that goes in concert with this matter of "Blessed are the peacemakers," is Jesus' teaching in Matthew 7:1-2 regarding "Do not judge," which is a direct reflection of the teaching of Hillel noted in *Abot* 1:6; 2:5, and *Kidushin* 81a.[65]

Yet, there are still so many Christian New Testament scholars who simply *do not* clearly understand this *fact*, and therefore, at times, make very erroneous assumptions and draw very erroneous conclusions because of their misunderstandings. As an example of this point, Bart Ehrman refers to the account in John 3[66] regarding Jesus' conversation with Nicodemus, and specifically about the part where it is stated, "You must be born again." Ehrman's conclusion regarding this matter is, "So it looks as though this conversation could not have happened – at least not as it is described in the Gospel of John." Now, while this statement by Ehrman may indeed be accurate in regards to the part, "at least not as it is described in the Gospel of John," the *fact* of the matter is that Ehrman has erroneously interpreted this entire incident with Nicodemus, and thus, such a conversation *is in fact* quite likely to have actually occurred. For the Greek words *gennethe anothen*, which get translated out as "born again," was actually a very

---

63   See the comments on this in *The Life and Teachings of Hillel*, Yitzhak Buxbaum, pp. 78-94.

64   *The Life and Teachings of Hillel*, Yitzhak Buxbaum, p. 78.

65   See the comments on these tractates in *The Life and Teachings of Hillel*, Yitzhak Buxbaum, pp. 103-104.

66   *Jesus Interrupted*, Bart D. Ehrman, p. 155.

common Jewish term that was used at the time of Jesus in regards to gentiles converting to Judaism.[67] Thus, when Jesus used this terminology in regards to a Jew, (and especially in regards to a Jew of the stature of Nicodemus),[68] this brought about Nicodemus' very sarcastic and confused response that is recorded in John 3. But Jesus here was referring to a "conversion" that even Jews must undergo, which brings about Jesus' lengthy explanation in John 3:5-21. In actuality, Jesus was actually giving Nicodemus a sarcastic chastising for not correctly understanding his remark. For Nicodemus knows that Jesus is an interpreter of Scripture, and in fact, it is recorded that Nicodemus even refers to Jesus as *didaskalos* ("interpreter"). Jesus' use of this terminology to a fellow Jew was in reality a reference to Ezekiel 36:25-27, which Nicodemus, being a Pharisee should have already known.[69] For it is more than probable that this is the *same* Nicodemus as the one referenced in *Gittin* 56a; *Ta'anit* 19b. Jesus is letting Nicodemus know that as a Jew, he must heed the "call to repentance," to "walk in His statutes," and "observe His ordinances." J. Dwight Pentecost[70] refers to John 3:5 as an indication that as long as one is being sinful and non-repentant, (even a Jew the stature of Nicodemus), then one cannot enter the Kingdom of Heaven. Furthermore, Jesus' words in John 3:13 are simply an echo to his earlier remarks found in John 1:51, which in reality are simply a reference to Jacob's Ladder (Genesis 28:12). The Hebrew word, *sullam* (translated out as "ladder" in Genesis 28:12) is a Hapax Legomenon, (meaning that it appears only this one time in Scripture), which derives from the root word, *salal*, which means, "a path," or "a Way," and is thus, indicating the "Way" one should live their life. Bart Ehrman's misunderstanding of this incident with Nicodemus simply demonstrates his lack of understanding of Jewish idioms used at the time of Jesus. Jules Isaac makes an excellent point, in regards to such errors made by scholars the caliber of Bart

---

67 See Kaufmann Kohler, "Birth, New," *Jewish Encyclopedia.*

68 See the comments of Schulim Ochser and Kaufmann Kohler, "Nicodemus," *Jewish Encyclopedia.*

69 See the comments regarding the Pharisaic teachings pertaining to "converts" to Judaism as opposed to individuals who were true descendants of Aaron and Israel in *The Life and Teachings of Hillel*, Yitzhak Buxbaum, pp. 69-77.

70 *The Words and Works of Jesus Christ*, J. Dwight Pentecost, p. 125, but see also the comments on this matter in *What Did Jesus Mean*, Ron Rhodes, p. 126.

Ehrman, when Isaac writes,[71] "That is why even today, 'aside from rare and moving exceptions,' Christians of all persuasions do not hesitate to pass a harsh verdict against first century Judaism – and why their judgment must be brought face to face with historic reality here, insofar as impartial investigation can lay that reality bare." As a great example for this, in Matthew 6:5 Jesus' teaching about not praying as the "hypocrites" do, was termed, (at the time of Jesus), *berakhah le-vatalah*, ("prayer that is pointless"), as found being stated and referred to in Mishnah *Berakhot* 9:3; *Berakhot* 60a.[72] Rabbi Joseph Telushkin comments on this by demonstrating how the contrasts between the teachings of Jesus and those of Hillel were very similar to the contrasts between the teachings of Hillel and those of Shammai,[73] and thus, proving that there *was not* one uniform Judaism at the time of Jesus, and therefore, the teachings of Jesus, in essence and in simplest terms, were neither different, nor better, nor worse than those of either Hillel or Shammai!

A very important point to make here in this chapter surrounds Matthew 2:23, to which many scholars have stated that they have searched high and low in the Hebrew Scriptures for *any* prophecy that clearly states, or indicates even remotely that the Messiah would be a "Nazarene."[74] St. Jerome though, referred to Isaiah 11:1 as being this very prophecy based on the fact that the word *nazar*, (the shortened form of *nazari*, i.e. "Nazarene"), is found being used as a messianic prophecy in this verse, and even Joseph A. Fitzmyer has this verse listed as being the verse referenced by Matthew 2:23 under the category of "Florilegia," or *Book of Testimonies*, (a matter

---

71   *Jesus and Israel*, Jules Isaac, p. 35.

72   See the comments on this in *Hillel*, Rabbi Joseph Telushkin, pp. 134-135; *The Life and Teachings of Hillel*, Yitzhak Buxbaum, pp. 190-192.

73   *Hillel*, Rabbi Joseph Telushkin, pp. 134-141.

74   See for example *Essays on the Semitic Background of the New Testament*, Joseph A. Fitzmyer, pp. 14-15. Other scholars though, will reference either Judges 13:5; 16:7, or 1 Samuel 1:11 (see for example *The Birth of the Messiah*, Raymond E. Brown, pp. 223-224), but see also Isaiah 60:21; Jeremiah 4:16; Daniel 11:7. Concerning Isaiah 60:21, Fitzmyer on p. 132 of *Essays on the Semitic Background of the New Testament* notes the Dead Sea Scroll referred to as the *Thanksgiving Psalms* (1QH), which references *natzar* and relates it not to Isaiah 11:1, but to Isaiah 60:21 thereby contradicting his own opinion, because the *Thanksgiving Psalms* is a reference to an entire community of "Nazarenes"!

---

that will be mentioned further in Chapter 6), which is in all reality a contradiction of Fitzmyer's own opinion![75] Now, it is true that this *is* the Hebrew word that did come to be used as a reference to Christians, and it is also true that Isaiah 11:1 *did* become and *was* interpreted as a messianic prophecy by a certain Jewish philosophy, (namely the Essens), as can be found in the Dead Sea Scroll fragment that is referred to as the *Pesher on Isaiah*, or *4QpIs*, which speaks of Isaiah 11:1 as a Messianic prophecy by way of the "Shoot of David."[76] But even more importantly to point out here is the fact that there was no known actual city named "Nazareth" at the time of Jesus as even modern archaeology has proven.[77] Yet, the fact remains though, that there is no *direct* written prophecy that clearly states and confirms what is stated in Matthew 2:23 concerning the Messiah. This particular Jewish philosophy's interpretation of Isaiah 11:1 is just another example of the very diversity of opinions and interpretations of not only the Torah, but other sacred ancient Jewish prophecies and texts at the time of Jesus. But to go further into this matter concerning the philosophical interpretation of Isaiah 11:1, the Hebrew word *nazar* is etymologically connected to the Hebrew word *natzar*,[78] which then means that both of these Hebrew words offer the meanings of, "separate," "consecrate," or "watchers,"[79] and thus, the very reason why there was a particular Jewish philosophy, (long before the time of Jesus, during the time of Jesus, and long after the time of Jesus), who interpreted Isaiah 11:1 as an indication that *THE* "Messiah" would be a "Nazarene." Joseph A. Fitzmyer offers numerous examples of how the Hebrew Scriptures were interpreted by the Qumran inhabitants, (i.e. the Essens), by what Fitzmyer calls "modernized," or "accommodated" interpretations.[80] Now, Acts 24:5 *clearly* denotes that there *were* first century Palestinian Jews referred to as "Nazarenes" and that

---

75 See *Essays on the Semitic Background of the New Testament*, Joseph A. Fitzmyer, pp. 63-64.

76 *Essays on the Semitic Background of the New Testament*, Joseph A. Fitzmyer, p. 120.

77 See *On Earth As It Is In Heaven*, D. C. Thielmann, p. 624, and n. 37-43, pp. 654-659; *The Myth of Nazareth: The Invented Town of Nazareth*, Rene Salm; Owen Jarus, "Jesus' House? 1st-Century Structure May be Where He Grew," *Live Science*, March 1, 2015.

78 See *A Comprehensive Etymological Dictionary of the Hebrew Language*, p. 424; *Etymological Dictionary of Biblical Hebrew*, pp. 160-161.

79 In regards to this word, "watchers," see the comments of Gary Wayne, "The Essenes."

80 *Essays on the Semitic Background of the New Testament*, Joseph A. Fitzmyer, pp. 21-58.

this Jewish faction existed long before the time of Jesus, and furthermore, this faction of "Nazarenes" *was* associated with the philosophy of the Essens![81] In Acts 21:23-26 we find it *clearly* being stated that Paul went through the rites of a *Nazarite* at the request of the head of the Jerusalem Church, James, which even Joseph Fitzmyer makes note of. Yet, Fitzmyer does not seem to be able to make the connection between Matthew 2:23, and the interpretation of the faction of the "Nazarenes" regarding Isaiah 11:1, and the Essens.[82] It must be further noted that in Acts 24:17-18 Paul then fully fulfills his *Nazarite* rites when he brings alms and offers sacrifices at the Temple.

At the time of Jesus therefore, there simply was no such thing as "one united Judaism." First century Palestinian Judaism was highly divided, and even the New Testament documents this division between the divergent philosophies of the Sadducees, and Pharisees, but of course there was even the unmentioned philosophy of the Essens, (who broke away from the Pharisees),[83] and as just noted above, the Pharisees were even divided into seven different factions, as well as there being different factions of the Essens as just noted! This *fact* that first century Palestinian Judaism was so highly divided has created problems within the scholarly world in regards to their depictions of the historical Jesus regarding his debates and criticism of both the Sadducees and Pharisees. Bart D. Ehrman, in fact, does a very poor job of accurately describing the different factions of the different Jewish philosophies mentioned in Mark's Gospel, especially regarding the "Scribes," the "Pharisees," and the "Sadducees," but also in his description of the "Herodians" *and* the "Chief Priests."[84] Ehrman is quite in error when he states that,[85] "The Pharisees were not numerous in the days of Jesus." Ehrman's error is derived from what Josephus states in

---

81   See Lost Christianity, "Jesus was an Essene and Nazareth did not exist"; Samuel Krauss, "Nazarenes," *Jewish Encyclopedia*.

82   See *Essays on the Semitic Background of the New Testament*, Joseph A. Fitzmyer, p. 280.

83   See Kaufmann Kohler, "Essenes," *Jewish Encyclopedia*.

84   See *The New Testament*, Bart D. Ehrman, Box 5.2, p. 71. But to see a more accurate depiction of the various Jewish sects at the time of Jesus see *How Jesus Became Christian*, Barrie Wilson, pp. 31-44.

85   *The New Testament*, Bart Ehrman, Box 5.3, p. 72; but see also the similar comments in *Conflict, Holiness & Politics*, Marcus Borg, pp. 59-61; *Jesus*, David Flusser, p. 53.

Antiquities 17:42 in which one finds Josephus giving an estimate of the number of Pharisees at 6000. But it seems that *many* scholars, (such as Ehrman), have missed the *fact* that this estimate given by Josephus is *only* in regards to the number of Pharisees living in Jerusalem at the time, to which Josephus also gives an estimate of the *total* population of Jerusalem at 20,000, thus meaning, that the Pharisees that lived *only in Jerusalem* was nearly one third of the *total* population of just *that particular city*. Furthermore, Josephus in *Antiquities* 18.20 gives the number of Essens living in Jerusalem at "more than 4000," and in *Antiquities* 18.17 Josephus states that the Sadducees living in Jerusalem were "but a few men"![86] These numbers given by Josephus are, of course, only estimates and they have been debated by scholars for centuries, but nonetheless, this estimate still puts the error to scholars claiming that "the Pharisees were not numerous in the days of Jesus." For these scholars seem to be completely ignoring the *fact* that the Pharisees lived in virtually every town and village in Palestine[87] as well as ignoring the Pharisees that lived in Babylon, (i.e. the very compilers of the Talmud Babli), and the place from which Hillel was born and raised from parents who were converts to Judaism.

Far too many modern Christian New Testament scholars fail to remember, take note of, and then point out the *fact* that the Pharisees and the Sadducees not only disagreed on interpretations of the Torah, but that they also disagreed politically. The Pharisees and the Sadducees were in *fact*, mortal enemies as clearly stated in Mishnah, *Qiddushin*, 66a; Talmud, *Sotah* 22b; *Pesahim* 57; *Niddah* 4:1-2; *Niddah* 31b; *Tosefta Teruma* 4:12; *Berakhot* 14b, but also by the historian Josephus, *Jewish Wars* 1.107-114; *Antiquities* 13.372-383; 13.288-298; 13.399-418; 18.11-17, and also as is found in the Dead Sea Scrolls *4QpNah* 1,[88] or in essence, there is *"multiple attestation"* to this *fact*, which once again, *"multiple attestation"* is one of the most essential criteria used by scholars as being one of *the* most important tools in determining *historical truth* of a matter! It is quite unfortunate though, that no Sadducean writings have survived, or have yet to be uncovered, although it has been debated by some scholars

---

86 See the comments on this in *Israel in Revolution*, David Rhoads, p. 32.

87 See "Origin of the Pharisees," *Bible History Online*; *Crime before Calvary*, Guy Schofield, p. 33.

88 See *Kosher Jesus*, Rabbi Shmuley Boteach, pp. 19-20.

that portions of the Dead Sea Scrolls were in fact remnants of Sadducean writings,[89] and one *could* consider 1 *Maccabees* as a Sadducean writing. It is also unfortunate that some scholars will claim that,[90] "Pharisean opinions alone are recorded," (i.e. the Mishnah and Talmud), and further claiming that, "opinions contrary" to basically the "majority" Pharisaic opinion, "were naturally excluded." If such a claim were in fact true though, then we would *not* find such accounts as those, for example, that are found in Babli *Yoma* 19b; Yerushalmi *Yoma* 1:5, 39a; *Tosephta Kippurim* 1:8; Babli *Berakhot* 61b! Many, many more examples *could be* offered, but it should not be necessary to offer *every* instance that provides *proof* that such claims simply are *not true* at all, as will be further proven below regarding how the "minority opinions" were very carefully recorded in the Mishnah and Talmud right alongside of the "majority opinions," even when those minority opinions might be derived, *not* from the Pharisaic philosophy, but from one of the other differing Jewish philosophies.

Now, the very name *Pharisee* means, "separate ones,"[91] but it must be *clearly* understood that this meaning of "separate ones," *did not* mean that they separated themselves from "the common people," (or what far too many Christian scholars call, the "*am ha-eretz*,"[92]). For as Hillel stated in *Abot* 2:5,[93] "Do not separate yourself from the community," (but see also what is stated in *Sotah* 5:7, 20c), and as E. P Sanders writes,[94] "We shall see that there is no evidence for full sectarianism, and the concerns which were peculiar to them were just enough to give them a feeling of group solidarity and distinction, not to make them isolated from the rest of Israel." The term *am ha-eretz*, as just noted, has been greatly misunderstood

---

89 See the comments on this in *Caiaphas*, Helen K. Bond, p. 13; *Jesus and Purity Halakah*, Thomas Kazen, p. 53; *Jewish Law from Jesus to the Mishnah*, E. P. Sanders, p. 37 who references the Dead Sea Scroll fragment 4QMMT; *On Earth As It Is In Heaven*, D. C. Thielmann, pp. 569-570 and the corresponding scholars notations to these pages.

90 See for example *Paul and Rabbinic Judaism*, W. D. Davies, p. 3.

91 See the comments in *Jesus before Christianity*, Albert Nolan, p. 12; *The Life and Teachings of Hillel*, Yitzhak Buxbaum, pp. 161-162.

92 See the comments on this term in *A Jewish Understanding of the New Testament*, Samuel Sandmel, p. 201.

93 See the comments on this in *The Life and Teachings of Hillel*, Yitzhak Buxbaum, pp. 193-196.

94 *Jewish Law from Jesus to the Mishnah*, E. P. Sanders, p. 236.

and abused by far too many Christian New Testament scholars[95] for far too long now, and E. P. Sanders is quite correct when he points out two examples, namely, Mishnah *Demai* 2:2-3; *Demai* 6:6, that get used and abused by such scholars.[96] For it was not until *after* the Council of Jamnia that this term became a widely used derogatory term by certain sages. *Originally*, the term *am ha-eretz*, was used *only* in regards to any *Jew* who was "willfully ignorant of the Torah," (*Abot* 2:5, which the sages based on 2 Kings 11:14, 18-20; Ezra 4:4), and after the destruction of the second Temple this in fact became far more true amongst the sages of the Talmud Babli than amongst the sages of the Talmud Yerushalmi,[97] and in *fact* one finds that in John 7:49 even Jesus is highly critical of those who were "willfully ignorant of the Torah," (i.e. the *am ha-eretz*)![98] But the term, (especially in its plural form, *ammei ha-aretzot*), *had been*, and *was still used* as a reference to "foreigners," (i.e. "*gentiles*," based on Genesis 23:7; Job 12:24; Nehemiah 9:10, 24, 30 for Scriptural examples that the Talmudic sages referenced as can be found in Mishnah *Hagigah* 2:7 contrary to the opinions of far too many scholars[99]), and which again, one finds Jesus also being highly critical of "gentiles," (i.e. "foreigners"), in Matthew 6:7; 18:17. For the Greek words, *ethnos, ethnon, ethnikoi*, or *ethnikos* can be considered as equivalents to the Hebrew *am ha-eretz*, (as it is gets used in regards to "foreigners"), in these incidents. Going further though, the term was also applied as well to "Samaritans," (Ezra 9:1), whom, once again we find Jesus likewise being indirectly critical of in Matthew 10:5-6. This is essential to understand in regards to the matter of associating with "tax collectors and sinners"[100] that will be discussed later in this chapter.[101] Now, Marcus

---

95   See the comments on this in *The Life and Teachings of Hillel*, Yitzhak Buxbaum, pp. 167-183.

96   See the comments on this in *Jewish Law from Jesus to the Mishnah*, E. P. Sanders, pp. 33, 155, and 202.

97   See Yoni Pomeranz, *Ordinary Jews in the Babylonian Talmud: Rabbinic Representations and Historic Interpretations*.

98   See the comments on this of Kaufmann Kohler, "Am Ha-Are<u>z</u>," *Jewish Encyclopedia*.

99   See the comments on this in *Galilee*, Sean Freyne, p. 306.

100   In regards to the translation of "tax collectors and sinners," see the comments in *Problems of New Testament Translation*, Edgar J. Goodspeed, pp. 28-29.

101   See also *Taanith* 11a; *Derekh Eretz Zuta* 5:5 and the comments in *Hillel*, Rabbi Joseph Telushkin, pp. 181-183.

Borg does though, rightly believe that the name "Pharisee" was derived from the Hebrew word, *parush*, or the Aramaic *parishaya*,[102] which again means, "set apart," or "separate ones."

Although it is true that there is simply no way of knowing *exactly when* the Pharisees, or for that matter the Essens as a philosophy originated, it is true that both of these philosophies claimed, (and many modern scholars today agree with this claim), to be able to trace their origin back to the *Hasidim* of the time of Ezra and Nehemiah.[103] In the Talmud, for example, (the Essens in particular), were referred to by various terms other than just *Hasidim*. They were referred to as *zenu'im*, (chaste ones), *anav* (humble ones), *kesherim* (blameless ones), *hashsha'im* (silent ones), *watikim* (men of firm principles), *kadoshim* (saints), *banna'im* (builders), *anshe ma'aseh* (men of miraculous deeds),[104] as well as, `*osey ha-Torah* ("observers of the Torah"). Yet, the fact remains that the main "separation" into the different philosophies known as the "Sadducees," "Pharisees" and "Essens" occurred after the Maccabean period when the Hasmoneans reneged on their promises to put in place a legitimate Zadokite priesthood and a legitimate Davidic king.[105] The Hasmonean-Seleucid war brought about a vast breakup of the Jews at that time into the three distinct philosophies noted by Josephus, and as Rabbi Joseph Telushkin states concerning this matter,[106] "One of the sadder ironies of Jewish history is that the Maccabees led a successful revolt against King Antiochus's anti-Semitic oppression only to turn into oppressors of the Jews themselves."

The first of these Jewish philosophies to really discuss are of course the Sadducees, who were the remnant of the Hasmoneans and those who assumed the High Priestly and kingship status, and who then later became collaborators with the Romans and Herodians. As Darrell L. Bock writes

---

102 *Conflict, Holiness & Politics*, Marcus Borg, p. 58.

103 See for example "Origin of the Pharisees," *Bible History Online*.

104 See the comments on this in *Jesus the Pharisee*, Harvey Falk, pp. 39-62.

105 See the comments in *The New Testament*, Bart D. Ehrman, pp. 232-234; *Jewish Literature Between the Bible and the Mishnah*, George W. E. Nickelsburg, pp. 117, 122-123; *A Jewish Understanding of the New Testament*, Samuel Sandmel, p. 21.

106 *Jewish Literacy*, Rabbi Joseph Telushkin, p. 110, but see also his further comments on this matter on p. 112.

concerning the Sadducees,[107] "The Annas clan would have justified its role in sending Jesus to Rome as a matter of ensuring an understanding of the priesthood's policy concerning the newly emerging, socially disturbing movement. Included in this would have been to reasons Jesus was taken before Pilate," (this is a matter that will be discussed in much greater detail in later chapters). The other two primary Jewish philosophies were of course the Pharisees, and also the Essens, (and it must be noted again, that it was the Essens who believed that *they* were the legitimate Zadokite priestly descendants as discussed previously in Chapter 2), and furthermore, both the Pharisees and Essens were loyal patriots of Israel.[108]

A further problem resides in the fact that Judas Maccabaeus made a peace treaty with the Romans in 160 BCE, and therefore, when the dispute broke out between the two Hasmonean brothers, (Aristobulus and Hyrcanus), in 63 BCE the Romans were quick to take advantage of the situation in order to expand their empire and stepped in and took control of Palestine not only ending the conflict between the two brothers, but also ending Jewish sovereignty of Palestine at that time.[109] Therefore, the implication found in the New Testament, and particularly in the Gospel accounts that the Sadducees and the Pharisees somehow collaborated together against Jesus is simply *historically* untrue! As Amy-Jill Levine writes concerning Matthew 28:11-15,[110] "The story makes no sense from any historical perspective. The 'chief priests and the Pharisees' who, according to Matthew (27:62), approach Pilate to request that a guard be placed at the tomb are a very odd combination. Matthew has lumped together two opposing groups in order to present a unified Jewish front against Jesus and his followers... All this suggests the scene is Matthew's composition, not a record of what 'really happened'." Also, as Rabbi Shmuley Boteach rightly points out,[111] "In the Gospels, the Pharisees and Sadducees are frequently described as acting in concert." (Rabbi Boteach cites Matthew 3:7 as an example and goes on to state), "How could this be? The Pharisees and Sadducees were

---

107   *Blasphemy and Exaltation in Judaism*, Darrell L. Bock, p. 196.

108   See the comments in *Bandits, Prophets, and Messiahs*, Richard A. Horsley and John S. Hanson, p. 24.

109   See the comments on this matter in *Revolution in Judaea*, Hyam Maccoby, pp. 25-28.

110   *The Misunderstood Jew*, Amy-Jill Levine, pp. 113-114.

111   *Kosher Jesus*, Rabbi Shmuley Boteach, pp. 19-20.

diametrically opposed, both religiously and politically. Yet Matthew has John the Baptist denouncing them as though they were one and the same. And this doesn't even address the fact that the Pharisees and Sadducees would *never* have gone together to see John the Baptist in the first place...." Boteach then notes Matthew 16:5-12 and writes, "...Anyone who lived during the era would have known the Pharisees and Sadducees were as different from one another as chalk and cheese. So why are they maligned as equal enemies of Jesus' efforts? Something is amiss. Somewhere along the line, the image of the Pharisees has been tampered with." Boteach goes on to state, "Furthermore, as we shall discuss later in greater depth, all allegations that the Pharisees or the supreme court, the Sanhedrin, were involved in Jesus' death were deliberate misrepresentations."

It is essential at this juncture in this chapter to make an important point regarding the *Birkat Ha-Minim*, or *Ha-Zaddukim*, which has for far too long been thought and taught by far too many Christian New Testament scholars that this was a curse by Jews against Christians that was instituted at the Council of Jamnia. But, the *historical fact* of the matter is that this was *originally* a prayer against Jewish "heretics," which became a prayer specifically directed against the "Sadducees," (i.e. "traducers," "informers," and "traitors"), or in essence, a prayer against those who collaborated with "foreign powers" *against* their own Jewish brethren. The usage of this prayer began during the Hasmonean-Seleucid war and was directed against those particular Jews who became "Hellenized"![112] Thus, the *Birkat Ha-Minim* was *never originally directed at Christians*, (for this prayer was in use *long before the time of Jesus*), nor was it even directed at gentiles! This prayer was directed *only* at "heretical" Jews who collaborated with "enemy foreign powers." This is *precisely* why the *Birkat Ha-Minim* began to be directed towards "Christians" after the Council of Jamnia! For scholars seemingly forget that the "*original*" followers of Jesus were Jews, and thus, when this "new movement" of Jews became known as "Christians," and

---

112   See Cyrus Adler and Emil G. Hirsch, "Shemoneh 'Esreh: Petitions against Enemies; Modifications in Birkat Ha-Minim," *Jewish Encyclopedia*; David Instone-Brewer, "The Eighteen Benedictions and the *Minim* before 70 CE," *The Journal of Theological Studies*, Volume 54, N.1, (2003), pp. 25-44; Ben-Zion Binyamin, "Birkat Ha-Minim and the Ein Gedi Inscription," *Immanuel* 21, (Summer 1987), pp. 68-79; *Jesus the Pharisee*, Harvey Falk, pp. 42-46, 70-78.

which included "gentiles" as well, this "movement" was perceived, in the exact same way as during the Hasmonean-Seleucid war, as "Hellenized collaborators with foreign powers," or "traitors" to their own Jewish heritage and brethren! The *original* meaning of the Hebrew word *min*, was "kinds," or "species," (see for example Genesis 1:11-25; 6:20; Leviticus 11:14-29; 19:19; Deuteronomy 14:13-18), and this word derives from the Hebrew root word, *manah*, meaning "apportion," "divide and limit," "split," or "to separate." Now, both of these words in Aramaic have *completely different* meanings, (which again, as was pointed out in the Preface, Hebrew *does not* always readily translate even into Aramaic), and thus, it was only in the post-Biblical time that the word *min* came to have a meaning of "heretic," or "sectarian."[113] There is another non-Biblical Hebrew word that was used in regards to "heretics" at the time of Jesus that began being used around the time of the Maccabees also, and this word being, *epikoros*, as noted in Mishnah *Sanhedrin* 10:1; *Sanhedrin* 13:5;[114] Josephus *Antiquities* 10.11.7.[115] This non-Biblical Hebrew word was derived from the Hebrew root word, *paqar*,[116] combined with the name of the Greek philosopher, Epicurus, and therefore, its usage came about as a result of Jews who had become overly influenced by "Hellenism," (a matter discussed previously in the Preface), or in essence, again, by the time of Jesus it was primarily directed towards the Sadducees and any other collaborators with the Romans. There is also one other final Hebrew word that was used before, during and after the time of Jesus in regards to Jewish "heretics," and this word being, *mumar*, or *mumarim*, "apostates," or "one who converted from Judaism to another religion,"[117] as can be found in *Hullin* 4b; *Tosefta Horayot* 1:5; *Eruvin* 69b; *Horayot* 11a; *Avodah Zarah* 26b. The main points being made here is to

---

113   See David Fouts, "The Meaning of *Min*," *Answers in Genesis* January 1, 2009, last featured June 1, 2011; *Judaism and the Origins of Christianity*, David Flusser, pp. 637-643.

114   See the comments of David M. Grossberg, "Is There a Doctrine of Heresy in Rabbinic Literature?" *The Gemara.com.*

115   See the comments on this in *Paul Was Not a Christian*, Pamela Eisenbaum, pp. 94-95; Gotthard Deutsch, "Apikoros (plural Apikorism)," *Jewish Encyclopedia.*

116   See *A Comprehensive Etymological Dictionary of the Hebrew Language*, p. 522.

117   See the comments on this of J. J. Petuchowski, "The *Mumar* – A Study in Rabbinic Psychology," *Hebrew Union College Annual* Volume 30 (1959), pp. 179-190; *A Comprehensive Etymological Dictionary of the Hebrew Language*, p. 325.

demonstrate how so many Christian New Testament scholars have for far too long now not only abused, misused, and distorted the *original* meaning of the *Birkat Ha-Minim*, but to also demonstrate the distaste that the Pharisees and Essens had in regards to the Sadducees, as well as any other Jew who was a "collaborator with a foreign power."

Now, Dale C. Allison writes this,[118] "The early Church, moreover, did not, as far as we know, engage the Sadducees in debate...." This statement and opinion alone should give *all* scholars a clear indication that the New Testament writings, as we have them today, (including even Paul's Epistles), are *all* products of a period *well after* the 66-73 revolt when the Sadducean philosophy was almost wiped out by the Zealots, and those of the Sadducean philosophy who *did* survive the 66-73 revolt became, in essence, were "absorbed" into Pharisaic/rabbinic Judaism. For as Allison further states,[119] "There is no evidence of real Christian debate with Sadducees in any of the four Gospels, and they are missing entirely from all the New Testament Epistles. They are only marginal in Acts (4:1-2; 5:17-18; 23:6-10)." Likewise, as Thomas Kazen writes,[120] "We should remember that the Tannaim were not heirs of the first-century Pharisees only, but other traditions were also incorporated in the emerging rabbinic movement after 70 CE.[121] The Qumran sectarians seem to have shared priestly perspectives with the Sadducees and expansionist concerns with the Pharisees." But the fact is though, that in all reality there are many instances in the Gospels in which the name "Pharisees" was substituted for the name "Sadducees" as if they were already one in the same philosophy,[122] again, something that would be true only *well after* the 66-73 revolt. As Hyam Maccoby rightly points out concerning this fact,[123] "A very plain example of the substitution of 'Pharisees' for 'Sadducees' is the remark about respect for parents, reported in Mark 7 and Matthew 15. Here Jesus reproves the 'Pharisees' for holding that a man might legally prevent his parents from

---

118 *Jesus of Nazareth*, Dale C. Allison, p. 53.

119 *Jesus of Nazareth*, Dale C. Allison, n. 184, p. 53.

120 *Jesus and Purity Halakah*, Thomas Kazen, p. 216.

121 *Jesus and Purity Halakah*, Thomas Kazen, n. 78, p. 216, *Jewish Contemporaries of Jesus: Pharisees, Sadducees, Essenes*, Gunter Stemberger, pp. 140-147.

122 See the comments in *Jesus and Purity Halakah*, Thomas Kazen, p. 45.

123 *Revolution in Judaea*, Hyam Maccoby, n. 13, p. 225.

benefitting from certain goods, by the device of dedicating the goods to the Temple. The actual ruling of the Pharisees on this point is the exact opposite (Mishnah, *Nedarim* 3:2). The Pharisees placed respect for parents much higher than respect for the Temple. The Sadducees, on the other hand, with their exaggerated respect for the Temple,[124] may have had the ruling described. Jesus is here undoubtedly urging a Pharisaic viewpoint; yet he is represented as urging it *against* the Pharisees." Furthermore, Lloyd Gaston makes an excellent point when he writes concerning Luke 16:14-15,[125] "As Manson,[126] points out, there are a number of traits in this chapter which indicate that the polemic was originally directed against the Sadducees. In general it simply is not true that the Pharisees were lovers of money (Luke 16:14), and the phrase, 'you are those who justify yourselves (*ha-tzedeq*)' (Luke 16:15).[127] However, in the only occurrence of the Hithpael of *zedek* in the Hebrew Bible, Genesis 44:16, Onkelos translates *zekiy*. This might be a play on the name *Sadducee*." Gaston also notes Luke 16:31, which again, it was *only* the Sadducees who did not believe in the resurrection of the dead, whereas the Pharisees did. Thus, this verse from Luke too, could *only be* pointed directly at the Sadducees!

Far too many Christian New Testament scholars have tried to claim that the Pharisees were "strict legal interpreters" of the Torah, and therefore, Jesus' disputes with the Pharisees, as they are outlined in the Gospels, demonstrate that Jesus taught a "relaxed attitude towards the Torah." But, as Rabbi Zelig Pliskin states,[128] "It should be kept in mind that in many instances the stories depict behavior that is praiseworthy and meritorious, but is not obligatory according to the letter of the law." Barrie Wilson likewise very rightly states,[129] "Yet, like the prophets and all Jewish leaders before him, Jesus did exactly that; he taught, debated, and practiced Torah. His earliest followers, under the leadership of his brother, James, also observed the law

---

124   James Dunn in *The Partings of the Ways*, p. 31 is quite in error when he asserts that the "political power" of the Temple lay solely within the Sadducees.

125   *No Stone on Another*, Lloyd Gaston, p. 318.

126   *No Stone on Another*, Lloyd Gaston, n. 3, p. 328, T. W. Manson, *The Mission and Message of Jesus*, pp. 587-593.

127   *No Stone on Another*, Lloyd Gaston, n. 4, p. 328.

128   *Love Your Neighbor*, Rabbi Zelig Pliskin, p. 15.

129   *How Jesus Became Christian*, Barrie Wilson, p. 63.

as Jesus himself had done. This meant keeping the Sabbath, observing the dietary laws, practicing circumcision, honoring the Ten Commandments, and all the other requirements of the law. In light of well-founded fears over Hellenistic assimilation and annihilation, no responsible Jewish leader of the time would have dared suggest abandoning the Torah."

We then find the very stunningly erroneous claim made by Joseph Ratzinger and Pope Benedict XVI that the "Messiah" was to somehow bring forth some sort of a "new" Torah.[130] Now at first, the word they use is *"renewed"* Torah, but in the end their opinion is that the "Messiah" would bring forth a *"new"* Torah, which begs the question to be asked; from where, and/or from what source, or from what verse of Scripture do they derive such an interpretation? For as Joel Carmichael so rightly points out,[131] repeatedly throughout Scripture, (Genesis 9:17; Genesis 17:11; Exodus 24:8; Jeremiah 31:31-39; Malachi 3:1 for examples), God *"renews"* a "covenant" with "His people," and in the majority of these examples it is by way of His Torah, which is *precisely* what Jesus was doing as well – i.e. *"renewing"* the "covenant" God made with His people Israel by way of God's Torah![132] Furthermore, as Gerhard von Rad points out concerning Jeremiah 31:31-32, (but see also Ezekiel 36:24-28), Jeremiah mentions a "new covenant," but which Jeremiah says that this "new covenant" would have as its basis of formation *the Torah*, and *not* a "new" Torah! As Gerhard von Rad writes,[133] "This *Torah* is also to stand in the center of the New

---

130   See the comments in *Jesus of Nazareth: Part One*, Ratzinger and Pope Benedict, pp. 99-106; but see also the similar comments in *The Theological Significance of Jesus' Temple Action in Mark's Gospel*, Emilio G. Chavez, pp. 47-56; *Paul and Rabbinic Judaism*, W. D. Davies, pp. 72-73, and pp. 147-176 in which Davies equates this notion of a "new" Torah as deriving from the teachings of Paul, which in essence, Davies is quite accurate, (as will be discussed in this chapter), since Paul deviated from the teachings of Jesus, but which Davies seems to not acknowledge, or recognize.

131   See the comments in *The Death of Jesus*, Joel Carmichael, p. 119.

132   See the comments in *The New Testament and the People of God*, N. T. Wright, pp. 299-301; *Jesus and the Spiral of Violence*, Richard A. Horsley, p. 265.

133   *The Message of the Prophets*, Gerhard von Rad, pp. 181-182, and see also his comments on p. 203.

Covenant which Yahweh is going to make with Israel 'in these days'."[134] Gerhard von Rad goes on to state that,[135] "According to their prophecies, the 'new things' will follow the pattern of the 'old' – a new exodus, a new covenant, a new David, etc. The old is thus renewed; it is present in the new, in the enigmatic dialectic of valid and obsolete." Gerhard von Rad concludes his comments on this matter by writing concerning *all* of the ancient prophets of Israel that,[136] "Yet, they also shared a common certainty that the new thing which they expected was already prefigured in the old, and that the old would be present in the new in perfect form." There have been, and it seems that there still are a great many scholars such as Ratzinger and Pope Benedict who seem to ignore what is stated in Deuteronomy 17:18-20, which *clearly* states that the one who "sits upon the throne of his kingdom" will not only "write for himself a copy of *this* (emphasis mine) Torah," but it should always "be with him, and he shall read therein all the days of his life" and "keep all the words of *this* (emphasis again mine) Torah," and these verses *do not* say that this will be some sort of "new" Torah![137] Furthermore, as Edgar Goodspeed points out regarding Matthew 26:28,[138] the word "new" *does not* appear in the oldest and best manuscripts of this verse, and thus, the verse simply reveals that Jesus was simply reiterating, "the blood of the covenant," the *original* covenant made at Sinai and *not* some "new" covenant! There is also though, the erroneous idea that somehow, "Jesus' improvisation on Jewish eschatology was the creation of a new religious identity based on a novel interpretation of the world in the light of Jewish tradition."[139]

Returning for a moment to the matter noted above about the scholars who portray Jesus as teaching a "relaxed attitude towards the Torah" while claiming that the Pharisees were "strict interpreters to the letter of the Torah," we now know from the Dead Sea Scrolls that the Essens were even "far more strict" in *their* legal interpretations of the Torah than even the

---

134 See further on this the comments in *On Earth As It Is In Heaven*, D. C. Thielmann, pp. 392-393 and the corresponding scholars notations to these pages.

135 *The Message of the Prophets*, Gerhard von Rad, pp. 238-239.

136 *The Message of the Prophets*, Gerhard von Rad, p. 266.

137 See the comments in *A Rabbi Talks with Jesus*, Jacob Neusner, p. 32.

138 *The Problems with New Testament Translation*, Edgar J. Goodspeed, pp. 40-41.

139 See for example the comments in *Jesus of Nazareth*, Dale C. Allison, p. 171.

Pharisees were.[140] Yet, *nowhere* in the New Testament, and a *fact*, which is virtually *never* mentioned by *any* of these scholars who claim that Jesus taught a "relaxed attitude towards the Torah," is the *fact* that we *never* read or hear anything in the Gospels about Jesus ever having similar disputes with any of the Essens over *their* even "far more strict" interpretations of the Torah,[141] *especially* in regards to the Essens strict adherence to the "purity" halakha, a matter even noted in *Avodah Zarah* 9:15 regarding the Essens.[142] Why, and why the failures on the part of so many Christian New Testament scholars to even mention this *fact*? If, as these mainline modern Christian New Testament scholars so often desire to claim that Jesus taught a "relaxed attitude towards the Torah," should we not then find Jesus likewise *chastising* the Essens – the strictest observers of the Torah amongst *all* of the Jewish philosophies at the time of Jesus? This *fact* that we never find Jesus chastising the Essens makes absolutely no sense whatsoever when stacked up against the claims being made about the "historical Jesus" by these mainline modern New Testament scholars! The Essens were no small or insignificant Jewish philosophy; for they even had their own special gate entering into the Temple called the "Gate of the Essens." Now, James Dunn[143] believes that he *does* see Jesus chastising the Essens in Luke 14:1-6, as well as elsewhere, which is in agreement with Pharisaic "oral law," yet is in disagreement in particular with the Dead Sea Scrolls *CD11* (*Damascus Document*), as well as some of the other scrolls and fragments found at Qumran. But, the *best* carbon dating evidence for the *Damascus Document* in particular, places it being written sometime

---

140   See the comments in *Bandits, Prophets, and Messiahs*, Richard A. Horsley and John S. Hanson, pp. 26 and 178-179; *The New Testament and Jewish Law*, James G. Crossley, pp. 11-13; *Jewish Law from Jesus to the Mishnah*, E. P. Sanders, p. 15; in *The Trial of Jesus*, Josef Blinzler, pp. 51-72 one finds a prime example of the erroneous depiction of the Pharisees as being the greatest "enemies" of Jesus; see further on the correct depiction of the Pharisees in *On Earth As It Is In Heaven*, D. C. Thielmann, pp. 885-886; *Israel in Revolution*, David Rhoads, pp. 34-46.

141   See the comments on this in *Jesus and Israel*, Jules Isaac, p. 82; *Jesus and His Contemporaries*, Etienne Trocme, p. 3.

142   See Kaufmann Kohler, "Essenes," *Jewish Encyclopedia*.

143   *The Partings of the Ways*, James Dunn, pp. 108, 112-113; but see also the similar comments in *The New Testament and Jewish Law*, James G. Crossley, p. 33.

around the time of the Maccabees, (which as noted in Chapter 1 already, at that time a much stricter Sabbath observance was in place). Thus, Dunn's conclusions are highly questionable as to their merit. Likewise, though, David Flusser perceives Luke 16:1-9 to be a criticism of the Essens by Jesus.[144] As proof texts to his claim, Flusser references Luke 16:10-12; Romans 15:26-27; 1 Corinthians 9:11; *Didache* 4:7-8. According to Flusser's claim, the Essens *only* conducted commerce with members of their own Palestinian philosophy, while in each of these examples that Flusser offers as proof that Jesus was criticizing the Essens one finds that commerce is being conducted with "gentiles," or in essence, individuals who were *outside* of the Palestinian Essen community. The *historical fact* is though, that the Essens only disapproved of commerce that was conducted for the purposes of one gaining wealth, or profit, or for the personal gain of worldly possessions[145] as noted by Josephus *Jewish Wars* 2.122, 137-138;[146] as well as by Philo *Every Good Man is Free* 12.75-87. Josephus, in *Contra Apion* 1:60 makes it quite clear that virtually *all* first century Palestinian Jews did very little commerce "outside of their philosophy," or especially, "outside of their fellow Jews," in essence, conducting any commerce with "gentiles," which thus, eliminates the probability that Luke 16:1-9 was directed *solely* at the Essens as Flusser claims. Furthermore, Dunn and Flusser, as well as other scholars who hold to similar opinions as theirs, seem to ignore the fact that the Church historian Eusebius, (*Ecclesiastical History* 2.17.11), *clearly* associates the Essens writings with the New Testament writings, stating, "The writings of ancient men were the founders of the sect referred to by Philo, may very well have been the Gospels and Epistles which were not yet written."[147] Thus, the many alterations made to the New Testament, (noted in the Preface), might very well have brought about certain statements by Jesus to appear to be contrary to what is found in the Dead Sea Scrolls. Therefore, since no *actual* mentioning of the Essens can be found *anywhere* in the New Testament, (unless, that is, scholars

---

144   *Judaism and the Origins of Christianity*, David Flusser, pp. 150-168.

145   See the comments on this of E. Planta Nesbit, "Christ, Christians and Christianity," *Jesus an Essene.*

146   See the comments of John C. Reeves, "The Essene Hypothesis," *Early Judaism.*

147   See the comments on this in *On Earth As It Is In Heaven*, D. C. Thielmann, n. 8, pp. 594-595.

desire to equate the Essens with the Nazoreans), then *no scholar* can make such claims as Dunn and Flusser make! For each and every time a scholar makes such a claim, one will then find the fact that these scholars, such as David Flusser, contradicting their own claims when they point out a great many similarities between Jesus and the Essens![148]

Going even further into this matter though, one finds the *fact* that around 20 BCE, Menachem the Essene, served as the *Ab Bet Din*, (a term that will be discussed in Chapter 5), of the Great Sanhedrin for a period of time during which Hillel was serving as the *Nasi*, (another term that will be discussed in Chapter 5), of the Great Sanhedrin as noted in Mishnah *Hagigah* 2:2. During this period, Menachem the Essene subjected himself to the rulings of the much more lenient Hillel.[149] Now, it has been suggested by several modern Jewish scholars that it was *this very Menachem the Essene*, (spoken about by Josephus in *Jewish Wars* 11.8.3; *Antiquities* 15.10.5), who *was* the "Teacher of Righteousness" referred to in the Dead Sea Scrolls,[150] while other Jewish scholars believe that it was only *after* Menachem the Essene had resigned from being the *Ab Bet Din*, (to which Shammai took his place), that Menachem even *became* an Essene.[151] In the Talmud though, it states that Menachem had a strong relationship with Herod the Great, (*Hagigah* 16b), simply because he had praised Herod the Great while Herod was a young boy in school, and the Talmud also states that Menachem became an apostate, (*Hagigah* 77d). But there is really no way for one to be certain whether or not Menachem was, or was not already an Essene while he served as the *Ab Bet Din*, and/or whether or not the Talmudic reference to Menachem becoming an apostate was due to his resigning from being the *Ab Bet Din* of the Great Sanhedrin. For as noted earlier in this chapter, both the Essens and the Pharisees claimed to be able

---

148   See the comments on this in *Jesus*, David Flusser, pp. 75-83; *Judaism and the Origins of Christianity*, David Flusser, pp. 23-87, 102-105, 169-172, 193-201.

149   See the comments on this in *Jesus the Pharisee*, Harvey Falk, pp. 6-7, and 157.

150   See the comments on this by Dr. Lizorkin Eyzenberg, "Jesus and Jewish Essenes," *Jewish Jesus*, January 5, 2018; Kaufmann Kohler, "Menahem the Essene," *Jewish Encyclopedia*; Kaufmann Kohler, "Essenes," *Jewish Encyclopedia*; *Jesus the Pharisee*, Harvey Falk, pp. 6-7, and 157.

151   See the comments of Rabbi Moshe Reiss, "The Dead Sea Scrolls," *Christianity: A Jewish Perspective*.

to trace their beginnings all the way back to the _Hasidim_ from the time of Ezra and Nehemiah. Yet, the main point being made here is to show that the Essens not only had a strong relationship with the Pharisees and shared much in common, but also to show that the Essens at times were willing to be just as lenient in regards to certain aspects of the "oral" Torah as were the Pharisees.

There have also even been some scholars who have attempted to claim that Jesus and his disciples _cannot_ "be likened to a religious community like that of Qumran or the Essenizing or Baptizing Brotherhoods."[152] But such claims actually get refuted by what Josephus tells us about the Essens in _Jewish Wars_ 2.124, and this being that, the Essens settled "not in one city" but "in large numbers in every town."[153] Thus, a "learned rabbi" of the Essens would need to wander from town to town teaching and preaching to his "fellow Essens," _especially_ if what that "learned rabbi" was bringing to them was the "Good News" that the "Kingdom of Heaven was at hand," _exactly_ as was done by Jesus and his disciples! Therefore, _all_ such claims that the "Jesus movement" _cannot_ "be likened to a religious community like that of Qumran" are simply _without merit!_ So, it is long past the time for these mainline modern Christian New Testament scholars to produce _indisputable, undeniable historical factual evidence_ that Jesus chastised the Essens over _their_ strict interpretations of the Torah in order to substantiate any such scholarly claims that Jesus taught a "relaxed attitude towards the Torah,"[154] or that his movement _cannot_ be likened to the Essens and Qumran! The very _fact_ though, that Jesus himself was indeed _very strict_ not only in his _own_ adherence to the Torah, but also in his teachings of the Torah, as can be seen in Matthew 5:20, which is a direct reflection of the Pharisaic teaching found in _Baba Metzia_ 30b; _Baba Metzia_ 83a; _Baba Metzia_ 108a regarding the fact that one "should go beyond the letter of the

---

152   See the comments in _Jesus and His Contemporaries_, Etienne Trocme, p. 37; and see also the similar comments in _The Partings of the Ways_, James Dunn, pp. 59-60.

153   See the comments in _The Apocalyptic Imagination_, John J. Collins, pp. 117-119.

154   See the comments in _The Jews and the Gospel_, Gregory Baum, pp. 56-59 who does an excellent job proving that Jesus _did not_ teach a "relaxed attitude towards the Torah"; see also the excellent refutations to such claims in _Jesus and Israel_, Jules Isaac, pp. 49-73, and 179-180.

law in our dealings with others,"[155] and in *fact*, Matthew 5:19 *clearly* states that "whoever then *relaxes* one of the least of these commandments and teaches men so, shall be called least in the Kingdom of Heaven," which is a *clear and direct* contradiction to *any* and *every* scholar who claims that Jesus either taught or preached a "relaxed attitude towards the Torah."

As Lloyd Gaston so rightly points out though, in regards to whether or not Jesus had a "relaxed attitude towards the Torah," that in Mark 11:16,[156] "The action of Jesus here reported is strange enough. That he would not allow anyone to carry a vessel (*skeuos*) through the Temple area goes beyond even the regulations of the Pharisees, for the prohibition in *Berakhot* 9:5 usually referred to in this connection speaks of staff, sandals, wallet, and dust on the feet but does not specifically mention a vessel at all." Gaston also quotes from the Dead Sea Scroll fragment *4 Qflor* I, 1-13 and states,[157] "The community is unmistakably called a 'Temple made of men' (*miqdash adam*) who offer as sacrifices deeds of the law." Gaston goes on to point out that the community at Qumran interpreted 2 Samuel 7 by way of Exodus 15:17 and the *miqdash Adonai* (Temple of God) to mean a "Temple of men," (i.e. the people of Israel) just as later Christians came to believe in regards to the Church as he notes regarding 1 Timothy 3:15.[158] Thus, it is quite refreshing to see such prominent scholars as Joseph Ratzinger and Pope Benedict XVI freely stating,[159] "… It appears that not only John the Baptist, but possibly Jesus and his family as well, were close to the Qumran community." For the moment though, let us just focus on whether or not the Pharisees *were* in fact such "strict legal interpreters of the Torah" as these mainline modern Christian New Testament scholars far too often try to claim.

Although several of these matters have already been briefly mentioned in previous chapters it is essential to mention them again here in this chapter simply as examples of the point being made. First, let us look at the matter of divorce spoken about by Jesus in Matthew 5:31-32, and Matthew 19:8-9, which, for some reason, has seemingly confused some

---

155   See the comments in *Love Your Neighbor*, Rabbi Zelig Pliskin, pp. 378-379.

156   *No Stone on Another*, Lloyd Gaston, p. 85.

157   *No Stone on Another*, Lloyd Gaston, pp. 163-164.

158   *No Stone on Another*, Lloyd Gaston, p. 197.

159   *Jesus of Nazareth: Part One*, Ratzinger and Pope Benedict, pp. 13-14.

scholars,[160] and one can only guess that it is because of the fact that these scholars have failed to do a thorough enough job of researching Jewish laws and customs from the time of Jesus! For this teaching by Jesus directly reflects the Pharisaic teaching that is found in Mishnah, *Gittin* 9:10, which notes the differences of interpretation between the schools of Hillel and Shammai.[161] As it states in regards to the opinion of the school of Shammai in *Gittin* 9:10, "A man should not divorce his wife unless he has found her guilty of some unseemly conduct." It is then further stated in *Gittin* 90b, "If a man divorces his wife, even the alter sheds tears."[162] Mary Douglas makes a very erroneous statement when she writes,[163] "The primitive church of the Acts in its treatment of women was setting a standard of freedom and equality which was against the traditional Jewish custom." But, as Amy-Jill Levine rightly states,[164] "To claim that Jesus 'liberated' women from a repressive Judaism by forbidding divorce and so protecting women's rights is false, wrong, and bigoted... Again, it is about time that Jews and Christians stopped bearing false witness against each other's traditions." Levine is quite correct here, for the fact is that the "liberation" of women goes all the way back to the time of Moses concerning the matter involving the five daughters of Zelophead that is recorded in Numbers 27:1-11 and further debated in Numbers 36:1-12, and then fulfilled in Joshua 17:3-4. As Rabbi Barry L. Schwartz writes concerning this matter,[165] "Judged by the standards of their time, the sisters won a significant victory in the battle of equality." Another good example that should be offered here as

---

160   See for example *Jesus Before the Gospels*, Bart Ehrman, pp. 200-202.

161   See the comments on this matter of debate over divorce in *The New Testament and Jewish Law*, James G. Crossley, pp. 67-76; *Jewish Literacy*, Rabbi Joseph Telushkin, p. 122.

162   See the comments in *The New Testament and Rabbinic Judaism*, David Daube, pp. 71-89.

163   *Purity and Danger*, Mary Douglas, p. 194; but see also the erroneous comments on this matter in *Mark*, Robert H. Gundry, pp. 528-543.

164   *The Misunderstood Jew*, Amy-Jill Levine, p. 141; but see also the comments on this matter in *The New Testament*, Bart D. Ehrman, p. 43; but to see a great deal more on this matter see the comments in *On Earth As It Is In Heaven*, D. C. Thielmann, pp. 401-407 and the corresponding scholars notations to these pages.

165   *Judaisms Great Debates*, Rabbi Barry L. Schwartz, p. 26; but see also the comments of Solomon Schecter and Judah David Eisenstein, "Etiquette," *Jewish Encyclopedia*.

well is Deborah the Prophetess in Judges 4-5, as well as the Prophetess Anna mentioned in Luke 2:36-37.

Also, we have the matter of Jesus saying in Matthew 6:24; Luke 16:13 that one cannot be a "slave of two masters." But comparisons to this saying, as well as certain aspects of Paul's teachings related to this saying of Jesus can be found, for example, in *Berakhot* 61a; *Eruvin* 18a; *Genesis Rabbah* 14.4; *Testament of Dan* 4:7; *Shabbat* 30a; *Shabbat* 151b; *Niddah* 61b. In these last three examples is where one finds the reflection of a Pauline theme, for as R. Yoḥanon is recorded as stating here, "It is written (Psalm 88:6, 'Free among the dead'; when a man dies, he becomes free from the law and the commandments; as Solomon said (Ecclesiastes 4:2), 'And I praise the dead who are already dead'." As David Flusser points out concerning this[166] man is freed from his own inclinations, and thus, a man belongs to and serves *only* the one true master – God!

Bart Ehrman, (as a result of his own *personally chosen* biased reasons), considers the parable found in Matthew 22:1-14 to be a "distorted memory" by the author of Matthew's Gospel.[167] Ehrman clearly notes his main reasoning for his opinion when he states that the ending of this parable (Matthew 22:14) is "confusing," and "a very strange ending" simply because, as Ehrman puts it, they were not wearing "the appropriate apparel." But it is quite obvious, (as happens far too often with far too many Christian, or in Ehrman's case, "agnostic," New Testament scholars), that Ehrman has failed to do enough research into ancient Jewish customs and teachings, not only from the time of Jesus, but dating from even long before the time of Jesus. For one finds a shorter, but almost identical parable to the one found in these verses from Matthew's Gospel, which contains a virtually identical ending to the one in Matthew's Gospel in *Shabbat* 153a![168]

Likewise, as previously mentioned, Jesus' association with "tax collectors and sinners" has somehow been interpreted as being "unique," or "unusual." As an example, C. Leslie Mitton writes,[169] "Among contemporary Jews it

---

166   *Judaism and the Origins of Christianity*, David Flusser, p. 170.

167   *Jesus Before the Gospels*, Bart Ehrman, pp. 202-204.

168   See the comments on this of Frere Olivier Catel, "The Parable – A Rabbinical Literary Genre," *The Jewish Sources of Christianity*, November 23, 2018.

169   *Jesus*, C. Leslie Mitton, p. 92; but see also the comments on this in *Mark*, Robert H. Gundry, pp. 123-131.

was incredible that anyone claiming to speak as a prophet of God would degrade himself and his message by such conduct." The scholars who make such assertions as these, quite often derive their thinking based on what is found being stated in the Mishnah and Talmud, *Avodah Zerah* 39a; *Bekharoth* 31a; *Shabbat* 78b; *Hagigah* 26a; *Shebiyth* 39a; *Sanhedrin* 25b-26a; *Baba Kamma* 10:1; *Baba Kamma* 113a; *Nedarim* 111:4; *Tohoroth* 7:6;[170] *Eruvin* 36b; *Demai* 3:4, all of which speak seemingly poorly about tax collectors, harlots, robbers, and sinners in general. But the misrepresentation of all of these Mishnaic and Talmudic tractates by these scholars simply demonstrates, as noted in an earlier chapter, their lack of the specialized training that is needed in order to properly understand the Talmud.[171] For in reality, all of these Mishnaic and Talmudic tractates are in fact no different than Jesus' own actions, which was, to bring such individuals to repentance for their conduct and to bring them back to living their lives according to the Torah,[172] just as can be found in Luke 3:12 being done by John the Baptist. As Ezekiel 33:11 states, "Say to them, 'As I live,' says the Lord God, 'I have no pleasure in the death of the wicked; but that the wicked turn from his way and live...'." It is quite erroneous, and blatantly unfair with the added problem of an extreme bias for *any* scholar to portray these Pharisaic teachings in any other manner. As Hyam Maccoby remarks, (as

---

170   See the comments on this tractate in *Ritual and Morality*, Hyam Maccoby, p. 150.

171   See for example *Who is Jesus*, Darrell L. Bock. pp. 48-59; *Studies of the Historical Jesus*, Ernst Fuchs, p. 36; in *The Partings of the Ways*, James Dunn, pp. 102-107, Dunn interprets these "sinners" to either be "gentiles," (based on Galatians 2:15), or "*apostate Jews*," (based on 1 Maccabees 1:34; 2:44, 48; Psalms of Solomon 3:3-7; 4:1, 8; 9:3 and certain parts of the Dead Sea Scrolls); *Jesus and the Laws of Purity*, Roger P. Booth, pp. 110-111.

172   See the comments in *Love Your Neighbor*, Rabbi Zelig Pliskin, p. 34; Kaufmann Kohler and Ludwig Blau, "Gehenna: Sin and Merit," *Jewish Encyclopedia*; Crawford Howell Toy and Joseph Jacobs, "Publican," *Jewish Encyclopedia*; Emil G. Hirsch and Eduard Konig, "Deep," *Jewish Encyclopedia*; Kaufmann Kohler and Max Schlesinger, "Repentance (Hebrew, 'teshuva')," *Jewish Encyclopedia*; *On Earth As It Is In Heaven*, D. C. Thielmann, p. 65 and n. 67, p. 100 as well as the entirety of Chapter 2; *God in Search of Man*, Abraham Joshua Heschel, p. 363; *A Heart of Many Rooms*, David Hartman, pp. 37, 46-47; *The Life and Teachings of Hillel*, Yitzhak Buxbaum, pp. 82-83, 108-109, and 114-124; *Jesus*, David Flusser, p. 18.

any Jew would remark),[173] "These wretches who were prepared to join in the organized robbery of their own countrymen for the sake of a percentage of the loot were regarded as criminals by their compatriots. These are the 'publicans' with whom Jesus consorted in order to reclaim them from sin. If they were social outcasts, it was for good reason. It was the measure of Jesus' optimism and faith that he hoped to reclaim even these most abandoned of torturers and extortionists." Maccoby also states,[174] "Many scholars, however, unlike Milgrom, have accepted uncritically that Leviticus 11:8 forbids the incurring of impurity. This has led to misinterpretations of the New Testament: for example, that Jesus' association with sinners and tax collectors showed that he flouted the laws of ritual purity. Since there was no law forbidding people to incur impurity, Jesus was not flouting any impurity law. What may have aroused criticism was his association with people who were real sinners, in the sense of being extortionate gangsters cooperating with Roman tax farmers. But Jesus, like many messianic claimants both before and since, hoped to induce repentance even in the most desperate sinners. The argument between Jesus and his critics thus had nothing to do with ritual impurity." Maccoby further clarifies this when he states,[175] "There are few overt references to ritual purity in the New Testament, but most of the ritual purity aspects which scholars read into the text are non-existent. For example, there is no basis for the idea that Jesus' association with sinners and tax gatherers was opposed by the Pharisees on ritual purity grounds. The text does not say so, and it would not make sense to say so."[176]

But taking this one step further, in order to point out just how wrong all of these scholars are in their interpretations, it seems that these scholars have all either missed, or ignored the *fact* that even Jesus himself criticizes certain *particular* "tax collectors" in Matthew 18:17,[177] pointing out that people should virtually avoid them, (see also Matthew 5:46 as well, which

---

173   *Revolution in Judaea*, Hyam Maccoby, p. 39.

174   *Ritual and Morality*, Hyam Maccoby, p. 69.

175   *Ritual and Morality*, Hyam Maccoby, p. 149.

176   See the further comments on this in *Ritual and Morality*, Hyam Maccoby, p. 150.

177   See the comments on this of Glenn G. Waddell, "The Meaning of Matthew 18:17B in its Historical and Literary Context and its Application in the Church Today," Charlotte, North Carolina, January 2014.

is an indirect criticism of "tax-collectors")! Likewise, in Matthew 17:24-27 Jesus *does not* criticize in any way the "Temple tax collectors" in *these* verses, but Jesus *does* criticize *only* the "tax collectors" for the "kings of the earth." The two key Greek words of importance in these verses as *proof* of this *fact* are the words *allotrion* (Matthew 17:25), meaning "foreign," "strange," or "belonging to another,"[178] and the Greek word *skandalisomen* (Matthew 17:27), meaning "an action that causes sin," "fault," "stain," "a stumbling block," (compare to the Hebrew word *mikshol* in Leviticus 19:14 for example), and which a form of this Greek word can also be found, for example, in Matthew 13:41; Romans 9:33 as well as elsewhere, for which it can also mean "hostility."[179] Furthermore, one can easily recognize that this Greek word is comparable to the English word, *scandalous*. Now, it has been suggested by some scholars that Jesus in these verses mentioned is claiming to be of the priesthood, (a matter discussed previously in Chapter 2), and therefore, he was exempt from having to pay the Temple tax,[180] as prescribed in Mishnah *Shekalim* 1:3. There is also further proof that Jesus' association with "tax collectors," etc. was nothing "unique" in regards to Jewish law, or first century Jewish practice. For we find in the Talmud, *Baba Batra* 143a; *Yoma* 1.2.39a; *Ketuboth* 10.5.34a that it speaks of an incident between two different tax collectors that got resolved by R. Judah I, which then *obviously* means that this Pharisee had to have some sort of *association* with these "tax collectors" in order to have resolved the dispute that occurred between them![181] But in reality, scholars are missing the biggest point of all, and this being namely, that Luke 3:12-13 clearly denotes that the majority of the "tax collectors" being referred to in the New Testament *are not* the "tax collectors" for the Romans – as far too many

---

178   See *BDAG Greek-English Lexicon*, pp. 47-48; *Liddell and Scott's Greek-English Lexicon*, p. 38.

179   See *BDAG Greek-English Lexicon*, p. 926; *Liddell and Scott's Greek-English Lexicon*, p. 731.

180   See for example *Jewish Law from Jesus to the Mishnah*, E. P. Sanders, pp. 50-51; David Daube, "Temple Tax," *Jesus, the Gospels, and the Church: Essays in Honor of William R. Farmer*, E. P. Sanders, pp. 121-134.

181   See the comments in *Studies in the History of the Sanhedrin*, Hugo Mantel, p. 203 and n. 208, p. 203.

scholars, for far too long now have been claiming,[182] nor were they the "tax collectors" for Herod Antipas as other scholars claim[183] - but instead they are the Temple "tax collectors"[184] who were highly respected for the most part. But now it is true that at times, there were a very *few* individuals who *were*, in fact, crooked in their Temple tax collecting responsibilities with their own Jewish countrymen,[185] and Leviticus 19:35 and 25:14 expressly forbid one from being "crooked" in dealings with others, and therefore the distaste against these particular "crooked tax collectors."[186] But also at times, these "tax collectors" who were crooked thieves ended up being punished even by the Romans because of their crooked dealings.[187] Yet, in Luke 19:2-10 we find a prime example of these crooked "tax collectors" repenting of their crooked dealings. There is another example from the New Testament that the scholars making these ridiculous claims about associating with "sinners" have either seemingly overlooked or deliberately paid no attention to, and this being, what is found being stated in 1 Corinthians 5:9-13. For in these verses one finds Paul teaching that one should avoid "sinners" who were *already* members or followers of the "Jesus movement," yet it was perfectly okay for one to associate with "sinners" who were *not* members of the community of followers of Jesus! In essence then, Paul, as just pointed out from 1 Corinthians 5:9-13, Jesus as noted

---

182 See for example, *The New Testament*, Bart D. Ehrman, p. 260; *Jesus and the Spiral of Violence*, Richard A. Horsley, pp. 7-8.

183 See for example *Jesus and the Spiral of Violence*, Richard A. Horsley, pp. 212-223 in which he does offer refutation for the general consensus opinion about these "tax collectors," yet his overall assertions are still quite in error in that he wrongly assumes that they are the "tax collectors" for Herod Antipas' tetrarchy and not the Romans.

184 See the comments in *Roman Society and Roman Law in the New Testament*, A. N. Sherwin-White, pp. 125-143.

185 See the comments on this in *The Death of Jesus*, Joel Carmichael, p. 168; Daniel Sperber, "Tax Gatherers," *Encyclopedia Judaica*; *Love Your Neighbor*, Rabbi Zelig Pliskin, pp 36-38, and on pp 76-77 Rabbi Pliskin discusses how one should pray diligently for others despite their shortcomings.

186 See the comments on this in *Love Your Neighbor*, Rabbi Zelig Pliskin, pp. 315-316 and 321-325.

187 See the comments on this by Joseph Jacobs and Isaac Broyde, "Sardinia: Under the Romans," *Jewish Encyclopedia*.

above, *and* the Pharisees were all in one accord in regards to attempting to bring "tax-collectors and sinners" to repentance,[188] which thus, *required* that one *associate* with said "tax collectors and sinners" in order to bring about said "repentance"!

Now, *the* most important point of all to understand in regards to the fact that Jesus' actions with "tax collectors" was nothing "unique" resides in the *fact* that the Greek word, *apostole*, was the term given to the money, or taxes for Palestine (i.e. the "Temple Tax"), and the word *apostoli*, (which means one who is "sent," or "sent forth"[189]), was the Greek word used to designate these individuals who were sent out to collect the "Temple Tax" including the collection of the "Temple Tax" from the Diaspora communities,[190] and these two Greek words correspond with the Hebrew word *m'shullaḥ*, "one who is sent," or *shaliaḥ*, "messenger,"[191] both of which derive from the Hebrew root word *shalaḥ*.[192] These *apostoli* were in fact, for the most part, highly respected individuals *except* when they became crooked (as just noted above). Furthermore, one can easily recognize that these two Greek words comprise the very term to which Jesus' disciples eventually came to be known as – i.e. "Apostles!"[193] The community at Qumran, as well as certain accounts in Acts, (such as Acts 5 regarding Ananias and Sapphira),[194] Romans 16, and 1 Corinthians 16 speaks of such matters! Thus, *all* of Jesus' disciples were in essence "tax collectors," (*apostoli*), for their community of followers, and as long as they were not "crooked" in their tax collections, there was nothing "unique," "unusual," or in violation of any Jewish law by Jesus' associating with them! Furthermore, one can find this very fact in the interpretation of saying #100 in the *Gospel of Thomas*,

---

188   See the comments on this in *Paul Was Not a Christian*, Pamela Eisenbaum, pp. 161-167.

189   See the comments in *Prophecy in Early Christianity*, David E. Aune, p. 202.

190   See the comments on this by Richard Gottheil and Alexander Buchler, "Apostole, Apostoli," *Jewish Encyclopedia*.

191   See *A Jewish Understanding of the New Testament*, Samuel Sandmel, p. 43.

192   See *A Comprehensive Etymological Dictionary of the Hebrew Language*, pp. 660-661; *Etymological Dictionary of Biblical Hebrew*, p. 263.

193   See the comments on this matter from Kaufmann Kohler, "Apostle and Apostleship," *Jewish Encyclopedia*.

194   See the comments on this in *On Earth As It Is In Heaven*, D. C. Thielmann, pp. 628-630 and the corresponding scholar's notations to these pages.

which parallels, (with slight difference), what is found, for example, in Mark 12:14-17,[195] (a matter that will be further discussed in Chapter 8). Now, the word, *publicani*, "publicans," was used to refer to the individuals who collected the taxes *only* for the Romans, but *not* for the Temple. These Roman "tax collectors" were also referred to as *telonion*, (Matthew 9:9; Mark 2:14; Luke 5:27 for example),[196] and this word *telonion* actually means "toll booth," or "tax booth." The *publicani* were actually individuals who "farmed out" or "sold the rights" to other individuals who were the highest bidder to be the ones collecting the taxes in these *telonion*, "toll booths," and the *publicani* held control over several different towns' *telonion* in which they collected the "taxes" on exported goods from each of these towns. Virtually *all* of these *publicani* and the individuals who bought the rights to sit in the *telonion* to collect the taxes on exported goods were pagan gentiles, (i.e. Roman citizens), or in essence, "*non-Jews*." But, there *were*, also, a few Jews who were *publicani*, and it was these few "Jews" who *were publicani*,[197] such as Zacchaeus in Luke 19:2 who were looked upon as "traitors" to their own brethren, and thus, the reason *why* the Gospel accounts so accurately note that these individuals were so hated by other Jews. Now, the Greek word *telos* was used in regards to the taxes that were paid to the Romans, as noted in *1 Maccabees* 10:31; 11:35; Romans 13:7. In regards to the Temple tax though, as it is found being stated in Mishnah *Shekalim* 1:3; Philo *Special Laws* 1.77-78; Josephus *Antiquities* 18.312 one could pay the Temple tax either directly at the Temple, *or* one could pay the Temple tax to an *apostoli* at a *telonion* in their own province, town, or village, and this Temple tax continued to be collected as such even *after* the destruction of the Temple in 70 CE,[198] yet the monies collected *after* the destruction of the Temple was used for other purposes as noted by Josephus *Jewish Wars* 7.218 and *Dio Cassius* 66.7. In Mishnah *Shekalim* 1:1 it states that on the first of the month of Adar, (or during leap years, Adar II), word was "sent out" by way of the *apostoli* that it was time for individuals to pay the annual Temple tax. Then on the fifteenth of Adar

---

195   See the comments in *Gnosis*, Kurt Rudolph, p. 267.

196   See the comments in *Pontius Pilate in History and Interpretation*, Helen K. Bond, pp. 16-17.

197   See the comments of Joseph Jacobs and Isaac Broyde, "Tax-Gatherers," *Jewish Encyclopedia*.

198   See the comments of Gotthard Deutsch and M. Seligsohn, "Poll-Tax," *Jewish Encyclopedia*.

telonion or "Temple tax booths" were set up in every province and even in individual cities or towns to collect the Temple tax.[199] Thus, since we *do not know exactly when in terms of what month*, Matthew was recruited by Jesus, and since Matthew was from a Levitical Priestly family, he most likely was a well-respected *apostoli* or *Temple* "tax collector" and *not* one of the much hated *publicani* or *telonioni* collecting taxes for the Romans *or* for Herod Antipas!

This brings us to the very matter of the "calling of Matthew," the "tax collector," to be a disciple of Jesus, for as just noted above, the fact that the generally accepted interpretation that Matthew was a "tax collector" for the Romans is a highly debatable matter. There is in fact though, much debate amongst scholars over the matters of the *publicani* and *telonioni* in regards to whether or not they were "tax collectors" (indirectly) for the Romans, or whether they were "tax collectors" for the Jewish aristocracy, or even "tax collectors" for Herod Antipas. But the greater problem lies in the fact, noted previously above, that in Matthew 18:17, (even though it was noted in the preface that the *actual* Gospel authors are unknown), Jesus criticizes and chastises these very *telonion*! If Matthew himself was supposed to be one of these *telonion* who had paid the highest price to a *publicani* in order to be able to sit in the *telonion* then why would he write about a supposed statement by Jesus that was so critical of him? This creates a rather peculiar contradiction and serious inconsistency, which begs for the questioning of whether or not Levi/Matthew was indeed one of the individuals who bought the right to sit in the *telonion* to collect the taxes on exported goods, or whether he was actually sitting in the *telonion* as an *apostoli* to collect the Temple tax from that town, especially since he was a "Levite," (which a portion of his name clearly indicates)? Something is quite amiss in this matter, and thus, whoever the actual author of the Gospel of Matthew may have been it is most probable that they clearly misunderstood the differences between *apostoli, publicani*, and *telonion*.

There is one further matter regarding "tax collectors and sinners" that must be noted here, and this being the matter pointed out by Arland Hultgren concerning Mark 2:15-17.[200] In this account in Mark 2:15-17, Hultgren points out a problem, and this problem being that Jesus

---

199   See the comments on this in *Galilee*, Sean Freyne, p. 280.

200   See *Jesus and His Adversaries*, Arland J. Hultgren, pp. 109-111.

is dining at "his house" in Capernaum, and thus, Hultgren rightly asks, "But why are the Pharisaic scribes there too (within the house), as the story presupposes?" Now, although Hultgren is correct in noticing that something is amiss in this account from Mark 2:15-17, Hultgren goes on to erroneously claim that, "The pious do not associate with such persons in table fellowship," and Hultgren erroneously cites as his proof, (a matter previously discussed already above), Mishnah *Demai* 2:3 as his proof for his claim. Yet, once again, we find a Christian New Testament scholar misrepresenting a Mishnaic or Talmudic tractate! For Mishnah *Demai* 2:3 *only* refers to "*hosting*" a *ḥaver*, ("close friend," and not to "*hosting*" an *am ha-eretz*, a term discussed earlier in this chapter), as a "guest while wearing his own garment." But as Hultgren points out, *it is Jesus who is* "*hosting*" *in* "*his house*" *in Capernaum*, and thus, Hultgren's overall assessment of these verses is quite erroneous based on these two facts – his misrepresentation of a Mishnaic tractate, and the fact that Jesus is in "*his house*" in Capernaum.

In Matthew 22:34-40; Mark 12:28-34; Luke 10:25-28, (and these verses from Luke's Gospel will be further expounded upon below), we find an account of a Pharisee, or "lawyer" approaching Jesus and asking him a question,[201] or as some may refer to it, "testing Jesus," to see if Jesus really was a "worthy teacher." Now, at the time of Jesus it was *essential* for people to recognize if someone was a "Torah scholar." For as it was taught at the time of Jesus, based on the interpretation of Leviticus 19:32, (noted in *Kidushin* 32b; *Yevamoth* 62b; *Makkoth* 22b; *Makkoth* 2:6), one was "obligated to honor Torah scholars and the aged."[202] As it is stated in Mishnah *Abot* 4:3, "Have contempt for no man."[203] Furthermore, it was not only standard Jewish practice, but it was also *expected* of every Jew to "question," or "test" someone who was portraying themselves as a "teacher of the Torah" to be certain that they not only understood correctly what

---

201   See the comments in *The New Testament and Rabbinic Judaism*, David Daube, pp. 141-150 who does an excellent job of demonstrating and showing how so many of Jesus' responses to such questions posed to him, while seemingly sounding or indicating one thing, Jesus would "privately" explain to his disciples what he actually meant. As Daube shows, this was not an uncommon Pharisaic/rabbinic practice.

202   See the comments of Solomon Schechter and Julius H. Greenstone, "Excommunication (Hebrew, 'niddui,' 'ḥerem'), *Jewish Encyclopedia*.

203   See the comments on this in *The Life and Teachings of Hillel*, Yitzhak Buxbaum, pp. 35-36.

the "Torah scholar" was teaching, but also to be certain that what they were learning from this "Torah scholar" was possibly a "new interpretation"[204] of a particular matter in the Torah. Furthermore, one was *expected* to place doubts of accuracy into the mind of this individual portraying themselves as a "Torah scholar" in order to make certain that this particular "Torah scholar" was *truly certain* about the validity of their teachings as can be found being stated in *Yevamoth* 79a; *Baba Metzia* 84a; *Abot* 2:5; *Ta'anit* 7a.[205] There were four different ways, in fact, in which one was supposed to "test" someone – *hokhmah*, "wisdom," (i.e. halakhic interpretations of the Torah), *borut*, "vulgarity," (i.e. ridicule of an interpretation of the Torah), *derekh eretz*, "the way of the land," (i.e. the principle of moral conduct), and *haggadah*, "legend," (i.e. the interpretation of prophetic texts),[206] and one can even find this *fact* concerning the "testing" of individuals being taught in 1 Corinthians 14:29; 1 Thessalonians 5:21; 1 John 4:1. As Moshe Chaim Luzzatto writes concerning "Torah scholars,"[207] "It is obvious that the higher the level of comprehension, the higher there will be the corresponding influence derived through it. An individual who understands only the language of a Biblical passage is therefore not equal to one who understands its meaning. Likewise, one who understands only its superficial meaning is not the same as one who delves more deeply. Furthermore, even when one does go into the deeper meaning, the more he delves, the higher will be his level." Therefore, "testing" someone, such as Jesus to be certain that he *was* in fact a "Torah scholar" to be honored was not out of place in the least![208] But as Yitzhak Buxbaum points out,[209] "It was never part of the ancient rabbinic tradition to focus on a single man, no matter how great he was or how profound his influence."

Now, Jesus' responses in each of these accounts on this matter of his being "tested" are a direct reflection of what is found in the Talmud

---

204 See the comments on this of Ray Vander Laan, "Rabbi and Talmidim," *That the World May Know.*

205 See the comments on this in *Hillel*, Rabbi Joseph Telushkin, pp. 156-160.

206 See the comments in *Essays on the Semitic Background of the New Testament*, Joseph A. Fitzmyer, p. 124.

207 *The Way of God*, Moshe Chaim Luzzatto, p. 257.

208 See the comments on this in *Love Your Neighbor*, Rabbi Zelig Pliskin, pp. 313-315.

209 *The Life and Teachings of Hillel*, Yitzhak Buxbaum, p. 5.

Yerushalmi, *Nedarim* 9:4.[210] Likewise, the teachings in Matthew 7:12 are directly reflected in the Talmud Babli, *Shabbat* 31a,[211] as well as Luke 6:37 being directly reflected in Mishnah, *Abot* 2:3-5, and the parable in Matthew 20:1-16 is a direct reflection of what is taught in Deuteronomy 24:15.[212] As Rabbi Shmuley Boteach rightly states,[213] "While the New Testament portrays these teachings as new and antithetical to Pharisaic instruction, they actually align perfectly with accepted wisdom derived from the Torah. Similarly, Christians often associate parables with Jesus to the extent that they presume he invented a new method of teaching. This wasn't the case; parables were a common, well established instructional tool drawn from the rabbinic tradition. Jesus' use of them was very much in keeping with his role as a rabbi in a rabbinic world,"[214] a fact that can even be found attested to in the minor Talmudic tractate *Masehet Soferim* 16:9.[215] As Yitzhak Buxbaum writes concerning this,[216] "A skillful teacher of religion will often use parables and similes to explain subtle spiritual concerns by means of more tangible physical images. We have seen earlier (*Soferim* 16:9) that Hillel was renowned for his knowledge of parables." Also, as George W. E. Nickelsburg points out[217] in regards to "parables" being a part of Jewish thinking, teaching, and literature, Chapters 37-71 of *1 Enoch* are in reality a "Book of Parables."[218] In Ezekiel 17:2 and 21:5 it

---

210   See the comments on this in *Love Your Neighbor*, Rabbi Zelig Pliskin, p. 19.

211   See the comments on this in *Jewish Literacy*, Rabbi Joseph Telushkin, pp. 49-50.

212   See the comments in *Love Your Neighbor*, Rabbi Zelig Pliskin, pp. 421-423.

213   See the comments in *Kosher Jesus*, Rabbi Shmuley Boteach, p. 26; but see also the similar comments in *Barabbas and Esther*, Roger David Aus, pp. 65-68.

214   *Kosher Jesus*, Rabbi Shmuley Boteach, n. 29, p. 232 for a detailed exploration of the rabbinic precedents for Jesus' parables and allegories, see Craig L. Blomberg, *Interpreting the Parable* [Downers Grove, Il.: Intervarsity Press, 1990], pp. 29-60.

215   See the comments on this in *The Life and Teachings of Hillel*, Yitzhak Buxbaum, pp. 20-21, and 224.

216   *The Life and Teachings of Hillel*, Yitzhak Buxbaum, p. 233.

217   *The Historical Jesus in Context*, George W. Nickelsburg, p. 91.

218   See further Nickelsburg's book, *Jewish Literature Between the Bible and the Mishnah: A Historical and Literary Introduction*; and see the further comments by Gary G. Porton in *The Historical Jesus in Context*, Levine, Allison Jr. and Crossan, pp. 206-221 but especially his comments on p. 209; *Revolution in Judaea*, Hyam Maccoby, Appendix 7, pp. 217-218.

very clearly states that people protested Ezekiel's using "parables," (*mashal* in Hebrew), in his prophecies and teachings, and this is also found in the *Wisdom of Sirach* 39:1-3. Far too many Christian scholars for far too long now have tried to claim that Jesus' teaching by way of parables was somehow "unique," or "unusual" in regards to Jewish thinking and teaching.[219] Some scholars though, such as Etienne Trocme, while pointing out that there was nothing "unique" about Jesus' teaching in parables, believes that the parables themselves as we have them in the Gospels went through a later Hellenized gentile Church alteration to make them appear to be more like classic "Greek rhetoric," which would thus make them only *appear* to be "unique" in regards to Jewish usage.[220] While this claim by Trocme might be true, the *fact* remains, as even Trocme admits, that there was nothing "unique" about Jesus' teaching in parables, and therefore, it is high time that the majority of Christian scholars finally come to accept and admit to this *fact*![221] As David Flusser rightly states,[222] "This does not mean that Jesus was unaware of the fact that his arguments would seem unusual to some of the conformists of his day – but even in these cases he would by no means be described as an innovator."

Now, Bart Ehrman is somewhat in error when he claims,[223] "that the Pharisees were not the 'power players' in Palestine in Jesus' day. That is to say, they appear to have had some popular appeal but no real political clout." To a certain extent this claim may be true since the Romans held the *real* "political clout." But amongst the Jews themselves Ehrman's claim is quite erroneous! For the Pharisees were held in high regard, even by the Romans, as being champions of the poor and those who were oppressed,[224] as can be

---

219   As an example, see the comments in *Jesus of Nazareth: Part One*, Ratzinger and Pope Benedict, pp. 183-217; *Jesus*, C. Leslie Mitton, pp. 141-147.

220   See the comments on this in *Jesus and His Contemporaries*, Etienne Trocme, pp. 81-96.

221   See the comments on this in *Jesus and Israel*, Jules Isaac, pp. 203-227; and see also the excellent comments and comparisons to this *fact* in *The Parable of the Wicked Tenants*, Klyne Snodgrass, pp. 22-26.

222   *Judaism and the Origins of Christianity*, David Flusser, p. 495.

223   *The New Testament*, Bart D. Ehrman, p. 236.

224   See the comments in *The Mythmaker*, Hyam Maccoby, p. 6; *Love Your Neighbor*, Rabbi Zelig Pliskin, pp. 30-33, and on pp. 75-76 he references *Shabbat* 133b, which talks about how, "failure to aid the poor is a most serious crime." But see further Rabbi Pliskin's

found stated in *Gittin* 61a, which even states that this held true for both Jewish and gentile poor. As Yitzhak Buxbaum writes,[225] "Hillel had a dim view of the urge to accumulate wealth, and was against a person's having a large household with many servants, since many possessions only lead to increased anxiety (*Abot* 2:8) … But considering Hillel's compassionate instincts and ideals, as well as his background of self-imposed poverty, we can understand how he became a champion of the poor and lower classes." Now it is true though, that many negative statements *against* gentiles *can be* found in both the Talmud Yerushalmi and the Talmud Babli, but this is *not* simply because they were non-Jews, but simply because gentiles were viewed by observant Jews as "idolaters." Yet at the same time, gentiles who of their own accord were righteously adhering to the Noahide commandments, or observed and studied the Torah of their own accord were viewed by Jews in a very favorable manner. Furthermore, the Pharisees were *always* very lenient[226] in their legal rulings as even Josephus notes in *Antiquities* 13.294,[227] so lenient in fact that in Mishnah *Kidushin* 1:10 it states that an individual "who performs a single commandment is bestowed with goodness." Josephus also writes in *Antiquities* 13.10.6, "… The Pharisees have delivered to the people a great many observances by succession from their fathers, which are not written in the laws of Moses; and it is for this reason that the Sadducees reject them, and say that we are to esteem those observances to be obligatory which are in the written word, but are not to observe what are derived from the tradition of our forefathers. And concerning these things it is that great disputes and differences have arisen among them, while the Sadducees are able to persuade none but the rich, and have not the populace obsequious to them, but the Pharisees have the multitude on their side." In regards to what Josephus states here, Hyam

---

comments on pp. 142-143, 331-333, and 385-405; and see also the comments on this in *Hillel*, Rabbi Joseph Telushkin, pp. 47-58, and 66-68; *The Literature of the Sages: First Part: Oral Torah, Halakha, Mishnah, Tosefta, Talmud, External Tractates*, Shmuel Safrai, p. 188.

225 *The Life and Teachings of Hillel*, Yitzhak Buxbaum, p. 51.

226 See the comments in *Paul Was Not a Christian*, Pamela Eisenbaum, pp. 116-131.

227 See the comments in *The Mythmaker*, Hyam Maccoby, p. 19 and n. 3, p. 212; see also further Josephus, *Antiquities* 17.41 where he calls the Pharisees, "thorns in the flesh" in regards to "political authorities."

Maccoby remarks,[228] "From the Talmud we learn that the leading Pharisees such as Hillel, Shammai, Hanina ben Dosa and Akiba, came from the working class, and even at the height of their fame worked as woodcutters, shepherds, carpenters, shoemakers, etc.," (see for example *Abot* 1:9; *Kidushin* 4:14, which each discuss the matter that "a man should teach his son a trade"). In essence then, because of the very *fact* that the majority of the leading Pharisees were among the "common Jewish people" and "lower classes," this is the very reason *why* they were "champions of the poor and oppressed," (see Mishnah *Horayot* 3:8; *Baba Metzia* 2:11),[229] and thus, held such "powerful sway" with the majority of the "common Jewish people."[230] As David M. Rhoads states,[231] "Pharisees were made up primarily of artisans and merchants from the middle and lower urban classes." This matter goes back to what was pointed out in Chapter 2 regarding the overall dislike of the High Priest by the people, and which will be further noted in Chapters 5 and 7. For as Maccoby further states,[232] "But it is very hard for Gentiles, such as the Greeks and the Romans, to understand that the religious official who wore the gorgeous robes and presided at religious ceremonies with pomp and circumstance was ultimately of no religious significance, and that the religious authority whom the Jews most revered might be some penurious village shoemaker who was the chief repository of the law." As an example of Maccoby's statement, Marcus Borg is quite in error when he claims that Jesus' teaching about "mammon"[233] in Matthew 6:19-24; Luke 12:33-34; 16:13, (which Borg seems to interpret as being pointed directly at the Pharisees), meant that, "apparently, Jesus perceived most of his contemporaries as centered in the finite," to which Borg interprets his usage of the word "finite" as being "opposite of serving God."[234] But Borg's

---

228   *Revolution in Judaea*, Hyam Maccoby, pp. 59-60.

229   *A Rabbi Talks with Jesus*, Jacob Neusner, pp. 47-50.

230   See the comments in *History of the Jewish People in the Time of Jesus Christ*, Emil Schurer, Part 2, 2:28.

231   *Israel in Revolution*, David Rhoads, p. 32.

232   *Revolution in Judaea*, Hyam Maccoby, p. 62; but see also the similar comments in *The Life and Teachings of Hillel*, Yitzhak Buxbaum, pp. 9-10, and 76.

233   Concerning this word "mammon" see Joseph Jacobs, "Mamon (Mammon)," *Jewish Encyclopedia*.

234   *Conflict, Holiness & Politics*, Marcus Borg, pp. 240-241.

statement is neither an accurate nor fair interpretation of Jesus' teaching by inferring that it somehow referred to Jesus' "contemporaries."[235] Going further though, as Jules Isaac rightly points out,[236] "The Sadducees, whom an already long tradition set in opposition to the Pharisees, constituted the political party confronting the religious party, opportunists antagonistic to any excess or fanaticism, conservative, old-fashioned believers wedded to the letter of the Law and hostile to any innovation, in the temporal domain as in the spiritual. But what was their influence on the religious life in Israel of the time? Almost nil."

Therefore, all attempts by *any* scholar, (such as Ehrman noted above), to try and portray the Pharisees in any other manner than the *fact* that they were very "lenient" in their legal rulings; that they did not impose those legal rulings onto others who were not of the Pharisaic philosophy; and that the Pharisees were "champions of the poor" and more highly respected than even the High priest, are nothing but futile attempts at *dishonest nonsense.* The Pharisees accepted a wide range of opinions, viewpoints, and interpretations of the Torah and they made certain that even minority opinions were held in high regard, just in case that minority opinion was later accepted as being the majority opinion. As Hyam Maccoby writes concerning this,[237] "Thus the assemblies of the sages (as the Pharisee leaders were called before the destruction of the Jerusalem Temple in AD 70, after which they became known as 'rabbis') made decisions, but did not invest these decisions with divine authority. The opinions of dissenting minorities were carefully recorded and included in the records such as the Mishnah, so that (as the Mishnah itself explains in *Eduyot* 1:5) it may become the basis of new decision in the future, if required (just as today the opinions of dissenting judges are recorded in the High Court and are cited as support if an attempt is made at a later date to bring in a new ruling)... 'According to the effort is the reward',"[238] and this ruling in *Eduyot* 1:5 is exemplified by what is found in Mishnah *Eduyot* 1:3-4 and *Shabbat* 15a where the opinions of both Shammai and Hillel were overruled and ignored and in

---

235 For a more accurate depiction of Jesus' "contemporaries" on such matters see the comments of Kaufmann Kohler, "Alms," *Jewish Encyclopedia.*

236 *Jesus and Israel*, Jules Isaac, p. 38.

237 *The Mythmaker*, Hyam Maccoby, pp. 21-22.

238 *The Mythmaker*, Hyam Maccoby, n. 5, p. 212, Mishnah, *Abot* 5:23.

which the actual majority ruling on the matter at hand in this tractate was arrived at based on the opinions of two simple weavers who had entered Jerusalem through the Dung Gate. Also, as David Daube writes,[239] "In the three centuries preceding the destruction of the Second Temple, different classes, schools and individuals held different views even on important questions. But those warring parties never considered one another as outside Judaism. They all based themselves on the Pentateuch: that made them belong to one religion." Now, W. D. Davies is partially in error when he states that,[240] "Moreover, it is clear that it was Pharisaism, and that of the Shammaite kind, that dominated first century Judaism." While it is true, as Davies states, that Pharisaism "dominated first century Judaism," he is quite in error in claiming that the "Shammaite kind" dominated. But, *if* what Davies is referring to though, is that there were a greater number of Pharisees at the time of Jesus who were associated with the school of Shammai, then Davies would be correct.[241] Yet, on the other hand, *if* what Davies is referring to are the halakha rulings then Davies is quite in error,[242] for as Samuel Sandmel writes,[243] "The rabbis could and did tolerate opposing legalistic opinions, as between the followers of Hillel and those of Shammai; and in ultimately preferring Hillel they could still describe the rejected Shammai as the 'voice of the Living God.' The rabbis were choosing between two forms of overt action, expressive of the same unexpressed, basic conviction. The Church, however, inclined very naturally to the division of doctrine into the true and the false, not out of zeal for mere division, but out of the direct confrontation by explicit doctrines. For the Church, heresy was a matter of wrong formulation or of wrong accentuation; it could not treat the divergent as the voice of the Living God, but only as the deceitful voices of living prophets." This statement by Sandmel still holds true today in regards to the majority of modern Christian New Testament scholars who desire to distance Jesus from his Judaism through

---

239   *The New Testament and Rabbinic Judaism*, David Daube, p. 92.

240   *Paul and Rabbinic Judaism*, W. D. Davies, p. 9.

241   See the comments on this in *Jesus the Pharisee*, Harvey Falk, p. 93.

242   See the comments on this in *Jesus the Pharisee*, Harvey Falk, pp. 93-104, 156-157.

243   *A Jewish Understanding of the New Testament*, Samuel Sandmel, p. 311; but see also the comments of Rabbi Jay Kegman, Eruvin 13b: Following Beit Shammai," March 29, 2013, *Torah in Motion*.

their *claimed* "historical" portraits of him, and by continuously attempting to try and find something in Jesus' teachings or actions that was somehow so completely contrary to first century Palestinian Judaism that it caused some sort of Jewish authorities to desire Jesus' death! This statement by Sandmel also goes right back to what was stated in the Preface regarding the differences between Jewish "oral traditions" recorded in the Mishnah and gentile "oral traditions" that became the Gospel accounts!

But going further into this matter of recognizing that Jesus' teachings were squarely in line with Pharisaic teachings and thinking, if we look at Matthew 10:39; Luke 9:29; 17:33; John 12:24-25 what is found is a direct reflection of the Pharisaic teaching found in the Talmud Babli, *Ta'anit* 32a, which says, "what shall a man do that he may live? They answered, 'let him kill himself.' Then the king asked, 'And what shall a man do that he may die?' to which the elders replied, 'Let him keep himself alive'." Also, as it states in *Sanhedrin* 97b, "All dates for the end have expired and the matter now depends solely on repentance and good works." If one then looks carefully at what is found being stated by Jesus in Matthew 25:31-46[244] and Luke 10:25-37, (see Mishnah *Nazir* 7:1 based upon Leviticus 21:1-4,[245] and compare this to the story found in Mishnah *Pe'ah* 1:1,[246] and see also Malachi 1:11), one will find another very clear comparison with Pharisaic teachings. Now, just to provide further examples, Matthew 7:1-2; Luke 6:37 is a direct equivalent reflection of the teaching of Hillel noted in the Mishnah, *Abot* 2:4-5; Matthew 6:34 is found being reflected in *Sanhedrin* 100b; *Berakhot* 9b; Matthew 12:38-39; Mark 8:11-12; Luke 11:29-30 are paralleled in *Sanhedrin* 98a-b,[247] and the teaching found in Matthew 7:7-8; Luke 11:9-10; Luke 12:36; Luke 13:25; Acts 12:13-16; Revelation 3:20 is a reflection of the teaching in *Baba Kamma* 33a; *Niddah* 16b, and *Ecclesiasticus* 21:22.[248]

---

244   See the comments on this verse in *Jesus: Apocalyptic Prophet of the New Millenium*, Bart D. Ehrman, p. 136; *We Have Seen the Lord*, William Barclay, p. 83.

245   See the comments on this in *Ritual and Morality*, Hyam Maccoby, pp. 27 and 68.

246   See the comments on this in *Ritual and Morality*, Hyam Maccoby, pp. 150-151.

247   See the comments in *Judaism and the Origins of Christianity*, David Flusser, pp. 526-534.

248   See the comments on this by Solomon Schecter and Judah David Eisenstein, "Etiquette," *Jewish Encyclopedia*. For even more examples that could be offered here see Solomon

In Matthew 9:20; Mark 6:56 it is very *clearly* noted that Jesus wore the traditional Jewish *tzitzit*,[249] or "prayer shawl," which had "fringes" as required in Numbers 15:37-40. But Jesus, in Matthew 23:5 seems to criticize those who wear "their fringes long." As Amy-Jill Levine writes concerning the fact that Jesus wore *tzitzit*,[250] "Jesus thus does not dismiss Torah, in the modern idiom; he 'wears it on his sleeve'." Amy-Jill Levine further states, "The Gospel preservation of this detail indicates that the Old Testament must be acknowledged as more than just an anticipation of the coming of the Messiah, after which it can be discarded or, more respectfully, put on the shelf next to the other antiques, to be admired but not used. By preserving the detail that Jesus wore fringes, the New Testament mandates that respect for Jewish custom be maintained and that Jesus' own Jewish practices is honored, even by the gentile church, which does not follow those customs." But the fact is that while it may be true that certain individuals *did* wear their "fringes long" simply as a statement of "status," not all who wore their "fringes long" did so for that same reason. There were quite a few very pious sages who deliberately wore "long fringes" in order to be able to tie coins to these long fringes, which would then drag behind them as they walked, which allowed for the poor and needy to run up behind them and untie the coins and take them as they needed.[251] But just prior to this matter in Matthew 23:5 we find in Matthew 23:2-3 Jesus stating, "The scribes and Pharisees sit on

Schechter, "Some Rabbinic Parallels to the New Testament," *The Jewish Quarterly Review*, Volume 12, No. 3 (April 1900), pp. 415-433.

249   In the Talmud, *Menahot* 40b it clearly states that the Essens were very scrupulous about wearing the *tzitzit*, see the comments of Kaufmann Kohler, "Essenes," *Jewish Encyclopedia*.

250   *The Misunderstood Jew*, Amy-Jill Levine, p. 24; and see also the comments in *The Partings of the Ways*, James Dunn, p. 101; *Jesus and the Laws of Purity*, Roger P. Booth, pp. 31, 109-110.

251   See the comments in *On Earth As It Is In Heaven*, D. C. Thielmann, pp. 716-717 where it is pointed out that very pious Pharisees deliberately would wear their "fringes" long in order to be able to tie coins to them so that the poor could run up behind them and take the coins without the individual knowing who was taking them, and thus, giving to the poor "in secret," a matter that can be found being taught in *Shekalim* 5:6; *Ketuboth* 67b, (see further on this the comments in *The Life and Teachings of Hillel*, Yitzhak Buxbaum, pp. 207-211).

Moses' seat; therefore, do whatever they teach you and follow it…" to which Barrie Wilson makes the very right comment that,[252] "Here Jesus recognized the validity of Pharisaic teachings. Surely this is one of the most overlooked passages in all of the New Testament, and it is powerful in its implications. A close bond exists between the teachings of Jesus and that of the Pharisees."

Another matter that far too many modern Christian New Testament scholars try to use as a point of contention that Jesus deviated from conventional first century Palestinian Jewish Pharisaic teaching and thinking comes from Jesus' teaching about the sharing of wealth.[253] But such scholarly claims can be thoroughly refuted simply by what is found being stated not only in Deuteronomy 15:7, but also by what Josephus states in *Contra Apion* 2.39.283, and in the Yerushalmi Talmud, *Pe'ah* 15d; Talmud Babli, *Baba Batra* 10a, as well as by way of many other scholarly sources.[254]

As pointed out above, the Pharisees and the Sadducees were mortal enemies. The main point of contention between these two philosophies was in regards to the validity of the "oral Torah," or in essence, how to interpret the Torah given to Moses at Sinai.[255] Hyam Maccoby writes concerning this that,[256] "The essential point at issue between the Pharisees and the Sadducees was the validity of the oral Law, but this point was far from academic, for it led to enormous differences of outlook on social and political questions, as well as in the practice of Religion." Maccoby goes on to point out that the Pharisees regarded the Sadducees as "heretics," (a matter discussed previously above). In the Mishnah, *Horayot* 3:8 it is found being stated by a Pharisee that, "A learned bastard takes precedence over an ignorant High Priest." But the historical fact is that there have

---

252 *How Jesus Became Christian*, Barrie Wilson, p. 186.

253 See for example the comments in *Jesus: Uncovering the Life, Teachings and Relevance of a Religious Revolutionary*, Marcus Borg, pp. 208-211.

254 See for example the comments in *The New Testament and Rabbinic Judaism*, David Daube, pp. 128-129; *On Earth As It Is In Heaven*, D. C. Thielmann, pp. 628-629 and the corresponding scholars notations to these pages.

255 See the comments in *The Death of Jesus*, Joel Carmichael, pp. 105-107; *The Partings of the Ways*, James Dunn, p. 99.

256 *The Mythmaker*, Hyam Maccoby, p. 22.

always been Jews who have rejected the validity of the "oral Torah,"[257] either as a whole, or rejecting only the validity of certain portions of the "oral Torah," (an example of which will be discussed further below, as well as in Chapter 5). Yet, there are some scholars,[258] who point out that even the Talmud records disputes between the Sadducees and the Pharisees over "oral interpretations" of the Torah,[259] which would thus tend to indicate that the Sadducees *did*, in fact, have their own "oral Torah," only that it *did not* coincide with the Pharisaic "oral Torah," (see for example, Mishnah *Yadayim* 4:6-8).

This brings us to another very important point of contention between the Pharisees and Sadducees noted earlier in this chapter, and this being that, although many of the Temple priests *were*, in fact, Pharisees,[260] the High Priest was a Sadducee – a political appointee of the Romans at the time of Jesus[261] - and for the Pharisees, the Temple played only a minor secondary role in regards to living according to the Torah.[262] So for *some* of the Pharisees at the time of Jesus, the purity teachings, which the Sadducees believed and contended only applied to the Temple priests,[263] there were a certain *few* Pharisees who believed, and began to teach that these Torah purity

---

257 See the comments of Kaufmann Kohler and Abraham de Harkavy, "Karaites and Karaism," *Jewish Encyclopedia*.

258 See for example *Caiaphas*, Helen K. Bond, p. 25.

259 *Caiaphas*, Helen K. Bond, n. 9, p. 165.

260 See the comments in *The Mythmaker*, Hyam Maccoby, p. 26. N. T. Wright in *The New Testament and the People of God*, pp. 209-213 is quite in error when he asserts that *all* of the Temple "priests" were of the sect of the Sadducees. But in regards to his claim that they were also "aristocrats," this could be considered true to a certain degree, but *not* in accordance with the common understood definition of the English word "aristocrat," (see the comments on this of Lorne Rosovsky, "Raise Your Hand if You're a Kohen," *Chabad.org*).

261 See the comments in *The Last Week*, Marcus Borg and John Dominic Crossan, pp. 19-20; *The Trial of Jesus: Cambridge Studies in Honour of C. F. D. Moule*, pp. 11-12.

262 See the comments in *The Mythmaker*, Hyam Maccoby, p. 23; *Hillel*, Rabbi Joseph Telushkin, pp. 168-169.

263 In regards to the matter of "priestly purity" see the comments in *The Idea of Purity in Ancient Judaism*, Jacob Neusner, pp. 26-31.

teachings should apply to *all* Jews.[264] As Jacob Neusner states concerning this matter,[265] "It may be shown, for example, that certain Mishnaic pericopae take for granted a priestly and cultic setting, while others assume the law is to be kept at home by ordinary people, not priests. These assumptions constitute two important and divergent interpretations of purity and probably indicate the laws derive from different sources." Thus, there are some scholars[266] who are in error in claiming that *all* Pharisees at the time of Jesus rigorously insisted on *all* Jews applying the purity teachings in their daily lives. For as just pointed out, the Temple played a very minor secondary role to the majority of the Pharisees, so in truth, it was not until *after* the destruction of the Temple during the 66-73 revolt that the Pharisees as a whole decided to put into place interpretations of both the Written Torah and the "oral" Torah that the purity teachings should be observed by *all* Jews,[267] and furthermore, as noted already above, *none* of the differing Jewish philosophies *imposed their interpretations* of the Torah onto other Jews who were outside of *their* philosophy!

Now, some scholars attempt to use the Gospel accounts of Jesus' "laying on of hands" or dining with "lepers" as an example that Jesus somehow violated the "purity" laws.[268] But this is hardly the *historically* accurate truth regarding this particular matter though![269] Furthermore, these same scholars will also attempt to use the accounts in Matthew 26:6-13; Mark 5:25-34; 14:3-9; Luke 7:36-50; John 12:1-8 as an example that Jesus' actions either disregarded, violated, or somehow abrogated these "purity halakha" regarding "bodily discharges."[270] Yet, these very scholars *admit* that at the time of Jesus the halakhic interpretations regarding all of these

---

264   See the comments in *On Earth As It Is In Heaven*, D. C. Thielmann, p. 920 and the corresponding scholars notations to this page.

265   *The Idea of Purity in Ancient Judaism*, Jacob Neusner, p. 72.

266   See for example, *The Partings of the Ways*, James Dunn, pp. 41-44; *Conflict, Holiness & Politics*, Marcus Borg, p. 58 and n. 44, n. 45, p. 300.

267   See the comments on this in *On Earth As It Is In Heaven*, D. C. Thielmann, n. 157, p. 784; *Jewish Law from Jesus to the Mishnah*, E. P. Sanders, pp. 131-254.

268   See for example the comments in *Jesus and Purity Halakah*, Thomas Kazen, pp. 98-127.

269   See Emil G. Hirsch, J. F. Schamberg, Joseph Jacobs, A. S. Waldstein, and Maurice Fishberg, "Leprosy," *Jewish Encyclopedia*.

270   See for example *Jesus and Purity Halakah*, Thomas Kazen, pp. 127-164.

matters were quite diverse[271] as noted in the Mishnah tractates *Niddah* and *Zavim*, and thus, as a result, (as occurs far too often with Christian New Testament scholarship), the very scholars who attempt to claim that Jesus was somehow "indifferent," "opposed to," or advocated "abrogation" of the Pharisaic "oral" Torah on these matters will then contradict their own claims in their conclusions. As an example of such a scholarly contradiction, Thomas Kazen after making the very claims just noted then writes,[272] "As I concluded in the previous chapter, it is highly implausible that Jesus was directly opposed to, or attempting to do away with, Jewish law and tradition. It is clear that he operated within a cultural and religious context, to which the purity paradigm belonged."

E. P. Sanders very rightly states concerning the debates and disagreements over the correct interpretations of the "purity" *halakha* at the time of Jesus that,[273] "Since they disagreed about immersion pools, one might expect the Pharisees and the priesthood to regard each other as being always impure. Yet this appears not to have been the case, and tolerance of each other's views prevailed." Sanders then goes on to state, and point out that,[274] "Pharisees disagreed among themselves about purity rules," and therefore, the Pharisees *did not* impose their "special rules" onto the "populace in general." In John 9:1-11 we find the mentioning of the "Pool of Siloam," which was a large Temple *miqvah* that was used for various reasons, but which had a very primary function during the Feast of Tabernacles to draw water for the Temple.[275] The Hebrew word *siloam* means "sent," or in essence, it was a *miqvah* where individuals were "sent" to be "purified" before they could enter the Temple, just as Jesus had "sent" the individual in the story in John 9:1-11 in order for this individual to be "purified" so that the individual in this account could enter the Temple. Now, the *actual* "Pool of Siloam" was discovered by archaeologists in 2004, but an

271   *Jesus and Purity Halakah*, Thomas Kazen, p. 219.

272   *Jesus and Purity Halakah*, Thomas Kazen, p. 198, but see also his additional comments on pp. 342-353.

273   *Jewish Law from Jesus to the Mishnah*, E. P. Sanders, p. 32.

274   *Jewish Law from Jesus to the Mishnah*, E. P. Sanders, p. 35.

275   See Judah David Eisenstein and the Executive Committee of the Editorial Board, "Water-Drawing, Feast of," *Jewish Encyclopedia*; *The Life and Teachings of Hillel*, Yitzhak Buxbaum, pp. 256-263.

inscription describing King Hezekiah's digging the tunnel to fill the Pool of Siloam was discovered in 1880. Thus, the *fact* that Jesus underwent the act of "ritual immersion" at the hands of John the Baptist along with the *fact* that Jesus' disciples performed the act of "ritual immersion" (a matter that will be further discussed in Chapter 9), *and* this *fact* that Jesus "sent" individuals to perform the act of "ritual immersion" simply demonstrates that Jesus *must have* followed Jewish *halakha* and used a *miqvah* himself after being in contact with each of the individuals mentioned in the above accounts. Modern Jewish archaeology has discovered, (near where the Church of St. James is located, and close to one of the walkways to the Essen Gate to the Temple in Jerusalem), a first century BCE to first century CE elaborate *miqvah* that has been presumed to be the very *miqvah* used by Jesus before his entrances to the Temple, (John 11:55 for example), and which for some unknown reason, this discovery is being kept secret from the world![276] Now, nowhere in *any* of the Gospels do we ever read about Jesus ever actually using a *miqvah*, but logically it *must be* acknowledged by *any* competent scholar that Jesus *must have, would have*, and actually *did use* a *miqvah* before ever entering into the Temple![277] Emmaus, well-known by Christians from Luke 24:13, was in fact a place that was widely used and well-known for its "ritual immersions" or "ritual bathing" because they had "warm baths"[278] as even noted by Josephus in *Antiquities* 18.2.3! Philo in *Special Laws* 1:259-266, (as well as Mishnah *Parah* 11:5), discusses the very matter of this "ritual purification" before one could enter the Temple, and in *Special Laws* 3.15.89 Philo speaks of how even individuals "who have done no wrong the Temple is still inaccessible until they have washed themselves, and sprinkled themselves, and purified themselves with the accustomed purifications." It was only from the Greek wording of the Septuagint, Philo, and Josephus that the gentile Christian concept of a "spiritualized purity," or "inner purity" developed out of the Jewish action of "ritual immersion" in a *miqvah* as well as from "ritual sacrifices" or

---

276   See Steven Ben-Nun, "The Miqvah that Yeshua/Jesus Used," *Israeli News Live*, November 17, 2016.

277   See the comments on this in *Jesus and Purity Halakah*, Thomas Kazen, p. 249.

278   See the comments of Cyrus Adler and Frederick de Sola Mendes, "Baths, Bathing," *Jewish Encyclopedia*.

"offerings."[279] Yet, it is quite true that the pagan Greek religions already held such concepts as that of "inner purity" long before the time of Jesus,[280] and thus, it should be easy for anyone to see how and why these former pagan gentiles who became the early Church could very easily take the Jewish practice of "ritual immersion" and alter it into a meaning of a "spiritualized inner purity." As Thomas Kazen states,[281] "At the same time, the Christian water rite, like the ablutions of the Qumran sectarians, was perceived as a method of purification," to which Kazen references Ephesians 5:26.

Therefore, in regards to this matter of "purity,"[282] and in particular, Jesus' teachings about such matters, Jonathan Klawans rightly points out that,[283] "An accurate understanding of these matters, including the distinction between ritual and moral defilement, is essential for fully understanding the New Testament. Various sayings attributed to Jesus use the terms 'pure' and 'impure' ... Too many modern readers – scholars included – have been reluctant to give these terms the time it takes to understand their meaning and message." As far back in Jewish history as the time of the writing of the Book of Chronicles, and specifically, 2 Chronicles 30:18-19, "ritual impurity" *was not* considered to be a "heinous sin," and ignoring, forgiving, and pardoning individuals who did not keep to "ritual purity" was commonplace throughout Jewish history as can be seen by way of these verses of 2 Chronicles 30:18-19.[284] Klawans then goes on further to state,[285] "One frequent error is the blind identification of impurity with sin: it is frequently assumed that sinners were considered defiling and were therefore excluded from the Temple ... Another frequent error is blind

---

279   *Jesus and Purity Halakah*, Thomas Kazen, p. 222; and see the comments of Kaufmann Kohler and Samuel Krauss, "Baptism," *Jewish Encyclopedia*.

280   See Andej Petrovic, *Inner Purity and Pollution in Ancient Greek Religion* Volume I.

281   *Jesus and Purity Halakah*, Thomas Kazen, p. 312, and n. 82, p. 312.

282   For an excellent reading about matters of "purity," see the entire book, *Purity and Danger* by Mary Douglas; and see the comments in *The New Testament and Jewish Law*, James G. Crossley, pp. 45-66.

283   See *The Historical Jesus in Context*, Levine, Allison Jr., and Crossan, p. 266.

284   See the comments on this in *The Idea of Purity in Ancient Judaism*, Jacob Neusner, pp. 12-17.

285   *The Historical Jesus in Context*, Levine, Allison Jr., and Crossan, p. 267; but see also the comments in *The New Testament and Jewish Law*, James G. Crossley, pp. 109-115.

identification of purity with status: it is assumed that not just sinners but others of low social or religious rank (such as women or gentiles) also would have been considered ritually impure.... A third frequent error is based on the previous misunderstandings: it often is supposed that the purity system was the tool by which the socially dominant Pharisees, or the priests who ran the Temple, asserted their power over those elements of society that they despised and wished to lord over ... A careful review of the evidence puts the lie to all three of these common assumptions." There was clear separation made between "ritual impurities" and "moral impurities" and "moral impurity" in contrast to "ritual impurity" was considered a defiling and heinous sin.[286] A noteworthy point to make here comes from Hyam Maccoby who rightly states,[287] "The conditions which produce impurity are in no way class-oriented. Menstruation, for example, cuts across all classes: a priest's wife who is menstruating causes just as much impurity to all who touch her as the wife of the poorest peasant, or (more to the point) of a slave or *mamzer*. None causes impurity just because he or she is a member of a certain class. While certain classes, or semi-castes do exist in the Biblical and even rabbinic systems, ritual purity has nothing to do with demarcation of those classes." Klawans again though, rightly states,[288] "Unfortunately, the last generation of scholarship on both early Judaism and the New Testament did not pay due attention to the Biblical distinction between ritual and moral defilements.... Once we begin to understand better the disputes among early Jewish groups regarding the relationship between ritual and moral impurity, we find a credible context for understanding Jesus' approach to these matters."[289] It is, therefore, *essential* to point out that Revelations 7:4; 15:6; 19:8, 14; 21:27; 22:14 *all* refer to the importance of "purity" in the future coming "Kingdom of God." Furthermore, as William Klassen rightly points out concerning the incident in John 13:5 of Jesus "washing the feet" of his disciples, this very incident demonstrates a *clear* indication that Jesus held to the Jewish

---

286   *The Historical Jesus in Context*, Levine, Allison Jr., and Crossan, pp. 268-269.

287   *Ritual and Morality*, Hyam Maccoby, p. 37.

288   *The Historical Jesus in Context*, Levine, Allison Jr., and Crossan, p. 270.

289   See also the comments on this entire matter in *Jewish Christianity Reconsidered*, Matt Jackson-McCabe, pp. 210-215, (Patrick J. Hartin commenting).

customs of "purity." As Klassen states concerning this matter,[290] "The theme of purity is important here as it is throughout the ministry of Jesus." Likewise, the accounts in Acts 9:18; 21:26 cannot just be dismissed since these verses *clearly* demonstrate that the Jewish customs of "purity" were still being performed *after* Jesus' ministry had ended.

The Gospels, and in fact the entire New Testament's depiction of the Pharisees is merely a reflection of the separation that occurred between the gentile followers of Jesus, who became the Church of Christianity, and the Jewish followers of Jesus who remained loyal to their Judaism and to the Synagogue.[291] Now, even though I am not in total agreement with Nils Dahl, he is somewhat correct when he writes,[292] "The historical Jesus is to be found at the crossroads where Christianity and Judaism begin separating from each other, although it only became gradually clear that the paths parted in such a way that Christianity appeared as a new religion alongside Judaism... On the other hand, we must view Jesus within the context of Palestinian Judaism." Also, Hyam Maccoby rightly notes[293] the differences in the accounts in Mark 12:28-34 and Matthew 22:34-40 and how these two divergent accounts are in reality merely a reflection of later Christian traditions that came about from the separation of the Church from the Synagogue, and as Samuel Sandmel so rightly puts it in regards to the First Epistle to the Corinthians,[294] "Its separation from Judaism, therefore, although well defined, is not complete. It may be put this way, that when one tears a paper in two, one first creases and then tears; in Paul's day the crease has been made, and the paper is divided by the crease – but the tearing is only commencing."

---

290 *Judas*, William Klassen, p. 151.

291 See the comments in *The Trial of Jesus: Cambridge Studies in Honour of C. F. D. Moule*, p. 11; *Jesus and Israel*, Jules Isaac, p. 391; *Jesus and His Contemporaries*, Etienne Trocme, p. 57; *Revolution in Judaea*, Hyam Maccoby, pp 176-187, and Appendix 8, pp. 218-219; *The Crucifixion of Jesus*, Gerard S, Sloyan, pp. 72-97; *The New Testament*, Bart D. Ehrman, pp. 408-425; *The Partings of the Ways*, James Dunn, pp. 1-4; *Jewish Christianity Reconsidered*, Matt Jackson-McCabe, pp. 10-11, and p. 157, (Warren Carter commenting and referencing Ignatius' *Letter to the Magnesians*), and pp. 181-201, (Raimo Hakola commenting); *Prophecy in Early Christianity*, David E. Aune, p. 16; *The History of the Synoptic Tradition*, Rudolf Bultmann, pp. 52-54; *Judaism and the Origins of Christianity*, David Flusser, pp. 617-644.

292 *The Crucified Messiah and other Essays*, Nils Dahl, p. 68.

293 *The Mythmaker*, Hyam Maccoby, pp. 30-31.

294 *A Jewish Understanding of the New Testament*, Samuel Sandmel, pp. 62-63.

Hyam Maccoby further points out in regards to these two accounts (i.e. Mark 12:28-34 and Matthew 22:34-40) that[295] Jesus' response in these accounts can be found mirrored in the Talmud Babli, *Berakhot* 13b. Now, the greatest portion of this parting between Church and Synagogue came about *after* the Council of Jamnia (refer back to Chapter 2 for a discussion about the Council of Jamnia).[296] Despite Jamnia bringing about the greatest portion of this parting, the very worst cause for this parting was the *Fiscus Judaicus*, which was a *humiliating* tax imposed upon *only* Jews, those who converted to Judaism, or those who just *lived* like they were Jews after the destruction of the Temple in 70 CE.[297] The matter of what resulted from this tax is noted by Suetonius, *Life of Domitian*, XII; Josephus, *Jewish Wars* 7.218; *Dio Cassius* 66.7.2. There has been great debate over the centuries, which still rages today amongst many scholars, whether or not both Jewish Christians *and* gentile Christians were exempt from this tax, or whether it was *just* gentile Christians who were exempt from this tax.[298] But the greatest *fact* is, (as just noted above from the Samuel Sandmel quote), that the first *real* parting of the two can be found being described in Acts 15, Galatians 2,[299] and Romans 9-11. As Walter Bauer writes,[300] "And it can hardly be doubted that they won a much greater number of adherents from the Hellenistic world than the other groups, whose Jewish Christian wing would increasingly be pushed into the background." Also, as Bart Ehrman states,[301] "Any author who thought that it was Jesus' teachings, rather than his death and resurrection, that ultimately mattered stood at odds with

---

295   *The Mythmaker*, Hyam Maccoby, n. 1, p. 212.

296   See the comments on this in *The Jews and the Gospel*, Gregory Baum, pp. 106-107.

297   See the comments on this in *Ancient Jewish Proselytism in Theory and in Practice*, David Rokeah, p. 206; Martin Goodman, "Proselytizing in Rabbinic Judaism," *Journal of Jewish Studies* 40, (1989), p.184; *A Jewish Understanding of the New Testament*, Samuel Sandmel, pp. 112-113.

298   See the comments on all of this matter in *The Scepter and the Star*, John J. Collins, pp. 200-201; *No Stone on Another*, Lloyd Gaston, pp. 3-4; *On Earth As It Is In Heaven*, D. C. Thielmann, p. 838 and the corresponding scholar's notations to this page.

299   See the comments on Galatians 2 in *Orthodoxy and Heresy in Earliest Christianity*, Walter Bauer, pp. 63-67.

300   *Orthodoxy and Heresy in Earliest Christianity*, Walter Bauer, p. 101.

301   *Jesus Before the Gospels*, Bart Ehrman, p. 280.

Paul." Yet, far too many scholars though, still attempt to use the Gospels and Epistles as evidence of overall Jewish hostility towards Jesus. John 7:49 and John 7:52 are quite often used as examples by scholars to substantiate such claims.[302] But again, these scholars fail to recognize these verses for what they truly are, and this being, simply *words from an evangelist author.* For the truth of the matter is that Isaiah 9:1-2 clearly refutes these verses from John and the Pharisees would have known this fact emphatically.[303]

In Matthew 23:15 there is found a somewhat unusual teaching attributed to Jesus about the "scribes and Pharisees" supposedly "crossing sea and land to make a single convert." The problem with this though, is that Jews at the time of Jesus *did not* conduct such "missionary" activity. It is true that John Hyrcanus performed *forced* conversions onto the Idumaeans, but this occurred over a century *before* the time of Jesus![304] The *only real* Jewish *axiom* that one should consider as being a "missionary" objective can be found in Isaiah 2:3; 49:6, which *is not* indicating that Jews should make "converts" out of all other peoples or nations. This simply instructs Jews to be a "light unto the nations" through their actions, and interactions with other peoples.[305] There *were* many, many individuals at the time of Jesus who *voluntarily* converted to Judaism, as even noted by the Roman satirist Juvenal in *Saturae* 14.96-106,[306] but the Jews *did not* go seeking out or "cross sea and land to make a single convert."[307] What the Jews, and particularly the Pharisees of the time of Jesus, *did do* was to make certain that gentiles were aware of the Noahide covenant, (a matter that will be discussed in the Epilogue), as noted in *Sanhedrin* 57a; *Avodah Zarah* 10b.[308] Thus, it is highly doubtful that this was in fact what was actually meant by Jesus'

---

302   See for example *Jesus Before Christianity*, Albert Nolan, p. 23.

303   For more on this matter concerning Galilee see *On Earth As It Is In Heaven*, D. C. Thielmann, n. 41, pp. 656-657.

304   See the brief comments on this matter in *Jewish Literacy*, Rabbi Joseph Telushkin, p. 120.

305   See the comments on this in *Jewish Literacy*, Rabbi Joseph Telushkin, p. 82.

306   See the comments on this in *Paul Was Not a Christian*, Pamela Eisenbaum, p. 110.

307   See the comments on this in *On Earth As It Is In Heaven*, D. C. Thielmann, p. 926 and the corresponding scholars notations to this page; Valerie S. Thaler, "Jewish Attitudes Toward Proselytes: The Second Temple Period," *My Jewish Learning*; Joseph Jacobs and Emil G. Hirsch, "Proselyte," *Jewish Encyclopedia*.

308   See the comments on this in *Jesus the Pharisee*, Harvey Falk, pp. 30-35.

statement. Now, Martin Goodman[309] believes that what Jesus was *actually* indicating by what he stated was that certain Jews were "converting" other Jews into a particular faction of the Pharisees, which seems to be far more plausible in regards to the *historical* truth of this matter.[310] Hillel, in one of his most famous quotes attributed to him in *Shabbat* 31a, (noted already above), accepted three gentile converts on very simple terms of conversion after Shammai had rejected each of these gentiles seeking to convert. Yet, neither Shammai, nor Hillel sought out these individuals by "crossing sea and land." So, could it be that it is to this very incident to which Jesus is referring? It is also true that Hillel used a long standing Jewish tradition of referencing Abraham, (just as Paul did likewise), as a tool to "bring people under the wings of the *Shekinah*," but this was true more in the sense of "bringing back Jews who have strayed" more so than "seeking out" gentiles to convert, although Hillel *did* openly welcome gentiles who desired of their own free will to convert to Judaism.[311] In essence, Jesus' practice was the same as that of Hillel as can be found in Matthew 10:5-6; 15:24; Luke 15:3-32. *Abot* 1:1 clearly states, "Raise up many disciples," which was interpreted differently by Shammai and Hillel with Shammai interpreting this to be indicating *only* "respectable people," whereas Hillel interpreted this to be indicating that one was to "teach all men." Now, at the time of Jesus there were two different types of individuals who were accepted as "converts" to Judaism, which were referred to as the *ger tzedek* and the *ger toshav*. The first term referred to converts who accepted upon themselves all 613 commandments of the Torah and were therefore recognized as being a "full Jew," whereas the second term referred to converts who accepted onto themselves *only* the seven Noahide commandments, (again, a matter that will be mentioned further in the Epilogue), and thus, the second type of individual was *not* counted as being a "full Jew," but only as one who was permitted to settle in the land of Palestine/Israel and which the Jewish

309   *Mission and Conversion*, Martin Goodman, pp. 70-73.

310   See also the comments on this in *The Jews among Pagans and Christians in the Roman Empire*, Judith Lieu, John North, and Tessa Rajak, pp. 53-78.

311   See the comments on this in *The Life and Teachings of Hillel*, Yitzhak Buxbaum, pp. 125-147.

community as a whole became liable to look after the well-being of this individual just as if they *were* a "full Jew."[312]

Also, there are still other scholars who while somewhat recognizing the evangelistic misrepresentations of first century Palestinian Judaism in the Gospels and Epistles, they will still attempt to portray Jesus as being some sort of combination between a Jew and a gentile – a "Hellenized" Jew, in other words. Marcus Borg, for example,[313] attempts to combine the Jewish understanding of "repent" with the pagan gentile Greek word, which means, "to go beyond the mind that you have." But as Gerard S. Sloyan rightly states,[314] "Often the most crucial scholarly declarations go undocumented and are accompanied by the scholar's weakest refuge, the adverb 'undoubtedly' or 'beyond question.' Gospel statements, in a word, are accepted when they fit the modern author's scheme and rejected when they do not. To say this is not to charge bias so much as to indicate that when anyone wishes to take a stand on what happened at any point in the interrogation and trial sequence, as distinct from what the Evangelists with their conflicting details maintain took place, he or she will do so on the basis of theory. Individual passages will then be argued in light of this theory."

Now, the portrait of Jesus that some scholars paint is based upon "Jewish literature of the period between the Testaments, beginning with the texts from Qumran."[315] But, as pointed out in the Preface, this is simply an erroneous way of trying to portray the "*historical*" Jesus! It seems that the greatest problem and error such scholars have in bringing about these erroneous depictions of Jesus derives from their genuine lack of understanding Jewish *metaphor* and how the Jews borrowed terms, ideas, and words from the languages of the pagan nations, cultures, and religions that they encountered or had dealings with, and utilized these terms and ideas *metaphorically* in their teachings and interpretations of the Torah and other Scriptures.[316] Far too often these scholars claim that Jewish *metaphoric* descriptions, (given even by Jews of today), contain "literal"

---

312   See the comments on this in *Jesus the Pharisee*, Harvey Falk, pp. 26-30.

313   *Jesus: Uncovering the Life, Teachings, and Relevance of a Religious Revolutionary*, Marcus Borg, pp. 219-220.

314   *Jesus On Trial*, Gerard S. Sloyan, p. 10.

315   See for example *Jesus and His Contemporaries*, Etienne Trocme, pp. 6-8.

316   See the comments in *The Apocalyptic Imagination*, John J. Collins, p. 17.

interpretations of Scripture.[317] This is hardly the truth of the matter, and as just stated, it simply demonstrates their lack of understanding of Jewish *metaphor*.[318] Chester Charlton McCown very rightly states in regards to scholars attempting to uncover the "historical" Jesus that,[319] "He must know the grammar and style so as to catch the finer shades of meaning. He must know the ancient society which produced the document, its ways of living and thinking, so that he may catch innumerable allusions and turns of expressions that otherwise he would miss, and so that he may not mistake figure for fact. He must know the language of his sources and the society which produced them so thoroughly that he thinks and feels as the ancient writers and the people they describe thought and felt."[320] Likewise, as N. T. Wright states,[321] "Even where a word is clearly univocal, we can never rule out possible metaphorical meanings, and in any case we only know the univocal meaning through experience of sentences in which it has become plain." The prime example that can be offered here is in regards to the Greek word *Angelos*, "Angels," which are *nowhere* to be found in ancient Jewish thought. But, after the Babylonian exile and the influences of their pagan beliefs, an adaptation to the interpretations of the ancient stories of Jewish history came about,[322] as can be found in the Biblical writings stemming from this period of Jewish history and in which thus, later became a major part of Jewish *metaphoric* teachings,

---

317　See for example, *Jesus of Nazareth*, Dale C. Allison, pp. 152-169.

318　See the comments in *On Earth As It Is In Heaven*, D. C. Thielmann, pp. 129-130 regarding the dangers of interpreting Jewish *metaphor* with "literal-mindedness"; and see also the entire book *The History of the Synoptic Tradition*, Rudolf Bultmann where Bultmann does an excellent job throughout this entire book of understanding and describing the Jewish "metaphors" in Jesus' teachings.

319　*The Search for the Real Jesus*, Chester Charlton McCown, p. 118.

320　For more on this matter see the comments in *On Earth As It Is In Heaven*, D. C. Thielmann, pp. 128-129 and the corresponding scholars notations to these pages.

321　*The New Testament and the People of God*, N. T. Wright, pp. 115-116, yet despite his right comments on these pages, Wright then erroneously reverts, (as most New Testament scholars seem to do), to claiming, on pp. 282-286, that these "metaphoric" terms were understood "literally" at the time of Jesus.

322　See the comments of Ludwig Blau and Kaufmann Kohler, "Angelology," *Jewish Encyclopedia*;

and even more so *after* the influence of Greek mythology on Palestine![323] As a result, many modern Christian scholars simply *do not* understand the Jewish "metaphoric" terminology regarding Jewish expectations surrounding *THE* "Messiah," especially in regards to such claims that the Jews expected a "supernatural cosmic judge of the earth,"[324] a matter that was briefly discussed in Chapter 2 regarding the Book of Daniel. Now, Michael Peppard believes that,[325] "Over time and through repeated use, metaphors die. A metaphor dies when its meaning becomes stable for its audience, when it stops being considered, when everyone knows what it means." Peppard's statement offers a great deal of truth in so far as the *fact* just stated above that there are far too many New Testament scholars who simply *do not* fully understand ancient Jewish "metaphors" even though they purport to understand these ancient Jewish "metaphoric" terminologies. As Peppard says, these "metaphors" have simply "died" to these many Christian New Testament scholars.

A great deal of the scholarly claims, misunderstandings, and misrepresentations of the Pharisees derives from the claim in Acts 22:3-6 that Paul was a Pharisee, and specifically, a student of Gamliel. But this claim in Acts is highly doubtful as being historical truth, and in fact, this claim has been thoroughly refuted.[326] For as Bart Ehrman points out about this matter,[327] "Since Paul himself makes neither claim, a historian might suspect Luke of attempting to provide superior credentials for his protagonist. Tarsus was the location of one of the most famous schools of Greek rhetoric, that is, a school of higher learning reserved for the social

---

323 See a thorough discussion on this matter in *On Earth As It Is In Heaven*, D. C. Thielmann, pp. 82-86 and the corresponding scholars notations to these pages; see also *The Way of God*, Moshe Chaim Luzzatto, pp. 75-87, 147-153, 157-161, 189-191, 199-211, and n. 33, pp. 409-410, n. 44, p. 411; *One God One Lord*, Larry W. Hurtado, pp.41-50, 71-92.

324 See for example the comments in *The New Testament*, Bart D. Ehrman, Box 5.1, p. 68; *The Apocalyptic Imagination*, John J. Collins, pp. 81-85 even though Collins clearly points out that the term "angels" meant "simply 'men'."

325 *The Son of God in the Roman World*, Michael Peppard, p. 3.

326 See the comments in *Kosher Jesus*, Rabbi Shmuley Boteach, pp. 112-116; *The Misunderstood Jew*, Amy-Jill Levine, pp. 79-81; *Christianity: A Jewish Perspective*, Rabbi Moshe Reiss, Chapter 9 Conclusions; the entire book *The Mythmaker*, Hyam Maccoby.

327 *The New Testament*, Bart D. Ehrman, p. 292.

and intellectual elite, something like an Ivy League University." Gamliel at the time of Jesus was *the* most highly respected, renowned and influential Pharisee as noted in the Mishnah, *Sotah* 9:15; *Gittin* 4:2-3; *Abot* 1:16. Gamliel, in Acts 5:34-39 even protects the followers of Jesus[328] by going so far as even chastising the Great Sanhedrin in defense of the followers of Jesus, whereas Paul, in Acts 8:1 clearly gives orders to kill Stephen and persecute the followers of Jesus. This clear contradiction in the Book of Acts between the actions of the renowned and highly respected teacher (Gamliel) and supposed student (Paul) *cannot*, and *must not* be ignored, downplayed, or distorted by *any* competent scholar! In regards to this, it is essential for scholars, theologians, and even the general Church laity to clearly recognize that Gamliel, (in his defense of the followers of Jesus), *clearly* perceived of the followers of Jesus as being in the *same category of movements* as those of the "insurrectionist movements against Roman tyranny" as those of Theudas, and Judas the Galilean![329]

Furthermore, Paul is clearly educated in only using the Septuagint,[330] and he rarely ever cites from the actual Hebrew of the Torah or prophets, which *no student* of Gamliel would *ever* have done! For as noted earlier in Chapter 2, by the time of Jesus the Pharisaic schools of Hillel and Shammai, (which Gamliel was the head of the school of Hillel by this time), the Septuagint was not even accepted as authoritative, plus students of Gamliel were even forbidden from using the Aramaic Targums as noted in the Yerushalmi Talmud, and Mishnah *Megillah* 4! As Jules Isaac rightly points out,[331] "In the last analysis, nothing allows us to believe and assert that the Pharisee master's, Judaism's true religious guides, the nation's spiritual elite, who alone may rightly be said to have been Israel's qualified representatives in certain respects, fought against Jesus, and even less that they wanted,

328   See the comments on this in *The Partings of the Ways*, James Dunn, p. 119; Solomon Schecter and Wilhelm Bacher, "Gamaliel I," *Jewish Encyclopedia*; Rabbi Louis Jacobs, "Rabban Gamaliel," *My Jewish Learning*.

329   See the comments in *Jesus of Nazareth*, Dale C. Allison, pp. 43-44.

330   See the comments on this in *The New Testament*, Bart D. Ehrman, p. 292; *A Jewish Understanding of the New Testament*, Samuel Sandmel, p. 44; *Paul and Rabbinic Judaism*, W. D. Davies, p. 12; Kaufmann Kohler, "Saul of Tarsus (known as Paul, the Apostle of the Heathen)," *Jewish Encyclopedia*.

331   *Jesus and Israel*, Jules Isaac, pp. 271-272.

demanded, and plotted his death." This contradiction *must be* recognized as to what it really indicates in historical reality, and this being, that Paul *was not* a student of Gamliel from the school of Hillel as is claimed in the Book of Acts.[332] Now, there have been some scholars who have tried to put forth claims that Paul *was*, in fact, a Pharisee but a Pharisee from the rival school of Shammai.[333] But such claims have likewise been thoroughly refuted as well.[334] As Samuel Sandmel states concerning Paul,[335] "He was deeply meditative, and his viewpoints about the nature of man and the nature of sin, and an impending end of the world which, mistakenly, he thought was soon to come, are based on assumptions which are diametrically opposed to the views which traditional Judaism has bequeathed to us. Indeed, to move from the rabbinic Jewish mode of thought to Paul's requires a radical shift." W. D. Davies refers to Paul's teachings regarding the difference between "flesh" and "spirit," and Davies refers to the Hebrew word *basar*, (which does generally get translated into English as "flesh"), and Davies cites as his proof texts for his opinion on this matter such verses as Isaiah 31:3; 40:6; Psalm 56:5 as well as several other verses, for where Paul derived *his* interpretations regarding the difference between "flesh" and "spirit."[336] But the fact is that the Hebrew word *basar*, *does not* always offer such a meaning in its contextual usage as Davies infers. For at times this Hebrew word means, and is referring to, "a perceptive person,"[337] as it is found being used in Isaiah 40:5, (just one verse prior to one of the verses Davies cites for his proof texts), and Psalm 65:3. Therefore, scholars must be cautious about ascribing to Paul rabbinic interpretations derived from Scripture just as Samuel Sandmel stated and just noted above. Now, it is true that the schools of Hillel and Shammai debated for more than two and a half

---

332   See the comments on how Paul's teachings so much go against the teachings of Gamliel and the School of Hillel in *Hillel*, Rabbi Joseph Telushkin, p. 131, n. 2, p. 224, and n. 1, pp. 230-231; *The Nine Questions People Ask about Judaism*, Dennis Prager and Rabbi Joseph Telushkin, pp. 78-83; *Jewish Literacy*, Rabbi Joseph Telushkin, p. 126.

333   See for example *Paul and the Torah*, Lloyd Gaston, pp. 18-19.

334   See the comments in *The Mythmaker*, Hyam Maccoby, pp. 54-55 and all of his scholar's notations to these pages.

335   *A Jewish Understanding of the New Testament*, Samuel Sandmel, pp. 37-38.

336   *Paul and Rabbinic Judaism*, W. D. Davies, p. 18.

337   See *Etymological Dictionary of Biblical Hebrew*, p. 33.

years whether or not it was good that man was created, as can be found in Babli *Eruvin* 13b; *Exodus Rabbah* 48, which even Davies rightly notes.[338] But in each of these tractates referred to this matter is being interpreted in regards to "regular people," but *not* in regards to a *zadakim*, or in essence, one who is referred to readily as "a perceptive person," (again, one of the possible meanings of the Hebrew word *basar*),[339] and something to which Davies even notes. Davies points out that there was a division of Jewish opinions upon this very matter,[340] thus, in essence, Davies is contradicting his own assertions about Paul. Also, there is a further point of proof to be offered here in regards to the matter of Paul *not* actually being a Pharisee, and this being what one finds in Philippians 3:5, a verse which generally gets translated out as, "... a Hebrew descended from Hebrews *according to* (emphasis mine) the law a Pharisee."[341] But the problem with such an interpretation surrounds the Greek word *kata* that so often gets translated as "according to." For this Greek word *kata* also offers a meaning of, "*against*" something, or "*opposed*" to something.[342] Thus, one *can actually* render out Philippians 3:5 as stating, "... a Hebrew descended from Hebrews *opposed to* the law of the Pharisee," meaning "*opposed to*" the "oral" Torah of the Pharisees exactly as the Sadducees were! This fact goes hand-in-hand with Paul's teachings regarding circumcision, which directly contradict Pharisaic teachings on this matter.[343] Now, it is true that under both Greek and Roman law, becoming circumcised was a violation of the

---

338 *Paul and Rabbinic Judaism*, W. D. Davies, p. 13.

339 See the comments on this of Rabbi Pesach Feldman of *Kollel Iyun Hadaf,* "Yerushalmi on *Eruvin* 13."

340 *Paul and Rabbinic Judaism*, W. D. Davies, p. 53.

341 See for example *Problems of New Testament Translation*, Edgar J. Goodspeed, pp. 175-176.

342 See the *Strong's Exhaustive Concordance* Greek Dictionary #2596; *Liddell and Scott's Greek-English Lexicon*, pp. 402-403; *BDAG Greek-English Lexicon*, p. 511, #2.

343 See the comments concerning Pharisaic teachings regarding "circumcision" of Emil G. Hirsch, Kaufmann Kohler, Joseph Jacobs, Aaron Friedenwald, and Isaac Broyde, "Circumcision," *Jewish Encyclopedia*; Matthew Thiessen, "Genealogy, Circumcision and Conversion in Early Judaism and Christianity," *Dissertation submitted in partial fulfillment of the requirements for the degree of Doctor of Philosophy in the Department of Religion in the Graduate School of Duke University,* (2010).

law,[344] which thus, since Paul was a Roman citizen, (as will be discussed in detail below), this fact quite possibly could have been a major factor in his teachings regarding circumcision.

Therefore, there have also been scholarly claims that Paul *was* actually a Sadducee.[345] For it clearly states in Acts 22:5 that Paul was dispatched by the High Priest, (i.e. a Sadducee). It is important to point out here that at that time of this supposed dispatching of Paul by the High Priest, the High Priest *did not* have any jurisdiction over affairs that occurred in the location that one typically identifies as "Damascus" (of Syria), especially since at that time Damascus was under the control of the Nabateans[346] as noted even in 2 Corinthians 11:32; Galatians 1:15-17, and which even Josephus points out in *Antiquities* 14.10; 24.5.2-3 that such matters were under the jurisdiction of the local Synhedria, (a matter that will be further discussed in Chapter 5). Furthermore, as pointed out earlier in this chapter, the High Priest (a Sadducee) and the Pharisees *never* collaborated together for *any* reason *after* the Hasmonean-Seleucid war ended and the Maccabees reneged on their promises, (a matter discussed previously above), which further puts the claim that Paul was a Pharisee in serious doubt! Now, in regards to this matter in Acts 22:5, there are some scholars who try to utilize *2 Maccabees* 1:10, 18; 2:214 to claim that legal rulings made by the Jerusalem Great Sanhedrin extended out to cover also *all* diaspora communities.[347] But the fact is that not only are these portions of *2 Maccabees* debated amongst scholars as to whether or not they are forgeries, nothing in these verses from *2 Maccabees*, in actuality, says anything that indicates that it is a

---

344   See Joseph Offord, "Restrictions of Circumcision under the Romans," *Proc R Soc Med* 1913;6 (Sect Hist Med): pp. 102-107; Frederick M. Hodges, "The Ideal Prepuce in Ancient Greece and Rome: Male Genital Aesthetics and Their Relation to *Lipodermos*, Circumcision, Foreskin Restoration, and the *Kynodesme*, *The Bulletin of the History of Medicine*, Volume 75, Fall 2001, pp. 375-405.

345   See the comments of Samuel Belkin, "The Problem of Paul's Background," *Journal of Biblical Literature* 54.1, (1935), pp. 41-60.

346   See the comments on this in *How Jesus Became Christian*, Barrie Wilson, p. 140; *The Other Side of the Jordan*, Nelson Glueck, pp. 19 and 193; *Deities and Dolphins*, Nelson Glueck, p. 40; *The Mythmaker*, Hyam Maccoby, pp. 85-86; *Caiaphas*, Helen K. Bond, p. 81.

347   See for example Shmuel Safrai and M. Stern, :Relations Between the Diaspora and the Land of Israel," *The Jewish People in the First Century*, pp. 184-215.

legal ruling that required that *all* diaspora communities, such as Damascus and/or Alexandria in Egypt for example, abide by a prescribed Palestinian Pharisaic practice or *legal ruling.*[348] But, it is also *essential* to point out here that the place name, "Damascus" was also used as a "code name" for the community now referred to as Qumran and to the sect of the Essens,[349] and which then, *this* particular community *was* located within Judea, and therefore, *this* particular community at Qumran *would have been* under the jurisdiction of the High Priest! Furthermore, *only* the High Priest and his fellow Sadducees as a whole had their own "police force" with the High Priest serving as "Chief of Police."[350] As Jacob Neusner writes concerning the High Priesthood at the time of Jesus, referencing the story in *Tosephta Kippurim* 1:12; *Tosephta Shavuot* 1:4; Mishnah *Yoma* 2:2; Babli *Yoma* 23a,[351] "One kills the other, showing that the priesthood was hot-headed and violent, just as Josephus says of the Sadducees."

Paul, in Romans 11:1 and Philippians 3:5, *claims* to be from the Tribe of Benjamin. But the *Jewish historical fact* is that by the time of Jesus, genealogical records other than for the descendants of Aaron, the Levites, and for the lineage of David were no longer being kept as noted in *Pesaḥim* 62b,[352] and as noted by Josephus in *Contra Apion* 2.190-194, (this holds true as well for what is found being stated in Luke 2:36).Furthermore, Paul also admits to being a Roman citizen in Acts 22:25-28,[353] and thus, Paul's allegiance would have also been to Roman authorities as well as to the High Priest's and other Sadducees. Now, it is true that there are some

---

348   See the lengthy comments on this matter in *Jewish Law from Jesus to the Mishnah*, E. P. Sanders, pp. 255-308.

349   See the comments on this in *The Apocalyptic Imagination*, John J. Collins, p. 61; *On Earth As It Is In Heaven*, D. C. Thielmann, p. 581 and the corresponding scholar's notations to this page.

350   See the comments in *The Mythmaker*, Hyam Maccoby, p. 58 and n. 3, p. 214; *Caiaphas*, Helen K. Bond, p. 42.

351   *The Idea of Purity in Ancient Judaism*, Jacob Neusner, p. 77.

352   See the comments on this from Kaufmann Kohler, "Saul of Tarsus (known as Paul, the Apostle of the Heathen)," *Jewish Encyclopedia*.

353   But see also Acts 16:37-40; 25:10-12 and see the comments in *Pontius Pilate in History and Interpretation*, Helen K. Bond, p. 141; *Roman Society and Roman Law in the New Testament*, A. N. Sherwin-White, pp. 144-162.

scholars who doubt the credibility of this claim in Acts 22 that Paul was a Roman citizen based on their belief that Paul never mentions being a Roman citizen in any of his letters.[354] But, *if* it is true though, (and it would seem that even Church traditions confirm this to be true), that Paul *was* in fact from Tarsus, (as even the Church Father, Jerome, in his *Commentary on Philippians 5* records a story of Paul's parents being former slaves in Tarsus who were freed), then, since Tarsus was a Roman "free city," one must understand that *under Roman law* there were several factors that *automatically* constituted one becoming a Roman citizen – one of these factors being that anyone who was *born* in a Roman "free city," such as Tarsus was, *or*, as a possible second factor, anyone who had once been a slave but who had been granted their freedom from being a slave, such as the story recorded by Jerome states *did* occur with Paul's family, then that "freed slave" *automatically* became a *Roman citizen* and was given a *Roman citizenship surname*! Therefore, the single greatest *proof* that Paul *was* in *fact* a Roman citizen comes from Paul's own writings, (as will be shown momentarily), and particularly from the letters which are now generally accepted by the majority of scholars as actually having been written by Paul. This *proof* derives from what is stated in Acts 13:9 – "Saul, the one also called Paul" – for as just noted above regarding a Roman "free city" as soon as one became a Roman citizen they were given a *Roman citizenship name*, yet *nowhere* in *any* New Testament writing - regardless of whether or not that writing was from Paul or any other New Testament author - *nowhere* is there *ever* any mention of a name change from "Saul" to "Paul"! While the name "Saul" may have, and most probably *was* his Jewish heritage name, "Paul" (Greek, *Paulos*, from the Latin, *Paulus*),[355] was his *Roman citizenship surname*, and in *all* of Paul's *legitimate* letters, (as believed by the majority of New Testament scholars), *Paul* refers to himself *by* his *Roman citizenship surname, Paulos* – "*Paul*"![356] Philippi was another Roman "free city" and in Philippians 3:20 one finds that Paul makes a *clear* reference to one's "citizenship" (*politeuma* – a Greek word that was used in regards to

---

354 See for example the comments in *Paul Was Not a Christian*, Pamela Eisenbaum, p. 141.

355 See the *BDAG Greek-English Lexicon*, p. 789; T. J. Leary, "Paul's Improper Name," *New Testament Studies* Volume 38, No. 3 (1992), pp. 467-469.

356 See the comments on this of Greg Lanier, "No, 'Saul the Persecutor' Did Not Become 'Paul the Apostle'," *The Gospel Coalition*, May 3, 2017.

one being a Roman citizen), and when one remembers that Paul is writing *to gentiles* of a Roman "free city," then it should become quite clear that Paul is referring to *their Roman citizenship*, and when one further sees that Paul in this verse states, "*our* citizenship" it is obvious that he is including his *own Roman citizenship* as well or else it would be found being stated, "*your* citizenship"!

Going further into this matter of Paul being a Roman citizen though, Josephus in *Antiquities* 13.251-252 states that Jews who were Roman citizens were "dismissed" from observing "the rites of the Jewish religion, on account of *their* religion," and *as* a Roman citizen, Paul was also protected by the *Lex Julia*.[357] In essence, this is precisely why we find Paul giving such teachings that have been interpreted to mean that Jesus' death abrogated the Torah! For Paul, being a "Roman citizen," was "dismissed" from having to observe "the rites of the Jewish religion,"[358] even though as noted above Paul underwent the full Nazarite rites, but he did so under false pretense, as Paul even admits in 1 Corinthians 9:19-23! As A. N. Sherwin-White writes concerning this,[359] "The provincial who became a Roman ceased to be a member of his native community, and to exercise any rights or to be required to perform any duties there." A. N. Sherwin-White goes further to point out that,[360] "Officially the Roman citizen may not practice any alien cult that has not received the public sanction of the State, but customarily he might do so as long as his cult did not otherwise offend against the laws and usages of Roman life, i.e. so long as it did not involve political and social crimes." Sherwin-White then points out that in each instance of Paul's arrests at Philippi, Ephesus, and Thessalonica (for example), those who arrested and "persecuted," or "punished" Paul were non-Jews, (i.e. gentile *Roman citizens*). Yet, despite all of the indications that Paul was a Roman citizen aligned with the Sadducees, there is one major overlying problem even with this claim, and this being what was noted earlier in this chapter that the Sadducees did not believe in the "resurrection of the

---

357 See the comments in *Roman Society and Roman Law in the New Testament*, A. N. Sherwin-White, pp. 58-70.

358 See the comments on this in *The New Testament and Jewish Law*, James G. Crossley, pp. 42-44.

359 *Roman Society and Roman Law in the New Testament*, A. N. Sherwin-White, p. 181.

360 *Roman Society and Roman Law in the New Testament*, A. N. Sherwin-White, p. 79.

dead," which Paul seems to clearly teach in his Epistles. So, we have clear evidence that Paul *was not* a Pharisee, and the matter of his teachings about the resurrection of the dead puts him at odds with the Sadducees, and thus, we have an unresolved matter that begs the question to be asked - what sort of a Jew *was* Paul? Now, W. D. Davies makes a very telling statement concerning Philo and Paul that must be noted here, for Davies states that,[361] "For example, how different Paul must have been from a Jew like Philo can be measured by the fact that Philo never discovered that the *Kupios* (kyrios) of the LXX represented the Hebrew *Yahweh*." Davies statement though, is quite in error in claiming that the Greek word *Kupios* was *always* being used in the LXX for the Hebrew *YHWH* (Yahweh),[362] a matter which Philo, (as Davies notes, but seems to not realize himself), *clearly knows*. Furthermore, Davies is also in error regarding Paul, for Paul *only* uses *Kupios* in regards to Jesus, but uses the word *Theos* in regards to God.[363] But despite this, the question still needs to be asked – what sort of a Jew *was* Paul?

Going even further though, Paul also admits to being related to the Herodians[364] as he clearly writes in Romans 16:10-11, and the Herodians likewise had their own henchmen and ruffians who kept control over malefactors. Paul even admits in 1 Corinthians 7:12; 7:25; 7:40; Galatians 1:1-24 to not teaching according to Jesus' teachings, but instead uses *his own* opinions and teachings![365] In addition to Paul teaching his own opinions, Paul quite often contradicts himself, and at times these contradictions are found between what Paul states in one Epistle and what he then states in a different Epistle. But at other times, one can find such contradictions within the *same* Epistle.[366] In 2 Peter 1:20-21, (a writing which most scholars believe was not actually written by the disciple named *Simon Peter*), even

---

361   *Paul and Rabbinic Judaism*, W. D. Davies, p. 12.

362   See *On Earth As It Is In Heaven*, D. C. Thielmann, p. 172 and n.14 – 20, pp. 203-206.

363   See the comments on this in *Paul Was Not a Christian*, Pamela Eisenbaum, pp. 177-189.

364   See the comments of Robert Eisenman, "Paul as Herodian," *JHC* 3/1 (Spring 1996), pp. 110-122.

365   See the comments on this in *Jesus*, C. Leslie Mitton, p. 49 who seemingly points out this fact unknowingly in regards to its full ramifications; *How Jesus Became Christian*, Barrie Wilson, pp. 1-6, 103, 131-149, 168-181, 237-253.

366   See the comments on this in *Paul Was Not a Christian*, Pamela Eisenbaum, pp. 27-31.

though it *clearly* states, "that no prophecy of Scripture is a matter of one's own interpretation," this writing then goes on to reference Paul's teachings, which as just noted, a great deal of Paul's teachings *came from his own opinions and interpretations!* Thus, given the fact of the disputes noted between Peter and Paul, this writing of 2 Peter *cannot* be an Epistle actually written by the apostle Peter,[367] for as Walter Bauer points out,[368] the Church at Rome, established by Peter, was the very center of activity attempting to control "heresies," (see again, the comments in the Preface on this matter), and "heretics" who "contradicted" the "orthodox" teachings of Jesus. Yet, as Georg Strecker points out,[369] the Jewish followers of Jesus, (who were also referred to as *Ebionites*, and the word *Ebionite* means "poor," such as is found in Romans 15:26; Galatians 2:10),[370] later came to be referred to as "heretics" themselves even though *they* were the *original* followers of the teachings of Jesus!. As a further note to this matter, Bart Ehrman believes that Galatians 2:6-9 is referring to two different individuals when Paul refers to "Peter" and "Cephas" separately, even though both names mean "rock."[371] One will also find that in 1 Corinthians 9:1-2 Paul even states that there were individuals who *did not* recognize him as being a *legitimate* "Apostle,"[372] and in 1 Corinthians 15:8 Paul even admits that he is, "unfit to be an Apostle."

In Galatians 1:1,12, 16-17 Paul distances himself from those who are the very "heads" of the Jesus followers in Jerusalem, and in Galatians 2:6 Paul actually then states in regards to these "leaders" of the Jesus movement that, "what they once were makes no difference to me," which again, clearly demonstrates that Paul was going out on his own, using his *own* "opinions

---

367   See the comments on this in *The New Testament*, Bart D. Ehrman, pp. 457-458.

368   *Orthodoxy and Heresy in Earliest Christianity*, Walter Bauer, pp. 229-240.

369   See *Orthodoxy and Heresy in Earliest Christianity*, Walter Bauer, with Georg Strecker commenting in Appendix 1.

370   See the comments on *Ebionite* in *Essays on the Semitic Background of the New Testament*, Joseph A. Fitzmyer, pp. 437-447.

371   See the comments on this in *The New Testament*, Bart D. Ehrman, Box 20.6, p. 335; but see also the comments on this in *Orthodoxy and Heresy in Earliest Christianity*, Walter Bauer, p. 115; *A Jewish Understanding of the New Testament*, Samuel Sandmel, pp. 159-160.

372   See the comments in *A Jewish Understanding of the New Testament*, Samuel Sandmel, pp. 84-85.

and teachings" in contradiction to not only Jesus, but also in contradiction to the very individuals who were the actual true *original* followers of Jesus and who *actually witnessed* Jesus' teachings, such as Peter, James and the other *legitimate* "Apostles!" This is exactly why the "split" between the "gentile Church" and the "Jewish Synagogue" actually started at such an early point in time after Jesus and still during the lifetime of the *original* disciples of Jesus. This "split" can ultimately be traced back to the "heretical teachings" of Paul that formed what eventually became the Church of today, and thus, the very key to what brought about the alterations in the Gospels and Epistles that distort the "historical" truth about Jesus as well as the "historically" erroneous portrait of the Pharisees.[373] Now, Walter Bauer is quite in error when he writes,[374] "The Paul of the Pastoral Epistles fights in union with 'the church' *against* the heretics." Bauer goes on then to identify these so-called "heretics" that he is referring to as "Jewish-Christians" who held fast to the Torah, Sabbath observance, and circumcision in opposition to Paul, which to Bauer, seemingly derived from the Apostle John.[375] Yet later, Bauer ends up rightly noting that the Church of Rome separated itself from any connection to Paul making Peter their basis because, "Peter provides the close tie to Jesus, which alone guarantees the purity of Church teaching."[376] James Dunn, on the other hand, admits that it was Paul who "undercut the self-understanding of Judaism as expressed in the Torah,"[377] and again, Jesus was wholly dedicated to the Torah as clearly pointed out in Chapter 3 as well as in this chapter. James Dunn rightly admits that Paul was "regarded as an apostate," i.e., a "heretic!"[378] Therefore, it is quite

---

373   See the comments on this in *Jewish Literacy*, Rabbi Joseph Telushkin, pp. 125-127.

374   *Orthodoxy and Heresy in Earliest Christianity*, Walter Bauer, p. 84.

375   See the comments on this in *Orthodoxy and Heresy in Earliest Christianity*, Walter Bauer, pp. 85-89, and 99.

376   *Orthodoxy and Heresy in Earliest Christianity*, Walter Bauer, pp. 113-114.

377   *The Partings of the Ways*, James Dunn, p. 140.

378   *The Partings of the Ways*, James Dunn, p. 233; *How Jesus Became Christian*, Barrie Wilson, pp. 101, 109-130, and 165 in which he references the writings known as the *Gospel of the Nazarenes*, the *Gospel According to the Hebrews*, the *Gospel of the Ebionites*, the *Homilies of Clement* (and for more on the *Homilies of Clement* see *On Earth As It Is In Heaven*, D. C. Thielmann, n. 2, pp. 423-424; *The Jesus Mysteries*, Timothy Freke and Peter Gandy, pp. 161-162), and the *Letter of Peter to James and its Reception*, all

erroneous for *any* scholar to claim that Paul *was not* instrumental in *any way* in altering or formulating the Christianity we have come to know today![379] James Dunn though, states,[380] "But it does mean that Paul's subsequent use of *nomos*[381] to sum up Israel's obligations as set out by Moses cannot be dismissed as a Hellenistic Jew's Septuagintal distortion of his heritage, and that Paul's theological argument was interacting with a very important strand of Jewish thought and life."[382] Also, as Edgar J. Goodspeed writes[383] "… Paul's letters have become for most readers of the standard versions a vast jungle of words, from which an intelligible idea only occasionally emerges. As Paul is the leading thinker among the writers of the New Testament, this has been in the highest degree disastrous." And a further statement of importance comes from Barrie Wilson, who writes,[384] "Simply put, the teachings of Jesus himself were smothered by the religion of Paul." Now, in regards to the matter of Paul's "Septuagintal distortion" mentioned just above, some scholars though, have claimed to find in the Dead Sea Scrolls certain Essen interpretations of Scripture that are derived from the Septuagintal reading of certain verses as opposed to the Hebrew reading of these same verses, and therefore, these scholars claim that one *should not* dismiss the Septuagintal readings such as Paul gives, as being "erroneous

---

of which are strongly opposed to the teachings of Paul as being "heretical" teachings! See also the similar comments regarding the *Letter of Peter to James*, and the *Homilies of Clement* regarding Paul being a "heretic" in *Jewish Christianity Reconsidered*, Matt Jackson-McCabe, pp. 285-304, (F. Stanley Jones commenting); *Essays on the Semitic Background of the New Testament*, Joseph A. Fitzmyer, pp. 447-453, and 463; *Paul and Rabbinic Judaism*, W. D. Davies, pp. 50-51.

379   See the comments, for example, in *The New Testament*, Bart D. Ehrman, Box 9.6, p. 147.

380   *The Partings of the Ways*, James Dunn, p. 24.

381   See the comments on this word *nomos* in *On Earth As It Is In Heaven*, D. C. Thielmann, pp. 128-129 and the corresponding scholars notations to these pages.

382   James Dunn then references in *The Partings of the Ways*, n. 32, p. 287, "See particularly S. Westerholm, "Torah, Nomos and Law: A Question of 'Meaning'," *Studies in Religion* 15, (1986), pp 327-336; Also, A. F. Segal, "Torah and *nomos* in Recent Scholarly Discussion," *Studies in Religion* 13, (1984), pp. 19-28, reprinted in *Other Judaisms*, pp. 131-145; and the earlier protest to the same effect by E. E. Urbach, *The Sages*, pp. 288-290."

383   *Problems of New Testament Translation*, Edgar J. Goodspeed, p. 3.

384   *How Jesus Became Christian*, Barrie Wilson, p. 255.

translations."[385] This point is well taken, but *if* this is true, then once again this *truth* will place the followers of Jesus closer to the Qumran sect of Essens than the majority of scholars are willing to admit!

Yet, despite all of this historical evidence that Paul was a "heretic,"[386] there are still far too many scholars who try to defend Paul.[387] Moshe Chaim Luzzatto gives a lengthy discussion on how one can easily recognize someone who has received a "false vision," and thus termed a "false prophet," or a "false witness."[388] Barrie Wilson also makes a very important point to make mention of here,[389] and this being that not long after Paul's conversion to being a follower of Jesus (Acts 9:9-19), Paul begins proclaiming Jesus in the synagogues in Damascus (Acts 9:20-22). But then Wilson points out that a plot to kill Paul was raised by "the Jews" and Paul was helped to escape by "*his* disciples" (Acts 9:23-25). Thus, Wilson very rightly states, "Some details here should set off alarm bells in the mind of a wary reader. Were there already members of the Jesus Movement so far from Jerusalem? Also, how was it that Paul already had disciples – where did they come from? Did Paul already have 'a movement'? Moreover, would any member of the Jesus Movement have referred to the worshippers in synagogues as 'the Jews' – as 'other' – or was this a reflection of a much later stance, when the Christian community was separating from Judaism? A lot of things do not ring true in this account." Wilson then points out that Galatians 1:16 contradicts this by stating that immediately after his conversion, Paul "*did not confer with any human being*," for a while, having first gone to Arabia (Galatians 1:17).

This fact regarding the claim that the Pharisees collaborated with the Herodians is also quite strange though, as noted already above, which is the very reason why the verses of Scripture were used as the title to this

---

385 See the comments in *Essays on the Semitic Background of the New Testament*, Joseph A. Fitzmyer, pp. 87-89.

386 See the comments in *The New Testament*, Bart D. Ehrman, p. 3.

387 See for example the comments in *The Crucifixion of Jesus*, Gerard S. Sloyan, p. 49 and n. 2, p. 49 where he references Terrance Callan, *The Origins of Christian Faith*, pp. 7-35.

388 *The Way of God*, Moshe Chaim Luzzatto, pp. 231-237.

389 *How Jesus Became Christian*, Barrie Wilson, pp. 138-140.

chapter. For as Hyam Maccoby rightly states,[390] "Yet so remote is the New Testament from the facts of the period that the Gospels sometimes represent the Pharisees and the Herodians as allies!" Also, as Lloyd Gaston rightly states,[391] "If Proto-Luke sometimes considers the Pharisees as enemies of the Gospel, at other times they are shown in a more friendly light... We can also refer to the statement that when Herod is seeking to kill Jesus, it is Pharisees who warn him to flee (Luke 13:31)." It seems very clear that this attitude of the Gospel authors towards the Pharisees parallels all of Paul's letters, (but primarily 2 Corinthians and Galatians), which speak negatively about those who "oppose" him, and it is clear from these letters that Paul is referring to the "Jewish leaders" or "pillars" of the Jerusalem Church, namely, Peter and James.[392]

Yet, there is still another very odd reference to a historically unlikely connection that can be found in Mark 2:18[393] where it refers to John the Baptist's disciples *and* the Pharisees fasting.[394] This is odd because Matthew 3:7 has John the Baptist referring to both the Pharisees and the Sadducees as a "brood of vipers." So, why would John's disciples be "fasting" at the same time as the members of this "brood of vipers"? Now, it is quite true that Matthew's Gospel seems to reword what is found in Mark 2:18, and thereby, eliminating a seeming referential connection, but nonetheless, something is amiss with Mark's reference, to which some scholars ascribe this supposed account by Mark to being the evangelist's attempt to separate Jesus from John as a representation of the separation of the church,

---

390   *Revolution in Judaea*, Hyam Maccoby, p. 71, and see also his comments on p. 99 in regards to how important it is to understand Luke 13:31; see further the comments in *The Crucifixion of Jesus*, Gerard S. Sloyan, pp. 30-31 and n. 51, p. 31, J. Saldarini, *Pharisees, Scribes, and Sadducees in Palestinian Society*, pp. 79-106.

391   *No Stone on Another*, Lloyd Gaston, p. 315.

392   See the comments on this in *Jewish Christianity Reconsidered*, Matt Jackson-McCabe, pp. 57-80, (Jerry L. Sumney commenting).

393   See the somewhat erroneous comments on this verse and matter in *Mark*, Robert H. Gundry, pp. 131-139.

394   On this matter of "fasting" see Isidore Singer and Jacob Zallel Lauterbach, "Megillat Ta'anit ('Scroll of Fasting')," *Jewish Encyclopedia*; Julius H. Greenstone, Emil G. Hirsch, Hartwig Hirschfeld and the Executive Committee of the Editorial Board, "Fasting and Fast Days," *Jewish Encyclopedia*.

(Christianity) from the synagogue, (Judaism).[395] In regards to this matter of "fasting" though, other than for the Torah commandment regarding the Day of Atonement, "fasting" just for the sake of "fasting" was a matter that was greatly debated between Shammai and Hillel as noted in *Eruvin* 13b; *Pesaḥim* 2:7a; *Berakhot* 31a. But "fasting," as a practice other than for the Day of Atonement was eventually denounced as noted in *Ta'anit* 11ab. Yet, despite this ruling there were still many who "fasted," but generally such "fasting" was over matters of destress, as noted in *Ketuvah* 104a; *Pesaḥim* 68a, and in fact after the destruction of the Temple in 70 CE there was a massive "fasting" by a great many Jews, as noted in *Baba Batra* 60b.[396] So again, something is amiss in these Gospel accounts regarding the Pharisees and John the Baptist "fasting"! In *Didache* 8:1 it speaks of "fasting," but not "with the hypocrites" who "fast on the second and fifth day of the week," for one should "fast on the fourth day and the Preparation day," so it is quite obvious that there *was* an early Church tradition regarding "fasting" only that this tradition differed from the Pharisaic tradition of "fasting," which is noted in Luke 18:12. Now, Mishnah *Ta'anit* 1:1-7 speaks of "fasting" during drought years and Mishnah *Ta'anit* 2:1-9 speaks of "fasting" for the Day of Atonement, but also, as just noted above, "fasting" was most often done during times of distress.[397]

With all that has been pointed out in this chapter, as well as what has been noted in previous chapters, it is now necessary to state once again that at the time of Jesus and during the century prior to the time of Jesus, there was not any uniformity amongst the Jews in regards to an expected *Messiah*.[398] Therefore, for any individual, whether scholar, theologian, or general laity to emphatically claim that "the Jews" rejected Jesus as a claimed Messiah would simply be *historically* untrue. This fact has though, not escaped the notice of the Catholic Church and Vatican scholars whom have begun to recant what had long been taught for centuries beginning with the *Lumen Gentium* ("Light of the Nations"), and the *Declaration On the Relation of the Church to Non-Christian Religions*, or *Nostra Aetate*

---

395   See the comments of Robert McFarlane, "The Gospel of Mark and Judaism," *Jewish-Christian Relations: Insights and Issues in the Ongoing Jewish-Christian Dialogue.*

396   See the comments of Kaufmann Kohler, "Ascetics," *Jewish Encyclopedia.*

397   See the comments on this in *Jewish Law from Jesus to the Mishnah*, E. P. Sanders, pp. 81-84.

398   See the comments in *The Jewish Messiah*, James Drummond, p. 273.

("In Our Time")[399] of the Second Vatican Council, 1962-1965, both of which culminated in Pope John Paul II's unequivocal statement in his *Allocution in Mainz,* November 17, 1980 that, "the Old Covenant has never been revoked." Since this time of Pope John Paul II's statement, several further Vatican statements have been released, such as that of Cardinal Joseph Ratzinger on January 17, 2002[400] and the statement released by the Vatican's Commission for Religious Relations, titled, "The Gifts and Calling of God are Irrevocable" released December 10, 2015. Therefore, the following chapters will now discuss the *true* "enemies" of Jesus and what actually led to his arrest, trial, and crucifixion.

---

399   See the comments on this in *The Partings of the Ways,* James Dunn, p. 15; *Jewish Literacy,* Rabbi Joseph Telushkin, pp 526-527.

400   See *Christianity: A Jewish Perspective,* Rabbi Moshe Reiss, Introduction A.

Chapter 5

"Jesus no longer walked openly among the Jews...."
(John 11:54)

I n this chapter we are going to examine the role of the Great Sanhedrin both in regards to its duties and responsibilities as the judges in cases involving violations of Jewish law, but also examine its role in a *supposed* "trial of Jesus" as described in the Gospels. First though, we must mention that the word "Sanhedrin" derives, *not* from a Hebrew word, but from the Greek word, *synedrion*, which has a primary meaning of, "council," or "assembly," but this word does also offer the meaning of, "governing body." Thus, as a result of this fact, Hugo Mantel rightly points out,[1] "Our knowledge of the Sanhedrin is derived from two sets of sources: the one Greek, the other Hebrew. Unfortunately, we are at once confronted with the problem of reconciling these two sets of sources, for they do not speak with a single voice. The account of the Sanhedrin in Josephus and the New Testament does not tally with the account to be found in the Talmud." Now, it has been suggested by some scholars that the Great Sanhedrin did not exist at all under Roman rule of Palestine.[2] But as will be proven in this chapter, such suggestions are without merit.

---

1   See *Studies in the History of the Sanhedrin*, Hugo Mantel, Introduction, p. xi.
2   See for example *Caiaphas*, Helen K. Bond, pp. 33-34 and n. 2, p. 167.

We must now closely examine the verse used as the title to this chapter in regards to one particular aspect of the overall role of the Great Sanhedrin as it pertains to Jesus and his ministry. For one of the very duties of the Great Sanhedrin was that it was required to issue what we today would call a "summons," or an order to appear before the court in regards to a particular complaint made by *any* individual. This is clearly found being stated in Mishnah, *Makkoth* 2:6; Talmud Babli, *Sanhedrin* 19a; and by Josephus in *Antiquities* 14.169. In other words, just as in our own justice system of today, say for example, one of our neighbors lodged a complaint against us in a court of law for some reason. The court would then issue us a "summons" requiring us to appear before the court in answer to this complaint regardless of whether or not the complaint was a valid, truthful complaint or an invalid and bogus complaint. If we fail to answer such a summons by failing to appear before the court in regards to the summons we were issued, but instead we "flee," we would then become a "fugitive from justice" and a "warrant" for our "arrest" would be issued. This is precisely what John 11:54 indicates that Jesus did – "flee" from a "summons" issued by the Great Sanhedrin.[3] John's Gospel (John 11:47-53) clearly places a gathering of the "council," or "Sanhedrin" long before the final Passover trial before Pilate. Now, there are some scholars who believe that this mentioning of a meeting of the Great Sanhedrin in John 11:47-53 is "unhistorical."[4] Yet, as will be shown, this account in John is *most probably* quite close to being *historically* true, yet *not* for the reasons for which most Christians, (whether scholar, theologian, or general church laity) might understand this *historical* truth! As Joseph Ratzinger and Pope Benedict XVI, for example, state concerning this,[5] "John dates it, incidentally, before 'Palm Sunday' and sees as its immediate occasion the

---

3 See the comments in *The Trial of Jesus: Cambridge Studies in Honour of C. F. D. Moule*, pp. 32-35; *The Trial of Jesus*, Josef Blinzler, pp. 56-57; *Herod Antipas*, Harold W. Hoehner, pp. 191, 199-202, and 320-330; *The Life of Jesus*, M. Goguel, pp. 354-392; *The Destroyer of Jesus*, V. E. Harlow, pp. 148-160; *The Last Journey of Jesus to Jerusalem*, W. H. Cadman, pp. 27-52; "Jesus and Herod Antipas," *Journal of Biblical Literature*, LXXIX, J. B. Tyson, pp. 239-246; *The Gospel History and its Transmission*, F. C. Burkitt, pp. 91-98 even though Burkitt admits in his 3rd edition, pp. xii-xiv that he may have overstated his case.

4 See for example the comments in *Barabbas and Esther*, Roger David Aus, p. 62.

5 *Jesus of Nazareth: Part Two*, Ratzinger and Pope Benedict, p. 168.

popular movement generated by the raising of Lazarus… Evidently John is preserving a historical memory here, to which the Synoptics also refer briefly (c.f. Mark 14:1; Matthew 26:3-4; Luke 22:1-2)." Also, as another example, Albert Nolan writes concerning this gathering mentioned in John's Gospel that,[6] "The details of this scene in John may not be, and were probably never intended to be, an accurate historical account of what transpired at the meeting. But the fact that there was some such conspiracy is attested by the independent account of it which we find in the other three Gospels (Mark 14:1-2; Matthew 26:3-5; Luke 22:2) and by the fact that at some stage Jesus became a fugitive." Although Nolan is correct in stating that Jesus became a "fugitive," there are certain matters to be disagreed with in regards to portions of his assessment that will be discussed later in Chapter 6. Yet, despite this *very probable historical fact* that a "warrant" for Jesus' "arrest" was issued by the Great Sanhedrin, (and once again, *not* for the reasons that the majority of Christians believe, as will be proven), it will also be proven that Jesus was *never* actually taken before the *Great Sanhedrin* for any trial![7]

In regards to this matter of Jesus' "fleeing," there have been scholars who have interpreted certain verses from the Gospels as further indications that Jesus knew that he was a "wanted fugitive."[8] As a prime example of this, Matthew 8:20 and Luke 9:58 regarding "The foxes have holes, the birds of the air have nests; but the son of man has nowhere to lay his head," has been interpreted to be a *clear* indication that Jesus knew that he was a "wanted fugitive" from justice. Furthermore, as Hyam Maccoby writes concerning other such interpretations of New Testament verses,[9] "An interesting indication of the hunted existence that Jesus and his disciples led is provided by a little understood passage dealing with corn-plucking on the Sabbath," (this was a matter already discussed in Chapter 1). As Maccoby goes on to state, "Jesus defends his disciples for plucking ears of corn by quoting an incident from Scripture. David, when fleeing for his life from Saul, broke the law forbidding the eating of sacred food by non-priests. The emergency and danger of starvation overrode such laws.

---

6 *Jesus Before Christianity*, Albert Nolan, p. 105.

7 See the comments in *Judaism and the Origins of Christianity*, David Flusser, pp. 588-592.

8 See the comments in *Revolution in Judaea*, Hyam Maccoby, p. 101.

9 *Revolution in Judaea*, Hyam Maccoby, n. 2, p. 228.

In a similar emergency the Pharisees permitted breaches of the Sabbath laws, and Jesus even cites the Pharisee maxim which covers such cases, 'The Sabbath was made for man, not man for the Sabbath.' But Jesus' citation of the case of David is apposite only if his own case was similar, i.e. he too was fleeing for his life. The Gospels suppress the fact that Jesus was on the run from Herod or the Romans, and represent Jews as *attacking* Pharisaic attitudes towards the Sabbath when he was in fact applying them."[10] Moshe Chaim Luzzatto points out something very important to note that relates to this matter when he writes,[11] "There are other details of laws which were not known from tradition, but which were derived from the Torah, either through logic or by means of specific formulas. It is possible, too, that there might be a dispute regarding these laws," (refer back to Chapter 4 regarding the many disputes not only between the different factions of Pharisees, but also between the Pharisees and other Jewish philosophies at the time of Jesus). "Even in such a case, however, the final decision is binding upon us, and we must abide by it. The fact that there is a dispute does not weaken the final decision at all. God commanded that every dispute involving Torah law should be decided by the Sanhedrin (Supreme Court), and that the decision of the Sanhedrin must be obeyed absolutely," (see Deuteronomy 17:11, which says, "You shall not stray from the word that they tell you, either to the right or to the left"). In *Shabbat* 17a we find an example of such a dispute between Hillel, (who at the time was the *Nasi* over the Sanhedrin), and Shammai in which the Sanhedrin voted in favor of the opinion of Shammai regarding this particular debate of an interpretation of the Torah. Thus, there *is* the possibility that Jesus' being "summoned" to appear before the Great Sanhedrin *was not* as a result of a violation of *any* Jewish law, but simply in regards to a debate that Jesus had with someone, (most likely a Pharisee), over a certain "interpretation" of the Torah, which would require then that such a dispute be taken before the Great Sanhedrin to settle as stated in the Mishnah and both Yerushalmi and Babli Talmud's, *Pesaḥim* 6:1; *Pesaḥim* 33a; *Pesaḥim* 66a; *Baba Metzia* 104a; *Ketuboth* 4:8, and 28d; *Tosefta Ketuboth* 4:9.

---

10 See the further comments upon this matter in *Who Did Jesus Think He Was*, J. C. O'Neill, p. 42.

11 *The Way of God*, Moshe Chaim Luzzatto, pp. 399-401.

But where exactly did Jesus "flee" *to*? For the Gospel accounts seem to be in somewhat of a disagreement on this matter. John 11:54, for example, seemingly has Jesus "fleeing" to the wilderness,[12] which was a very common refuge for "wanted fugitives" to flee as noted in *II Maccabees* 6:11; Josephus *Antiquities* 4.220; 15.266. Now, Matthew's Gospel though, seems to indicate that Jesus' "fleeing" occurred right after the death of John the Baptist,[13] as does Luke 9:3-9. But, John 6:1 and John 6:15 seems to indicate that Jesus' flight was in regards to the desire of the people to make him king. So then, instead of the summons being as a result of a disagreement over an interpretation of the Torah, (noted just above), could the complaint *possibly* then have been issued against Jesus by Herod Antipas? We do not know for certain, for the Gospels are not entirely clear on this matter. Matthew 15:1-20; Mark 7:1-23 seem to indicate that Jesus fled to Gennesaret, which was a place, located still within Herod Antipas' tetrarchy.[14] Yet, both Mark 6:53 and Matthew 14:34 use the words, "crossed over" the Sea of Galilee, and the Sea of Galilee was also referred to as "Lake Gennesaret," and therefore, the seeming inference to Jesus' going to Gennesaret may be a mistaken indication that Jesus actually "crossed over Lake Gennesaret" to a location in the wilderness, which would have then been outside of Herod Antipas' tetrarchy, but which would then put this matter totally in line with what was just noted above from John 11:54.

In regards to this matter of a "summons" being issued for Jesus to appear before the Great Sanhedrin, there are some scholars who have asserted that the "letters" carried by Paul in Acts 9:2 were in fact either a "summons" or an "arrest warrant" issued by the Great Sanhedrin, (a matter briefly mentioned in Chapter 4). The problem though, lies in the fact that Paul is said to be headed to Damascus, (again, already pointed out in Chapter 4, but necessary to reiterate in this chapter), which as is known from 2 Corinthians 11:32; Galatians 1:15-17, the most commonly known Damascus was the city in Syria, and thus, a location that *was not* under the

---

12   See the comments in *Maccabees, Zealots, and Josephus*, W. R. Farmer, pp. 116-122.

13   See the comments on this in *Herod Antipas*, Harold W. Hoehner, Appendix ix, pp. 317-318; *Jesus and Israel*, Jules Isaac, p. 99.

14   See the comments in *Herod Antipas*, Harold W. Hoehner, Appendix ix, p. 320.

jurisdiction of the Great Sanhedrin at that time.[15] But as we know from the Dead Sea Scroll called the *Damascus Document* 6:19; 19:33-34, (of which no less than ten copies were found amongst the Dead Sea Scrolls, and which was first discovered in a Cairo Synagogue in 1896), the community now known in the scholarly world as Qumran, referred to their community as "Damascus in the wilderness," based on 1 Kings 19:15. Therefore, Qumran, which *was* located within the jurisdiction of the Great Sanhedrin at that time, is most likely the actual place where Paul was carrying these "letters," or if one prefers, "summons," or "arrest warrants."

Now, before any individual could be brought to trial, or, even before a summons or an arrest warrant could be issued, an individual had to first be "warned" that they were committing some offense,[16] *except*, if as just noted above, one was being "summoned" to appear before the Great Sanhedrin in regards to a disagreement over an interpretation of the Torah. Ezekiel 3:17-18 (and see also Ezekiel 3:19), clearly states, "Son of man, I have made you a watchman to the house of Israel: and when you shall hear a word at My mouth, you shall give warning from Me. When I say to the wicked man, you shall surely die; and you give them not warning, nor speak to warn the wicked from their wicked ways, to save their life; the same wicked man shall die in his iniquity: but his blood will I require at your hand." This matter goes back to the point that was made in Chapter 4 about Jesus' association with "tax collectors and sinners," and more will be said in Chapter 7 regarding Jesus' usage of this very term, "son of man" that is *clearly* used in this passage from Ezekiel. But this warning was to be given so that no one could use the plea of "ignorance for the law" at their trial, which was a very commonly used plea, as noted in the Talmud, *Sanhedrin* 8b; 72b; 41a and this was derived from both Leviticus 19:17, 26:37 where it was interpreted from these verses that "we are obligated to correct others when they transgress," but we are *not* to "embarrass them" by

---

15 See the comments in *The Other Side of the Jordan*, Nelson Glueck, pp. 19 and 193; *Deities and Dolphins*, Nelson Glueck, p. 40; *The Mythmaker*, Hyam Maccoby, pp. 85-86.

16 See the comments on this in *On Earth As It Is In Heaven*, D. C. Thielmann, pp. 63-65 and the corresponding scholars notations to these pages; *The New Testament and Jewish Law*, James G. Crossley, p. 42; Joseph Jacobs and Judah David Eisenstein, "Rebuke and Reproof," *Jewish Encyclopedia*; *Jewish Literacy*, Rabbi Joseph Telushkin, pp. 610-612.

that correction or "warning."[17] This is also *precisely* what Matthew 18:15-17 refers to and there are some scholars who miss this fact and as a result they end up erroneously interpreting these verses from Matthew's Gospel.[18] Jesus also points out in these verses the necessity of "two witnesses" to any further violations, just as was prescribed by Jewish law, *after* one had been first given this "warning" that they were violating a particular law. But after such a warning had been given, if the individual continued to commit whatever illegal activity they may be accused of, and *if* they *were* seen by at least "two witnesses" committing the same offense again, then a "summons" or "arrest warrant" was handed to the *hazzan*[19] ("law enforcement" or possibly the "Temple police") to be presented to that individual,[20] and a written "warrant for arrest" was required by Jewish law as noted in the Mishnah, *Sanhedrin* 1:5.[21] Now, even the Roman authorities could issue a complaint or an "arrest warrant," but *only* if the warrant was in regards to a capital offense in violation of *Roman law* committed by a Jewish citizen, and even then, the process for issuing such an "arrest warrant" still had to go through the local Jewish court, or Great Sanhedrin.[22]

Therefore, to briefly summarize what has already been stated here in this chapter, a complaint was presented to the Great Sanhedrin against Jesus by *someone*, and as to who exactly the individual was who made the complaint against Jesus is unclear, nor is the exact reason for the complaint made clear in the Gospel accounts. The complaint could have been made by Herod Antipas, or even by Pontius Pilate, or by both separately, or

17   See the comments on this in *Love Your Neighbor*, Rabbi Zelig Pliskin, pp. 278-295, and 336; *Hillel*, Rabbi Joseph Telushkin, n. 2, p. 232 who references *Baba Metzia* 58a which states that one should not shame his neighbor publicly, and *Baba Metzia* 58b states that one who does forfeits his share in the world to come, and *Baba Kamma* 86a-b even extends this to include not shaming children publicly.

18   See for example *Studies of the Historical Jesus*, Ernst Fuchs, pp. 152-153; *Jesus and the Spiral of Violence*, Richard A. Horsley, pp. 276-279; Jacob Voorsanger and Kaufmann Kohler, "Anathema," *Jewish Encyclopedia*.

19   See the comments of Cyrus Adler, Max Schloessinger, Joseph Jacobs, and Alois Kaiser, "Hazzan," *Jewish Encyclopedia*.

20   See the comments in *The Trial of Jesus from Jewish Sources*, Rabbi A. P. Drucker, p. 6.

21   See the comments in *The Trial of Jesus*, Josef Blinzler, p. 70.

22   See the comments in *The Trial of Jesus*, Josef Blinzler, n. 53, p. 71.

again as noted above, it could have even been made by some unknown individual in regards to a dispute over an interpretation of the Torah, but nonetheless, the Gospels seemingly indicate that a "summons" to appear before the Great Sanhedrin was issued against Jesus, but instead of answering the summons at the appointed time that Jesus was to appear before the Great Sanhedrin, Jesus instead "fled," and thus, a "warrant for his arrest" as a "fugitive" was issued.

Now, the search for a "fugitive," such as Jesus became, could have involved the Temple police alone, or in concert with Roman soldiers,[23] which again, the Gospels are in disagreement over this matter as can be found in Matthew 26:47; Mark 14:43; Luke 22:52; John 18:3, 12, and even Acts 5:17 could be utilized as an example. Joseph Blinzler believes that it was *only* Temple police who were involved in the actual arrest[24] of Jesus along with "court servants" citing Josephus, *Jewish Wars* 1.33.4; *Antiquities* 16.8.1 as to his reasoning. These "court servants" are also noted in the Talmud, *Pesaḥim* 57a; *Tosefta Menahot* 13.21, as well as in Matthew 5:25. Blinzler though, *does* mention[25] that the Gospel of John does *clearly* speak of a Roman cohort also, but Blinzler believes it to be "extremely improbable" even though he freely notes[26] that Josephus, *Antiquities* 18.3.2; *Jewish Wars* 2.9.4; *Middot* 1:2; *Shabbat* 6:4 all consider "clubs," "sticks," "torches," "wooden staves" as weapons sometimes carried by Roman soldiers and other "armed individuals." Joel Carmichael points out[27] concerning this mentioning of Romans being involved, and specifically, John 18:12, that this verse uses the Greek word *chiliarchos* in regards to the individual who is leading the arresting party. This is a word, which generally gets translated as, "tribune," but which actually means, "Captain," a word that is more often than not associated with Roman soldiers. The fact is though, that it *is highly probable* that a Roman cohort *was* amongst the search and

---

23 See the comments in *Pontius Pilate*, Ann Wroe, pp. 64-65; *The Last Week*, Marcus Borg and John Dominic Crossan, p. 124; *Judas Iscariot and the Myth of Jewish Evil*, Hyam Maccoby, pp. 76-77 and 79; *Revolution in Judaea*, Hyam Maccoby, pp. 154-155; *Jesus and Israel*, Jules Isaac, pp. 298-301.

24 *The Trial of Jesus*, Josef Blinzler, pp. 62-70.

25 *The Trial of Jesus*, Josef Blinzler, pp. 64-65.

26 *The Trial of Jesus*, Josef Blinzler, n. 36, p. 64.

27 *The Death of Jesus*, Joel Carmichael, pp. 21-22.

arresting party against Jesus despite the fact that they are not specifically called such in the Synoptic Gospels. For as Josephus notes in *Jewish Wars* 2.224, part of the duties of the cohort of Roman soldiers that were stationed in Jerusalem was to carry out "police duties in both the Temple Mount and the city itself."[28] A. N. Sherwin-White also points out that,[29] "The Equestrian Governors had military forces under their command. Though their troops were not normally legionary troops, but local auxiliaries, their commanders and often their centurions were Romans." The "Herodian ruffians," (mentioned in Chapter 4), were one of these branches of the Roman soldiery known as the *speculatores* as noted in Mark 6:27 and by Tacitus *Histories* 1.24-25; 2.73.[30] Thus, the combination of "Temple police" *and* individuals referred to as Roman soldiers being involved in the search for the "fugitive" Jesus and involved in Jesus' arrest is most probably the *historical* truth!

Now, similarly to the opinion of Blinzler just noted above, Gerard S. Sloyan doubts that Romans were involved in the arrest of Jesus[31] referencing *Judith* 14:12; *2 Maccabees* 8:22; 12:20, 22; Josephus, *Antiquities* 17.215 [17.9.3]; *Jewish Wars* 2.578 [2.20.7] for his opinion. Sloyan makes the unusual remark[32] that the evangelists, (Gospel authors, that is), "did not know which soldiery, Roman or Jewish, visited what cruelties on Jesus." The "Temple Police," first off, *were not* "soldiers," and secondly, *if* the "Temple Police" *had*, in fact, "visited" *any* "cruelties" upon Jesus, it would have been a major violation of Jewish law! Sloyan thus, rightly questions John 18:3 about the mentioning of "Pharisees" in this verse, but he erroneously equates this to not being able to determine if Romans were involved as a result of this false mentioning of the "Pharisees" having *any* "guards."[33] But despite all of this debate as to who exactly was involved in the arresting

---

28 See the comments in *Pontius Pilate in History and Interpretation*, Helen K. Bond, p. 13.

29 *Roman Society and Roman Law in the New Testament*, A. N. Sherwin-White, p. 8, but see also his additional comments on this on p. 10.

30 See the comments in *Roman Society and Roman Law in the New Testament*, A. N. Sherwin-White, pp. 109-110, and 124.

31 *Jesus on Trial*, Gerard S. Sloyan, pp. 33, 88 and n. 11, p. 136; but see also, *The Trial of Jesus*, David R. Catchpole, pp. 148-150.

32 *The Crucifixion of Jesus*, Gerard S. Sloyan, p. 12.

33 *The Crucifixion of Jesus*, Gerard S. Sloyan, p. 36.

party of Jesus, no one, (whether scholar, theologian, or general laity), *can*, or *should* blame the Great Sanhedrin for acting as it was required to do *by law* just the same as if any one of us today were to have a "summons" or "arrest warrant" issued against us, we *could not* or *should not* blame the court for fulfilling its required responsibility for the issuance of such. Thus, Donald Juel is quite correct when he writes,[34] "If the verdict of the Jewish court is not the direct cause of Jesus' death however, we must look elsewhere for its function in the story."

It is essential now to take a close examination of this term, *Sanhedrin*, (which as was explained above derives from a Greek source), and understand who and what comprised the "Sanhedrin," and how much power and/or authority did this "assembly" actually have at the time of Jesus. Now, many scholars believe that the "Great Sanhedrin," (which consisted of only 70 individuals, who for the most part, were the leading rabbis of the time, and which was overseen by the *Nasi*), had been abolished in 40 BCE and was not again re-established until 42 CE by Herod Agrippa I.[35] But as will be mentioned below, Herod the Great *did not* actually abolish the Great Sanhedrin. Herod the Great only briefly, (until his death in 4 BCE, that is), changed the overall members who were judges on the Great Sanhedrin when he had 45 of the judges killed and replaced by judges who, should we say, Herod the Great believed would *conform* to *his* will, and the majority of these 45 judges who were killed were Hasmonean rivals to Herod the Great and Sadducees, but *not* the Pharisee members of the Great Sanhedrin of that time.[36] Now, Josef Blinzler[37] references Mishnah, *Sanhedrin* 1:6; Josephus, *Antiquities* 4.5.4; *Jewish Wars* 2.18.6, and it is *historically* known that Gamliel (as even Blinzler admits),[38] was the *Nasi* of the Sanhedrin at the time of Paul, as well as at Peter's trial, and possibly also at the time of Jesus' *supposed* trial before the Sanhedrin as well, (or it could even have been Gamliel's dad, R. Shimon ben Hillel who was the *Nasi* at the time of

---

34   *Messiah and Temple*, Donald Juel, p. 66.

35   See the *Jewish Encyclopedia*, Volume 6, "Herod"; *History of the Jews*, Heinrich Graetz, Volume 2, Chapter IV; Talmud, *Baba Batra* 3a; *The Trial of Jesus from Jewish Sources*, Rabbi A. P. Drucker, p. 5.

36   See the comments on this in *The Life and Teachings of Hillel*, Yitzhak Buxbaum, p. 66.

37   *The Trial of Jesus*, Josef Blinzler, p. 91.

38   *The Trial of Jesus*, Josef Blinzler, p. 97.

Jesus' *supposed* trial before the Sanhedrin, since Gamliel replaced his dad as *Nasi* in approximately 30 CE, or around the approximate time that the majority of scholars believe that Jesus was crucified as mentioned in the Preface). We also know from Acts 5:37-38 that Gamliel was a sympathizer and protector of Jesus and his movement just as Joseph of Arimathea was as well, (who again, Blinzler admits that Joseph of Arimathea was *also* a member of the Great Sanhedrin).[39] Therefore, with Blinzler also rightly admitting[40] that Nicodemus, (known from John 3:1-21), was *also* a member of the Great Sanhedrin and a known supporter and protector of Jesus and his movement as well, we therefore have three "*No*" votes already sitting as members of the Great Sanhedrin, and it took thirty seven or more votes to convict an individual accused of any crime, especially in "capital offense" cases. But, *if* there was *not* a *single* "*No*" vote to acquit someone in regards to capital offense cases then, as Rabbi Joseph Telushkin rightly explains it,[41] "When a capital case came before it, the Sanhedrin's head would appoint different judges, some to investigate evidence pointing to the defendant's guilt, others to probe evidence pointing to his innocence. The examining judges then reported the results of their inquiries to their colleagues. Unlike contemporary prosecutors or defense attorneys, the Sanhedrin judges had no vested interest in developing a good record of convictions, or enabling guilty defendants to be acquitted. A peculiar provision of the Sanhedrin regulated that if its members voted unanimously to convict a defendant in a capital case, the person was not executed; the very unanimity of the vote made the rabbis fearful that no judge had actually sought exonerating evidence." Thus, it would be *impossible* for a "capital offense trial," such as a *supposed* trial of Jesus before the Great Sanhedrin, to be conducted as quickly as the Gospel accounts record that it occurred. For it took quite some time for these appointed judges to investigate the evidence of either the guilt or innocence of the accused.

Thus, there has been great confusion and debate amongst scholars over the matters of not only who comprised the Great Sanhedrin at the time of Jesus, but also confusion over who presided over the Great Sanhedrin, as well as confusion over exactly how the Great Sanhedrin actually functioned.

---

39   *The Trial of Jesus*, Josef Blinzler, p. 95.

40   *The Trial of Jesus*, Josef Blinzler, p. 96.

41   *Jewish Literacy*, Rabbi Joseph Telushkin, pp. 118-119.

This was why I have utilized the word *nasi* several times already in this chapter, as well as in an earlier chapter. For the term *nasi, was in fact* the term used for the individual presiding over the Great Sanhedrin.[42] This term *nasi* is used at various times in Scripture in regards to individuals who were "chief men," a "king," a "tribal chief," or for an "important man of a congregation." There were also two secondary terms that were at times also used either alongside, or in place of the term *nasi*, and these two terms are, *Ab Bet Din*, ("Chief of the Court"), or *Rosh Bet Din*, ("Head of the Court").[43] Now, at times in Jewish history these terms *did* get applied to the High Priest as noted by Rashi's commentary on the usage of the term in Ezekiel 45:17. At the time of Ezekiel's writing in Jewish history the Davidic King and the High Priest, were the *Zugot* ("two heads") of the Great Court. As such, the High Priest ruled on "religious matters," and the King ruled on "political matters" as noted in *Sanhedrin* 14b. Ezekiel 45:16 and 46:2-13 further note such, but far too many scholars have tried to apply this fact to the time of Jesus.[44] But the historical *fact* of the matter is that the High Priest serving as one of the *Zugot* occurred *only* during pre-Maccabean times, and even then the High Priest served as one of the *Zugot only on special occasions.*[45] Yet, *after* the Maccabean period it is an *historical fact* that the Great Sanhedrin still had the *Zugot* ("Two Heads"), but the *Zugot* consisted *only* of the leading members of the Pharisees,[46] with the possible exception of Menahem the Essen, (spoken of in Chapter

---

42 See the comments on this in *Studies in the History of the Sanhedrin*, Hugo Mantel, pp. 1-2, 176-179, and 244-253; *Hillel*, Rabbi Joseph Telushkin, p. 213; Solomon Schecter and Wilhelm Bacher, "Gamaliel I," *Jewish Encyclopedia*; Rabbi Louis Jacobs, "Rabban Gamaliel," *My Jewish Learning*; Joseph Jacobs and Kaufmann Kohler, "Nasi," *Jewish Encyclopedia*; Solomon Schechter, "Some Rabbinic Parallels to the New Testament," *The Jewish Quarterly Review*, Volume 12, No. 3 (April 1900), pp. 415-433.

43 See the comments in *Studies in the History of the Sanhedrin*, Hugo Mantel, pp. 102-129 where he points out that the *Ab Bet Din* was the "junior head" of the *Zugot* for the Sanhedrin.

44 See for example the comments in *Historyah shel ha-Bayit he-Sheni*, Joseph Klausner, Volume I, pp. 110-111.

45 See the comments on this in *Studies in the History of the Sanhedrin*, Hugo Mantel, n. 26, p. 5; *Toledot ha-Halakah*, Chaim (Rav Zair) Tchernowitz, Volume III, pp. 55-59.

46 See the comments on this in *The Life and Teachings of Hillel*, Yitzhak Buxbaum, pp. 16, 20-32.

4). It is true though that at the time of Jesus there were two consecutive occasions in which the Sanhedrin only had a *Nasi*, but no *Ab Bet Din*,[47] which would have meant that the *Nasi* of the Great Sanhedrin was from either the school of Hillel, or from the school of Shammai,[48] and more often than not he was from the school of Hillel. As Hugo Mantel states concerning this *historical fact*,[49] "In the days of the Temple, the Nasi was not the Political head of the nation; he was merely the President of the Sanhedrin." The *only* time that the High Priest became involved in any such matters pertaining to the Great Sanhedrin was if the matter at hand was one that dealt with the "appointed king," (i.e. at the time of Jesus, one of the Herods in other words), and the High Priest would *not* consult the Great Sanhedrin on the matter of a king's violation of a law, but instead he used the Urim and Tummim, (Exodus 28:30; Leviticus 8:8; Numbers 27:21; Deuteronomy 33:8; 1 Samuel 28:6; Ezra 2:63; Nehemiah 7:65), to decide the matter as noted in *Yoma* 73b; *Sanhedrin* 16b.[50]

To go a bit further with this though, the Talmud, *Sanhedrin* 19a; 2:1, 19d clearly indicate that none of the Herodians (as "client" kings for Rome), nor *any* of the "appointed" Roman puppet High Priests, (i.e. Annas, Caiaphas, etc.),[51] "had any seat on the Great Sanhedrin, nor on the board for the intercalation of the year," yet the High Priest *was* required to be present at *every session* of the Great Sanhedrin as stated in *Horayot* 4b[52] even though the High Priest held no power whatsoever over the matters brought before the Great Sanhedrin. In regards to this matter in the Talmud, Hugo

---

47 See the comments of Jacob Zallel Lauterbach and the Executive Committee of the Editorial Board, "Rabban (Literal 'our teacher,' 'our master')," *Jewish Encyclopedia*.

48 See the comments in *Studies in the History of the Sanhedrin*, Hugo Mantel, pp. 48, 53; n. 290, p. 53, (Ezekiel 45:17); n. 291, p.53; *Hillel*, Rabbi Joseph Telushkin, p. xvii who points out that even Hillel was once the *Nasi* over the Great Sanhedrin; and see also the comments in *Judaisms Great Debates*, Rabbi Barry L. Schwartz, p. 47 who also points out that Hillel was once the *Nasi* of the Great Sanhedrin.

49 See *Studies in the History of the Sanhedrin*, Hugo Mantel, p. 19.

50 See the comments on this of Joseph Jacobs and Kaufmann Kohler, "Nasi," *Jewish Encyclopedia*.

51 See the brief comments on Caiaphas by Richard Gottheil and Samuel Krauss, "Caiaphas or Caiphas, Joseph," *Jewish Encyclopedia*.

52 See the comments of Joseph Jacobs and Kaufmann Kohler, "Nasi," *Jewish Encyclopedia*.

Mantel writes,[53] "We conclude that the rule which made the intercalation of the year dependent upon the Nasi's approval can only have referred to the Learned Head of the Sanhedrin." Thus, from this *clear* statement from the Talmud, and from Mantel's conclusion we *know* that the Head of the Great Sanhedrin at the time of Jesus *was not* Caiaphas![54] Caiaphas and Annas were both members of the Sadducees and therefore, as Hugo Mantel points out in regards to what Josephus *clearly* writes in *Antiquities* 18.1.4 [17], "The Sadducees participated as magistrates in the Judicial system only 'unwillingly and by force'."[55] Thus, Donald Juel is quite in error when he states,[56] "However popular and influential the Pharisees might have been within the Jerusalem establishment, the Sadducees represented an extremely important element and their opinions on legal matters were certainly reflected in the conduct of the High Court."[57] Likewise, Richard A. Horsley is also quite in error when he bundles the Sanhedrin with the High-Priestly Administration, writing,[58] "Jerusalem along with the rest of Judea was governed by the royal or the High-Priestly Administration, including the Sanhedrin." There is one other erroneous scholarly quote that needs to be noted here, and this quote being from David M. Rhoads, who makes reference to Josephus *Antiquities* 20.200, and states that,[59] "The High Priest was also head of the Jewish high council, or Sanhedrin." It is quite obvious that Rhoads did not read this excerpt he references from *Antiquities* in its entirety before making his erroneous statement! For as Josephus goes on to state here, the actions of the High Priest in this instance, aroused the people and made them "most uneasy at the breach of the laws," and "that what he had already done was not to be justified" because "it was not lawful for Ananus to assemble a Sanhedrin," which resulted in Ananus being removed as High Priest! Thus, as is being pointed out here in this chapter, and as it was pointed out earlier in Chapter 4,

---

53   See *Studies in the History of the Sanhedrin*, Hugo Mantel, pp. 25-26.

54   See also the comments in *Revolution in Judaea*, Hyam Maccoby, p. 45.

55   See the comments in *Studies in the History of the Sanhedrin*, Hugo Mantel, p. 85.

56   *Messiah and Temple*, Donald Juel, pp. 60-61.

57   Juel references as his source in *Messiah and Temple*, n. 4, p. 60, *The Mishnah*, H. Danby, xiv-xv.

58   *Jesus and the Spiral of Violence*, Richard A. Horsley, p. 94.

59   *Israel in Revolution*, David Rhoads, p. 29.

the *historical truth* is that the Sadducees held *very little* power in regards to the Jewish legal system as just noted previously regarding the *Zugot!*[60]

Despite all of the historical evidence that Caiaphas *never* headed the "Great Sanhedrin," some scholars conclude that at the time of Jesus there must have been two courts in place in Jerusalem – the Great Sanhedrin, and a "political puppet" court headed by the Roman "political puppets" of Herod Antipas and Caiaphas.[61] As Hugo Mantel writes,[62] "According to the Gospels the trial of Jesus took place before the Sanhedrin with the High Priest presiding;[63] yet according to rabbinic tradition the presiding officer of the Sanhedrin was a Pharisaic scholar, not the High Priest.[64] In our first chapter we pointed out that there is no reason to doubt the trustworthiness of this tradition, while in the second we found that the Synedrion of the Gospels is not identical with the Sanhedrin in the Hall of Gazit. The one was a political, the other a religious body. So, there is no contradiction between the rabbinic sources and the New Testament concerning the court before which Jesus was tried. The difficulty lies rather in the Gospel accounts of the circumstances of Jesus' trial, especially the day on which it occurred, on the one hand, and the nature of the charges brought against him on the other." A further interesting note to mention here is the fact that many scholars have commented on the fact that in Mark's Gospel Caiaphas is *never* specifically named, but instead, Mark only uses the reference, "the High Priest," and these scholars offer many interpretations as to the reason *why* Mark has omitted the specific mentioning of Caiaphas.[65]

When one looks at the list that Jewish sources have in regards to the *Nasi, Ab Bet Din,* or *Rosh Bet Din,* dating from even before the time of the Maccabees up until approximately 425 CE, neither the names Caiaphas,

---

60 See the comments of Joseph Jacobs and Jacob Zallel Lauterbach, "Zugot ('pairs')," *Jewish Encyclopedia.*

61 See the comments on this in *Studies in the History of the Sanhedrin*, Hugo Mantel, pp. 92-101.

62 See the comments in *Studies in the History of the Sanhedrin*, Hugo Mantel, p. 254.

63 *Studies in the History of the Sanhedrin*, Hugo Mantel, n. 1, p. 254, Matthew 26:59; Mark 14:53; Luke 22:66.

64 See *Studies in the History of the Sanhedrin*, Hugo Mantel, n. 2, p. 254, where Mantel references his own book pp. 1 and 176-179.

65 See *Caiaphas*, Helen K. Bond, pp. 100-108 for a brief discussion of this matter.

or Annas can be found *anywhere* on this list as *ever* presiding over the Sanhedrin![66] Thus, although Caiaphas, as a Roman "political appointee" *may* have been present during a gathering of the Great Sanhedrin, as required under Jewish law of the time, he would have been nothing more than just an "observer for the Romans," but he *never* would have actually presided *over* the Great Sanhedrin. Hugo Mantel rightly points out concerning this,[67] "Given the precision of the Mishnah with regards to such things as the structure of the Temple,[68] the rules of the various offerings, [69] as well as the procedure of the *Bikkurim*,[70] and even customs that were 'not with the consent of the sages,'[71] there appears to be little justification for the theory that it invented the title *Nasi* for the Head of the Great Sanhedrin."[72] Now, Josephus mentions "The High Priest, the prophet and the council of elders," in *Antiquities* 4.8.14. [218]; *Contra Apion* 2.23.194, but Josephus here is referring to the way the judicial system was established by Moses, as noted by what is stated in *Antiquities* 4.8.1 and Josephus *is not* referring to how the Great Sanhedrin functioned *after* the time of the Maccabees. Furthermore, nowhere does Josephus say anything in *Antiquities* 4.18.14 about the High Priest "presiding over," i.e. being the *Nasi* of the court at the time of Jesus, nor does Josephus mention the High Priest even being present at such prominent trials as that of Hyrcanus, son of Baris, Anan, the son of Anan, or James, the brother of Jesus, as well as many other such prominent trials.[73] James Dunn is quite in error in associating the "Chief court, the Sanhedrin," with the Temple aristocracy and in claiming that it had much wider legislative and executive power under Roman rule, as

---

66 See the comments on this in *Studies in the History of the Sanhedrin*, Hugo Mantel, n. 4, p. 2; *Sanhedrin*, Wikimedia Foundation.

67 See *Studies in the History of the Sanhedrin*, Hugo Mantel, pp. 11-12.

68 See *Studies in the History of the Sanhedrin*, Hugo Mantel, n. 63, p. 12, referencing tractate *Middot*.

69 See *Studies in the History of the Sanhedrin*, Hugo Mantel, n. 64, p. 12, the tractates *Zebahim, Menahot, Tamid*, etc.

70 See *Studies in the History of the Sanhedrin*, Hugo Mantel, n. 65, p. 12, the tractate *Bikkurim*.

71 *Studies in the History of the Sanhedrin*, Hugo Mantel, n. 66, p. 12, Mishnah, *Menahot* 10:5.

72 See further on this the comments in *Studies in the History of the Sanhedrin*, Hugo Mantel, pp. 41-45.

73 See the comments on this in *Studies in the History of the Sanhedrin*, Hugo Mantel, pp. 65-68.

if to further assert that the Romans and Sadducees "controlled" the Great Sanhedrin.[74] It must be pointedout though, that when utilizing what Josephus writes on these matters, one must remember that while Josephus was writing historical accounts *after* the destruction of the Temple when there was no longer a need for the Temple priests, he at times though, also wrote from a "personal standpoint" of these historical accounts simply because he *had been* one of those Temple priests. For by the time that Josephus wrote, the High Priest no longer existed because again, Josephus was writing *after* the destruction of the Temple in the 66-73 revolt. Thus, we find, for example, Josephus writing in *Contra Apion* 2.21.185, "Could there be a finer and more equitable polity, than one which sets God at the head of the universe, which assigns the administration of the highest affairs to the whole body of priests, and entrusts to the supreme High Priest the direction of the other priests." Yet, the simple *fact* is that even Acts 23:1-10 *clearly* seems to indicate that the High Priest *was not* the *Nasi* over the Great Sanhedrin but merely an observer. Many scholars have therefore concluded that the *only* real authority that the High Priest had in regards to the Great Sanhedrin was in his ability to issue a "summons" to someone to appear before the Great Sanhedrin,[75] which again, goes back to the very matter discussed above about a "summons" being issued for Jesus to appear before the Great Sanhedrin.

There was also another very important member of the Sanhedrin who was referred to as the *Mufla*. The *Mufla* on the Sanhedrin was a *specific* individual on the court who was an "expert instructor" regarding *all* judicial matters. The *Mufla*, therefore, also served as the "advocate" for the accused who offered "appeals" on behalf of the accused from rulings derived from any of the "lower," "minor," or "Lesser Sanhedrin" courts (i.e., "local city courts" generally consisting of only 3 members,[76] or the "Lesser Sanhedrin" consisting of a quorum of only 23 members), to bring the matter before the full "Greater Sanhedrin,"[77] as even noted by Josephus *Antiquities* 4.8.14;

---

74   See *The Partings of the Ways*, James Dunn, p. 31.

75   See the comments on this and the sources cited on this matter in *Studies in the History of the Sanhedrin*, Hugo Mantel, p. 70.

76   See the comments on this in *Jewish Literacy*, Rabbi Joseph Telushkin, p. 118.

77   See the comments in *Studies in the History of the Sanhedrin*, Hugo Mantel, pp. 135-139; "The Right of Appeal in Talmudic Law," *Case Western Reserve Journal of International*

Mishnah *Yoma* 7, 71b.[78] Thus, if the *Mufla* was *not present* or available to appear at a particular time, then *no case against any individual* could be brought before even one of the "Lesser Sanhedrin," consisting of *only* the 23 members, or even before the "smaller city, town or village courts." In Mishnah *Sanhedrin* 4:1 it *does* state that a Lesser Sanhedrin consisting of 23 members *could* try a capital offense case, but, in Mishnah *Sanhedrin* 5:5; *Sanhedrin* 17a it is found being stated that *if* an individual was found guilty of a death sentence in one of the Lesser Sanhedrin consisting of only 23 members, that death sentence *could not* be carried out *until all 71 members of the Greater Sanhedrin were brought together in order for the required 37 guilty votes of the full 71 member Greater Sanhedrin could be gathered,* (as noted already above), *in order for that individual, who had been sentenced to death by the Lesser Sanhedrin of 23, could be confirmed as warranting a death sentence under Jewish law,* and such bringing together of all 71 members of the Greater Sanhedrin *could not* have been accomplished within the short time span that is described in the Gospels.

So, for a moment, it is essential to point out some of the confusion that far too many scholars have over these matters and they must be discussed a little deeper. Now, according to the Talmud, *Tosefta Sukkah* 4.6 the Sanhedrin set up in Alexandria had 71 seats, which is not inconsistent with what was just pointed out above about the High Priest, at times, sitting in during sessions of the Great Sanhedrin in the Chamber of Hewn Stone in Jerusalem, but the High Priest *was not* considered to be one of the 70 actual members of the Great Sanhedrin. There have been some scholars who claim though, that a quorum of the Great Sanhedrin could consist of only 23 members.[79] But such scholars are completely wrong here for this was the number that made up what was referred to as the *Lesser Sanhedrin* and *not* the *Great Sanhedrin*, and there *was* a difference between the two as noted in the Mishnah, *Sanhedrin* 1:4.[80] It is clearly stated in Mishnah, *Sanhedrin* 1:5.4 that *only the Great Sanhedrin of 71* could set up a *legal Lesser Sanhedrin*

Law, Volume 6, Issue I, (1973), Arthur Jay Silverstein, p. 38.

78   See the comments of Joseph Jacobs and Kaufmann Kohler, "Nasi, *Jewish Encyclopedia.*

79   See for example the comments in *The Trial of Jesus*, Josef Blinzler, pp. 91-97.

80   For a brief breakdown of the contents of the tractate *Sanhedrin* see the comments of Wilhelm Bacher and Jacob Zallel Lauterbach, "Sanhedrin," *Jewish Encyclopedia*, (two separate articles under this same title).

of 23. Thus, Caiaphas could not have called a quorum consisting of only 23 members *on his own* as some scholars have erroneously tried to claim! For as just pointed out above, Caiaphas *was never* the *nasi of the Sanhedrin,* which was held consistently by the leading Pharisees as stated in *Shabbat* 15a; Mishnah *Hagigah* 2:2; Babli *Hagigah* 16b; Yerushalmi *Hagigah* 77d. It is true, as was noted already above in regards to the *Zugot,* that in past Jewish history (see 2 Chronicles 19:11 for example) the High Priest *did* rule on "religious matters," and thus again, at one time in Jewish history the High Priest *had served* as one of the *Zugot.* But again, this ended long before the time of Jesus during the period of the Maccabees.[81]

Before going on with this matter being discussed, it is essential to point out something interesting from Luke's Gospel, and specifically, Luke 10:1-24, but particularly Luke 10:1. In these verses from Luke's Gospel we have an account of Jesus appointing "seventy elders" (and it must be noted that in some of the ancient manuscripts this actually reads "seventy two"). As Lloyd Gaston comments, it would seem that this,[82] "Refers rather to the 70 elders of Exodus 24:1; Numbers 11:16." But Gaston seems to leave out mentioning Exodus 18:21-27.[83] If this is in fact a historically accurate matter and not a later Evangelistic creation, then for all intents and purposes it would appear that Jesus was intending and attempting to create his own "new" *Great Sanhedrin!*

In regards to the *Lesser Sanhedrin* though, there have been many scholars who have long believed that there were in fact 3 separate *Lesser Sanhedrin* – one High Priestly, one Levitical, and one an Israelite (or Pharisaic) common peoples' court – and that each of these three different courts dealt with different legal matters that involved *only* breaches of Jewish law pertaining to these specific separations.[84] In essence, each of the three had certain rules and regulations that governed them – i.e. the High Priests

---

81   See the comments in *Studies in the History of the Sanhedrin,* Hugo Mantel, pp. 29-32.

82   *No Stone on Another,* Lloyd Gaston, p. 318; but see also the comments in *Jews Greeks and Christians,* (Edited by Roger Hammerton-Kelly and Robin Scroggs), David Daube commenting, pp. 151-163.

83   See the comments in *Love Your Neighbor,* Rabbi Zelig Pliskin, pp. 151-153.

84   See the comments on all of the various scholarly opinions on this in *Studies in the History of the Sanhedrin,* Hugo Mantel, pp. 54-101; Wilhelm Bacher and Jacob Zallel Lauterbach, "Sanhedrin," *Jewish Encyclopedia.*

had certain rules and regulations that they must follow, likewise the Levites had certain other rules and regulations that pertained *only* to them, and the common people had certain rules and regulations that pertained to them as well, and thus, the separation into these three *Lesser Sanhedrin* to specialize in the legal matters pertaining to each of the three separately. *But*, according to the majority opinion of these scholars that hold to this belief that three *Lesser Sanhedrin* existed at the time of Jesus, when it came to a matter of a "political" case then these three separate courts were brought together to form the *Great Sanhedrin* with the *Nasi* presiding (in other words, three courts of 23, brought together equaling 69, presided over by the *Zugot Nasi* who became the 70th member of the *Great Sanhedrin* and observed by the 71st member, i.e. the High Priest). Some other scholars though, believe that at times only two, of the three *Lesser Sanhedrin*, got together at certain "political" trials based on what is found being stated in Josephus, *Antiquities* 15.5-10 regarding when Herod the Great, (after being taken to trial), killed 45 judges, already discussed above. As an example of some of these opinions regarding a "political" *Lesser Sanhedrin*, Lloyd Gaston comments,[85] "The grave historical difficulties which the Synoptic accounts of this trial give to anyone considering it in the light of Jewish jurisprudence are well known…[86] Many of them can be avoided when we assume that the Sanhedrin was not involved at all but rather only the High Priest and his counselors."[87] Now, Mishnah *Sanhedrin* 11:2 *does* refer to three different courts, but that two of these courts, or *Lesser Sanhedrin* were inferior to "the Great Court in the Chamber of Hewn Stone," and thus, one could make an appeal, (by way of the *mufla* noted above), to the *Great Sanhedrin* in regards to a ruling delivered by one of the *Lesser Sanhedrin* as noted in Mishnah *Eduyot* 1:5; *Megillah* 2a.

Each of the individual Tetrarchy's had a "Lesser Sanhedrin" that served as a type of "appeals court," and in every little city, town, or village there were minor courts, or "minor Sanhedrin," noted already above, a matter which is spoken of by Josephus, *Antiquities* 13.338;[88] *Jewish Wars* 2.571, as well as even being mentioned in Luke 18:2, and these "smaller city courts"

---

85   *No Stone on Another*, Lloyd Gaston, p. 67.

86   See the sources Lloyd Gaston lists in *No Stone on Another*, n. 1, p. 67.

87   See the sources Lloyd Gaston lists in *No Stone on Another*, n. 2, pp. 67-68.

88   See the comments in *Herod Antipas*, Harold W. Hoehner, pp. 84-86 and 102.

is derived from Numbers 25:3-4 as it is interpreted in *Sanhedrin* 35a; Yerushalmi *Sanhedrin* 10:2, 28d.[89] As Hugo Mantel writes concerning this that,[90] "The local Bet Din in each city was the authority on all religious and civil matters, deciding which customs to retain and which to innovate." The Galilean Tetrarchy "Lesser Sanhedrin" had originally been in Sepphoris, but after the minor revolt in 6 CE in which the city of Sepphoris was devastated, (even though Sepphoris was later rebuilt by Herod Antipas), the Galilean "Lesser Sanhedrin" was moved to Tiberias,[91] which created somewhat of a very serious problem as was discussed in Chapter 4 regarding the city of Tiberius being built atop a graveyard. The evangelists who wrote the Gospels do not really seem to be aware of all of these facts concerning all of these various different courts in first century Jewish jurisprudence, nor do they seem to know who made up each of these various different Sanhedrin courts. This fact is made clear by way of the manner that the Gospel authors refer to these members as, "chief priests," or "Temple custodians," "elders and scribes," and even "Pharisees."[92] As Hyam Maccoby writes concerning this,[93] "The Sanhedrin, therefore, continued to function, as did the minor courts in every town, in all of which the Pharisees were dominant... The High Priest was, in effect, a police official whose job, as a Roman appointee, was to look out for signs of sedition against the occupying authority." This is essential to understand as will be further noted later in this chapter, but also in the following chapters as well.

Now, the Mishnah and Talmud, *Sanhedrin* 1:1; 7.2; *Sanhedrin* 18a; 24b; *Sotah* 6:3 all state that the ability of the Great Sanhedrin to pass a death sentence upon anyone had been taken away from them by the Romans some forty years prior to the destruction of the Temple. Josephus, *Jewish Wars* 5.5.2 (193); *Antiquities* 15.11.5 (417) as well as Philo, *Ad Gaium* 31, (212) confirm this fact as well.[94] Some scholars though, interpret Mishnah

---

89   See the comments in *"Caught in the Act,"* Roger David Aus, p. 36.

90   See *Studies in the History of the Sanhedrin*, Hugo Mantel, p. 86.

91   See Josephus, *Jewish Wars* 2.639-641; *The Life of Flavius Josephus*, 64, 69, 168-169, 284, 296, 300, 313, 381; *Herod Antipas*, Harold W. Hoehner, pp. 96-97.

92   See the comments in *Jesus On Trial*, Gerard Sloyan, pp. 13-14.

93   *Revolution in Judaea*, Hyam Maccoby, p. 70.

94   See the comments in *On Earth As It Is In Heaven*, D. C. Thielmann, n. 70, pp. 337-339; *Messiah in Context*, Jacob Neusner, p. 112; *Roman Society and Roman Law in the New*

Sanhedrin 9:6 as stating that the ability of the Sanhedrin to pass a death sentence had been taken away as early as 7 CE with the short exception of a period of time under Agrippa I, and as a result an actual "death sentence" was left in the hands of "zealots," (sort of like "vigilante justice"), such as the story in Numbers 25 concerning Phinehas.[95] This means then, that the Great Sanhedrin *did not* have any authority to pass a death sentence upon *anyone* at the time of Jesus' *supposed* trial before the Great Sanhedrin, which occurred, according to the majority of scholarly opinions, *after* this time that this authority to pass death sentences had been removed. This is one of the reasons why we find it being stated in John 18:31 that the Jewish court was not permitted to pass a sentence of death. But going further with this matter of death sentences, the Pharisees had made many reforms to Jewish law making the laws far more humane and far more difficult for the Great Sanhedrin to even pass a death sentence upon *any* individual.[96] But one might ask the question though, if in fact it is historically true that the authority to pass a death sentence had been removed, then how does one account for the killing of James recorded in Acts 12:1-2, as well as by Josephus, *Antiquities* 20.200, andEusebius *Ecclesiastical History* 2.23.16? Does this fact concerning the killing of James then bring into question whether or not Jesus *did* have an actual Sanhedrin trial in which a death sentence was passed? The truthful answer to this matter is an emphatic, *no it does not*! For when one looks at the account of the killing of James one finds that James was killed by a sword at the hands of some of the "Herodian henchmen" without *any* trial whatsoever being conducted![97] Now, Darrell L. Bock[98] attempts to use the fact of Josephus' referencing of the killing of James as proof for the Gospel accounts about a *supposed* "trial of Jesus" before the Great Sanhedrin simply because Josephus knows of this incident regarding James. But as has just been demonstrated, James

---

Testament, A. N. Sherwin-White, pp. 32-43 although Sherwin-White believes that the Sanhedrin *did* still hold the right to certain "death sentences" when it involved matters of the Temple.

95   See the comments on this in *"Caught in the Act,"* Roger David Aus, pp. 16-18, 30-32, and 43.

96   See the comments on this matter in *Revolution in Judaea*, Hyam Maccoby, Appendix 5, pp. 210-215.

97   See the comments on this in *Jesus and Israel*, Jules Isaac, p. 272.

98   *Blasphemy and Exaltation in Judaism*, Darrell L. Bock, pp. 196-197.

did not have a trial before the Sanhedrin, but was simply killed, *without a trial of any kind,* by "vigilante henchmen"! Thus, Bock's attempted point that he is trying to make is baseless!

In regards to this *fact* of how James was killed though, it is essential to point out the remarks on this matter of Hugo Mantel:[99] "First of all, there was no fixed punishment, certainly no capital punishment, for merely speaking against traditional observances.[100] Secondly, according to Tannaitic Literature, it is only 'the murderer and the inhabitants of an Apostate City' who are liable to decapitation...[101] James' words may have sounded like a call to revolt, and the penalty for such revolt, as the Talmud derives it from Scripture, is the sword."[102] One more essential point to make here is that we never read from *any* source, (not the Gospels, or Josephus, or even any other Jewish source such as the Mishnah), about John the Baptist *ever* having a "trial" of *any kind* before the Great Sanhedrin! This fact is quite similar in some respects to the matter noted by Josephus in *Antiquities* 14.167 and *Jewish Wars* 1.209 where the Jews protested against Herod the Great and were thus murdered as a result. The leading Jews in Jerusalem at that time are reported to have said that what Herod the Great had done by his murdering of these protestors violated Jewish law, "which forbids us to slay a man, even an evildoer, unless he has first been condemned by the Sanhedrin to suffer this fate."[103] This matter of one being first given a trial before they are put to death can even be found in the Gospel of John 7:51 where it is reported that Nicodemus rightly asks Jesus, "Our law does not judge people without first giving them a hearing to find out what they are doing, does it?"

It is essential to make a point about a certain fact, which will also be further commented upon later, and this being, the matter of the four different supposed trials found in the New Testament – the trial of Jesus,

99   See *Studies in the History of the Sanhedrin*, Hugo Mantel, p. 74.

100   See *Studies in the History of the Sanhedrin*, Hugo Mantel, n. 119, p. 74 and he references his book Chapter 6, n. 134.

101   See *Studies in the History of the Sanhedrin*, Hugo Mantel, n. 120, p. 74 Mishnah, *Sanhedrin* 9:1.

102   See *Studies in the History of the Sanhedrin*, Hugo Mantel, n. 122, p. 74, *Sanhedrin* 49a, based on Joshua 1:18.

103   See the comments on this in *"Caught in the Act,"* Roger David Aus, p. 142.

Peter, Stephen and Paul. In regards to these supposed trials Hugo Mantel rightly points out and asks,[104] "Were Jesus, Paul and others tried before the Sanhedrin, as the New Testament states? The fact is that nowhere does the New Testament explain precisely what Jewish laws the defendants were charged with violating. Nor does it explain why they were tried before a court presided over by the High Priest. What was the competence of this High-Priestly Synedrion, which is not so much as mentioned in the Hebrew sources?"

Under Jewish law *only* stoning was the prescribed legal form of execution for someone who committed "blasphemy," (a matter that will be discussed in greater detail in Chapter 7), and for the profaning of the Sabbath (see Leviticus 24:14-16; Numbers 15:35; 1 Kings 21:10, 13 and as noted also in the Talmud, *Sanhedrin* 6.16c; 6.3; 6.4; 6.5abc; 6.7abc; and 6.8). Therefore, we must ask about the death of Stephen recorded in Acts 6:8-7:60, who not only seems to have had some sort of a trial before one of the "smaller town courts," but it also seems quite clear that the stoning of Stephen was the result of "vigilantes" and *not* as a result of a sentence of death passed by the court, and we do *know* that such vigilante attempts to stone people without cause or trial *did* occur during and after the time of Jesus from the story concerning Mary Magdalene in John 8, but also, we find an account in John 10:31-32 where Jesus himself is threatened to be stoned by "vigilantes."

The only other legal forms of execution under Jewish law, as noted in the Mishnah, *Sanhedrin* 7:1 were burning, beheading, and strangling. Crucifixion *was not* a form of Jewish punishment for *any* crime. Crucifixion was used *only* by pagans as noted in *Sifre Deuteronomy* 21(1146), Talmud Babli, *Sanhedrin* 46b; *Midrash Tannaim* 132.7. Now, in the Talmud, *Makkoth* 3.2 scourging was also sometimes used as a form of Jewish punishment, but for only minor offences. But to hang someone up as an example for others, (such as crucifixion was in reality), was something which occurred under Jewish law *only after* an individual had first been put to death by one of the other previously described legal forms of execution as clearly noted and stated in *Koheleth Rabbah* 89b to 7:26; *Esther Rabbah* to 1:12

It is now essential that we examine closely the Gospel accounts of a *supposed* trial of Jesus before the Great Sanhedrin. In doing so, it must first

---

104　See *Studies in the History of the Sanhedrin*, Hugo Mantel, Introduction, p. xiv.

be stated that because of the many discrepancies in these Gospel accounts regarding a supposed trial of Jesus before the Great Sanhedrin it is finally becoming quite clear to the majority of Christian New Testament scholars that one should have quite a few doubts as to the historical accuracy of these accounts.[105] As a simple example, Matthew 26:3-5; Mark 14:1-2; Luke 22:1-2 all refer to the Jewish authorities who had been seeking the arrest of the "fugitive" Jesus (noted earlier in this chapter), being afraid to arrest Jesus around the time of the festival out of fear that the people might riot. Yet, not only *do* the authorities arrest Jesus around the time of the festival, but they do so by way of "stealth" using the cover of darkness, and also by using a "betrayer," (a matter that will be elaborated upon in detail in Chapter 6). Now, N. T. Wright makes a very unusual interpretation of these matters,[106] in fact, it is a rather bizarre interpretation of Luke 22:53. Wright associates the Greek word *skotus*, "darkness," with somehow indicating "Satan." But such an interpretation is completely taken out of context, for as the verse clearly states, "day after day in the Temple you did not lay hands on me," indicating that they would not arrest Jesus in broad daylight in front of the crowds, but instead they had to use "stealth" and the cover of the "darkness" of night time. Trying to stick a meaning of "Satan" into this makes absolutely no sense whatsoever! Now, it is true though, that at the time of Jesus night time *was* interpreted as being the time "when the forces of evil are given authority and proliferate in the world,"[107] but nonetheless, such an interpretation as Wright's makes absolutely no sense at all!

Going further though into this matter of some sort of Jewish authorities at first being afraid to arrest Jesus around the time of the festival, these authorities then put Jesus out onto a public trial *before* the very people whom they feared would riot! Concerning this matter, Bart Ehrman writes,[108] "Some readers have wondered if this narrative sequence makes sense. The leaders don't want to arrest him during the festival, but they do anyway.

---

105 See for example the comments in *Jesus: Uncovering the Life, Teachings, and Relevance of a Religious Revolutionary*, Marcus Borg, p. 263; *Studies in the History of the Sanhedrin*, Hugo Mantel, pp. 254-268 and all of his scholar's notations to these pages.

106 *Simply Jesus*, N. T. Wright, p. 126.

107 See the comments on this in *The Way of God*, Moshe Chaim Luzzatto, pp. 307-311.

108 *The Lost Gospel of Judas Iscariot*, Bart D. Ehrman, p. 21, and n. 11, p. 182.

And they are afraid that the crowds will riot in Jesus' support, but at his trial they have no trouble stirring up the crowds against him. But why would the crowd riot at his arrest but not at his trial? Is Mark giving us an historical account?" Also, as Marcus Borg and John Dominic Crossan write,[109] "In a tradition that goes back centuries, Christians have most often portrayed the Jewish crowd against Jesus during his last days as rabidly and violently against him... What these portrayals fail to ask however is this, why, if the Jewish crowd was so against Jesus, was it necessary to arrest him in the darkness of night with the help of a traitor from amongst Jesus' followers?" They cite Mark 14:48-49 and they further note that John 11:48 clearly denotes that the priestly clan was afraid of both the Romans destroying them for allowing Jesus to continue his teachings, as well as afraid of the crowds destroying them for stopping/preventing Jesus from continuing his teachings. Borg and Crossan also note that Josephus, *Antiquities* 18.116-119 reports that it was Herod Antipas who was afraid of the crowds around John the Baptist.[110] So in essence, the very crowds who were feared would riot over Jesus' arrest, and whom the Gospels speak of as triumphantly welcoming Jesus on his entry into Jerusalem for the festival, (another matter that will be elaborated upon in a later chapter), are now the very same crowd that calls for the crucifixion of Jesus during a public trial! This makes absolutely no sense whatsoever as will be noted in a later chapter. It is true though, that some scholars claim that these were in fact two completely different crowds. As Cardinal Ratzinger and Pope Benedict XVI write regarding this matter,[111] "All three Synoptic Gospels, as well as Saint John, make it very clear that the scene of Messianic homage to Jesus was played out on his entry into the city and that those taking part were not the inhabitants of Jerusalem, but the crowds who accompanied Jesus and entered the Holy City with him," and they reference Matthew 21:10-11 here. Ratzinger and Pope Benedict XVI go on further then to state, "The crowd that paid homage to Jesus at the gateway to the city was not the same crowd that later demanded his crucifixion." But Mark 11:18-19 and John 12:12, both seemingly put the error to this claim, as well as what is found being stated in Luke 21:37-38.

---

109   *The Last Week*, Marcus Borg and John Dominic Crossan, pp. 87-88.

110   See further the comments on this in *Creation Continues*, Fritz Kunkel, p. 284.

111   *Jesus of Nazareth: Part Two*, Ratzinger and Pope Benedict, p. 8.

Another discrepancy, which seems to be ignored by most scholars, or it seems to be one that they view as simply being a minor discrepancy, is found in what is stated in Mark 15:42-46, which refers to Joseph of Arimathea as being a member of the Sanhedrin whereas Matthew 27:51-59 seems to strip Joseph of Arimathea of this distinction.[112] But this matter is in reality a major problem based on factors noted above. The other factors that raise problems with this matter resides in what is stated in the Talmud, *Sanhedrin* 11b that it is expressly forbidden to pass a judgment upon *any* judicial matter at night,[113] which the Gospels seem to indicate is precisely what occurred since Jesus was arrested in the stealth of darkness and quickly carted off to a *supposed* trial before the Great Sanhedrin at night. Now the Gospels, which clearly note the true *fact* that the Pharisees *did* make up a majority portion of the members of the Great Sanhedrin, and whom the Gospels portray as being *sticklers for the law*, most *certainly* then would have *forbidden* such a trial from being conducted at night! Furthermore, *Sanhedrin* 32b forbids *any* capital judgments from being made on the eve of a festival, which though is a matter of debate as to precisely *when* Jesus was arrested. Rabbi Shmuley Boteach rightly compares the Gospel accounts to,[114] "…The United States Supreme Court agrees on short notice to meet on Christmas Eve because a young troublemaker had burned an American flag outside the Washington monument." Also, as Amy-Jill Levine rightly states,[115] "The synoptic Gospels suggest that the entire Jewish council, the Sanhedrin, met on the first night of Passover to determine Jesus' fate – this would be tantamount to gathering all of the members of the Supreme court, Congress, and the White House press corps together late on Christmas eve to debate a minor case of law. If the story of Barabbas, the insurrectionist released from custody, has any credibility … then the story makes no sense given the synoptics' timing: he would

---

112   See the comments in *Kosher Jesus*, Rabbi Shmuley Boteach, p. 92.

113   See the comments in *"Caught in the Act,"* Roger David Aus, p. 36.

114   *Kosher Jesus*, Rabbi Shmuley Boteach, p. 92; see also the comments in *A Jewish Understanding of the New Testament*, Samuel Sandmel, pp. 128-129.

115   *The Misunderstood Jew*, Amy-Jill Levine, pp. 208-209.

have been released too late to celebrate Passover.... John's dating does not violate the Mishnaic teaching, the synoptics' does."[116]

Now, Mishnah, *Sanhedrin* 4:1 and 7:5 both give clear reference to the conducting of a Great Sanhedrin trial, and therefore, *if* a *supposed* trial of Jesus were conducted in the manner that is described in the Gospels as having occurred before the Great Sanhedrin, such then, would have made such a trial a clear violation of both of these Jewish laws. Josephus, *Antiquities* 16.162-165 clearly states that no Sanhedrin trials could occur, *by law*, "after the ninth hour" on a day *before* a Sabbath or a festival,[117] (see also the Talmud Babli, *Sanhedrin* 35a).[118] Caesar Augustus had even given approval to this matter concerning the Jewish courts stating, "That they need not give bond (to appear in court) on the Sabbath or on the day of preparation for it after the ninth hour."[119] As Ann Wroe writes concerning this,[120] "Some formal respect was shown to them" (she is speaking here of the Jewish people). "According to a decree of Augustus, Jews could not be made to appear in court on the Sabbath, which was understood to start at three o'clock on Friday afternoons; and their sacred money from the 'first fruits' was always sent to receivers in Jerusalem and never touched by Romans. The law also dictated that 'anyone caught stealing their holy books, or their sacred money, whether out of synagogues or from the men's apartments, shall be deemed a sacrilegious person.' Tiberius, too, was actually solicitous for these Jews, allowing them to come a day late to claim the distributions of money or corn that were made on the Sabbath." But, *if* an individual were being prepared to appear before a trial that was

---

116   For more on these matters, see the comments in The *Trial of Jesus: Cambridge Studies in Honour of C. F. D. Moule*, p. 58; *The Trial of Jesus from Jewish Sources*, Rabbi A. P. Drucker, pp. 10-11; *The Trial of Jesus*, Josef Blinzler, pp. 76-77.

117   See the comments in *Jesus of Nazareth: Part Two*, Ratzinger and Pope Benedict, pp. 106-109.

118   See the comments on this in *Jesus and Israel*, Jules Isaac, p. 312; "Tract 13c, The Hebrew Trials of Christ – Supplement to Lesson 13," *Champions of Truth: The Open-Door Church*.

119   See the comments in *The Trial of Jesus: Cambridge Studies in Honour of C. F. D. Moule*, p. 58; E. P. Sanders, "Common Judaism and the Synagogue in the First Century," *Jews, Christians, and Polytheists*, p. 2.

120   *Pontius Pilate*, Ann Wroe, pp. 61-62.

to be conducted by the Roman governor, then *neither* of these *Jewish* laws applied.

Furthermore, Mishnah, *Sanhedrin* 10:2 and the Talmud, *Sanhedrin* 36b both state that it was required that at least two scribes be present at *any* Sanhedrin trial in order to accurately record the preceding. But the Talmud further states in *Shabbat* 73 that it was forbidden for scribes to do any writing activity during a festival time, plus, it was considered a desecration of the festival day to even hold court *on, or before* a festival day, or a Sabbath day, (i.e. on the "Day of Preparation," a matter discussed previously in the Preface).[121] Also, according to the Gospel accounts, the High Priest Caiaphas asked the other judges, "What do you think," or "What is your verdict," (Matthew 26:66; Mark 14:64 for example). But this was a clear violation of Jewish law, for there was no voting at a Sanhedrin trial "en bloc." After a period of deliberation and discussion, each judge was then required to rise independently, state their opinion and their reasons for their individual decision as clearly noted in Mishnah, *Sanhedrin* 4:1; *Gittin* 59a; Talmud *Bal Taschit* 32a. If such a violation as this actually occurred, as claimed by the Gospels at a *supposed* trial of Jesus, then under Jewish law this was considered a "conspiracy," and "the criminal was required to be set free immediately" as stated in the Talmud, *Sanhedrin* 17a! It is important to quote here, Rabbi A. P. Drucker:[122] "If one of the judges, by some mistake, participated in the preparation of the case, the procuring of witnesses, or the obtaining of testimony; or if one happened to express an opinion before the trial, or if he were an enemy or a relative of the accused, he was not allowed to sit in judgment on the case (Mishnah, *Sanhedrin* 3:3)."

Also, as a further matter to be noted, no Great Sanhedrin trial, such as the supposed trial of Jesus, could be conducted outside of the *Lischas Hagoris*, (the "Hewn Chamber," which was also called the *Hall of Gazit* mentioned earlier in this chapter), within the Temple itself as stated in *Sanhedrin* 86b, 88b; *Avodah Zora* 8b. Yet, the Gospels claim that the trial of Jesus took place at the house of Caiaphas.[123] It is true, that this could

---

121   See the comments in *The Trial of Jesus from Jewish Sources*, Rabbi A. P. Drucker, pp. 10-11.

122   *The Trial of Jesus from Jewish Sources*, Rabbi A. P. Drucker, p. 7.

123   See the comments in *The Trial of Jesus*, Josef Blinzler, pp. 112-114 where he tries to pinpoint exactly where the supposed trial of Jesus by the Sanhedrin took place.

be an error on the part of the Evangelists, for according to Theodosius Archidiaconus, (*Nuovo Bull. Di Arch. Crist* vi.184),[124] Caiaphas' palace was only one hundred paces from the "Hewn Chamber." Now, in regards to the matter of the striking of Jesus, as the Gospels claim occurred at this *supposed* Sanhedrin trial, (and similarly to what is found in Acts 23:2 involving a *supposed* trial of Paul), this would also have been a further violation of Jewish law as clearly stated as well in *Sanhedrin* 58b, 86b, 88b; *Avodah Zora* 8b,[125] which was derived directly from Exodus 2:13; Deuteronomy 25:2-3. *Anyone* committing such an act was automatically *invalidated* from serving in a Jewish court, or even being a "witness" in a Jewish court as clearly stated in *Ketuboth* 25a,[126] and if such were committed by the *nasi* of the Sanhedrin, (even though Caiaphas was never the *nasi*, as noted already above), or by one of the "chief rabbis," this would have resulted in that particular "chief rabbi" or *nasi* being excommunicated for a day.[127]

It is now essential to mention the matter of "witnesses" at the *supposed* trial of Jesus as described in the Gospels.[128] There are vast discrepancies in the Gospel accounts concerning any *reliable* "witnesses" against Jesus at this supposed trial, and in fact, the Gospels clearly note that there was even difficulty in *finding any* "witnesses" to testify *against* Jesus whatsoever. Deuteronomy 17:6-7 clearly states, and insists, that at least two witnesses *must be* in complete agreement on a matter before *anyone* could be sentenced to death,[129] and Proverbs 21:28 is another example of warning

---

124   See the comments on this by Richard Gottheil and Samuel Krauss, "Caiaphas or Caiphas, Joseph," *Jewish Encyclopedia*.

125   See the comments in *The Trial of Jesus from Jewish Sources*, Rabbi A. P. Drucker, pp. 8-9.

126   See the comments in *Love Your Neighbor*, Rabbi Zelig Pliskin, pp. 132-133, and 424-425.

127   See the comments of Solomon Schechter and Julius H. Greenstone, "Excommunication (Hebrew, 'niddui,' 'herem'), *Jewish Encyclopedia*; Jacob Voorsanger and Kaufmann Kohler, "Anathema," *Jewish Encyclopedia*; Morris Jastrow, Jr., Kaufmann Kohler, and Marcus Jastrow, "Banishment," *Jewish Encyclopedia*.

128   For an in depth discussion on the matter of "witnesses" at the supposed trial of Jesus before the Sanhedrin, see *No Stone on Another*, Lloyd Gaston, pp. 68-74; *On Earth As It Is In Heaven*, D. C. Thielmann, pp. 301-306 and the corresponding scholars notations to these pages.

129   See the comments in *The Trial of Jesus: Cambridge Studies in Honour of C. F. D. Moule*, p. 82; Haim Cohn, "Witness," *Encyclopedia Judaica, Jewish Virtual Library*.

an individual about being a "false witness." The fact that reliable witnesses are such a discrepancy in the Gospel accounts of a *supposed* trial of Jesus before the Sanhedrin creates a serious historical problem in regards to *any* scholarly claims that such a trial actually occurred.[130] Furthermore, there are many scholars who erroneously attempt to claim that women were *never* considered to be "reliable witnesses" according to Jewish law at the time of Jesus.[131] These scholars primarily derive their claims from the Gospel accounts of Jesus' resurrection where only women found the empty tomb, and also, by what is stated by Josephus in *Antiquities* 4.219, as well as how they interpret what is stated in the Mishnah and Talmud *Yevamoth* 16:7; *Ketuboth* 2:5; *Eduyot* 3:6. But the *truth* of the matter is that women were not considered as "reliable witnesses" *only* when a matter required "two *kosher* witnesses" such as in matters of law regarding monetary issues, capital crimes, and sexual crimes.[132] But going further into this matter of "witnesses" or "accusers" it is essential to bring up the matter of Paul's supposed trial in Acts in relation to Jesus' supposed trial before Pilate, and specifically, the matter of Acts 24:18-19 in which the "accusers" against Paul, (i.e. Asian Jews), according to this account, seemingly disappear from Paul's actual trial and Paul ends up requesting that his *actual* "accusers" be present at his trial before the Roman Governor. Thus, as A. N. Sherwin-White states concerning this matter,[133] "In the hearing before Felix, Paul objects, rightly, that they ought to be present to make their charges. The Roman law was very strong against accusers who abandoned their charges." This is *essential* to understand in that these *supposed* "witnesses/accusers" at the *supposed* trial of Jesus before the Great Sanhedrin, likewise *never* appear at Jesus' trial before Pilate! As Sherwin-White then further points out, "The disappearance of one set of accusers may mean the withdrawal of the charge with which they were particularly associated." This matter is important to understand and remember when reading Chapter 8.

There have been many scholars who have tried to claim that an actual trial of Jesus before the Sanhedrin *can* be found recorded in the Talmud.

---

130   See the comments in *Jesus On Trial*, Gerard S. Sloyan, p. 60.

131   See for example the comments in *Who is Jesus*, Darrell L. Bock, pp. 198-199.

132   See the comments on this by Tirzah Meacham, "Obligation of Women in Commandments," *Legal-Ritualistic Status of the Jewish Female*.

133   *Roman Society and Roman Law in the New Testament*, A. N. Sherwin-White, p. 52.

But such scholars are simply and completely unfamiliar with the Talmud as noted in previous chapters, for such claims by such scholars have been thoroughly refuted.[134]

There are simply far too many discrepancies and violations of Jewish law in regards to the proper conducting of *any* Sanhedrin trial as found recorded in the Gospels in regards to a *supposed* trial of Jesus before the Great Sanhedrin for such to have *any historical truth*![135] It is far more likely that these accounts in the Gospels were fabricated sometime *after* the split between the gentile Church followers of Jesus, and the Jewish Synagogue followers of Jesus.[136] As Hyam Maccoby rightly states,[137] "But we see on two occasions in Acts that the High Priest was outvoted by the Pharisees in the Sanhedrin; on both occasions, the Pharisees were *opposing* an attempt to persecute the followers of Jesus; so the representation of High Priest and Sanhedrin as having identical aims is of the suspect features of these accounts." Maccoby then goes on further to note Acts 23:1-10 and to rightly point out and state,[138] "Many of the details of this account are manifestly unhistorical. The Sanhedrin was a dignified body, not an unruly mob, and conducted its affairs with great decorum, in accordance with the provisions of the law: it is extraordinary how the New Testament, while complaining that the Jews and particularly the Pharisees showed over-zealous attachment to the law, portrays them on occasion as flouting it outrageously." This statement by Maccoby, although referring to an account in Acts involving Paul, *must*, and in fact *does* relate to the Gospel accounts of a *supposed* trial of Jesus before the Great Sanhedrin as well! For as Maccoby goes on to write,[139] "In the four trials described in the New Testament – those of Jesus, Stephen, Peter, and Paul – all purporting to be before the Sanhedrin, only two, those of Peter and of Paul, can be regarded

---

134 See the comments in *Kosher Jesus*, Rabbi Shmuley Boteach, pp. 219-223; David Instone-Brewer, *Jesus of Nazareth's Trial in the Uncensored Talmud*; Gil Student, *The Jesus Narrative in the Talmud: The Real Truth about the Talmud*.

135 See the comments in *The Trial of Jesus*, Josef Blinzler, p. 6; *Blasphemy and Exaltation in Judaism*, Darrell L. Bock, pp. 189-190.

136 See the comments in *The Misunderstood Jew*, Amy-Jill Levine, pp. 82-86.

137 *The Mythmaker*, Hyam Maccoby, p. 10.

138 *The Mythmaker*, Hyam Maccoby, pp. 165-166.

139 *The Mythmaker*, Hyam Maccoby, pp. 165-166.

as genuine Sanhedrin trials, and in both of them the Pharisees were on the side of humanity and tolerance." But going even further into this though, Maccoby refers to Acts 24:1-9 and states,[140] "This speech of the High Priest is valuable further evidence of the standpoint of the Nazarene movement, as argued in this book, showing that the Jerusalem Jesus movement had strong political aims."

Hugo Mantel though, takes this matter a step further by pointing out that,[141] "In Acts there is an account of Paul's trial before the 'chief priests and all the council' at which, we are told, 'the chief captain' and 'soldiers' were present.[142] The presence of these Romans at Paul's trial shows that it could not have taken place before the Great Sanhedrin in the Hall of Gazit. For no gentiles were ever allowed within the precincts of the Temple."[143] Mantel goes on though, to point out that[144] this alone does not rule out the possibility that Paul indeed was brought before the Great Sanhedrin because some scholars claim that the Sanhedrin had moved from the Hall of Gazit approximately forty years prior to the destruction of the Temple, or in other words, roughly around the very time of the trial of Jesus.[145] The actual claim is that the Great Sanhedrin had been moved to a different location on the Temple Mount referred to as _Hanut_, (_Shabbat_ 15a; _Avodah Zerah_ 8b; _Sanhedrin_ 41a; _Sanhedrin_ 1.1.18c, 2.1.24b), or in other words, what was referred to as the Temple "Trade Hall," but that it is believed that the Great Sanhedrin moved back to the Hall of Gazit during the time of Herod Agrippa. But the _fact_ is that other scholars point out the error in these claims by offering _proof_ that what is actually stated is that this move occurred only _four years_, and _not_ forty years prior to the

---

140   _The Mythmaker_, Hyam Maccoby, pp. 169-170.

141   See _Studies in the History of the Sanhedrin_, Hugo Mantel, p. 290.

142   See _Studies in the History of the Sanhedrin_, Hugo Mantel, n. 346, p. 290, Acts 22:30, 23:10.

143   See _Studies in the History of the Sanhedrin_, Hugo Mantel and the very lengthy _proof_ he offers, n. 347, p. 290.

144   See _Studies in the History of the Sanhedrin_, Hugo Mantel, pp. 290-291.

145   See for example the comments in _The Jews and the Gospel_, Gregory Baum, p. 86; _Messiah in Context_, Jacob Neusner, pp. 194-196.

destruction of the Temple, or in other words roughly near the beginning of the 66-73 revolt.[146]

But now, *if* a trial of a Palestinian Jewish citizen such as Jesus had been called for by the Roman governor, or in other words, by Pontius Pilate, for a violation of *Roman law*, then under the Roman codes and laws at the time of Jesus, (a matter that will be discussed further in a later chapter), certain leading members of the Great Sanhedrin would have been *required* to serve as "defense attorneys" for the accused Jewish citizen – i.e. Jesus (which was a matter noted above concerning the role of the *Mufla*). Despite what has been pointed out in this chapter and in earlier chapters, and while it *is* true, (as was pointed out in Chapter 4), that *some* matters covered in the Talmud, (yet not so much in the Mishnah), *did in fact* derive from the period *after* the destruction of the second Temple, there are still far too many scholars, whom for far too long now, have tried to claim that one *cannot* utilize the Mishnah, or Talmud in any way, shape, or form in order to arrive at any accurate conclusions regarding the conducting of a trial of Jesus before the Sanhedrin,[147] and more often than not these scholars will erroneously use Jacob Neusner's *opinions* as their source.[148] For Neusner erroneously asserted[149] that there is no evidence of an "oral Torah," (such as what the Mishnah and Talmud became), *prior to* 200 CE! So how then did Neusner ever explain Haggai 2:10-13, (for example), or Nehemiah 8:7-8, which uses the Hebrew words *meviniym*, "interpreters," *meforesh*, "explained," and *sakal*, "instructed"?[150] Yet, Neusner himself points out

---

146　See the comments on this in *Studies in the History of the Sanhedrin*, Hugo Mantel, pp. 291-300 and all of his corresponding scholar's notations to these pages.

147　See for example the comments in *Jesus of Nazareth: Part Two*, Ratzinger and Benedict, pp. 175-176; *The Crucifixion of Jesus*, Gerard S. Sloyan, p. 44; *The Partings of the Ways*, James Dunn, p. 13 even though later in this book Dunn contradicts himself as will be noted below; *Messiah and Temple*, Donald Juel, p. 60; *The Search for the Real Jesus*, Chester Charlton McCown, p. 137; *Jesus Before the Gospels*, Bart Ehrman, pp. 66-69.

148　*The Rabbinic Traditions About the Pharisees Before AD 70*, Jacob Neusner; *Development of a Legend*, Jacob Neusner.

149　*Messiah in Context*, Jacob Neusner, p. 5.

150　See John J. Parsons, *"Torah sheba'al Peh* – The Oral Torah and Jewish Tradition; *The Sages*, Binyamin Lav, 3 Volumes; Samuel Fleischacker, "Hearing God's Voice: Two Models for Accepting the Torah."

and cites various Mishnah tractates that refer to "oral traditions" from Israel's history that had been passed down from generation to generation, in essence, contradicting his own claim,[151] and which is even noted in *Hagigah* 9b and *Menahot* 99a.[152] As Jacob Neusner himself even admits,[153] "My claim is not, and cannot be, that if a saying is first attributed to a given authority, it must begin with him, or that ideas appearing for the first time in a later stratum cannot have been available to the authorities in an earlier one. We do not know that as fact." Neusner also further admits,[154] "We can hardly be surprised by the evidences of the greater antiquity, the longer pre-history, of Ohalot, as compared to the pre-history of Kelim." In Chapter 4 it was pointed out that there have always been Jews who have rejected the "oral Torah," either in whole or just portions of it, and therefore, it is essential to point out a particular matter pertaining to Jacob Neusner's erroneous opinions and conclusions regarding the Mishnah and Talmud that so many Christian New Testament scholars have come to utilize, and this matter being that, Jacob Neusner was born to Reform Jewish parents, and which then, Neusner later became an ordained Conservative Jewish rabbi. The importance of pointing this matter out derives from what was just stated above, and in Chapter 4 regarding how there have *always* been Jews who have rejected the "oral Torah" either in whole or in part. For as Rabbi Joseph Telushkin states,[155] "The differing views of Orthodox and Conservative Judaism on both the antiquity and binding nature of the Oral Law are one of the major, perhaps *the* major, issues separating them," and therefore, it is quite right for one to conclude that Neusner's opinions and conclusions concerning the Mishnah and Talmud are, and have been *tainted* by *a personal bias*, which *no genuine objective scholar* should *ever* have! For scholars should *always* be *open-minded*, never allowing any *personal biases* to interfere with their studies and conclusions! Now, Jacob Neusner studied the Mishnah and Talmud at the *Jewish Theological Seminary* under the tutelage of the renowned Jewish scholar, Saul Lieberman. After Jacob

---

151   See for example *Messiah in Context*, Jacob Neusner, pp. 42-53.

152   See the comments on this in *The Life and Teachings of Hillel*, Yitzhak Buxbaum, pp. 33-36, and 163.

153   *The Idea of Purity in Ancient Judaism*, Jacob Neusner, p. 76.

154   *A History of the Mishnaic Law of Purities*, V, *Ohalot*, Jacob Neusner, p. 243.

155   See *Jewish Literacy*, Rabbi Joseph Telushkin.

Neusner put forth his erroneous opinions and conclusions regarding the Mishnah and Talmud, Neusner's *own teacher*, Saul Lieberman, (who was also affectionately referred to as, *Gra'sh*, (*Gaon Rabbeinu Shaul*), wrote a very famously scathing criticism of his *own student*, Jacob Neusner, stating this,[156] "… One begins to doubt the credibility of the translator [Neusner]. And indeed, after a superficial perusal of the translation, the reader is stunned by the translator's ignorance of Rabbinic Hebrew, or Aramaic grammar, and above all, of the subject matter with which he deals… I conclude with a clear conscience: the right place for [Neusner's] English translation is the waste basket." But Lieberman was not the only highly acclaimed scholar to write a scathing criticism of Jacob Neusner's erroneous opinions and conclusions regarding the Mishnah and Talmud.[157]

Thus, such claims that one *cannot* use the Mishnah and Talmud in regards to the matters of the trial of Jesus are simply *historically untrue*[158]

156 See Saul Lieberman, "A Tragedy or a Comedy?" *Journal of the American Oriental Society*, Volume 104(2), April/June 1984, pp. 315-319.

157 See for example, Shaye J. D. Cohen, "Jacob Neusner, Mishnah and Counter-Rabbinics," *Conservative Judaism*, Volume 37(1) Fall 1983, pp. 48-63; Craig A Evans, "Mishnah and Messiah 'In Context'," *Journal of Biblical Literature*, 112/2 1993, pp. 267-289; Hyam Maccoby, "Jacob Neusner's Mishnah," *Midstream*, 30/5 May 1984, pp. 24-32; Hyam Maccoby, "Neusner and the Red Cow," *Journal for the Study of Judaism*, 21, 1990, pp. 60-75; John C. Poirier, "Jacob Neusner, the Mishnah and Ventriloquism," *The Jewish Quarterly Review*, 87, Nos. 1-2, July-October 1996, pp. 61-78; E. P. Sanders, *Jewish Law from Jesus to the Mishnah*; Solomon Zeitlin, "A Life of Yohanan ben Zakkai: A Specimen of Modern Jewish Scholarship," *Jewish Quarterly Review*, 62, 1972, pp. 145-155; Solomon Zeitlin, "Spurious Interpretations of Rabbinic Sources in the Studies of the Pharisees and Pharisaism," *Jewish Quarterly Review*, 62, 1974, pp. 122-135; Evan M. Zuesse, "The Rabbinic Treatment of 'others' (Criminals, Gentiles) According to Jacob Neusner," *Review of Rabbinic Judaism*, Volume 7, 2004, pp. 191-229; Joseph M. Baumgarten, "The Pharisaic-Sadducean Controversies about Purity and Qumran Texts," *Journal of Jewish Studies* 31.2, (Autumn 1980), pp. 169-170.

158 See the comments in *On Earth As It Is In Heaven*, D. C. Thielmann, pp. 305-306 and the corresponding scholars notations to these pages; but see also the comments in *Jews, Greeks and Christians*, (Edited by Roger Hammerton-Kelly and Robin Scroggs), E. E. Urbach commenting, pp. 112-128; *"Caught in the Act,"* Roger David Aus, p. x; Jacob Zallel Lauterbach and the Executive Committee of the Editorial Board, "Mishnah," *Jewish*

and only serve to show either *an apologetic bias*, or *a lack of complete study on this particular matter* on the part of such scholars making these claims, and *any and every* scholar *must be* willing to admit that *no one* knows *all* there is to know about Scripture and ancient Jewish history, and therefore, *every* scholar makes errors, (a matter pointed out in the Preface to *always remember*)! Scripture itself, (Numbers 15:34, as well as 1 Kings 3:16-28), gives us early examples of the "oral Torah," (or in other words, that which constitutes the Mishnah and Talmud), and Exodus 18:21-25 describes the very first "*Sanhedrin*," which had all of its decisions passed down "from father to son from then on," (Psalm 78:1-6; Proverbs 1:8; Proverbs 4:1; Proverbs 5:7-14; Proverbs 22:6; Isaiah 38:19).[159] But the greatest offer of *proof* that there *had to be* an "oral Torah" passed down "from father to son from then on" resides in the *fact* that the Hebrew alphabet contains no vowels, nor did ancient Hebrew writings contain any sentence punctuation, nor was there division between words in the ancient Hebrew manuscripts,[160] and thus, *there had to be an "oral Torah" (i.e. "oral Teaching") passed down from generation to generation regarding the most accurate wording of the "Written Torah."*[161] Thus, *any* scholar attempting to claim that one *cannot* rely upon, or utilize the Mishnah and/or Talmud in regards to the matters of a better understanding of whether or not a trial of Jesus took place before the Great Sanhedrin are only demonstrating a *personally chosen prejudicial bias*! James Dunn very rightly points out[162] that the practices found in the Mishnah "predates the Mishnah," and thus, even predates Jesus in the very fact that both the school of Hillel and the school of Shammai predate Jesus, and the rulings of these two individuals who pre-date Jesus are *clearly* noted in the Mishnah! But in all truthfulness and reality, such claims by these

---

Encyclopedia; *Jesus and Purity Halakah*, Thomas Kazen, pp. 51-55, and 342; and see the entire book *Jewish Law from Jesus to the Mishnah*, E. P. Sanders.

159 See the comments on this in *Ever Since Sinai*, J. J. Petuchowski, pp. 4-13; *On Earth As It Is In Heaven*, D. C. Thielmann, n. 27, p. 153, and p. 697.

160 See the comments on this in *On Earth As It Is In Heaven*, D. C. Thielmann, pp. 131-132 and the corresponding scholars notations to these pages.

161 See the comments on this by Gil Student, "The Oral Law": "The Course of Tradition: A Timeline of the Oral Law," *Chabad.org*.

162 *The Partings of the Ways*, James Dunn, p. 99, which contradicts his earlier noted opinion above.

scholars then, are really no different than if I were to state that, "trying to derive anything from the much later Gospel accounts, Epistles, or the much later historical accounts of Josephus, Tacitus, etc., in order to arrive at any accurate historical conclusions about the historical Jesus...." In essence, such claims by these scholars are simply moot and nonsense! Yet, despite making such erroneous claims, some of these very same scholars will still rightly admit that a *supposed* trial of Jesus before the Sanhedrin *was not* a "proper trial," according to Jewish law at the time of Jesus! As Joseph Ratzinger and Pope Benedict XVI (for a prime example), state,[163] "It now seems reasonable to assume that what took place when Jesus was brought before the Sanhedrin was not a proper trial, but more of a cross-examination that led to the decision to hand him over to the Roman Governor for sentencing." Likewise, as Donald Juel writes,[164] "When measured by rabbinic legal standards, the trial as described by Mark is highly irregular if not downright illegal." These scholars *could not* have derived these statements from anywhere else *except* from an understanding of the legal rulings found in the Mishnah and Talmud!

Furthermore, there are some scholars who use Acts 13:27 to claim that Jesus *did* have an actual "trial" before the Great Sanhedrin.[165] They reference this verse from Acts simply because it utilizes a similar Greek word to that which is found in Mark 14:64, and this Greek word used in Acts 13:27 is, *krinantes*, which derives from the Greek word, *krino*, and which gets usually translated into English in Acts 13:27 as "condemned." But the fact is that this Greek word *also* offers a meaning of, "to be brought to trial," and thus in actuality the verse in Acts 13:27 can therefore be *clearly* understood as indicating that the Sanhedrin *did not* "try" or "condemn" Jesus, but that they simply "brought him" before Pilate "to be tried" *by* Pilate! This then, just as in our own justice system today, would mean that the accused had been given his right and opportunity to meet with his "attorney(s)" – i.e. the members of the Sanhedrin – *prior to* any trial before

---

163   *Jesus of Nazareth: Part Two*, Ratzinger and Benedict, pp. 175-176.

164   *Messiah and Temple*, Donald Juel, p. 59.

165   See for example the comments in *Blasphemy and Exaltation in Judaism*, Darrell L. Bock, p. 192.

the Roman Governor,[166] a matter discussed above that would have been required by both Roman, and Jewish law of that time and place in history!

---

166 See the comments of Otto Betz, "Jesus and the Temple Scroll," in *Jesus and the Dead Sea Scrolls*, pp. 87-88; *On Earth As It Is In Heaven*, D. C. Thielmann, n. 76, p. 340.

Chapter 6

"Do quickly what you are going to do."
(John 13:27)

I n this chapter we are going to examine the individual disciple of Jesus, Judas Iscariot, and his *supposed* role as "betrayer" in the arrest, and trial of Jesus as he is portrayed in the New Testament. The importance of writing this chapter derives from the simple fact that there are far too many discrepancies[1] surrounding the New Testament accounts pertaining to this individual. There are even questions that have been raised by some scholars as to whether or not such an individual named, *Judas Iscariot,* actually existed historically. Such questions surround and derive from the designated title name, "Iscariot," which has brought about a vast amount of scholarly debate as to its *true* meaning,[2] such as for example, that the name indicates that Judas was one of the "Sicarii," or that he was from

---

1 See the comments in *The Lost Gospel of Judas Iscariot,* Bart D. Ehrman, pp. 31 and 33; *Jesus Interrupted,* Bart D. Ehrman, pp. 45-47.

2 See for example the comments in *Judas Iscariot and the Myth of Jewish Evil,* Hyam Maccoby, pp. 128-140; *The Trial of Jesus,* Josef Blinzler, p. 60; *The Lost Gospel of Judas Iscariot,* Bart D. Ehrman, pp. 145-146, and n. 5, p. 187; *Judas and the Gospel of Jesus,* N. T. Wright, p. 45; *The Death of Jesus,* Joel Carmichael, p. 19; *On Earth As It Is In Heaven,* D. C. Thielmann, n. 131, pp. 775-776; *Judas,* William Klassen, pp. 29-34.

some location referred to as "Iscariot," etc. Despite these various factors and discrepancies surrounding this individual named, Judas Iscariot, it nevertheless became an *historical* fact that this individual ended up representing an anti-Semitic symbol of "Jewish evil."[3]

Rabbi Joseph Telushkin makes a very accurate statement when he writes that,[4] "The Jews are depicted very critically by the prophets... Indeed, Medieval Christian theologians often cited the prophets to prove the eternally evil character of the Jews. But this is naïve; it is as if a scholar five hundred years from now were to write a history of the world during the 1960's based exclusively on *Pravda's* panegyrics to communism and *The New York Times* exposes of corruption in the United States, and conclude that Russia was a much better place to live than America... The New Testament and Koran do not have a large body of statements denouncing evil behavior by early Christians or Muslims. Thus, we must conclude that either the early Christians and Muslims were overwhelmingly righteous, or they did not have a tradition of self-criticism."[5] But there have been some scholars who have attempted to counter this fact of using Judas Iscariot as a symbol of "Jewish evil" by offering a "unique" interpretation surrounding the matter of Judas Iscariot's supposed "betrayal" of Jesus.[6] The claim is that this "betrayal" symbolizes people of even the Church of today "betraying" being a true follower and believer in Jesus. As Cardinal Ratzinger and Pope Benedict XVI write,[7] "The breach of friendship extends into the sacramental community of the Church, where people continue to take 'his bread' and to betray him. Jesus' agony, his struggle against death, continues until the end of the world as Blaise Pascal said, on the basis of similar considerations (c.f. Pensees VII, 553)." While such a "unique" attempt at reinterpreting the many centuries that the Church used Judas Iscariot as a symbol of not only "Jewish evil," but also, "Jewish

---

3   See the comments in *Judas Iscariot and the Myth of Jewish Evil*, Hyam Maccoby, p. 29 and the corresponding scholars note to this page; *The Lost Gospel of Judas Iscariot*, Bart D. Ehrman, p. 42; *The Death of Jesus*, Joel Carmichael, p. 19.

4   *Jewish Literacy*, Rabbi Joseph Telushkin, p. 90.

5   See the further comments on this in *Jewish Literacy*, Rabbi Joseph Telushkin, pp. 515-526.

6   See for example the comments in *Jesus of Nazareth: Part Two*, Ratzinger and Pope Benedict, pp. 65-68.

7   *Jesus of Nazareth: Part Two*, Ratzinger and Pope Benedict, p. 68.

rejection of Jesus," such an interpretation as this simply does not hold water in regards to how the Gospel accounts have portrayed the matters surrounding Judas Iscariot!

Let us begin by looking at Matthew 19:28 and Luke 22:30 where both of these verses have Jesus speaking to and about his twelve disciples, (which *includes* even Judas Iscariot), sitting as judges at the end of days, judging the twelve tribes of Israel.[8] It is essential to point this matter out along with how the Epistle of James 1:1 starts off with the address, "To the twelve tribes in the dispersion,"[9] and combining this with what is stated in Revelations 7:1-10.[10] In regards to this, Joel Carmichael points out that what Jesus is saying to his disciples in these verses in conjunction with Jesus' calling gentiles "dogs" in Mark 7:26-27; Matthew 15:25-27; Matthew 7:6, is thus, as Carmichael believes, a demonstration that Jesus' teachings *only applied* to Jews entering the *Kingdom of Heaven*![11] Lloyd Gaston also comments on this matter of Jesus' disciples sitting on "thrones" believing that it is derived from Daniel 7:9,[12] (a verse referred to previously in Chapter 2). Gaston further notes that even the rabbis in the Talmud had difficulty interpreting Daniel 7:9, so thus, the question needs to be asked, is Jesus' statement regarding his disciples sitting on "thrones" similar to Jesus' appointing of "seventy elders" noted in Chapter 5?

Going further into this matter though, Mark 3:13, 19 and Mark 14:20 clearly state that Judas Iscariot had the same purpose and responsibilities as the other eleven disciples.[13] William Klassen makes an excellent point

---

8   See the brief but excellent discussion in regards to the scholarly debate over the historicity of this matter in *Jesus of Nazareth*, Dale C. Allison, pp. 101-102, but on pp. 141-145 Allison interprets this though, as "ruling," and not "judging." James Dunn in *The Partings of the Ways*, p. 117 interprets this as indicating a "reconstituted Israel"; see also the comments on this in *Jesus and the Spiral of Violence*, Richard A. Horsley, pp. 199-208.

9   See the comments on this in *Jewish Christianity Reconsidered*, Matt Jackson-McCabe, pp. 207-210, (Patrick J. Hartin commenting).

10   See the comments on this in *Jewish Christianity Reconsidered*, Matt Jackson-McCabe, pp. 251 and 254, (John W. Marshall commenting).

11   See the full comments on this in *The Death of Jesus*, Joel Carmichael, pp. 102-103.

12   *No Stone on Another*, Lloyd Gaston, pp. 406-407.

13   See the comments in *How Jesus Became God*, Bart D. Ehrman, p. 109; *Understanding the Difficult Words of Jesus*, David Bivin and Roy Blizzard, pp. 60-61; *On Earth As It Is*

regarding this matter of *all* of Jesus' disciples having the same purpose and responsibilities by noting how Judas is portrayed in John's Gospel.[14] For John 6:64 clearly states that Jesus knew all along who would "betray" him, and then in John 6:70 Jesus calls this disciple that he knew would "betray" him, "a devil." The point being made, and which clearly needs to be understood here in regards to the matter of *all* of Jesus' disciples serving the same purpose and having the same responsibilities surrounds the matter of the "casting out of demons," (Matthew 10:8; Luke 9:1-2 for example). For this begs the question to be asked then, how could this be true based on what was just noted from John 6:70? For if Jesus "knew" that Judas was "a devil" (John 6:64, 70 again), and Judas was sent forth with the other disciples to, at times when necessary, "cast out demons," this then would be a *direct contradiction* to Jesus' own words, "how can Satan cast out Satan," (Matthew 12:26; Luke 11:18)![15] Something is totally amiss in regards to the portrayal of Judas in John's Gospel! For there is an even more important contradiction found in Matthew 26:50 where Jesus refers to Judas Iscariot as his "friend!"[16]

There are some scholars though, who question whether or not Jesus actually stated anything about the disciples judging the twelve tribes,[17] while other scholars are emphatic in their belief that Jesus' statement regarding this matter is in fact historical.[18] Therefore, the question begs to be asked, does this mean that Judas Iscariot is going to be one of these twelve judges just as Jesus is reported to have stated despite a supposed "betrayal" of Jesus by Judas Iscariot? This is a very important question and matter to ask about for the simple fact that in 1 Corinthians 15:5 Paul states that the risen Jesus was seen by *all twelve disciples*, meaning that the risen

---

In Heaven, D. C. Thielmann, n. 193, p. 367.

14 See *Judas*, William Klassen, pp. 1-2.

15 See the comments in *Jesus and His Adversaries*, Arland J. Hultgren, pp. 100-106; but see also Morris Jastrow, Jr. and J. Frederick McCurdy, "Baal-Zebub," *Jewish Encyclopedia*; Kaufmann Kohler, "Beelzebub or Beelzebul," *Jewish Encyclopedia*.

16 See *Judas*, William Klassen, pp. 46, and 103-104.

17 See for example the comments in *Creation Continues*, Fritz Kunkel, p. 244.

18 See for example the comments in *Jesus before Christianity*, Albert Nolan, p. 106; *The Lost Gospel of Judas Iscariot*, Bart D. Ehrman, p. 152; *Jesus Interrupted*, Bart D. Ehrman, pp. 159-160; *The Crucifixion of Jesus*, Gerard S. Sloyan, p. 50.

Jesus was even seen by Judas Iscariot *prior to* the death of Judas Iscariot![19] Also, in the Gospel of Peter 15:59 it states, "We, the twelve disciples of the Lord, were weeping and were in sorrow."[20] Virtually every scholar agrees that Paul's letters were first written prior to *any* of the Gospels being written. Thus, what is found being stated in Matthew 28:16 concerning only eleven disciples going to Galilee can *only* mean that the excluding of Judas Iscariot from this narrative indicates that the matter surrounding Judas Iscariot was a late developing church tradition. For the replacement of Judas Iscariot, found in Acts 1:15-26, only occurred *after* the account of Jesus' ascension into heaven noted in Acts 1:9-11.[21]

When one carefully examines each of the four Gospels it becomes very clear that the matters concerning Judas Iscariot changed, evolved, and morphed into the traditional place in Church history that they represent today.[22] As an example, both Mark 13:14-19 and Matthew 10:2-4 mention only one "Judas" in regards to Jesus' closest followers. But then in Luke 6:16; Acts 1:13; John 14:22; John 13:2, 26, 29 one finds the mention of a second and possibly even a third individual with the name "Judas."[23] This second "Judas" mentioned though, was in fact a relative of Jesus, the "brother of James," whom was the "brother of Jesus" as even stated in the *Apostolic Constitution* 7:46.[24] Mark 6:3 also indicates that Jesus had a brother named "Judas," and according to scholarly interpretations of the *Gospel of Thomas*, this brother of Jesus named "Judas" was actually a "twin brother."[25] John 13:26 though, is one of the most peculiar verses that mentions an individual named "Judas." For the actual Greek texts exclude the words

---

19   See the comments on this matter in *Judas Iscariot and the Myth of Jewish Evil*, Hyam Maccoby, pp. 24-25; *The Lost Gospel of Judas Iscariot*, Bart D. Ehrman, pp. 15-16; Anastasios Kioulachoglou, "Judas' Death and its Timing," *The Journal of Biblical Accuracy*.

20   See the comments in *Revolution in Judaea*, Hyam Maccoby, p. 152.

21   See the comments in *Judas Iscariot and the Myth of Jewish Evil*, Hyam Maccoby, pp. 87-88.

22   See the comments in *Judas Iscariot and the Myth of Jewish Evil*, Hyam Maccoby, p. 22.

23   See the comments in *Judas Iscariot and the Myth of Jewish Evil*, Hyam Maccoby, pp. 34-45, 51, 153, and n. 2, p. 175, n. 3, pp. 177-178).

24   See the comments in *Judas Iscariot and the Myth of Jewish Evil*, Hyam Maccoby, pp. 155-156.

25   See the comments on this in *The New Testament*, Bart D. Ehrman, Box 12.2, p. 202; *Essays on the Semitic Background of the New Testament*, Joseph A. Fitzmyer, pp. 369-370.

"son of," and therefore, for one to translate this verse as, "Judas Iscariot, son of Simon," is actually quite misleading and inaccurate.[26] The actual *best* reading and translation of this verse should be, "Judas Simon Iscariot," or in essence, could this simply be another reference to, "Simon the Zealot," since, (as was noted above concerning the designated "title name," *Iscariot*), the Sicarii were a branch of the Zealots? So, the question now becomes which *Judas* actually "betrayed" Jesus, if in fact such a "betrayal" by *any* Judas, did in *historical* reality actually occur? Also, then, which *Judas* was actually the one replaced in the account in the Book of Acts? For as William Klassen points out,[27] there are in fact *eight* different individuals with the name, "Judas," in the entire New Testament!

This now brings us to the discrepancies in the New Testament surrounding the matter of the demise of a supposed individual named "Judas Iscariot." For although there are some similarities in the accounts given in the Gospels, especially that of Matthew and Acts concerning the death of Judas Iscariot, there are also conflicting matters in these two accounts.[28] There have been many attempts made over the centuries to try and rectify the differences between these two accounts,[29] including Papias, the Bishop of Asia Minor in his work, *Exposition of the Lord's Sayings*, (which only survives today in fragments). But all of these attempts actually fail to rectify these differences, which simply put, *cannot* be rectified.[30] As

---

26 See the comments in *Judas Iscariot and the Myth of Jewish Evil*, Hyam Maccoby, p. 74.

27 *Judas*, William Klassen, p. 30.

28 See the comments in *The Lost Gospel of Judas Iscariot*, Bart Ehrman, p. 38; *The New Testament*, Bart D. Ehrman, Box 9.5, p. 141; *Jesus Before the Gospels*, Bart Ehrman, pp. 28-29; *Judas Iscariot and the Myth of Jewish Evil*, Hyam Maccoby, pp. 2-3, 57, and n. 5, p. 178; Anastasios Kioulachoglou, "Judas' Death and its Timing," *The Journal of Biblical Accuracy*.

29 See the comments in *Judas Iscariot and the Myth of Jewish Evil*, Hyam Maccoby, n. 3, p. 180 who notes several of these attempts.

30 See the comments in *Judas Iscariot and the Myth of Jewish Evil*, Hyam Maccoby, pp. 82-84; in the Preface it was mentioned that there are some scholars who claim that the discrepancies in the Gospels surrounding the matter of the trial of Jesus *can be* reconciled, and Max Radin was noted as being one of these scholars, yet Radin contradicts himself when he admits on p 159 of *The Trial of Jesus of Nazareth* that this matter regarding the demise of Judas Iscariot *cannot* be rectified.

William Klassen rightly states,[31] "Attempts to harmonize the accounts cannot succeed."

It is necessary now to look closely at some of these mentioned discrepancies in the accounts of Judas Iscariot's demise.[32] Acts 1:16-26 seems to combine Psalm 69:26 (or 69:25 in the general English translations) with Psalm 109:8. But the problem with this lies in the fact that the *best* rendering of Psalm 109:8 actually says, "take his possessions," and *not*, "take his place." Furthermore, the description given in Acts 1:18 looks more like it resembles what is found in 2 Chronicles 25:12. Thus, the account in Acts sounds more like Judas Iscariot was *executed* and *not* that he committed suicide, which then is quite in keeping with matters found being outlined in the Dead Sea Scrolls. For as it is stated in the *Damascus Zadokite Document*, CD–A, Column IX, 1, "Every man who gives over to anathema (that is, dooms him) shall be executed according to the laws of the gentiles."

In regards to the matter described in the Gospels about Judas Iscariot supposedly being given "thirty pieces of silver," (as stated in Matthew 27:9-10, for example), it is important to point out that Mark's Gospel omits that Judas' supposed "betrayal" of Jesus was done for money.[33] Mark's Gospel only says that Judas was *promised something* in return for his "betrayal" of Jesus,[34] but as to *what* he was *promised* we do not know from Mark's Gospel. We do not find the mention of any "money" being given to Judas until, as just noted above, the tradition changed by the time that Matthew's Gospel was written, and thus, we find in Matthew 16:15, Judas asks, "what will you give me?" This price of "thirty pieces of silver" was the "average price for a slave" as found in Exodus 21:32[35] and it was enough to provide food for an individual for about five months.[36]

---

31   *Judas*, William Klassen, p. 171.

32   See the excellent comments on this matter in *The Last Week*, Marcus Borg and John Dominic Crossan, p. 126.

33   See the comments in *The Lost Gospel of Judas Iscariot*, Bart D. Ehrman, p. 42.

34   See the comments in *The Last Week*, Marcus Borg and John Dominic Crossan, p. 105.

35   See the comments in *Judas Iscariot and the Myth of Jewish Evil*, Hyam Maccoby, p. 39; *The Lost Gospel of Judas Iscariot*, Bart D. Ehrman, pp. 26-27.

36   See the comments in *Judas Iscariot and the Myth of Jewish Evil*, Hyam Maccoby, n. 4, p. 175.

Many scholars have tried to rectify the obviously fabricated error of Matthew 27:9-10, which simply cannot be done.[37] Therefore, it is essential to go into much more detail about not only the matter of the "thirty pieces of silver" Judas was supposedly given, and, exactly what became of these "thirty pieces of silver," but also the matter of the term used in the Gospel of Matthew, "field of blood." But first, it is essential to point out that even though silver coins *were* still accepted as currency in matters of commerce by Jews in Palestine at the time of Jesus, the *historical* fact is that "silver coins" had not been as readily used in Palestine for over 300 years, (a matter that will be further discussed in Chapter 9). Even the weighing of silver for use as money was no longer as prevalent in Palestine, "for coins needed to be counted once they had been minted."[38] The Romans though, did still mint and use silver denarii, so while Palestinian Jews would quite likely have been familiar with this particular coin, and may possibly have accepted it in matters of individual commerce with gentiles, this coin was *forbidden* to be used, or accepted to pay the Temple Tax into the Temple Treasury! The Temple Tax coin and the Temple Treasury coins were primarily *gold*,[39] (see Ezra 2:69; Mishnah *Baba Metzia* 4:2; *Baba Metzia* 44a-b; *Baba Kamma* 97a-b), but also, the poor *could use* copper, brass, or bronze coins,[40] (see Luke 21:1-4). The term "shekel" simply was a measure of weight, (in today's terminology what would constitute approximately a weight of somewhere varying between 8.4 grams, and 10.52 grams),[41] and thus, the term, "shekel," *was not* the name for a particular coin, and

---

37   See the comments concerning these failed scholarly attempts at rectifying this matter in *Judas Iscariot and the Myth of Jewish Evil*, Hyam Maccoby, p. 57 and n. 5, p. 178; *On Earth As It Is In Heaven*, D. C. Thielmann, pp. 309-310 and the corresponding scholars notations to these pages.

38   See the comments on this in *Judas*, William Klassen, p. 197; *Wer war Schuld an Jesu Tod*, P. E. Lapide, pp. 23-25; Dov Genachowski, "Ancient Jewish Coins," *Encyclopedia Judaica: Coins and Currency*.

39   See the comments of Emil G. Hirsh and Wilhelm Nowack, "Shekel," *Jewish Encyclopedia*; Wilhelm Bacher, Jacob Zallel Lauterbach, "Shekalim," *Jewish Encyclopedia*.

40   See the comments in "The Money of the Jewish Temple," *Ministry: International Journal for Pastors*, September 1984.

41   See "Ancient Jewish History: Weights, Measures & Coins of the Biblical and Talmudic Periods," *Jewish Virtual Library*.

therefore, a "shekel" could be made out of gold, silver, bronze, brass, or copper with each differing in size in order to equal the "weight" required to qualify *as* a "shekel," (see for example what is stated in *Kiddushin* 12a). But usually, bronze, brass, and copper coins were considered to be of a lesser value, (i.e. A "lesser measure of weight"), similarly to the modern penny being of lesser value than that of a nickel coin. During the time of the return from the Babylonian exile, payment of the Temple Tax was reduced to one-third of a "shekel," (see Nehemiah 10:32), but by the time of Jesus the payment of the Temple Tax had been restored to one-half of a "shekel" in accordance with Exodus 30:11; 2 Kings 12:5, and this also can be found clearly being stated in Matthew 17:24 when Jesus pays the Temple Tax for both himself and Peter by way of what might possibly have been a *stater* coin, which was the Greek equivalent of the "shekel," which was the value of two *drachma*, and in which the word, *didrachma*, (or that which constituted two *drachma*), is the Greek word used in Matthew 17:24. For a *drachma*, or in Hebrew, *beka*, (which again, is another term indicating a "weight" as noted in Genesis 24:22; Exodus 38:26),[42] was the required amount to pay one's Temple Tax,[43] and since Jesus, in this verse from Matthew's Gospel, is paying for both his and Peter's Temple Tax, this is the precise reason the Greek word *didrachma* is used in this verse. Now, modern archaeology *has* discovered a few silver Tyrian shekels in Palestine. But these coins were primarily used by diaspora Jews, and therefore, they were accepted in commerce by Palestinian Jews, (as noted in *Tosefta Ketuboth* 13:20), but yet again, these coins *were not* used as payment of the Temple Tax into the Temple Treasury,[44] especially since, as just noted above, the Temple Tax by the time of Jesus was only one-half a shekel, and therefore, it not only is inconsistent with the *historical* truth of the matter, it is also illogical for *any* scholar to claim that it was the Tyrian Shekel that was the coin used to pay the Temple Tax when the Temple Tax at the time of Jesus was only *half* a shekel. Virtually all coins minted for usage in Palestine at

---

42 See "Ancient Jewish History: Weights, Measures & Coins of the Biblical and Talmudic Periods," *Jewish Virtual Library*.

43 See Sebastian Selven, "The Privilege of Taxation: Jewish Identity and the Half-shekel Temple Tax in the Yerushalmi Talmud," *University of Cambridge*.

44 See the comments of Joseph Jacobs and Theodore Reinach, "Numismatics," *Jewish Encyclopedia*.

the time of Jesus were minted either in brass, bronze, or copper, including the Temple Tax coinage. The Jews had, at one time in ancient Israelite history, minted coins in silver, but the largest denomination of a Jewish silver coin minted in silver was a *drachma*, but primarily they only minted silver *oboloi*, or *hemi-oboloi* as modern archaeology has uncovered. The *first* Jewish *shekel* coins *ever* minted in silver did not occur until just prior to the 66-73 revolt, and *only* Jewish minted coins were *ever* accepted into the Temple Treasury.[45] Thus, the main point being made here is that "thirty pieces of silver" *did not* necessarily mean, or indicate "thirty Tyrian shekels" from the "Temple Treasury" as the majority of scholars attempt to claim in regards to this account concerning what Judas may, or may not have been paid for "handing over" Jesus.

In Matthew's Gospel this "field of blood" was given this term because it was supposedly purchased by the Chief Priests with the "blood money" that Judas had returned, or thrown back down into the Temple precincts treasury, and as just noted in the paragraph above, the *only* silver coins that were available at the time of Jesus were *forbidden* to be used as a part of the Temple treasury. Yet, in Luke's version, there is nothing said about Judas ever returning the money. In fact, Luke's version has Judas himself using the money as "the wages of his unrighteous act" to buy the field for himself, and therefore, this field is called the "field of blood" not because the money was used to purchase the field with money tainted by the blood of an innocent man (i.e. Jesus), but because this was the field where Judas himself experienced his *own* bloody demise.[46] Matthew 27:3 though, *clearly* gives the indication that Judas *never* expected that Jesus would be condemned to death. So, what are we to make of all of these discrepancies in the Gospel accounts surrounding the demise of Judas Iscariot?

It is therefore necessary to examine the historical and Scriptural accuracy of the usage of this term "field of blood."[47] This "field" is found being mentioned in Nehemiah 11:29; Jeremiah 7:31; 32:35; Isaiah 31:9 and it is

---

45   See Dov Genachowski, "Ancient Jewish Coins," *Encyclopedia Judaica: Coins and Currency.*

46   See the comments in *The Lost Gospel of Judas Iscariot*, Bart D. Ehrman, p. 38.

47   For very detailed descriptions of this matter see the comments in *On Earth As It Is In Heaven*, D. C. Thielmann, pp. 627-628 and the corresponding scholars notations to these pages; "Matthew," in *Peake's Commentary on the Bible*, Krister Stendahl, eds. Matthew Black and Harold H. Rowley, London, Nelson (1962), p. 796, Section 694b; *Jesus on Trial,*

referred to as *Gei ben-Hinnom* and later referred to as *Gehenna*. Originally, as noted in Jeremiah and Isaiah, this field was used as a place for offering sacrifices to the pagan deities Ba'al and Molech, but later became a burial ground for non-Jews, or gentiles in other words. Another Biblical term used for this field was, *Topeth*, as found for example in 2 Kings 23:10, and this term, as noted by Jeremiah and Isaiah, meant "contempt," or "willful disobedience to," or "open disrespect of the valid rules, orders, or processes." Thus, the entire accounts in the Gospels and Acts concerning not only this "field of blood," but also in regards to Judas Iscariot in general resembles something more like what is derived straight out of pagan gentile religious beliefs than it does something that would come out of the Jewish religious teachings and beliefs of Jesus and his disciples, *including* Judas Iscariot![48] Yet, some scholars believe that there was a collection of writings, (refer back to what is stated in the Preface concerning 2 Timothy 4:13), that are referred to as a *Book of Testimonies*, or "Florilegia" that were a collection of Old Testament verses that were used as sources to describe certain events, such as the matter of the "thirty pieces of silver"[49] already discussed above. Although this might be quite true, the fact remains that this belief does not have any substantial proof, and this collection would be no different than say, the Dead Sea Scrolls were to the Qumran community of Essens, and thus, this very collection these scholars are referring to could just as easily be a collection of *those writings* that we now refer to *as* the "Dead Sea Scrolls"!

This then brings us to the actual matter of the "betrayal" of Jesus by Judas, and what exactly *was* this "betrayal." The first and best place to find the *accurate* reason for this "betrayal" is found in Acts 1:18, which as it is generally translated out reads that Judas "burst open" spilling out his guts.[50] Now, Papias told a story about Judas Iscariot that claimed that after Judas had "betrayed" Jesus, Judas' body "swelled up" until "his innards"

Gerard S. Sloyan, p. 62; *Judas Iscariot and the Myth of Jewish Evil*, Hyam Maccoby, pp. 46, 48 and n. 13, pp. 176-177.

48   See the comments in *Judas Iscariot and the Myth of Jewish Evil*, Hyam Maccoby, pp. 45-47.

49   See the comments on this in *Essays on the Semitic Background of the New Testament*, Joseph A. Fitzmyer, p. 63.

50   See for example *Problems of New Testament Translation*, Edgar J. Goodspeed, pp. 123-126.

poured out.[51] But the actual *best* understanding of the Greek words used in the context of this verse from Acts is more in line with a meaning of, "he began babbling," or "speaking out," or in essence, "he told about who Jesus really was." We have all heard the modern phrase, or perhaps even used this modern phrase our self, "he spilled his guts," in regards to someone telling others the truth about something that was supposed to be kept "secret," or "held in confidence" between just a few people. This term derived from the Ancient Greek term, "spilled the beans." For the Ancient Greeks, beginning around 500 BCE, used either colored "pebbles," (Greek, *psephos*, a word found being used, for example in Acts 26:10[52]), or colored "beans" to cast secret votes during jury trials. If the bowl in which the *psephos* or beans were placed was inadvertently overturned, then this "secret voting" would be revealed, or, if someone were to inadvertently vocalize how they had voted, such actions thus brought about the terms, "to spill the beans," or he "spilled his guts" by revealing what was supposed to be kept "secret."[53] This then, is *precisely* what Acts 1:18 *actually* means, for if we look, for example, at Mark 8:27-30; Luke 9:21, Jesus "sternly ordered and commanded them not to tell anyone" that he *was* in fact the Messiah,[54] (but see also Mark 1:24; 1:34; 3:11-12; 1:43-44; 5:43; 7:36; 9:9; Matthew 8:4; 9:30; 12:16; 17:9; Luke 4:41; 9:36). This order was given to all twelve disciples, including Judas Iscariot. This is though, *exactly* what Judas went and did – he told others that Jesus *was* the Messiah, and where he could be found, remembering what was noted in Chapter 5 that Jesus was a "wanted fugitive"![55] This reason then, holds squarely in line

---

51   See the comments on this in *Jesus Before the Gospels*, Bart Ehrman, p. 29.

52   See *Strong's* Greek-English dictionary section #5586; *BDAG Greek-English Lexicon*, p. 1098; *Liddell and Scott's Greek-English Lexicon*, p. 901.

53   See Annelisa Stephen, "Voting with the Ancient Greeks: One of the Earliest Artistic Depictions of Voting, 490 B. C." November 6, 2012; Jeremy James Patterson, "Elections: How the Greeks and Romans did them and why lots can be better than votes," *University of St. Andrews, Ancient and Modern Rhetoric.*

54   For a brief analysis on the various opinions on this matter see *Who is Jesus*, Darrell l. Bock, pp. 93-106; *Jesus and the Laws of Purity*, Roger P. Booth, p. 27.

55   See the comments in *The Lost Gospel of Judas Iscariot*, Bart D. Ehrman, pp. 162-165; *How Jesus Became God*, Bart D. Ehrman, p. 122; *The New Testament*, Bart D. Ehrman, Box 16.10, p. 272; *The Search for the Real Jesus*, Chester Charlton McCown, p. 250.

with what was taught in Pharisaic Jewish law at the time of Jesus. For as it states in the Mishnah, *Abot* 1:10, "Love work and hate mastery, and make not yourself known to the government." Now, under Jewish law at the time of Jesus, it was expressly forbidden to repeat something to others that had been expressly told should *not* be repeated, or told to others, as found in *Yoma* 4b. *But,* if someone were to give their permission to repeat what had first been expressly told "privately" not to repeat to others, this then *was not* a violation of Jewish law. Therefore, when Jesus expressly says to Judas, "Do quickly what you are going to do," (John 13:27, the title verse to this chapter for example), Jesus had thus given Judas permission to repeat what had been told to Jesus' disciples "privately," thereby nullifying any violation of Jewish law![56] J. C. O'Neill though, quite erroneously believes that it was this very fact that Judas went and "told" others who Jesus was that brought about the charge of "blasphemy" based on Mishnah *Sanhedrin* 11:5.[57] But as will be proven in Chapter 7, such a claim by O'Neill is erroneous and without merit.

Joel Carmichael though, chooses to interpret the matter of Judas Iscariot in this way:[58] "If we try to explain his treachery either psychologically or functionally on the basis of the present Gospel account, it remains altogether enigmatic, while if we take as our starting point the existence of an armed contest between an insurrectionary force and the powerful institutions it was assaulting we can begin to see its point." Yet, as Jules Isaac points out,[59] in *all* of the Gospel passages, just noted above it is clearly stated that people *did not* keep silent, but on the contrary, openly proclaimed Jesus to be *THE* "Messiah," or "son of David," which was likewise a *clear* "messianic" reference! But it is essential to notice that *none* of the Gospel references noted come from John's Gospel! For in John's Gospel, Jesus makes no

---

But in *The Trial of Jesus*, Josef Blinzler, p. 59, Blinzler lists several possible reasons for Judas' "betrayal" of Jesus.

56 See the comments on this in *Love Your Neighbor*, Rabbi Zelig Pliskin, pp. 216-218.

57 See the comments on this in *Who Did Jesus Think He Was*, J. C. O'Neill, pp. 52-54.

58 *The Death of Jesus*, Joel Carmichael, p. 150.

59 *Jesus and Israel*, Jules Isaac, pp. 148-151; *Jesus and His Contemporaries*, Etienne Trocme, p. 101.

"effort to keep his identity secret nor does Jesus command others to keep silent as to his being *THE* "Messiah".[60]

There is a major problem though, with the use of the English words "betrayed," or "betrayal" in regards to the accounts of Jesus' arrest. For the Greek words, *paradidemi*, or *paredidoto* are better understood to have a meaning of, "to hand over," or "handed over," especially when we remember again that Jesus was a "wanted fugitive."[61] William Klassen points out that only in Luke's Gospel, (Luke 6:16), is the Greek word for "traitor," (*prodotes*) ever used in regards to Judas![62] Paul, in 1 Corinthians 11:23-24 indicates that he knows *of* this "handing over" of Jesus, but Paul does not specifically name *who* was involved in this "handing over" of Jesus as if Paul does not know *who* precisely was involved in the "handing over" of Jesus, nor does Paul even refer to this "handing over" as being some sort of a "betrayal." In fact, in Romans 8:32 Paul seems to indicate that it was God Himself who "handed over" Jesus to the arresting party. Yet, in 1 Peter 2:23, it seems to indicate that Jesus "handed over" himself to the arresting officers. In essence then, there really is no indication of an actual "betrayal," per se, in contrast to the common perception of such! For Mark 14:44 indicates, by way of the Greek wording, that Judas wanted the arresting officers to take Jesus away "safely," as if to emphatically ensure that no harm were to come to Jesus.[63] Therefore, could this be the very reason why Judas gave Jesus a "kiss" as Jesus was being arrested?[64]

John's Gospel, above any of the Synoptic Gospels, seems to indicate that Jesus had foreknowledge that someone would "hand him over." In fact, again, as already noted above, John 6:70 implies that Judas had been "chosen" from the very beginning as the one who would "hand over"

60   See the comments in *The New Testament*, Bart D. Ehrman, pp. 159-160.

61   See the comments in *Judas Iscariot and the Myth of Jewish Evil*, Hyam Maccoby, p. 24; *Jesus Before Christianity*, Albert Nolan, pp. 131-132; *The Lost Gospel of Judas Iscariot*, Bart D. Ehrman, pp. 15-16; *The New Testament*, Bart D. Ehrman, p. 215; *Judas*, William Klassen, pp. 22-23, 44, 47-58, 62-74, 77-78, and 202-203; *The Death of the Messiah*, Raymond E. Brown, pp. 1399-1401.

62   See *Judas*, William Klassen, p. 116.

63   See the comments in *The Lost Gospel of Judas Iscariot*, Bart D. Ehrman, pp. 23, and 166.

64   See the comments in *Judas Iscariot and the Myth of Jewish Evil*, Hyam Maccoby, pp. 37, and 42.

Jesus.[65] But some scholars, (while agreeing that Jesus had some sort of pre-arranged foreknowledge), will use Mark 14:11 as an indication that Jesus made "clandestine arrangements for the Passover meal" while Judas was off arranging for Jesus' "betrayal."[66] This theory comes from the fact that in this verse from Mark's Gospel, Judas is visiting the High Priest while we do not find the actual meal arrangements being made until two verses later, Mark 14:13-16. But *if* this scholarly opinion were true, then how would Judas Iscariot himself have known *where* this "clandestine Passover meal" was being held in order for Judas Iscariot to even be present at this meal also? Likewise, *if* this theory were true, then would Mark 14:17 not then have had such wording as, "one of you *has already* betrayed me"? But the wording of Mark 14:17 is "*will betray* me," which indicates that a supposed "betrayal" had not yet occurred. In Mark's Gospel Jesus clearly knows *what will* happen, even though the wording in Mark's Gospel indicates that it had *already happened!* Something is totally amiss in this entire account in Mark's Gospel!

Regarding the Gospel accounts of what Jesus is reported to have said at the Last Supper in regards to Judas, some scholars have pointed to Psalm 41:10 (41:9 in Christian translations), and Proverbs 21:6 as the basis for the evangelists words.[67] These scholars are correct in assuming that these words were placed onto the lips of Jesus by the evangelists and not something which Jesus actually spoke. For taking these two verses one at a time, the common translation in Christian Bibles of Psalm 41:10 (41:9 in Christian translations), this verse is generally rendered as saying, "Even my bosom friend in whom I trusted, who ate my bread, has lifted the heels against me." But the *better* rendering of the *actual* Hebrew of this verse in regards to the overall context of Psalm 41 is, "Even everyone's well-being He confirmed to my trust, therein consumed, I did battle with the deceivers."[68] Likewise, in regards to Proverbs 21:6, which is commonly translated as, "Well meant

---

65 See the comments in *Judas Iscariot and the Myth of Jewish Evil*, Hyam Maccoby, p. 64.

66 See for example the comments in *The Last Week*, Marcus Borg and John Dominic Crossan, p. 111.

67 See for example the comments in *The Lost Gospel of Judas Iscariot*, Bart D. Ehrman, pp. 26-27.

68 See and use *Etymological Dictionary of Biblical Hebrew*, and *A Comprehensive Etymological Dictionary of the Hebrew Language* for this *better* rendering of the contextual Hebrew.

are the wounds a friend inflicts, but profuse are the kisses of an enemy." Yet again, the actual *better* rendering of the contextual Hebrew of Proverbs 21:6 should actually be understood to say, "The getting of treasures by a lying tongue is a fleeting vapor: they lead to death."[69] The point being made here, as stated already earlier in this chapter, is that the matter and accounts of a "betrayal" of Jesus by an individual named "Judas Iscariot" is one of a late developing tradition by the gentile church in order to place *all* of the blame for the arrest, trial and crucifixion of Jesus upon the Jews! As Gerard S. Sloyan writes concerning this,[70] "Jesus' earliest followers, all of them Jews, proclaimed this tortured death among Jews, who might have been open to a particular tale of cruelty at the hands of the Roman oppressor. But Jesus' crucifixion was never presented on those terms. If anything, Roman responsibility was deemphasized in favor of Jewish." Now, even though Samuel Sandmel understands that the majority of scholars do not believe that Paul actually wrote 2 Thessalonians, Sandmel still makes an excellent point in regards to 2 Thessalonians 2:15 when he writes,[71] "Nowhere else does Paul speak in such bitter accusation about Jews. His tone elsewhere, as in Romans, is one of regret that the Jews have failed to see what they might have seen. Nowhere else does he charge them with responsibility for the crucifixion; indeed, from Paul's standpoint the crucifixion was something chosen by the Christ, and not forced on him… Many scholars, therefore, regard this passage as the result of editing and interpolation by the later church, in the interest of an accrued bitterness which had developed between Jews and Christians."

This then brings us to several important matters, and questions that must be asked in regards to not only Judas' supposed "betrayal" leading to Jesus' arrest, but also in regards to the trial accounts of Jesus in the Gospels. First is the matter of the *Gospel of Judas Iscariot*, a document first discovered in Coptic in the 1970's near Beni Masar, Egypt, which had long thought to be lost.[72] Irenaeus in *Against Heresies* 1.31.1 mentions this very

---

69   See and use again, *Etymological Dictionary of Biblical Hebrew*, and *A Comprehensive Etymological Dictionary of the Hebrew Language* for this *best* rendering.

70   *The Crucifixion of Jesus*, Gerard S. Sloyan, p. 13.

71   *A Jewish Understanding of the New Testament*, Samuel Sandmel, p. 83.

72   See the comments on this in *The Lost Gospel of Judas Iscariot*, Bart D. Ehrman, p. 3.

Gospel,[73] but the question is, why would there even have been a Gospel written about Judas Iscariot's relationship and perspective of Jesus if in fact Judas had actually been a "betrayer" of Jesus? But an even better question to ask is, if Judas Iscariot died shortly after Jesus' crucifixion, then how could Judas have gained any followers such as Peter, the other disciples, and Paul did in order to give this account from Judas' standpoint? One other important point to mention along with this comes from Mark 14:50-51, which mentions a "young man" as being the *true* "betrayer" of Jesus, and which some scholars then relate to the prophecy of Amos 2:15 (2:16 in most Christian Bibles).[74] In regards to this "unnamed" individual, in John 18:15-16, (verses mentioned previously in Chapter 2), these verses clearly state that a certain "unnamed"[75] disciple of Jesus is "known to the High Priest," and thereby, "went with Jesus into the courtyard of the High Priest." This "unnamed" disciple then "brought Peter in." So, who could this "unnamed" disciple possibly be who was "known to the High Priest"? If this one "unnamed" disciple was certainly "*known*" to the High Priest, then the question begs to be asked, why were *all* of the other disciples of Jesus also not "known to the High Priest" as a result of this seemingly intimate relationship between this "unnamed" disciple and the High Priest that is hinted at in these verses from John? Is it thus, *possibly* being hinted at that this "unnamed" disciple was in *fact* some disciple *other than* Judas Iscariot? For as was noted in Chapter 4, Matthew, (by way of his name Levi), was a Levite and most probably a Temple tax collector who then quite possibly could have been "known to the High Priest"! Therefore, for *any* scholar to use the claim "that Judas did betray Jesus is almost certain,"[76] simply because "it is multiple attested" to, *does not* take into consideration *all* of the discrepancies and other factors and facts surrounding these *supposed* "multiple attestations" of this matter! If a matter has no congruency within the supposed "multiple attestations," then the matter *cannot be* considered as being "almost certain." We *can be* certain through "multiple attestation" that Jesus *was* "handed over" by *someone*, but we *cannot be* certain about

---

73   See the comments in *The Lost Gospel of Judas Iscariot*, Bart D. Ehrman, p. 63.

74   See the comments in *Revolution in Judaea*, Hyam Maccoby, pp. 152-153.

75   See the comments in *Caiaphas*, Helen K. Bond, pp. 134-135, yet her identification of this "unnamed" disciple as that of Judas Iscariot is highly questionable.

76   See for example, *The New Testament*, Bart D. Ehrman, p. 271.

whom it was that "handed Jesus over," or about what happened to that particular individual *after* they "handed over" Jesus!

But let us look at a matter that is *only* found in the Gospel of John 18:8, and once again, according to virtually *all* scholars, the Gospel of John *was* the last Gospel to be written. *Only* in John's Gospel do we find that Jesus says to the arresting party, "Let these men go away," or in other words, Jesus was telling the arresting officers to let his disciples go free. Yet, in the three Synoptic Gospel accounts, not only is it reported that Jesus' disciples "fell asleep" while on their "watch" for an arresting party, but it is also reported that they "*fled*"[77] when Jesus was arrested. This differs from what is found being stated in the Gospel of Judas in regards to these matters. For would Judas have also "fled" or have been referred to also by Jesus when he said, "Let these men go" if Judas had been the one who actually brought the arresting party?[78] Furthermore, it is reported that Jesus had asked his disciples if any of them were carrying "swords," to which they answered that they had "two." So, the *only* logical conclusion that can be drawn from this particular matter is that Jesus *expected to be* arrested, and, that Jesus was ready for conflict and resistance *to ensue at* his arrest.[79]

In retrospect of what we have in the Gospel accounts, all of Jesus' disciples "fled" *after* using one of the "swords" that they had with them to lop off an individual's ear. So, who was present amongst Jesus' followers to be able to give *any* eyewitness account of a *supposed* trial before the Great Sanhedrin?[80] The *only* disciple of Jesus who could possibly have been present at a *supposed* trial before the Great Sanhedrin would have been the *only* disciple who *did not*, possibly, "flee" as did all of the remaining other disciples because *he* was amongst the arresting party, and therefore, it is most likely that this disciple was also taken along with Jesus to serve as a "witness," and this disciple could either be Judas Iscariot, as "Church tradition" has it, or it could have been this "*unnamed* disciple" mentioned above.

---

77   See the comments in *The Last Week*, Marcus Borg and John Dominic Crossan, p. 125.

78   See the comments in *The Lost Gospel of Judas Iscariot*, Bart D. Ehrman, p. 97.

79   See the comments in *Understanding the Difficult Words of Jesus*, David Bivin and Roy Blizzard, p. 69.

80   See the comments in *The Last Week*, Marcus Borg and John Dominic Crossan, p. 128.

Therefore, in closing this chapter on Judas Iscariot it is essential to ask two important questions that go to the very heart of certain Christian doctrines and theology. First, if Jesus did in fact have foreknowledge of a "betrayal" by one of his disciples, and this "betrayer" had been "chosen" from the beginning, then how can Judas Iscariot be portrayed as being "evil" and someone to be punished for all eternity?[81] For Acts 2:23 clearly states that this had been God's plan from the very beginning. So, *if,* according to standard Christian theology, Jesus was *supposed to be* "handed over" by Judas Iscariot to die for our sins, then how can Judas Iscariot be viewed in any other way than as an individual who was doing God's will?[82]

---

81 See the comments in *Judas Iscariot and the Myth of Jewish Evil*, Hyam Maccoby, pp. 70-71 and n. 4, p. 179.

82 See the comments in *The Lost Gospel of Judas Iscariot*, Bart D. Ehrman, p. 138 and n. 10, p. 186; *Judas and the Gospel of Jesus*, N. T. Wright, pp. 48-49.

Chapter 7

"And the High Priest tore his garment and said,
'He has blasphemed'!"
(Matthew 26:65).

I n this chapter we are going to take a close examination of the charge
of "blasphemy" that was *supposedly* leveled against Jesus, which many
scholars, theologians, and even the general church laity have believed
was in fact the final verdict reached by a *supposed* trial before the Great
Sanhedrin that convicted Jesus to a death sentence.[1] This matter of a
supposed charge of "blasphemy" against Jesus has caused a great deal of
debate amongst scholars, many of whom admit that the Jews have suffered
greatly at the hands of Christians over the centuries as a result of the
erroneous assumptions put forth concerning this matter. Yet, it seems that
some of the very scholars who admit that erroneous assumptions have been
made about this matter of a "guilty verdict" given at a *supposed* trial of Jesus
before the Great Sanhedrin, these very same scholars have put forth *their
own* erroneous assumptions in regards to this supposed "guilty verdict" of
"blasphemy" that was *supposedly* committed by Jesus![2] What is even more

---

1   See for example the comments in *The Trial of Jesus*, Josef Blinzler, pp. 24-28; Steven L.
    Cox in *Journal for Baptist Theology and Ministry*, Vol. 2, No. 2, (Fall 2004), pp. 64-84.
2   See the comments for example in *Jesus On Trial*, Gerard S. Sloyan, p. 97.

amazing though, is the *fact* of how many modern Christian scholars today simply *do not* understand Jewish *metaphoric* terminology that was used, not only at the time of Jesus, but also long before the time of Jesus, and which in *fact*, is still used by Jewish scholars today! But, as will be shown in this chapter, the entire account regarding a supposed "guilty verdict" for "blasphemy" is nothing but a later gentile church fabrication, which, I might add, has already been thoroughly demonstrated and proven, by quite a few other scholars, to be nothing but an early church fabrication simply as a way to blame the Jews for Jesus' crucifixion.[3] Nevertheless, the matter of Jesus *ever* committing any form of "blasphemy" is *still* a very highly debated matter amongst Christian New Testament scholars, as will also be shown in this chapter, and it seems to remain such a highly debated matter simply because the majority of Christian New Testament scholars *have to* find *some sort of reason* to throw guilt and blame onto the Jews in general in regards to Jesus' crucifixion! It is also necessary to point out here early in this chapter that *nowhere* in John's Gospel is there *any* reference to a charge of "blasphemy" against Jesus, nor does there appear to be *any* reference whatsoever to *any* trial of Jesus before the Great Sanhedrin.[4] Helen K. Bond very rightly states,[5] "The historical accuracy of the trial narratives in the Gospels is highly questionable, and few New Testament scholars would maintain that the Gospel reports are transcripts of the actual proceedings."

It is essential to point out that the English word "blasphemy" derives from the two Greek words, *blapto* and *pheme*. The word *blapto* means, "to hinder," and the word *pheme*, comes from the same root as does the words *phos*, "light," and the word *phaino*, "to lighten," or "to shine." Thus, the Greek word, *blasphemia*, (from which we derive our English word "blasphemy"), in its *best* English meaning actually means, "a hindering of light that brings injury," but in a more broad representative sense of the pagan gentile origins of this word, it is usually used as a "misrepresented

---

3   See for example the comments in *The Mythmaker*, Hyam Maccoby, pp. 72-81 in which he does an excellent job demonstrating this fabrication by utilizing Acts 7 and the trial accounts of Stephen as a comparison to the Gospel accounts of the supposed trial of Jesus; and see also the comments in *Pontius Pilate in History and Interpretation*, Helen K. Bond, p. 148.

4   See the comments on this in *The New Testament*, Bart D. Ehrman, p. 159.

5   *Caiaphas*, Helen K. Bond, p. 17.

image that brings injury to you by hindering the light that reveals God."[6] In essence, this pagan gentile concept is *precisely* what is portrayed by what is stated in Matthew 5:14-16. Yet, these verses have absolutely nothing whatsoever to do with any "blasphemous" actions or words that would warrant a death sentence for anyone. Thus, in reality the Greek meanings and concepts are hardly an accurate depiction of the many Hebrew terms that are used that get too often translated into English as "blasphemy." Furthermore, at the time of Jesus many Jews *did not* believe that "blasphemy" even applied to gentiles in any way.[7] Yet, it is true that there *were* still other Jews at the time of Jesus who *did* believe that "blasphemy" applied to both Jews and gentiles alike, and that "blasphemy" *could be* committed by gentiles under the Noahide covenant.[8]

So, what exactly constituted a charge of "blasphemy" in Jewish law at the time of Jesus? There have been many scholars who have simply misused and misunderstood the Talmud and all of its different references to "blasphemy" when attempting to answer this very question![9] Although it is true that in the Talmud these many references to "blasphemy" take many forms, and the punishments outlined for *each* of these different forms of the offence of "blasphemy" differ greatly. Yet, there was *only one* form of "blasphemy" that constituted a "death sentence," to which the punishment for *that* particular offense came by way of stoning to death the individual who committed this particular "blasphemy." The *only* offense of "blasphemy" that resulted in this death sentence was the "reviling"[10] of the Ineffable Name of God

---

6 In *Thayer's Greek-English Lexicon of the New Testament,* one finds that this gets defined as "detraction," which is a *"malicious discrediting of someone's character and accomplishments."*

7 See for example Piero Stefani, "What Does 'Blasphemy' Mean in Judaism?" *Freedom and Democracy,* February 21, 2014.

8 See for example the comments on this in *Blasphemy and Exaltation in Judaism,* Darrell L. Bock, pp. 77-78, and 101-102; *Torah for Today: What Does the Torah Say about ... Blasphemy?* Rabbi Jeremy Lawrence.

9 See for example the comments in *The Trial of Jesus,* Josef Blinzler, pp. 104-111; *Blasphemy and Exaltation in Judaism,* Darrell L. Bock, p. 72 in regards to his interpretation of *Megillah* 3.41.

10 The English word "revile" means, "to subject to verbal abuse: address or assail with opprobrious (meaning 'grossly wrong or vicious' and usually public) language: rail at: to

– i.e. the Tetragrammaton.[11] Now, simply uttering the Ineffable Name of God *did not* constitute "blasphemy" punishable by death as far too many scholars and theologians have claimed,[12] and in fact, if one looks at what is stated in *Kidushin* 71a one will find that at least once every seven years the sages of Israel would simply utter the Ineffable Name of God to their students in order that the correct pronunciation would get passed along from generation to generation. As Exodus 20:21 *clearly* states, "… In every place where I allow My Name to be mentioned, I will come to you and bless you."[13] A division of the Essens known as the *Hemerobaptists* would undergo "ritual immersion" (see again, Chapter 4 concerning the matter of "ritual purity halakha"), every morning in order to be "ritually pure" enough to be able to pronounce the Ineffable Name of God.[14] It is true though, that in Mishnah *Sanhedrin* 10:1 it states that "He who pronounces the Divine Name as it is spelled out," will not share in a portion of the world to come, and in *Abot* 1:13 it states that, "He who makes use of the Crown will pass away," which was interpreted to mean that a "commoner," (or in essence, someone not "learned" in the *appropriate pronunciation and usage* of the Divine Name), *should not* attempt to make use of the Divine Name,[15] but neither of these two Mishnah tractates says anything about this being a form of "blasphemy." But Jesus was hardly someone who was not "learned" in the appropriate usage of the Divine Name of God! Now,

---

use contemptuous or opprobrious language: synonym see *scold*."

11   See the comments in the *Jewish Encyclopedia*, "Blasphemy," Kaufmann Kohler and David Warner Amram; *Jewish Virtual Library*, "Blasphemy"; Mishnah, *Sanhedrin* 6:4; 7:5; *The Mythmaker*, Hyam Maccoby, p. 67; *On Earth As It Is In Heaven*, D. C. Thielmann, p. 314 and n. 158, p. 362 and n. 159, pp. 362-363.

12   See the comments of Solomon Schechter and Julius H. Greenstone, "Excommunication (Hebrew, 'niddui,' 'ḥerem')," *Jewish Encyclopedia*; Morris Jastrow, Jr., Kaufmann Kohler, and Marcus Jastrow, "Banishment," *Jewish Encyclopedia*; "Jewish Practices & Rituals: Excommunication," *Jewish Virtual Library*; *The Gifts of the Jews*, Thomas Cahill, pp. 109-110; *On Earth As It Is In Heaven*, D. C. Thielmann, n.18, p. 206.

13   See the comments in *The Way of God*, Moshe Chaim Luzzatto, pp. 199-211.

14   See the comments on this of Kaufmann Kohler, "Hemerobaptists: 'Morning Bathers'," *Jewish Encyclopedia*.

15   See *The Way of God*, Moshe Chaim Luzzatto, pp. 205 and 223.

Darrell L. Bock does rightly reference Mishnah *Sanhedrin* 7:5.[16] Yet, Bock does not believe that Jesus ever actually uttered the Ineffable Name of God, but instead, Bock's opinion is that this matter is simply "a piece of early Church rhetoric and propaganda."[17] Darrell Bock goes on further though to write, "There is little discussion of formal judicial examples of blasphemy. Trials for blasphemy are not present in these texts… It possessed ambiguities that made defining blasphemy, especially where euphemisms were used, a subject of some rabbinic debate."[18] Bock then erroneously states, "The official rabbinic position is that use of the Divine Name constitutes the only clear case of capital blasphemy (Mishnah, *Sanhedrin* 7:5)."[19] Bock makes further erroneous claims regarding this,[20] which results from his misunderstanding and misrepresentation of Mishnah, *Sotah* 7:6, and Mishnah *Yoma* 6:2, and this despite the fact that[21] he references Craig Evans,[22] who clearly points out that "Uttering the Divine Name, especially in the context of quoting Scripture and with all proper reverence, is not blasphemous." Therefore, Bock's interpretation is simply untrue as will be proven in this chapter, for the "capital offense of blasphemy" regarding the "Divine Name" *only* involved "defiling," or "reviling" the Divine Name of God. Period!

Thus, since it was *only* an act of "reviling" the Ineffable Name of God, which constituted a sentence of death, it has been strongly proven that Jesus *never* committed such an act.[23] Furthermore, at the time of Jesus Leviticus 22:32 was interpreted to indicate that "a Torah scholar's behavior must be beyond reproach,"[24] and as pointed out in Chapter 4,

---

16 *Blasphemy and Exaltation in Judaism*, Darrell L. Bock, p. 2; but see also *Messiah and Temple*, Donald Juel, p. 97.

17 *Blasphemy and Exaltation in Judaism*, Darrell L. Bock, n. 1, p. 2 where he cites *The Trial of Jesus*, Simon Legasse, who likewise holds a similar opinion.

18 *Blasphemy and Exaltation in Judaism*, Darrell L. Bock, p. 110.

19 *Blasphemy and Exaltation in Judaism*, Darrell L. Bock, p. 11.

20 *Blasphemy and Exaltation in Judaism*, Darrell L. Bock, pp. 198-199.

21 See *Blasphemy and Exaltation in Judaism*, Darrell L. Bock, n. 38, p. 199.

22 *Jesus and His Contemporaries*, Craig Evans, p. 413.

23 See the comments in *On Earth As It Is In Heaven*, D. C. Thielmann, n. 160, p. 363; *The Crucifixion of Jesus*, Gerard S. Sloyan, pp. 31 and 51.

24 See *Love Your Neighbor*, Rabbi Zelig Pliskin, pp. 317-318.

Jesus was "tested" to make certain that he was indeed a "Torah scholar," (i.e. a "learned rabbi beyond reproach"), and as *Abot* 4:12 states regarding the conduct of a "Torah scholar," "Let the honor of your students be as clear as your own." Also, based on Deuteronomy 6:5, (as interpreted in the Talmud, *Yoma* 86a; *Shabbat* 23b), a "Torah scholar" *must* "behave in a manner that will cause the Name of Heaven to be beloved."[25] Thus, as Rabbi Shmuley Boteach writes,[26] "…Jesus' statement contains absolutely nothing blasphemous. Indeed, Jews would view a statement like this as being quite virtuous insofar as it expresses what millions of Jews have aspired to throughout their lives, namely, to be at the right hand of God. The Talmud is replete with similar statements by great rabbis who wished that when they died, they would be beside God's throne. So where is the blasphemy? …But even had Jesus claimed to be God (which is different from claiming to be divine and thus another god), he would not have been charged with blasphemy. Unlike Christianity, Judaism does not associate blasphemy with a person claiming to be God… In Judaism, blasphemy involves *cursing* God, not claiming to be God. If you curse God, and you do it in front of a minimum of two witnesses, that is a circumstance under which you can incur the penalty of death." But *this is not* what happens in the Gospel accounts, and therefore, no such charge of "blasphemy" would have been found in *any* of the words of Jesus that are recorded in the Gospels.[27] It is essential to point out that in 1 Peter 2:22 it clearly says that, "no guile was found in his mouth." Furthermore, even *if* Jesus *had* in fact committed such an act of "blasphemy," such an offence *would not* have been a matter that would have involved Pilate and the Romans carrying out the "death sentence" *on behalf* of a request by the Great Sanhedrin. Therefore, many scholars have erroneously tried to claim that *two* trials were conducted,[28] which as was strongly proven in Chapter 5 is simply *not true historically* at all.

It is important here to point out that Jesus in Mark 3:29 clearly warns people about committing "blasphemy" against the spirit because it was an

---

25   See *Love Your Neighbor*, Rabbi Zelig Pliskin, p. 376.

26   *Kosher Jesus*, Rabbi Shmuley Boteach, pp. 102-103.

27   See further though, the comments in *The Trial of Jesus From Jewish Sources*, Rabbi A. P. Drucker, pp. 16-20.

28   See for example the comments in *The Trial of Jesus*, Josef Blinzler, p. 168.

"unforgivable sin,' and this was based on the account from Mark 2:7, which then in essence, sets up a sort of debate or "battle of the blasphemies," between Jesus' interpretation of "blasphemy" and the interpretations of what constituted "blasphemy" by other Jewish sages of the time. But such debates between sages, as noted in earlier chapters, was nothing unusual, for it was simply *standard* Jewish practice to debate interpretations of the Torah. So, the question begs to be asked here, since Jesus clearly knows and understands what constituted "blasphemy," and he even *warns* others not to commit "blasphemy," then why would Jesus himself have *ever* committed *any* form of "blasphemy"? This is virtually the very question we find Jesus himself asking in Mark 15:29!

Since there have been scholars who have gone to great lengths to study and write about the matter of what constituted "blasphemy" in Jewish law at the time of Jesus, and in particular, the matter of "cursing," or "reviling" the Name of God, it is essential at this time to examine some of these scholarly opinions about this matter.

First, in matters of trials that involved someone having been accused of "cursing/reviling" God's Name it is claimed that witnesses were encouraged to actually avoid repeating the utterance, while at the same time trying to describe the utterance that they claim to have heard even though Leviticus 19:16 instructs that, "we are sometimes obligated to relate derogatory information."[29] Also, there are scholarly claims that "blasphemy" constituted not only speaking, but actions as well that "cursed/reviled" the Name of God. But again, as noted above, the fact is that there actually is no precise Hebrew word for "blasphemy."[30] Thus, since there is no actual Hebrew word, "blasphemy," scholars have looked at the various different Hebrew words that quite often get translated out as "blasphemy."[31] Yet, despite such great efforts by these scholars to carefully examine all of the Hebrew words that get translated into English as "blasphemy," they simply fail to prove that Jesus ever actually violated *any* law in such a manner as that of "cursing/reviling" the Ineffable Name of God. Now, Darrell L. Bock[32]

---

29   See the comments on this in *Love Your Neighbor*, Rabbi Zelig Pliskin, pp. 270-271.

30   See the comments in *Blasphemy and Exaltation in Judaism*, Darrell L. Bock, p. 30 for examples of each of these mentioned opinions.

31   See for example *Blasphemy and Exaltation in Judaism*, Darrell L. Bock, pp. 31-35.

32   *Blasphemy and Exaltation in Judaism*, Bock, p. 36-37.

refs to a specific incident in Leviticus 24:10-23, and primarily Leviticus 24:11 as a supposed incident of someone cursing the Ineffable Name of God, YHWH. Bock utilizes[33] a desired translation of the Hebrew in regards to a particular idiomatic terminology claiming that *his* interpretation is the *real* interpreted meaning. But again, such *does not* prove anything in regards to Jesus committing such an act.[34] Such scholarly claims as these even go so far as to claim that the "cursing/reviling," or even just "insulting" of a Jewish "king" or other Jewish "leader" (such as the High Priest, for example), was in essence, equivalent to "cursing/reviling" the Ineffable Name of God, and thus, such an act constituted "blasphemy"[35] punishable by death. Darrell L. Bock, for example,[36] cites 1 Kings 21:13; Job 2:9-10; Isaiah 8:21; 2 Kings 19:3; Isaiah 37:3 Ezekiel 35:12; Nehemiah 9:18, 26 in regards to such an opinion. Bock then further states concerning this that,[37] "The Hebrew Scriptures indicate that blasphemy represents speech or action that shows disrespect to God, by insulting His power, uniqueness, or goodness. In such speech or action, God is reviled, insulted, or taunted. To attack those who are God's anointed leaders or even His people can also be seen as indicative of disrespect for God." Even *if* this were in fact true, it still *would not* constitute a death sentence. Furthermore, Bock seems to not realize that neither the High Priest, nor any of the Herodians at the time of Jesus were an actual "anointed" *appointee* of God, and in fact, as shown in an earlier chapter, they were very much despised by the people in general as "political *appointees*" of Rome.

Taking this a step further though, in Numbers 12 both Moses' sister and brother speak against Moses, exactly in a manner that Bock is claiming, yet the *only* punishment that resulted was that Moses' sister contracted a

33 *Blasphemy and Exaltation in Judaism*, Darrell L. Bock, n. 12-14, p. 36.

34 See further on this though from Moshe J. Bernstein, "Ki-qelelath elohiym thalowiy (Deuteronomy 21:23): A Study in Early Jewish Exegesis," *Jewish Quarterly Review* 74, (1983), pp. 21-45.

35 See for example *Caiaphas*, Helen K. Bond, p. 136.

36 *Blasphemy and Exaltation in Judaism*, Darrell L. Bock, p. 39.

37 *Blasphemy and Exaltation in Judaism*, Darrell L. Bock, p. 42.

skin disease.[38] Thus, Bock's entire claims on this matter are a moot point,[39] and the primary reason that this is a moot point is because Bock himself[40] admits that such "blasphemy" could *only* occur against a "legitimate" king or High Priest, which again, neither Caiaphas, nor Herod Antipas constituted a "legitimate" High Priest or king at the time of Jesus! Now, an important matter to note here comes from Mark 14:71 where it seems to clearly indicate that Peter "cursed" (*anathema*), Jesus,[41] which according to Paul in 1 Corinthians 12:3, Paul warns individuals not to do. For *if* Jesus *was indeed THE* "legitimate Messiah," (i.e. the *legitimate* "king"), then Peter *also* would have been guilty of such a "blasphemous" offense noted by Bock. But the simple fact is that such *was not* equivalent to "cursing/reviling" the Ineffable Name of God, and thus, such *did not* warrant a "death sentence." Let us take as an example, for a moment, what is found in Exodus 22:27 (22:28 in most Christian translations), which speaks of "reviling a judge." But this verse says *nothing* about the *Nasi*, or Head of the Court, (noted in Chapter 5). As Hugo Mantel points out concerning this,[42] "The Baraita argues: 'Now the case of a judge is not analogous to that of a Nasi, for thou art commanded to obey the ruling of a judge, but not of a Nasi; whilst the case of a Nasi is not analogous to that of a judge, for it is only against the decree of a Nasi that thou art enjoined not to rebel,' (*Sanhedrin* 66a)."[43] Furthermore, based upon what is stated in Leviticus 19:14, it was even forbidden to "revile the deaf," which was interpreted

---

38 See the comments on this in *Love Your Neighbor*, Rabbi Zelig Pliskin, pp. 343-347 and how this relates back to what was discussed in Chapter 3 about the *lashon ha-ra*; but see also the comments on this in *Jews, Greeks and Christians*, (Edited by Robert Hammerton-Kelly and Robin Scroggs), Jacob Neusner commenting, pp. 103-104; *The Idea of Purity in Ancient Judaism*, Jacob Neusner, pp. 24, 83-84; *Jewish Literacy*, Rabbi Joseph Telushkin, p. 46; *Ritual and Morality*, Hyam Maccoby, pp. 120-121.

39 See also his further comments on this *Blasphemy and Exaltation in Judaism*, Darrell L. Bock, p. 111.

40 *Blasphemy and Exaltation in Judaism*, Darrell L. Bock, p. 207.

41 Concerning this particular matter see the comments of Jacob Voorsanger and Kaufmann Kohler, "Anathema," *Jewish Encyclopedia*.

42 See the comments in *Studies in the History of the Sanhedrin*, Hugo Mantel, pp. 43-44.

43 *Studies in the History of the Sanhedrin*, Hugo Mantel, n. 246, p. 43; *Love Your Neighbor*, Rabbi Zelig Pliskin, pp. 189-190.

by the Pharisees of Jesus' time as indicating that if the deaf, who cannot even hear your "reviling" them was forbidden, how much more then must it be forbidden to "revile" *anyone* who *could* hear! Thus, even "reviling a common individual" was a violation of Jewish law at the time of Jesus,[44] but yet, if one were to commit such an offense, it *would not* be an offense that warranted a "death sentence."

Therefore, we must now examine some of the other statements that Jesus made, which many scholars have pointed to and claimed were other forms of "blasphemy." The first of these statements by Jesus to be briefly discussed is Jesus' stating, "I am," such as is found for example in, Matthew 27:43; Mark 14:62; Luke 22:70; John 18:37. Now, there have been some scholars who have referred to John 10:30 as being an indication that this was a form of "blasphemy" because it states, "I and the Father are one." As an example of this, Bart D. Ehrman writes concerning this,[45] "His Jewish listeners appear to have known full well what he was saying: they immediately pick up stones to execute him for blasphemy." But such a statement by Jesus *is not* "blasphemous" in the least! For many of the prophets, including Moses, used this phrase in their prophecies, which was derived from what is stated in Deuteronomy 18:19 (italics mine), "And it shall come to pass, that whoever will not hearken to *My words* which he shall speak *in My Name*, I will require it of him." Likewise, the meaning that Jesus is implying is made quite clear in his statement just prior to this, "My Father, who gave them me, is greater than *all*." In essence, Jesus is only stating, just as the prophets of old, that his purpose is to do God's will as is demonstrated further by what is found in John 17:22; John 8:29; Acts 2:22.[46] This phrase simply indicated that the individual prophet was speaking *for* God in the *Name* of God![47] In fact, Jesus himself clearly points

---

44 See the comments on this in *Love Your Neighbor*, Rabbi Zelig Pliskin, pp. 252-253.

45 *Jesus Interrupted*, Bart D. Ehrman, p. 80; but as another example Darrell L. Bock, *Blasphemy and Exaltation in Judaism*, pp. 224-230 makes the erroneous claim that Jesus' usage of the term "son of man," and other such similar terminology usages in Scripture, constitutedone saying "I" or "I am."

46 See the comments on this matter by Gerald Sigal, "Jesus Says, 'I and the Father are One,' Doesn't this show that they are one in Essence?" *Jews for Judaism*.

47 See the comments in *Kosher Jesus*, Rabbi Shmuley Boteach, pp. 47-48; *Jesus: Uncovering the Life, Teachings, and Relevance of a Religious Revolutionary*, Marcus Borg, p. 103; *The*

out in Matthew 27:4; Mark 13:6; Luke 21:8 that there would be "*many who will come saying 'I am'.*"[48]

Gerhard von Rad, commenting upon Ezekiel 2:8-3:3, (but see also Jeremiah 15:16; 30:1-2), that Ezekiel's being told to "eat that which I give you," and to "eat that scroll,"[49] compares this to the Gospel of John 1:14 writing,[50] "(We may ask whether this entry of the word into a prophet's bodily life is not meant to approximate to what the writer of the Fourth Gospel says about the word becoming flesh)." Now, while von Rad's interpretation may in fact have possibly been the *original* intended interpretation of John 1:14, it most certainly became something quite distorted by way of later pagan gentile interpretations! For as it is noted in Jeremiah 28:12; 42:7; Ezekiel 3:15; Daniel 8:27; 10:8-10; Isaiah 21:1-10; Habakkuk 3:16 it clearly states that when an individual was given a prophecy that it not only effected them "spiritually," (i.e. such as being "awe struck"), but it also effected them "physically," (i.e. such as being "sick for days"). In essence, they experienced a *bat qol*, (i.e. an "altered state of consciousness"). At times the prophet would even take on the very aspects and attributes of God Himself, and as Jeremiah 6:11; 15:17; 20:9 all indicate, this then meant that the prophet would sometimes "pour out wrath," or "anger" upon his listeners in God's stead! Thus, it has long been a part of Jewish prophetic history that the term "I am" was associated with "prophets!" David E. Aune even points out this very common Jewish prophetic practice of using "I am" when he references Revelation 1:17-20; 3:20; 16:15; 22:12.[51]

There is another scholarly opinion that must be mentioned here in regards to the term "I am" possibly being used by Jesus, and this being the opinion that, at times in the Gospel accounts where the term "son of man" gets used, (a term that will be discussed further below), it is believed that this was in reality an Evangelist's interpolation replacing Jesus' actually using an "I" or "I am" phrase. These same scholars likewise believe that at

---

Message of the Prophets, Gerhard von Rad, pp. 33-38, and 57; *Judaism and the Origins of Christianity*, David Flusser, pp. 509-525.

48   See the comments in *The New Testament and Rabbinic Judaism*, David Daube, p. 325.

49   See the comments in *The Way of God*, Moshe Chaim Luzzatto, pp. 217-237, 239-243, 381-385.

50   *The Message of the Prophets*, Gerhard von Rad, p. 70.

51   *Prophecy in Early Christianity*, David E. Aune, pp. 233-235.

other times the reverse has occurred, or in other words, a Gospel author's use of an "I am" phrase was interpolated in place of Jesus' usage of a "son of man" phrase.[52] Furthermore, there are still other scholars who are of the belief that such a phrase as, "I am," could never have been actually spoken by Jesus.[53]

But as some scholars have pointed out, when Jesus is asked by the High Priest if he is the Christ, the translators into English have reversed the order in which the Greek words are actually written,[54] and thus, Jesus' response instead of being the statement of, "I am," should actually be interpreted as being a question of, "Am I?"[55] Matthew's Gospel account though, (Matthew 26:64), completely eliminates this response. But even *if* Jesus had indeed said, "I am," and even *if* such a statement *had* been considered a "blasphemous" statement under Jewish law, then, as clearly stated under Jewish law in *Sanhedrin* 9b; 25a; *Ketuboth* 18a; *Yevamoth* 25a, (italics mine), "*No man can incriminate himself*," and therefore, such *would not* have brought about a "guilty verdict" from a *supposed* trial before the Great Sanhedrin![56] Furthermore, *if* an individual did in fact incriminate one's self, then as clearly stated in the Talmud Babli, *Sanhedrin* 43a, it was *required* that the individual be given a forty day interval in order to find points in the law that may exonerate that individual.[57] This clearly is a matter nowhere found being described in the Gospel accounts, and thus, the matter of Jesus stating "I am," *cannot*, in any way, be claimed by *any* competent scholar as being the reason for some sort of "guilty verdict" against Jesus on the charge of "blasphemy."

This then brings us to the matter of whether or not referring to one's self as the "Messiah," or "son of God," or even the term "son of man" constituted

---

52   See the comments on this in *Jesus and His Contemporaries*, Etienne Trocme, p. 34; *Jesus of Nazareth*, Dale C. Allison, Jr., p. 29; *The Partings of the Ways*, James Dunn, p. 173.

53   See for example *Who Did Jesus Think He Was*, J. C. O'Neill, p. 3.

54   See the comments in regards to this matter and the problems such causes in properly understanding what is really being said and meant by what is being said in *On Earth As It Is In Heaven*, D. C. Thielmann, pp. 132-133.

55   See the comments in *The Last Week*, Marcus Borg and John Dominic Crossan, p. 24.

56   See the comments in *The Trial of Jesus from Jewish Sources*, Rabbi A. P. Drucker, p. 13; *The Trial of Jesus: Cambridge Studies in Honour of C. F. D. Moule*, p. 30.

57   See the comments in *Love Your Neighbor*, Rabbi Zelig Pliskin, pp. 42-43.

a charge of "blasphemy." Each of these terms need to be examined not only individually, but also collectively since they are in essence, and at some points in time, related to each other in usage.

Taking the term "Messiah" first, it must be pointed out right up front that for any individual making a claim of being THE "Messiah" *did not* constitute any form of "blasphemy" under Jewish law.[58] Now, it has been asserted by many modern Christian New Testament scholars, (utilizing many verses from the Gospels as attempts to offer proof texts for their assertions), that Jesus went out of his way to avoid referring to himself as "Messiah," (i.e. "Christ").[59] But it has also been clearly proven that despite these assertions that Jesus possibly *never directly* referenced himself as being THE "Messiah," the fact is that many of the very remarks that Jesus made, and some of his actions as well, *did* in fact reflect *his own personal belief* that he *was* indeed THE "Messiah."[60] Darrell L. Bock, while speaking about Jesus' actions of specifically choosing twelve disciples, rightly states concerning this,[61] "As we discuss this historical detail, we will come upon a key point this study as a whole makes – that Jesus often revealed more about who he was by what he did than by what he said." Now, although Bock is quite accurate by what he states and it is quite true that Jesus' actions quite often revealed more about who he was "historically" than his words sometimes reveal, Bock fails to correctly interpret Jesus' actions. Warren Carter also rightly points out that,[62] "While titles may contribute to this picture, so do his actions, words, interactions with other characters, and sections of the Gospel in which no titles appear." Carter goes on to point

---

58 See the comments in *Jesus On Trial*, Gerard S. Sloyan, p. 46; *Kosher Jesus*, Rabbi Shmuley Boteach, pp. 96-97; and see also the comments in *The Scepter and the Star*, John J. Collins, p. 2; *The Death of Jesus*, Joel Carmichael, pp. 38-39.

59 See the comments regarding the scholars who make such assertions in *Jesus Before Christianity*, Albert Nolan, p. 120; *Jesus*, C. Leslie Mitton, pp. 61 and 74; *Who Did Jesus Think He Was*, J. C. O'Neill, pp. 23-24 and 44; *On Earth As It Is In Heaven*, D. C. Thielmann, p. 174.

60 See the comments in *On Earth As It Is In Heaven*, D. C. Thielmann, pp. 680-681 and the corresponding scholars notes to these pages; *Who Did Jesus Think He Was*, J. C. O'Neill, pp. 42-54, 117-135; *The Parable of the Wicked Tenants*, Klyne Snodgrass, p. 109.

61 *Who is Jesus*, Darrell L. Bock, pp. 39-47.

62 *Matthew and Empire*, Warren Carter, pp. 58-59.

out the error that far too many scholars make in not understanding this matter when he writes,[63] "Investigations of the title 'Christ' or 'Messiah,' for example, have invariably discussed Jewish Messianic expectations (or non-expectations). But in observing the term's basic meaning of 'anointing' as an expression of being commissioned for a task, it has neglected the key 'commissioned' figure who dominates late first-century society, the Roman Emperor or who is commissioned to rule by the gods." Warren Carter further points out that the word/title "Emmanuel," was a title that had even been claimed and used as a "divine title" by the gentile Antiochus IV Epiphanes long *before* the time of Jesus! Thus, at times, actions, and words/titles, were representations of a particular claim *by someone* to *be* something, such as, for example, a claim to be *THE* "Messiah." But Jules Isaac makes an excellent point that must be mentioned here. Isaac goes to great lengths to prove that the Jews *never* rejected Jesus[64] writing at the beginning of his long remarks, "In any case, no one has the right to declare that the Jewish people rejected Christ or the Messiah, that they rejected the son of God, until it is proved that Jesus revealed himself as such to the Jewish people 'as a whole' and was rejected by them as such. But the Gospels give us good reason to doubt that this ever happened." Also, as Etienne Trocme rightly points out,[65] "Nowhere does Jesus appear as a true public figure, for example on the scale of the Jewish nation of Palestine. He remains a provincial prophet, without any apparent hold over the majority of the population of the country." But now, Jules Isaac does go on to point out concerning Luke 4:18-21[66] that Jesus *did* in fact allow people to clearly understand that he *was THE "Messiah"* despite what was discussed in Chapter 6 about Jesus instructing people "not to tell anyone."

There have even been though, some very ridiculous claims made by many modern Christian scholars that Jesus was never even referred to as *THE* "Messiah" until after his death.[67] But all such ridiculous claims not

---

63   *Matthew and Empire*, Warren Carter, pp. 58-59.

64   *Jesus and Israel*, Jules Isaac, pp. 132-176.

65   *Jesus and His Contemporaries*, Etienne Trocme, p. 110.

66   *Jesus and Israel*, Jules Isaac, pp. 154-155.

67   See for example *No Stone on Another*, Lloyd Gaston, pp. 282 and 295-296; and see *The Crucified Messiah and other Essays*, Nils Dahl, pp. 10-36, which seems to be his overall conclusion as well.

only *can be*, but already *have been* thoroughly refuted, and even Scripture itself clearly refutes such nonsensical claims as found in Psalm 30:9; 6:5; 115:17.[68] As John J. Collins writes concerning this,[69] "It is unlikely that Jesus' followers would have given him such a politically inflammatory title after his death if it had no basis in his life." Likewise, as David Flusser states,[70] "It is quite certain that in his own lifetime Jesus became accepted by many – not just Peter – as the Messiah. Had it not been so, Pilate would not have written above the cross of Jesus: 'King of the Jews'." But the fact is though, that if we utilize one of the most popular criteria that is used by modern New Testament scholars as proof that either an action, or a saying of Jesus is "historically" true, and this being namely the criteria referred to as "embarrassing to the Church," or to "gentiles" in particular, then we *must* look very closely at the account in Mark 7:26-29 and its parallel in Matthew 15:21-28. In this account we have a "gentile" woman coming to Jesus because she "had heard about him," (Mark 7:25), or in essence she came shouting, "have mercy on me, Lord, son of David," (Matthew 15:22). Yet, in both of these accounts we find the Jew, Jesus, referring to this "gentile" woman as a "dog," (verses briefly mentioned in Chapter 6), which at that time and place in history was a known derogatory remark about "gentiles," and which is a *clear* "embarrassment to the gentile Church," and thus, according to this very majority New Testament scholarly piece of criteria, this *must be* an "historically" truthful account to some degree! Thus, as David Flusser so rightly states in regards to this matter,[71] "As far as the sources allow us to judge, Jesus had a poor opinion of the non-Jews, the gentiles." It is essential to go further though, in regards to this matter of Jesus referring to "gentiles" as "dogs." For there are some scholars who attempt to soften these accounts, (as well as to try and soften Paul's reference to "dogs" in Philippians 3:2[72]), by claiming that since the Greek word used in Mark 7:27, *kunariois*, (which is the diminutive form of the Greek word, *kuon*), is best understood as "little dogs," or "house dogs," as opposed to "field

---

68 See the comments in *On Earth As It Is In Heaven*, D. C. Thielmann, pp. 707-708 and the corresponding scholars notations to these pages.

69 *The Scepter and the Star*, John J. Collins, p. 204.

70 *Jesus*, David Flusser, p. 103.

71 *Jesus*, David Flusser, pp. 61-62.

72 See for example *Paul and Rabbinic Judaism*, W. D. Davies, pp. 69-70.

dogs," therefore, as these few scholarly claims go, Jesus is compassionately referring to this "gentile woman" almost like she is a "puppy," or a "pet." But the *fact* is, which *no scholar* can get around regardless of how clever they try to interpret this matter, this Greek word and its usage is actually very similar to the English slang term, "small potatoes," or in other words, it is a reference to *something or someone who has little or no significance*, or to the Jews, such as Jesus, it was a reference to someone who was "unclean," "unqualified," or "unworthy"![73] Nevertheless, the *primary fact* to observe in this account is that even "gentiles" had become familiar with the claims that Jesus was the "son of David," i.e. *THE* "Messiah!"[74]

As a further example that some of Jesus' actions demonstrated that he *was* making a claim to be *THE* "Messiah," Hyam Maccoby very rightly points out[75] that the Mount of Olives was a significant location to Jews in regards to one claiming to be, or actually being *THE* "Messiah," (see for example, 2 Samuel 15:30-32; Ezekiel 11:23). Therefore, such actions by Jesus as his "Sermon on the Mount," his retreating to the Mount of Olives after his "cleansing of the Temple," and his "anointing by oil" in Bethany, which was a city located on the Mount of Olives, all point to the fact that Jesus believed himself to be *THE* "Messiah." Furthermore, as it is known from Zechariah 14:4,[76] the Mount of Olives *would be* the place from which *THE* "Messiah" would place his feet before defeating the enemies of Israel, and thus, we have the one last all important action, and this being, the fact that Jesus was arrested in the Garden of Gethsemane, which is located on the Mount of Olives, and what is even more important to understand about this is that *gethsemane* means, "valley of oil," as in the "anointing oil" for *THE* "Messiah"![77] Adding to this matter though, some scholars[78] interpret Jesus' statement to "let those in Judaea flee to the mountains…"

73   See *BDAG Greek-English Lexicon*, pp. 575, and 579; *Liddel and Scott's Greek-English Lexicon*, pp. 456 and 459.

74   See the comments on this in *The Jews and the Gospel*, Gregory Baum, p. 40.

75   See the comments in *Revolution in Judaea*, Hyam Maccoby, p. 140 and n. 1, p. 235.

76   See the comments on this verse in *The Theological Significance of Jesus' Temple Action in Mark's Gospel*, Emilio G. Chavez, pp. 63 and 84.

77   See the comments in *Revolution in Judaea*, Hyam Maccoby, p. 146.

78   See the comments in *Jesus of Nazareth: Part Two*, Ratzinger and Pope Benedict, pp. 28-29; *Prophecy in Early Christianity*, David E. Aune, pp. 311-312.

(Mark 13:14) as being an indication that Jesus was instructing his followers to "flee from the fighting" that would besiege Jerusalem and the Temple. Now, while these scholars are somewhat correct that this was in regards to the Abomination of Desolation, they are quite in error, as just pointed out regarding the significance of the Mount of Olives in Jewish Messianic prophecy and understandings, and thus, the *true* interpretation of Jesus' statement should be for one to understood that Jesus is instructing his followers that this is the place for everyone to "flee" to in order to "assemble the forces" to *fight* alongside *THE* "Messiah."

There have also been many scholars, and theologians as well, who have claimed that Jesus' acts of "forgiving one's sins" was a form of "blasphemy," because, as the claims go, *only* God can "forgive sin," and thus, for any individual to have done so would constitute a proclamation by one that they were God themselves, which they believe was a form of "blasphemy." Marcus Borg and John Dominic Crossan, for example, are quite in error when they state,[79] "John's baptism was for the 'forgiveness of sins.' But the forgiveness was a function that Temple theology claimed for itself, mediated by sacrifice in the Temple. For John to proclaim forgiveness apart from the Temple was to deny the Temple's role as the essential mediator of forgiveness and access to God." But this simply is not true at all and shows a lack of knowledge and understanding from scholars the caliber of Borg and Crossan in regards to the *miqvah*, which *did not* need to occur at the Temple. For as we know from the Dead Sea Scrolls the Essens believed that ritual immersion in a *miqvah* accompanied by genuine repentance constituted "forgiveness of sins." So certainly no scholar will attempt to claim that the entire philosophy of the Essens was "blasphemous," and thus, they were all destined to be put to death simply as a result of their interpreted beliefs![80] Furthermore, Borg and Crossan seem to ignore not only 2 Samuel 12:13, but also the *Prayer of Nabonidus* in the Dead Sea

---

79   *The Last Week*, Marcus Borg and John Dominic Crossan, p. 21; but see also the erroneous comments in *The Partings of the Ways*, James Dunn, pp. 45-46; *Mark*, Robert H. Gundry, pp. 110-123.

80   See the comments on this in *Jesus*, David Flusser, p. 28.

Scroll *4QNab* 1-5.[81] Borg and Crossan[82] go on to note Mark 2:7 and the claim of "blasphemy" leveled against Jesus for healing and referring to it as "forgiveness of sin" apart from the Temple. Now, Rudolf Bultmann believed that this matter is just a reflection of the later Church belief that only the Church had the right to "forgive sins."[83] But as was discussed in Chapter 1 and will be further shown here, this is hardly accurate either! For healing individuals *was not* forbidden under Jewish law and at the time of Jesus. "ailments," and "diseases" were considered to be something that came about in an individual's life as a result of some "sin" or "transgression" committed by that individual.[84] Therefore, to heal someone, was in essence, the "forgiving the individual of their sins," and thus, *not* a "blasphemous" act in other words. But Jesus himself even instructs individuals to go to the Temple and offer a sacrifice (Matthew 5:23; 8:4; Mark 1:44;[85] Luke 5:14 for example), which directly refutes Borg's and Crossan's claims. The fact is though, as is clearly stated in Jewish law, Talmud Babli, *Sanhedrin* 98a.5; 98b.39, "The diseases that the people ought to have suffered because of their sins are borne instead by the Messiah." This interpretation in Jewish law was based not only on Leviticus 13, but also on Isaiah 53:4. As Moshe Chaim Luzzatto writes,[86] "As a result of this principle, suffering and pain may be imposed on a *tzaddik* (righteous person) as atonement for his entire generation. The *tzaddik* must then accept this suffering with love for the benefit of his generation, just as he accepts suffering imposed upon him for his own sake. In doing so, he benefits his generation by atoning for it, and at the same time is himself elevated to a very great degree. For a *tzaddik* such as this is made into one of the leaders in the Community

---

81 See the comments on this in *Who Did Jesus Think He Was*, J. C. O'Neill, p. 151.

82 But see also the similar erroneous comments in *Jesus and His Adversaries*, Arland J. Hultgren, pp. 106-109.

83 See *The History of the Synoptic Tradition*, Rudolf Bultmann, pp. 15-16.

84 For more on this matter see the comments in *On Earth As It Is In Heaven*, D. C. Thielmann, pp. 292-293 and pp. 938-944 and the corresponding scholars notations to these pages.

85 See the erroneous comments and conclusions of this verse from Mark's Gospel in *The Theological Significance of Jesus' Temple Action in Mark's Gospel*, Emilio G. Chavez, pp. 35-40.

86 *The Way of God*, Moshe Chaim Luzzatto, p. 123; but see also the comments in *Judaism and the Origins of Christianity*, David Flusser, pp. 535-542.

of the Future World, as discussed earlier. Such suffering also includes cases where a *tzaddik* suffers because his entire generation deserves great punishments, bordering on annihilation, but is spared via the *tzaddik's* suffering. In atoning for his generation through his suffering, this *tzaddik* saves these people in this world and also greatly benefits them in the World-to-Come."[87] Therefore, claiming to be *THE* "Messiah" in order to bear the sins of others, *and* having the authority to forgive sins as a result *was not* a violation of *any* Jewish law, or in other words, this *would not* have constituted "blasphemy."[88] One can also find it being stated in Jewish law, *Berakhot* 5a, "Sufferings wash away the sins of man,"[89] but one should also see what is stated in *Nedarim* 41a; *Sanhedrin* 98a, and furthermore, the Essens as well held strongly to such similar interpretations as these as noted by Josephus, *Jewish Wars* 2.8.8 [144].[90] This *fact* is further confirmed by what is found being stated in *1 Maccabees* 6:26; 17:20-22. Now, there are some apologetic scholars who will attempt to utilize Isaiah 53:10-12[91] as a basis for their claims despite the noted points here that this was in no way a form of "blasphemy," which in all reality is a huge mistake for their desired intent, for by attempting to utilize these verses from Isaiah they actually only end up providing further *proof* that Jesus was an "insurrectionist" against Roman oppression![92]

In Chapter 5 was mentioned the "false witnesses," or difficulty in finding any "witnesses" to testify against Jesus at a supposed trial before the Great Sanhedrin. There have been some scholars who have put forth nonsensical claims that these "false witnesses" were "pre-arranged" by the Great Sanhedrin in order to force Jesus to admit to a claim of being *THE*

---

87 See further in *The Way of God*, Moshe Chaim Luzzatto, and all of the Mishnaic, Talmudic, and other Rabbinic sources he references in n. 33, pp. 413-414, and n. 35, p. 414; *Paul and Rabbinic Judaism*, W. D. Davies, pp. 270-273.

88 See the comments on this in *Studies in the History of the Sanhedrin*, Hugo Mantel, p. 269.

89 See *Studies in the History of the Sanhedrin*, Hugo Mantel, n. 117, p. 269.

90 See the comments in *Studies in the History of the Sanhedrin*, Hugo Mantel, n. 118, p. 269.

91 See for example *The Theological Significance of Jesus' Temple Action in Mark's Gospel*, Emilio G. Chavez, p. 28.

92 See the comments on this in *On Earth As It Is In Heaven*, D. C. Thielmann, n. 107, pp. 552-560.

"Messiah," or "Christ." Fritz Kunkel writes concerning this,[93] "Matthew, however, calls him Christ instead of Messiah. The two words have the same meaning, 'the anointed one,' but their historical implications are as different as night and day," (Kunkel is referring here to Matthew 1:1).[94] But as is being proven here in this chapter, a claim of being *THE* "Messiah" *was not* "blasphemy" nor was it a violation of *any* Jewish law.[95] There were many claimants to being the "Messiah" before, during, and even after the time of Jesus. Yet, *none* of these other claimants were ever charged with "blasphemy" or any other violation of Jewish law![96] At worst, Jesus would have been asked to produce his "credentials" for claiming to be *THE* "Messiah" just as all of the other claimants were asked. This is *precisely* what we find in the Gospel accounts occurring, which have so often, and so wrongly been interpreted as "confrontations with the Pharisees," (a matter already noted in Chapter 4 concerning Jesus' being "tested"). Now, John J. Collins points out an essential matter to understand in regards to why a claim to be *THE* "Messiah" *was not* "blasphemous" when he writes,[97] "There is also the perennial problem of terminology. The word *moshiah* – messiah – can refer to prophets and priests as well as to kings, and to figures from the past as well as the future." But virtually all of these individuals who were would be messianic claimants, including Jesus; either had, or believed that they had undergone what was termed a *bat qol.*[98]

---

93   *Creation Continues*, Fritz Kunkel, p. 22.

94   See further comments on this in *Creation Continues*, Fritz Kunkel, p.291; *Pontius Pilate*, Ann Wroe, p. 331.

95   J. C. O'Neill is quite in error in *Who Did Jesus Think He Was*, pp. 48-49 when he asserts that anyone claiming to be *THE* "Messiah" was committing "blasphemy."

96   See the comments in *Kosher Jesus*, Rabbi Shmuley Boteach, p. 101; *Jesus On Trial*, Gerard S. Sloyan, p. 46.

97   *The Scepter and the Star*, John J. Collins, p. 56.

98   For more on this term *bat qol* see the comments in *On Earth As It Is In Heaven*, D. C. Thielmann, p. 174; *The Misunderstood Jew*, Amy-Jill Levine, p. 204; *Prophecy in Early Christianity*, David E. Aune, p. 104; *Jesus: Uncovering the Life, Teachings, and Relevance of a Religious Revolutionary*, Marcus Borg, p. 121; *The Life and Teachings of Hillel*, Yitzhak Buxbaum, pp. 248-249. In *Who is Jesus*, Darrell L. Bock, pp. 36-38, even though he never actually uses this term *bat qol*, he describes it precisely and does so in such a way as if Bock is totally unaware of this Jewish term and its usage in Jewish history.

This now brings us to the terms, "son of God," and "son of man" and whether or not the use of either of these terms constituted "blasphemy." The very first thing that needs to be noted in regards to these two terms concerns the matter of the idioms of the Hebrew word that gets generally translated into English as, "son." For while the Hebrew word does offer such a possible translation as "son," this word also offers such possible meanings as, "a male offspring," "descendant," "citizen," "member," and even "disciple."[99] Furthermore, many scholars also simply do not understand the idioms surrounding the Jewish terms, "the Blessed One," or "Blessed be He,"[100] which in Jewish liturgy were used as a substitute for the Tetragrammaton. Thus, the very question found in Mark 14:61, for example, is in all reality the *exact* same as if the question were asked, "Are you the son of YHWH?"

Now, amongst the gentile nations, referring to one's king, or prince, or even the Emperor of Rome, (i.e. Caesar) as the "son of god" was commonplace.[101] In regards to this *fact*, Joseph Ratzinger and Pope Benedict XVI point out[102] that the Greek word *euaggelion*, which is generally translated as "good news," (i.e. the "Gospels"), is thus, exactly why the Gospel authors were referred to as, "evangelists." But, this was also a term used by the Roman Emperors under the Latin word *evangelium*, and both the Greek word and the Latin word correspond to the Hebrew term

---

99 See the comments in *Understanding the Difficult Words of Jesus*, David Bivin and Roy Blizzard, p. 53.

100 See for an example *Messiah and Temple*, Donald Juel, pp.78-80 even though he notes in n. 5, p. 78, 1 Enoch 77:1; Mishnah *Berakhot* 7:3; Yerushalmi *Berakhot* 7:11c; Babli *Berakhot* 50a all of which are *clear* examples of these terms being used as substitutes for the Tetragrammaton.

101 See the comments in *On Earth As It Is In Heaven*, D. C. Thielmann. P. 171 and the corresponding scholar's notes to this page; *How Jesus Became God*, Bart D. Ehrman, pp. 12-17, 49, and 53; *The Last Week*, Marcus Borg and John Dominic Crossan, p. 3; *"Caught in the Act,"* Roger David Aus, pp. 117-126; *Jesus of Nazareth: Part One*, Ratzinger and Pope Benedict, pp. 335-339; *The Son of God in the Roman World*, Michael Peppard, pp. 31-49; *The Historical Jesus in Context*, Levine, Allison Jr., Crossan, p. 26 and pp.42-44 where they note ancient artifacts and coins that contain this phrase in Latin.

102 See the comments in *Jesus of Nazareth: Part One*, Ratzinger and Pope Benedict, pp. 46-47.

besura toba.[103] The difference between these two – the "Gospel" authors and the Roman Emperors – is why Joseph Ratzinger and Pope Benedict XVI point out that this translation of "good news" actually "falls short" of its *true* meaning. For the Roman Emperor's *evangelium*[104] was not *always* "cheerful and pleasant," but nonetheless, it was intended to serve as "a saving message." The point being made here is to demonstrate the further intent of the Gospel authors to try and contrast the Roman Emperor being called the "son of god" with Jesus' likewise being referred to as the "son of God."[105] As some scholars point out,[106] "It is clear that the Greek sense of a 'divine being,' differing in substance from common mortals influenced the Christian use of the title even before the end of the first century: the infancy narratives, and particularly that of Luke, confirm this." But Robert Gundry rightly points out that the usage of this term "son of God," (at least in Mark's Gospel), "does not necessarily imply Divinity, much less preexistence in Heaven."[107] Now, Donald Juel is quite in error when he writes,[108] "But the title 'son of God' is rarely used as a messianic designation in extant Jewish literature...." Juel is in error for the simple reason that in ancient Israel, the Davidic king or "Messiah" was referred to as the "son of God" repeatedly in Scripture, the Apocryphal and Pseudepigraphic

---

103   See the comments in *A Jewish Understanding of the New Testament*, Samuel Sandmel, p. 4; *Mark the Evangelist*, Willi Marxsen, pp. 136-137.

104   It is necessary to note here that in, *What are the Gospels*, Richard A. Burridge, pp. 192-195, Burridge tries to use this Greek word *euaggelion* to claim that the Gospels are "biographies." But as pointed out in the Preface, and by what is being pointed out here in regards to this Greek word, it simply makes it *impossible* for one to refer to the Gospels as "biographies."

105   See also the comments in *Matthew and Empire*, Warren Carter, pp. 57-74 for a much broader comparison of how the Roman Emperor was portrayed in regards to how Jesus is portrayed in like manner, primarily in Matthew's Gospel, with Jesus being the "Heavenly" opposite to the "earthly" Emperor.

106   See for example *Jesus and His Contemporaries*, Etienne Trocme, p. 61.

107   *Mark*, Robert H. Gundry, p. 34.

108   *Messiah and Temple*, Donald Juel, p. 78, yet on p. 82 Juel admits that the usage of this term *must be* "clearly a part of the royal ideology."

writings, as well as the Dead Sea Scrolls.[109] *The Psalms of Solomon* 18:4 is a prime example of this *fact*.[110] Scriptural verses that can *clearly* be cited as examples are 2 Samuel 7:14; 1 Chronicles 17:13. As John J. Collins writes,[111] "The king becomes the son of God by adoption but the paternity of the human father is also essential to the ideology. Nonetheless, the oracle reflects the common assumption throughout the Near East that the king enjoys special status in the divine world… While the king was not to be confused with the Almighty, he was evidently exalted above the common rank of humanity."[112] But under Jewish understandings and interpretations of Scripture at the time of Jesus, it was believed that it was God Himself who would be the one who would announce who His "anointed Messiah" (i.e. son of God") would be. This seems though, to be precisely what John 10:36 is indicating! Therefore, to some at the time of Jesus, any *self-proclamation* as being *THE* "Messiah," "son of God" prior to any such pronouncement of such by God could have constituted a charge of "blasphemy." But again, as noted above already, such was not a form of "blasphemy" that would have been punishable by death. Therefore, while Luke 22:69; Mark 14:62; Matthew 22:64; Acts 7:55 could all be seen by some as a basis for a claim that Jesus was charged with "blasphemy" at a *supposed* trial before the Great Sanhedrin, *The Psalms of Solomon* 17:22, which is echoed in Matthew 11:25-27; Luke 10:21-22 eliminates this possibility from actually being historically true.[113] Furthermore, as Hyam

---

109   See *A Wandering Aramean*, Joseph A. Fitzmyer, pp. 91-94 and 102-107 concerning the usage of "son of God" in the Dead Sea Scrolls.

110   See the comments in *The Jewish Messiah*, James Drummond, p. 142; *The Scepter and the Star*, John J. Collins, pp. 163-169; *Messiah and Temple*, Donald Juel, pp. 108-114; *The Parable of the Wicked Tenants*, Klyne Snodgrass, pp. 85-87, 98, and 107.

111   *The Scepter and the Star*, John J. Collins, pp. 22-23.

112   *The Scepter and the Star*, John J. Collins, n. 19, p. 42, "see further the classic account of Israelite kingship in its ancient Near Eastern context by Mowinckel, *He That Cometh*, pp. 21-95 and *The Psalms in Israel's Worship*, pp. 50-60; *King and Messiah: The Civil and Sacral Legitimation of the Israelite Kings*, pp. 254-293."

113   See the comments in *The Trial of Jesus: Cambridge Studies in Honour of C. F. D. Moule*, pp. 74-77; *Jesus Interrupted*, Bart D. Ehrman, p. 140.

Maccoby points out,[114] "It used to be thought that the Gnostic sects, of which there were many, were all heresies derived from Christianity, but it seems probable that Gnostic sects existed before Christianity began, and it may be closer to the facts to explain Christianity in terms of Gnosticism than reverse. In Gnosticism there was a Savior (in Greek, 'Soter') who was one of a Trinity of divine beings. This Savior was also called the 'son of God'." The fact that adds weight to Maccoby's statement is found in the very "gnostic" style teachings that one sees in Ephesians 5:14; 2 Corinthians 5:16; John 1:14; John 1:1-5; John 1:9-12; John 6:53; Philippians 2:6-8; Colossians 1:15-20; 2:13-15; 1 Corinthians 15:12; 15:50; Romans 6:3; 2 Timothy 2:18.

God can elevate *any* individual at *any time* to be called "His son," which was something that was even a common understanding in the pagan gentile world, especially in regards to the Romans.[115] In fact, God can even elevate an entire nation or even an entire race of people to be called "His sons," or "His children,"[116] (Exodus 4:22; Deuteronomy 14:1, for example). The *best* interpreted reading of Matthew 5:9 clearly states this fact. As Fritz Kunkel writes,[117] "The Greek says clearly, 'They will be ranked sons of God.' Moffatt's translation is correct. The Authorized Version, in order to preserve the title 'Son of God' for Jesus alone, says, 'They shall be called the children of God,' which is not quite fair to Matthew's text. This problem unfolds its depths throughout the Gospel." But what if someone elevated or "exalted" one's self? Did such constitute a form of "blasphemy" punishable by death? Some scholars believe that such does, referencing

---

114 See *Revolution in Judaea*, Hyam Maccoby, pp. 88 and 97; but see also the comments in *Gnosis*, Kurt Rudolph, pp. 84-106, 118-134, 139, 141, 144, 147, 189-191, 209, 276-282, 291-294, 298-308.

115 See the comments on this in *The Son of God in the Roman World*, Michael Peppard, pp. 70-73, 105-112.

116 See the comments in *Jesus Interrupted*, Bart D. Ehrman, pp. 245-249; *Blasphemy and Exaltation in Judaism*, Darrell L. Bock, p. 183; *The Jews and the Gospel*, Gregory Baum, p. 177; *The Scepter and the Star*, John J. Collins, pp. 160-161; *On Earth As It Is In Heaven*, D. C. Thielmann, pp. 924-925 and the corresponding scholar's notations to these pages.

117 See *Creation Continues*, Fritz Kunkel, p. 67. See also the comments on this in *Jesus of Nazareth: Part One*, Ratzinger and Pope Benedict, p. 85.

Numbers 16:30 as a proof text.[118] But this simply is not true whatsoever, for this was *precisely* what got Moses into trouble with God, which instead of constituting a sentence of death it only resulted in the prevention of Moses from being allowed to enter the "Promised Land."[119] As Moshe Chaim Luzzatto points out,[120] "A prophet does not attain this highest level all at once. He must elevate himself, step by step until he actually attains full prophecy. Prophecy therefore requires a course of apprenticeship, just as in the case of other disciples and crafts, where one must advance step by step until he masters them thoroughly. This explains what Scripture means when it speaks of the 'sons of the prophets'."[121] Although a prophet "must elevate himself," as Luzzatto states, it was also taught that he *must* remain humble as well, (Babli *Pesaḥim* 66b), and it was further taught by both Shammai (*Abot* 1:10) and Hillel (*Abot* 1:13) that he *must not* ever exalt himself. Jesus even taught on this very matter, as noted in Matthew 23:12, which is a direct reflection of Hillel's teaching found in *Abot* 2:6, which states, "My humiliation is my exaltation; my exaltation is my humiliation."[122] This teaching of Hillel was further elaborated on in *Eruvin* 13b, which states, "This teaches us that whoever lowers himself, the Holy One, blessed be He, exalts, and whoever exalts himself, the Holy One, blessed be He, lowers."[123]

There is another important verse from the New Testament that needs to be mentioned here, and this being, John 1:18. The necessity in mentioning this verse derives from how Joseph Ratzinger and Pope Benedict XVI have chosen to interpret this verse.[124] They have quite erroneously translated this verse out as stating, "No one has ever seen God; it is the only Son, who is nearest to the Father's heart, who has made him known." But the *fact* of

---

118   See for example the comments in *Blasphemy and Exaltation in Judaism*, Darrell L. Bock, p. 41.

119   See the comments regarding this fact in *On Earth As It Is In Heaven*, D. C. Thielmann, pp. 923-924.

120   *The Way of God*, Moshe Chaim Luzzatto, p. 221.

121   *The Way of God*, Moshe Chaim Luzzatto, n. 41, p. 424 referencing 1 Kings 20:35; 2 Kings 2:3; 2:5; 2:7; 2:15; 4:1; 4:38; 5:22; 6:1; 9:1.

122   See the comments on this in *The Life and Teachings of Hillel*, Yitzhak Buxbaum, p. 178.

123   See the comments on this in *The Life and Teachings of Hillel*, Yitzhak Buxbaum, p. 212.

124   See *Jesus of Nazareth: Part One*, Ratzinger and Pope Benedict, p. 6.

the matter is that they fail to point out that the portion of this verse that they translate as stating, "It is the only Son," is in reality a very late addition that was made to the text by some unknown redactor. So, in essence, all this verse actually stated *before* this later redacting was, "*No one has ever seen God*," which would then include even Jesus himself.

This now brings us to Jesus' reference to God as *Abba* in his prayer recorded in Mark 14:33-36. Did such constitute Jesus elevating himself to being God's *only* "son," or "Messiah"? The fact is that it *did not* in any way whatsoever, nor was this usage of *Abba* a form of "blasphemy."[125] Many scholars have made very erroneous claims in regards to the usage of the term *Abba*.[126] As a prime example, Mary Rose D'Angelo in a chapter titled, "*Abba* and Father: Imperial Theology in the Contexts of Jesus and the Gospels,"[127] writes in regards to Mark 14:33-36 that, "In fact, the evidence that the word *abba* was important to or even used by Jesus is, at best, extremely slender. This word occurs only once in the Gospels, in a scene for which the evangelist provides no witnesses (Mark 14:35-36) … The scene reflects the theology of the evangelist, writing sometime between the late 60's and early 80's (probably after the fall of Jerusalem in 70) rather than a historical event." Why does she believe that Jesus' possible usage of this term is "at best, extremely slender"? For the fact is that the term *abba* was very often used as an address of respect, especially in regards to a "learned teacher" or "rabbi."[128] But, D'Angelo goes on to claim[129] that, "Rabbinic Literature is significantly later than the career of Jesus and the New Testament and cannot be used as direct evidence for the Judaism of the earlier period." This is not only a highly biased statement; it simply demonstrates a lack of genuine understanding of "Rabbinic Literature," (as was pointed out and discussed in Chapter 5 regarding scholars who claim that the Mishnah and Talmud cannot be used in order to get an accurate understanding of the trial of Jesus). Likewise, Darrell L. Bock

---

125   See the comments in *The Last Week*, Marcus Borg and John Dominic Crossan, p. 123.

126   See the comments in *Jesus of Nazareth: Part One*, Ratzinger and Pope Benedict, p. 344 and *Jesus of Nazareth: Part Two*, Ratzinger and Pope Benedict, pp. 161-162; *Jesus*, C. Leslie Mitton, pp. 140-141 for example.

127   See *The Historical Jesus in Context*, Levine, Allison Jr., and Crossan, p. 64.

128   See the comments in *Jesus*, David Flusser, p. 20.

129   See *The Historical Jesus in Context*, Levine, Allison Jr., and Crossan, pp. 70-71.

writes,[130] "*Second, coherence* would apply, as almost all scholars accept that Jesus spoke of God as his Father in a way unprecedented for Judaism (Mark 14:36 = Matthew 26:39 = Luke 22:42; Matthew 11:25-27 = Luke 10:21-22)." Bock's claim, (as well as his referencing the fact regarding "almost all scholars"), that Jesus' referencing of God as Father was somehow "unprecedented," (i.e. "unique"), is simply *untrue* "historically!" Bock's statement, as with the claims by so many other *Christian New Testament scholars*, once again simply demonstrates how many of these Christian New Testament scholars have failed to do enough homework into Jewish studies! As Dale Allison rightly points out,[131] "I remember W. D. Davies once advising me never to use the word *unique* in connection with Jesus. His reason was very simple: How can we claim anything to be without parallel when so little is known about antiquity. The recent publication of old Palestinian prayer texts which address God as 'my Father' (4Q372 and 4Q460) has vindicated the wisdom of his warning... Joachim Jeremias's confident and influential conclusions about Jesus' use of *abba*, conclusions built upon a claim to distinctiveness, have been discredited." Also, there is the simple fact and "historical" truth found stated in the Talmud Babli, *Ta'anit* 23a that Honi the Circle Maker quite often referred to God as *Abba*, "Father," which is an *essential* point in this regard especially when his usage was *never* considered as "blasphemous," or as elevating one's self to being God's "*only* son."[132] Philo, *On the Birth of Abel and the Sacrifices Offered by Him and His Brother* 18.68; Josephus, *Antiquities* 2.6.8; 4.8.24; *Tobit* 13:4; *Wisdom of ben Sirach* 26:1 and 51:10, for just a few examples, all attest to the fact that referring to God as *Abba* long before, during, and even after the time of Jesus was quite common amongst Jews.[133] As Etienne Trocme writes,[134] "There are too many indications of Jesus' certainty of being the 'son of God' in the Jewish sense, beginning with his use in prayer of 'Father' in the familiar form *abba*, for it to be possible to dismiss this idea in his case." Notice the fact that Trocme rightly states "*familiar form*" of "*abba*"! But what really proves that D'Angelo's and Bock's claims are erroneous is

---

130 *Who is Jesus*, Darrell L. Bock, p. 37.

131 *Jesus of Nazareth*, Dale C. Allison, p. 5.

132 See the comments in *The Parable of the Wicked Tenants*, Klyne Snodgrass, pp. 82-84.

133 See the comments on this of Kaufmann Kohler, "Abba," *Jewish Encyclopedia*.

134 *Jesus and His Contemporaries*, Etienne Trocme, p. 62.

what can be found in Malachi 2:10; Psalm 89:27 (89:26 in most Christian translations); Jeremiah 31:8; Isaiah 64:7; Isaiah 63:16; Deuteronomy 32:6; 1 Chronicles 29:10; Jeremiah 3:19; Malachi 1:6; Proverbs 3:12; Psalm 103:13, for each of these verses are *all* examples which *prove* that God has been called "Father" by *many Jews*, (and at times "privately" called "Father" *without any witnesses*), throughout *all* of Jewish history! For the Hebrew words *ab, abi,* and the Aramaic *abba,* as well as the Arabic *abu* all mean, "father" and were *all* used at times to refer to God. Thus, *any* individual Jew respectfully using *Ab, Abi,* or *Abba* in reference to God *would not* be out of place, "unique," "unusual," or even "blasphemous"! But Romans 8:15 and Galatians 4:6-7 alone should suffice as *proof* of this *fact* for *any* and *every* scholar!

It is therefore, essential to point out here now, that Josephus, in *Jewish Wars* 5.6.3 states that during the retaking of Jerusalem by the Romans in the 66-73 revolt, the Romans used white stones in their catapults that had the very mocking words written on them, "the son cometh."[135] This is a very important matter to note for the simple fact that this demonstrates that the term "son of God" was so widely used and accepted as a "messianic" term, that even the Romans were aware of its usage, and thus, it could hardly have been construed as being "blasphemous" because of its widely known usage.[136] Now, Joel Carmichael does an excellent job of demonstrating how the Jewish understanding of the term "son of God," became distorted into the pagan Christian concept of this term, and it is this pagan Christian concept, which in all reality *could* quite possibly be construed as being "blasphemous."[137] Also, as James Dunn rightly states,[138] "At the time of Jesus, in Jewish thinking of the early first century, 'son of God' was not a specific title or description." Dunn further points out that this term "son of God" was used collectively about the people of Israel as a whole, in regards to a "heavenly council," *or* in regards to a "singular king," but going beyond Dunn's references, there were even times that the term "son of God" was

---

135   See the comments in *On Earth As It Is In Heaven,* D. C. Thielmann, p. 172; *The Parable of the Wicked Tenants,* Klyne Snodgrass, pp. 115-116.

136   See the comments on the *fact* that the term "son of God" was not "blasphemous" in *The Scepter and the Star,* John J. Collins, pp. 154-172; *Jesus and Israel,* Jules Isaac, pp. 142-144.

137   See the comments on this matter in *The Death of Jesus,* Joel Carmichael, pp. 252-256.

138   *The Partings of the Ways,* James Dunn, p. 170.

used for a very "pious" individual as noted in the Mishnah *Abot* 3:14; Yerushalmi *Qiddushin* 1:7. Dunn then further rightly points out that the term "son of God" was used to denote someone "commissioned by God" for a specific purpose.[139]

But again, as noted already above, the consensus scholarly opinion holds that Jesus went clearly out of his way to avoid referring to himself as the "son of God," opting instead for the term, "son of man,"[140] which while many scholars do not believe that this title was widely recognized or used by many people at the time of Jesus as a messianic reference, the historical fact is though, that this term *was* used as a messianic reference as can even be found in the Talmud Babli *Hagigah* 14a; *Sanhedrin* 38b.[141] This goes back to what was pointed out in Chapter 2 about the concept that some Jews at the time of Jesus had in regards to the "preexistence" of *THE* "Messiah" as well as what was pointed out in Chapter 4 about how the Jews borrowed terms, words, and concepts from their neighbor pagan nations and used these terms, words, and concepts *metaphorically* as teaching lessons. For this concept of the "son of man" being a "preexisting messiah," or "savior of the world" was historically originally an ancient Babylonian, Assyrian, and Tyrean concept from which the Jews borrowed from even before their Babylonian captivity,[142] which serves as the *proof* that by the time of Jesus the term "son of man" was known to be a "messianic" title! Now, it is true that some scholars believe that Jesus *did not* use this title, "son of man," as a reference to himself, but instead, Jesus used this title as a reference to some *future coming* "son of man."[143] But this term, "son of man," merely referred to a "mere mortal human being" and *not* to someone being a "deified being."[144] At the time of Jesus there were in fact

139 *The Partings of the Ways*, James Dunn, p. 171.

140 See the comments in *On Earth As It Is In Heaven*, D. C. Thielmann, p. 174.

141 See the comments on this in *Who Did Jesus Think He Was*, J. C. O'Neill, p. 123.

142 See the comments on this in *The Son of Man in Myth and History*, Frederick Borsch, pp. 89-113, 143-145, 151-156, 167-231.

143 See for example *Prophecy in Early Christianity*, David E. Aune, pp. 181-184.

144 On a minor point to note, Darrell Bock in, *Blasphemy and Exaltation in Judaism*, p. 225 states that the term "son of man" is used 82 times in the New Testament, but in the all-important comments to understand on the whole matter of the usage of "son of man" by Emil G. Hirsch, "Son of Man," *Jewish Encyclopedia* states that the term is used only 81

three different Hebrew terms used for the English term, "son of man" – *ben-adam* or *ha-adam*, *ben-ish*, and *ben-anosh*, and one Aramaic term *bar-nasha* or *bar-nosh*. Numbers 23:19 is the first place in Scripture in which this term "son of man" is found being used. This term in Jewish history was used most often to distinguish between different human beings as it can be found being used, for example, in Job 16:18-21; 25:1-6; 35:6-8; Psalm 8:5-6; 80:15-19; 144:3-4; 146:1-4; Isaiah 51:11-13; 56:1-2.[145] Yet, Ezekiel uses this term 94 times as a personal pronoun. In essence, Ezekiel used the term as a *title* "*I*," or in other words, precisely the same way in which Jesus most often used this term![146] Therefore, Bart Ehrman is quite in error when he claims that the term "son of man" had connotations of being someone "divine."[147] This goes back to what was pointed out in Chapter 4, and also noted again at the beginning of this chapter about how far too many Christian, (or "agnostic") New Testament scholars simply *do not* understand Jewish "metaphoric" terminology! But Ehrman *is* partially correct in stating that Jesus *did not* commit "blasphemy" by anything he said or did, yet Ehrman is in error in interpreting that Jesus was somehow claiming to be "divine" by his use of the term "son of man," and therefore, Jesus *was* "blasphemous."[148] Mark 8:38 though, seems to clearly differentiate Jesus from being the *coming* "son of man."[149]

There have been though, many scholars who have tried to claim that this term "'son of man' was not *used as a title* at the time of Jesus,"[150] or any

---

times in the New Testament; but on the particular matter prompting this notation see the comments in, *A Wandering Aramean*, Joseph A. Fitzmyer, pp. 143-155; *Jewish Literature Between the Bible and the Mishnah*, George W. E. Nickelsburg, p. 215; *On Earth As It Is In Heaven*, D. C. Thielmann, n. 38, pp. 209-210.

145 See the comments on this in *The Son of Man in Myth and History*, Frederick Borsch, pp. 22-32.

146 See the comments on this in *The Son of Man in Myth and History*, Frederick Borsch, p. 35.

147 See *The New Testament*, Bart D. Ehrman, Box 5.5, p. 77, and his erroneous comments and understandings of Jewish "metaphor" on pp. 265-269.

148 See the comments in *The New Testament*, Bart D. Ehrman, Box 5.6, p. 79.

149 See the comments in *The Lost Gospel of Judas Iscariot*, Bart D. Ehrman, pp. 144-148 and n. 2, p. 187.

150 See for example the comments in *Jesus of Nazareth: Part One*, Ratzinger and Pope Benedict, pp. 321-335; *No Stone on Another*, Lloyd Gaston, pp. 374-375; *A Wandering*

other time in Jewish history, especially in regards to it being a "Messianic" sort of title for an individual. But the *fact* is that Psalm 80:15-20, as well as Acts 7:56,[151] puts the error to such claims by demonstrating that this phrase *had*, at times, such an intended usage even *if* it might be true that those times were rare in Jewish history, and this also demonstrates that it was in use *long before the time of Jesus*. Now, Jules Isaac points out that in the majority of the Hebrew Scriptures the term "son of man" had nothing to do with any Messianic claim, but that by the time of Jesus the usage of the term had developed into a quite common "Messianic" term and claim.[152] Yet once again though, we find that some of the very scholars, who make the claims that the term "son of man" had no "Messianic" connotations, turn right around and contradict themselves. As an example of this *fact*, Joseph Ratzinger and Pope Benedict XVI, while making such a claim then freely admit that one finds a "hint of it in the Book of Daniel's vision," and they also admit that the "Messianic hope" usages of this term are also found in *4 Ezra*, and the Ethiopian Book of Enoch. Such contradictory conclusions by scholars are not only illogical, but they are also difficult to understand in regards to how such scholars arrive at their conclusions, and even more so, one finds that these scholars even have difficulty trying to explain *how* they arrived at their conclusions. Now, some scholars doubt that the *Similitudes* section of the Book of Enoch, which contains the references to the "son of man," even existed at the time of Jesus, and the primary reason for such claims by these scholars is based on the lack of finding them included in the Dead Sea Scrolls copies of the Book of Enoch.[153] Still other scholars

---

Aramean, Joseph A. Fitzmyer, pp. 153-155.

151   See the comments on Acts 7:56 and this matter in *The Partings of the Ways*, James Dunn, p. 171.

152   See the comments on this in *Jesus and Israel*, Jules Isaac, pp. 144-148; Joseph Jacobs and Moses Buttenweiser, "Messiah: The Heavenly Messiah: In Rabbinic Literature," *Jewish Encyclopedia*; *One God One Lord*, Larry W. Hurtado, p. 12, and n. 37, p. 135; *Jesus Son of Man*, B. Lindars, pp. 1-16; *Son of Man*, M. Casey; *Who Did Jesus Think He Was*, J. C. O'Neill, pp. 122-132; *Jews, Greeks and Christians*, (Edited by Robert Hammerton-Kelly and Robin Scroggs), Matthew Black commenting, pp. 51-73; *Prophecy in Early Christianity*, David E. Aune, pp. 123-124; *The Apocalyptic Imagination*, John J. Collins, pp. 147-154, 209-210; *Paul and Rabbinic Judaism*, W. D. Davies, pp. 159-160.

153   See for example *Conflict, Holiness & Politics*, Marcus Borg, pp. 223-227.

though, while admitting that the *Similitudes* section of the Book of Enoch was an addition to the *original* form of the Book of Enoch, they will still date this addition to sometime between the first century BCE and the early first century CE.[154] But what might be the greatest surprise of all is the fact that these scholars fail to even try to explain the usages of this term "son of man" as a Messianic title that are found in some of the *other* Dead Sea Scrolls.[155] Andres A. Tejada-Lalinde has done an excellent job proving that this term *was in fact* a known "Messianic" title and claim at the time of Jesus.[156] Daniel 7:9[157] and Daniel 7:13 were discussed in Chapter 2, but it is essential to discuss these verses further here by making the point that by the time of Jesus the term "son of man" had been "reinterpreted" and came to be understood by some Jews, (and especially Jews from one particular first century Jewish philosophy, namely, the Essens), to be a "Messianic" term and claim, and some scholars reference Revelation 13 as proof of this fact.[158] As John J. Collins rightly states in regards to this *fact*,[159] "It is natural enough, then, to infer that the figure on the clouds is the king of a restored Jewish Kingdom."[160] Now it is true though, that still other scholars interpret this as indicating a "restored Israel."[161]

---

154   See for example *The Old Testament Pseudepigrapha and the New Testament*, James H. Charlesworth, p. 89; *Paul and Rabbinic Judaism*, W. D. Davies, pp. 278-283; *The Son of Man in Myth and History*, Frederick Borsch, pp. 145-148.

155   See the comments in *The Son of Man in Myth and History*, Frederick Borsch, pp. 219-223.

156   See Andres A. Tejada-Lalinde, "Jesus as the Son of Man in Mark," *Florida International University Electronic Theses and Dissertations*, (3-24-2014), pp. 11-18; and see also the comments in *Matthew and Empire*, Warren Carter, p. 68; *The Scepter and the Star*, John J. Collins, p. 12; *One God One Lord*, Larry W. Hurtado, pp. 53-54; and see the entirety of *The Son of Man in Myth and History*, Frederick Borsch.

157   See the comments on this verse in *The Way of God*, Moshe Chaim Luzzatto, p. 155.

158   See the comments in *Jewish Literature Between the Bible and the Mishnah*, George W. E. Nickelsburg, pp. 212, 216-217, 222-223, 292.

159   *The Scepter and the Star*, John J. Collins, pp. 36 and 173-194.

160   *The Scepter and the Star*, John J. Collins, n. 92, p. 46, Paul Mosca, "Ugarit and Daniel 7: A Missing Link," *Biblica* 67, (1986), pp. 496-517 and Collins further comments on pp. 142-143.

161   See for example *The New Testament and the People of God*, N. T. Wright, pp. 291-297 and 319.

This then brings us to another all-important matter to mention in regards to the Gospel accounts of a trial of Jesus before the Great Sanhedrin which resulted in a conviction for "blasphemy," and this being, the account of the High Priest "rending his garments." Now, Donald Juel is quite in error when he writes,[162] "... Mark's description of the response to blasphemy in 14:63 indicates his knowledge of at least certain aspects of Jewish legal practice." So, let me now point out what makes this statement by Juel so erroneous. The first thing to be pointed out in regards to this supposed Gospel account comes from the *fact* noted in an earlier chapter, and this being, that even though the Sadducees, the philosophy of which the High Priest belonged, rejected the *oral Torah* of the Pharisees, the Sadducees were still sticklers to the written Torah of Moses. Therefore, for the High Priest to have "rent his garments" in front of the entire Sanhedrin, as the Gospel accounts claim, would have clearly violated Leviticus 10:6; 21:10, which forbid the High Priest from *ever* "rending his garments" *especially* at a festival time such as Passover, which is *precisely* when this incident supposedly occurred according to the Gospel accounts.[163] Such an action, if it had actually occurred, would have brought about the immediate ire of the other members of the Great Sanhedrin, both from the Pharisees, but even more so from the few Sadducee members of the Sanhedrin! Now it is true though, that if one hears "blasphemy" being committed by another individual then one was to "rend their garments,"[164] as can be found for example in Numbers 14:6, 11, 23; Genesis 37:29; Judges 11:35 2 Samuel 1:11. But, *if* such a "blasphemous" statement had in fact been made by Jesus, then *we would have*, or at least *we should* have the Gospel accounts stating that *each and every member* of the Great Sanhedrin – *all of them* – "rending their garments." But this *is not* what we find being stated in *any* of the Gospel accounts.

---

162 *Messiah and Temple*, Donald Juel, p. 64.

163 See the comments in *The Trial of Jesus From Jewish Sources*, Rabbi A. P. Drucker, p. 12; *Caiaphas*, Helen K. Bond, p. 126. But see also the erroneous interpretations, claims, and comments on this matter in *Jesus of Nazareth: Part Two*, Ratzinger and Pope Benedict, pp. 181-182 who claim that this matter is historically accurate.

164 See the comments in the *Jewish Encyclopedia*, "Blasphemy"; *Blasphemy and Exaltation in Judaism*, Darrell L. Bock, p. 40.

The "rending of garments" was referred to as *keriah*, or "tearing," and it was more often than not used, or done as a symbol of grief and mourning for the loss of a beloved individual,[165] or an expected passing away of a beloved individual as can be found in Genesis 37:29, 34; Genesis 49:13; 2 Samuel 1:11; 2 Kings 2:12; Ezekiel 24:17; 24:21; Job 1:20. This reason is found in the Talmud Babli, *Moed Qatan* 26a right beside the reason given for "rending the garments" in regards to hearing a "blasphemy" committed, as clearly stated in the Talmud, *Moed Qatan* 25a and b; Mishnah, *Sanhedrin* 7:5.[166] As stated in Joel 2:12-13, the *keriah* was done as a symbol of exposing one's heart to demonstrate the immortality of the soul.

Josephus, in *Jewish Wars* 2.237; 2.321, 323; 2.397, 400; 2.421; 5.345; 6.301 repeatedly speaks of how the Romans threatened to take drastic actions against the entire people of Palestine in regards to the matter of an "unlawful" action committed by a single individual. The Romans also threatened to take action against the High Priestly families, the very "puppet appointees" of the Romans, simply because of the actions committed by a single individual such as Jesus. Thus, the statement found in John 11:50 is quite likely an historically accurate statement. So remembering what was noted in earlier chapters, we have the "fugitive" Jesus being "handed over" to some sort of arresting party, who in turn knew that they *must* "hand him over" to Pilate, and therefore, the more logical and reasonably accurate *historical* reason for a "rending of the garments" being mentioned in the Gospel accounts is because the last thing that *any* Jew would have wanted to see was one of their very own fellow Jews, (especially one who was beloved by so many people), being executed by the Romans.[167] Thus, *if* there *was* an act of the "rending of the garments" it most likely *was not* done by the High Priest, nor was it most likely done as a result of any "blasphemy" being committed by Jesus! For such an act, *if* it actually *did* occur *historically*, was most likely done as an act of "mourning" because

---

165   See the comments in *Ritual and Morality*, Hyam Maccoby, p. 125.

166   See the comments in *Blasphemy and Exaltation in Judaism*, Darrell L. Bock pp. 97 and 103-104.

167   See the comments in *Jesus On Trial*, Gerard S. Sloyan, pp. 4-5; Haim Cohn, "Reflections on the Trial of Jesus," *Judaism 20*, (1971), pp. 18-19.

they knew that this beloved Jew, Jesus, was inevitably going to be executed by the Romans.[168]

Therefore, in closing this chapter, it has been *clearly* demonstrated that Jesus *never* committed *any* act of "blasphemy," and especially the *only* act of "blasphemy" which constituted a death sentence by stoning, *before* being "hanged on a gibbet" ("stake," or "tree").[169] Furthermore, as is clearly stated in *Tosefta Sanhedrin* 9:5, based on Deuteronomy 21:23, "those who are put to death by the court have a share in the world to come." Thus, ultimately in the end, *nothing* that Jesus said or did constituted "blasphemy." *All* of Jesus' actions and statements were *only* "political" matters that would have aroused *only* the ire of the Romans, Herodians, and the "politically appointed" High Priestly families.[170] Joseph Ratzinger and Pope Benedict XVI use an apologetically biased opinion when they attempt to claim that Jesus was in no way "political." Yet, they *do* make a quite accurate conclusion, which puts the error to their own claims when they write,[171] "So the circle of accusers who instigate Jesus' death is precisely indicated in the Fourth Gospel and clearly limited: it is the Temple aristocracy – and not without certain exceptions, as the reference to Nicodemus (John 7:50-52) shows." Joseph Ratzinger and Pope Benedict XVI make a further error when they claim that the reason that Jesus was convicted was because,[172] "He seemed to be putting himself on an equal footing with the living God Himself. This was what the strictly monotheistic faith of the Jews was unable to accept." But how Joseph Ratzinger and Pope Benedict arrive at such a conclusion, they in reality actually struggle very badly to try and explain! Even their *own* statement in this quote of, "*he seemed to be*," in regards to the notion that Jesus was "putting himself on an equal footing with the living God," *clearly demonstrates* that they themselves even have doubts about what they are attempting to claim. In the end, their claim is nothing more than an apologetically biased contention and not one that is based on the actual *historical facts* of the matter! Gerard S. Sloyan makes an excellent point

---

168   See the comments of Haim Cohn, "Reflections on the Trial of Jesus," *Judaism 20*, p. 22.

169   See the comments in *Jewish Law from Jesus to the Mishnah*, E. P. Sanders, pp. 57-67.

170   See the comments in *The Mythmaker*, Hyam Maccoby, pp. 36-40; *Jesus and Israel*, Jules Isaac, pp. 264-284.

171   *Jesus of Nazareth: Part Two*, Ratzinger and Pope Benedict, p. 185.

172   *Jesus of Nazareth: Part One*, Ratzinger and Pope Benedict, pp. 303-305.

when he writes,[173] "Two self-evident conclusions follow from the above truisms as they apply to Jesus of Nazareth. One is that Pilate must have become convinced, perhaps in very short order, that Jesus and the two men crucified with him constituted a serious threat to the peace of the empire. The other is that there is little likelihood that Jesus' disputes with other religious teachers, or even the charge that he spoke blasphemously, was the immediate cause of his death." But Joel Carmichael makes the *best* statements to appropriately end this chapter with when he writes,[174] "The trial before the Sanhedrin, in fact, appears to be nothing but an artificial device; it was introduced in order to make the Jews responsible for the death of Jesus, just as the celebrated episode of Barabbas, which we shall come to in a moment, was put in for the purpose of making the Roman procurator the guarantor of Jesus' innocence." Also, as Carmichael writes,[175] "There must after all, have been other Jews in those turbulent times roving about with their own interpretations of the Jewish law; the Temple authorities could hardly have reacted with the malice reported in the Gospels to the presence of a mere chatterbox calling upon the Jews to do no more than improve themselves morally so as to be ready for the Kingdom of God whenever it suited the good Lord to establish it."

---

173 *The Crucifixion of Jesus*, Gerard S. Sloyan, p. 20.

174 *The Death of Jesus*, Joel Carmichael, p. 31.

175 *The Death of Jesus*, Joel Carmichael, p. 128.

Chapter 8

"… They bound Jesus, led him away, and handed
him over to Pilate."
(Mark 15:1)

"… Having learned he was under Herod's
jurisdiction, he sent him off to Herod…."
(Luke 23:7)

In this chapter we are going to examine not only the role of Pontius
Pilate in the trial of Jesus, but also, the manner in which Pilate is
portrayed in the Gospel accounts. We will also include a brief look at
the role and relationship of Herod Antipas to Pontius Pilate in regards to
the trial of Jesus.

It has long been well-established by critical scholars of the New
Testament that the overall image of Pilate, as he is portrayed in the Gospels,
is a very clear "whitewashing" of not only his true character, but also in
regards to his role in the trial of Jesus.[1] Pilate began to be portrayed, (even

---

1   See for example the comments in *On Earth As It Is In Heaven*, D. C. Thielmann, pp. 298-301
    and the corresponding scholars notations to these pages; *Bandits, Prophets, and Messiahs*,
    Richard A. Horsley and John S. Hanson, pp. 66 and 164; *Jesus Before Christianity*, Albert
    Nolan, p. 128; *How Jesus Became God*, Bart D. Ehrman, pp. 161-164; *Kosher Jesus*, Rabbi

as early as the mid second century by the early Christians), as feeling regret, and sorrow over his actions taken against Jesus, even portraying Pilate to such a point that caused many of these Christians to claim that Pilate converted to being a follower of Jesus, as noted in Tertullian's *Apology* 21-24.[2] Yet, despite this well-established fact that Pilate has been "whitewashed," there *are* still a few scholars who attempt to defend this "whitewashing" with blatant apologetic bias.[3] There are also, still other scholars, who while admitting that the image of Pilate in the Gospels has been "whitewashed," they attempt to claim that the images of Pilate portrayed by the historians Josephus and Philo are "unjustifiable."[4] But, *if* it were true, as these particular scholars claim, that the image and accounts of Philo and Josephus regarding Pilate are "unjustifiable," then one *must* point out to such scholars the *fact* that there were four Procurators of Judea *prior to* Pilate that Josephus, for example, talks about – Coponius, Marcus Ambivius, Annius Rufus, and Valerius Gratus. Yet, taking our example of Josephus, he makes no mention of *any* evil deeds perpetrated upon the people of Judea by *any one of these four prior Procurators* such as he relates in regards to Pilate! Therefore, *if* the scholars who desire to claim that Josephus' images of Pilate are "unjustifiable," then these scholars *must justify their claims* by answering the question of *why* Josephus would *only* record evil deeds perpetrated upon the Jewish people of Palestine *by*

Shmuley Boteach, p. 50; *Pontius Pilate*, Ann Wroe, p. 253; *The Trial of Jesus from Jewish Sources*, Rabbi A. P. Drucker, pp. 21-32 and 41-44; *Jesus On Trial*, Gerard S. Sloyan, pp. 21-22; *Revolution in Judaea*, Hyam Maccoby, pp. 18-19 and n. 2, p. 222; *The Death of Jesus*, Joel Carmichael, pp. 40-41; *Jesus and Israel*, Jules Isaac, pp. 314-320 and 343-347; *Jesus and the Spiral of Violence*, Richard A. Horsley, p. 100; *Jewish Literature Between the Bible and the Mishnah*, George W. E. Nickelsburg, p. 201; *Judaism and the Origins of Christianity*, David Flusser, pp. 593-603; *Jewish Literacy*, Rabbi Joseph Telushkin, p. 123.

2   See the comments on this in *Jesus Before the Gospels*, Bart Ehrman, pp. 29-32.

3   See for example the comments in *Jesus of Nazareth: Part Two*, Ratzinger and Pope Benedict, p. 188.

4   See for example the comments in *The Trial of Jesus*, Josef Blinzler, pp. 177-180 and 182-183; *Herod Antipas*, Harold Hoehner, pp. 181-182. In *Matthew and Empire*, Warren Carter, pp. 145-146, and notations 4-12, p. 216 points out *all* of the various different ways that Pilate has been interpreted and portrayed throughout history.

Pilate!⁵ N. T. Wright though, is quite correct as an answer to such scholars when he writes,⁶ "The fact that a human mind has to organize and arrange material does not 'falsify' the history. This is simply what 'history' is. At the same time, Thucydides and the rest were every bit as aware as we are of the historian's solemn duty to strive towards intellectual honesty and severe impartiality." Wright also refers to Josephus as well in this context and Wright further states, "Thus, on the one hand, ancient historians as well as modern ones were aware of the historian's obligation to do the best not to stand in his own light... Inventing 'history' by a backwards projection of ideology is as much if not more a modern phenomenon as it is an ancient one. It is something from which New Testament scholars are not exempt."⁷ The ancient historian Dionysius stated in *Ancient History of Rome*, Book I, Chapter I that there were certain "principles" that an historian was obligated to follow when making a written historical record, and amongst these "principles" was that an historian had to ensure that they were utilizing "proper sources," which W. R. Farmer, (the same as N. T. Wright), believes that Josephus did indeed use such "proper sources" when he wrote his historical accounts.⁸ It is true though, that one's own *interpretations* of the *historical accounts* offered by Josephus *could be* viewed as being "unjustifiable" in regards to Pilate, but it must also be pointed out that such scholarly *interpretations* on such matters are simply *personal opinions*, and quite often, and in fact far too often, such scholarly opinions are tainted by *personal biases*. This fact goes right alongside of the fact noted in earlier chapters about the scholars who *must* still attempt to try and find some sort of Jewish law that Jesus violated to such an extent that would have caused some sort of "Jewish authorities" to desire the death penalty for Jesus!Also though, even though the matter of the actual crucifixion of Jesus is not a matter discussed in any detail in this book, the fact that the crucifixion of Jesus has been mentioned, (previously in Chapter 5), demands that *this* particular matter *must be* reiterated in this chapter, and this being, the matter regarding crucifixion being *only* a gentile form

---

5   See the comments on this in *Crime before Calvary*, Guy Schofield, pp. 83-84; *The Trial of Jesus of Nazareth*, Max Radin, pp. 183-184.

6   *The New Testament and the People of God*, N. T. Wright, p. 85.

7   See also the comments in *Pontius Pilate in History and Interpretation*, Helen K. Bond, p. 78.

8   See the comments in *Maccabees, Zealots, and Josephus*, W. R. Farmer, pp. 3-6.

of punishment despite the fact that some scholars have claimed that the Jews did in fact utilize crucifixion as a form of punishment. Such claims by such scholars are, at times, primarily derived from an interpreted meaning of one text from the Dead Sea Scroll referred to as the *Pesher Nahum*, as well as an interpreted meaning of Leviticus 24:16.[9] Still other scholars attempt to us the Septuagint reading of Esther 7:9 and 8:12 as a claim that these verses can be utilized in relation to Jesus' crucifixion.[10] But the *fact* that has been pointed out already in earlier chapters is that the Septuagint had many additions and alterations made to it, (and again, many of these additions and alterations were made by *non-Jews*), *and* the *fact* that the Book of Esther *did not* become a part of the Jewish canon until after 90 CE, (a matter that will be further discussed in Chapter 10), causes one to highly question the interpretations offered by these scholars of the Greek translation of Esther 7:9 and 8:12. For the Hebrew of Esther 7:9 in particular contains the Hebrew word, `*ez*, which means, "tree," or "gallows" for "hanging" someone to death. But, this Hebrew word *does not* offer a meaning of "crucifixion."[11] Even Josephus in *Antiquities* 11.208, 246 and 280, commenting on this matter from Esther, uses the Greek word *kremannumi*, which means, "to hang," or "to be hung,"[12] (and this despite Paul's usage of this same word in Galatians 3:13), for again, this word *does not* offer a meaning of "crucifixion." As further clarification for this *fact*, Josephus states that the "tree" that was used was approximately 70 to 80 feet tall (Esther 5:14; 7:9). Can *any* competent scholar then, even logically imagine one attempting to try and erect a "cross" to be used for "crucifixion" that was 70 to 80 feet tall?

Going even further into this matter though, there have even been claims by scholars that the Talmud Babli, *Sanhedrin* 45b makes a reference to "crucifixion" being permissible under Jewish law.[13] But such claims, once again as pointed out in Chapter 5, are simply very bad misinterpretations

---

9   See for example *Blasphemy and Exaltation in Judaism*, Darrell L. Bock, p. 37, and n. 20, p. 37 where Bock cites David J. Halperin, "Crucifixion, the Nahum Pesher, and the Rabbinic Penalty of Strangulation," *Journal of Jewish Studies* 32. (1981), pp. 32-46.

10   See for example *Barabbas and Esther*, Roger David Aus, p. 10.

11   See *A Comprehensive Etymological Dictionary of the Hebrew Language*, p. 479.

12   See *Liddell & Scott's Greek-English Lexicon*, p. 449; *BDAG Greek-English Lexicon*, p. 566.

13   See for example *Blasphemy and Exaltation in Judaism*, Darrell L. Bock, p. 80.

and misrepresentations of Talmudic texts by these scholars! For crucifixion was *never* used by Jews as a form of punishment.[14] As Hyam Maccoby rightly states,[15] "To the Jews, crucifixion was a loathsome and horrifying form of inhumanity. It was outlawed in Jewish law to such an extent that it was forbidden to crucify a dead body (see Deuteronomy 21:23)." But these supposed references to Jews using crucifixion that are cited by these scholars as proof that Jews used crucifixion are sources that make reference to Alexander Jannaeus' (103–76 BCE) and his *supposed* use of "crucifixion" to eliminate 800 of his political opponents. These references though, have been questioned and challenged by other scholars in regards to the accuracy of such "interpretations" (i.e. "translations") that attempt to prove that Jews used crucifixion. For the *fact* of the matter is that the words "hang from a tree," which are so often believed by these scholars to be an indication that "crucifixion" was permissible in Jewish law, simply *does not*, in any way, "translate" into a meaning of "crucifixion,"[16] and this is true despite the general translation of the Greek word, *xulon*, that is used, for example, in Acts 5:30; 10:39. For this Greek word *xulon* simply meant something "made out of wood," such as "staves," as it is found being used in Matthew 26:47, 55; Mark 14:43, 48; Luke 22:52 As further proof, the word *xulon* also means "stocks," as in the case of like handcuffs, or feet cuffs, as it is found being used in Acts 16:24. But once again for emphasis, the Greek word *xulon* simply meant something which was "*made*," or "*fabricated* out of wood" as proven by its usage, for example, in 1 Corinthians 3:12; 2 Timothy 2:20; Revelations 9:20; 18:12, and thus, a cross for crucifixion was simply another item "made," or "fabricated out of *wood*"!

To proceed now into the matter of the depiction of Pilate, the *only* canonical Gospel that offers even a very small accurate account of Pilate's *true* character and nature can be found in Luke 13:1-3. Therefore, it is necessary to examine in greater detail the actual *true* nature of the character of Pontius Pilate from an *historical* standpoint in order to correctly understand the *accurate historical reality* of Jesus' trial before Pontius Pilate. The biggest problem though, with attempting to gain such an accurate historical

---

14   See the comments in *The Crucifixion of Jesus*, Gerard S. Sloyan, pp. 21-23.

15   *Revolution in Judaism*, Hyam Maccoby, p. 36, but see also his comments on p. 73.

16   See Geza Vermes, "Was Crucifixion a Jewish Penalty," (April 2013); "Crucifixion," *Jewish Encyclopedia*, Kaufman Kohler and Emil G. Hirsch.

depiction of this matter lies in the fact that *all* of the documentation and written records that Roman provincial governors were *required* to keep, regarding such trials and matters as that of the trial of Jesus, have disappeared along with two chapters of Tacitus' historical records, which cover the approximate years of 30-31CE, or in other words, records from the very period of history that the *majority* of scholars believe that the trial and crucifixion of Jesus occurred.[17] Josef Blinzler notes that[18] Justin Martyr, *Apology* 1.35.9; 1.38.7; 1.48.3; Tertullian, *Apology* 5.2; 21.20; Eusebius, *Ecclesiastical History* 2.2, (the essential scholarly criteria of "multiple attestation" in other words), all state that Pontius Pilate *did in fact* send a record or report to Tiberius about Jesus' trial and crucifixion just as was required under Roman law. Blinzler points out though,[19] that Eusebius, *Ecclesiastical History* 9.5.1; 9.7.1 claimed that this report that Pilate sent to Tiberius was full of blasphemous lies against Jesus, and that Eusebius seems to have erroneously shifted the date of this trial to the year 21CE, which would have been impossible because that was before Pilate had even become Procurator of Judea. Blinzler clearly states that,[20] "Hence we see that official Roman documents concerning Pilate's proceedings against Jesus have not been preserved for us." Now, Gerard Sloyan, on the other hand, believes that it is highly, "doubtful that *any*, correspondence from Pilate to Rome" was "important enough to report" in regards to a trial of Jesus.[21] Therefore, we are left with Josephus' writings, Philo, a few snippets from the Dead Sea Scrolls, and hints from the Talmudic sources, plus one letter from Herod Agrippa I to the emperor Caligula dating from around 36-37 CE,[22] to try and derive the most accurate *historical* depiction of the *true* character of Pontius Pilate in regards to a trial of Jesus of Nazareth before this Governor/Procurator.

The first real historical clue we should look at in regards to the true character of Pontius Pilate derives from the very name, "Pilate." This name

---

17　See the comments in *Pontius Pilate*, Ann Wroe, pp. xii, 66-67, 93, and 100; *Jesus Interrupted*, Bart D. Ehrman, p. 148.

18　*The Trial of Jesus*, Josef Blinzler, n. 2, p. 22.

19　*The Trial of Jesus*, Josef Blinzler, n. 3, p. 22.

20　*The Trial of Jesus*, Josef Blinzler, p. 23.

21　*The Crucifixion of Jesus*, Gerard S. Sloyan, p. 6.

22　See the comments concerning this letter in *Kosher Jesus*, Rabbi Shmuley Boteach, p. 83.

is the masculine form of the Latin word *Pilatus*, which means, "one skilled with the javelin." As Ann Wroe states,[23] "It may have been during these years – if Pilate did not earn the name himself later – that the cognomen 'Pilatus,' 'skilled with the javelin,' became attached to his family. Javelin-throwing was thought to have come from the Samnites anyway, and the Oscan version of 'Pilatus,' *eh-peilatus*, has been found on an inscription from Capua. It is another clue to Pilate's origins: an indication of the violent past that beat, however faintly, behind him." Thus, we know that Pilate had the military experience of being a fearless warrior leader. It is true though, that there are some scholars who believe that there is no way to know for certain from what, or from where the origins of the name "Pilate" was derived.[24]

Another essential historical fact to understand about Pilate is that Pilate was specifically chosen and then appointed to be governor of Judea by Sejanus, (who was a very "anti-Jewish" military friend and confidant of the emperor Tiberius), and Sejanus' deliberate appointment of Pilate was done in order to have Pilate deliberately try to instigate and provoke the Jewish people of Palestine into open revolt and rebellion simply to give the Romans an excuse to crush the Jews.[25] But here again, there is debate amongst scholars over whether or not this is in fact the *historically* true reason as to *why* Pilate was appointed as governor of Judea.[26]

We must now look at the historical accounts of Josephus in regards to the matter of Pontius Pilate raiding the Temple treasuries in order to build an aqueduct, which resulted in a protest raised by the Jews. During this rather "peaceful" protest, according to Josephus, Pontius Pilate ordered

23   *Pontius Pilate*, Ann Wroe, p. 16.

24   See for example the comments on this in *Crime before Calvary*, Guy Schofield, p. 48.

25   See P. L. Maier, "Sejanus, Pilate and the Date of the Crucifixion," *Church History* 37, pp. 8-9; *The Catholic Encyclopedia*, Volume 12, p. 614; Harold W. Hoehner, "Chronological Aspects of the Life of Christ, Part V: The Year of Christ's Crucifixion," *Bibliotheca Sacra* 131, (October-December, 1974), p. 341; Harold W. Hoehner, "Pilate," *Dictionary of Jesus and the Gospels*, pp. 172-183; *From Pompey to Diocletian*, E. M. Smallwood, pp. 160-170; *Crime before Calvary*, Guy Schofield, p. 47.

26   See the comments in *Pontius Pilate in History and Interpretation*, Helen K. Bond, pp. xiii-xvi.

the execution of these protestors.[27] Philo as well documents the ruthless, violent nature of Pilate, and the Dead Sea Scrolls refer to Pontius Pilate as "the Young Lion of Wrath."[28] But what is really important to understand about these historical depictions of Pontius Pilate is that none of these accounts mentions anything about Pontius Pilate consulting, or using the Great Sanhedrin in any way as was required under the *Pax Romana*, and which was required *prior to any provincial governor* taking such violent actions against the people of a Roman province. Yet, it was the very *fact* that Pilate *was indeed* a very violent and brutal governor in regards to his actions against the people of Judea, which brought about his removal *as* the governor of Judaea, as noted by Josephus in *Antiquities* 18.4.1(88); 18.4.3(124).[29] Therefore, how can so many scholars then attempt to "whitewash" this *true historical* character of Pilate, or even attempt to claim that the historical accounts about Pilate's *true* character that we *do have* are somehow "unjustifiable"?

It is important now, to provide a clear understanding of the *Pax Romana* in regards to how this relates not only to Pontius Pilate and his actions, but also to Herod Antipas, and therefore as a result, provide an overall accurate understanding of the trial of Jesus. *Pax Romana* means, "The Peace of Rome," and it was first established after Octavian (or Augustus Caesar) defeated Marc Antony in the battle of Actium, September 2, 31 BCE. It was established in order to bring about peace, not only within Rome itself, but also within all of the Roman provinces as well.[30] The *Pax Romana* gave certain rights to the inhabitants of the Roman Provinces such as Palestine, and amongst those rights was the fact that the citizens *of* these provinces

---

27 See the comments in *On Earth As It Is In Heaven*, D. C. Thielmann, p. 299; *The Misunderstood Jew*, Amy-Jill Levine, p. 128, and n. 5, p. 235; *Jesus and the Spiral of Violence*, Richard A. Horsley, pp. 105-108.

28 See the comments in *Pontius Pilate*, Ann Wroe, p. 175.

29 See the comments in *On Earth As It Is In Heaven*, D. C. Thielmann, pp. 509 and 524; *The New Testament and the People of God*, N. T. Wright, p. 174 who lists seven *known* incidents in the ten years Pilate was in Judea.

30 See the comments in *Ancient History Encyclopedia*, "Pax Romana," Donald L. Wasson, December 8, 2015; *The Historical Jesus in Context*, Levine, Allison Jr., Crossan, p. 45; *Blasphemy and Exaltation in Judaism*, Darrell L. Bock, p. 193; *Matthew and Empire*, Warren Carter, pp. 30-33; *How Jesus Became Christian*, Barrie Wilson, pp. 86 and 133.

were not considered to be Roman citizens, unless, of course, as was noted in Chapter 4, one was either born in, or a freed slave of a Roman "free city," and thus, one remained a citizen *of* that particular province. As A. N. Sherwin-White points out,[31] *only* "the Provincial Roman citizen was protected against summary execution by clauses of the *Lex Julia* concerning riots, or *Vis Publica.*" Also though, under the *Pax Romana* all lower classed individuals (i.e. what so many scholars term, "peasants," or individuals such as Jesus would have been considered), that had to be taken to trial before the Procurator of a province, were termed, *Extra Ordinum*, or "Outside the List [of State Judgments]," and their trials were referred to as, *cognition*, whereas though, people of a higher status were granted a full tribunal or jury trial as noted by Pliny, *Epistles* 10.29-30.[32] One consequence of the *Pax Romana* though, was that the Romans installed "client kings" in these Roman provinces, and in Palestine this began with Herod the Great, and then after his death the province was divided into the tetrarchs headed by Herod Archelaus, Herod Philip, and of course, Herod Antipas.

The Herodians though, *were not* considered by the Jews to be *true* Jews, or in essence, *genuinely* of Jewish lineage as noted in Mishnah *Sotah* 7:8. This is because of the fact that Herod the Great was actually born in Idumea and his father was an Edomite who only *claimed* to have converted to Judaism, and thus, the Jews of Palestine considered both he, and *all* of his offspring to be "foreigners" as well as collaborators with the Romans.[33]

Before continuing further into the topic of the role that both Pontius Pilate and Herod Antipas played in the trial of Jesus there is one all important question that needs to be asked that derives from the historical accounts written by Josephus, and this question being, who is the *Antipas* that Josephus mentions in *Jewish Wars* 4.139-141? For Josephus seems to indicate that this individual *was* one of the Herodians. But the *Herod Antipas* of history and Gospel fame had long since been exiled to Gaul by Caligula by this point of time in history that Josephus refers to this individual in

---

31 *Roman Society and Roman Law in the New Testament*, A. N. Sherwin-White, p. 1.

32 See the comments on this in *Who is Jesus*, Darrell L. Bock, p. 180.

33 See the comments in *Herod Antipas*, Harold W. Hoehner, pp. 233-235; *The Other Side of the Jordan*, Nelson Glueck, pp. 166-167; *On Earth As It Is In Heaven*, D. C. Thielmann, pp. 511-512.

this section of *Jewish Wars*. So, who exactly is this *Herod Antipas* to which Josephus is referring?[34]

Now, the Herodians had their own gangs of "ruffians,"[35] or one might even refer to these "ruffians" as being sort of "body guards," or "secret police," as is noted, or hinted at in Matthew 22:16; Mark 3:6; 12:13 for example, (but see also the fact that these "ruffians" are mentioned in the Talmud Babli, *Pesahim* 57a).[36] So, it was *only* the High Priest and the Sadducees who had the "Temple police," the Herodians who had their "ruffians," and the Romans with their "soldiers," all of whom were collaborators with each other in regards to "keeping the peace" and keeping control over the remainder of the people of Palestine, while the Palestinian general populace only had as *their* protection the "bandits," "brigands," "lestai," "Zealots," and the "Sicarii" all of whom were loyalist patriots in regards to a "legitimate" *independent* Israel. As Richard A. Horsley and John S. Hanson write,[37] "The High Priestly families, Herodians, and much of the wealthy aristocracy, of course, were engaged in mutually beneficial collaboration with the Roman imperial system in maintaining control in Jewish Palestine."[38] Paul was a member of these "police," as can be clearly determined from Acts 8:1 and Acts 22:3-6. Josephus in *Jewish Wars* 2.430-431; 4.325-327; 5.440-441 clearly points out, the "Zealot revolt" of 66-73 attacked not only the High Priestly families and the "Temple police," but also the Herodian "ruffians" as well.

The Jews loyal to Israel, such as Jesus was, were fearless in regards to these "pretend" authorities of the Romans, Sadducees, and the Herodians. There are a great many stories found in the Talmud about many Pharisaic

---

34   See the comments in *Bandits, Prophets, and Messiahs*, Richard A. Horsley and John S. Hanson, pp. 223-229.

35   See the comments on this in *Jesus and the Spiral of Violence*, Richard A. Horsley, pp. 44 and 46.

36   See the comments on this in *Jesus and Israel*, Jules Isaac, pp. 275-276; *Hillel*, Rabbi Joseph Telushkin, p. 186.

37   See the comments in *Bandits, Prophets, and Messiahs*, Richard A. Horsley and John S. Hanson, p. 42.

38   For a very thorough and excellent commentary laying out this matter of Roman Imperial governing of its provinces, see the comments in *Matthew and Empire*, Warren Carter, pp. 9-17.

sages standing up courageously against these authorities only to be brutally tortured and murdered.[39] As noted in an earlier chapter, the Pharisees warned Jesus to take flight from the Herodian "ruffians" out of concern for *his* safety.

This then brings us to what we find being stated in Mark 8:15-17. In these verses of Mark's Gospel, we find partly truth, and partly evangelistic later interpolations. For as we find it being stated in these verses, "Beware of the leaven of the Pharisees and the leaven of Herod."[40] Many scholars have very badly misrepresented, and misinterpreted what is being stated in these verses as well as missing the inaccuracy of the statement "leaven of the Pharisees."[41] For example, Marcus Borg interprets this to be indicating "bad teaching."[42] Now, according to Borg's claims, the association of "leaven" with "evil" (which will be discussed just below), derived from a much later time than Jesus, (i.e. roughly the third century CE). Yet, Hillel, (who again died when Jesus was only somewhere between eight and twelve years old), as noted in Mishnah *Pesaḥim* 1:1, (*if* one *correctly* interprets what is stated in this Mishnaic tractate that is), puts the error to Borg's claim.[43] Thus, the idioms of the usage of the term "leaven" in Hebrew referred not only to something being "sour," or "fermented," it also indicated something that was filled with "violence." Therefore, Jesus' statement actually meant "beware of the *violence* of ...." But as just pointed out above, *only* the Sadducees, the Herodians, and the Romans had "ruffians," "police,"[44] and "soldiers" capable of inflicting the "violence" to which Jesus was referring. The Pharisees, Essens, and even the followers of Jesus, again had *only* "loyal patriots" of Israel on their side, again in the form of the "Zealots," "bandits," and "Sicarii" and while it is quite true that each of these groups were very capable of being "violent," Jesus *does not* refer to *any* of these individuals

---

39 See the comments in *Kosher Jesus*, Rabbi Shmuley Boteach, p. 71.

40 See the comments on this by Kaufmann Kohler, "Herodians," *Jewish Encyclopedia*.

41 See for example the comments in *Herod Antipas*, Harold W. Hoehner, pp. 202-213.

42 See *Conflict, Holiness & Politics*, Marcus Borg, pp. 111-113.

43 See Jeffrey Spitzer, "The Birth of the Good Inclination," *My Jewish Learning*; "In Search of (the Meaning of) Chametz," *Torch*; Solomon Schechter and Julius H. Greenstone, "Leaven," *Jewish Encyclopedia*; Shalom Kantor, "Taming the Beast: The Yetzer Ha Ra and the Yetzer Ha Tov," *Sefaria*.

44 See the comments in *Conflict, Holiness & Politics*, Marcus Borg, p. 69.

in *any way* in these verses from Mark's Gospel! Therefore, this reference to the "leaven of the Pharisees" can *only be* a later evangelistic interpolation reflecting the separation of gentile church from Jewish synagogue noted in earlier chapters, or possibly another instance in which the name "Pharisees" was substituted for the name "Sadducees" as noted in Chapter 4.

This usage of the idiom "leaven" also holds true for the parable found in Matthew 13:33; Luke 13:21, and also Luke 12:1 as can be found noted, for example, in the Talmud Babli, *Berakhot* 17a where it is used in reference to the *yetzer ha-ra*, (the "evil inclination"). But this term is used in this Talmudic reference in conjunction with Israel being subjected to the control of "foreign powers." Thus, the idioms of this term "leaven" also indicated that "inner force within all of us," as it is found being used in Jeremiah 6:11.[45] The Pharisees, as clearly pointed out in an earlier chapter, as well as again in this chapter, along with the Essens, and as well as Jesus and his followers, were all "loyal patriots" of Israel. Thus, it must be clearly stated again that this statement in Mark 8:15-17 about the "leaven of the Pharisees" *can only be* a later evangelistic interpolation. For even Jesus surrounded himself with these "loyal patriots" of Israel as pointed out in an earlier chapter – i.e. "Simon the Zealot," the "Thunder brothers," and "Judas Iscariot," for example. In regards to "Simon the Zealot," Joel Carmichael writes,[46] "In short, the presence of an avowed Zealot among the disciples of Jesus is illuminating. There must have been something about Jesus' movement that was attractive to this extremist wing of the opposition to Rome." Also, it is essential to point out here that in Matthew 16:17 the word "barjona" is a derivative of the Aramaic word *baryona*, which means, "outlaw," and thus we not only have an individual named "Simon the Zealot," or as it is found in Matthew 10:4; Mark 3:18, "Simon the Canaan" or "Canaanite," (which the names "Canaan" or "Canaanite"

---

45 For more on this term *yetzer ha-ra* and this "inner force within us" see the comments in *On Earth As It Is In Heaven*, D. C. Thielmann, pp. 58-60; Joseph Jacobs and the Executive Committee of the Editorial Board, "Yezer Ha-Ra," *Jewish Encyclopedia*; *Paul and Rabbinic Judaism*, W. D. Davies, pp. 20-35; *Judaism and the Origins of Christianity*, David Flusser, pp. 214-225.

46 *The Death of Jesus*, Joel Carmichael, p. 156; see also the comments in *Jesus and Israel*, Jules Isaac, p. 37, and the notations 10-11, p. 37.

were synonymous with "Zealot"),[47] we also have another individual named, "Simon the Outlaw," (or in other words, a "bandit," or "brigand," one of the branches, or factions of the "Zealot" philosophy). Furthermore, as Hyam Maccoby points out, (referencing the Talmud Babli, *Gittin* 56a which clearly notes the meaning of *baryona*),[48] "The singular form of this word is *bariona*, which means 'outlaw, rebel or freedom-fighter' – in other words, a *Zealot*. It seems then that Simon Peter, like Judas Iscariot and Simon the Zealot, was previously a member of the Zealot party and retained a nickname to mark his affiliation." Now, David Flusser, (and Brad Young), believe that *barjona* (Baryona), is actually a misspelling or mispronunciation of *bar-Johna*, or in essence, "the son of Yohanan" (John), which according to John 1:42 was the name of Peter's father, (i.e. *Yohanon*), and which Flusser believes that at the time of Jesus the shortened form of *Yohanon* was *Yohna*, the misspelled/mispronounced form of the Hebrew word *yona*,[49] and which this Hebrew word means "depriving someone of possessions," "extorting," "to oppress," or "mistreat"[50] others. Thus, the single most important *fact* that all *competent* New Testament scholars *cannot*, and *must not* attempt to avoid, or try to "*cleverly*" get around by way of *any* attempt to "whitewash" this *fact*, is the *fact* that between just these three specific individual disciples, plus the "Thunder Brothers," Jesus had chosen out, and then surrounded himself with "freedom fighters"![51] As Samuel Sandmel so rightly states concerning this,[52] "The greater the zeal to overthrow Rome, the more ready were the extreme 'nationalists' to accept and embrace a messianic claimant." Now, Joseph Ratzinger and Pope Benedict XVI[53] try to apologetically deny that the "Thunder Brothers" had

47 See the comments on this fact in *Jesus of Nazareth: Part One*, Ratzinger and Pope Benedict, pp. 177-178.

48 *Judas and the Myth of Jewish Evil*, Hyam Maccoby, pp. 144-146. See also though, the comments on this in *The Death of Jesus*, Joel Carmichael, p. 157.

49 See the comments on this in *Judaism and the Origins of Christianity*, David Flusser, p. 292 and n. 27, p. 292.

50 See *Etymological Dictionary of Biblical Hebrew*, p. 105; *A Comprehensive Etymological Dictionary of the Hebrew Language*, p. 260.

51 See the comments in *Jesus and His Contemporaries*, Etienne Trocme, p. 119.

52 *A Jewish Understanding of the New Testament*, Samuel Sandmel, p. 30.

53 *Jesus of Nazareth: Part One*, Ratzinger and Pope Benedict, pp. 177-178.

anything to do with being "freedom fighters." Yet, there is no escaping the *fact* that Jesus was surrounded by "freedom fighters" and *any* apologetic attempts from *biased* scholars who try and deny this *fact* in their portrayals of the *historical* Jesus are futile! *This factual truth must figure into any and all scholarly attempts to define the historical Jesus!* It is very welcoming to see Joseph Ratzinger and Pope Benedict XVI *admitting* that Jesus *was* surrounded by "freedom fighters"[54] even though they do try to downplay this fact by way of an apologetic bias claiming that these individuals, "*had been,*" (past-tense, in other words), one time "freedom fighters." But, as Hyam Maccoby rightly states,[55] "Nicknames seem inappropriate to the usual conception of Jesus' band of disciples as engaged on a pacifist, otherworldly religious cause, but they seem perfectly compatible with the comradery of men aiming at the overthrow of an occupying power and the restoration of national liberty." Maccoby further notes Josephus, *Antiquities* 12.266 as an example of this essential point to understand. Also, as Ann Wroe writes concerning all of this,[56] "The man began to gather disciples of his own, who also began to baptize. To a Roman governor, the names of some of those disciples were disturbing: two brothers who were called Sons of Thunder and a man called Simon the Zealot. Perhaps these titles had no political connotation to the disciples or to Jesus, but they carried echoes of rebellion, which Pilate would not have missed." Also, as Gerhard von Rad points out,[57] names to the Jews held a *major* significance, as he states, "This kind of thing is done all the more easily in Hebrew in that the Hebrew speaker, even when he is using language noetically, is in general far less concerned with linguistic precision and the avoidance of ambiguity than we can assume. If in prophetic diction a phrase or word could have several possible references, so much the better, for the saying was thereby enriched."

One must be further reminded of the *fact* that *some* of Jesus' disciples were even carrying swords! As Hyam Maccoby states concerning this *fact*,[58] "Only Luke, of the Gospel-Writers, has retained the incident of the swords.

54   *Jesus of Nazareth: Part One*, Ratzinger and Pope Benedict, pp. 12-13.

55   *Judas and the Myth of Jewish Evil*, Hyam Maccoby, pp. 144-146.

56   *Pontius Pilate*, Ann Wroe, p. 139.

57   *The Message of the Prophets*, Gerhard von Rad, pp. 63-64.

58   *Revolution in Judaea*, Hyam Maccoby, pp. 142-143.

He could have had no possible motive in inventing it, for it goes against the whole grain of his narrative." Peter even uses one of these swords at the time of Jesus' arrest only to then "flee" afterwards as noted in Chapter 6. But in Acts 2:36; 3:13; and 5:30 there is this seeming attempt to exonerate Peter's actions. We then find it being stated in 1 Peter 2:13, "Respect all human authority, whether the king as head of state or the officials [God] has appointed,"[59] which basically contradicts what is stated in Acts 5:29, although it is quite true that if one notices that this *clearly* states, "*the officials [God] has appointed*," noting what was discussed in Chapter 7 about "blasphemy" against such individuals being an offense *only* against *God's* "*legitimate*" appointees. Thus, as noted in Chapter 4 the Pharisees had warned Jesus to "flee" because the Herodian "ruffians" sought to seize him and do him harm. So, how and why would Jesus then *warn others* to "beware of the *leaven* of the Pharisees" that was discussed above?

This now brings us to the important question of who, between Pontius Pilate and Herod Antipas, actually had jurisdiction over the matter of a trial of Jesus. At the same time, it is essential here to reiterate a point that was made in several earlier chapters in regards to a *supposed* trial of Jesus before the Great Sanhedrin. As was pointed out in these earlier chapters, there is absolutely *nothing* that can be found in *any* of the Gospel accounts that can be utilized by *any* competent scholar to justify *any* claim that Jesus violated *any Jewish* law. Some scholars though, have asserted, based on what is found being stated in Luke 23:2; John 18:19, that Jesus *was* convicted by the Great Sanhedrin on the charge of "leading Israel astray," a matter covered in the Talmud Babli, *Sanhedrin* 43a.[60] The laws of Deuteronomy 13:15; 17:4 regarding one whom is accused of "misleading" or "leading astray" others of Israel *required* that a diligent and thorough investigation into the truth of such a charge be conducted. Yet, *nowhere* in the New Testament can one find such a *required* "thorough investigation" of such a charge be found being recorded. Thus, this also *cannot* be the *supposed* verdict of the Great Sanhedrin against Jesus because there are absolutely *no witnesses* to

59 See also Romans 13:1-7, and the comments on this matter in *Jesus Interrupted*, Bart D. Ehrman, pp. 97-98.

60 See the comments in *Historical Tradition In the Fourth Gospel*, C. H. Dodd, p. 95; *The Trial of Jesus: Cambridge Studies in Honour of C. F. D. Moule*, pp. 8-11; *Jesus On Trial*, Gerard S. Sloyan, p. 19.

such a charge being found recorded in *any* of the Gospels, or *any* of the Epistles, and the Pharisees, but even more so the few Sadducees who were also members of the Sanhedrin, are again, portrayed in the Gospels as being sticklers for abiding by the "oral" and "written" Torah! But the *fact* that is being overlooked by the scholars making this claim is that Luke 23:14 *does* clarify what is actually meant by this supposed charge against Jesus. In this verse from Luke is found the Greek word *apostrepho*, which in *Hellenized* communities had a meaning of, "perverting the people."[61] In *Hellenized* communities this was considered to be one of the forms of "blasphemy," a matter already covered in Chapter 7 that has been proven that Jesus *never* committed. Thus, since we *are not* speaking about a *Hellenized* diaspora Jewish community, (as was so *clearly* noted in the Preface*)*, but instead we are speaking about a Palestinian Jewish community wholly dedicated to Israel and the Torah, then the *only* logical alternative *must be found* in one of the *other* possible meanings of this Greek word *apostrepho* that is being referred to in Luke 23:14, and the *only* logical alternative meaning *must be* the meaning, "inciting to revolt."[62] It is easy to arrive at this *best* logical conclusion based on what is found in Luke 23:2 and the "render unto Caesar ..." statement of Jesus and the accusation of "forbidding to pay taxes," which are in essence, contradictions, unless, that is, there are scholars who believe that paying taxes with Jewish coinage of the time was somehow wrong as opposed to only using accepted Roman coinage,[63] (a matter already discussed previously in Chapter 6). Now, Hyam Maccoby offers an interesting opinion on this matter when he writes,[64] "Jesus' actual words on the tribute may have been correctly reported in the Gospels, but if so, they have been misinterpreted... The accusation made against Jesus when he was handed over to Pilate, that he was 'forbidding to give tribute to Caesar,' was the literal truth, the necessary corollary of his preaching the 'Kingdom of God' and claiming the Messiahship." Also, Maccoby writes further in a footnote to this,[65] "S. G. F. Brandon has argued that Jesus meant, 'Let Caesar go back to Rome where he belongs, and leave God's

---

61   See the comments in *Jesus On Trial*, Gerard S. Sloyan, p. 78.

62   See the *BDAG Greek-English Lexicon*, p. 123.

63   See the comments in *Pontius Pilate*, Ann Wroe, pp. 141-142.

64   *Revolution in Judaea*, Hyam Maccoby, p. 100.

65   *Revolution in Judaea*, Hyam Maccoby, p. 100.

land to the People of God.' In other words, he meant to forbid the giving of tribute not to allow it." The matter and importance of understanding Maccoby's remarks here will be made clearer in Chapter 9 in regards to understanding the term "Kingdom of God."

Acts 13:27-28 *very clearly* states that the Great Sanhedrin *never* found Jesus guilty of *any* crime worthy of death! These verses in Acts use the Greek word *krinantes*, which quite often gets translated into English as, "condemning," which *can be* implied by the actual meaning of this Greek word. But this implied meaning tends to distort the *actual* contextual meaning of this Greek word, and thus, causes many scholars, theologians, but mostly the general church laity to wrongly interpret the actions of the Great Sanhedrin. For this Greek word actually should be interpreted as indicating that the Great Sanhedrin "*brought* him to trial" *before* Pontius Pilate. Thus, as was already noted in earlier chapters, and again in this chapter, Jesus was *never* actually taken before the Great Sanhedrin, nor did the Great Sanhedrin *ever* pronounce Jesus guilty of violating *any* Jewish law! But, even *if* the Great Sanhedrin *had indeed* found Jesus guilty of some matter that violated Jewish law, Acts 18:15; 23:29; 25:18-20 all *very clearly* point out that the Romans *never* involved themselves in matters that pertained *only* to violations of Jewish laws![66] As Joel Carmichael writes concerning this *fact*,[67] "The Romans are well known to have taken pains to avoid meddling in the religious affairs of their subjects, and while they disliked the Jews for a variety of reasons – perhaps chiefly because of their stubborn devotion to an incomprehensible, disembodied deity – there is no reason to think they would have been disturbed by a purely religious movement within the Jewish community." Now, according to the way that the earliest followers of Jesus perceived of these matters, the Great Sanhedrin *was only guilty of* "handing over" Jesus to Pontius Pilate to be tried under Roman law. Mark 8:31; 9:31; 10:33; Luke 9:22; 9:44; 18:32 *all* make this point very clear.[68] As Hugo Mantel writes concerning this,[69] "So it appears from the Synoptic Gospels that Jesus was tried for his life

---

66 See the comments on this in *Israel in Revolution*, David Rhoads, pp. 30-31.

67 *The Death of Jesus*, Joel Carmichael, p. 127.

68 See the comments in *The Trial of Jesus: Cambridge Studies in Honour of C. F. D. Moule*, pp. 48-58.

69 See *Studies in the History of the Sanhedrin*, Hugo Mantel, p. 254.

twice,[70] although Roman law forbade placing a man in jeopardy twice for the same offense."[71] Thus, the scholarly claims that Jesus had *two* trials – one before the Great Sanhedrin, and one before Pilate – would have been a *clear violation of Roman law by Jesus being twice placed in jeopardy*!

At this point it is important to refer back to a matter that was mentioned in several earlier chapters in regards to Jesus being "handed over" to Pilate, and this being what is stated in John 11:50. It is in this verse in John's Gospel that we find it stating that it is better to "hand over" one individual then to have "the entire nation perish." Now, Gerard S. Sloyan erroneously comments on this verse that,[72] "This can be taken as either the callous comment of one who favors sacrificing an individual for the greater good or, in a supreme expression of irony, as unconscious affirmation of Jesus' death as a boon to Israel." But, in order to demonstrate the error in Sloyan's comment one must look to 2 Samuel 20:20-22 to find the example that was utilized in Jewish law requiring that one individual accused of wrongdoing be "handed over" to someone who was threatening to destroy an "entire city," or "town," for failing to "hand over" said individual, and in Jewish law, this was broadened to cover "the whole nation," or even simply just "the Temple."[73] But did Jewish law also include "handing over" an individual Jewish citizen to a "foreign power," i.e. the Romans? William Klassen believes that at the time of Jesus "handing over" a fellow Jew to a "foreign power" was a very serious crime.[74] But this seems to be a matter that is unclear, and thus, the possible reason for the followers of Jesus attempting to place the blame for his crucifixion onto the Sanhedrin. In *Genesis Rabbah* 94.9[75] on

---

70 *Studies in the History of the Sanhedrin*, Hugo Mantel, n. 3, p. 254, Matthew 26:57, 27:11; Mark 14:53-15:15; Luke 22:54-23:25; John 18:19-19:16.

71 See *Studies in the History of the Sanhedrin*, Hugo Mantel, n. 4, p. 254, where he cites *The Prosecution of Jesus*, R. W. Husband, p. 9 and *The Legal Procedure of Cicero's Time*, A. H. J. Greenidge, pp. 499-500 who points out that second trials became obsolete during the period Cicero lived.

72 *The Crucifixion of Jesus*, Gerard S. Sloyan, p. 70.

73 See the comments in *Barabbas and Esther*, Roger David Aus, pp. 45-56.

74 See the comments in *Judas*, William Klassen, p. 162; J. D. M. Derrett, "The Iscariot, Mesira, and the Redemption," *Journal of the Study of the New Testament* 8, (1980), p. 4.

75 See the comments on this by Richard Gottheil and Samuel Krauss, "Caiaphas or Caiphas, Joseph," *Jewish Encyclopedia*.

46:26; *Tosephta Terumoth* 7:20; Talmud Yerushalmi, *Terumoth* 46b all note an account of how R. Joshua ben Levi "handed over," or more accurately, convinced a wanted criminal to "hand himself over" to a "foreign power."[76] But the Talmud Babli *Sanhedrin* 43b clearly speaks about those who are called, *masar* ("betrayers," or "denouncers"),[77] derived from the account of Achan in Joshua 7, and this applies to the "handing over" of one to a "foreign power" as being a *masar*. As David Daube writes concerning this,[78] "However, as we shall have more occasion to note, (n. 4, p. 8, see below pp. 13ff., Chapter 2, p. 27, Chapter 6, pp 72ff.), the rabbis frequently discriminate between more and less direct modes of producing an effect; in their eyes, forthright action may be one thing, to let things take their course towards a predetermined end quite another." This is, in essence, *precisely* what we find in Acts 5:34-39 is the Pharisaic position of Gamliel, *the* most prominent member of the Great Sanhedrin around the time of Jesus' trial, (as previously noted in earlier chapters). This word *masar* also has the meanings of, "delivered," or "handed over," such as is found in Numbers 31:5, or even can mean, "to discipline," as it is found being used in Ezekiel 20:37.[79] David Daube goes on further though to point out that,[80] "The word for 'to surrender' is *masar*, a terrible action. The phrase 'a soul from Israel' is reminiscent of the statute in Deuteronomy declaring it a capital crime for a man to steal and sell abroad 'a soul from his brethren the children of Israel,' (n. 1, p. 19, Deuteronomy 24:7). 'They shall not give up a single soul from Israel': this is unconditional, not admitting of sophisticated distinctions... However, if the demand is for a named individual like Sheba son of Bichri, (2 Samuel 20) then, in order to avoid wholesale slaughter, he should be surrendered." Now, one can find that after the Bar Kochba revolt that R. Elazar b. R. Shimon *did* in fact "seize thieves and robbers" and "hand them over" to the Romans as noted in *Baba Metzia* 83b. Furthermore, one needs to also look at what is found in Judges 15:9-15. But, in this account in Judges 15, Samson *agreed* to be "handed

---

76   See the comments on this in *Collaboration with Tyranny*, David Daube, pp. 6-7.

77   See *Judas*, William Klassen, pp. 48, 58, and 62-74.

78   *Collaboration with Tyranny*, David Daube, pp. 8-9.

79   See *Etymological Dictionary of Biblical Hebrew*, p. 142; *A Comprehensive Etymological Dictionary of the Hebrew Language*, p. 363.

80   *Collaboration with Tyranny*, David Daube, p. 19.

over," and then freed himself and slew 1000 Philistines with the jawbone of an ass. Also though, when David was fleeing from Saul certain cities were willing to "hand over" David, whereas other cities would not (see 1 Samuel 21:1; 22:9-11; 23:6-15).[81] Now, the Talmud Yerushalmi, *Shebiyth* 35a; Yerushalmi *Terumoth* 8:4; *Sanhedrin* 21b; Talmud Babli, *Pesaḥim* 25b; *Sanhedrin* 74a all speak of the matter of "handing over" a "certain *named* individual*," even though it *might be* considered a "sin" to do so by some Jews, it *was* still permissible if doing such meant the difference between preserving one's own threatened life, and the life of the specifically *"named* individual."* Therefore, as it states in the Talmud, "Is your blood redder than his?" Thus, "handing over" a "specifically named individual" *was permitted* under Jewish law and doing such was referred to by the Hebrew word *nathan*, "to give over,"[82] such as one can find this word being used in the account of 2 Samuel 20 just noted above. So whereas in the case of Jesus, certain Jews may have referred to Jesus' being "handed over" to Pilate as being *nathan*, while other Jews (namely the followers of Jesus), it appears, referred to this matter of "handing over" Jesus to Pilate by way of the Hebrew word *masar*, which in essence, would be nothing more than another example of the common first century Palestinian Pharisaic/ Rabbinic matters of debating interpretations of the Torah! In fact, David Daube rightly points out that this very matter was nothing more than a debate over "interpretation," (i.e., whether it was *nathan* or *masar*), which depended entirely on whether one "admired" and "collaborated" with the Romans, or simply "obeyed" Roman demands out of fear of total destruction of the Jewish people of Palestine, or whether one looked at the Romans as being "tyrants," (see for example what is stated in the Talmud Babli, *Shabbat* 33b).[83] Also, if one was found to have committed murder, then one *could be* "handed over" to a "foreign court" as noted in *Nida* 61a. But regardless of which interpretation one used, before one could be "handed over" one *must be* found to be "deserving of death" *and* this must first have been *confirmed* by "two witnesses" in a *Jewish court*, (i.e. the Great Sanhedrin),

---

81   See the comments on this in *Collaboration with Tyranny*, David Daube, pp. 23-24.

82   See *Etymological Dictionary of Biblical Hebrew*, p. 165; *A Comprehensive Etymological Dictionary of the Hebrew Language*, p. 431; and see the comments on this in *Collaboration with Tyranny*, David Daube, pp. 26-27.

83   See the comments on this in *Collaboration with Tyranny*, p. 39.

as deserving of such *before* being "handed over" to a "foreign court," or even before one could even be subpoenaed to *appear* for judgment before a "foreign court."[84] But as was *proven* already in several earlier chapters, Jesus not only was *never* found guilty for *any* crime by *any Jewish* court, he was also *never* even taken for a trial before the Great Sanhedrin *Jewish court*! Thus, in all reality, what we find occurring in the Gospel accounts is that Jesus was *not* "handed over" *by* the Great Sanhedrin, but instead we find that Jesus was "handed over" to the Romans *by Caiaphas* out of fear that the Romans were threatening to destroy *all* of Palestine, and/or there is also the possibility that the Romans threatened *only* to remove Caiaphas as High Priest, (the same as they had done with previous Roman appointed High Priests), *if* Caiaphas *did not* "hand over" Jesus!

A further example in Jewish law of "handing over" someone to a "foreign power" is found in *Leviticus Rabbah* 19 on 15:25, which refers to the matter of King Jehoiakim who rebelled against the orders of the Babylonian King Nebuchadnezzar (2 Kings 23:36-24:7; 2 Chronicles 36:5-8), which points out that the Sanhedrin warned Jehoiakim of the pending destruction of the Temple if he was not "handed over" (which actually uses another Hebrew word here, *daḥa*, meaning "to push away"), to Nebuchadnezzar as a result of this rebellion by King Jehoiakim.[85] The case reported in *Genesis Rabbah* though, also more closely resembles the actions surrounding Jesus, the Sanhedrin, and Pilate. There is though, one last Hebrew word that must be mentioned here in regards to the matter of "handing over" someone, and this being the Hebrew word *hisgir*, which referred to a "fugitive slave" and the "handing him back" to his master, but this hardly can be applied to the matter of Jesus.[86] So as one can clearly see, the matter of "handing over" a Jew to a "foreign power" was a very complicated legal matter, which had many varying interpretations of Jewish law at the time of Jesus. Therefore, Helen K. Bond is quite in error when she asserts that attempts "to remove the Jewish leaders from *any* complicity

---

84   See the comments on this in *Collaboration with Tyranny*, pp. 44-48 where he references Matthew 5:22 as confirmation of this interpretation of Jewish law at the time of Jesus.

85   See the comments on this in *Collaboration with Tyranny*, David Daube, pp. 49-68; *Barabbas and Esther*, Roger David Aus, pp. 31-44.

86   See the comments on this in *Collaboration with Tyranny*, David Daube, pp. 56-57.

in Jesus' death are difficult to substantiate."[87] But, as is being proven here, the *fact* that Jesus was "handed over" to Pilate hardly proves "complicity" on the part of *any* Jewish "authorities." For as noted in Chapter 4, the High Priest, (i.e. Caiaphas), had absolutely zero real "authority" amongst the Jewish people of Palestine.

But once again for emphasis, Jesus said or did nothing to violate *any* Jewish law, and thus, one can *only* logically conclude that Jesus was tried *only* by Pilate under Roman law for "political" reasons.[88] Yet, there have been many scholars who while recognizing that Jesus *must* have been tried by Pilate for "political" reasons, these very same scholars then contradict their own opinions by attempting to claim that trying Jesus for "political" reasons while doing nothing about his disciples does not make any sense.[89] But these scholars seem to forget, or they have paid little or no attention to the *fact* noted in earlier chapters that Jesus' disciples "fled" at his arrest, which was in compliance with Jesus' very orders to them in Matthew 10:23, when he said that they would have to "flee from city to city," and as Acts 5:17-33 makes quite clear, *all* of the Apostles of Jesus were arrested and imprisoned. Furthermore, we also know from Acts that Paul "pursued" and "persecuted" these very followers and disciples. Thus, such claims that Pilate "did nothing" are not exactly, precisely, or necessarily true!

This then brings us to the heart of the matter of who actually had jurisdiction over the trial of Jesus – Herod Antipas, or Pontius Pilate? We find such scholarly comments to this matter as,[90] "The only course open to the Jews was to hand Jesus over to the Roman governor on the political charge implicit … since the religious charge would not lead to execution." But this seems to be more of an evangelistic theology as opposed to what was actual "historical" *fact* especially under the agreement between Roman law and the local provincial authorities noted above. In essence, it was

---

87 *Caiaphas*, Helen K. Bond, p. 62 and n. 15, p. 176.

88 See the comments in *The Trial of Jesus: Cambridge Studies in Honour of C. F. D. Moule*, pp. 48 and 79.

89 See the comments in *The Trial of Jesus: Cambridge Studies in Honour of C. F. D. Moule*, p. 8; and see also the erroneous comments on this in *The Crucifixion of Jesus*, Gerard S. Sloyan, p 32.

90 See the comments in *The Trial of Jesus: Cambridge Studies in Honour of C. F. D. Moule*, p. 79.

required that they "hand over" for trial and/or execution anyone accused of "political" crimes against Roman authority under the Roman threat of utter destruction of the entire nation. Also, as Gerard S. Sloyan points out in regards to Pilate's authority regarding "capital offense" cases,[91] "capital sentences could not be delegated."[92] Yet, A. N. Sherwin-White states regarding this,[93] "But the provincial novelty – the implication that Pilate adopted, or was willing to adopt, the sentence of the Sanhedrin – is entirely within the scope of the Procurator's *imperium*," that is, of course, *if* the crime committed was a "capital offense" crime that was also considered to be a *Roman* "political capital offense." But, as was pointed out in Chapters 5 and 7, no trial of Jesus actually ever occurred before the Great Sanhedrin especially a trial that involved a "capital offense" crime, and thus, this matter noted by Sherwin-White is a moot point! Now, Sloyan goes on to state,[94] "The only law that limited their power," (i.e. Roman governors), "was the law against extortion.[95] For the rest they could do as they pleased... The power that an official like Pilate had in criminal cases was called *coercitio* if it fell within the crimes listed in the statutes designated as public laws, for example, adultery, forgery, murder, bribery, and treason.[96] ... Juries were not known in Roman trials whereas counselors were." Furthermore, as Warren Carter points out,[97] "It is crucial for twenty-first-century readers to realize that in the Roman world there was no separation between the religious and political spheres."[98] Carter also points out in regards to the many "Conflict Stories" in the Gospels that Jesus has with, what Carter

---

91   *The Trial of Jesus*, Gerard S. Sloyan, p. 19.

92   *The Trial of Jesus*, Gerard S. Sloyan, n. 16, p. 118 Sherwin-White, *Roman Society*, 4, 5, 9, quoting *Digesta Iuris Romani* i.16; i.18.89 in *Corpus Iuris Civilis*, and Theodor Mommsen in the French edition of *Römisches Staatsrecht, Le droit Publique Romain*, trans. P. F. Girard, [Paris: Thorin et Fils, 1893] 3:280-281.

93   *Roman Society and Roman Law in the New Testament*, A. N. Sherwin-White, p. 47.

94   *The Trial of Jesus*, Gerard S. Sloyan, p. 19.

95   See further concerning this matter of "extortion" in *Roman Society and Roman Law in the New Testament*, A. N. Sherwin-White, pp. 1 and 3.

96   *The Trial of Jesus*, Gerard S. Sloyan,n. 17, Sherwin-White, *Roman Society* 13.

97   *Matthew and Empire*, Warren Carter, p 20.

98   See also the comments on this in *The New Testament*, Bart D. Ehrman, pp. 29-31; *Jesus and the Spiral of Violence*, Richard A. Horsley, Introduction, p. xi.

terms, "religious leaders" that,[99] "… Religious matters are not separate from social and political issues in the imperial world. No conflict is 'just' or 'simply' a religious one. The conflicts have social, political, and economic dimensions also. Knowing these two factors – that religious leaders are part of the ruling elite, and that religious matters are intertwined with social, political, and economic matters – casts the conflict between Jesus and the religious leaders in new light."

When Jesus was "handed over" to Pilate, and then Pilate learned during his questioning of Jesus, that Jesus was "Galilean," (Luke 23:6 for example), Pilate sends Jesus to Herod Antipas. As Rabbi Shmuley Boteach states concerning Luke 23:2,[100] "This statement in Luke indicates that corrupt priests delivered Jesus to his oppressors, the Roman administration, because he was a rebel against Roman rule pure and simple. Because it is so different from other statements throughout the rest of the Gospels, which take great pains to make Jesus non-political, it is an obvious piece of real history that slipped through, contrary to the intent of editors pushing Paul's concept of a strictly spiritual Jesus." Now, in regards to this matter of the question about Jesus being a "Galilean," at face value this seems to be an error. For according to the Gospels, and especially according to Matthew 2:11, Joseph and Mary had a "house" in Bethlehem, and according to later Church tradition as well, Jesus being born in Bethlehem of Judaea would make Jesus Judean and *not* Galilean, exactly the same as Luke's account regarding Joseph, (Luke 2:1-4). Thus, this fact that Pilate would send Jesus to Herod seems more like a matter of *where* did the *supposed* crime of "stirring up the crowds" occur, or in other words, a matter of who had jurisdiction over the trial of Jesus,[101] because Galilee did not become a Roman Province until the death of Agrippa I in 44 CE, and thus, if the crime occurred in Galilee it would have been a matter under the jurisdiction of Herod Antipas and not Pilate![102] For we know from Acts 23:34–24:26, it did not matter where someone was from, but where did the offense actually occur, as noted by the case brought against

---

99   *Matthew and Empire*, Warren Carter, p. 35.

100   *Kosher Jesus*, Rabbi Shmuley Boteach, p. 51.

101   See the comments in *The Trial of Jesus: Cambridge Studies in Honour of C. F. D. Moule*, n. 10, p. 85.

102   See *Roman Society and Roman Law in the New Testament*, A. N. Sherwin-White, p. 124.

Paul in these verses from Acts. Galilee was also known to be a "hotbed for political insurrectionists" against both Herod and the Romans, and furthermore, during the reign of Tiberius trials for what was referred to as "treason" or "insurrection" increased significantly.[103] As Hyam Maccoby writes concerning this,[104] "The Jews of Galilee disliked and despised him (Herod Antipas). They were famous for their fierce Jewish patriotism, and the events in Judaea affected them deeply… Even though Galilee itself was not under direct rule, Jesus grew up in an atmosphere more patriotic and anti-Roman than if he had been born in Jerusalem itself." In regards to this fact that Galilee was such a "hotbed for political insurrectionists," Gerard S. Sloyan rightly asks,[105] "Why both Jewish and Roman authority would have wondered, would large crowds have been assembling in Galilee to hear this man if not with a view to an uprising?" Also, the fact is that Galileans were very much against the illegitimacy of the High Priest as well for being a collaborator with the Romans,[106] as noted previously in Chapter 2. Now some scholars though, believe that it *was not* Galilee but Judea that was the "hotbed for political insurrection."[107] While it is quite true that most of the "insurrectionary" activities occurred in Judea, and primarily surrounding matters involving the Temple, and although these "insurrectionary" activities involved a wide cross section of Jews, (as pointed out in Chapter 2), the *fact* remains though, that the main *leaders* of these "insurrectionary" actions came from Galilee![108]

There are in fact a few scholars who claim that Pilate was under no obligation whatsoever to send Jesus to Herod Antipas. These scholars believe that Pilate's reason for doing so was simply to try and improve his relations with Herod Antipas, which had been strained by certain previous actions

---

103   See the comments on this in *Pontius Pilate in History and Interpretation*, Helen K. Bond, pp. 43-44.

104   *Revolution in Judaea*, Hyam Maccoby, p. 38.

105   *The Crucifixion of Jesus*, Gerard S. Sloyan, p. 40.

106   See the comments in *Herod Antipas*, Harold W. Hoehner, pp. 56-57; *Kosher Jesus*, Rabbi Shmuley Boteach, p. 3.

107   See for example the comments in *Conflict, Holiness & Politics*, Marcus Borg, pp. 45 and 48.

108   See the comments on this in *Galilee*, Sean Freyne, pp. 245-247.

that had been taken by Pilate in regards to the Jewish populace.[109] Justin Martyr in his *Dialogue with Trypho* 103.4, likewise states this very same thing that Pilate was under no obligation to send Jesus to Herod Antipas.

Since it has been shown in earlier chapters, and again mentioned in this chapter, that Jesus violated no Jewish laws and was therefore, not convicted of any crime by the Great Sanhedrin, but was simply "handed over" to Pilate to be tried under "Roman law," it is necessary here to now speak of certain matters regarding trials by Roman law, as they pertain to this matter of Pilate sending Jesus to Herod Antipas. But it must first be noted that Pontius Pilate's primary residence in Judea was at Caesarea and he only came to Jerusalem during the time of the Jewish festivals in order to oversee that things remained peaceful. For it was during such festival times that quite often minor little unrests occurred.[110] This then brings us to several key words of Roman law, and these words being, *Forum Domicilii*, (trial conducted in a provincial domicile, such as Palestine), *Forum Apprehensionis*, (where a prisoner was caught, or arrested), and *Forum Delecti*, or *Forum Originis*, (where the crime was committed).[111] Therefore, this then goes back to a matter mentioned in earlier chapters in regards to Jesus being a "fugitive" and Jesus being "warned" by the Pharisees that "Herod sought Jesus." So then, who actually made the complaint to the Great Sanhedrin that brought about the "summons" for Jesus to appear before the Great Sanhedrin that was discussed in Chapter 5, and thus, what then brought about the formal "warrant" for Jesus' arrest as a "fugitive" – was it Pontius Pilate, or Herod Antipas, or again, as mentioned in Chapter 5, was Jesus "summoned" to appear before the Great Sanhedrin in regards to a debate over an interpretation of the Torah? The most logical conclusion though, based on the overall evidence in the Gospels is that it was either Pilate, or

---

109   See the comments in *The Trial of Jesus: Cambridge Studies in Honour of C. F. D. Moule*, p. 88; *Herod Antipas*, Harold W. Hoehner, pp. 182-183 and 236; *Pontius Pilate*, Ann Wroe, p. 246.

110   See the comments in *Pontius Pilate*, Ann Wroe, p. 77; *Pontius Pilate in History and Interpretation*, Helen K. Bond, p. 7.

111   See the comments in *Pontius Pilate*, Ann Wroe, p. 246; *Herod Antipas*, Harold W. Hoehner, pp. 233-239; *Roman Society and Roman Law in the New Testament*, A. N. Sherwin-White, pp. 28-31.

Herod Antipas that registered the complaint that resulted in a "summons" being issued by the Great Sanhedrin.

There are some scholars who believe that it was actually Herod Antipas who convicted Jesus, and Herod Antipas only sent Jesus back to Pilate in order to have Pilate carry out the actual execution of Jesus.[112] In fact, an essential point to make here comes from the non-canonical *Gospel of Peter*, (a fragment of which was discovered in 1886, and which it must be stated, does contain a sort of "bias" that needs to be considered regarding credibility[113]). For it states in the *Gospel of Peter* that it was Herod Antipas, along with his Sadducee collaborators, who actually ordered Jesus to be crucified, and thus, Antipas sent Jesus back to Pilate to carry out this order.[114] Yet, some of these very same scholars who make these claims offer evidence that refutes their very own claims. For instance, in Luke 23:11 Herod Antipas places a robe onto Jesus in a very mocking gesture as if to say, "So *you* are the king and not I, eh?" Thus, just from this verse alone we know that Herod Antipas was given some knowledge from somewhere that Jesus had been pronounced "King of the Jews," and this despite the claims by so many *modern* scholars that such *never* occurred until *after* Jesus was dead, (a matter noted already in an earlier chapter). This mocking gesture is also reflected in Acts 12:21, and by Josephus, *Antiquities* 19.344. Therefore, Herod Antipas sending Jesus back to Pilate *was not* because Herod had found Jesus "guilty," but for the simple reason noted above concerning the *Pax Romana* and the fact that it was the Roman governors that decided *who* the provincial "client kings" were to be. In essence then, Herod Antipas sent Jesus back to Pilate mockingly saying, "Pilate you decide whether I am the appointed ruler of Galilee, or is this Jesus of Nazareth to be the appointed king over *all* of Palestine."[115] Klaus Wengst writes concerning the Lord's Prayer that it,[116] "Amounts to a questioning of the *Pax Romana*: anyone who prays for the coming of the

---

112   See for example the comments in *Herod Antipas*, Harold W. Hoehner, p. 230; *The Trial of Jesus of Nazareth*, M. Rodin, p. 175.

113   See the comments on this in *The New Testament*, Bart D. Ehrman, p. 218.

114   See the comments on this in *The New Testament*, Bart D. Ehrman, p. 199.

115   See the comments in *Herod Antipas*, Harold W. Hoehner, pp. 244-249; *The Last Week*, Marcus Borg and John Dominic Crossan, p. 146.

116   *Pax Romana and the Peace of Jesus Christ*, Klaus Wengst, p. 55.

Kingdom of God (Matthew 6:10), expects it very soon, and has no faith in the imperial good tidings of a pacified world and human happiness in it." Warren Carter also writes concerning this,[117] "But it is more than a questioning, it is a challenge that subverts imperial claims and creates an alternative empire and way of life."[118]

It is therefore now, essential to point out here a somewhat erroneous statement made by Joseph Ratzinger and Pope Benedict XVI when they write,[119] "As Prefect, Pilate represented Roman law, on which the *Pax Romana* rested – the peace of the empire that spanned the world. This peace was secured, on the one hand, through Rome's military might. But military force alone does not generate peace. Peace depends on justice. Rome's real strength lay in its legal system, the juridical order on which men could rely. Pilate – let us repeat – knew the truth of the case, and hence he knew what justice demanded of him." But, as was clearly pointed out above, it was Pilate's *own violent actions*, which violated and disregarded the provisions of the *Pax Romana* that got Pilate removed as governor, and thus, the very reason why such an apologetically biased statement in regards to Pilate by Ratzinger and Pope Benedict XVI is just another example of a "whitewashing" in regards to the "historical" and *factual* truth surrounding Pilate's true character as Procurator!

Another claim that has been made in regards to it being Herod Antipas, instead of Pilate, who actually convicted Jesus revolves around the belief that there are two possible "eyewitnesses" to both John the Baptists' episode with Herod Antipas and Jesus' episode with Herod Antipas, and these supposed *possible* "eyewitnesses" are first, Joanna, the wife of Chuza mentioned in Luke 8:3 and Luke 24:10. For Chuza was the "steward of Herod Antipas." The second possible "eyewitness" is Manaen, an intimate friend of Herod Antipas and a member of Herod's court mentioned in Acts 13:1.[120] But *modern* scholarship, which relies so heavily now on what is called "multiple attestation," brings such claims into question since these individuals are

---

117 *Matthew and Empire*, Warren Carter, p. 61.

118 See also the comments on this in *How Jesus Became Christian*, Barrie Wilson, pp. 93, 256, ans 263-265.

119 *Jesus of Nazareth: Part Two*, Ratzinger and Pope Benedict, pp 200-201.

120 See the comments in *Herod Antipas*, Harold W. Hoehner, Appendix VI, pp. 303-305; *Crime before Calvary*, Guy Schofield, pp. 66-67, and 136-137.

only mentioned by the author of Luke/Acts and therefore, doubts as to the historical reliability of these individuals as being actual "eyewitnesses" to a conviction of Jesus rendered by Herod Antipas must also be questioned. The other point that brings further doubt that it was Herod Antipas who convicted Jesus derives from the historian Tacitus, *Annals* 15:44. Tacitus was no friend of the followers of Jesus[121] and Tacitus *clearly* states that it was *Pontius Pilate* who convicted Jesus and *not* Herod Antipas, *nor* does Tacitus say that it was the Jewish Great Sanhedrin who convicted Jesus.

There are two different matters mentioned in the Gospels that prove that Pontius Pilate alone judged, and convicted Jesus of violating *only* Roman law.[122] The first of these matters derives from what is found being stated in John 19:13 by way of the Greek words *lithostroton*, "mosaic pavement," or Aramaic *gabbatha*, "raised platform," and the Greek word *bematos*, "judgment seat," or "tribunal bench."[123] Josephus in *Jewish Wars* 2.301[2.14.8] mentions this very bench in regards to Pilate's successor taking "his seat" in this same location to conduct a tribunal. The location of this "judgment seat" was, according to Josephus, and Mark 15:16, by way of the Greek word *aule*, at Herod's Palace near the Jaffa Gate, or west hill.[124]

The second fact that proves that Pontius Pilate alone tried and convicted Jesus for "political crimes" under Roman law derives from the *fact* that all four Gospels, Matthew 27:37; Mark 15:26; Luke 23:38; John 19:19 ("multiple attestation" in other words), clearly state that Jesus was convicted for being the *assumed* "King of the Jews."[125] Crimes committed under Roman law that were "capital offenses" punishable by public execution required what was called, *Titulus Qui Causam Poenae Indicat*, "A Title Indicating the Cause of Punishment."[126] Under the *Lex Julia Maiestates*

---

121   See the comments in *Kosher Jesus*, Rabbi Shmuley Boteach, pp. 83-84.

122   See the comments in *The Trial of Jesus*, Josef Blinzler, pp. 30-32.

123   See the comments in *"Caught in the Act,"* Roger David Aus, p. 140; *Roman Society and Roman Law in the New Testament*, A. N. Sherwin-White, p. 24.

124   See the comments in *Jesus On Trial*, Gerard S. Sloyan, pp. 26-27.

125   See the comments in *Roman Society and Roman Law in the New Testament*, A. N. Sherwin-White, pp. 24-26; *On Earth As It Is In Heaven*, D. C. Thielmann, pp. 307-308 and the corresponding scholars notations to these pages.

126   See Suetonius *Domitianes* 10,1; "The Trial of Jesus," *Trivium*, P. Winter, (1967), p. 109; *Jesus and the Origins of Christianity*, M. Goguel, Volume II, n. 2, p. 521; *The Trial and*

of Roman law, anyone claiming to be the "king" of a Roman province whom had not been *appointed* by the Roman Governor or Procurator of that Roman province *to be* the "king" of that Roman province was guilty of "high treason" against Rome![127]

The general belief by so many scholars, theologians, and church laity is that Jesus went out of his way to avoid not only claiming to be the *messiah* (i.e. "King of the Jews"), but also resisted others trying to proclaim his being such.[128] But such claims make absolutely no sense whatsoever given the "multiply attested" *Titulus* judgment rendered by Pilate! Mark 15:12 offers a prime example of this *fact* that such claims make no sense. For why would this verse, for example, be stating, (italics mine), "Then what shall I do with the man *whom you call* the King of the Jews?"[129] Why would Jesus have been arrested, tried, and convicted by Pilate under the charge placed on the *Titulus Qui Causam Poenae Indicat* of "King of the Jews" if Jesus himself had not in some way, manner, or action *clearly* indicated or claimed to be such? As Joel Carmichael rightly states,[130] "Summed up, a Roman governor crucifies a Jew who is politically inoffensive for what is, at one point, said to be an offense against the Jewish religion. At another point an offense against Rome is also mentioned, but this is expressly declared to be imaginary. Yet it is ultimately for just this offense against Rome, as a pretender to power ('King of the Jews'), that Jesus is crucified. This contradiction at the very crux of the Gospel account is an indispensable

---

Death of Jesus, H. Cohn, p. 171; *Jesus of Nazareth*, Gunther Bornkamm, p. 165; *Pontius Pilate*, Ann Wroe, p. 66; *On Earth As It Is In Heaven*, D. C. Thielmann, n. 112, p. 353; *Jesus Interrupted*, Bart D. Ehrman, pp. 43-45; *Who is Jesus*, Darrell L. Bock, p. 111.

127 See the comments in "The Roman Law of Treason Under the Early Principate," *Journal of Roman Studies*, 45 (1955), C. W. Wilton, pp. 73-81; *Pontius Pilate*, Ann Wroe, pp. 207-208; *Jesus Interrupted*, Bart D. Ehrman, p 169; *Revolution in Judaea*, Hyam Maccoby, p. 14; *Matthew and Empire*, Warren Carter, pp. 160-163; *How Jesus Became Christian*, Barrie Wilson, p. 193; *On Earth As It Is In Heaven*, D. C. Thielmann, pp. 307-308 and the corresponding scholars notations to these pages.

128 See for example the comments in *Pontius Pilate*, Ann Wroe, pp. 207-208; *The Lost Gospel of Judas Iscariot*, Bart D. Ehrman, pp. 158 and 162.

129 See the comments in *On Earth As It Is In Heaven*, D. C. Thielmann, n. 110, pp. 352-353; *You Take Jesus, I'll Take God*, Samuel Levine, p. 72.

130 *The Death of Jesus*, Joel Carmichael, pp. 9-10.

signpost for the reconstruction it clamors for."[131] Also, as other scholars have rightly pointed out, the matter of the "politically" charged conviction noted on the *Titulus* would *not* have been invented by either the Jerusalem Church *or* the later gentile Christians.[132]

Eusebius in his *Ecclesiastical History* 3:12 and 3:19:1-3; 20:7 traces the "Messianic claim" for the entire family of Jesus as followed by the Jerusalem Church.[133] This then brings us to the all-important statement made by Jesus himself in answer to Pilate's question, and this being, Jesus' response, "You say so!"[134] This statement alone is a bold slap in the face of Pilate by Jesus! It is essential to point out here before discussing the matter of this statement made by Jesus, that the use of this phrase, (or a similar phrase), was a very common Pharisaic/rabbinic practice of affirming something to be true as found noted in Yerushalmi *Kilaim* 9:3; Babli *Ketuboth* 104a; *Koheleth Rabbah* 7:12; *Tosefta Kelim* 1.1.6.

The account we have in John's Gospel is of great value in regards to the matter of determining the very cause of Jesus' conviction by Pilate. To be more specific here, we must take a closer look at what is stated in John 18:36-37 and John 19:10-12. Looking closely first at John 18:36-37 it must be pointed out that what is stated here by Jesus is a very clear Jewish "eschatological" and "Messianic" statement, that although some scholars believe that Pilate may have misunderstood this statement by Jesus, the fact is that any and *all* Jews would clearly have understood the statement to *clearly* be an "eschatological Messianic" statement. Rabbi Moshe Reiss writes concerning John 18:36,[135] "This is an eschatological statement.

---

131   See further on this the excellent comments in *The Death of Jesus*, Joel Carmichael, pp. 12-13.

132   See the comments on this in *Jesus and His Contemporaries*, Etienne Trocme, pp. 74-75.

133   See the comments in *Judas Iscariot and the Myth of Jewish Evil*, Hyam Maccoby, pp. 156-159 and n. 13-15, pp. 189-190.

134   See the comments in *Jesus and Israel*, Jules Isaac, pp. 322-324; *Jesus: Uncovering the Life, Teachings, and Relevance of a Religious Revolutionary*, Marcus Borg, p. 264 who believes that this response by Jesus to Pilate "suggests contempt" towards Pilate, while on the other hand, Edgar J. Goodspeed in *Problems of New Testament Translation*, pp. 64-68 interprets this to be a direct simple statement by Jesus of, "yes I am."

135   *Christianity: A Jewish Perspective*, Rabbi Moshe Reiss, 2 "Jesus Comes From the Jewish Tradition," IX "Jesus the Crucified Messiah."

Many scholars believe Jesus was unwilling to state his Messiahship, thus his 'You said it.' William Wrede and Rudolf Bultmann, write that neither Jesus nor his disciples thought he was the messiah. 'The proclaimer became the proclaimed.'[136] Those who proclaimed the coming of the age of heaven became the messiah. On the other hand, J. C. O'Neill disputes that in a famous article.[137] A major part of his contention is all the Gospels say that Pilate executed the 'King of the Jews.' Who is the King of the Jews if not the Messiah? For Pilate a 'King of the Jews' was simply a kingly pretender. It is certain that Pilate would not understand 'my kingdom does not belong here' (John 18:36). That eschatological statement would only be understood by Jewish apocalypts." There are other scholars though who believe Pilate *did* clearly understand the statement as a "messianic" claim, which in essence then Pilate *clearly* understood that Jesus' statement *was* a claim to being "King of the Jews."[138] But these same scholars believe that Pilate *did* misunderstand Jesus' meaning that he expressed in these verses from John in regards to the "Kingdom of Heaven."[139] For the Greek words, *ek tou kosmou toutou* are not intended to be translated and interpreted as meaning, "my kingdom is not *of this* world," but are *better* interpreted as meaning, "my kingdom is *for* this world."[140]

This then brings us to what we find being stated in John 19:10-12. Now, in these verses of John's Gospel both the Greek nouns and the Greek verbs that are used offer several possible meanings, and thus, several different possible ways of interpreting what is being stated in these verses. For example: The Greek word *emoi* can mean, "To me," or it can also mean, "Against me," and therefore, Pilate's statement, "*To me* won't you speak?"

---

136   *Christianity: A Jewish Perspective*, Rabbi Moshe Reiss,n. 130, *The Theology of the New Testament*, R. Bultmann [Edinburgh University Press, Edinburgh 1957], p. 32. See also, *The Messianic Secret*, W. Wrede, [J. Clark, Cambridge 1971], and *Jesus of Nazareth*, Gunther Bornkamm, [Harper and Row, NY 1960].

137   *Christianity: A Jewish Perspective*, Rabbi Moshe Reiss, n. 131, "The Silence of Jesus," *New Testament Studies* 15, J. C. O'Neill.

138   See the comments in *Judas and the Gospel of Jesus*, N. T. Wright, pp. 85-87; *Simply Jesus*, N. T. Wright, pp. 69 and 85-86.

139   See the comments in *Simply Jesus*, N. T. Wright, pp. 144-145.

140   See the comments in *Judas and the Gospel of Jesus*, N. T. Wright, p. 88 and n. 1, p. 152 (the italics are N. T. Wright's).

and Jesus' response, "*Against me*, you are powerless," is such an emphatically clear statement and *admission* by Jesus of his "Kingship" that Pilate most certainly *would not* have missed this *fact!*[141] Thus, Pilate's reaction to being accused of "not Caesar's friend," or what was referred to as *Caesaris Amicus* would then be totally plausible as believed by some scholars.[142] There are some scholars though, who have claimed that what is stated in John 19:8 about Pilate being "afraid" is legitimate.[143] But not only are such claims a further attempt at "whitewashing" Pilate, they simply make absolutely no sense given what has just been pointed out in regards to the verses that follow in John 19:10-12. Also, though, as pointed out in Chapter 7, Roman Emperors were referred to as "son of god," so why would Pilate be "afraid" of hearing such a term being used by anyone? The only possible "historical" reaction that a Roman governor would have had upon hearing such a claim coming from a "*provincial lower class*" individual in regards to themselves would be that it was a mocking affront to Caesar!

There is one last aspect of the accounts in John's Gospel that must be mentioned, and this being what is found in John 19:15. In all intents and purposes this *must be* understood as a very late gentile Church interpolation to simply make the Jews look guilty and Pilate and the Romans look innocent. As Barrie Wilson writes,[144] "The tendency to exonerate Roman authorities and to fix the blame on the Jews increased with time as early Christianity moved into the Mediterranean arena." Despite the fact that Herod the Great had erected three temples in various cities in Palestine to commemorate the Roman emperor Augustus,[145] it is simply ridiculous to conceive of *any first century Palestinian Jew*, (whether Pharisee, Essen, or even Sadducee, or regardless of whether they were Judean or Galilean, and regardless of whether they were from the Jewish lower classes, or from the Jewish aristocracy), *completely forsaking God or the "Messianic hope*," to such a point so as to state, "We have no king but Caesar." As Joseph Ratzinger

---

141 See the comments in *Pontius Pilate*, Ann Wroe, p. 269.

142 See the comments in *Pontius Pilate*, Ann Wroe, p. 97; *Roman Society and Roman Law in the New Testament*, A. N. Sherwin-White, p. 47.

143 See for example the comments in *Jesus of Nazareth: Part Two*, Ratzinger and Pope Benedict, p. 195.

144 *How Jesus Became Christian*, Barrie Wilson, p. 233.

145 *The Son of God in the Roman World*, Michael Peppard, pp. 92-93.

and Pope Benedict XVI state concerning this,[146] (and it must be stated that their comment here is virtually a quite accurate statement), "... This only *appears* to be a renunciation of Israel's Messianic hope...." This statement of *fact* is the very reason why John 19:15 is clearly a late interpolation! For the Jewish "hope" for the Messiah has *never* been abandoned! There were many different interpretations of this hope, but it has *never* been abandoned by Jews! Now it is true though, that in Philo's writings Philo states that the Jews would refer to the Roman emperor as "master," but Philo *never* states that the Jews *ever* referred to the Roman emperor as "king."[147]

From these accounts in John's Gospel we are now brought to what we find being stated in, 1 Timothy 6:13. In this verse it *clearly* states that Jesus testified "before Pontius Pilate and made the good confession." Donald Juel writes concerning this "confession,"[148] "For Mark, the true meaning of the Passion can only be understood in terms of the confession of Jesus as Messiah, son of God." Now, as noted in an earlier chapter, one's own confession *could not* be the grounds for one's conviction under *Jewish law*. But, under *Roman law*, one's own confession *was* sufficient for a conviction,[149] and in fact if one was to remain "silent" and said nothing in regards to their own defense, then likewise, under Roman law this silence "was counted in the same way as if they had pleaded guilty."[150] This verse of 1 Timothy 6:13 then corroborates the *Titulus Qui Causam Poenae Indicat* noted earlier in this chapter as the reason for Jesus' conviction because Jesus himself *admitted* to Pilate that *he was* the true "King of the Jews" despite all of the attempts by so many modern New Testament scholars who try to claim that Jesus *never* claimed to be such. This then also answers why we have the Gospel accounts noting that the Roman soldiers, after Jesus' conviction by Pilate, were playing a game referred to as *Basilinda*, "The King" game, in other words, which was played with knucklebones, and in which such a convicted prisoner as Jesus, was taken out and had a crown

---

146   *Jesus of Nazareth: Part Two*, Ratzinger and Pope Benedict, p. 197.

147   See the comments on this in *Pontius Pilate in History and Interpretation*, Helen K. Bond, pp. 37-48.

148   *Messiah and Temple*, Donald Juel, p. 211.

149   See the comments in *Jesus On Trial*, Gerard S. Sloyan, p. 17; *How Jesus Became God*, Bart D. Ehrman, pp. 122-124.

150   *Pontius Pilate in History and Interpretation*, Helen K. Bond, p. 108.

of thorns placed upon their head, and then that prisoner was robed before being lead off to be crucified.[151]

For all intents and purposes then, the *only* supposed trial of Jesus in the Gospel accounts that can be said or claimed by *anyone* to have been conducted in a legitimately correct manner under either Jewish law or Roman law, which could have resulted in a conviction punishable by a death sentence of crucifixion, was Jesus' trial before Pontius Pilate![152] As Bart Ehrman writes,[153] "From a Roman administrative point of view, Pontius Pilate was altogether justified in condemning Jesus to death as a public nuisance. People like Pilate were expected to deal with cases like this with justice when possible and severity when necessary." But, as Roger David Aus points out,[154] "None of Jesus' followers were eyewitnesses to Pilate's interrogation of Jesus, if one occurred at all. Pilate was well-known for constantly ordering executions (including crucifixion) without a trial (Philo, *Embassy to Gaius* 302)."

---

151   See the comments in *Pontius Pilate*, Ann Wroe, p. 199.

152   See the comments in *Pontius Pilate*, Ann Wroe, p. 227; *The Lost Gospel of Judas Iscariot*, Bart D. Ehrman, pp. 162-163 and n. 13, p. 188; *Jesus: Uncovering the Life, Teachings, and Relevance of a Religious Revolutionary*, Marcus J. Borg, p. 271; *Jesus*, C. Leslie Mitton, p. 88.

153   *The New Testament*, Bart D. Ehrman, p. 428.

154   *"Caught in the Act,"* Roger David Aus, p. 165.

Chapter 9

"But you have made it a den of thieves"
(Matthew 21:13).

The most important aspect of Jesus' entire ministry to correctly interpret in regards to understanding the ultimate reason as to *why* Jesus was brought to a trial of *any* kind surrounds the Temple incident that is reported in all four Gospels. There are though, differences between the four Gospels, not only in regards to exactly *what* occurred at this Temple incident, but also in regards to exactly *when* this incident occurred. For example, did Jesus just "drive out" the moneychangers (Luke's version), or did he both "drive out" *and* "overturn the tables" of the moneychangers (Matthew, Mark, and John's version)?[1] As Joseph Ratzinger and Pope Benedict XVI write concerning this,[2] "It was this action – the cleansing of the Temple – that contributed significantly to Jesus' condemnation to death...." This Temple incident, (in conjunction with the fact noted in earlier chapters that Jesus was already a "wanted fugitive"), can then, basically, be described as the "final straw" in Jesus'

---

1 See the comments in *Kosher Jesus*, Rabbi Shmuley Boteach, p. 22; and see the very thorough covering of all of the varying opinions regarding the Temple incident in *Who is Jesus*, Darrell l. Bock, pp. 122-136.

2 *Jesus of Nazareth: Part Two*, Ratzinger and Pope Benedict, p. 148.

ministry that prompted his arrest.[3] As will be discussed in this chapter, even though this incident has the all-important criteria of "multiple attestation," with only slight differences as to *what* exactly occurred, there *is* though, a major discrepancy in the Gospel accounts as to exactly *when* the Temple incident actually occurred during Jesus' ministry, which therefore, creates the possibility that it was this Temple incident that caused Jesus to become a "wanted fugitive" in the first place. Yet, it is also essential to point out that outside of the Gospels, we really have no other source, whether an "historical" source, such as Josephus, Tacitus, or Philo, nor do we find anything in the Mishnah and Talmud that attests to this Temple incident by Jesus of *Nazareth*, (a matter that will be discussed further below), nor do we even find anything in *any* of Paul's letters, or in *any* of the other New Testament Epistles.

Now, Hyam Maccoby may make the best overall statement in regards to this matter of the Temple incident when he writes concerning the incident of Jesus' disciples "plucking corn" on the Sabbath (discussed in Chapter 1, but is necessary to refer to again here because of its connection to the Temple incident),[4] "Why then, was the element of emergency removed from the story as we have it in the Gospels, thus reducing the whole episode to nonsense? The answer is: for the same reason that the element of emergency has been removed from the whole of the Gospels, which portray Judaea and Galilee as peaceful areas under benign Roman rule, instead of what they were in historical reality at this time, areas of bitter unrest and constant rebellion against the savage oppression of the Romans and the depredations of the tax-farmers (or publicans). If the sense of emergency had been retained in the story, not only would it have to be revealed that Jesus was not flouting Pharisee law but also that he was a hunted man, wanted by Herod and the Romans, and in rebellion against them." Also, Marcus J. Borg writes concerning the importance of this matter in the context of the social world that Jesus lived that,[5] "To apply this to Jesus, it is impossible to see his significance without setting his life and public activity in the context of his social world. It would be

---

3   See the comments in *Pontius Pilate*, Ann Wroe, p. 211.

4   *The Mythmaker*, Hyam Maccoby, p. 42.

5   *Jesus: Uncovering the Life, Teachings, and Relevance of a Religious Revolutionary*, Marcus J. Borg, pp. 78-79.

like trying to understand the significance of Abraham Lincoln's speeches without setting them in the context of the Civil War, or Martin Luther King Jr.'s words and deeds without locating them in the mid-twentieth-century struggle over civil rights. Words and deeds have their meaning in the cultural context, the social world, in which they are said and done."

There are many scholars who have chosen to interpret Jesus' overturning of the moneychangers' tables as being simply a "symbolic" action that indicated that the Temple "no longer had a purpose,"[6] or that it "symbolized" the replacing of an "economically exploitive and politically oppressive system."[7] The same scholars that make such preposterous assertions that Jesus' action in the Temple incident was *only* a "symbolic" action love to use the term, "cleansing of the Temple," and they will quite often make reference to such verses as Malachi 3:1-3 for example, to justify their assertions. But the Hebrew word *teher*, "purify," used in Malachi 3:3 indicates both a "moral" *and* "ritual purity," as well as indicating that something is being made "free of foreign elements,"[8] (and the matter of Jesus' attitude towards such "purity" halakha was discussed previously in Chapter 4), which thus, in essence and in all reality, contradicts the very intent of the preposterous claims being made by these scholars! There are also other scholars who believe that while the charge against Jesus regarding his supposed claim to "destroy this Temple ... and after three days I will build another," is a "false charge," because, as they claim, "Jesus never made such a statement." These very scholars who hold to *this* particular opinion though, will still claim that this matter of the overturning of the moneychanger's tables had sort of a "symbolic" truth to it. As Donald Juel writes, for example,[9] "The charge reflects Mark's view of the relationship between the Christian

---

6   See for example the comments in *Simply Jesus*, N. T. Wright, pp. 127-135; *The Partings of the Ways*, James Dunn, pp. 47-49; *Caiaphas*, Helen K. Bond, pp. 66-70; and see the entire book *The Theological Significance of Jesus' Temple Action in Mark's Gospel*, Emilio G. Chavez.

7   See for example the comments in *Jesus: Uncovering the Life, Teachings, and Relevance of a Religious Revolutionary*, Marcus J. Borg; *The Last Week*, Marcus J. Borg and John Dominic Crossan, pp. 28 and 47; *Jesus Interrupted*, Bart D. Ehrman, pp. 166-168.

8   See *Etymological Dictionary of Biblical Hebrew*, p. 94; *A Comprehensive Etymological Dictionary of the Hebrew Language*, p. 240.

9   *Messiah and Temple*, Donald Juel, pp. 57-58.

movement and the Temple establishment. The Church is characterized as a spiritual Temple made without hands and is viewed as a replacement of the Jewish Temple." But such claims only beg for a question to be asked, and this question being, if Jesus never made such a statement, then how could *any* competent scholar justify this matter by claiming that it contains *any* sort of *truth*, (whether "symbolic" or otherwise), in regards to the trial narratives? There is an *historical fact* that is too often overlooked by scholars, and this being that on two separate occasions in Jewish history – during the Babylonian exile, and between the years 168-165 BCE, (as stated in *1 Maccabees* 1:54; 4:52) – the valid Temple practices were discontinued. These two *historical facts* alone *should be* sufficient proof that such scholarly claims and assertions about Jesus' actions at the Temple are without merit! For such a belief as they are claiming had already been amongst the majority of Jews *long before* the time of Jesus going all the way back in history to the time of the Babylonian exile, and this belief being that, *"prayer, repentance, and charity"* were far more important as a substitute for the Temple rituals, as it is *clearly* noted in Mishnah *Ta'anit* 2:1; 65b. Therefore, far too many scholars have put forth these absurd notions and claims that the early Church perceived of Jesus' Temple incident as being some sort of a "permanent end" to the Temple.[10] Yet, these scholars seem to ignore the very *fact* that the New Testament Books of Acts (Acts 15:16) and Revelations references a *third Temple* (Revelations 3:12-13; 7:15; 11:1-2; 11:19), and they also seem to not take into account the prophecies of Ezekiel, and the other ancient prophets, or take into account *1 Enoch* 90:28-36, or even the *Temple Scroll* and fragment *4Q174* found amongst the Dead Sea Scrolls,[11] all of which reference a restored *third Temple* complete with *all* of the Temple "rituals" and with a restored "legitimate" Priesthood returning at some point in time in the future. In other words, these scholars are ignoring the references to a restored Third Temple, even the references to a restored Third Temple found in the New Testament, that will occur during the period of time in the future which gets generally referred to, even *by* the early Church, as "the end times." Now, in regards to the references

---

10   See for example the comments in *The Partings of the Ways*, James Dunn, pp. 95-97.

11   See the comments on the *Temple Scroll* in *Jesus and the Spiral of Violence*, Richard A. Horsley, pp. 291 and 295; *The Theological Significance of Jesus' Temple Action in Mark's Gospel*, Emilio G. Chavez, pp. 110-111.

in the Book of Revelations just noted, many apologetic New Testament scholars, as well as the general church laity, believe that these references to a "third Temple" in the Book of Revelations are indicating a "Temple in Heaven," or in essence, a "*spiritual* Temple" and *not* an actual earthly materially rebuilt Temple. But such interpretations are simply without merit, as will be pointed out. For the term "Kingdom of Heaven" was an indication of God's presence here on earth, such as is found in the Lord's Prayer![12] As an example of what is meant by what is being stated here, Donald Juel discusses the Jewish "historical" tradition of a *third Temple*,[13] and Juel makes the comment that this *third Temple*, mentioned in the *Temple Scroll* was, (in his opinion), as he believes that it is being interpreted by the Qumran sectarians (i.e. the Essens), was indicating just a "community" of "individuals,"[14] to which Juel then connects this "community" imagery with "messianic" expectations.[15] But again, this is just another example of a scholar misunderstanding Jewish "metaphor," and thus, the main point to be made here is that there *were* expectations, even among the Essens that the second Temple would be destroyed and replaced by an "earthly" *third Temple* during the "*messianic era*."[16]

There is still one more scholarly opinion that must be mentioned here, and this being, that there are some scholars who believe that Jesus' Temple incident is a "Markan fabrication,"[17] meaning that these scholars believe that no such incident instigated by Jesus ever actually occurred. This is an opinion that seems highly unlikely given the scholarly criteria of "multiple attestation," although *some* of the scholars who hold to *this* particular opinion believe that the criteria of "multiple attestation" should simply

---

12 See the comments on this in *Judaism and the Origins of Christianity*, pp. 464-465.

13 *Messiah and Temple*, Donald Juel, pp. 150-152; but see also the comments in *Messiah in Context*, Jacob Neusner, pp. 108-110, 183.

14 *Messiah and Temple*, Donald Juel, pp. 159-168; but see also the similar comments in *The Theological Significance of Jesus' Temple Action in Mark's Gospel*, Emilio G. Chavez, pp. 112-114.

15 *Messiah and Temple*, Donald Juel, pp. 172-209.

16 See the comments on this in *Judaism and the Origins of Christianity*, David Flusser, pp. 88-98.

17 See for example *A Myth of Innocence*, Burton L. Mack, p. 292; Neil Godfrey, "Why the Temple Act of Jesus is Almost Certainly Not Historical," February 13, 2010, *Vridar*.

be ignored in regards to this one particular matter. Now, the main basis for the claim by these scholars that Jesus' Temple incident is a "Markan fabrication" is derived from the similarities of the Gospel accounts to the account in Josephus *Jewish Wars* 6.300-309, (which will be mentioned again below), regarding an individual named Jesus son of Hananiah, or also known as, Jesus ben Ananus (or Ananias). As the claim goes, the author of Mark's Gospel, (again, the Gospel believed by the majority of scholars to be the first written), *borrowed* this account from Josephus and "fabricated" a similar account concerning the actions of Jesus of Nazareth. *If* these scholarly claims *are* in fact the *historical truth* regarding the Temple incident attributed to Jesus, then in all reality all that this fact will do is to lend real *proof* to what was pointed out in the Preface that the Gospels, as we know them today, *could not* have been written until *after* Josephus' writings were completed, or in other words, until sometime during the second century CE!

Many scholars also claim that there is absolutely no evidence in the New Testament that either Jesus or any of his immediate followers participated in *any* of the Temple "rituals."[18] Such claims though, only go to demonstrate a total lack of understanding of what constituted the Temple "rituals" at the time of Jesus! Lloyd Gaston, for example, even though he rightly quotes Josephus *Antiquities* 18.19,[19] which states in regards to the Essens, "Although they send votive gifts to the Temple, they do not offer sacrifices, because of what they consider to be superior purifications, and therefore, abstaining from the common sanctuary, they offer their sacrifices by themselves." This is *precisely* what is mentioned in Acts 21:26 (a verse that will be noted again just below), and such an "offering" of a "votive gift" at the Temple *was in fact* a part of the Temple "rituals" that Gaston erroneously tries to claim that no evidence can be found being mentioned *anywhere* in the New Testament, (one needs also to look at Luke 21:5 and

---

18   See for example the comments in *No Stone on Another*, Lloyd Gaston, pp. 97-102.

19   *No Stone on Another*, Lloyd Gaston, pp. 120-121; but see also the comments in *Essays on the Semitic Background of the New Testament*, Joseph A. Fitzmyer, pp. 466-467.

the Greek word *anathemasin*[20]). Such "votive offerings"[21] are described in Leviticus 22:21-23, and are in fact even referenced by Jesus in Mark 7:11-13; Matthew 15:5 as *korban!*[22] Joseph A. Fitzmyer is quite in error in his seeming assertion that this word *korban* is an Aramaic word!²³ For this word *korban* is strictly speaking, a *Hebrew* word²⁴ that derives from the *Hebrew* root word *qarab!*²⁵ But going further into this matter, these offerings were called, *nedabah*, "free will offerings,"²⁶ which even Gaston refers to on his own as being described in the Dead Sea Scrolls,²⁷ but one should also note Josephus *Antiquities* 4.72-73! Gaston then writes concerning Paul, and Paul's activities, and all of Paul's writings (but primarily Gaston refers to what is reported in Acts 21:28; 24:5), that,²⁸ "In any case, the charge of opposition to the Temple is not justified by anything Paul himself said or did, in Jerusalem or elsewhere, but it is made because it is simply assumed that Christians would be against the Temple." Bart Ehrman also, writes concerning "Jewish-Christian adoptionists,"²⁹ that they believed that, "Jesus

20 See the comments of Jacob Voorsanger and Kaufmann Kohler, "Anathema," *Jewish Encyclopedia.*

21 See further on these "votive offerings" in *Mosaic Sacrifice in the New Testament*, Avraham Yehoshua, pp. 2-8; *Unger's Bible Dictionary*, Merrill F. Unger, p. 487 based on Acts 21:17-26 and Paul taking the Nazarite vow.

22 See the comments on this word *korban* and its use in Mark 7:11-13 in *Jesus and the Laws of Purity*, Roger P. Booth, pp. 94-96; Joseph Jacobs and Kaufmann Kohler, "Korban ('an offering')" *Jewish Encyclopedia*; *Problems with New Testament Translation*, Edgar J. Goodspeed, pp. 60-62; *The New Testament and Jewish Law*, James G. Crossley, pp. 81-83; *Jesus and the Spiral of Violence*, Richard A. Horsley, p. 107; *Jewish Law from Jesus to the Mishnah*, E. P. Sanders, pp. 52-53.

23 See *A Wandering Aramean*, Joseph A. Fitzmyer, p. 11 and n. 56, p. 24.

24 See *A Comprehensive Etymological Dictionary of the Hebrew Language*, p. 591.

25 See *Etymological Dictionary of Biblical Hebrew*, p. 233.

26 See Morris Jastrow, Jr. and Ira Maurice Price, "Free-Will Offering ('nedabah')," *Jewish Encyclopedia.*

27 *No Stone on Another*, Lloyd Gaston, pp. 122-123; and see also the lengthy comments on this in *Essays on the Semitic Background of the New Testament*, Joseph A. Fitzmyer, pp. 93-100.

28 *No Stone on Another*, Lloyd Gaston, p. 144.

29 *The New Testament*, Bart D. Ehrman, p. 3.

taught that his followers must continue to obey the entire law (except the law that required animal sacrifice – for them, Jesus himself was the perfect sacrifice) in all its details – and not just the Ten Commandments!"

But all such claims by these scholars have in *fact* been thoroughly refuted and proven to be in strong error,[30] and it seems that not only have these scholars either forgotten, or *clearly do not understand* what is *clearly* stated in Acts 21:26 that even the followers of Jesus *still* went to the Temple and performed most, if not *all* of the "ritual" acts that were required under Jewish law even *after* Jesus' crucifixion![31] These scholars also seem to ignore what is stated in Matthew 5:24;[32] Matthew 23:37-38 and Luke 13:34-35;[33] Luke 24:52-53;[34] Acts 2:46; 3:1; 5:42.[35] Furthermore, John 2:17 *clearly* indicates that the actions of Jesus at the Temple were because, "zeal for your House will consume me,"[36] (meaning Jesus himself), which is a reference to Psalm 69:10. As Cardinal Ratzinger and Pope Benedict XVI write,[37] "Inasmuch as it belonged to the Father, Jesus loved the Temple (Luke 2:49) and taught there gladly… Regarding the relationship of the earliest community to the Temple, the Acts of the Apostles has this to say: 'Day by day, attending the Temple together and breaking bread in their homes, they partook of food with glad and generous hearts' (Acts 2:46)." But furthermore, some of these scholars who make such erroneous claims about Jesus teaching that the Temple "no longer served a purpose," etc., eventually end up making

---

30   See for example *The Misunderstood Jew*, Amy-Jill Levine, pp. 153-155; *Bandits, Prophets, and Messiahs*, Richard A. Horsley and John S. Hanson, p 62; *The Mythmaker*, Hyam Maccoby, pp. 119-120; *Who is Jesus*, Darrell L. Bock, pp. 127-128; *On Earth As It Is In Heaven*, D. C. Thielmann, pp. 716-717 and the corresponding scholars notations to these pages.

31   See the comments on this in *Jewish Christianity Reconsidered*, Matt Jackson-McCabe, p. 51, (Craig C. Hill commenting).

32   See the comments on this in *The Jews and the Gospel*, Gregory Baum, p. 39.

33   See the comments on this in *Jesus of Nazareth: Part Two*, Ratzinger and Pope Benedict, p. 24.

34   See the comments on this in *The Death of Jesus*, Joel Carmichael, pp. 221-223.

35   See the comments in *The Jews and the Gospel*, Gregory Baum, p. 138.

36   See the comments on this verse in *Problems of New Testament Translation*, Edgar J. Goodspeed, pp. 101-102.

37   *Jesus of Nazareth: Part Two*, Ratzinger and Pope Benedict, pp. 35-36.

the grave mistake of contradicting their own opinions.[38] Therefore, Jesus' actions at the Temple regarding the overturning of the moneychangers' tables *must be* interpreted correctly in order to properly understand what Jesus' overall teachings and actions were all about.[39]

Once again, as stated already above, one of *the* most essential points to understand about Jesus' incident at the Temple is in regards to *when* the incident actually occurred within Jesus' ministry. It is generally believed that the incident occurred in the final week of Jesus' ministry, as it is seemingly indicated by what is stated in the three Synoptic Gospels. But the Gospel of John places this incident very near the *beginning* of Jesus' ministry, and thus, this discrepancy as to exactly *when* the incident occurred plays a very significant role in regards to many other matters,[40] such as the matter noted in earlier chapters about Jesus being a "wanted fugitive." It seems also that this then causes some scholars to believe that Jesus was arrested some lengthy period of time *after* the incident at the Temple. For example, as Bart Ehrman writes concerning this,[41] "Why wasn't Jesus arrested on the spot, but only a week later?" Also, as Etienne Trocme writes,[42] "...The Chronology of the Gospel narratives is even more questionable than had been thought, and that the Last Supper and the arrest of Jesus may have preceded the crucifixion by a longer period than the Gospels suggest." Ehrman's question, and Trocme's comments begs the question to be asked in return, from where does such an opinion derive that Jesus was arrested "a week later," or at "a longer period than the Gospels suggest" after the "Temple incident"? For according to the Synoptic Gospel accounts Jesus was arrested merely two days after the Temple incident, not a week later. It is *only* John's Gospel that places Jesus' arrest a couple of years after the Temple incident and not two days, or even one week after the Temple incident.[43] But yet, the majority of scholars, including Ehrman, tend to disregard virtually

---

38 See for example the comments in *The Last Week*, Marcus Borg and John Dominic Crossan, pp. 42-43.

39 See the comments in *The Mythmaker*, Hyam Maccoby, pp. 126-127; *How Jesus Became God*, Bart D. Ehrman, p. 6.

40 See the comments in *Jesus Interrupted*, Bart D. Ehrman, pp. 6-7.

41 *Jesus Interrupted*, Bart D. Ehrman, pp. 168-169.

42 *Jesus and His Contemporaries*, Etienne Trocme, p. 70.

43 See the comments of Doug Bookman, "Passion Week."

anything written in John's Gospel, and thus, we have an inconsistency within such scholarly opinions! As a result of this discrepancy in the four Gospel accounts, and the resulting debate amongst scholars over how long after the incident Jesus was actually arrested, there arises such scholarly claims that,[44] "The issue is not simply one of political whitewash obscuring the historical details of the event; the fact is that the whole tradition of Jesus' last week in Jerusalem would have to have been radically altered."[45] But the facts *do indeed* point to such a "radical alteration," especially in regards to the *Barabbas* matter, which will be discussed in Chapter 10!

In order to correctly understand Jesus' actions at the Temple regarding the overturning of the moneychanger tables one must realize that this was a premeditated action on the part of Jesus as is *clearly* noted by what is found being stated in Mark 11:11 and 11:15.[46] So, an important question to ask here is, what were the moneychangers' tables, and what purpose did they serve at the Temple? The answer is that *only* a specific, *legitimate Jewish minted coin* was permissible for the Temple Treasury, and since each Palestinian Tetrarch had their own coinage,[47] and, several Palestinian cities also minted their own coinage, added to the fact that people were coming to the Jewish pilgrimage festivals from all parts of the Diaspora with coinage from these foreign lands, these "foreign coins" therefore, needed to be exchanged for the legitimate Temple coinage.[48] Furthermore, as noted in Mishnah *Shekalim* 1:3, the moneychanger's tables for the Passover festival were only set up in the Temple from 25 Adar thru Passover. Now, there is a very important matter to point out about this legitimate Temple coin, and this being the fact that this Temple coin *was not* the Tyrian shekel, as far too many scholars believe,[49] (a matter mentioned in an earlier chapter

---

44   *The Partings of the Ways*, James Dunn, p. 47.

45   In *The Partings of the Ways*, James Dunn, he cites as his source in n. 42, p. 291 E. Bammel and C. F. D. Moule, *Jesus and the Politics of His Day*.

46   See the comments in *Gospel Truth*, Russell Shorto, p. 181; *Jesus: Uncovering the Life, Teachings, and Relevance of a Religious Revolutionary*, Marcus J. Borg, pp. 233-234; *On Earth As It Is In Heaven*, D. C. Thielmann, n. 224, pp. 802-803.

47   See the comments in the *Israel Exploration Journal* 1, 166.

48   See the comments in *Herod Antipas*, Harold W. Hoehner, p. 99; *Pontius Pilate*, Ann Wroe, p. 92; William Bacher and Jacob Zallel Lauterbach, "Shekalim," *Jewish Encyclopedia*.

49   See for example the comments on this matter in *Galilee*, Sean Freyne, p. 181.

but which is an important matter to mention again here in this chapter). The Tyrian shekel *had* at one time been minted in silver by the Romans, that is though, until the Romans closed down the Tyre silver minting of this coin roughly fifty years *before* the time of Jesus, and therefore, by the time of Jesus there was a scarcity of the Tyrian Shekels being in existence even in commerce. But the Jews minted their own coins, as noted in Chapter 6, and it was *forbidden* under Jewish law to *use* these Tyrian silver coins, (when they were prevalent in usage), to pay the Temple tax, for the Temple tax was to be paid, primarily, with gold coinage, as noted in Exodus 30:13; Leviticus 27:25; Numbers 3:47.[50] But it *was* acceptable under Jewish law for the poor to use the more commonly minted copper, brass, or bronze coins to pay the Temple tax, (as can even be seen being mentioned in Mark 12:42), but also, one could use jewelry, or other items of value, for again, the term *shekel* simply indicated a unit of "weight" and as long as items of value totaled the weight of one-half "shekel" they were accepted as payment for the Temple Tax. Therefore, as a result of the destruction of the Temple during the 66-73 revolt, and the fact that the Romans carted away virtually *all* of the Temple Treasury that remained after its destruction, in all reality then, *no one* really knows *precisely* what the acceptable, legitimate Jewish Temple coinage looked like. Thus, what makes this matter so important to understand is the fact that the Tyrian Shekel coin, as well as some of the various Jewish minted coins, had the image of a pagan deity stamped onto one side, which then could be the very reason why Jesus gave his famous words, "Render unto Caesar...."[51] For attempting to use a coin with a pagan deity stamped onto it in the Temple of God at the time of Jesus was sacrilege to many, especially to the Essens as noted in *Pesaḥim* 104a; Yerushalmi *Avodah Zerah* 3.42c, 43b,[52]

---

50 See the comments of Emil G. Hirsch, Immanuel Benzinger, Joseph Jacobs, and Jacob Zallel Lauterbach, "Weights and Measures," *Jewish Encyclopedia*; Emil G. Hirsch and William Nowack, "Shekel" *Jewish Encyclopedia*; William Bacher and Jacob Zallel Lauterbach, "Shekalim," *Jewish Encyclopedia*; Joseph Jacobs and Theodore Reinach, "Numismatics," *Jewish Encyclopedia*.

51 See the comments in *Who is Jesus*, Darrell L. Bock, p. 129; *Jesus and the Spiral of Violence*, Richard A. Horsley, pp. 306-317.

52 See the very interesting and enlightening comments regarding "money" in *Purity and Danger*, Mary Douglas, p. 86; Kaufmann Kohler, "Essenes," *Jewish Encyclopedia*.

and furthermore, the Essens believed that the Temple Tax should *only* be paid once in an individual's entire life as is found being stated in the Dead Sea Scroll fragment *4Q Ordinances*! Now, Pilate only minted pagan coins during the years 29-31 CE, but Jewish coinage was being minted before, during, and after this period and the Romans *did not* interfere with the Jewish minting of coinage.[53] Now, many of these "moneychangers" were using an unbalanced measuring weight for their scales that was tilted in favor of the "moneychanger," thereby, *gouging* the unknowing individual paying the Temple Tax. Going further though, these moneychanger tables had been illegitimately sold, by the illegitimate High Priestly collaborators with the Romans to the highest bidders as noted in the Yerushalmi Talmud, *Pe'ah* 6:1.[54] In fact, these "moneychangers" were interrelated with the "tax collectors" discussed in Chapter 4.[55] Now, many scholars are divided on this matter of the "moneychanger's tables" being illegitimately sold seemingly unaware of this "fraudulent" activity noted in the Yerushalmi Talmud,[56] and these scholars must likewise be unfamiliar with Mishnah *Kerithoth* 1:7, which discusses a reduction in the price for a pair of doves at the Temple by 99% because of the "price-gouging" that was occurring, and in which Mark 11:15 *specifically* notes that along with the "moneychangers' tables" being overturned, so were "the seats of those who sold doves"! Yet, despite the scholars who are seemingly unaware of these *facts* noted in the Mishnah and Yerushalmi Talmud, Jesus' *premeditated* actions at the Temple were a direct *political action* against the illegitimacy regarding *how* such activities as these were being conducted at the Temple. Thus, Helen K. Bond is quite in error when she asserts that, "there is no evidence that anyone was doing anything improper... Nor is there any indication that corruption was particularly rife amongst the Temple traders."[57] Another matter of importance to note is that the amount noted in Chapter 6 that

---

53   See the comments in *Pontius Pilate in History and Interpretation*, Helen K. Bond, pp. 19-23.

54   See the comments in *The Trial of Jesus From Jewish Sources*, Rabbi A. P. Drucker, p. 48; *Jesus of Nazareth: Part Two*, Ratzinger and Pope Benedict, pp. 12-13; *Mark*, Robert H. Gundry, pp. 644-645.

55   See the comments on this by Daniel Sperber, "Money Changers," *Encyclopedia Judaica*.

56   See for example *The Theological Significance of Jesus' Temple Action in Mark's Gospel*, Emilio G. Chavez, pp. 72-73 and n. 35, p. 72.

57   *Caiaphas*, Helen K. Bond, p. 65.

was *supposedly* given to Judas Iscariot, which equaled the price that was to be paid to one who had been "gored by an ox," (Exodus 21:30), and it was the price to be "paid to redeem a poor kinsman's property," (Leviticus 25:24; 25:26; 25:51-52; 27:31),[58] and this amount *was not*, as some scholars have asserted, the amount equaling the Temple Tax.

Lloyd Gaston makes an important comment to note here in regards to correctly interpreting what is stated in Mark 13:14-19. Gaston writes concerning this portion of Mark's Gospel,[59] "The writer does not expect the death of Caligula and warns that when the statue is set up, then 'they' (the Christians, the Jews? It is doubtful if a distinction can be made. We have only the fact this verse is in the Gospel to make us think that it is of Christian origin. But is it then so inconceivable that at least a section of the Jerusalem Church should have so sympathized with their fellow countrymen as to share their horror at Caligula's attempt)[60] should flee to the mountains, just as the Maccabees did, to prepare for guerilla warfare?"[61]

It is very important to now take a close examination of Jesus' words at the Temple that are used as the title to this chapter. Specifically, we are going to look at the words that are generally translated out as, "You have made this a den of thieves." The first word to look at is the word translated out as, "thieves," which is the Greek word, *lestai*, or *lestes*. These two Greek words are actually *better* understood to mean, "brigand," or "rebel,"[62] and to the Romans this word meant, and referred to, "insurrectionists" as noted quite often in the historical writings of Josephus. This is the exact same Greek word that is used for the two individuals who were crucified

---

58 See the comments on this in *The Theological Significance of Jesus' Temple Action in Mark's Gospel*, Emilio G. Chavez, p. 29.

59 *No Stone on Another*, Lloyd Gaston, p. 25.

60 *No Stone on Another*, Lloyd Gaston, n. 3, p. 25.

61 *No Stone on Another*, Lloyd Gaston, n. 4, p. 25, "compare 1 Maccabees 2:23ff. Tacitus speaks of preparations for war even before the statue was to have been set up."

62 See the comments in *On Earth As It Is In Heaven*, D. C. Thielmann, p.308 and n. 113, p. 353; *The Origin of Satan*, Elaine Pagels, p. 7; *The Last Week*, Marcus Borg and John Dominic Crossan, p. 51; *Bandits, Prophets, and Messiahs*, Richard A. Horsley and John S. Hanson n. 9, p. 87; *Messiah and Temple*, Donald Juel, p. 132; *The Mythmaker*, Hyam Maccoby, n. 1, pp. 214-215; *Revolution in Judaea*, Hyam Maccoby, p. 17 states that it most accurately meant, "freedom fighter."

next to Jesus.[63] Furthermore, these *lestai* had become quite popular with the general first century Palestinian Jewish people as "heroes," and "loyal patriots" of Israel.[64] This has already been noted in Chapter 3 regarding the erroneous conclusions about "viable families," as well as in regards to Jesus' popularity,[65] but as pointed out in that earlier chapter, Galilee was hardly a bastion for a great many peasants. But nevertheless, the more accurate comments of Richard A. Horsley and John S. Hanson need to be pointed out here when they write,[66] "Significantly, the period of most interest with regard to popular movements and popular leaders such as Jesus of Nazareth is framed by large-scale peasant uprisings: the outbursts following the death of Herod in 4 BCE and the massive revolt against Rome in 66-73 CE, followed by a second major revolt against Rome in 132-135 CE." Horsley and Hanson then further write,[67] "One is forced to ask why so many hundreds, even thousands, of Jewish peasants were prepared to abandon their homes to pursue some prophet into the wilderness, or to rise in rebellion against their Jewish and Roman overlords when the signal was given by some charismatic 'king,' or to flee to the hills to join some brigand band. Peasants generally do not take such drastic action unless conditions have become such that they can no longer simply pursue the traditional patterns of life." Horsley and Hanson go on to note[68] that these so-called "peasants" that they are referring to were not against the tithing and Temple taxing, but became alarmed over the "double taxing" imposed by the Romans noted in Josephus, *Antiquities*, 14.202-203

---

63   See the comments in *The Last Week*, Marcus Borg and John Dominic Crossan, p. 147; *Jesus: Uncovering the Life, Teachings, and Relevance of a Religious Revolutionary*, Marcus Borg, p. 215.

64   See the comments in *Bandits, Prophets, and Messiahs*, Richard A. Horsley and John S. Hanson, pp. 73 and 93.

65   See further on this the erroneous comments in *Jesus: Uncovering the Life, Teachings, and Relevance of a Religious Revolutionary*, Marcus Borg, p. 207.

66   *Bandits, Prophets, and Messiahs*, Richard A. Horsley and John S. Hanson, p. 30.

67   *Bandits, Prophets, and Messiahs*, Richard A. Horsley and John S. Hanson, p. 50; but see also the similar comments in *Maccabees, Zealots, and Josephus*, W. R. Farmer, pp. 175-177.

68   *Bandits, Prophets, and Messiahs*, Richard A. Horsley and John S. Hanson, pp. 51-56.

that amounted to over forty percent.[69] Horsley and Hanson then further point out that,[70] "Large numbers of people, inspired and convinced of the imminence of God's action, abandoned their work, homes, and villages to follow their charismatic leaders out into the wilderness." Finally, Horsley and Hanson comment[71] on Acts 5:33-42 and they note Acts 21:38 where Paul is mistaken as being a part of a revolt that is noted even by Josephus, *Antiquities* 20.169-171, and *Jewish Wars*, 2.261-263, which was an uprising that even though Josephus may have over-estimated its size as being 30,000, the size of this uprising, nonetheless, was in the thousands, and thus, they write,[72] "Moreover, the frequent appearance among the peasantry of actual movements shaped according to this pattern is significant in the attempt to understand Jesus of Nazareth and his movement. Whether or not the early church was (or was conscious of itself as) such a movement, it was certainly aware of its 'competition'," and they cite as their examples Mark 13:22 and Matthew 24:26.[73] Yet, despite these correct statements by Horsley and Hanson, Richard A. Horsley is quite in error when he tries to assert that these *lestai*, or "brigands," as Horsley also refers to them, (especially by way of his references to the writings of Josephus), were somehow *not* violent "insurrectionists" against Roman rule, nor were they in any way associated with the Zealots and Sicarii.[74]

The fact is though, that the *lestai* were a faction of the philosophy known as the "Zealots," which were the primary individuals involved in the 66-73 Jewish revolt. In Chapter 4 it was pointed out that the school

69 See also the comments in *Herod Antipas*, Harold W. Hoehner, p. 79; *Matthew and Empire*, Warren Carter, p. 18 concerning this forty percent taxing.

70 *Bandits, Prophets, and Messiahs*, Richard A. Horsley and John S. Hanson, p. 162.

71 *Bandits, Prophets, and Messiahs*, Richard A. Horsley and John S. Hanson, pp. 165-172.

72 *Bandits, Prophets, and Messiahs*, Richard A. Horsley and John S. Hanson, p. 172.

73 But see also their comments in *Bandits, Prophets, and Messiahs*, Richard A. Horsley and John S. Hanson, p. 199.

74 See the comments in *Jesus and the Spiral of Violence*, Richard A. Horsley, pp. 37-43. But for a more accurate assessment see the comments in "Social World of Bandits," *American Bible Society Resources*; Lawrence Ronald Lincoln, *A Socio-Historical Analysis of Jewish Banditry in First Century Palestine: 6-70CE*, November, 2005; *Pontius Pilate in History and Interpretation*, Helen K. Bond, p. 4; *Prophecy in Early Christianity*, David E. Aune, p. 174.

of Hillel and the school of Shammai at times were engaged in "knock-down-drag-out-fights" over the interpretations of the Torah. But at times these "disagreements" also involved their differing opinions and attitudes towards the Roman authority after the banishment of Archelaus, noted by Josephus in *Jewish Wars* 2.111, 117. The school of Hillel, (beginning with Hillel himself), believed in waiting for "divine intervention," (and as will be pointed out further below, belief in "divine intervention" is *Jewish metaphorical* terminology), whereas the school of Shammai, (beginning with Shammai himself), "openly supported the Zealots."[75] But, *Gittin* 56a appears to indicate that the school of Shammai eventually broke away from this "*open* support" of the Zealots. This is precisely why it was noted in Chapter 4 that Gamliel, (who became the head of the school of Hillel and *nasi* of the Great Sanhedrin), is reported to have defended the followers of Jesus found in Acts 5 because he was following in the footsteps of the teaching and understanding that his grandfather Hillel had taught! As Yitzhak Buxbaum states concerning this matter,[76] "According to Josephus (*Antiquities* 18.1.16), it was their negative attitude to political violence that in later years separated the Pharisees, with whom Hillel was identified, from the Zealots, who rebelled against Rome. Otherwise, their religious views were largely the same." Now it is true though, that the son of Gamliel *did* take part in the 66-73 revolt against the Romans.[77] Thus, going further with this matter, Josephus, *Antiquities* 18.23 refers to the followers of Jesus as being a "school" which "agrees in all respects with the opinions of the Pharisees, except that they have a passion for liberty that is almost unconquerable," or in other words and in simplest terms, that which one could and *should* label as, "Zealots!" Thus, Richard A. Horsley is quite in error when he writes,[78] "Unfortunately for these studies and for the concerns of their authors, 'the zealots' as a movement of rebellion against Roman rule did not come into existence until the winter of 67-68 C.E. – that is, until the middle of the great revolt. The recent move to less

75   See the comments on this in *Jesus and the Laws of Purity*, Roger P. Booth, p. 167; *Jesus the Pharisee*, Harvey Falk, pp. 152-153; *Israel in Revolution*, David Rhoads, p. 54.

76   *The Life and Teachings of Hillel*, Yitzhak Buxbaum, p. 65.

77   See Solomon Schecter and Wilhelm Bacher, "Gamaliel I," *Jewish Encyclopedia*.

78   *Jesus and the Spiral of Violence*, Richard A. Horsley, Introduction, pp. x-xi; but see also the similar comments in *Israel in Revolution*, David Rhoads, pp. 2 and 174-181.

specific labels such as 'resistance fighters' or 'the activist element,' however, does not change the fact that there is simply no evidence for an organized movement of violent resistance that agitated for armed revolt from 6 to 66 C. E. Jewish reaction to Roman rule was far more complex than the old 'Zealots' concept allowed, and social unrest took a variety of social forms. It is obviously necessary to reexamine the view that Jewish Palestine was a hotbed of violent resistance during the time of Jesus."[79] Horsley *is* partially correct in his stating that, "social unrest took a variety of forms,"[80] but Horsley is quite in error in his overall assessment regarding the *historical* truth surrounding the "Zealots,"[81] as just noted above regarding the debates over the "Zealots" between the schools of Hillel and Shammai, which *predate* the ministry of Jesus and which falls *precisely* during the time period that he claims that there is no evidence of "organized violent resistance that agitated for armed revolt" – i.e. from 6 to 66 C.E. The "Zealots" were quite active, as were the fierce branch of the "Zealots" referred to as the "Sicarii," long before, and long *after* the time of Herod the Great as referred to by way of the Hebrew word, *kanna'im*, noted in the Mishnah and Talmud, *Sanhedrin* 9:11; *Sanhedrin* 82a and b; Yerushalmi *Sanhedrin* 9:27; *Abot de-Rabbi Nathan* 6 for just a few examples of this fact.[82] The faction referred to as the "Sicarii" are even specifically mentioned in the Mishnah *Bikkurim* 1:2; 2:3; *Gittin* 5:6; *Makshirin* 1:6 by the Hebrew word, *sicaricon*, "robbers," "bandits," "assassins," or "murderers."[83] Horsley does refer to the violent uprising that came about by way of the "Zealots" (*kanna'im*) after the death of Herod the Great![84] Yet, Horsley seems to ignore the fact that the very sons of the supposed originator of the Philosophy referred

---

79   See the further similar comments on this in *Jesus and the Spiral of Violence*, Richard A. Horsley, pp. 77-89, 116-129, 297, and 318.

80   See the comments in *Conflict, Holiness & Politics*, Marcus Borg, pp. 2-3, 30, 34, 64-68.

81   See the more accurate assessment of the "zealots" in *Pontius Pilate in History and Interpretation*, Helen K. Bond, pp. 61-65, 71-73, 76-77.

82   See the comments on this by Kaufmann Kohler, "Zealots (Hebrew, Kanna'im)," *Jewish Encyclopedia*; *Maccabees, Zealots, and Josephus*, W. R. Farmer, p. 178.

83   See *A Comprehensive Etymological Dictionary of the Hebrew Language*, p. 445; Richard Gottheil and Samuel Krauss, "Sicarii (Greek, 'assassins,' 'dagger men')," *Jewish Encyclopedia*.

84   See *Jesus and the Spiral of Violence*, Richard A. Horsley, pp. 43-44, 50-54, 71-77.

to as the "Zealots," Judas the Galilean, (and these sons being, James and Simon), were crucified as "Zealots" for their continuation of their father's rebellious actions against the Romans sometime between 46 and 48 CE as noted by Josephus, *Antiquities* 20.102,[85] and another of Judas the Galilean's sons, Mena<u>h</u>em, was the head of the Sicarii as noted by Josephus *Jewish Wars* 2.17.8-9.[86] Furthermore, Josephus in *Jewish Wars* 2.14.1 talks about how "the enterprises of the seditious at Jerusalem were very formidable" during the reins of both Felix and Albinus, both of whom served *prior to* the 66-73 revolt! Josephus further states in *Jewish Wars* 6.6.2(329), "You who from the first, ever since Pompey reduced you by force, never ceased from revolution, and have now ended by declaring open war with the Romans...." Thus, in essence, and quite contrary to the claims of Horsley, we find the ancient historian Josephus *clearly* stating that there *was in fact* a certain philosophy of Jews, (i.e. "Zealots") who had "never ceased from revolution" for 130 years, meaning that all during that very time period in which Horsley claims that there is "no evidence" that the "Zealots" existed (i.e. 6 CE – 66 CE), and/or that the very "revolutionary" activity that characterized this Jewish philosophy of individuals was based on their "zeal for the Torah," or in which they were "zealous for the Torah," the very words found in Acts 21:20-22, a verse which will be mentioned again, and discussed further below.[87] Therefore, as Rabbi Joseph Telushkin rightly states,[88] "At the beginning of the Common Era, a new group arose among the Jews: the Zealots (in Hebrew, *Ka-na-im*). These anti-Roman rebels were active for more than six decades, and later instigated the Great Revolt. Their most basic belief was that all means were justified to attain political and religious liberty."

Marcus Borg as well, asserts that there is no evidence of "Zealots" prior to 66 CE.[89] But Borg's greatest error in his claim though, derives from his referring to the "Zealots" as a "party" and *not* as a "philosophy." In essence, Borg attempts to perceive of the "Zealots" as an *ideology* instead

---

85   See the comments in *Israel in Revolution*, David Rhoads, p. 54.

86   See the comments of Kaufmann Kohler and M. Seligsohn, "Judas the Galilean," *Jewish Encyclopedia*.

87   See the comments on this in *Maccabees, Zealots, and Josephus*, W. R. Farmer, pp. 49-83.

88   *Jewish Literacy*, Rabbi Joseph Telushkin, p. 130.

89   See *Conflict, Holiness & Politics*, Marcus Borg, pp. 36, 43-44, 64.

of a *philosophy*, and there is a vast difference between the meanings of these two words, which is why Josephus places the "Zealots" into the category of a "philosophy." Yet, Borg's own summary conclusions[90] that he offers on this matter demonstrates that the "Zealots" were indeed a "philosophy" and *not* an "ideology," to which Borg, later, rightly refers to the "Zealots" *as* a "philosophy,"[91] and thereby, contradicting his earlier classification of the "Zealots" as a "party." The matter surrounding the Gospel accounts concerning a *supposed* individual named, "Barabbas," (a matter that will be discussed in Chapter 10), and in particular, Mark 15:7 *clearly* indicates that violent actions were being committed by individuals who were well organized by way of a particular "philosophy" *long before* the 66-73 revolt!

This reference to the "Zealots" by way of the Hebrew word *kanna'im* though, was derived from the usage of this word as one of the Names of God in Exodus 20:5; 34:14; Deuteronomy 4:24; 5:9; 6:15; Joshua 24:19.[92] Now, Horsley himself even references the Hebrew word *kanna'im*,[93] yet not only does Horsley fail to mention any of the references to the *kanna'im* in the Mishnah and Talmud, he also fails to recognize and/or acknowledge that the *kanna'im* are the *same* "philosophy" that Josephus refers to as the "fourth philosophy," which Josephus states was founded by Judas the Galilean, but in *historical* reality actually existed since the time of the Maccabees as proven by the fact that the father of Judas the Galilean, (Hezekiah), already had an organized band of assassins during the reign of Herod the Great, which *again*, is noted in the Mishnah and Talmud! So, once more for emphasis, Horsley is quite in error, (as well as the other scholars who hold to similar opinions), when claiming that there is no proof for the existence of an organized group, or "philosophy" of "Zealots" who used "violence" against the Romans and their installment of "illegitimate client kings," (i.e. "Herodians"), and "illegitimate High Priests," (i.e. Annas and Caiaphas for example), at the time of Jesus, or at *any time* prior to the 66-73

---

90   *Conflict, Holiness & Politics*, Marcus Borg, pp. 48-49.

91   *Conflict, Holiness & Politics*, Marcus Borg, p. 56.

92   See *Etymological Dictionary of Biblical Hebrew*, p. 229; *A Comprehensive Etymological Dictionary of the Hebrew Language*, p. 583.

93   *Jesus and the Spiral of Violence*, Richard A. Horsley, p. 123.

revolt![94] But going even further into the erroneous opinions of Richard A. Horsley regarding the "Zealots," Horsley writes,[95] "So far as we know, none of the Jewish resistance movements produced any literature; at least none is extant." Horsley seems to be completely ignoring *The War Scroll* discovered amongst the Dead Sea Scrolls, which Horsley even makes reference to, yet, he fails to acknowledge that it represents "Jewish resistance movement literature"![96] Now, David Flusser rightly discusses the comparison between the *War Scroll* and portions of the prayers in Luke's Gospel referred to as *"the Magnificat"* and *"the Benedictus."*[97] Thus, Horsley's entire analogy of Jewish apocalyptic literature demonstrates, once again, a scholar lacking in the understanding of Jewish *metaphoric* terminology! Jewish apocalyptic *metaphor always* referred to actual war and the fighting between men, and *not* to some fighting between some "spiritual Heavenly hosts,"[98] which one can even find being stated in 2 Corinthians 10:4! As Paul William Roberts correctly writes,[99] "People did their duty, fought with absolute 'zeal for the law.' What more could Zealots have done? And there was no difference between Zealots, Essens, Ebionites, Nazoreans, or Nazarites, et.al. These distinctions are more obfuscation of a truth the Church has been reluctant to face: the purpose of Jesus' life was to prevent such a Church, such an institutionalization of spirituality, from ever existing."[100] As an example of what Roberts is referring to, W. D. Davies[101] distorts what is *actually* stated in several Talmudic tractates, such as Babli *Megillah* 14a, claiming that this tractate states, "Iskah is Sarah; why is Sarah called Iskah? Because she looked by the Holy Spirit." But the actual *best* English rendering of this

---

94   See the comments in *Caiaphas*, Helen K. Bond, pp. 26-28; *Jewish Literature Between the Bible and the Mishnah*, George W. E. Nickelsburg, p. 203; *"Caught in the Act,"* Roger David Aus, pp. 18-21.

95   *Jesus and the Spiral of Violence*, Richard A. Horsley, p. 132.

96   *Jesus and the Spiral of Violence*, Richard A. Horsley, pp. 135 and 186.

97   See the comments in *Judaism and the Origins of Christianity*, David Flusser, pp. 126-149.

98   See the comments in *A Jewish Understanding of the New Testament*, Samuel Sandmel, pp. 27-28.

99   *In Search of the Birth of Jesus*, Paul William Roberts, p. 359.

100   See further on this in *On Earth As It Is In Heaven*, D. C. Thielmann, n. 15, p. 1036 and the entirety of Chapter 12B; Kaufmann Kohler, "Essenes," *Jewish Encyclopedia*.

101   *Paul and Rabbinic Judaism*, W. D. Davies, p. 184.

tractate should be understood as stating, "Iskah is in fact Sarah. And why was she called Iskah? For she saw (*sakhta*) by means of *Divine Inspiration*," (italics mine).[102] Although the Hebrew words *rua<u>h</u> ha-kodesh* are far too often rendered into English as, "Holy Spirit," Judaism, (even at the time of Jesus), interpreted this to mean, "Divine Inspiration."[103] As George Foot Moore states,[104] "If 'spirit' were taken in the Biblical sense, there would be no other objection to the phrase than its aberrations. But in modern use spirit is the contrary of matter, and 'spiritual' equivalent to 'immaterial.' In this sense the spirituality of God is a philosophical theory derived from Greeks, not a doctrine of Judaism in Biblical times or thereafter, any more than Jewish monotheism is a doctrine of the unity of God in the metaphysical sense."

Thus, regardless of whether one chooses to refer to the "fourth philosophy" spoken of by Josephus as "bandits," "brigands," "insurrectionists," (i.e. *lestai*), "Sicarii," or as the "*kanna'im*,"[105] or as some scholars rightly point out, that they were at times even referred to as "Galileans,"[106] or also "Canaanites," (as noted in Chapter 8 that Galilee was a "hotbed for insurrection" and as even stated as being such by Josephus in *Jewish Wars* 3.3.2; Mishnah *Nedarim* 5:5; Yerushalmi *Ketuvim* 4,29b; Babli *Nedarim* 48a), they were *all* a "faction" of one in the same "philosophy!" There were even timeswhen the "Essens" were also referred to as being a faction of the "Zealots."[107] Thus, there is in all actuality an *undeniable historical fact* that still remains, and this *undeniable fact* being, that regardless of which of these various terms just noted that one might use, they were *all* from the same "*fourth philosophy*" known from the writings of Philo and Josephus as the "*Zealots*" who did "violence" against not only the Romans and Herodians,

---

102 See *The William Davidson Talmud, Megillah* 14a.

103 See *On Earth As It Is In Heaven*, D. C. Thielmann, p. 138 and the corresponding scholars notations to this page.

104 *Judaism in the First Centuries of the Christian Era*, George Foot Moore, Volume I, p. 233.

105 See the brief comments of examples of "Zealots" in *Jewish Literature Between the Bible and the Mishnah*, George W. E. Nickelsburg, pp. 277-278; *Galilee*, Sean Freyne, pp. 209-211, 218-219.

106 See the comments in *The History of the Synoptic Tradition*, Rudolf Bultmann, pp. 54-55; *Galilee*, Sean Freyne, pp. 68-78.

107 See the comments on this by Kaufmann Kohler, "Essenes," *Jewish Encyclopedia*.

but also even against their own Jewish brethren who were collaborators *with* the Romans and Herodians *long before the 66-73 revolt!*[108] Josephus in *Jewish Wars* 2.264-265 *clearly* states that *each* of these various factions just mentioned above had been "banding together"![109] *Any* and *all* scholarly attempts to try and claim otherwise are nothing but attempts to distort the *historical reality of this fact!* For this *fact* is in all intents and purposes no different from the *fact* pointed out in Chapter 4 that the Pharisees had seven *different* "factions," yet these different factions were *all* part of the *one* "philosophy" called, "Pharisees"! This *historical reality* regarding the "Zealots" can be further compared to the twentieth and twenty first century references to "Islamic Extremism," (i.e. "Jihadists," or "terrorists" as other terms), which have many *different* factions ranging from "Hamas," to "Al Qaeda," to "Ansar Al-Sharia," to "Boko Haram," to "Hezbollah," etc., yet all of these different factions have the same basic goals, motives and are of the *same overall philosophy* just as the seven different factions of *Pharisees* and the many different factions of the philosophy of the *Zealots!*

The *Zealots* derived their very name for themselves from Numbers 25:13.[110] As Hyam Maccoby points out in regards to this,[111] "The Zealots took their name from Phinehas the Zealot, the son of Aaron, who 'was zealous for his God' (Numbers 25:13) with sword in hand. It was believed that Phinehas, as a reward for his violent zeal, had never died and was identical with the prophet Elijah who would come back one day to act as the fore-runner of the Messiah (Malachi 4:5). The choice of this name as the watchword of the movement had, therefore, messianic overtones." At the time of Jesus, based on the interpretation of Numbers 25:10-11, it was believed that, "only someone with *Ahavos Yisroel* ('love of his fellow Jew') could be zealous for God's honor, and His Torah," and such a leader, (based on the interpretation of Numbers 27:16-17), was "expected to be at the forefront of the battle."[112] Acts 21:20-22 clearly notes this very fact that Jesus and his immediate Jewish followers were *Zealots* who were

---

108 See the comments in *Barabbas and Esther*, Roger David Aus, p. 69.

109 See the comments in *Israel in Revolution*, David Rhoads, pp. 54-60, 159-173.

110 See the comments in *Kosher Jesus*, Rabbi Shmuley Boteach, p. 22.

111 *Revolution in Judaea*, Hyam Maccoby, pp. 65-66.

112 See *Love Your Neighbor*, Rabbi Zelig Pliskin, pp. 361-367.

"zealous for the Torah."[113] These same words are also found in *1 Maccabees* 2:22-27,[114] and as Cardinal Ratzinger and Pope Benedict XVI rightly point out concerning this that,[115] "From that moment, the slogan 'zeal' (in Greek, *zelos*) became the byword for readiness to stand up for Israel's faith with force, to defend Israel's law and freedom by treading the path of violence." Yet, Ratzinger and Pope Benedict XVI go on further[116] to demonstrate a theological apologetic bias by erroneously claiming that Jesus *never* taught such *zeal* to his followers, and in fact, some scholars even erroneously try to claim that Jesus taught *against Zealots*.[117] But such a claim makes absolutely no sense whatsoever given what was just pointed out concerning what is written in Acts 21:20-22! Furthermore, Edgar J. Goodspeed rightly interprets 1 Corinthians 13:1 about the matter of a "clanging cymbal" to be indicating "to raise the war cry," "to shout for victory," or "a war cry."[118] Likewise, in 1 Corinthians 14:8 Paul refers to the "blowing of the trumpet" and the "call to war" that was used by the ancient Israelites after their exodus from Egypt,[119] (but see also Romans 11:26 and 2 Thessalonians 2:4-8[120]), and again, for the benefit of Richard Horsley, Paul wrote about these "calls to war" *prior to* the 66-73 revolt.

This brings us to the next Greek word to look closely at from the verse used as the title of this chapter, which gets generally translated out as "den." This Greek word is the word, *spelaion*, which is *better* understood by its

---

113　See the comments in *Christianity: A Jewish Perspective*, Rabbi Moshe Reiss, 2.IV; *Judas Iscariot and the Myth of Jewish Evil*, Hyam Maccoby, n. 1, p. 178; *On Earth As It Is In Heaven*, D. C. Thielmann, n. 60, p. 336, n. 220, pp. 799-800, n. 221, p. 800, n. 223, pp. 801-802.

114　See the comments on this in *Conflict, Holiness & Politics*, Marcus Borg, p. 62; *Paul and Rabbinic Judaism*, W. D. Davies, pp. 263-264.

115　*Jesus of Nazareth: Part Two*, Ratzinger and Pope Benedict, p. 14.

116　*Jesus of Nazareth: Part Two*, Ratzinger and Pope Benedict, pp. 15-23, and pp. 169-171.

117　See for example *No Stone on Another*, Lloyd Gaston, pp. 425-426; *Conflict, Holiness & Politics*, Marcus Borg, p. 234.

118　See *Problems of New Testament Translation*, Edgar J. Goodspeed, pp. 160-161.

119　See the comments on this in *On Earth As It Is In Heaven*, D. C. Thielmann, pp. 677-678, and n. 1, pp. 733-734; *Maccabees, Zealots, and Josephus*, W. R. Farmer, pp. 159-172.

120　See the comments on these verses in *The Crucified Messiah and other Essays*, Nils Dahl, p. 47.

meanings of, "a hiding place," or "a refuge," or even "a stronghold." Thus, *the most important* Greek word to correctly understand in this verse used as the title to this chapter becomes the word, which is generally translated out as, "you have made." This Greek word is *pepoiekate*, which is *best* understood in the context of its usage in this verse as meaning, "*you have caused the actions.*" Therefore, the *best way* for *anyone* (whether scholar, theologian, or general church laity) to understand Jesus' words in this verse, (and the reminder must be stressed here that Jesus spoke in *Hebrew*, but his words that we have *now* were written down in a translated language of Greek), are therefore, (italics mine), "*You have brought about the actions of turning this into a stronghold for insurrection!*"[121]

Despite the historical facts of the conditions, the sentiments, and the eagerness of the people of first century Palestine to get back to living according to the Torah, far too many modern Christian scholars either ignore all of these factors, or they choose to engage in their own personal bias's in order to portray Jesus in a way that contradicts his very words and actions. Dale C. Allison is quite in error when he writes,[122] "It is precarious to urge that we can find the truth about Jesus on the basis of a few dozen sayings determined to be authentic if those sayings are interpreted contrary to the general impression conveyed by the early tradition in its entirety. If Jesus was, for example, either a violent revolutionary or a secular sage, then the tradition about him is so misleading that we cannot use it for investigation of the pre-Easter period – and so we cannot know that Jesus was either a violent revolutionary or a secular sage. Here skepticism devours itself. The conclusion refutes the premises." Let me now demonstrate precisely *why* Allison's statement is so erroneous by listing off, and then strongly suggesting that everyone think carefully about just three matters that virtually *all* New Testament scholars agree are *undeniable historical facts*, which namely are, first; that Jesus was condemned to crucifixion by Pontius Pilate;[123] second; that the required *Titulus*[124] that names the crime for which Pontius Pilate

---

121   See the comments in *Who is Jesus*, Darrell L. Bock, p. 123 and n. 3, p. 228; *No Stone on Another*, Lloyd Gaston, pp. 84-86; *Mark*, Robert H. Gundry, p. 644; *Conflict, Holiness & Politics*, Marcus Borg, pp. 174-175..

122   *Jesus of Nazareth*, Dale C. Allison, p. 45.

123   See the comments in *Pontius Pilate in History and Interpretation*, Helen K. Bond, p. xi.

124   See the comments on this in *The Partings of the Ways*, James Dunn, p. 167.

found Jesus guilty of a death sentence by crucifixion was, "*King of the Jews*," (and as pointed out already in Chapter 8, this was a *Roman* verdict regarding *insurrection*),[125] and the third *undeniable historical fact is*; that Jesus *did in fact* instigate some sort of a *violent incident* at the Temple by his "driving out," and "overturning the tables of the money changers"! Thus, *all* of the "*historical*" sayings of Jesus, *must be* interpreted in such a manner that coincides with these three *undeniable historical facts*! Therefore, *if* the sayings of Jesus, that are deemed by scholars to be authentic, *are not* being interpreted in such a manner to coincide with these three *undeniable historical facts*, then the *only* logical conclusion that *anyone* should make is that the "traditions" about Jesus that convey a "general impression" of Jesus that is "contrary" to these three *undeniable historical facts* could *only* have come about in order to try and "whitewash" the image of Jesus from being any sort of "insurrectionist"!

Far too many scholars are attempting to portray Jesus as a "pacifist" instead of what he actually was in historical reality – an "*activist*." Marcus Borg, for example,[126] refers to Matthew 5:39 and the Greek word in this verse, *antistenai*, which is generally translated out as "resist," or "oppose." But this Greek word also offers a meaning that even Borg rightly notes that is its most often used meaning, and this being, to "resist with violence." Yet, Borg attempts to claim, even despite his pointing out the appropriate meaning of this Greek word, that Jesus is *somehow*, advocating "*non-violence*."[127] But this Greek word *antistenai* in Matthew 5:39 is actually a combination of two different Greek words, which *actually* is *better* understood in the context of its usage in this verse to mean, "Do not requite with a verbal scolding." Therefore, this response by Jesus has absolutely nothing whatsoever to do with "non-violence." Likewise, Jesus' response about "turn to him the other," the Greek word *strepson* actually means, "to turn around in revolt," or in other words, to "turn around and give the same back." The whole notion of some scholars to try and "whitewash" Jesus' teachings and actions as

---

125 See the comments in *A Jewish Understanding of the New Testament*, Samuel Sandmel, p. 130.

126 *Jesus: Uncovering the Life, Teachings, and Relevance of a Religious Revolutionary*, Marcus Borg, pp.248-249.

127 Borg cites his sources for his opinion in n. 19, p. 329, *Jesus and Non-Violence*, Walter Wink, pp. 9-14; *Engaging the Powers*, Walter Wink, pp. 184-189.

being those of a "pacifist" is actually a disgrace to their professed dedication to "objective scholarship!"[128] For example, many scholars will admit that the saying of Jesus that is most often translated as, "love your enemies," is greatly *abused, misrepresented, misused,* and *misunderstood.* Yet, these very same scholars will also themselves *misunderstand, misrepresent, misuse,* and *abuse* this saying, (Matthew 5:43-44 is the best example to be utilized in regards to this very point being made here).[129] For the *best* interpretation of the Greek words used in this matter of "turn to him the other," is that Jesus is actually saying, "Show brotherly love to those who have enmity towards your fellow countrymen." Thus, while far too many scholars try to claim that this saying is a direct statement of "non-violence" on the part of Jesus, and basically a chastising of those such as the "Zealots," in actuality the *best* interpretation of this saying of Jesus is that Jesus is teaching that one should *embrace* the "violence" of those such as the "Zealots"![130] As Rabbi Moshe Reiss points out concerning Matthew 5:39 that the "turn to him the other" cheek is actually a matter found in Lamentations 3:30 and in this verse in Lamentations it refers to one receiving punishment for one's transgressions (Lamentations 3:39), and it was done in order to bring one "back to the Lord" (Lamentations 3:40). For as Lamentations 3:63-64 goes on to state, "Render to them recompenses, O Lord, according to their work of their hands." Jesus' teaching that Marcus Borg is referring to is in reality a matter that comes straight out of these teachings in Lamentations.[131] Furthermore, as John J. Collins rightly points out,[132] "Exhortation to pacifism is distinctly different from exhortation to violence, and either may be the function of a given text." We do find though, even some apologetic theologians who *do* recognize that Jesus was in fact an "activist," such as

---

128 See as an example of this fact *Jesus Before the Gospels*, Bart Ehrman, pp. 167-171.

129 See for example the comments in *Jesus and the Spiral of Violence*, Richard A. Horsley, pp. 261-273.

130 See the definitions of the Greek words, *agapate, echthrous,* and *son* in the *BDAG Greek-English Lexicon*, pp. 5-6, 419, and 934; *Liddell and Scott's Greek-English Lexicon*, pp. 4, 340, and 737.

131 *Christianity: A Jewish Perspective*, Rabbi Moshe Reiss, 6 "The Torah and the Gospel of Matthew." See also the comments in *The New Testament and Rabbinic Judaism*, David Daube, pp. 254-265; *Revolution in Judaea*, Hyam Maccoby, p. 110.

132 *The Apocalyptic Imagination*, John J. Collins, p. 19.

Ruth N. Koch and Kenneth C. Haugk, who write,[133] "Many Christians may think that Jesus' loving, self-sacrificing attitude and lifestyle mark him as a passive individual, pushed around by life, taken advantage of by countless people, and finally killed. Few people realize how genuinely assertive Jesus was."

At times though, it is quite strange to find so many of these scholars such as Marcus Borg contradicting their own opinions.[134] As another example of this *fact* let me quote here Ernst Fuchs who tries to deny that Jesus offered a "political program," while at the same time admitting that a "political element" was "always certainly inherent." Fuchs writes,[135] "That Jesus did not offer a political program is apparent from the sternness of his proclamation with its almost impossible demands; although the political element which was always certainly inherent in the idea of the rule of God induced men to interpret him in this way. But Jesus did go up to Jerusalem. The sight of his followers could, in fact, make this appearance look like an insurrection. Indeed, the attitude of the authorities suggests that they *did* regard the whole business as an uprising. Scenes like the cleansing of the Temple could hardly be called anything else." But Warren Carter does an excellent job presenting the truth of the matter that Jesus *did in fact* put forth a "political" movement when he states,[136] "In his actions and teachings, Jesus manifests God's sovereignty or empire in which he and God, not Rome, share 'all authority in heaven and on earth' (Matthew 28:18), an empire that prefers egalitarian structures rather than Rome's hierarchy (Matthew 23:8-12)... An Empire that emphasizes service not Rome's domination (Matthew 20:24-28), that values inclusion not the elite's exclusion (Matthew 9:9-13), mutuality not patriarchy (Matthew 19:3-9; 23:9), healing not sickness (Matthew 4:23-25), food and plenty not lack for the majority (Matthew 12:1-8; 14:13-21; 15:32-39), the marginal not the center (Matthew 19:13-15), inclusive love not privilege (Matthew 5:45), mercy not intimidating violence (Matthew 9:13; 26:52),

---

133   *Speaking the Truth In Love: How To Be An Assertive Christian*, Ruth N. Koch and Kenneth C. Haugk, p. 53.

134   See for example *Jesus: Uncovering the Life, Teachings, and Relevance of a Religious Revolutionary*, Marcus Borg, pp. 78-79.

135   *Studies of the Historical Jesus*, Ernst Fuchs, p. 24.

136   *Matthew and Empire*, Warren Carter, p. 61.

God not Caesar (Matthew 22:15-22). These actions and teachings negate any attempt to argue that God's Empire is somehow 'spiritual' or 'individual' in its sovereignty, and poses no political threat." Likewise, other scholars have pointed out that many of the parables in Mark's Gospel have long been misinterpreted by far too many scholars regarding their "political" connotations that they contain. As a prime example of this is Mark 12:1-12, as pointed out by Gregory Baum when he writes,[137] "The deputation of the Sanhedrin understood that God's vineyard was Israel, and that the wicked vine-dressers were the leaders to whom the community of salvation had been entrusted. They were to be removed and done away with, and the leadership was to pass into the hands of more faithful shepherds. The Parable did not indicate who should replace the traditional hierarchy, but the reader of the Gospel understands that Jesus was thinking of the Twelve whom he had prepared for this role."

In regards to this matter of Jesus' choosing of twelve primary disciples, (a matter discussed previously in Chapter 6), an important point needs to be mentioned that derives from the interpretation of this fact by Joseph Ratzinger and Pope Benedict XVI.[138] Referring specifically to Mark 3:14 they compare this to the account in 1 Kings 12:31-33 writing, "In reality, these words of the Evangelist take up the Old Testament terminology for appointment to the priesthood (cf. 1 Kings 12:31; 12:33) and thus characterize the apostolic office as a priestly ministry." Now although it is quite true, as pointed out in Chapter 2 that the "Jesus movement" was disillusioned with the High Priest just as many other first century Palestinian Jews were, Joseph Ratzinger and Pope Benedict XVI are quite in error in their interpretation here, for as it clearly states in 1 Kings 12:30, "this thing became a sin."

Thus, Jesus and his actions and teachings fall smack dab in the middle of all of the groups that these scholars themselves point out are "violent" groups. Therefore, it is of major importance to point out one very glaring fact that derives from Josephus' historical accounts. This fact being that Josephus *only* references three different "Jewish philosophies," and then adds a fourth "Jewish philosophy" consisting of the Zealots and Sicarii. Yet

---

137   *The Jews and the Gospel*, Gregory Baum, pp. 33-37.

138   See *Jesus of Nazareth: Part One*, Ratzinger and Pope Benedict, pp. 170-171.

nowhere does Josephus *ever* mention a *fifth* "*pacifist* Jewish philosophy,"[139] and by the time that Josephus wrote his historical accounts the Jesus movement had indeed spread out to the diaspora and become quite widely known, since even Josephus himself mentions not only Jesus, but also his brother James. As David E. Aune rightly states,[140] "Within the brief span of twenty years early Christianity had spread quickly throughout the Mediterranean world until house churches were located in virtually every major urban center. Thessalonica itself was situated in Macedonia, nearly a thousand miles (as the crow flies) from Jerusalem, where Christianity began 'in a corner' in A.D. 29." Therefore, just as Josephus so adequately described the other *four* "Jewish philosophies," why would Josephus then so blatantly ignore describing some *fifth* "pacifist Jewish philosophy" that had arisen and spread so "quickly" when Josephus is writing some *fifty to seventy years after* the rise of this *supposedly* "new" *fifth* "pacifist Jewish philosophy" that so many Christian New Testament scholars try to claim was the very backbone motive of the "Jesus movement"? This *fact* is one that *cannot*, nor *should not* and *must not* be ignored by *any* legitimate scholar, and thus, it *must be* considered in an *unbiased and objective manner by all* New Testament scholars! As Joel Carmichael rightly states,[141] "Hence, even if he (Jesus) did not think himself the actual Messiah his role was certainly martial. It would have corresponded with the then current Jewish conception of the Warlike Messiah, and since there was no room in Jewish Messianic belief for a Pacific Messiah an apologia was eventually bound to be called for in the evolution of Christian belief as soon as it became necessary to tone down the political aspects of Jesus' career."

N. T. Wright, while referring to the *Martyrdom of Polycarp* 9.1-3, which occurred, by the way, in about 155-156 CE, Wright states concerning this that,[142] "In particular, it is assumed that Christians are members of a subversive sect. They do not believe in the normal pagan gods, and so have incurred the charge of atheism that was sometimes levelled at the Jews.

---

139   See the comments in *The New Testament*, Bart D. Ehrman, pp. 41-44; *The Partings of the Ways*, James Dunn, pp. 18-19; *Essays on the Semitic Background of the New Testament*, Joseph A. Fitzmyer, n. 11, p. 276.

140   *Prophecy in Early Christianity*, David E. Aune, p. 190.

141   *The Death of Jesus*, Joel Carmichael, p. 191.

142   *The New Testament and the People of God*, N. T. Wright, pp. 347-348.

In particular, they do not owe allegiance to Caesar, and refuse to swear by his genius. Christ is seen as a rival monarch, a king to whom is due an allegiance which allows no room for the dictatorship of the emperor. Already it is clear that the Christianity to which Polycarp (and/or his biographer) had given allegiance was rooted in Judaism." Wright then goes on to refer to the incident with James,[143] which as just noted above Josephus even writes about stating how the Pharisees were incensed over this matter of the killing of James, and thus, *proving* that Josephus is *clearly* aware of Jesus, his followers, and his "movement!" Yet again for emphasis, the *fact* that Josephus *does not* refer to this "Jesus movement" as being some sort of *fifth* "*pacifist*" philosophy *must be* clearly understood by *all* scholars!

If history has taught us anything it is that the organizing of middle and lower classes of a people into uprisings against an oppressive aristocratic, and/or militaristic domination system of governing a people have been commonplace![144] Hyam Maccoby makes an excellent point,[145] which *every* legitimate New Testament scholar needs to clearly understand. Maccoby rightly states, "Anyone familiar with Jewish history around the time of Jesus must find this very puzzling," (Maccoby is here referring, of course, to the very scanty references in the Gospels to the Romans and their military occupation of Palestine at the time of Jesus). Maccoby then goes on to state, "The overriding political fact of the period was the Roman occupation of Judaea where the last remnant of political independence had ceased only very recently, (6 CE, when Jesus was about 12 years old). Yet in the Gospels the Roman occupation is treated as a matter of no interest or importance. It is as if someone were to write about France in the years 1940-1945 without mentioning that it was under the occupation of Nazi Germany... In the whole of the four Gospels the word 'Romans' occurs only once (in John 11:48). This is an extraordinary fact which requires

---

143 *The New Testament and the People of God*, N. T. Wright, pp. 353-354.

144 See the comments in *Bandits, Prophets, and Messiahs*, Richard A. Horsley and John S. Hanson, Introduction, p. XVII.

145 *Revolution in Judaea*, Hyam Maccoby, p. 20; and see also the comments in *The Death of Jesus*, Joel Carmichael, p. viii; *The Search for the Real Jesus*, Chester Charlton McCown, p. 124.

explanation."[146] Maccoby is quite correct, and the world's *supposedly* foremost New Testament scholars need to step forth and give *logical* and *unbiased* explanations in regards to this matter! But Maccoby goes on further to state,[147] "Jesus, however, is portrayed in the Gospels as oblivious to the occupation."

Two matters need to be mentioned at this time together, the first being what has just been noted above about middle and lower class uprisings in history, and the fact that far too many scholars portray Jesus as a "pacifist," plus the matter of Jesus' speaking of the destruction of the Temple and its replacement with a "new Temple." The parable Jesus gives in Mark 12:1-12 offers a lesson derived from Isaiah 5:1-7. But when one closely examines what is stated in this parable one sees the clear *violence* that is being depicted in this parable. Yet here again, far too many scholars, even though admitting to the violence depicted in this parable, attempt to utilize this parable in such a manner as to claim that Jesus taught "non-violence."[148] But this entire matter of Jesus' going to Jerusalem *when* he did as a "wanted fugitive" to overturn the tables of the moneychangers was all about the very matter of provoking a *violent* confrontation of some kind.[149]

In regards to Jesus' prediction, or if one prefers, his prophecies[150] and teachings about the destruction of the Temple, was this sufficient in and of itself to warrant his arrest, trial, and crucifixion? The simple answer to this question is an emphatic, *NO!* For far too long now, far too many scholars have tried to claim that this was in fact a sufficient reason to have Jesus arrested and convicted.[151] Yet, examples of prophetic warnings of the

---

146   See also the brief comments in *Pontius Pilate in History and Interpretation*, Helen K. Bond, pp. xvii-xix.

147   See *Revolution in Judaea*, Hyam Maccoby, p. 23 and his further comments on pp. 94-97.

148   See for example the comments in *Jesus: Uncovering the Life, Teachings, and Relevance of a Religious Revolutionary*, Marcus J. Borg, p.237; *Bandits, Prophets, and Messiahs*, Richard A. Horsley and John S. Hanson, p. 3.

149   See the comments in *Jesus: Uncovering the Life, Teachings, and Relevance of a Religious Revolutionary*, Marcus J. Borg, p. 141.

150   See the comments in *Jesus Before Christianity*, Albert Nolan, p. 15.

151   See for example, *The New Testament*, Bart D. Ehrman, p. 258. Yet in Box 16.6 on p. 260 Ehrman does though, note Jeremiah, and thus, he refers to the Temple incident by Jesus as "an enacted parable," or "symbolic action" of future events. But such does not quite fit

destruction of not only the First Temple, but also the Second Temple as well can be found in the Hebrew Scriptures themselves. As a few examples of the many that could be offered, see, 1 Kings 9:7-8; Jeremiah 7:14-15; Ezekiel 9:9-10, and Ezekiel 40:2-4. Likewise, the two Talmud's are replete with examples of the prediction of the destruction of the Temple, such as, *Gittin* 56a-b; *Avodah Zerah* 8b; *Yoma* 39b; *Yoma* 5:2, 43c; *Bikkurim* 56a.[152] Even Josephus, *Jewish Wars* 6.300-309 gives a lengthy description about an individual named, Jesus son of Hananiah, who came to the Temple for seven years railing and ranting about the destruction of the Temple, and who at times even disturbed some of the activities at the Temple. As Lloyd Gaston so rightly states concerning Acts 6:13,[153] "Why then should Stephen be brought to trial for such a statement when others were not?" But yet, Gaston then goes on later to erroneously state that,[154] "Jesus was not interested in destroying the Jerusalem Temple, and the statement that he would do so seems to have been transmitted as part of the anti-Christian Jewish polemic." Such a statement as this is nothing more than a very anti-Semitic biased statement, which has no basis in *fact* and which has no place in genuine scholarship! Now, James Dunn[155] puts sort of a challenge to the words of Stephen in that Dunn claims that "the role of the Temple was called into question" and that Stephen was "enabled" by Jesus' previous similar words. But this is highly doubtful for the simple fact that there are so many discrepancies in Stephen's discourse in Acts

---

with all of the accounts before, during, or afterwards in regards to what happened, such as, withdrawing only a short distance and his disciples armed with swords! Ehrman does rightly note though in Box 16.7, p. 263 that Jesus *was not* the only individual of his time to predict the destruction of the Temple.

152   See the comments in *The Trial of Jesus: Cambridge Studies in Honour of C. F. D. Moule*, p. 22; *Jesus On Trial*, Gerard S. Sloyan, p. 59 and n. 2, p. 130; *Kosher Jesus*, Rabbi Shmuley Boteach, p. 104; *Jesus: Uncovering the Life, teachings, and Relevance of a Religious Revolutionary*, Marcus Borg, p. 243; *No Stone on Another*, Lloyd Gaston, pp. 140-161; Craig Evans, "Predictions of the Destruction of the Herodian Temple in the Pseudepigrapha, Qumran Scrolls, and Related Texts," *Journal for the Study of the Pseudepigrapha* 10, (1992), pp. 89-147.

153   *No Stone on Another*, Lloyd Gaston, p. 156.

154   *No Stone on Another*, Lloyd Gaston, p. 242.

155   *The Partings of the Ways*, James Dunn, p. 50.

about Jewish history! As just one example of this fact, Stephen claims that Jacob's tomb is in *Shechem*, (Acts 7:16), despite the *fact* that Jacob only purchased land in *Shechem*, (Genesis 33:19). Jacob's *actual* burial tomb is in *Machpelah* in *Hebron*, (Genesis 50:13). The fact that there are such errors in Stephen's discourse recorded in Acts, (which also then includes the supposed reference to Jesus' words about destroying the Temple), puts the entire discourse attributed to Stephen into great question as to its *historical* truth![156] Therefore, the *only* logical conclusion that *any* unbiased scholar should come to is that it was Jesus' "violent actions" of overturning the tables and chasing people with a whip that brought about the "final straw" noted above for his arrest, trial, and crucifixion as a *lestai*, "insurrectionist."[157] Now, it is true though, that in Mark's Gospel, (Mark 14:57-59), the claims that Jesus predicted the destruction of the Temple is attributed to statements made by "false witnesses,"[158] *exactly* the same as with Stephen in Acts 6:13-14. There is also one more crucial point to make regarding the statements attributed to both Stephen and Jesus regarding the destruction of the Temple, and this being the matter surrounding the Gospel's attributed claims that Jesus stated that it would be "raised" in "three days." The point to be made here is that in Jewish *metaphoric* terminology, the Hebrew word that generally gets translated into English as "day," *did not* always indicate a "literal" *day* as one might think. One needs to consider what is stated in 2 Peter 3:8 and Psalm 90:4 for example, and thus, Jesus, as well as Stephen may have been intending for their words to be understood *metaphorically* as indicating 3000 years! In the *Epistle of Barnabas* 16:3 it is found being stated that the ones who destroyed the Temple, (i.e. the Romans), would be the ones who would rebuild the Temple.[159] But David Flusser rightly points out that Luke 22:69, (a verse discussed earlier in Chapter 7 regarding the supposed charge of "blasphemy" against Jesus), is a reflection of a very common first century

---

156 See the comments on this in *The Son of Man in Myth and History*, Frederick Borsch, pp. 233-235.

157 See the comments in *The Mythmaker*, Hyam Maccoby, pp. 45 and 157.

158 See the comments on this in *Jesus of Nazareth*, Dale C. Allison, pp. 52, 98-101, but most specifically, pp. 99-100.

159 See the comments on this in *Judaism and the Origins of Christianity*, David Flusser, pp. 99-101.

Palestinian Jewish belief, based on the interpretation of Zechariah 6:12, and this interpretation being that it would be *THE* "Messiah" who would have the Temple rebuilt. Thus, as Flusser points out, Jesus' statement in Luke 22:69 is a direct claim to being *THE* "Messiah!"[160]

In order for anyone, (whether they are a scholar, a theologian, or a member of the general church laity), to correctly understand Jesus' actions at the Temple one must first correctly understand Jesus' teachings and actions in other matters noted in the Gospels, and even as described in the Epistles. It is therefore important that we look at a few specific examples of Jesus' teachings and actions, by starting with the comments of Albert Nolan.[161] Nolan references Luke 13:6-9 and the parable of the fig tree that does not produce. But Nolan fails to mention the *fact* that the last Greek word used in Luke 13:9, has generally and continuously been left *untranslated*. It is the Greek word *auten*, which means, "by a shout," or by "crying out." In other words, then, the parable is actually *best* understood to be saying, "Bring it about with *loud proclamation.*" Thus, this then begs the question of whether this is not a matter related to what is stated in Mark 11:13-21?

Also, the comments of Marcus Borg need to be noted here,[162] for Borg refers to Matthew 28:18-20 and then writes, "They are to teach them 'to obey everything that I have commanded you.' Following Jesus is about obedience, not belief." Borg goes on further on to state,[163] "To take Jesus seriously is to follow him. To follow him is to participate in his passion. And his passion was God and the Kingdom of God." But as Borg rightly notes earlier in his book, this term "Kingdom of God" meant *here* "on earth as it is in heaven," and this is precisely what Jesus believed and taught, and thus, the reasons for the Temple incident.

Yet, possibly *the* most important example of a verse to closely look at is Luke 16:16 in which we find the Greek word *biazetai* repeatedly being translated in a manner that is simply misleading and disingenuous

---

160   See the comments on this in *Judaism and the Origins of Christianity*, David Flusser, pp. 301-305.

161   *Jesus Before Christianity*, Albert Nolan, p. 85.

162   *Jesus: Uncovering the Life, Teachings, and Relevance of a Religious Revolutionary*, Marcus Borg, p. 285.

163   *Jesus: Uncovering the Life, Teachings, and Relevance of a Religious Revolutionary*, Marcus Borg, p. 292.

to its accurate *true* meaning. This verse from Luke's Gospel, when this Greek word *biazetai*, (which in fact is the same word found being used in Matthew 11:12), is understood by its *best* meaning, actually says, (bold, underlined italics mine), "The Kingdom of God is proclaimed, and it will be **_taken by force_**!"[164] In essence, the Greek word *biazetai* means, "to use force," or "thru acts of violence."[165] Christian apologists, and even the world renowned *supposedly* moderate scholars from the late 1980's to 2005 *Jesus Seminar*, and those who have followed in their footsteps who attempt to claim to be unbiased, *fail miserably at being truthful in regards to the fact of what Luke 16:16 actually states!*[166] Furthermore, Luke 16:16 is merely a reiteration of what is found being stated in Jesus's Sermon on the Mount, and specifically Matthew 5:5,[167] and Matthew 5:5 is merely a statement reflecting what is found being stated in *Jubilees* 23:46-48!

But going further though, in Luke 3:7-14 we find here that it very *clearly* refers to John the Baptist performing his baptism upon "soldiers!" Well, this then begs the question to be asked, since John the Baptist only performed his baptism upon Jews, then who are these "Jewish soldiers?" For the Greek word *strateuomenoi*, which is used in these verses from Luke's Gospel, actually means, "combatants," and thus, these verses are clearly referring to "combatants" *against* the Romans, Herodians, and Sadducean oppressors. Furthermore, John's Baptism *must* therefore, be perceived as being an "initiation"[168] into being one of these "combatants," (see Joshua 3:1-4:24 for example, and see Numbers 31:19-24 concerning such after one has been to battle), and since Jesus was amongst those who were "initiated" by John, is it not then *logical* to conclude that Jesus was likewise a "combatant" against these hated enemies of the "loyal patriots

---

164   See the comments in *Jesus of Nazareth*, Dale C. Allison, p. 146.

165   See the comments in *Christianity: A Jewish Perspective*, Rabbi Moshe Reiss, 2 "Jesus Comes From the Jewish Tradition"; *The New Testament and Rabbinic Judaism*, David Daube, pp. 285-300; *The Death of Jesus*, Joel Carmichael, pp. 164-165.

166   See for example *Jewish Christianity Reconsidered*, Matt Jackson-McCabe, p. 128, (William Arnal commenting).

167   See the comments on Matthew 5:5 in *On Earth As It Is In Heaven*, D. C. Thielmann, pp. 691-693 and the corresponding scholar's notations to these pages.

168   See the comments on this in *The Son of Man in Myth and History*, Frederick Borsch, pp. 218-225.

of Israel?"[169] Yet, one of the most essential points to understand regarding this lies in the fact that despite the Christian ritual of "baptism" being such an important part of becoming a Christian, *nowhere* in the Gospels, (except for the brief exception in John 3:22), do we find it specifically stating that Jesus ever once performed a "baptism" upon *anyone*! Even in this one verse of John 3:22 it *does not* specifically state that it was Jesus who was performing these baptisms.[170] Also though, regarding this verse, it is very strange that the very next verse, (John 3:23), states that John the Baptist was also still baptizing in the very same locale! Why would there be the need for both John the Baptist and his followers, and Jesus and his followers, to be performing baptisms in the same locale at the same time *if* such baptizing was *not* being done as an "initiation" into becoming a "combatant"?[171] Dale C. Allison is quite in error when he claims that one possible difference between Jesus and John the Baptist was,[172] "that John was more ascetic than Jesus." As *the* supposed "world's expert on the Gospel of Matthew," has Allison so missed what is stated in Matthew 6:25-34? For these verses in Matthew's Gospel, (attributed to having been spoken by Jesus and *not* John the Baptist), are the *epitome* of the teachings of an ascetic! Yet, Allison goes on to provide comparative parallels between John the Baptist and Jesus in the fact that the early church adopted "baptism" as a practice,[173] and in fact, Allison also clearly places Jesus *as* an "ascetic,"

---

169   See the comments on this in *The Death of Jesus*, Joel Carmichael, pp. 167-168; *Jewish Christianity Reconsidered*, Matt Jackson-McCabe, pp. 269-270, (Jonathan A. Draper commenting on "baptism" as it is described in the *Didache*, and on pp. 270-273 Draper points out that the *Didache* references the *Eucharist* as an "initiation" or "incorporation of the gentiles into Israel, which requires the ritual purity of the participant"); but see also *The Jewish Antecedents of the Christian Sacraments*, Frank Gavin, pp. 26-58; *The Origin and Significance of the New Testament Baptism*, Herbert G. Marsh, p. 81; *The Beginnings of Christianity: The Acts of the Apostles*, F. J. Foakes Jackson and Kirsopp Lake, Volume I, pp. 332-342.

170   See the comments on this in *Jesus and Purity Halakah*, Thomas Kazen, pp. 231-255.

171   See the comments on this in *On Earth As It Is In Heaven*, D. C. Thielmann, pp. 517-518 and the corresponding scholars notations to these pages.

172   *Jesus of Nazareth*, Dale C. Allison, p. 104; but see also the similar comments in *Jesus and His Adversaries*, Arland J. Hultgren, pp. 79-80.

173   *Jesus of Nazareth*, Dale C. Allison, pp. 111, and n. 70, p. 111.

while still trying to claim that he was not the same sort of "ascetic" as John the Baptist.[174] But the very fact that we know so very little about John the Baptist places such claims upon very *flimsy* evidence, and in fact, a great deal about John the Baptist in Christian tradition has been altered.[175] Furthermore, as Samuel Sandmel writes about Paul,[176] "Far from being license, Paul's special kind of freedom is ascetic in nature." But the genuine *fact* of the matter is that "ascetics," and "asceticism" was totally contrary to Jewish thinking and the concept of "asceticism" is in all reality something of non-Jewish origin.[177]

This fact regarding John the Baptist though, is then rather strange in regards to *why* Christians go so far out of their way to insist upon this ritual of "baptism" when this was never once an actual teaching or practice of the founder of their very faith – i.e. Jesus![178] As Richard A. Horsley writes,[179] "There were no special name, rites (other than table fellowship; baptism was initiated by John and not distinctive to Jesus' followers), and organization separate from the rest of Jewish society." Going further into this matter though, N. T. Wright claims that,[180] "Our earliest evidence for Christian baptism involves the *name* of Jesus (and sometimes a larger formula) and the *death* and *resurrection* of Jesus," and Wright cites as his examples, Matthew 28:19; Acts 2:38; 8:16; 10:48; 19:5; Romans 6:2-11. But Wright seems to just simply ignore these earlier baptisms just noted above that were being performed by John the Baptist, and Jesus' disciples (John 3:22), which *were not* being done in "the *name* of Jesus," nor were they being performed *after* his "*death* and *resurrection*!" Therefore, when Wright further claims that,[181] "the subversion in question was not that of the ordinary political revolutionary," he is quite in error!

---

174   See *Jesus of Nazareth*, Dale C. Allison, pp. 172-216.

175   See *On Earth As It Is In Heaven*, D. C. Thielmann, Chapter 9.

176   *A Jewish Understanding of the New Testament*, Samuel Sandmel, p. 71.

177   See the comments on this matter of Kaufmann Kohler, "Ascetics," *Jewish Encyclopedia*;
      Kaufmann Kohler and Emil G. Hirsch, "Asceticism," *Jewish Encyclopedia*.

178   See the comments on this matter in *The Death of Jesus*, Joel Carmichael, p. 171; *How Jesus Became Christian*, Barrie Wilson, pp. 259-260; *The Jesus Dynasty*, James D. Tabor, p. 142.

179   *Jesus and the Spiral of Violence*, Richard A. Horsley, p. 211.

180   *The New Testament and the People of God*, N. T. Wright, p. 447, and n. 11, p. 447.

181   *The New Testament and the People of God*, N. T. Wright, p. 449.

Matthew 12:29; Mark 3:27 are the next verses to look at as examples. These verses, which are generally read as, "How can one spoil a strong man's goods except he first binds him?" There are two key Greek words found in these verses to take note of, and these being the words, *arpasai*, and *diarpasei*. These two Greek words indicate an *actual action* of "plundering," or "stealing," or in other words, the very actions associated with one being a "*lestai*," a "brigand," or a "bandit" noted above![182]

Luke 19:27, by no stretch of anyone's imagination can be considered as the actions or words of a "pacifist." Jesus saying to others regarding anyone rejecting him, "Bring them here and execute them before me," *are not* the words of a "pacifist," and by one of the most essential "criteria" that modern New Testament scholars like to use – i.e. an "embarrassment to the church" – why would the later church have placed such words as these onto the lips of Jesus? But the most telling words, actions, and/or event in the ministry of Jesus, besides the Temple incident, that demonstrates that Jesus was not a "pacifist" in the manner that he is so often portrayed is derived from Luke 22:36-49.[183] Why would a "pacifist" instruct his followers to buy swords? But even more telling is the fact that his followers *already had swords and staves*, both of which are things *not carried* by "pacifists." All four Gospels, Matthew 26:51; Mark 14:47; Luke 22:50; John 18:10 or in other words, "multiple attestation" all report this matter that is in all reality a direct reflection of "*violent*" intentions. We also find in Matthew 26:53 Jesus saying that he could "appeal to my Father" and be provided "twelve legions," which again, *are not* the words and actions of a "pacifist" but the words of an "activist" prepared for "*violence!*" To make the point further in regards to the matter of "staves" being used as a "weapon," during the protest incident following Pilate's raiding of the Temple treasury to build an aqueduct, (as described by Josephus), Pilate had the Roman soldiers disguise themselves as civilians dressed in Jewish clothes, and then, Pilate had them mingle amongst the crowd of protestors carrying only "staves" as their "weapons," to which the Roman soldiers then used these "staves" to beat the protestors to death. In Chapter 4 it was pointed out that the

---

182   See the comments in *The New Testament and Rabbinic Judaism*, David Daube, p. 286; *Pontius Pilate*, Ann Wroe, p. 204.

183   See the comments in *Judas Iscariot and the Myth of Jewish Evil*, Hyam Maccoby, p. 154; *The Mythmaker*, Hyam Maccoby, p. 53.

term, "Damascus" was a "code name" for the community at Qumran and the Essens, and it has been repeatedly demonstrated throughout this book that the Essens were, in simple terms, the forerunners of Christianity, (i.e. the Jerusalem Church). Now, the philosophy of the Essens actually existed long before the time of the Maccabees, (as already mentioned in Chapter 4, although some scholars attempt to debate the truth of this matter[184]). Prior to the time of the Maccabees they were referred to as the *Hasidim*, or "the pious ones," and these "pious ones" *were most assuredly not* "pacifists"![185]

The next essential teaching of Jesus to really understand in regards to interpreting Jesus' overall actions as being those of a "political activist" comes from his repeated references to the "Kingdom of Heaven." There have been some scholars who have tried to claim that Jesus' usage of this term was "not characteristic of Judaism."[186] But such claims can be, and already have been thoroughly refuted![187] At the time of Jesus the use of the word "heaven" was often utilized as a synonym for the Tetragrammaton – the Ineffable Name of God. Thus, the phrase "Kingdom of Heaven" indicated and meant, the "Kingdom of God."[188] As Moshe Chaim Luzzatto writes,[189] "Our sages thus taught us, 'The Kingdom of Heaven resembles an earthly kingdom'," (*Berakhot* 58a). So, what exactly constituted the "Kingdom of God" in the minds of first century Palestinian Jews such as Jesus? The answer to this question is multi-fold. For the term, "Kingdom of God," not only meant a legitimate Temple with a legitimate priesthood and High Priest, but it also meant a legitimate Davidic king and not one appointed by a foreign power such as the Herodians were as the "client kings" over a Roman province. But most of all it indicated the land of Palestine itself

---

184   See for example *The Apocalyptic Imagination*, John J. Collins, pp. 61-63.

185   See the comments in *The Apocalyptic Imagination*, John J. Collins, p. 62.

186   See for example the comments in *Jesus*, C. Leslie Mitton, pp. 139-140.

187   See Kaufmann Kohler, "Kingdom of God ('Malkuta de-Adonai')," *Jewish Encyclopedia*.

188   See the comments in *Understanding the Difficult Words of Jesus*, David Bivin and Roy Blizzard, p. 59; *The Jewish Messiah*, James Drummond, pp. 320-322; *Revolution in Judaea*, Hyam Maccoby, pp. 83-91, and 111-124; *Jesus of Nazareth: Part One*, Ratzinger and Pope Benedict, p. 55; *The Death of Jesus*, Joel Carmichael, p. 83; *The Search for the Real Jesus*, Chester Charlton McCown, pp. 247 and 254-255.

189   *The Way of God*, Moshe Chaim Luzzatto, p. 155.

being in the controlling hands of the Jewish people.[190] As Leviticus 25:23 clearly states, "The land shall not be sold in perpetuity, for the land is Mine; with Me you are but sojourners and tenants." Thus, at the time of Jesus this was most certainly not occurring in accordance with the Torah! For with the Romans in control, the Herodians as "client kings," and the Jewish aristocracy of the Sadducees collaborating with the Romans as the High Priestly families and wealthy "landowners," the result was an oppressive system on the people who were the most loyal to God and his Torah![191]

The sages of the time of Jesus, which also included Jesus, interpreted Genesis 25:23 as a reference to Rome. In essence, in the Talmud "Edom" was interpreted as indicating Rome, as can be found for example in, Talmud Babli, *Megillah* 6a.[192] Also, Babylon came to be used as a reference to Rome as noted in Revelations 14:8; 16:9; 18:2; *4 Ezra* 3; *2 Baruch* 10.[193] Therefore, Jesus' teachings regarding the "Kingdom of Heaven" as well as Jesus' Temple incident were in regards to a "political" and *not* a "spiritual" new Kingdom.[194] The modern concept of the "Kingdom of Heaven" being a "spiritual new Kingdom" derived from the misunderstandings of Paul's usage of the flawed Septuagint.[195] As Hyam Maccoby rightly

---

190   See the comments on all of this in *The Partings of the Ways*, James Dunn, pp. 31-35; *Jesus Before the Gospels*, Bart Ehrman, p. 54; Paula Fredriksen, "Judaism, the Circumcision of Gentiles, and Apocalyptic Hope: Another Look at Galatians 1 and 2," *Journal of Theological Studies* New Series 42, No. 2 (1991), p. 544; *Jesus and the Spiral of Violence*, Richard A. Horsley, pp. 167-208, although Horsley does make some errors in his comments on these pages that stem from his misunderstandings of Jewish metaphoric terminology.

191   See the comments in *Jesus: Uncovering the Life, Teachings, and Relevance of a Religious Revolutionary*, Marcus Borg, p. 100.

192   See the comments in *The Jewish Messiah*, James Drummond, p. 95 who references *Koren Talmud Babli: Taanith – Megillah*, Commentary by Adin Steinsaltz, Volume 12, pp. 224-225, Jerusalem Koren Publishers, (2014); *Hillel*, Rabbi Joseph Telushkin, p. 209.

193   See the comments on this in *The New Testament*, Bart D. Ehrman, pp. 470-473.

194   See the comments in *Judas and the Gospel of Jesus*, N. T. Wright, pp. 90-91, and n. 6, p. 152 where he cites Romans 8:18-27 as his proof text; *Jesus: Uncovering the Life, Teachings, and Relevance of a Religious Revolutionary*, Marcus Borg, pp. 143-144, and pp. 186-190; *Jesus Before the Gospels*, Bart Ehrman, p. 54.

195   See the comments in *The Misunderstood Jew*, Amy-Jill Levine, p. 79; *Kosher Jesus*, Rabbi Shmuley Boteach, p. 207; *Christianity: A Jewish Perspective*, Rabbi Moshe Reiss,

states, [196] "From previous chapters we can understand what it meant in first-century Palestine to proclaim the 'Kingdom of God' and to assume the title of 'Messiah.' These were not (as they later became in the Gentile-Christian Church) purely 'spiritual' expressions. They were political slogans which put those who used them in danger of their lives from the Roman and pro-Roman authorities, just as the use of expressions such as 'the dictatorship of the proletariat' would attract police attention in Tsarist Russia. They were expressions of revolutionary content." Also, as Moshe Chaim Luzzatto writes,[197] "What a person must understand here is that the world is rectified only by man, and not by itself." Likewise, as Joel Carmichael rightly states,[198] "As Jesus never explains what he means by the 'Kingdom of God,' we are left to assume he was using a phrase or an idea that was part of current Jewish thought, and thus, could be understood by anyone in his audience. We must accordingly deduce its meaning from the general background of his time and in conjunction with various hints in the Gospels. The coming Kingdom of God is a part of conventional Judaism; it is repeated even nowadays by pious Jews three times daily (in the prayer called *Shemonah Esreh*, No. 17)." Furthermore, as W. D. Davies states,[199] "But Paul's experience at Thessalonica soon proved to him that however suitable the term *basileia* had been in Palestine, its political connotation made it equally unsuitable for use in the Greco-Roman world, for the announcement of the arrival of another *basileia*, however spiritual, might and actually did lead to trouble with the Roman authorities.[200] Political considerations, therefore, compelled Paul to seek other ways to describe what the Synoptics called 'the arrival of the Kingdom of God'." Unknowingly, it seems, Davies demonstrates a matter discussed earlier in this chapter about *how* the "politically insurrectionary" teachings of Jesus became something that caused Jesus to appear to be "non-political" and

---

2 "Jesus Comes From the Jewish Tradition," conclusion; *The Last Week*, Marcus Borg and John Dominic Crossan, p. 28; *On Earth As It Is In Heaven*, D. C. Thielmann, Chapter 7.

196   *Revolution in Judaea*, Hyam Maccoby, pp. 93-94.

197   *The Way of God*, Moshe Chaim Luzzatto, p. 283.

198   See his full comments in *The Death of Jesus*, Joel Carmichael, pp. 82-98.

199   *Paul and Rabbinic Judaism*, W. D. Davies, pp. 36-37.

200   *Paul and Rabbinic Judaism*, W. D. Davies, n. 14, p. 36 citing W. L. Knox, *St. Paul and the Church of Jerusalem*, p. 7, and nn.7-8, Acts 17:7-8.

"non-insurrectionary" through Paul's seeking "other ways to describe" what Jesus was about, and therefore, ended up "spiritualizing" what Jesus had *actually* been all about, a matter already discussed previously in Chapter 4 regarding Paul's teachings!

Mark 4:26-29 is a primary example that Jesus taught "activism" and not "pacifism," (and this verse actually relates to Joel 3:13).[201] For the ones in this parable who "plant the seed," are *also* the very ones who "goes in with his sickle, because the harvest has come." Far too many scholars and theologians have misinterpreted this parable as somehow indicating that it is God who "puts in the sickle." But God uses men and nations to accomplish *His* work, as the Jews have long known, yet such has *always* been referred to by Jews *metaphorically*. As the *best* example that can be given in this regard to demonstrate this point, God used the Assyrians to punish the ten northern tribes of Israel, and God used the Babylonians to punish the tribes of Judah and Benjamin as we are clearly told by the writings of the prophets of Israel.

The final matter to be looked at in regards to Jesus' actions at the Temple concerns Jesus' triumphant entry into Jerusalem, which in reality was a very "political" action on the part of Jesus and his closest followers. In regards to this "triumphant entry," Hyam Maccoby makes a very important point to understand when he writes that,[202] "Luke alone suggests that the crowd of Palm Sunday was a *different* crowd from that of the Barabbas incident (Luke 14:37, where the crowd of Palm Sunday consists of 'disciples'). The other Gospels stress that both crowds consisted of the Jewish masses; and Luke, like the rest, stresses the representative character of the crowd who condemned Jesus. John *at first* says that it was only the 'chief priests and their henchmen' who shouted 'Crucify him!' But soon alters this designation to his usual blanket expression 'the Jews.' Modern scholars (e.g. Eduard Meyer) have suggested that the crowd before Pilate consisted only of Barabbas supporters, but there is no ground for this theory in the texts.

---

201   See the comments in *Studies of the Historical Jesus*, Ernst Fuchs, pp. 132-136; *On Earth As It Is In Heaven*, D. C. Thielmann, pp. 683-685 and the corresponding scholars notations to these pages.

202   *Revolution in Judaea*, Hyam Maccoby, n. 1, p. 221; but see also the comments in *The Theological Significance of Jesus' Temple Action in Mark's Gospel*, Emilio G. Chavez, p. 66 and n. 14, p. 66.

Whatever may have been the historical facts, the intention of the texts is to incriminate the Jews as a whole for Jesus' crucifixion. (Matthew and Luke use the Greek word 'laos' [people, nation] instead of Mark's word 'ochlos' [crowd]; see Matthew 27:25, and Luke 23:13)." More will be said about this word and matter of the Greek words, *ochlos* or *ochloi* in Chapter 10. But Maccoby goes on further to state, "A more 'liberal' interpretation (such as that of Vatican Council II), while intended to exonerate the majority of the Jews, has the incidental effect of whitewashing the Gospels."

Now, Jules Isaac believes that above all else that Jesus did – his teachings, his healings, etc. – this one event alone, (the "triumphant entry into Jerusalem"), demonstrated *clearly* a claim by Jesus to being *THE* "Messiah."[203] There has been a great deal of scholarly debate about whether or not the Gospels accurately depict this final entry by Jesus into Jerusalem upon a donkey.[204] But regardless of whether or not Jesus made his final entry into Jerusalem exactly as depicted in the Gospels, the fact remains, Jesus *did* make some sort of final entry into Jerusalem *with* his closest immediate followers. Three of the four Gospels, Matthew 21:9, 21:15; Mark 11:9-10; John 12:13 all report this entry into Jerusalem by Jesus to the accompanying shouts of, "Hosanna!"[205] Matthew's Gospel has the crowd basically quoting Psalm 118:25, which thus, have the shouts being, "Save, please, the son of David."[206] Many scholarly opinions are now quite in agreement that "this looks like a planned political demonstration,"[207] and such scholars are quite correct in these assertions. Therefore, scholars who attempt to claim that, "there is little if anything in the Gospel portrait

---

203   See the comments on this in *Jesus and Israel*, Jules Isaac, pp. 170-175.

204   See the comments on this matter in *On Earth As It Is In Heaven*, D. C. Thielmann, pp. 294-295 and the corresponding scholars notations to these pages; but see also the partially correct comments in *Jesus of Nazareth: Part Two*, Ratzinger and Pope Benedict, p. 5 where they rightly note the political aspect, but yet through apologetic bias erroneously try to separate such from having any "zealot" appearances or connotations.

205   See the comments on the translation of this word "Hosanna" in *Problems of New Testament Translation*, Edgar J. Goodspeed, pp. 34-35.

206   See the comments in *On Earth As It Is In Heaven*, D. C. Thielmann, n. 124, p. 356.

207   See the comments in *The Last Week*, Marcus Borg and John Dominic Crossan, p. 4; *Revolution in Judaea*, Hyam Maccoby, pp. 125-137; *Who is Jesus*, Darrell L. Bock, pp. 107-121; *The Death of Jesus*, Joel Carmichael, pp. 183-186.

of Jesus that accords with the Jewish expectation of a militant Messiah,"[208] are most assuredly in error for either some unknown biased reasoning, or for a simple lack of doing a full and complete analysis of Jesus' actions and words from the standpoint of the Hebrew and Jewish idioms used in first century Palestinian Judaism! For to the Romans, the slogan *Hosanna* was a term used by Jewish revolutionaries – "insurrectionists" (*lestai* in other words) – against Roman authority,[209] and the use of palm fronds had been declared by Caesar himself to be a symbol of a warrior's "victory," as well as to symbolize the bringing about of victorious "peace."[210] Originally to the Jews, "palm fronds" represented the "light of God shining upon and engulfing Israel." But after the time of the Maccabees, (as known from *1 Maccabees* 13:51), the use of "palm fronds" *became a symbol of Jewish nationalistic restoration and victory.* Thus, as Deuteronomy 28:10 says, (which the Jews related to this matter of the "palm fronds"), "All the nations of the earth shall see that God's Name is called upon you and they shall fear you," and thus the waving of the "palm fronds" also signified such prophecies as that of Isaiah 49:23, and Isaiah 60:14.[211]

Now, Hyam Maccoby points out a very important matter to understand regarding these shouts of "Hosanna," and this being, that Maccoby doubts that this incident of Jesus' "triumphant entry" into Jerusalem occurred at the time when the Gospels claim that it occurred.[212] Maccoby contends that this "triumphant entry" *actually* occurred *six months before Jesus' arrest*, or in other words, *during the Feast of Tabernacles*, (which would then support the scholarly claims noted above about Jesus being arrested well after his Temple incident which would thus, contradict the Gospel accounts). Now, Maccoby's supportive evidence to his claim is quite impressive, and Maccoby's first piece of evidence comes from the facts surrounding

---

208   See for example, *The Scepter and the Star*, John J. Collins, p. 204 and n. 55, p. 213.

209   See the comments on this in *Jesus of Nazareth: Part Two*, Ratzinger and Pope Benedict, pp. 7-8.

210   See the comments in *Pontius Pilate*, Ann Wroe, p. 210; *The Theological Significance of Jesus' Temple Action in Mark's Gospel*, Emilio G. Chavez, p. 66 and n. 15, p. 66.

211   See the comments on this in *The Way of God*, Moshe Chaim Luzzatto, pp. 343-345.

212   See the comments on this matter in *Revolution in Judaea*, Hyam Maccoby, pp. 132-135.

the shouting of "Hosanna," which as he notes,[213] "The alternative form 'Hoshiya-na' occurs, not prominently, in the Hallel of every Festival. Scholars, however, have failed to note the difference between the two forms, and have thus underestimated the uniqueness of 'Hosanna' in relation to Tabernacles."[214] The "Hallel" came about after the time of Mordecai and Esther[215] and this is known because it contains some Aramaic, (Mishnah *Pesaḥim* 117a, and a matter that will be discussed further in Chapter 10), and it was something, which was a cause of great rallying by the Jewish people for "liberation" from "foreign" control. Maccoby goes on further to point out though,[216] "According to John's story (John 7), which is contained in no other Gospel, Jesus was urged to go up to Jerusalem by his brothers at the time of 'the Feast of the Tabernacles.' Jesus refused to go, saying, 'My time is not yet come.' Yet he did go after all, 'not openly, but as it were in secret.' Despite this intention of secrecy, a disturbance arose among the people about him; and 'about the midst of the Feast,' Jesus appeared openly in the Temple, preaching boldly. Some of the people declared him to be 'the very Christ.' When the rulers tried to arrest him, he disappeared, 'because his hour was not yet come.' The story appears to be an intermediate version of the Triumphal Entry – that came later, at Passover. The Tabernacles visit is represented as merely preliminary; and in the other Gospels, it drops out altogether." Furthermore, as Maccoby goes on to point out concerning this matter,[217] "It was Jesus' confidence and faith that had betrayed him to the Romans. He had been convinced that the great miracle would occur on that very night. Why was he so sure? Zechariah had said that the miracle would occur during the Feast of Tabernacles, but the Festival lasted eight days. Which of the eight days

---

213   *Revolution in Judaea*, Hyam Maccoby, n. 4, p. 233; but see also the comments of Rabbi Isaiah Wohlgemuth, "Hallel," *My Jewish Learning*; Cyrus Adler, Lewis N. Dembitz, and Francis L. Cohen, "Hallel," *Jewish Encyclopedia*; Kaufmann Kohler, "Hosanna," *Jewish Encyclopedia*; Cyrus Adler and Lewis N. Dembitz, "Hosha'na Rabbah," *Jewish Encyclopedia*.

214   See also the comments on this matter in *Jesus of Nazareth: Part Two*, Ratzinger and Pope Benedict, pp. 6-7.

215   See Isadore Singer, M. Seligsohn, and Wilhelm Bacher, "Mordecai," *Jewish Encyclopedia*.

216   *Revolution in Judaea*, Hyam Maccoby, n. 7, p. 234.

217   *Revolution in Judaea*, Hyam Maccoby, p. 153.

was to be the day of deliverance? The obvious answer would have been the seventh day, known in Jesus' time as 'the day of Hosanna' (nowadays called by Jews 'the Great Hosanna')." Robert Gundry though,[218] is of the opinion that because of the story of the "cursing of the fig tree," (Mark 11:11-14; Matthew 21:17-19), Gundry claims that this then prevents this from being at the time of the "Feast of Tabernacles," (September-October). Gundry believes that the story only fits with "the season of Passover." But Gundry uses as his proof for his claim, Zechariah 14:20-21 in regards to Jesus' actions in Mark 11:16, (a matter briefly mentioned already in Chapter 4). But Zechariah 14:20-21 is a matter that is in regards to the "Feast of Booths," or in other words, the "Feast of Tabernacles," as *clearly* stated in Zechariah 14:17-19. Thus, Gundry is quite in error in his assertions!

Going further into this matter of the "Feast of Tabernacles" actually being *when* Jesus made his "Triumphant entry" into Jerusalem, Hyam Maccoby goes on further to point out another important piece of information regarding the matter referred to as the "Last Supper."[219] Maccoby writes, "We now come to the incident known as the Last Supper. It follows from the argument of the last chapter that this took place not at Passover time but during the Feast of Tabernacles... No trace is revealed of any of the special rites of a Passover 'Seder,' such as the eating of unleavened bread, the eating of the Paschal lamb, the bitter herbs, and the relating of the Exodus from Egypt. The only special right of Tabernacles, as regards eating, is taking of meals in the Succah, or Booth (from which the festival takes its name). Of this there is some trace in the odd reference to an 'upper room,' described in Mark 14:15 as 'strewn over' (Greek, *estromenon*), and in Jerusalem, the ritual booths or 'tabernacles' were often constructed on the roofs of houses, so the 'upper room' may in fact have been a 'tabernacle' which was 'strewn over' with tree-branches in the prescribed manner."[220] All four Gospels confirm what Maccoby points out here. For in each Gospel, (Matthew 26:26; Mark 14:22; Luke 22:19; John 13:18), the Greek

---

218   *Mark*, Robert H. Gundry, pp. 638-643.

219   *Revolution in Judaea*, Hyam Maccoby, p. 141.

220   See also the comments in *The History of the Synoptic Tradition*, Rudolf Bultmann, pp. 264-266.

word *arton* (or *artos*), "bread,"[221] is used, which *is not* the Greek word for "unleavened bread" that would be eaten at a Passover meal! The Greek word for "unleavened bread" is *azumos*,[222] which again, *is not* the Greek word that is used either in regards to the Last Supper in the Gospels or in the Eucharist description in 1 Corinthians! Darrell Bock's comments[223] as well, lend further weight to Maccoby's claims, and the wording in the *Didache* 9-10 lends even further weight to what Maccoby claims regarding the "Last Supper."[224] There is absolutely *nothing* in the Gospel accounts of the Last Supper that demonstrate that Jesus and his disciples were doing *anything* according to what is specifically prescribed in Numbers 9:13 regarding the Passover meal![225] In Mark 14:26; Matthew 26:30 it states that right after the Last Supper meal was eaten, they all "sung a hymn." Most interpreters assume this hymn to be the "traditional" singing of Psalms 113-118.[226] But at *Sukkot* ("The Feast of Tabernacles") there were hymns sung as well, especially on the final day of *Sukkot*, and one of those hymns that got sung *was* "The Great Hosanna!" Furthermore, as even Cardinal Ratzinger and Pope Benedict XVI point out on this matter,[227] "Jesus' final meal – whether or not it was a Passover meal – was first and foremost an act of worship." Now, David Daube though,[228] points out that, "… From earliest times guests, and especially such as had reason to be inconspicuous, were accommodated in an attic,[229] 2 Kings 4:10 Rahab concealed the spies on the roof; Joshua 2:6…." *If* this then is the actual reason as to why Jesus and his disciples ate in a "strewn over" "upper room," then this would lend weight to what was pointed out about Jesus being a "wanted fugitive."

---

221   See *BDAG Greek-English Lexicon*, p. 136; *Liddell and Scott's Greek-English Lexicon*, p. 121.

222   See *BDAG Greek-English Lexicon*, p. 23; *Liddell and Scott's Greek-English Lexicon*, p. 16.

223   *Who is Jesus*, Darrell L. Bock, pp. 141-151.

224   See the comments on this from Kaufmann Kohler, "Lord's Supper," *Jewish Encyclopedia*.

225   See the comments in *Hillel*, Rabbi Joseph Telushkin, p. 13.

226   See for example *Problems of New Testament Translation*, Edgar J. Goodspeed, pp. 62-63.

227   See the comments in *Jesus of Nazareth: Part Two*, Ratzinger and Pope Benedict, pp. 103-145.

228   *Collaboration with Tyranny*, David Daube, p. 6.

229   *Collaboration with Tyranny*, David Daube, n. 4, p. 6.

From Jesus' "Triumphant entry" into Jerusalem, whenever that may have actually occurred, to his overturning the tables of the moneychangers, *all* of Jesus' actions and his teachings were a direct reflection of his own *"political feelings"* about the Romans, the Herodians, the High Priest, and the illegitimate and fraudulent activities occurring at the Temple! *Period!* Jesus most certainly knew what the consequences of his actions at the Temple would be, and this very *fact* that Jesus knew what those consequences would be should be quite telling, in and of itself, in regards to any *genuine "historical" depiction of Jesus by any competent scholar!* For as W. R. Farmer states, (citing Josephus *Jewish Wars* 2.10.1-5(184-203); *Antiquities* 18.8.1-6(257-288); Philo *On the Embassy to Gaius* 31, (207) as his proof texts),[230] "Working backwards in time we notice first that when Petronius attempted to erect Caius Caligula's statue in the Jerusalem Temple, great multitudes of Jews were ready to die rather than see the National Sanctuary defiled," and thus, one *must* conclude that Jesus' "violent" actions at the Temple came about as a direct result of his observing the "defilement" of the "National Sanctuary" by these "moneychangers."

---

230   *Maccabees, Zealots, and Josephus,* W. R. Farmer, p. 123.

Chapter 10

"Release unto us Barabbas!" (Luke 23:18)

To begin this chapter on the supposed Gospel character, (who actually plays a very minor role in the Gospel accounts at the end of Jesus' trial), whom is so named, *Barabbas*, we must start by taking a very close look at this *supposed* name. This supposed name, *Barabbas*, is actually a combination of two untranslated Aramaic words – *bar* and *abba[s]*, (or *abba[n]*, as it is found in Mark's Gospel), and this change in suffix that is found in Mark's Gospel only, changes the meaning of this Aramaic word *abba* into the first person plural possessive, as will be pointed out just below.[1] We do know, from several sources, including the New Testament, such as Mark 10:46 and Acts 4:36, that it was quite common to combine the Aramaic word *bar* with someone's name, or at times one's "nickname," which resulted in someone being called, *bar so-and-so*, such as *Bartimaeus* of Mark 10:46. But in each of these instances where we find such in the New Testament what we actually find is a combination of both an Aramaic word that has been left untranslated *and* a word or term that while partially left untranslated its meaning has been badly rendered out

---

1   See the comments in *On Earth As It Is In Heaven*, D. C. Thielmann, pp. 308-309; and see John J. Parsons, "Hebrew For Christians," *Hebrew4Christians.com*.

into Greek terminology.[2] Therefore, we know that this *supposed* name, *Barabbas*, actually means, "son of the Father," (or also as just noted above regarding the first person plural possessive suffix in Mark's Gospel, "son of *our* Father"),[3] or it can even be interpreted as being, "son of the teacher," or "disciple of the teacher," or even most importantly of all since God Himself is referred to by the word *Abba*, (as was discussed in Chapter 7), this name *can even be* interpreted as being, "son of God!"[4]

Jules Isaac points out that over the centuries many scholars have tried to reinvent and reinterpret this name *Barabbas* so as to try and eliminate it from resembling "son of the father."[5] Now, as an example, using what was just stated above that the so-called name, *Barabbas*, can mean, "son of the teacher," Roger David Aus attempts to offer an ingenious explanation that *Barabbas* actually meant, *Bar Rabban*, or "son" of a prominent "teacher," and that this individual was quite possibly the "son" of either Judas the Galilean or Matthias, (the infamous leaders of the insurrection against Herod the Great, and as noted in Chapter 3 these two individuals were beloved as "educators of the youth," and as noted in Chapter 9 they were crucified sometime around 46 to 48 CE). Yet, even with this ingenious claim regarding *Barabbas*, Aus rightly states, and admits that,[6] "If correct, this means that there never was a real person, Barabbas, who was imprisoned at 'the' insurrection during the period shortly before Jesus' crucifixion.

---

2   See the comments in *On Earth As It Is In Heaven*, D. C. Thielmann, n. 119, pp. 353-354; *A Myth Of Innocence*, Burton L. Mack, n. 2, p. 297; *Community of the New Age*, Howard C. Kee, p. 101.

3   See *The Theological Significance of Jesus' Temple Action in Mark's Gospel*, Emilio G. Chavez, p. 25.

4   See the comments in *On Earth As It Is In Heaven*, D. C. Thielmann, pp. 308-309, n. 120, pp. 354-355 and n. 124, p. 356; *Honest to Jesus*, Robert W. Funk, pp. 208 and 235; *Jesus and His Times*, H. Daniel-Rops, p. 517; *Pontius Pilate*, Ann Wroe, p. 249; *The Misunderstood Jew*, Amy-Jill Levine, p. 99; *Jesus On Trial*, Gerard S. Sloyan, p. 50; *Judas Iscariot and the Myth of Jewish Evil*, Hyam Maccoby, n. 2, p. 186; *Jesus of Nazareth: Part One*, Ratzinger and Pope Benedict, pp. 40-41; *Jesus of Nazareth: Part Two*, Ratzinger and Pope Benedict, p. 197; *Strong's Exhaustive Concordance*, p. 18 of "The Greek Dictionary of the New Testament," #912.

5   See the comments on this in *Jesus and Israel*, Jules Isaac, pp. 341-342.

6   *"Caught in the Act,"* Roger David Aus, pp. 156-158.

There are absolutely no other Jewish, Jewish Christian, Greek, or Roman sources for such an insurrection at this time...." (exactly the same, as was pointed out in Chapter 9, that there are no other sources, other than the Gospels, for Jesus' Temple incident). Furthermore, Aus goes on to rightly point out that there are also no known sources – absolutely none – "for the custom of a Roman governor's releasing of a prisoner in Jerusalem to the crowds at the Festival of Passover. The entire episode is rather a Palestinian Jewish Christian creation designed to express definite religious truths." The *only* possible incident that could prompt *any* objectionable scholar to perceive that some sort of an "insurrection" occurred around the time of Jesus' arrest and crucifixion is the very matter discussed in Chapter 9 concerning the Gospel accounts involving Jesus' "overturning" the "moneychangers tables"! *Period!* But Aus also offers another very different, but also quite ingenious interpretation for the name *Barabbas*. Aus borrows from Josephus *Antiquities* 11.207 where Josephus is giving a brief narration of the Book of Esther in which Josephus refers to an individual that he calls, "Barnabazos," which in Aramaic can be shortened to, "Barnabaz." Therefore, as Aus writes concerning this,[7] "For a Jewish Christian describing the circumstances of Jesus' crucifixion in light of Judaic traditions on the Esther narrative, it would have been only a small step to drop the nun and exchange samek for zayin in Barnabaz: *Bar Abas*, similar to the frequently found Bar Abba." Thus, we find Aus offering two completely ingeniously different and contradictory means by which one can conclude that the name *Barabbas* was contrived by the Gospel authors.

Now, even though the word *abba* was briefly discussed in Chapter 7, it is essential to say more about it here in this chapter, for there has been a great deal of scholarly debate over the correct understanding of the Aramaic word *abba*.[8] It has been suggested by some scholars that the word *abba* was a very "affectionate" term and a very familiarly used term indicating not "father," but "daddy," or even "dear daddy."[9] But other scholars disagree

---

7   *Barabbas and Esther*, Roger David Aus, pp. 17-18.

8   See the discussion on this matter in *On Earth As It Is In Heaven*, D. C. Thielmann, n. 120, pp 354-355.

9   See the comments in *Resurrection, Myth or Reality*, John Shelby Spong, p. 268; *Jesus: An Unconventional Biography*, Jacques Duquesne, p. 161; *Meeting Jesus Again for the First Time*, Marcus Borg, pp. 35-36.

with this assertion believing that between the periods of 200 BCE – 200 CE the Aramaic term used by a child addressing its "father" was actually, '*abi*.[10] Still other scholars assert that at the time of Jesus it would have been quite unique and unusual for *anyone* to use *Abba* in a manner that addressed God, such as Jesus does.[11] But such claims that this usage was "unique" have been thoroughly refuted as noted already in Chapter 7.[12]

This then brings us to a very important question that arouses great debate amongst scholars, and this question derives from what is believed to be the *original* text of Matthew 27:16-17. In this supposed *original* text of Matthew 27:16-17 the given name of this supposed individual called *Barabbas* was, *coincidently*, "*Jesus.*"[13] So the question is: was Jesus of Nazareth and Jesus Barabbas one in the same individual?[14] It is true that there have been scholars, who have pointed out that even the Talmud mentions several individuals referred to as *Barabbas*.[15] But as noted above already, these two Aramaic words were used as an affectionate reference to an individual as being the "son of the teacher," or "disciple of the teacher." Therefore, in essence, the Talmudic references are really not an actual individual's "name" per se.[16] So, the scholars that try to claim that there

---

10 See the comments in *The Death of the Messiah*, Raymond E. Brown, p. 173, and n. 16, p. 173; J. Barr, "Abba Isn't Daddy," *Journal of Theological Studies*, NS 39 (1988), pp. 28-47.

11 See for example the comments in *The Central Message of the New Testament*, J. Jeremias, pp. 21, 30.

12 See for example the comments in *The Lord's Prayer and Jewish Liturgy*, Petuchowski and Brocke, p. 131 who cite from *Pirke Abot* 5:3; *Studies In Pharisaism*, I. Abrahams, n. 3, p. 104; Kaufmann Kohler, "Abba," *Jewish Encyclopedia*; *On Earth As It Is In Heaven*, D. C. Thielmann, n. 121, p. 355; *The Real Jesus*, Luke Timothy Johnson, p. 119; *The Five Gospels*, Robert W. Funk, pp. 28 and 149.

13 See the comments in *On Earth As It Is In Heaven*, D. C. Thielmann, n. 126, p. 357; *The Jesus Scroll*, Donovan Joyce, p. 97 who points out that even the Early Church Father Jerome knew of this *fact* as late as the 4th century CE.

14 See the comments on this matter in *Revolution in Judaea*, Hyam Maccoby, pp. 159-168, and 189-195.

15 See for example the comments in *The Death of the Messiah*, Raymond E. Brown, pp. 799-800; *On Earth As It Is In Heaven*, D. C. Thielmann, n. 125, pp. 356-357.

16 See the comments in *Judaism in the First Centuries of the Christian era*, G. F. Moore, Volume III, p. 17, notes to Volume I, p. 43, I, 30-44, 1.1f.

was an actual individual *named Barabbas*[17] are quite in error, for they have been thoroughly refuted by far too many other scholars already.[18] Thus, as I will do my best to attempt to show in this chapter, it is far more likely, as some other scholars have already very clearly stated, that Jesus of Nazareth and Jesus Barabbas *were in fact*, one-in-the-same individual.[19]

There are some scholars who will utilize the Book of Esther in great detail in regards to the Barabbas incident in the Gospels, as well as using the Book of Esther in regards to the overall trial of Jesus in the Gospel narratives.[20] While it is quite true that the Book of Esther was quite popular with many first century Palestinian Jews, (just as the Book of Daniel was, as noted in Chapter 2), the Book of Esther, (just as with the Book of Daniel), was not brought into an accepted Jewish canon until Jamnia, sometime after 90 CE. Furthermore, just as with the book of Daniel, the Book of Esther accepted at Jamnia had many late alterations, and therefore, it *was not* the same book as it was in its *original* form! Many scholars, theologians, and especially the general laity are simply unaware of the *fact* that many additions and alterations had been made to the *original* writing of what is now referred to as the Book of Esther. The *original* Hebrew writing was referred to as either, *The Dreams of Mordecai*, or *The Book of Mordecai* and the final additions and alterations to this writing were not completed until sometime around 30 BCE, although some scholars believe that the additions were completed by no later than 100 BCE.[21] Thus, scholars *should be* very cautious in attempting to utilize the Book of Esther in regards to interpretations that they offer regarding the Barabbas matter and the overall trial of Jesus because of the fact that by making such references to the Book of Esther scholars seem to be unknowingly giving further weight to the *fact* that Jesus and his disciples were of the particular Jewish philosophy known

17 See for example the comments in *The Death of the Messiah*, Raymond E. Brown, pp. 811-814.

18 See for example the comments in *Studies in Pharisaism*, I. Abrahams, miscellaneous note (d), pp. 201-202.

19 See the comments in *The Mythmaker*, Hyam Maccoby, n. 1, pp. 214-215; "Jesus and Barabbas," *New Testament Studies* 16, (1968), pp. 55-60, Hyam Maccoby; *Kosher Jesus*, Rabbi Shmuley Boteach, pp. 86-87.

20 See for example *Barabbas and Esther*, Roger David Aus, pp. 4-25.

21 See Emil G. Hirsch and Carl Siegfried, "Esther, Apocryphal Book of," *Jewish Encyclopedia*.

as the *"Zealots,"* as will be demonstrated and proven here. The matter of the debate over the inclusion of Esther into the Jewish canon is found being discussed in *Megillah* 7a[22] where it *clearly* states that this debate over the inclusion of the Book of Esther into an accepted Jewish canon was because it was a writing that dealt with the defeat of Israel's gentile enemies, and thus, there was concern that the inclusion of Esther would bring about (at first, prior to the time of the Maccabees) the ire of the Greeks, and then at Jamnia, that it would bring about the ire of the Romans. For the Book of Esther was *known*, (even by the Romans), to be beloved by *all* of the various factions of the "Zealots" discussed in Chapter 9, (i.e. the *Sicarii*, the *lestai*, the *Essens*, the Galileans, and the *Nazirites*).[23] After the decision to include the Book of Esther into the canon, the celebration of *Purim*, (which derived from the story of Esther), even aroused gentile Christian anger because it was believed that this was just a disguised Jewish attempt to ridicule Jesus and his crucifixion, and those who were followers of Jesus.[24] *The Dreams of Mordecai*, the *Story of Mordecai*, or the *Book of Esther* was *always* perceived by Jews as a writing that heralded Jewish/Israeli nationalism and victory over the gentile enemies who either persecuted or oppressed the Jewish people. Thus, *any scholar* who asserts that the Book of Esther was beloved and highly utilized by Jesus and his earliest followers only adds further weight to the *fact* that the Jesus movement was a *wholly political movement* more closely aligned to the Essens and "Zealots" than the majority of Christian New Testament scholars desire to admit!

Going further into this matter of the Book of Esther though, even Josephus in *Antiquities* 11:184-296 notes that the Book of Esther was utilized for much of its *Haggadic* material. But this goes further into *why* scholars should be cautioned about attempting to utilize the Book of Esther in regards to the trial of Jesus *if* said scholars desire to maintain that Jesus *was not*, in *any way*, associated with the "Zealots." For as was pointed out in Chapter 9, the question of whether or not the Last Supper was actually a Passover Seder has been raised by some scholars. We also know that for

---

22   See Emil G. Hirsch, John Dyneley Prince, and Solomon Schechter, "Esther," *Jewish Encyclopedia*.

23   See the comments of Jacob Hoschander, "Esther in the Light of History: Chapter IV," *Jewish Quarterly Review*, Volume 10, No. 1, (July 1919), pp. 81-119.

24   See Kaufmann Kohler and Henry Malter, "Purim," *Jewish Encyclopedia*.

quite some time after the discovery of the Dead Sea Scrolls scholars were puzzled by the fact that no portions of the Book of Esther could be found among the Dead Sea Scrolls. Yet, there was one very badly stained scroll, which was completely unreadable that the scholars working on the scrolls had stored away awaiting some new technology to come along that might someday reveal the contents of this badly stained scroll. New technology has in fact now emerged and by use of this new technology it was found that in fact this badly stained scroll *was* in fact the Book of Esther, which matched the *majority* of what is now the current Masoretic text of the Book of Esther. But, there *are* several differences in this scroll from our current Masoretic text as well, including references to the Dead Sea Scroll known as the *War Scroll!*[25] So once again, the fact that the Book of Esther was highly regarded and utilized, especially by one particular first century Jewish philosophy, just as was the Book of Daniel, thus, begs *any* scholar to be cautious in attempting to interpret the Book of Esther in regards to relating it to the Barabbas accounts in the Gospels, and in regards to the overall trial of Jesus! This is simply because of the *fact* that both the *Feast of Purim*, (which again, is derived from the story in the Book of Esther), and the *Feast of Passover*, (derived from the Exodus of the Israelites from Egyptian slavery), were interpreted as examples of God's bringing about the end of the "oppression of Israel" from "foreign control," such as the Romans had at the time of Jesus, (see for example, Yerushalmi *Megillah* 4:1, 74d; Babli *Megillah* 21b), which is *precisely why* the Book of Esther was beloved by the "Zealots"!

This then brings us to the next most important aspect of the Barabbas matter to examine in the Gospel accounts, and this being, a supposed tradition of releasing a prisoner at the Jewish Festival of Passover. Countless scholars have commented on the fact that no such known tradition can be found in regards to the releasing of *any* prisoner with complete amnesty under Roman law at the time of Jesus.[26] Now, the historian Josephus *does*

---

25   See Rabbi Asher Tov-Lev, "Newly Deciphered Qumran Scroll Revealed to be *Megillat Esther*," *The Torah: A Historical and Contextual Approach*.

26   See for example the comments in *On Earth As It Is In Heaven*, D. C. Thielmann, n. 118, p. 353; *Who Killed Jesus*, John Dominic Crossan, p. 111; *The Misunderstood Jew*, Amy-Jill Levine, p. 99; *The Last Week*, Marcus Borg and John Dominic Crossan, p. 143; *Jesus: A Revolutionary Biography*, John Dominic Crossan, p. 141; *Kosher Jesus*, Rabbi Shmuley

refer to prisoners being released by the governor Albinus, but *only* criminals who were being held "for trifling matters," and even then it was only done in exchange for cash.[27] There are also some scholars who will refer to where Josephus discusses a "release" of "insurrectionists" by Archelaus as justification for a belief that it is possible that there *was* such a matter as the "release" of Barabbas.[28] Yet, these scholars seem to overlook the fact that Archelaus was "reproached" by Caesar over this "release" of "insurrectionists,"[29] and thus, any attempt by scholars to relate this "release" by Archelaus to a justification for a "release" of Barabbas by Pilate falls quite short of their goal. For as a result of this "release" of insurrectionists" by Archelaus a *new* "insurrection" occurred, which was led by these very "insurrectionist" individuals who had been "released," and which resulted in Archelaus killing about 3000 innocent people.[30] So again, there is no known tradition for the releasing of such notorious wanton criminals, as "Barabbas" is portrayed to be in the Gospel accounts, at festivals that *were not* Roman festivals or special occasions.[31] *Barabbas* was, (even in the Gospel account depictions of him), a "bandit," a "rebel," or an "insurrectionist," who committed "murder" during his insurrection,[32] and he is even referred to as such in Mark 15:7; Matthew 27:16; Luke 23:19, as well as even being referred to as a "distinguished notable"[33] for his "revolutionist" heroics, and thus, it is completely unthinkable that the Romans would just voluntarily release

---

Boteach, pp. 81-82 and 86-87; *Jesus and Israel*, Jules Isaac, pp. 325-343; *The Theological Significance of Jesus' Temple Action in Mark's Gospel*, Emilio G. Chavez, p. 25; *Jesus Before the Gospels*, Bart Ehrman, pp. 171-173; *Revolution in Judaea*, Hyam Maccoby, p. 19 and n. 3, p. 222, and n. 4, p. 222, and even see Philo in *Against Flaccus*,81-84.

27 See the comments in *Pontius Pilate in History and Interpretation*, Helen K. Bond, p. 77.

28 See the comments on this in *"Caught in the Act,"* Roger David Aus, pp. 147-152.

29 See the comments in *"Caught in the Act,"* Roger David Aus, p. 149.

30 *"Caught in the Act,"* Roger David Aus, pp. 152-153.

31 See the comments in *Pontius Pilate*, Ann Wroe, p. 247.

32 See the comments in *"Caught in the Act,"* Roger David Aus, p. 136; *Barabbas and Esther*, Roger David Aus, p. 1.

33 See the comments in *Revolution in Judaea*, Hyam Maccoby, pp. 159-160 and n. 1, p. 237. See also the comments in *Jesus of Nazareth: Part One*, Ratzinger and Pope Benedict, pp. 40-41; *"Caught in the Act,"* Roger David Aus, p. 137.

such an individual with complete amnesty![34] In regards to the verses that refer to Barabbas as a "distinguished notable," Joel Carmichael comments that,[35] "No commentator has ventured to explain as yet this simple phrase in an intelligible, 'nonpolitical' way."

It is true though, that under Roman law there was a provision called the *Abolitio*, or "suspension of a suit." But this provision in Roman law *did not* involve a complete amnesty or "release" of a prisoner and it *only* occurred on festivals that were given for the *Roman* gods.[36] Yet, this *Abolitio* was done en masse and not simply for *just one* prisoner.[37] But this is *far different* again from a full amnesty release for an "insurrectionist" such as *Barabbas* is portrayed in the Gospels. It is also true that in the Assyrian-Babylonian Calendar Tablets found by archaeologists, that the king could release a prisoner on the sixth, sixteenth, and twenty sixth day of the eighth month.[38] But once again, this is hardly the same as what we have in the Gospel accounts regarding *Barabbas*, and thus, it is a futile attempt by *any* scholar to try and use any of these examples in order to justify the Gospel accounts surrounding *Barabbas*. If though, the Gospel accounts of a "releasing of a prisoner" are claimed to be, *in fact*, historically true, then the questions that are begged to be asked are; why were the two prisoners who are reported to have been crucified alongside of Jesus *also* not being offered up to the crowd to be "released"? Why are Jesus of Nazareth and a supposed individual named *Jesus Barabbas* the *only ones* being *supposedly* offered up to the crowd to be released?

Possibly the most puzzling aspect of the Gospel accounts surrounding *Barabbas* though, is in regards to Pilate even asking the crowds about releasing

---

34 See the comments in *Who Killed Jesus*, John Dominic Crossan, p. 112; *On Earth As It Is In Heaven*, D. C. Thielmann, n. 123, pp. 355-356.

35 *The Death of Jesus*, Joel Carmichael, p. 146.

36 See the comments in *Jesus On Trial*, Gerard S. Sloyan, p. 50; *The Trial of Jesus*, Josef Blinzler, p. 207.

37 See for example the comments by J. Merkel, "Die Begnadigung am Passahfeste," *ZNW* 6 (1905), pp. 293-316; *Light From the Ancient East*, Adolf Deissmann, 2nd Edition, p. 269; *Jesus and Israel*, Jules Isaac, p. 340.

38 See the comments of S. Langdon, "The Release of the Prisoner at the Passover," *Expository Times* 29, Edinburgh, (1918), pp. 328-330.

any prisoner.[39] In regards to this matter I offer the suggestion to readers to first look carefully at the apologetically biased comments offered by Joseph Ratzinger and Pope Benedict XVI.[40] After reading these comments from Joseph Ratzinger and Pope Benedict XVI, it is then suggested that one then reads the more accurate comments of David Bivin and Roy Blizzard[41] where they point out that the Greek word *ochloi*, (a word briefly discussed in an earlier chapter), is a Greek word that generally gets translated into English as, "multitudes," or "crowd," (such as it is found in Matthew 27:20; Mark 15:11). But this Greek word *ochloi* is actually *best* understood in English to mean, "those standing nearby," as derived from the Hebraic standpoint of first-century Palestinian Jews. Now, under the Roman law called the *Lex Valeria, only a Roman citizen* facing a death penalty could make an appeal for his life,[42] and neither Jesus of Nazareth *nor* Jesus *Barabbas* were Roman citizens. Furthermore, under the Roman law *Leges Duodecim Tabularum*, or *Duodecim Tabulae*, the "Law of the Twelve Tables," which Pilate was quite aware of, it is clearly stated concerning crowds asking for an individual's release that, "When they want to absolve a heinous crime or condemn an innocent man, the crowd's empty voices must not be listened to."[43] Now it is true though, that Cicero, who wrote before the time of Pilate's birth, writes that, "No one learns that law nowadays." But yet, as Helen K. Bond rightly points out concerning the incident described by Josephus in which the Jewish leaders go to Caesarea to protest an action taken by Pilate that was not only offensive to the Jews, but was also in violation of Jewish laws, Pilate left the protestors peacefully stand outside for five days not listening to their protests until finally Pilate gave in to these protestors because he

---

39 See the comments in *The Last Week*, Marcus Borg and John Dominic Crossan, p. 143; *"Caught in the Act,"* Roger David Aus, pp. 139-140; *Barabbas and Esther*, Roger David Aus, p. 23.

40 *Jesus of Nazareth: Part Two*, Ratzinger and Pope Benedict, pp. 185-188.

41 *Understanding the Difficult Words of Jesus*, David Bivin and Roy Blizzard, Forward; but see also the similar comments to this *fact* in *No Stone on Another*, Lloyd Gaston, pp. 331-333; *Jesus and Israel*, Jules Isaac, p. 349.

42 See the comments in *Pontius Pilate*, Ann Wroe, pp. 248-249.

43 See the comments in *Pontius Pilate*, Ann Wroe, pp. 248-249; *The Trial and Death of Jesus*, Haim Cohn, p. 158 who notes also the *Codex Justinianus* IX, 47, 12; *Jesus and His Times*, H. Daniel-Rops, p. 524; *On Earth As It Is In Heaven*, D. C. Thielmann, n. 123, pp. 355-356.

was astonished at their resilience.[44] This fact not only demonstrates, but also *proves* that Pilate *was not* easily moved by "the crowd's empty voices."

Under Jewish law though, as stated in the Mishnah, *Pesaḥim* 8:6, there *is* a provision concerning "prisoners who were *promised* to be released from prison on *Passover eve*," but this was *only* a *temporary* release to allow the prisoner to take part in the Passover feast. It is from this Mishnaic law that many scholars have tried to justify the Gospel accounts concerning the release of an individual named *Barabbas*.[45] But the Talmud Babli, *Pesaḥim* 91a makes it quite clear that these promised releases *only came from Jewish authorities* and *not* from *any* gentile authority! For as it is also made quite clear in this tractate the gentile authorities, "could not be trusted." Likewise, the *Codex Theodosius* 9.38.3-8 *cannot* be used to justify the Gospel accounts even though this Roman law *does* speak of releasing prisoners at Easter, for this Roman law was not enacted until roughly 370-385 CE, or in essence, three and a half centuries *after* the time of Jesus.[46]

There seems to be only one logical conclusion for the Gospel accounts leaving two Aramaic words untranslated, and thereby, having these two words appear to be an individual's name, and thus, fabricating a story regarding the "releasing of a prisoner" that surrounded these two untranslated words, and this reason being, in order to shift the blame for Jesus' crucifixion away from the gentile Romans and place this blame squarely onto the shoulders of the Jewish people.[47] As noted in earlier chapters, a division arose between the Jewish followers of Jesus and the gentile followers of Jesus, and after the destruction of the Temple during the 66-73 revolt it became easy for these gentile followers to assume that all of the covenants promised by God to the Jews had now shifted to the gentiles. Eusebius in *Demonstratio Evangelica* 8.362-365 even discusses this very Early Church thinking and tradition. Combining this fact with the seemingly obvious anti-Jewish teachings of Paul it then became even easier to write accounts

---

44 *Pontius Pilate in History and Interpretation*, Helen K. Bond, pp. 57-59, 74-75, 83-85.

45 See for example the comments of D. Flusser, "Mishpat Yeshu," *Tarbitz*, Volume 31, (1960), n. 41, p. 117; *Jerusalem und Rom im Zeitalter Jesus Christi*, E. Stauffer, p. 110.

46 See the comments in *The Trial and Death of Jesus*, Haim Cohn, pp. 165-169 who lists ten excellent arguments refuting the legitimacy of the Gospel accounts about releasing an individual named *Barabbas*.

47 See the comments in *Barabbas and Esther*, Roger David Aus, p. 3.

about Jesus that not only portrayed him as being contrary to the Judaism of his time,[48] but also that portrayed him as being "non-political," or as just a "pacifist," (a matter discussed already in Chapter 9).

Many modern scholars refer to these fabricated stories as "prophecy historicized."[49] Yet, many of these very same scholars who admit that many of these Gospel accounts *are* in fact "prophecy historicized," will still use an apologetic bias to try and claim that these stories are mere reflections of actual historical truth in order to simply try and portray Jesus in a manner in accordance with their own personally chosen biases.[50] This portrait of Jesus that these scholars are attempting to put forth places the Jews in general as rebellious advocates for "violence" while Jesus advocated "non-violence," (again, a matter discussed in Chapter 9). But these scholars who portray Jesus in such a manner are becoming, should we say, "dinosaurs" in their attempts to portray Jesus in such a manner as this. For Jesus' own words, "the Kingdom of Heaven is *at hand*," which even these very scholars admit Jesus spoke, *prove* that Jesus *was not* an advocate of "non-violence."[51] As Hyam Maccoby rightly states,[52] "If we could really understand the Barabbas episode we would understand the Gospels as a whole; for this episode contains in miniature not only the elements that go to make the Gospel story but also the Gospel orientation and attitude towards the life and death of Jesus." Maccoby then goes on to ask a very important question that *all* scholars *must* consider when he writes,[53] "Was the Barabbas incident

---

48 See the comments in *Judas Iscariot and the Myth of Jewish Evil*, Hyam Maccoby, pp. 27-28; *Jesus On Trial*, Gerard S. Sloyan, pp. 91-92.

49 See for example the comments in *The Trial of Jesus*, Josef Blinzler, pp. 40-44; *The Last Week*, Marcus Borg and John Dominic Crossan, p. 157.

50 See for example the comments in *The Last Week*, Marcus Borg and John Dominic Crossan, p. 144.

51 See for example the comments in *Understanding the Difficult Words of Jesus*, David Bivin and Roy Blizzard, pp. 62-65; *On Earth As It Is In Heaven*, D. C. Thielmann, pp. 682, 689-690, 724-727, n. 50, p. 747, n. 55, p. 748, n. 60, pp. 748-749, n. 93, pp. 760-765, n. 160, p. 785, n. 162, pp. 785-786.

52 *Revolution in Judaea*, Hyam Maccoby, p. 13.

53 *Revolution in Judaea*, Hyam Maccoby, p. 18.

---

simply an invention inserted into the record in order to discredit the Jews and saddle them with the corporate responsibility for Jesus' death?"

Epilogue

The matter of correctly understanding the betrayal, arrest, trial, and crucifixion of Jesus of Nazareth in its historical reality is more important in today's modern society than ever before in history. The reason being is that the Jewish people in general have suffered much at the hands of Christians over the centuries since these events of the early first century CE occurred simply because of *how* these events came to be portrayed in the New Testament, and interpreted throughout the centuries since. In essence, it is pointless to debate whether or not the New Testament contains Anti-Semitism![1] For the fact remains that the damage has already been done as a direct result of *how* the New Testament has been interpreted by the Church, which ultimately caused the Anti-Semitic events to unfold throughout the history of the Church *since* the time of Paul and the writing of the Gospels.[2] But since the discovery of the Dead Sea Scrolls combined with the change in the Catholic Church's doctrines, (beginning

---

1 See the comments in *The Misunderstood Jew*, Amy-Jill Levine, p. 88; *Jesus the Pharisee*, Harvey Falk, pp. 111-137; *Judaism and the Origins of Christianity*, David Flusser, pp. 552-574.

2 See the comments in *Judas Iscariot and the Myth of Jewish Evil*, Hyam Maccoby, pp. 80-81; *Revolution in Judaea*, Hyam Maccoby, pp. 50-51; *Jesus On Trial*, Gerard S. Sloyan, p. 12; *Pontius Pilate*, Ann Wroe, pp. 229-230, 233-234 and 329; *Kosher Jesus*, Rabbi Shmuley

in the 1960's, as discussed in Chapter 4), the damage done by the church over the centuries, and the relationship between Christians and Jews has begun to be repaired.

As pointed out in the Preface of this book, the Gospels as we have them today went through a great deal of editorial alteration and revision. As a result, a great deal of what we find being stated in the Gospel accounts are very bad misrepresentations of the historical truth of what actually occurred, which has caused a great deal of misunderstandings, even amongst scholars, to which even the more modern translations of the New Testament have not yet rectified. For example, one of the most badly misunderstood statements found in the Gospels is Matthew 27:25 where it states, "His blood be on us and on our children."[3] This statement in Matthew's Gospel is quite similar to the statements found in Jeremiah 26:15; 51:35; Acts 18:6. The misunderstanding of this statement has led to the erroneous conclusion and belief that the Jews accepted responsibility for the trial and crucifixion of Jesus.[4] But, as Gerard Sloyan so rightly states concerning this Jewish expression,[5] "The Expression, far from being a self-inflicted curse, is a strong statement of innocence. Its meaning is, 'If we had anything to do with it, let our descendants share the guilt. But we do not!' This statement found in Matthew 27:25, or statements very similar to this, appear in later Mishnaic form in the Talmud tractate *Sanhedrin* 37a, where in capital cases the witness used this invocation as proof that their testimony was truthful.[6] In essence, if the witness was lying, they

---

Boteach, pp. 58-59; *Jesus Interrupted*, Bart D. Ehrman, pp. 237-245; *The Crucifixion of Jesus*, Gerard S. Sloyan, pp. 213-214; *Jesus the Pharisee*, Harvey Falk, pp. 103.

3   See for example the comments in *How Jesus Became Christian*, Barrie Wilson, pp. 232-233; *Messiah and Temple*, Donald Juel, p. 2; *Pontius Pilate in History and Interpretation*, Helen K. Bond, p. 125; *Caiaphas*, Helen K. Bond, p. 123; *Barabbas and Esther*, Roger David Aus, p. 2.

4   See the comments in *On Earth As It Is In Heaven*, D. C. Thielmann, p. 863 and the corresponding scholars notations to this page.

5   See *Jesus On Trial*, Gerard S. Sloyan, p. 64; and see also the comments in *The Jews and the Gospel*, Gregory Baum, pp. 66-73; *The New Testament*, Bart D. Ehrman, pp. 107-108.

6   See Mishnah *Sanhedrin* 4:1 as proof of this fact, for it states here that during "capital offense" cases a "witness" was required to use this statement to ensure that their testimony would be

---

were willing to have the blood of the accused fall on themself and their offspring until the end of the world. This Jewish phrase was *always* a claim of innocence, and has *never* been an expression of guilt. The scholarly world could do a great service by proclaiming long and loud what this phrase Matthew took from the Bible actually means, even though the erroneous understanding of this phrase that has caused the Jewish people so much pain and persecution throughout the centuries cannot be undone."

The teachings of Paul, which contain such noticeable anti-Jewish emphasis, are what the predominant thinking of the Church became.[7] Paul emphasized that it was the belief in Jesus' death and resurrection that brought about one's salvation.[8] As an example, Paul states in 1 Corinthians 15:20 that Jesus is "the first fruits of those who have died." But this very statement in this verse clearly forgets and ignores 1 Samuel 28:3-19. Yet it is quite true though, that *not all* of the later followers of Jesus held to this belief that Paul tried to promote.[9] It is such an error as this in Paul's teachings that brought about the very separation of Jew from gentile in regards to understanding not only the very teachings of Jesus, but also, the overall teachings of the whole of the Hebrew Scriptures. This separation in understanding is what then brought about the belief that the Jews "rejected" Jesus, and thus, that which ultimately brought about the doctrinal thinking that the Jews "rejected" Jesus even *during* his years of ministry, and therefore, "the Jews" were the cause for Jesus' arrest, trial, and crucifixion.[10] But this simply *is not* the historical truth of this matter! As Rabbi A. P. Drucker writes concerning this,[11] "It is high time that those who consider themselves followers of Jesus should know the truth about their master, and follow his

---

truthful as an "eyewitness."

7   See the comments in *The Lost Gospel of Judas Iscariot*, Bart D. Ehrman, pp. 127, 129, and 132-133; I also highly recommend that one reads the excellent comments on this matter in *Jesus and Israel*, Jules Isaac, pp. 101-131; *The Partings of the Ways*, James Dunn, pp. 140-162.

8   See the comments in *The Lost Gospel of Judas Iscariot*, Bart D. Ehrman, pp. 155-156; *The Last Week*, Marcus Borg and John Dominic Crossan, pp. 102-103, and 155.

9   For more on this see what is pointed out in *The Lost Gospel of Judas Iscariot*, Bart D. Ehrman, pp. 92, 112-113, 128, and 136.

10   As an example of the fact that such thinking is still prevalent even today, see the comments in *Simply Jesus*, N. T. Wright, p. 5.

11   *The Trial of Jesus From Jewish Sources*, Rabbi A. P. Drucker, p. 64.

example in endeavoring to bring about a true knowledge of God and to eradicate prejudice and substitute tolerance and kindness toward all men; in giving up hatred, and preaching, instead love; and in teaching the whole world of the Fatherhood of God and the Brotherhood of Man." Also, as Rabbi Shmuley Boteach writes,[12] "Fundamentally, we understand Jesus as a foreign deity, a man worshipped by people. The Torah instructs us never to mention the names of other gods, as no other god exists except God. We also understand Jesus to be as anti-Jewish as his followers. Was he not the Jew who rebelled against his people? Was he not the one who instructed his followers to hate the Jews as he did, instigating countless cruelties against those with whom God had established an everlasting covenant? Was he not also the man who had abrogated the law and said that the Torah is now mostly abolished? In truth, Jesus was not that man. The more I studied the matter, the more I discovered Jesus had done none of these things. The people who represented him in this way had a vested interest in doing so. They superimposed onto Jesus their own antipathy toward Jews. They ripped a Jewish patriot away from his people." But yet, we still find today very prominent Christian, (or agnostic), New Testament scholars whose comments, although while being somewhat accurate, they appear to still be throwing blame toward the Jews, such as, for example, the comments of Bart Ehrman, who writes,[13] "The Christ of Nicea is obviously a far cry from the historical Jesus of Nazareth, an itinerant apocalyptic preacher in the backwaters of rural Galilee who offended the authorities and was unceremoniously crucified for crimes against the state. Whatever he may have been in real life, Jesus had now become fully God." The question must be asked here in regards to Ehrman's statement, to which "authorities" is Ehrman referring? For it seemingly appears that he is referring to some sort of "Jewish authorities," and *not* to "Roman authorities."

Now, there are some scholars[14] who like to try and utilize Josephus' statement in *Antiquities* 18.63-64) as proof that the Jews *did* in fact have a role in Jesus' crucifixion, (even though these very same scholars freely admit that there *have been* "Christian additions and alterations" made to this statement and account by Josephus). For according to this account in

---

12   *Kosher Jesus*, Rabbi Shmuley Boteach, Preface, p. ix.

13   *How Jesus Became God*, Bart D. Ehrman, p. 352.

14   See for example the comments in *Who is Jesus*, Darrell L. Bock, pp. 175-176.

Antiquities 18:63-64, (at least in the accounts as we have them today, that is), it seemingly appears that Josephus states that, "… The leading men among us condemned him to the cross." But the sheer *fact* that such scholars try to use this statement to claim "historical accuracy," (while at the same time clearly admitting that Christian additions and alterations were made to this statement), only demonstrates an *apologetic bias*, to which *proves* that such scholars have failed miserably to do a thorough investigation into *all* of the "historical" evidence that contradicts this statement and *proves* that this statement is indeed an addition made to the text in order to justify not only the Anti-Semitic doctrines that the Church adopted, but also to seemingly attempt to justify their own personally chosen Anti-Semitic biased opinions!

There are many, many doctrines and dogmas of the gentile Church that developed over time, even centuries after the time of Jesus, which were then, somehow, attributed to Jesus as the founder of these doctrines and dogmas. A prime example of a late developing doctrine is the doctrine of the Trinity, which did not become fully developed until the fourth century, or in other words, roughly three hundred years *after* the time of Jesus. The development of the Trinity doctrine actually went through several phases and steps beginning with Justin Martyr, *Apology*, and *Dialogue With Trypho*, then on to Novation in *Trinity*, then to Dionysius, and then finally to the controversial debate between Alexander and Arius.[15] The end result was founded, *not by Jesus*, but by the *Council of Nicea* where only 20 of the 318 Bishops disagreed with the Trinity doctrine as it has now come to be known.

The point being made here by referring to the development of the Trinity doctrine is to demonstrate *how* the notion to blame the Jews for the arrest, trial, and crucifixion of Jesus likewise developed. The notion that somehow God had replaced His covenant with Israel, (the covenant, which Christianity chooses to call the "Old Covenant"), with a "New Covenant" specifically for Christians, and *only* for Christians (see for example Hebrews 8:13), as a result of the death of Jesus was *never* what Jesus himself intended or taught would happen. As Amy-Jill Levine rightly points

---

15   See the comments in *A Brief History of the Doctrine of the Trinity In the Early Church*, Franz Dunzel, London: T&T Clark, (2007); *The Ecumenical Councils of the Catholic Church: A History*, Liturgical Press, Collegeville, MN, (2009); *Nicea and Its Legacy: An Approach to Fourth Century Trinitarian Theology*, Lewis Ayres, Oxford University Press, (2004).

out[16] concerning the depictions of the differences between the supposed "Old" and "New Testament" images of a "Messiah" or "Messianic Era" are that one is supposedly a "God of war" (Old Testament) and the other is supposedly a "God of Peace" (New Testament) to which Levine writes, "Nevertheless, it is not only incorrect but also heretical for Christians to distinguish between the God of the Old Testament and the God of the New. What must be noted first is that, according to Christian teaching, both Testaments depict the same God. There is no personality shift as the text moves from Malachi to Matthew, for the same bellicose deity appears in explicitly Christian texts. The Book of Revelation, which is replete with military imagery, offers the unpleasant image of the angel who 'swung his sickle on the earth and gathered the vintage of the earth, and threw it into the great wine press of the Wrath of God....'"[17] Furthermore, the so-called "Old Testament" was written over a period of some 1500 years, and thus, if one were to write a *similar* first 1500 year history of the Church one would find a "God of war" imbedded within that Church history!

Furthermore, it is essential to point out to *all* Christians, (whether critical scholar, theologian, or general laity), what the prophet Samuel said in 1 Samuel 8:18 regarding one being more beholding to a "Messiah" (an "anointed king" in other words) than to God when Samuel states, "And you will cry out on that day because of your king which you shall have chosen you; and the Lord will not hear you on that day." But modern Christian scholarship is finally beginning to recognize, and admit to the fact of this matter that Jesus never intended, or taught that the "Old Covenant" was being replaced by a "New Covenant." As Amy-Jill Levine writes concerning this,[18] "In the 1970's, the language of Biblical studies changed in the academy and in liberal churches. Instead of studying the 'Old Testament,' students and congregations were now to speak of the 'Hebrew Bible,' 'Hebrew Scriptures,' 'First Testament,' or even 'Jewish Testament'." Also, as Rabbi Moshe Reiss points out,[19] "Professor Didier Pollefeyt of the Catholic University of Leuven (the oldest continual Catholic University in the world) stated his view at the Cathedral Notre Dame in

---

16   *The Misunderstood Jew*, Amy-Jill Levine, p. 128.

17   See also the comments on this matter in *Kosher Jesus*, Rabbi Shmuley Boteach, pp. 170-206.

18   *The Misunderstood Jew*, Amy-Jill Levine, p. 193.

19   *Christianity: A Jewish Perspective*, Rabbi Moshe Reiss, Introduction A.

October 1996 as follows: 'The way Jesus will come as the Christ and the Redeemer of the world will depend on the way Christians re-present Him in the present. When Christians are not able to bring His redemption to the world today, especially in relationship with the Jewish people, I'm afraid that at the end of times, they will not meet a triumphalizing Messiah, but what I would call a 'weeping Messiah,' a Messiah weeping for the injuries and the unredeemedness Christians caused, especially to His own people. Then it could end with the fact that indeed not Christians, with their triumphalistic Messianic perceptions, but the Jews will be able to recognize as the first one's the Messiah as the 'Savior of the World'." Rabbi Reiss goes on further to write, "At a pre-Christmas service in 2001 Father Dr. Reimund Beiringer, also of the Catholic University of Leuven, began his sermon with the following opening remarks: 'When Jesus comes back he will be circumcised, he will not be able to eat at my home because it is not kosher and will look at this church and ask the rabbi where can he find a Synagogue'." Marcus Borg as well,[20] who while referring to John 4:6 believes that this verse is erroneously understood by people in that they interpret it to mean that *only Christians* are saved. But Borg interprets this verse to mean *anyone* who is beholding to "a life radically centered in God is saved." Borg then comments upon[21] a Hindu professor speaking on this verse from John at a Christian Seminary teaching how this resonates with *all* people of *all* religions and that this teaching is not a "...Unique revelation of a way unknown anywhere else...." Thus, this verse should actually be *best* understood to mean that *all* who are beholding to God are saved. This is the scholarly understanding which is, in fact, quite accurate. Borg also points out[22] that the same holds true for John 3:16. Yet, despite the efforts of such scholarly statements as these, this fact is slow in being brought to the full attention of the general church laity. But the church laity should be able to begin to realize and recognize this *fact* on their own simply by looking carefully at just a few of Jesus' teachings, such as Matthew 7:15-16. In these

---

20 *Jesus: Uncovering the Life, Teachings, and Relevance of a Religious Revolutionary,* Marcus Borg, p. 222.

21 *Jesus: Uncovering the Life, Teachings, and Relevance of a Religious Revolutionary,* Marcus Borg, n. 24, p. 328.

22 *Jesus: Uncovering the Life, Teachings, and Relevance of a Religious Revolutionary,* Marcus Borg, p. 223.

verses Jesus clearly warned about "false individuals" becoming some of his followers, and we would "know them by their fruits." Even more than this though, is the essential teaching in Matthew 7:21-22. In these verses we find Jesus very clearly stating that, "Not everyone who says to me, 'Lord, Lord,' will enter the Kingdom of Heaven, but only the one who does the will of my Father in Heaven." Jesus goes on to point out that "miracles" count for nothing, not even his own supposed "miracles," in other words.

Over the many centuries since the time of Jesus' ministry the church has desperately sought, and tried to maintain in its teachings to the general laity that they, and they alone represent the inheritors of the "true covenants" that God had made, not only with Israel, but also with mankind as a whole. Many scholars have noted Matthew 16:17-19, and specifically Matthew 16:18 and the Greek word *ekklesia*, which literally means "meeting," but which more often than not gets translated out as, "Church." The growing belief in the scholarly world surrounding this Greek word being translated as "Church," is that it is a later interpolation made by individuals of the later Church to try and give justification to itself in the Gospels.[23] One of the greatest sources for proof of this derives from the very *fact* that this word *ekklesia* is synonymous, (as noted already in the Preface but is essential to note again here), with another Greek word – *synedrion*, i.e. "Sanhedrin" – and that both of these Greek words were used as translations of the Hebrew word, `edah, meaning, "assembly," or "congregation."[24] Furthermore, as Jules Isaac points out[25] the Greek word *sunagoge*, "Synagogue," is likewise synonymous with the word, *ekklesia*, for again, both of these words mean, "assembly," or "meeting." Thus, the separation of these words in the New Testament into seemingly different meanings of, "Church" (*ekklesia*, indicating "Christians," and primarily gentile "Christians"), and "Synagogue" (*sunagoge* indicating "Jews," and/or "Judaizing Christians"), is simply a further reflection of the matter noted throughout this book about how much the separation between gentile

---

23   See for example the comments in *Creation Continues*, Fritz Kunkel, p. 218.

24   See the comments on this in *Studies in the History of the Sanhedrin*, Hugo Mantel, Appendix B, p. 308.

25   *Jesus and Israel*, Jules Isaac, p. 44; but see also the comments on this of Ralph J. Korner, "*Ekklesia* as a Jewish Synagogue Term: Some Implications for Paul's Socio-Religious Location," *Journal of the Jesus Movement in its Jewish Setting* No.2, (2015), pp. 53-78.

Church and Jewish Synagogue became hostile towards each other deriving from what began in the accounts noted in Acts 15.[26] This fact can be seen very clearly, for example, in John 9:22; 12:42 even though these two verses are contradicted in John's own Gospel by what is written in John 18:20.[27] The two greatest errors and problems that arose from this was first and foremost arrogance by the church, which was passed down to the general laity, and secondly this arrogance became the very cause for the Anti-Semitic blaming of the Jews for the arrest, trial, and crucifixion of Jesus. As Fritz Kunkel rightly states,[28] "Nevertheless, our self-righteousness prompts us to give advice and teach and preach all day long. We send missionaries or go on missions, and present our contaminated message as the pure truth. People believe us, follow our leadership, and are excluded from the Kingdom by our misuse of the keys." It became standard belief that the destruction of the second Temple and the scattering of the Jews into the diaspora were the indication of Jewish guilt for killing Jesus and that God had thereby forsaken His people. As Jules Isaac rightly states concerning this,[29] "For eighteen hundred years it has been generally taught throughout the Christian world that the Jewish people, in full responsibility for the crucifixion, committed the inexpiable crime of deicide. No accusation could be more pernicious – and in fact none has caused more innocent blood to be shed."[30] Likewise, as Gerard S. Sloyan rightly states,[31] "By the second century in the Greco-Roman world these believers were interpreting symbolic narrative as history. They had lost the Semitic skill of spotting a story crafted in Biblical style. Christians have been misreading their own holy books ever since, often making Jews pay the price of their incomprehension."

Even prior to this though, Paul tried to indicate such was going to occur by what he states in Romans 9:21. But, at the same time even Paul, the "heretic" that he was, warned about becoming arrogant such as how

26   See the comments in *Jewish Christianity Reconsidered*, Matt Jackson-McCabe, p. 169, (Warren Carter commenting).

27   See the comments on this in *Jesus and Israel*, Jules Isaac, p. 46.

28   *Creation Continues*, Fritz Kunkel, p. 264.

29   For the full comments see *Jesus and Israel*, Jules Isaac, pp. 233-263.

30   See also the comments on this in *The Crucifixion of Jesus*, Gerard S. Sloyan, p. 2.

31   *The Crucifixion of Jesus*, Gerard S. Sloyan, p. 29.

the later Church became. But everyone should very carefully study what Scripture itself says about becoming *arrogant* in ones beliefs, such as for example, what is stated in 1 Samuel 2:3, which says, "Do not keep talking so proudly or let your mouth speak such arrogance; for the Lord is a God who knows, and by Him deeds are weighed." But every Christian also needs to see further on this matter by reading and understanding *clearly* what is stated in, Isaiah 2:11; 2:17-18; 5:15; 13:11; Jeremiah 48:29-30; 50:31-32; Ezekiel 7:8-10; Malachi 3:15; Psalm 75:2-4; 94:4; 140:5; Proverbs 8:13; 27:2; Daniel 5:20; Nehemiah 9:10; Luke 18:9-14; Romans 12:3; Titus 1:6-9. This bad habit of Christians to boldly and arrogantly proclaim, "I know that I am saved by the blood of Jesus," need to all very carefully understand the comments of Amy-Jill Levine concerning her interpretation of John 14:6, when she writes,[32] "When the Johannine Jesus states, 'No one comes to the Father except through me,' he can even be seen as precluding any individual Christian or any Church from determining soteriological verdict. If Jesus is the Way, then *only* he determines entrance to Heaven." Also, though, these same arrogant individuals need to read what is stated in Mishnah, *Abot* 1:3, which states, "Do not be one of those people who serve God in order to receive a reward."

Although great strides have been made over the past nearly full century in repairing Christian and Jewish relations, as long as the church, and in particular the scholars of Christianity, continue to promote the erroneous notion that the Jews had and were *in some way* even the slightest bit responsible for the death of Jesus, then the relations between Christians and Jews will always remain strained. This is despite the fact of the quite noticeable rapid rise of Islam while there has been a decline in the followers of Christianity over this same period of history. Christians now admit to many of the mistakes that it made in centuries past, and admit that they need the Jews in their continuance, but yet find it difficult to accept that the Jews in general played no role in the arrest, trial, and crucifixion of Jesus.[33] As a further, even more difficult matter for Christians to come to the acceptance of is the reality that Jesus' arrest, trial, and crucifixion plays no role whatsoever as a salvific event for mankind. Jesus himself taught this in Matthew 5:10, and for one to *best* understand what Jesus meant by

---

32   See *The Misunderstood Jew*, Amy-Jill Levine, p. 91.

33   See the comments in *Judas Iscariot and the Myth of Jewish Evil*, Hyam Maccoby, p. 127.

his teaching found in this verse is to do so from the idioms of the Hebrew language of which Jesus spoke when he taught. Thus, we find Jesus teaching, "How blessed are those who pursue righteousness, for of these is the Kingdom of Heaven." In essence, this verse says absolutely nothing about anyone having to go through persecutions, trials, tribulations, martyrdom, or even a sacrificial death by crucifixion in order to achieve the salvation of the Kingdom of Heaven. This teaching of Jesus in Matthew 5:10 is a mirror of what is taught in Isaiah 51:1 where the Hebrew word *radaf* does not mean, "persecute," but instead means, "pursue," thus indicating in Isaiah 51:1 that one should, "pursue righteousness."[34] Joseph Ratzinger and Pope Benedict XVI make a statement that needs to be noted here when they write,[35] "All in all, it would be good for the Christian world to look respectfully at this obedience of Israel, and thus to appreciate better the great commandments of the Decalogue, which Christians have to transfer into the context of God's universal family and which, as the 'new Moses,' has given to us." Although it is quite right to note this statement of Ratzinger and Pope Benedict it must also be noted that a hint of their Christian bias shows through in this statement by way of their reference to Jesus as a "new Moses," similar to what was noted in Chapter 4 regarding their comments about a "new" Torah.

God already made a covenant with *all* of mankind separate from the covenant He made specifically with the Jewish people. This covenant for *all* of the gentile world is referred to as the Noahide Covenant. It was only *after* this covenant was made with *all* of mankind that God made a special covenant with the people of Israel alone – *two covenants* in other words, and thus, *Two Ways* of finding salvation in the Kingdom of Heaven, one for the Jew, and one for *all* other peoples,[36] (see *Sanhedrin* 56a-59b; 105a). There has never been a need since the time of these two events in history –

---

34 See the comments in *Understanding the Difficult Words of Jesus*, David Bivin and Roy Blizzard, pp. 75-77.

35 *Jesus of Nazareth: Part One*, Ratzinger and Pope Benedict, p. 122.

36 See the comments in *The New Testament and Rabbinic Judaism*, David Daube, p. 98; *No Stone on Another*, Lloyd Gaston, pp. 309-310; *The Way of God*, Moshe Chaim Luzzatto, pp. 141-143; *How Jesus Became Christian*, Barrie Wilson, pp. 142-143; *Paul and Rabbinic Judaism*, W. D. Davies, pp. 112-121; *Jesus the Pharisee*, Harvey Falk, pp. 4-6, 13-23, 83-91; *Judaism and the Origins of Christianity*, David Flusser, p. 508; *Ritual and Morality*,

the Great Flood, and the revelation at Sinai – for the establishment of *any other* "New Covenant," and the life, teachings, arrest, trial, and crucifixion of Jesus *must be* understood in the context of this very fact! Jesus rightly taught us all in the Lord's Prayer about God's ultimate plan for mankind *here*, in the "physical realm" of being "on earth" and not in some "spiritual realm."[37] As Jesus' words state, "on earth as it is in heaven," and as Psalm 115:16 states, "The heavens are for the Lord and the earth for the children of men." Let us all learn to understand the life, teachings, and death of Jesus of Nazareth in its proper and *historically* truthful context and "pursue righteousness" here on earth.[38]

Hyam Maccoby, p. 9; *On Earth As It Is In Heaven*, D. C. Thielmann, pp. 1028-1029 and the corresponding scholars notions to these pages.

37 See the comments in *Revolution in Judaea*, Hyam Maccoby, pp. 111-124.

38 See the comments in *The Mythmaker*, Hyam Maccoby, p. 49.

Bibliography

Abelson, J. – *The Immanence of God in Rabbinic Literature*, Hermon Press, New York, (1969).

Abrahams, Israel – *Studies in Pharisaism and the Gospels, First Series*, Cambridge University Press, (1917).

——— *Studies in Pharisaism and the Gospels, Second Series*, Cambridge University Press, (1924).

Adler, Cyrus and Dembitz, Lewis N. – "Hosha'na Rabbah," *Jewish Encyclopedia*, http://jewishencyclopedia.com/articles/7900-hosha-na-rabbah .

Adler, Cyrus, Dembitz, Lewis N., and Cohen, Francis L. – "Hallel," *Jewish Encyclopedia*, http://jewishencyclopedia.com/articles/7109-hallel.

Adler, Cyrus and de Sola Mendes, Frederick – "Baths, Bathing," *Jewish Encyclopedia*, http://jewishencyclopedia.com/articles/2661-baths-bathing .

Adler, Cyrus and Deutsch, Gotthard – "Hebra Kaddisha (more correctly Habura), *Jewish Encyclopedia*, http://jewishencyclopedia.com/articles/7442-hebra-kaddisha.

Adler, Cyrus and Hirsch, Emil G. – "Shemoneh ʿEsreh: Petitions against Enemies; Modifications in Birkat Ha-Minim," *Jewish Encyclopedia*, http://www.jewishencyclopedia.com/articles/13561-shemoneh-esreh.

Adler, Cyrus, Schloessinger, Max, Jacobs, Joseph, and Kaiser, Alois – "Hazzan," *Jewish Encyclopedia*, http://jewishencyclopedia.com/articles/7426-hazzan .

Allison, Dale C. Jr. – *The Sermon on the Mount*, the Crossroad Publishing Company, New York, (1999).

————. *Jesus of Nazareth: Millenarian Prophet*, Minneapolis: Fortress Press, (1998).

———— "Divorce, Celibacy, and Joseph," *Journal for the Study of the New Testament* 49, (1993), pp. 3-10.

Alter, Robert and Kermode, Frank – *The Literary Guide to the Bible*, The Belknap Press of Harvard University Press, Cambridge, Mass., (1987).

Altizer, Thomas J. J. *Oriental Mysticism and Biblical Eschatology*, Philadelphia, The Westminster Press, (1961).

Altmann, Alexander – *Biblical and Other Stories*, Harvard University Press, Cambridge, Mass. (1963).

American Bible Society Resources – "Social World of Bandits," bibleresources. americanbible.org/resource/social-world-of-bandits .

American Heritage – *The American Heritage Dictionary of the English Language*, Fifth Edition, Houghton Mifflin Harcourt Publishing Company, (2016).

Amram, David Werner – *The Jewish Law of Divorce According to Bible and Talmud: With Some Reference to its Development in Post-Talmudic Times*, Philadelphia, London, (1896-1897).

Ariel, Dr. David S. – *Spiritual Judaism: Restoring Heart and Soul to Jewish Life*, Hyperion, New York, (1998).

Armstrong, Karen – *A History of God*, Alfred A. Knopf, Inc., (1993).

Atwill, Joseph, Braunheim, Steve, Eisenman, Robert – *Redating the Radiocarbon Dating of the Dead Sea Scrolls*, Leiden, Brill, (2004).

Aune, David E. – *Prophecy in Early Christianity and the Ancient Mediterranean World*, Eerdmans, Grand Rapids, Michigan, (1983).

Aus, Roger David – *"Caught in the Act," Walking on the Sea and the Release of Barabbas Revisited*, Scholars Press, Atlanta, Georgia, (1998).

————. *Barabbas and Esther and Other Stories in the Judaic Illumination of Earliest Christianity*, Scholars Press, Atlanta, Georgia, (1992).

Avi-Jonah, M. – "The Foundation of Tiberius," *Israel Exploration Journal*, Volume 1, No. 3, (1950-1951), pp. 160-169.

Bacchiocchi, Samuele – *From Sabbath to Sunday: A Historical Investigation of the Rise of Sunday Observance in early Christianity*, The Pontifical Gregorian University Press, Rome, (1977).

Bacher, Wilhelm "Targum," *Jewish Encyclopedia*, http://www.jewishencyclopedia.com/articles/14248-targum.

———. "Academies in Palestine," *Jewish Encyclopedia*, http://www. jewishencyclopedia.com/articles/711-academies-in-palestine

Bacher, Wilhelm and Lauterbach, Jacob Zallel – "Shekalim," *Jewish Encyclopedia*, http://jewishencyclopedia.com/articles/13534-shekalim .

———. "Sanhedrin," *Jewish Encyclopedia*, (two separate articles under this same title), http://jewishencyclopedia.com/articles/13179-sanhedrin .

Bacon, B. W. – "Pharisees and Herodians in Mark," *Journal of Biblical Literature* 39, (1920), pp. 102-112.

Baeck, Leo – *The Essence of Judaism*, Schocken Books, New York, (1948).

Baigent, Michael and Leigh, Richard – *The Dead Sea Scrolls Deception*, Summit Books, New York, (1991).

Bailey, Sherwin D. – *Sexual Relations in Christian Thought*, New York, Harper, (1959).

Bamberger, B. – "The Dating of Aggadic Materials," *Journal of Biblical Literature* 68, (1949), pp. 115-123.

Bammel, E. and Moule, C. F. D. – *Jesus and the Politics of His Day*, Cambridge University, (1984).

Barclay, William – *We Have Seen the Lord: The Passion and Resurrection of Jesus Christ*, Westminster John Knox Press, (1998).

Bar-Ilan, Meir - "Literacy among the Jews in Antiquity: A Review of *Jewish Literacy in Roman Palestine: Texts and Studies in Ancient Judaism 81*, by Catherine Hezser," *Hebrew Studies* 44, (2003), pp. 217-222.

Barker, Kenneth L. and Kohlenberger, John R. III – *Zondervan NIV Bible Commentary*, 2 Volumes, Zondervan Publishing House, (1994).

Barr, Reverend Jack – "Claim: Pharisees and Sadducees were not Priest and Levites and Scribes: There were seven types of Pharisees," http:// www.barr-family.com/godsword/claim5.htm .

Barr, James – "Abba Isn't Daddy," *Journal of Theological Studies* ns 39, (1988), pp. 28-47.

Barton, J. – *Oracles of God: Perceptions of Ancient Prophecy in Israel after the Exile*, Oxford: Oxford University Press, (1986).

Bartsh, Hans-Werner – "Brethren Life and Thought," *New Theology* 6, (1969), pp. 185-198.

Bauer, Walter – *Orthodoxy and Heresy in Earliest Christianity*, Second German Edition, with added Appendices, By Georg Strecker, Translated by a team from the Philadelphia Seminar on Christian Origins, and Edited by Robert A Kraft and Gerhard Krodel, Fortress Press, Philadelphia, (1971).

Baum, Gregory – *The Jews and the Gospel: A Re-Examination of the New Testament*, The Newman Press, Westminster Maryland, Bloomsbury Publishing Co. Ltd. (1961).

Baumgarten, Joseph M. – "The Pharisaic-Sadducean Controversies about Purity and Qumran Texts," *Journal of Jewish Studies* 31.2, (Autumn 1980), pp. 169-170.

Beasley-Murray, G. R. – "The Interpretation of Daniel 7," *Catholic Biblical Quarterly* 45, (1983), pp. 44-58.

Beckwith, R. – *The Old Testament Canon of the New Testament Church and its Background in Early Judaism*, Grand Rapids: Eerdmans, (1985).

Belkin, Samuel – *Philo and the Oral Law*, Harvard University Press, (1942).

————. "The Problem of Paul's Background," *Journal of Biblical Literature* 54.1, (1935), pp. 41-60.

Ben-Nun, Steven – "The Miqvah that Yeshua/Jesus Used," *Israeli News Live*, November 17, 2016.

Benner, Jeff A. – "Biblical Word of the Month – Savior," *Ancient Hebrew Research Center Biblical Hebrew E-Magazine*, Issue # 020, October, 2005, http://www.ancient-hebrew.org/emagazine/020.html .

Bernstein, Moshe J. - "Ki-qelelath elohiym thalowiy (Deuteronomy 21:23): A Study in Early Jewish Exegesis," *Jewish Quarterly Review* 74, (1983), pp. 21-45.

Bernstein, Rabbi Steven – "Traditions of the Elders," *Aydat HaDerekh*, https://www.aydathaderekh.com/rabbi-steves-blog.html?post_id=81768.

Betz, Otto – *Jesus and the Dead Sea Scrolls*, Edited by James H. Charlesworth, New York, Doubleday, (1992).

Bible History Online – "Origin of the Pharisees," https://www.bible-history.com/pharisees/PHARISEESOrigin.htm .

Bickerman, Elias – *Four Strange Books of the Bible: Jonah/Daniel/Koheleth/Esther*, Schocken Books, New York, (1967).

Binyamin, Ben-Zion – "Birkat Ha-Minim and the Ein Gedi Inscription," *Immanuel* 21, (Summer 1987), pp. 68-79.

Bivin, David and Blizzard, Roy Jr. – *Understanding the Difficult Words of Jesus: New Insights From a Hebraic Perspective*, Revised Edition, Destiny

Image Publishers, Center For Judaic-Christian Studies, Dayton, Ohio, (2001).

Black, Matthew – *An Aramaic Approach to the Gospels and Acts*, 3rd Edition with Appendix by Geza Vermes, Oxford, Clarendon Press, (1967).

———. *The Scrolls and Christian Origins*, Charles Scribner's Sons, New York, (1961).

Blau, Ludwig and Kohler, Kaufmann – "Bat Kol," *Jewish Encyclopedia*, http://jewishencyclopedia.com/articles/2651-bat-kol .

———. "Angelology," *Jewish Encyclopedia*, http://www.jewishencyclopedia.com/articles/1521-angelology .

Blech, Rabbi Benjamin – *The Secrets of Hebrew Words*, Northvale, NJ.: Jason Aronson Inc., (1991).

Blinzler, Josef – *The Jewish and Roman Proceedings Against Jesus Christ Described and Assessed From the Oldest Accounts By Josef Blinzler, Translated From the Second Revised and Enlarged Edition By Isabel and Florence McHugh*, The Mercer Press Ltd., (1959).

Blizzard, Roy – "Mishnah and the Words of Jesus," *Bible Scholars: Question and the Answers*, https://www.biblescholars.org/2013/05/mishnah-and-the-words-of-jesus.html .

Blomberg, Craig L. – *Interpreting the Parables*, Downers Grove, Ill.: InterVarsity Press, (1990).

Bock, Darrell L. – *Blasphemy and Exaltation in Judaism: The Charge against Jesus in Mark 14:53-65*, Baker Books, Grand Rapids, Michigan, (1998).

———. "Luke 9:51-24:53," *Baker Exegetical Commentary on the New Testament*, 3b, Grand Rapids: Baker, (1996), pp. 1630-1641.

———. *Who is Jesus?: Linking the Historical Jesus with the Christ of Faith*, Howard Books, A division of Simon & Schuster, Inc., (2012).

Bond, Helen K. – *Pontius Pilate in History and Interpretation*, Cambridge University Press, (1998).

———. *Caiaphas: Friend of Rome and Judge of Jesus?* Westminster John Knox Press, Louisville, London, (2004).

Bookman, Doug – "Passion Week," www.jesus.org.

Booth, Roger P. – *Jesus and the Laws of Purity: Tradition, History, and Legal History in Mark 7*, Journal for the Study of the New Testament, Supplement Series 13, (1986).

Borg, Marcus J. – *Jesus: Uncovering the Life, Teachings, and Relevance of a Religious Revolutionary*, Harper San Francisco, (1989).

————. *Meeting Jesus Again for the First Time: The Historical Jesus & the Heart of Contemporary Faith*, Harper San Francisco, (1994).

————. *Conflict, Holiness & Politics in the Teachings of Jesus*, Studies in the Bible and Early Christianity Volume 5, The Edwin Mellen Press, New York and Toronto, (1984).

Borg, Marcus J. and Crossan, John Dominic – *The Last Week: The Day-By-Day Account of Jesus' Final week In Jerusalem*, Harper San Francisco, (2006).

Borg, Marcus J. and Wright, N. T. – *The Meaning of Jesus: Two Versions*, Harper Collins, (1998).

Bornkamm, Gunther – *Jesus of Nazareth*, Translated by Irene and Fraser McLuskey with James M. Robinson, New York: Harper, (1960).

Borowitz, Eugene B. and Schwartz, Francis Weinmann – *The Jewish Moral Virtues*, The Jewish Publication Society, Philadelphia, (1999).

Borowitz, Eugene B. – *Contemporary Christologies: A Jewish Response*, Paulist Press, New York, (1980).

Borsch, Frederick Houk – *The Son of Man in Myth and History*, The Westminster Press, Philadelphia, (1967).

Borysenko, Joan Ph.D. – *The Ways of the Mystic: Seven Paths to God*, Hay House Inc., Carlsbad, Ca. (1997).

Boteach, Rabbi Shmuley – *Kosher Jesus*, Gefen Publishing House, Jerusalem/New York, (2012).

Brandon, S. G. F. – "Jesus and the Zealots: Aftermath," *Bulletin of the John Rylands Library*, Volume 54, Issue 1, pp. 47-61.

————. *Jesus and the Zealots: A Study of the Political Factor in Primitive Christianity*, Manchester University Press, (1967).

Brichto, Herbert Chanon – "Blasphemy," *Encyclopedia Judaica*, (2008), https://www.jewishvirtuallibrary.org/jsource/judaica/ejud_0002_0003_0_03059.html.

Brown, Raymond E. and Meier, John P. - *Antioch and Rome: New Testament Cradles of Catholic Christianity*, Paulist Press, New York, (1983).

Brown, Raymond E. – *The Death of the Messiah*, 2 Volumes, Doubleday, New York, (1994).

————. *The Birth of the Messiah: A Commentary on the Infancy Narratives in Matthew and Luke*, Doubleday & Company Inc., Garden City, New York, (1977).

Brownlee, William H. – "A Comparison of the Covenanters of the Dead Sea Scrolls with Pre-Christian Jewish Sects," *The Biblical Archaeologist*, Volume xiii, no. 3, September, (1950).

Brueggemann, Walter – *The Prophetic Imagination*, Philadelphia, Fortress Press, (1978).

Buber, Martin – *Moses*, Harper Collins, (1958).

————. *Kingship of God*, Harper & Row, New York, (1967).

————. *At the Turning*, Farrar, Straus and Young, New York, (1952).

————. *I and Thou*, Translated with Prologue and notes by Walter Kaufman, a Charles Scribner's Sons Book, MacMillan Publishing Co., New York, (1970).

————. *On the Bible*, New York: Schocken Books, (1968).

————. *Paths in Utopia*, Translated by R. F. C. Hull, Introduction by Ephraim Fischoff, Beacon Press, Boston, (1966).

Bultmann, Rudolf – *The History of the Synoptic Tradition*, Harper & Row, Publishers, New York (1963).

————. *The Theology of the New Testament*, Edinburgh University Press, Edinburgh, (1957).

Burkitt, F. Crawford – *The Gospel History and its Transmission*, Edinburgh, T & T Clark, (1907).

Burney, C. F. – *The Aramaic Origin of the Fourth Gospel*, Oxford, Clarendon Press, (1922).

Burridge, Richard A. – *What are the Gospels: A Comparison with Graeco-Roman Biography*, Cambridge University Press, Cambridge, New York, (1992).

Burrows, Millar – *The Dead Sea Scrolls: With Translations by the Author*, New York, Viking Press, Inc., (1955).

Buss, Martin J. – *Encounter with the Text: Form and History in the Hebrew Bible*, Philadelphia/Missoula, Mont., Fortress Press/Scholars Press, (1979).

Buxbaum, Yitzhak – *The Life and Teachings of Hillel*, Jason Aronson Inc., New Jersey, London, (1973).

Cadman, William Healey – *The Last Journey of Jesus to Jerusalem: Its Purpose in the Light of the Synoptic Gospels*, London, Oxford University Press, H. Milford, (1923).

Cahill, Thomas – *The Gifts of the Jews*, Doubleday, New York, (1998).

Caird, G. B. – *The Language and Imagery of the Bible*, London: Duckworth, (1980).

Callan, Terrance – *The Origins of Christian Faith*, New York, Paulist Press, (1994).

Carmichael, Joel – *The Death of Jesus: With 'A New View,' Constituting a Fundamental Revision of the History of the Origins of Christianity*, Horizon Press, New York, (1982).

Carrier, Richard – "Why Do We Still Believe in Q?" https://www.richardcarrier.info/archives/12352 .

Carter, Warren – *Matthew and Empire: Initial Explorations*, Trinity Press International, (2001).

———. *Matthew and the Margins: A Socio Political and Religious Reading*, The Bible and Liberation Series, Maryknoll, N.Y.: Orbis Books, (2000).

Casey, Philip Maurice – *Son of Man: Interpretation and Influence of Daniel 7*, London: SPCK, (1979).

———. *From Jewish Prophet to Gentile God: The Origins of New Testament Christology: The Edward Cadbury Lectures at the University of Birmingham, 1985-86*, Cambridge J. Clarke; Louisville, Ky.: Westminster/John Knox Press, (1991).

Catchpole, David R. – *The Trial of Jesus*, Leiden: E. J. Brill, (1971).

Catel, Frere Olivier – "The Parable – A Rabbinical Literary Genre," *The Jewish Sources of Christianity*, blog.na4.org/2018/11/23/the-parable-a-rabbinical-literary-genre .

The Catholic Encyclopedia, New York, Appleton Co., (1911), Volume 12, p. 614.

Chabad.org – "The Course of Tradition: A Timeline of the Oral Law," www.chabad.org/library/article_cdo/aid/2074/jewish/The-Course-of-Tradition.htm.

Chambers – *Chambers Twentieth Century Dictionary*, Edinburgh, London: W & R Chambers, (1972).

Champions of Truth: The Open-Door Church – "Tract 13c, The Hebrew Trials of Christ – Supplement to Lesson 13," http://www.champs-of-truth.com/lessons/tract_13c.htm .

Charette, Blaine – "'To Proclaim Liberty to the Captives': Matthew 11:28-30 in the Light of OT Prophetic Expectation," *New Testament Studies* 38, pp. 290-297.

Charlesworth, James Hamilton – *The Old Testament Pseudepigrapha and the New Testament*, Philadelphia, Trinity Press International, (1998).
———. *The Messiah*, New York, Doubleday, (1991).
Charlesworth, James Hamilton and Brownson, J. – *The First Princeton Symposium on Judaism and Christian Origins: The Messiah; Developments in Earliest Judaism and Christianity*, Minneapolis: Fortress, (1992).
Chavez, Emilio G. – *The Theological Significance of Jesus' Temple Action in Mark's Gospel*, Toronto Studies in Theology Volume 87, The Edwin Mellen Press, (2002).
Chilton, Bruce D. – "The Glory of Israel: The Theology and Provenance of the Isaiah Targum," *Journal for the Study of the Old Testament*, 23, (Sheffield 1983), pp. 283-286.
———. "God in Strength: Jesus' Announcement of the Kingdom," Studien zum Neuen Testament und seiner Umwalt I, (Freistadt 1979), pp. 77-81.
Clark, Albert – *The Descent of Manuscripts*, Oxford, The Clarendon Press, (1918).
———. *Journal of Theological Studies*, 16, (1915), p. 233.
———. *The Primitive Text of the Gospels and Acts*, Oxford, the Clarendon Press, (1914).
Clark, Rabbi Matityahu – *Etymological Dictionary of Biblical Hebrew*, Based on the Commentaries of Rabbi Samson Raphael Hirsch, Feldheim Publishers, Jerusalem/New York, (1999).
Cohen, Abraham – *Everyman's Talmud*, Introduction by Professor Boaz Cohen, Schocken Books, New York, (1975).
Cohen, Boaz – "The Rabbinic Law Presupposed By Matthew 12:1 and Luke 6:1," *Harvard Theological Review*, Volume 23, (1923), pp. 91-92.
Cohen, Rabbi J. Simcha – *How Does Jewish Law Work*, Jason Aronson Inc., Northvale, New Jersey, (1993).
Cohen, Shaye J. D. – "The Ways that Parted: Jews, Christians, and Jewish-Christians ca. 100-150 C.E.", *Ways that Parted*, scohen@fas.harvard.edu .
———. "Jacob Neusner, Mishnah and Counter-Rabbinics," *Conservative Judaism*, Volume 37(1) Fall 1983, pp. 48-63.
Cohn, Haim – *The Trial and Death of Jesus*, Harper & Row Publishers, New York, (1967, 1971).
———. "Reflections on the Trial of Jesus," *Judaism* 20, (1971), pp. 18-19.
———. "Witness," *Encyclopedia Judaica, Jewish Virtual Library*, https://www.jewishvirtuallibrary.org/witness .

Cohn-Sherbock, Dan – *The Crucified Jew: Twenty Centuries of Christian Anti-Semitism*, Grand Rapids, Mich.: W. B. Erdmans, (1997), Originally Published; London, Harper Collins, (1992).

Collins, John J. – *The Scepter and the Star: The Messiahs of the Dead Sea Scrolls and Other Ancient Literature*, Doubleday, New York, *The Anchor Bible Reference Library*, (1995).

———. *Ideal Figures in Ancient Judaism: Profiles and Paradigms*, Ed. John J. Collins and George W. E. Nickelsburg, Chico, Calif.: Scholars Press, (1980).

———. *The Apocalyptic Imagination: An Introduction to the Jewish Matrix of Christianity*, Crossroad, New York, (1984).

Cornfield, Gaalyah – *The Historical Jesus: A Scholarly View of the Man and His World*, MacMillan Publishing Co., Inc., New York, (1982).

Cox, Steven L. – "A Consideration of the Gospel Accounts of the Charge of Blasphemy against Jesus," *Journal for Baptist Theology and Ministry*, Volume 2, No. 2, (Fall 2004), pp. 64-84.

Cross, Frank M. – *Canaanite Myth and Hebrew Epic: Essays in the History of the Religion of Israel*, Harvard University, Cambridge, Mass., (1973).

Crossan, John Dominic – *Jesus: A Revolutionary Biography*, Harper San Francisco, (1994).

———. *The Birth of Christianity*, Harper, San Francisco, (1998).

———. *In Parables: The Challenge of the Historical Jesus*, Harper & Row Publishers, New York, (1973).

———. *Who Killed Jesus?: Exposing the Roots of Anti-Semitism in the Gospel Story of the Death of Jesus*, Harper San Francisco, (1995).

———. *The Historical Jesus: The Life of a Mediterranean Jewish Peasant*, Harper San Francisco, (1991).

Crossley, James G. – *The New Testament and Jewish Law: A Guide for the Perplexed*, T&T Clark International, (2010).

Curtis, Michael – *Anti-Semitism in the Contemporary World*, Westview Press, Boulder Col., (1986).

Dahl, Nils Alstrup – "The Origin of Baptism," *Norsk Teologisk Tideskrift* 56, (1955), p. 36.

———. *The Crucified Messiah and other Essays*, Augsburg Publishing House, Minneapolis, Minnesota, (1974).

Danby, Herbert – *The Mishnah*, London, Oxford University Press, (1964).

Daniel-Rops, H. – *Daily Life in the Time of Jesus*, Translated by Patrick O'Brien, Hawthorn Books Inc., Publishers, New York, (1962).

Danielou, Cardinal Jean – *The Dead Sea Scrolls and Primitive Christianity*, Translated by Salvatore Attanasio, Baltimore, Helicon Press, (1958).

Danker, Frederick William – *BDAG: A Greek-English Lexicon of the New Testament and other Early Christian Literature*, 3rd Edition, Revised and Edited by Frederick William Danker Based on Walter Bauer's *Griechisch-deutsches Worterbuch zu den Schriften des Neuen Testaments und der fruhchristlichen Literatur*, sixth edition, ed. Kurt Aland and Barbara Aland, with Viktor Reichmann and on previous English editions by W. F. Arndt, F. W. Gingrich, and F. W. Danker, The university of Chicago Press, Chicago and London, (2000).

Daube, David – *The New Testament and Rabbinic Judaism*, Arno Press, New York, (1973).

———. *Collaboration with Tyranny in Rabbinic Law: The Riddell Memorial Lectures; Thirty-Seventh Series Delivered at the University of Newcastle upon Tyre, on 9, 10, and 11 November 1965*, London, Oxford University Press, (1965).

———. "Mark 1:22 and 27," *Journal of Theological Studies* 39, no. 153, (January 1938), pp. 45-59.

Davies, W. D. – *Paul and Rabbinic Judaism: Some Rabbinic Elements in Pauline Theology*, London, SPCK, (1965).

Deissmann, Adolf – *Light from the Ancient East; the New Testament Illustrated by Recently Discovered Texts of the Graeco-Roman World*, New York, George H. Doran Co., (1927).

Deutsch, Gotthard – "Apikoros (plural Apikorism)," *Jewish Encyclopedia*, http://www.jewishencyclopedia.com/articles/1640-apikoros .

Deutsch, Gotthard and Seligsohn, M. – "Poll-Tax," *Jewish Encyclopedia*, http://jewishencyclopedia.com/articles/12444-poll-tax .

Derrett, J. D. M. – "The Iscariot, *Mesira*, and the Redemption," *Journal of the Study of the New Testament* 8, (1980), pp. 2-23.

Dibelius, Martin – *Jesus*, Translated by Charles B. Hendrick and Frederick C. Grant, Philadelphia: Westminster, (1949).

———. *From Tradition to Gospel*, New York: Scribner, (1965).

Dimont, Max I. – *Jews, God and History*, New York, Signet Books, (1962).

DiscloseTV – "Jesus Was a Buddhist Monk BBC Documentary," *DiscloseTV*, www.disclosetv/bbc-documentary-proves-jesus-was-a-buddhist-monk-named-issa-314782 .

Dodd, C. H. – *The Founder of Christianity*, MacMillan Publishing Co., Inc., New York, (1970).

Donahue, John R. – *Are you the Christ? The Trial Narrative in the Gospel of Mark*, Missoula, Mont.: Society of Biblical Literature, (1973).

Donahue, John R. and Harrington, Daniel J. - *The Gospel of Mark*, Sacra Pagina Series, Collegeville, Minnesota: Liturgical Press, (2006).

Douglas, Mary – *Purity and Danger: An Analysis of Concept of Pollution and Taboo*, London and New York, Routledge and Kegan Paul, (2006).

Drachman, Bernard and Kohler, Kaufmann – "Ablution," *Jewish Encyclopedia*, http://jewishencyclopedia.com/articles/338-ablution .

Drane, John W. – *Jesus and the Four Gospels*, Harper & Row Publishers, New York, (1979).

Driver, S. R. – *A Critical and Exegetical Commentary on Deuteronomy*, 3rd Edition, Edinburgh: T. &C. Clark, (1902).

Drucker, Rabbi A. P. – *The Trial of Jesus From Jewish Sources*, New York, Bloch Publishing Company, (1907).

Drummond, James – *The Jewish Messiah: A Critical History of the Messianic Idea among the Jews from the Rise of the Maccabees to the Closing of the Talmud*, London, Longmans, Green, and Co. (1877).

Drury, John – *The Parables in the Gospels: History and Allegory*, New York: Crossroad, (1985).

Dunn, James D. G. – *The Partings of the Ways: Between Christianity and Judaism and their Significance for the Character of Christianity*, SCM Press, London, Trinity Press International, Philadelphia, (1991).

Duquesne, Jacques – *Jesus: An Unconventional Biography*, Translated by Catherine Spencer, Triumph Books, Ligouri Missouri, (1996).

Durant, Will – *The Story of Civilization: Part III – Caesar and Christ*, Simon and Schuster, New York, (1944).

Edersheim, Alfred – *The Life and Times of Jesus the Messiah*, Revised Edition, 2 Volumes, 35th printing, New York, Longmans, Green, (1952).

Ehrman, Bart D. – *How Jesus Became God: The Exaltation of A Jewish Preacher From Galilee*, Harper Collins, (2014).

————. *Jesus Interrupted: Revealing the Hidden Contradictions in the Bible (And Why We Don't Know About Them)*, HarperOne, Harper Collins, New York, (2009).

————. *The Lost Gospel of Judas Iscariot: A New Look At Betrayer and Betrayed*, Oxford University Press, (2006).

————. *The New Testament: A Historical Introduction to the Early Christian Writings*, Third Edition, New York, Oxford, Oxford University Press, (2004).

————. *Jesus: Apocalyptic Prophet of the New Millenium*, Oxford University Press, (1999).

————. *Jesus Before the Gospels: How the Earliest Christians Remembered, Changed and Invented Stories of the Savior*, HarperOne, Harper Collins Publishers, (2016).

Eisenbaum, Pamela – *Paul Was Not a Christian: The Original Message of a Misunderstood Apostle*, HarperOne, Harper Collins Publishers, (2009).

Eisenman, Robert H. – *Maccabees, Zadokites, Christians, and Qumran*, Leiden, (1983).

————. "Paul as Herodian," *JHC* 3/1 (Spring 1996), pp. 110-122.

Eisenstein, Judah David and the Executive Committee of the Editorial Board – "Water-Drawing, Feast of," *Jewish Encyclopedia*, http://jewishencyclopedia.com/articles/14794-water-drawing-feast-of .

Emerton, J. A. – "The Origin of the Son of Man Imagery," *Journal of Theological Studies* n. s. 9 (1958), pp. 225-242.

Encyclopedia Britannica – *Encyclopedia Britannica*, Encyclopedia Britannica, Inc., (1973).

Enslin, M. S. – *Christian Beginnings*, 4th Edition, New York; London: Harper & Brothers, (1938).

Evans, Craig A. – *Jesus and His Contemporaries: Comparative Studies*, Leiden, E. J. Brill, (1995).

————. "Predictions of the Destruction of the Herodian Temple in the Pseudepigrapha, Qumran Scrolls, and Related Texts," *Journal for the Study of the Pseudepigrapha* 10, (1992), pp. 89-147.

————. "Jesus' Action in the Temple: Cleansing or Portent of Destruction?" *Catholic Bible Quarterly* 51, (1989), pp. 237-270.

————. "Mishnah and Messiah 'In Context'," *Journal of Biblical Literature*, 112/2 1993, pp. 267-289.

Ewing, Upton Clary – *The Prophet of the Dead Sea Scrolls*, Philosophical Library, Inc., New York, (1963).

Eyzenberg, Dr. Lizorkin – "Jesus and Jewish Essenes," *Jewish Jesus*, January 5, 2018, https://israelstudycenter.com/jesus-and-jewish-essenes/ .

Fackenheim, Emil L. – *What Is Judaism?* Summit Books, New York, (1987).

Falk, Harvey – *Jesus the Pharisee: A New Look at the Jewishness of Jesus*, Paulist Press, New York, (1985).

Falk, Ze'ev W. – *The Divorce Action by the Wife in Jewish Law*, Jerusalem: Institute for Legislative Research and Comparative Law, (1973).

Farmer, William Reuben – *Maccabees, Zealots, and Josephus: An Inquiry into Jewish Nationalism in the Greco-Roman Period*, Greenwood Press, Publishers, (1956).

Fasman, Oscar Z. – *Judaism in a Changing World*, Edited by Leo Jung, New York, Oxford University Press, (1939).

Feldman, Rabbi Pesach – *Kollel Iyun Hadaf*, "Yerushalmi on *Eruvin* 13," dafyomi.co.il/eruvin/points/ev-ps-013.htm.

Finkelstein, L. – *Akiba- Scholar, Saint and Mrtyr*, New York, Meridian Books, (1962).

Fischel, Henry Albert – "Rabbinic Knowledge of Greek and Latin Languages," *Encyclopedia Judaica*, https://www.jewishvirtuallibrary.org/rabbinical-knowledge-of-greek-and-latin-languages .

Fitzmyer, Joseph A. – *A Christological Catechism: New Testament Answers*, New York, Paulist Press, (1981).

———. *Scripture and Christology: A Statement of the Biblical Commission with a Commentary*, London: Geoffrey Chapman, (1986).

———. *Essays on the Semitic Background of the New Testament*, Scholars Press, (1974).

———. *A Wandering Aramean: Collected Aramaic Essays*, Scholars Press, (1979).

Fleischacker, Samuel – "Hearing God's Voice: Two Models for Accepting the Torah," *The Torah: A Historical and Contextual Approach*, thetorah.com/two-models-for-accepting-the-torah .

Flusser, David – *Jesus*, New York, Herder and Herder, (1969).

———. "Mishpat Yeshu," *Tarbitz*, Volume 31, (1960), n. 41, p. 117.

———. *Judaism and the Origins of Christianity*, The Magnes Press, The Hebrew University, Jerusalem, (1988).

Ford, Josephine M. – *A Trilogy on Wisdom and Celibacy*, University of Notre Dame Press, (1967).

Fouts, David – "The Meaning of *Min*," *Answers in Genesis* January 1, 2009, last featured June 1, 2011.

Fredriksen, Paula – *Jesus of Nazareth, King of the Jews: A Jewish Life and the Emergence of Christianity*, Alfred A. Knopf, New York, (1999).

———. *From Jesus to Christ: The Origins of the New Testament Images of Jesus*, New Haven: Yale University Press, (1988).

———. "Judaism, the Circumcision of Gentiles, and Apocalyptic Hope: Another Look at Galatians 1 and 2," *Journal of Theological Studies* New Series 42, No. 2 (1991), p. 544.

Freke, Timothy and Gandy, Peter – *The Jesus Mysteries: Was the "Original Jesus" A Pagan God?* Harmony Books, New York, (1999).

Freyne, Sean – *Galilee: From Alexander the Great to Hadrian, 323 B.C.E. to 135 C.E.: A Study of Second Temple Judaism*, Co-Published by Michael Glazier Inc. and the University of Notre Dame Press, (1980).

Friedlander, Gerald – *The Jewish Sources of the Sermon on the Mount*, London, G. Routledge & Sons; New York, Bloch Pub. Co., (1911).

Friedmann, Meir – *Seder Eliahu Rabba and Seder Eliahu Zuta: Tanna d'be Eliahu; Pseudo-Seder Eliahu Zuta*, Jerusalem: Wahrmann Books, (1969).

Friedman, Richard Elliot – *Who Wrote the Bible*, Summit Books, New York, (1987).

Fuchs, Ernst – *Studies of the Historical Jesus*, Alec R. Allenson, Inc. (1964).

Funk, Robert W. – *Honest To Jesus: Jesus for a New Millenium*, Harper San Francisco, (1996).

Funk, Robert W. and Hoover, Roy W. – *The Five Gospels: The Search for the Authentic Words of Jesus*, MacMillan Publishing Company, New York, (1993).

Gager, John G. – *The Origins of Anti-Semitism: Attitudes Toward Judaism in Pagan and Christian Antiquity*, New York: Oxford University Press, (1983).

Gaster, Theodor H. – *The Dead Sea Scriptures: In English Translation*, Anchor Books, (1976).

Gaston, Lloyd – *Paul and the Torah*, Vancouver: University of British Columbia Press, (1987).

———. *No Stone on Another: Studies in the Significance of the fall of Jerusalem in the Synoptic Gospels*, Leiden, E. J. Brill, (1970).

Gavin, Frank – *The Jewish Antecedents of the Christian Sacraments*, New York and Toronto: The MacMillan Co., (1928).

Genachowski, Dov - "Ancient Jewish Coins," *Encyclopedia Judaica: Coins and Currency*, https://www.jewishvirtuallibrary.org/coins-and-currency .

Gikatilla, Rabbi Joseph – *Gates of Light: Sha'are Orah*, Translated with an Introduction by Avi Weinstein, Forward by Arthur Hertzberg and an Historical Introduction by Moshe Idel, Bronfman Library of Jewish Classics, Harper Collins Publishers, (1994).

Gilat, Yitzhak Dov – "Soferim," *Jewish Virtual Library*, https://www. jewishvirtuallibrary.org/soferim .

Ginzberg, Louis – *On Jewish Law and Lore*, Philadelphia, the Jewish Publication Society of America, (1955).

———. *The Legends of the Jews*, 7 Volumes, Philadelphia, The Jewish Publication Society, (1925).

———. *Students, Scholars, and Saints*, University Press of America, (1985).

Girzone, Joseph F. – *A Portrait of Jesus*, Doubleday, New York, (1998).

Glatzer, Nahum N. – *The Essential Philo*, New York, Schocken Books, (1971).

Glinert, Lewis – *The Story of Hebrew*, Princeton University Press, (2017).

Glueck, Nelson – *Deities and Dolphins*, Ambassador Books, Ltd., Toronto, (1965).

———. *The Other Side of the Jordan*, American Schools of Oriental Research, Cambridge Mass., (1970).

———. *Hesed in the Bible*, Translated by Alfred Gottschalk with Introduction by Gerald A. Larue, KTAV Publishing House Inc., (1975).

Godbey, Allen H. – *The Lost Tribes: A Myth*, Prolegomenon by Morris Epstein, KTAV Publishing House, Inc., New York, (1974).

Godfrey, Neil - "Why the Temple Act of Jesus is Almost Certainly Not Historical," February 13, 2010, *Vridar*, https://vridar.org/2010/02/13/ why-the-temple-act-of-jesus-is-almost-certainly-not-historical/ .

Goldin, Hyman E. – *The Case of the Nazarene Reopened*, New York, Exposition Press, (1948).

Goguel, Maurice and Wyon, Olive – *The Life of Jesus*, New York, the MacMillan Company, (1949, c 1933).

Goguel, Maurice – *Jesus and the Origins of Christianity*, New York: Harper Torch Books, (1960).

Goldstein, Rabbi Morris – *Jesus in the Jewish Tradition*, New York, the MacMillan Company, (1950).

Goodacre, Mark – *The Case against Q: Studies in Markan Priority and the Synoptic Problem*, Harrisburg, Pa.: Trinity Press International, (2002).

Goodenough, Erwin R. – *By Light, Light: The Mystic Gospel of Hellenistic Judaism*, New Haven: Yale University Press, (1935).

Goodman, Martin – *Mission and Conversion: Proselyting in the Religious History of the Roman Empire*, Oxford, Clarendon Press, (1994).

———. "Proselytizing in Rabbinic Judaism," *Journal of Jewish Studies* 40, (1989), pp. 175-185.

Goodspeed, Edgar J. – *Problems of New Testament Translation*, University of Chicago Press, (1945).

Gottheil, Richard and Bacher, William – "Aramaic Language Among the Jews," *Jewish Encyclopedia*, http://jewishencyclopedia.com/articles/1707-aramaic-language-among-the-jews .

Gottheil, Richard and Buchler, Alexander – "Apostole, Apostoli," *Jewish Encyclopedia*, http://jewishencyclopedia.com/articles/1658-apostle-apostoli .

Gottheil, Richard and Krauss, Samuel – "Caiaphas or Caiphas, Joseph," *Jewish Encyclopedia*, http://jewishencyclopedia.com/articles/3903-caiaphas .

———. "Greek Language and the Jews," *Jewish Encyclopedia*, http://www.jewishencyclopedia.com/articles6868-greek-language-and-the-jews .

———. "Sicarii (Greek, 'assassins,' 'dagger men')," *Jewish Encyclopedia*, http://jewishencyclopedia.com/articles/13630-sicarii .

Graetz, Heinrich – *History of the Jews*, Philadelphia: The Jewish Publication Society of America, (1939).

Grant, Frederick C. – *Ancient Judaism and the New Testament*, New York, MacMillan, (1959).

Greek Mythology.com – "Nephele," http://www.greekmythology.com/Other_Gods/Minor_Gods/Nephele/nephele.html .

Greenidge, A. H. J. – *The Legal Procedure of Cicero's Time*, London, New York, 1901.

Greenstone, Julius H., Hirsch, Emil G., Hirschfeld, Hartwig – "Fasting and Fast-Days," *Jewish Encyclopedia*, Executive Committee of the Editorial Board, http://jewishencyclopedia.com/articles/6033-fasting-and-fast-days.

Griffith-Jones, Robin – *The Four Witnesses: The Rebel, the Rabbi, the Chronicler, and the Mystic*, Harper San Francisco, (2000).

Grossberg, David M – "Is There a Doctrine of Heresy in Rabbinic Literature?" *The Gemara.com*, http://www.thegemara.com/is-there-a-doctrine-of-heresy-in-rabbinic-literature/ .

Guggenheimer, Heinrich W. – *The Jerusalem Talmud*, Edition, Translation, and Commentary by Heinrich W. Guggenheimer, Berlin; New York: Walter De Gruyter, (2000-2015).

Guillet, Jacques – *Jesus Christ Yesterday and Today: Introduction to Biblical Spirituality*, Translated by John Duggan, S. J. Franciscan Herald Press, Chicago, (1965).

Gundry, Robert H. – *Mark: A Commentary on His Apology for the Cross*, Eerdmans, Grand Rapids, Michigan, (1993).

Halevi, Judah – *The Kuzari*, Introduction by Henry Slonimsky, Schocken Books, New York, (1964).

Halperin, David J. – "Crucifixion, the Nahum Pesher, and the Rabbinic Penalty of Strangulation," *Journal of Jewish Studies* 32, (1981), pp. 32-46.

Hammerton-Kelly, Robert and Scroggs, Robin – *Jews, Greeks and Christians: Religious Cultures in Late Antiquity; Essays in Honor of William David Davies*, Edited by Robert Hammerton-Kelly and Robin Scroggs, Leiden: E. J. Brill, (1976).

Hanson, James M. – "Was Jesus a Buddhist?" *Buddhist-Christian Studies*, Annual 2005, v25, pp.75-89, www.thezensite.com/non_Zen/Was_Jesus_Buddhist.html .

Harlow, Victor E. – *The Destroyer of Jesus: The Story of Herod Antipas, Tetrarch of Galilee*, Oklahoma City: Modern Publishers, (1954).

Hartman, David – *A Heart of Many Rooms: Celebrating the Many Voices within Judaism*, Jewish Lights Publication, Woodstock, Vermont, (1999).

Hastings, James – *A Dictionary of the Bible*, with co-operation of John A Selbie, and with the assistance of John C. Lambert and Shailer Mathews, New York, C. Scribner's Sons, (1909).

Hengel, Martin – *Victory over Violence: Jesus and the Revolutionists*, Translated by David E Green, Introduction by Robin Scroggs, Philadelphia: Fortress Press, (1973).

Henry, Matthew – *Commentary on the Whole Bible: Complete and Unabridged in One Volume*, Hendrickson Publishers, (1997).

Heschel, Abraham Joshua – *God In Search of Man*, Jason Aronson, (1987).

———. *The Sabbath: Its Meaning for Modern Man*, Farrar, Straus & Company, New York, (1951).

———. *The Insecurity of Freedom*, The Noonday Press, a Division of Farrar, Strauss & Giroux, (1967).

———. *The Earth Is the Lord's*, Henry Schuman, Inc., New York, (1950).

Hezser, Catherine – *Jewish Literacy in Roman Palestine*, Tubingen: Mohr Siebeck, (2001).

Hirsch, Emil G. – "Son of Man," *Jewish Encyclopedia*, www. jewishencyclopedia.com/articles/13913-son-of-man .

———. "Heave Offering," *Jewish Encyclopedia*, http://jewishencyclopedia. com/articles/7439-heave-offering .

Hirsch, Emil G., Benzinger, Immanuel, Jacobs, Joseph, and Lauterbach, Jacob Zallel, "Weights and Measures," *Jewish Encyclopedia*, http:// jewishencyclopedia.com/articles/14821-weights-and-measures .

Hirsch, Emil G., Blau, Ludwig, Kohler, Kaufmann, and Schmidt, Nathaniel – "Bible Canon," http://www.jewishencyclopedia.com/ articles/3259-bible-canon .

Hirsch, Emil G., Buhl, Frants, and Schechter, Solomon – "Galilee," *Jewish Encyclopedia*, http://jewishencyclopedia.com/articles/6475-galilee .

Hirsch, Emil G., and Casanowicz, I. M. – "Swine," *Jewish Encyclopedia*, http://jewishencyclopedia.com/articles/14148-swine .

Hirsch, Emil G, Gottheil, Richard, Kohler, Kaufmann, Broyde, Isaac – "Demonology," *Jewish Encyclopedia*, http://www.jewishencyclopedia. com/articles/5085-demonology .

Hirsch, Emil G. and Kohler, Kaufmann – "Consecration or Dedication," *Jewish Encyclopedia*, http://www.jewishencyclopedia.com/articles/4612-consecration .

Hirsch, Emil G., Kohler, Kaufmann, Jacobs, Joseph, Friedenwald, Aaron, and Broyde, Isaac - "Circumcision," *Jewish Encyclopedia*, http:// jewishencyclopedia.com/articles/4391-circumcision .

Hirsch, Emil G. and Konig, Eduard – "Deep," *Jewish Encyclopedia*, http:// www.jewishencyclopedia.com/articles/5044-deep .

Hirsch, Emil G. and Krauss, Samuel – "Corpse," *Jewish Encyclopedia*, http://jewishencyclopedia.com/articles/4674-corpse .

Hirsch, Emil G and Nowack, Wilhelm – "Shekel," *Jewish Encyclopedia*, http://jewishencyclopedia.com/articles/13534-shekalim .

Hirsch, Emil G., Prince, John Dyneley, and Schechter, Solomon – "Esther," *Jewish Encyclopedia*, http://jewishencyclopedia.com/articles/5872-esther.

Hirsch, Emil G., Schamberg, J. F., Jacobs, Joseph, Waldstein, A. S., and Fishberg, Maurice – "Leprosy," *Jewish Encyclopedia*, www.jewishencyclopedia.com/articles/9774-leprosy .

Hirsch, Emil G. and Siegfried, Carl – "Esther, Apocryphal Book of," *Jewish Encyclopedia*, http://jewishencyclopedia.com/articles/5873-esther-apocryphal-book-of .

Hirsch, Samson Raphael – *Timeless Torah*, Edited by Jacob Breuer, New York, Feldheim, (1957).

History.com Editors – "Greek Mythology," *History.com*, December 2, 2009, https://www.history.com/topics/ancient-history/greek-mythology .

Hodges, Frederick M. - "The Ideal Prepuce in Ancient Greece and Rome: Male Genital Aesthetics and Their Relation to *Lipodermos*, Circumcision, Foreskin Restoration, and the *Kynodesme, The Bulletin of the History of Medicine*, Volume 75, Fall 2001, pp. 375-405.

Hoehner, Harold W. – *Herod Antipas: A Contemporary of Jesus Christ*, Zondervan Publishing House, Cambridge University Press, (1972).

————. "Chronological Aspects of the Life of Christ, Part V: The Year of Christ's Crucifixion," *Bibliotheca Sacra* 131, (October-December, 1974), p. 341.

————. "Pilate," *Dictionary of Jesus and the Gospels*, Downers Grove/Leicester: Intervarsity, (1992), pp. 172-183.

Horowitz, Isaiah – *The Generations of Adam*, Translated, Edited and with Introduction by Miles Krassen, Preface by Elliot R. Wolfson, Paulist Press, New York, (1996).

Horsley, Richard A. – *Jesus and the Spiral of Violence: Popular Jewish Resistance in Roman Palestine*, Harper & Row, Publishers, San Francisco, (1987).

Horsley, Richard A. and Hanson, John S. – *Bandits, Prophets, and Messiahs: Popular Movements in the Time of Jesus*, Winston Press, (1985).

Hulen, Amos B. – "The Dialogues with the Jews' as Sources for the Early Jewish Argument against Christianity," *Journal of Biblical Literature*, 51, (1932), pp. 58-71.

Hultgren, Arland J. – *Jesus and His Adversaries: The Form and Function of the Conflict Stories in the Synoptic Tradition*, Augsburg Publishing House, Minneapolis, (1979).

Hurtado, Larry W. – *One God One Lord: Early Christian Devotion and Ancient Jewish Monotheism*, Philadelphia, Fortress Press, (1988).

Husband, W. R. – *The Prosecution of Jesus: It's Date, History, and Legality*, Princeton, University Press, (1916).

Hyde, Orson – *Journal of Discourses Brigham Young* 2, (1854), pp. 79-83.

Instone-Brewer, David – "The Eighteen Benedictions and the *Minim* before 70 CE," *The Journal of Theological Studies*, Volume 54, N. 1, (2003), pp. 25-44.

———. *Jesus of Nazareth's Trial in the Uncensored Talmud*, http://www.tyndale.cam.ac.uk/Tyndale/staff/Instone-Brewer/prepub/07_InstoneBrewer.pdf .

Isaac, Jules – *Jesus and Israel*, edited and with a Forward by Claire Huchet Bishop, and Translated by Sally Gran, Holt, Rinehart and Winston, (1971).

Jackson, F. J. Foakes, and Lake, Kirsopp – *The Beginnings of Christianity: The Acts of the Apostles*, Five Volumes, Grand Rapids, Michigan: Baker Book House, (1979).

Jackson-McCabe, Matt – *Jewish Christianity Reconsidered: Rethinking Ancient Groups and Texts*, Minneapolis, Fortress Press, (2007).

Jacobs, Joseph – "Mamon (Mammon)," *Jewish Encyclopedia*, http://jewishencyclopedia.com/articles/10339-mamon-mammon .

Jacobs, Joseph and Adler, Cyrus – "Calendar, History of," *Jewish Encyclopedia*, www.jewishencyclopedia.com/articles/3920-calendar-history-of .

Jacobs, Joseph and Broyde, Isaac – "Herod I (Surnamed The Great)," *Jewish Encyclopedia* 6, (1965).

———. "Sardinia: Under the Romans," *Jewish Encyclopedia* 6, (1965).

———. "Tax-Gatherers," *Jewish Encyclopedia*, http://www.jewishencyclopedia.com/articles/14273-tax-gatherers .

Jacobs, Joseph and Buttenweiser, Moses – "Messiah: The Heavenly Messiah: In Rabbinic Literature," *Jewish Encyclopedia*, http://jewishencyclopedia.com/articles/10729-messiah .

Jacobs, Joseph and Eisenstein, Judah David – "Rebuke and Reproof," *Jewish Encyclopedia*, http://www.jewishencyclopedia.com/articles/12613-rebuke-and-reproof .

Jacobs, Joseph and the Executive Committee of the Editorial Board – "Yezer Ha-Ra," *Jewish Encyclopedia*, http://jewishencyclopedia.com/articles/15083-yezer-ha-ra

Jacobs, Joseph and Hirsch, Emil G. – "Proselyte," *Jewish Encyclopedia*, www.jewishencyclopedia.com/articles/12391-proselyte .

Jacobs, Joseph and Kohler, Kaufmann – "Korban ('an offering')," *Jewish Encyclopedia*, http://jewishencyclopedia.com/articles/9468-korban .

———. "Nasi (literally 'Prince')," *Jewish Encyclopedia*, http://www.jewishencyclopedia.com/articles/11330-nasi .

Jacobs, Joseph and Krauss, Samuel – "Tombs," *Jewish Encyclopedia*, www.jewishencyclopedia.com/articles/14441-tombs .

Jacobs, Joseph and Lauterbach, Jacob Zallel – "Zugot ('pairs')," *Jewish Encyclopedia*, http://jewishencyclopedia.com/articles/15293-zugot .

Jacobs, Joseph and Reinach, Theodore – "Numismatics," *Jewish Encyclopedia*, http://jewishencyclopedia.com/articles/11621-numismatics .

Jacobs, Rabbi Louis – *A Tree of Life: Diversity, Flexibility, and Creativity in Jewish Law*, New York: Oxford University Press, (1984).

———. "Rabban Gamaliel," *My Jewish Learning*, https://www.myjewishlearning.com/article/Rabban-Gamaliel/ , reprinted from *The Jewish Religion: A Companion*, Oxford, New York, Oxford University Press, (1995).

Jarus, Owen – "Jesus House? 1st-Century Structure May Be Where He Grew," *Live Science*, March 1, 2015, https://www.livescience.com/49997-jesus-house-possibly-found-nazareth.html .

Jastrow, Marcus and Friedlander, Michael – "Bezah ('Egg')," *Jewish Encyclopedia*, http://jewishencyclopedia.com/articles/3237-bezah .

Jastrow, Morris Jr., and Kohler, Kaufmann, and Jastrow, Marcus – "Banishment," *Jewish Encyclopedia*, http://jewishencyclopedia.com/articles/2441-banishment .

Jastrow, Morris, Jr. and McCurdy, J. Frederick – "Baal-Zebub," *Jewish Encyclopedia*, http://jewishencyclopedia.com/articles/2255-baal-zebub .

Jastrow, Morris Jr. and Price, Ira Maurice – "Free-Will Offerings ('nedabah')," *Jewish Encyclopedia*, http://www.jewishencyclopedia.com/articles/6338-free-will-offering .

Jeremias, Joachim – *Jerusalem in the Time of Jesus*, Translated by F. H. and C. H. Cave, Philadelphia, Fortress, (1969).

———. *The Prayers of Jesus*, London: S. C. M. Press, (1967).

———. *The Central Message of the New Testament*, New York, Charles Scribner's Sons, (1965).

Jewett, P. K. – *Lord's Day: A Theological Guide to the Christian Day of Worship*, Grand Rapids, Mich., W. B. Eerdmans Publishing Co., (1971).

Jewish Virtual Library – "Jewish Practices & Rituals: Excommunication," *Jewish Virtual Library*, https://www.jewishvirtuallibrary.org/excommunication .

———. "Ancient Jewish History: Weights, Measures & Coins of the Biblical and Talmudic Periods," *Jewish Virtual Library*, https://www.jewishvirtuallibrary.org/weights-measures-and-coins-of-the-biblical-and-talmudic-periods .

Johnson, Luke Timothy – *The Real Jesus: The Misguided Quest for the Historical Jesus and the Truth of the Traditional Gospels*, Harper San Francisco, (1996).

———. *The Writings of the New Testament: An Interpretation*, London: SCM, (1986).

Johnson, Paul – *The Quest for God*, Harper Collins, New York, (1996).

Jones, A. H. M. – *The Herods of Judaea*, Oxford Clarendon Press, (1938).

Josephus, Flavius – *The Works of Flavius Josephus*, 4 Volumes, Translated with Footnotes and Comments, William Whiston, A.M., Forward by Charles F. Pfeiffer, 18th Century.

Joyce, Donovan – *The Jesus Scroll*, New American Library, A Signet Book, (1972).

Juel, Donald – *Messiah and Temple: The Trial of Jesus in the Gospel of Mark*, Scholars Press: The Society of Biblical Literature, (1977).

Jull, A. J. Timothy, Donahue, Douglas J., Broshi, Magen, Tov, Emanuel – "Radiocarbon Dating of Scrolls and Linen Fragments from the Judean Desert," *Radiocarbon*, Vol. 37, No. 1, 1995, pp. 11-19.

Kadushin, Max – *The Rabbinic Mind*, Appendix By Simon Greenburg, Bloch Publishing Company, New York, (1972).

———. *Worship and Ethics: A Study in Rabbinic Judaism*, Northwestern University Press, (1964).

———. *Organic Thinking: A Study in Rabbinic Thought*, Bloch Publishing Company, New York, (1976).

Kahana, Kopel – *The Theory of Marriage in Jewish Law*, Leiden: E. J. Brill, (1966).

Kantor, Shalom – "Taming the Beast: The Yetzer Ha Ra and the Yetzer Ha Tov," *Sefaria*, https://www.sefaria.org/sheets/2384.?lang=bi .

Kaplan, Rabbi Aryeh – *Meditation and Kabbalah*, Samuel Weiser, York Beach, Maine, (1982).

Katz, Michael and Schwartz, Gershon – *Swimming in the Sea of Talmud*, The Jewish Publication Society, (1998).

Kaufman, Yehezkel – *The Religion of Israel: From Its Beginnings to the Babylonian Exile*, Translated and Abridged by Moshe Greenberg, The University of Chicago Press, (1960).

Kazen, Thomas – *Jesus and Purity Halakah: Was Jesus Indifferent to Impurity?* Winona Lake, Indiana, Eisenbrauns, (2010).

Kee, Howard Clark – *Jesus in History: An Approach to the Study of the Gospels*, Harcourt Brace Jovanovich, Publishers (1977).

———. *Community of the New Age: Studies in Mark's Gospel*, Philadelphia: Westminster Press, (1977).

Kegman, Rabbi Jay – "Eruvin 13b: Following Beit Shammai," March 29, 2013, *Torah in Motion*, https://www.torahinmotion.org/discussions-and-blogs/eruvin-13b-following-beit-shammai .

Kelley, Aidan – "Jesus was a Rabbi on the Hillel Side," *The Teachings of Jesus*, September 19, 2006, http://theteachingsofjesus.blogspot.com/2006/09/jesus-was-rabbi-on-hillel-side.html .

Kennedy, D. James – *Solving Bible Mysteries: Uncovering the Perplexing and Troubling Passages of Scripture*, Thomas Nelson Publishers, (2000).

Kenyon, Frederick George – *The Text of the Greek Bible: A Students Handbook*, London, Duckworth, (1937).

———. "The Western Text in the Gospels and the Acts," *Proceedings of the British Academy*, 24, (1938), pp. 287-315.

Kioulachoglou, Anastasios – "Judas' Death and its Timing," *The Journal of Biblical Accuracy*, https://www.jba.gr/judas-death.htm .

Kirby, Peter – "Historical Jesus Theories," *Early Christian Writings*, 7 January, 2019, *Didache*, http://www.earlychristianwritings.com/text/didache-roberts.html .

Klassen, William – *Judas: Betrayer or Friend of Jesus*, Minneapolis, Fortress Press, (1996).

Klausner, Joseph – *The Messianic Idea in Israel: From its beginning to the Completion of the Mishnah*, Translated from the Third Hebrew Edition by W. F. Stinespring, The MacMillan Company, New York, (1955).

———. *Jesus of Nazareth: His Life, Times, and Teaching*, Translated by Herbert Danby, the MacMillan Company, (1959).

————. *Historyah shel ha-Bayit he-Sheni*, 3rd Edition, 5 Volumes, Jerusalem, (1952).

Klein, Rabbi Dr. Ernest David – *A Comprehensive Etymological Dictionary of the Hebrew Language for Readers of English*, Foreword by Haim Rabin, The Hebrew University of Jerusalem, MacMillan Publishing Company, New York, (1987).

Klein, Isaac – *A Guide to Jewish Religious Practice*, The Jewish Theological Seminary of America, New York, (1979).

Kleist, James A. – *The Didache*, New York, Newman Press, (1988).

Klink, Edward W. III – "Expulsion from the Synagogue? Rethinking a Johannine Anachronism," *Tyndale Bulletin* 59.1, (2008), pp. 99-118.

Knox, W. L. – *The Sources of the Synoptic Gospels*, Cambridge, I, (1953), II, (1957).

————. *St Paul and the Church of Jerusalem*, Cambridge, (1925).

Koch, Ruth N. and Haugk, Kenneth C. – *Speaking the Truth in Love: How to Be An Assertive Christian*, Stephen Ministries, St. Louis, Missouri, (1992).

Kohler, Kaufmann – "Kingdom of God ('Malkuta de-Adonai')," *Jewish Encyclopedia*, http://www.jewishencyclopedia.com/articles/9328-kingdom-of-god .

————. "Herodians," *Jewish Encyclopedia*, http://jewishencyclopedia.com/articles/7605-herodians .

————. "Apostle and Apostleship," *Jewish Encyclopedia*, http://jewishencyclopedia.com/articles/1655-apostles-and-apostleship .

————. "Zealots (Hebrew, Kanna'im)," *Jewish Encyclopedia*, http://jewishencyclopedia.com/articles/9193-kanna-im .

————. "Sadducees," *Jewish Encyclopedia*, http://jewishencyclopedia.com/articles/12989-sadducees .

————. "Hosanna," *Jewish Encyclopedia*, http://jewishencyclopedia.com/articles/7893-hosanna .

————. "Essenes," *Jewish Encyclopedia*, http://jewishencyclopedia.com/articles/5867-essenes .

————. "Birth, New," *Jewish Encyclopedia*, http://jewishencyclopedia.com/articles/3321-birth-new .

————. "Agape," *Jewish Encyclopedia*, http://jewishencyclopedia.com/articles/888-agape .

————. "Burial," *Jewish Encyclopedia,* www.jewishencyclopedia.com/articles/3842-burial .

————. "Alms," *Jewish Encyclopedia,* http://jewishencyclopedia.com/articles/1295-alms .

————. "Hemerobaptists: 'Morning Bathers'," *Jewish Encyclopedia,* http://jewishencyclopedia.com/articles/7551-hemerobaptists .

————. "Ascetics," *Jewish Encyclopedia,* http://jewishencyclopedia.com/articles/1888-ascetics .

————. "Binding and Loosing (Hebrew, 'asar we-hittir'; Aramean, 'asar we-shera')," *Jewish Encyclopedia,* http://jewishencyclopedia.com/articles3307-binding-and-loosing .

————. "Menahem the Essene," *Jewish Encyclopedia,* http://jewishencyclopedia.com/articles/10625-menahem-the-essene .

————. "Beelzebub or Beelzebul," *Jewish Encyclopedia,* https://jewishencyclopedia.com/articles/2732-beelzebub .

————. "Hanukkah," *Jewish Encyclopedia,* http://jewishencyclopedia.com/articles/7233-hanukkah .

————. "Lord's Supper," *Jewish Encyclopedia,* http://jewishencyclopedia.com/articles/10113-lord-s-supper .

————. "Abba," *Jewish Encyclopedia,* http://www.jewishencyclopedia.com/articles/121-abba .

————. "Saul of Tarsus (known as Paul, the Apostle of the Heathen)," *Jewish Encyclopedia,* http://jewishencyclopedia.com/articles/13232-saul-of-tarsus .

————.- "Am Ha-Arez," *Jewish Encyclopedia,* http://jewishencyclopedia.com/articles/1356-am-ha-arez .

Kohler, Kaufmann and Amram, David Werner - "Blasphemy," *Jewish Encyclopedia,* http://jewishencyclopedia.com/articles/3354-blasphemy.

————. "Abba," E. Shurer, I.i.298 *Jewish Encyclopedia,* www.jewishencyclopedia.com/articles/121-abba .

Kohler, Kaufmann and Blau, Ludwig – "Gehenna: Sin and Merit," *Jewish Encyclopedia,* http://www.jewishencyclopedia.com/articles/6558-gehenna .

————. "Preexistence," *Jewish Encyclopedia,* http://www.jewishencyclopedia.com/articles/12339-preexistence .

Kohler, Kaufmann and Ginzberg, Louis – "Boethusians," *Jewish Encyclopedia,* http://jewishencyclopedia.com/articles/3467-boethusians .

Kohler, Kaufmann and de Harkavy, Abraham – "Karaites and Karaism," *Jewish Encyclopedia*, http://jewishencyclopedia.com/articles/9211-karaites-and-karaism .

Kohler, Kaufmann and Hirsch, Emil G. – "Crucifixion," *Jewish Encyclopedia*, www.jewishencyclopedia.com/articles/4782-crucifixion .

———. "Asceticism," *Jewish Encyclopedia*, http://jewishencyclopedia.com/articles/1887-asceticism .

Kohler, Kaufmann and Krauss, Samuel – "Baptism," *Jewish Encyclopedia*, http://jewishencyclopedia.com/articles/2456-baptism .

Kohler, Kaufmann and Malter, Henry – "Purim," *Jewish Encyclopedia*, http://jewishencyclopedia.com/articles/12448-purim .

Kohler, Kaufmann and Margolis, Max L. – "Celibacy," *Jewish Encyclopedia*, http://jewishencyclopedia.com/articles/4166-celibacy .

Kohler, Kaufmann and Schlesinger, Max – "Repentance (Hebrew 'teshuvah')," *Jewish Encyclopedia*, http://www.jewishencyclopedia.com/articles/12680-repentance .

Kohler, Kaufmann and Seligsohn, M., - "Judas the Galilean," *Jewish Encyclopedia*, http://www.jewishencyclopedia.com/articles/9032-judas-the-galilean .

Kohler, Kaufmann and Willner, Wolf – "Second Day of Festivals," *Jewish Encyclopedia*, http://www.jewishencyclopedia.com/articles/13370-second-day-of-festivals .

Korner, Ralph J. - "*Ekklesia* as a Jewish Synagogue Term: Some Implications for Paul's Socio-Religious Location," *Journal of the Jesus Movement in its Jewish Setting* No.2, (2015), pp. 53-78.

Kraeling, C. H. – *John the Baptist*, Charles Scribner's Sons, New York, (1951).

Krauss, Samuel, and the Executive Committee of the Editorial Board – "Nazarenes," *Jewish Encyclopedia*, http://jewishencyclopedia.com/articles/11393-nazarenes .

Kummel, Werner George – *Promise and Fulfillment: The Eschatological Message of Jesus*, Translated by Dorothea M. Barton, S. C. M. Press Ltd., London, (1957), Vanderville, Ill., A. R. Allenson, (1957).

Kunkel, Fritz – *Creation Continues: A Psychological Interpretation of the First Gospel*, Charles Scribner's Sons, New York, (1947).

Kushner, Rabbi Lawrence – *The Book of Words*, Jewish Lights Publishing, Woodstock, Vermont, (1991).

Laan, Ray Vander – "Rabbi and Talmidim," *That the World May Know*, https://www.thattheworldmayknow.com/rabbi-and-talmidim .

Lane-Fox, Robin – *Pagans and Christians*, New York, Knopf, (1987).

Langdon, S. – "The Release of the Prisoner at the Passover," *Expository Times* 29, Edinburgh, (1918), pp. 328-330.

Lanier, Greg – "No, 'Saul the Persecutor' Did Not Become 'Paul the Apostle'," *The Gospel Coalition*, May 3, 2017, www.thegospelcoalition. org/article/no-saul-the-persecutor-did-not-become-paul-the-apostle/ .

Lapide, P. E. – *Wer war Schuld an Jesu Tod*, 2nd Edition, Gutersloh: Mohn, (1989).

Lauterbach, Jacob Zallel. – "The Pharisees and Their Teachings," *Hebrew Union College Annual* 6, (1930), p. 74, n. 7.

––––––. "Mishnah," *Jewish Encyclopedia*, The Executive Committee of the Editorial Board, http://jewishencyclopedia.com/articles/10879-mishnah .

Lauterbach, Jacob Zallel and the Executive Committee of the Editorial Board – "Rabban (Literal 'our teacher,' 'our master')," *Jewish Encyclopedia*, http://jewishencyclopedia.com/articles/12491-rabban .

Lav, Binyamin – *The Sages*, 3 Volumes, Jerusalem, Maggid Books, (2013).

Lawrence, Rabbi Jeremy – *Torah for Today: What Does the Torah Say about ... Blasphemy?* http://jewishness.timesofisrael.com/torah-today-torah-says-blasphemy/ .

Leaney, A. R. C. – *The Rule of Qumran and its Meaning*, Westminster Press, Philadelphia, (1966).

Leary, T. J. – "Paul's Improper Name," *New Testament Studies* Volume 38, No. 3 (1992), pp. 467-469.

Legasse, Simon – *The Trial of Jesus*, London: SCM Press, (1997).

Legrand, Lucien – *The Biblical Doctrine of Virginity*, New York, Sheed and Ward, (1963).

Leiman, S. Z. – *The Canonization of Hebrew Scripture*, Hamden, CT: Archon Books, (1976).

Levine, Amy-Jill – *The Misunderstood Jew: The Church and the Scandal of the Jewish Jesus*, Harper Collins, (2006).

Levine, Amy-Jill, Allison, Dale C. Jr., and Crossan, John Dominic – *The Historical Jesus in Context*, Editors, Princeton Readings in Religions, Princeton University Press, Princeton and Oxford, (2006).

Levine, Samuel – *You Take Jesus, I'll Take God*, Hamorah Press, Los Angeles, Calif., (1980).

Levinthal, Israel Herbert, L. H. D. – *Judaism: An Analysis and an Interpretation*, Funk & Wagnalls Company, New York and London, (1935).

Lewis, J. P. – "What do we mean by Jabneh?" *Journal of Bible and Religion* 32, (1964), pp. 125-132.

Liddell and Scott's – *Greek-English Lexicon*, Oxford University Press, (1997).

Lieberman, Saul – *Hellenism in Jewish Palestine*, New York, The Jewish Theological Seminary of America, (1950).

———. "A Tragedy or a Comedy?" *Journal of the American Oriental Society*, Volume 104(2), April/June 1984, pp. 315-319.

Lietzmann, Hans – *Synopsis of the First Three Gospels*, Translated by F. L. Cross, 9th Revised Edition, Oxford: Basic Blackwell, (1968).

Lieu, Judith, North, John, and Rajak, Tessa – *The Jews among Pagans and Christians in the Roman Empire*, Abingdon, Oxon Taylor and Francis, (2013).

Lightfoot, R. H. - *The Gospel Message of St. Mark*, Oxford: Clarendon, (1968).

Lincoln, Lawrence Ronald – *A Socio-Historical Analysis of Jewish Banditry in First Century Palestine: 6 to 70CE*, Thesis submitted in partial fulfillment of the requirements for the degree of MPhil (Ancient Cultures) at the University of Stellenbosch, November 2005, Supervisor, Professor Johann Cook.

Lindars, B. – *Jesus Son of Man: A Fresh Examination of the Son of Man Sayings in the Gospels in the Light of Recent Research*, London: SPCK, (1983), Grand Rapids: Eerdmans, (1984).

Lohmeyer, E. – *Das Evangelium des Markus*, Gottingen, (1959).

Lord, Albert Bates – *The Singer of Tales: A Study in the Processes of Composition of Yugoslav, Greek, and Germanic Oral Narrative Poetry*, Cambridge, Harvard University, (1949).

Lost Christianity – "Jesus was an Essene, and Nazareth did not Exist," https://lostchristianity.wordpress.com/2012/06/03/jesus-was-an-essene-and-nazareth-did-not-exist/ .

Louth, Andrew – *Early Christian Writings: The Apostolic Fathers*, Translated by Maxwell Staniforth, Penguin Classics, (1987).

Luzzatto, Moshe Chaim – *The Way of God: An Essay on Fundamentals*, Translated and Annotated by Aryeh Kaplan, Emended by Gershon Robinson, Sixth, Extensively Revised Edition, Feldheim Publishers, Jerusalem and New York, (1997).

Maccoby, Hyam – *The Mythmaker: Paul and the Invention of Christianity*, Barnes &Noble, (1986).

————. *Judas Iscariot and the Myth of Jewish Evil*, The Free Press, New York, (1992).

————. "Jesus and Barabbas," *New Testament Studies* 16, (1968), pp. 55-60.

————. *Revolution in Judaea: Jesus and the Jewish Resistance*, Taplinger Publishing Company, New York, (1981).

————. "Jacob Neusner's Mishnah," *Midstream*, 30/5 May 1984, pp. 24-32.

————. "Neusner and the Red Cow," *Journal for the Study of Judaism*, 21, 1990, pp. 60-75.

————. *Ritual and Morality: The Ritual Purity System and its Place in Judaism*, Cambridge University Press, (1999).

Mack, Burton L. – *A Myth of Innocence: Mark and Christian Origins*, Philadelphia: Fortress Press, (1988).

Maier, P. L. – "Sejanus, Pilate and the Date of the Crucifixion," *Church History* 37, (1968), pp. 3-13.

Malan, Gert J. – "Is Rewritten Bible/Scripture the Solution to the Synoptic Problem?" *HTS Theological Studies*, Volume 70, n. 1, Pretoria, January 2014.

Malina, Bruce J. – *The Palestinian Manna Tradition: The Manna Tradition in the Palestinian Targums and Its Relationship to the New Testament Writings*, Leiden, E. J. Brill, (1968).

Manson, T. W. – *The Mission and Message of Jesus*, New York, E. P. Dutton, (1938).

Mantel, Hugo – *Studies in the History of the Sanhedrin*, Harvard Semitic Series XVII, Harvard University Press, (1961).

Margolis, Max Leopold and Marx, Alexander – *A History of the Jewish People*, Philadelphia: The Jewish Publication Society of America, (1956).

Marsh, Herbert G. – *The Origin and Significance of the New Testament Baptism*, Manchester University Press, (1941).

Marxsen, Willi and Boyce, James - *Mark the Evangelist: Studies on the Redaction History of the Gospel*, Nashville, New York, Abingdon, (1969).

Maxey, Al – "A Cloud of Witnesses: An Analysis of Hebrews 12:1," *Reflections*, Issue #241, March 25, 2006, http://www.zianet.com/maxey/reflx241.htm

McArthur, Harvey – "Celibacy in Judaism at the Time of Christian Beginnings," *Andrews University Seminary Studies*, summer 1987, Volume 25, No. 2, pp. 163-181.

McCown, Chester Charlton – *The Search for the Real Jesus: A Century of Historical Study*, New York, Charles Scribner's Sons, (1940).

McFarlane, Robert – "The Gospel of Mark and Judaism," *Jewish-Christian Relations: Insights and Issues in the Ongoing Jewish-Christian Dialogue*, www.jcrelations.net .

McLeman, James – *The Birth of the Christian Faith*, Oliver and Boyd, Edinburgh and London, (1962).

Meacham, Tirzah – "Obligations of Women in Commandments," *Legal-Religious Status of the Jewish Female*, https://jwa.org/encyclopedia/article/legal-religious-status-of-jewish-female .

Mead, G. R. S. – *Did Jesus Live 100BCE?* Theosophical Publishing Society, (1903).

Meier, John P. – *A Marginal Jew: Rethinking the Historical Jesus*, 5 Volumes, Doubleday, *The Anchor Bible Reference Library*, (1991-2016).

Merkel, J. – "Die Begnadigung am Passahfeste," *ZNW* 6, (1905), pp. 293-316.

Mettinger, T. N. D. – *King and Messiah: The Civil and Sacral Legitimation of the Israelite Kings*, Lund: Gleerup, (1976).

Metzger, Bruce M. – *The Text of the New Testament: Its Transmission, Corruption, and Restoration*, New York; Oxford: Oxford University Press, (1992).

Ministry – "The Money of the Jewish Temple," *Ministry: International Journal for Pastors*, September 1984.

Mitton, C. Leslie – *Jesus: The Fact behind the Faith*, Grand Rapids, Michigan, Eerdmans, (1974).

Moloney, Francis J. - *The Gospel of Mark: A Commentary*, Peabody, Ma: Hendrickson, (2004).

Montefiore, Canon Hugh – *For God's Sake: Sermons from Great St. Mary's*, Philadelphia: Fortress Press, (1969).

Montefiore, Claude G. – *Some Elements of the Religious Teaching of Jesus*, London, MacMillan and Co., (1910).

————. *Rabbinic Literature and Gospel Teachings*, London, MacMillan, (1930).

————. *Lectures on the Origin and Growth of Religion as Illustrated by the Religion of the Ancient Hebrews*, London, Williams and Norgate, (1892).

————. *The Synoptic Gospels*, 2nd Edition, London, MacMillan, (1927).

Moore, George Foot – *Judaism in the First Centuries of the Christian era: The Age of the Tannaim*, 3 Volumes, Cambridge, Harvard University Press, (1966).

Mosca, Paul – "Ugarit and Daniel 7: A Missing Link," *Biblica* 67, (1986), pp. 496-517.

Moule, C. F. D. – *The Trial of Jesus: Cambridge Studies in Honour of C. F. D. Moule*, Edited By Ernst Bammel, Alec R. Allenson Inc. (1970).

Mowinckel, Sigmund – *He That Cometh*, Translated by G. W. Anderson, Abingdon Press, (1956).

————. *The Psalms in Israel's Worship*, Nashville: Abington, (1967).

Muller, Wayne – *Sabbath: Restoring the Sacred Rhythm of Rest*, Bantam Books, New York, (1999).

Nesbit, E. Planta – "Christ, Christians and Christianity," *Jesus an Essene*, www.sacredtexts.com/chr/jae/jae03.htm .

Nelson, Wendy – "Sexuality in Judaism," (1999), http://www.mesacc.edu/~thoqh49081/StudentPapers/JewishSexuality.html .

Neusner, Jacob – *Invitation to the Talmud*, Harper San Francisco, (1989).

————. *From Politics to Piety: The Emergence of Pharisaic Judaism*, Prentice-Hall, Inc., Englewood Cliffs, New Jersey, (1973).

————. *The Rabbinic Traditions about the Pharisees Before AD 70*, Leiden Brill, (1971).

————. *Development of a Legend: Studies on the Traditions Concerning Yohanon ben Zakkai*, 2nd Edition, Leiden, (1970).

————. *A Rabbi Talks with Jesus: Intermillennial Interfaith Exchange*, Doubleday, New York, (1993).

————. *Messiah in Context: Israel's History and Destiny in Formative Judaism*, Philadelphia, Fortress Press, (1984).

————. *The idea of Purity in Ancient Judaism: The Haskell Lectures, 1972-1973*, With a Critique and a Commentary by Mary Douglas, Wiff & Stock Publishers, Eugene Oregon, (1973).

————. *A History of the Mishnaic Law of Purities*, V, *Ohalot*, E. J. Brill, Leiden, (1975).

————. "First Cleanse the Inside," *New Testament Studies* 22, (1976), pp. 486-495.

Nickelsburg, George W. E. – *Jewish Literature between the Bible and the Mishnah: A Historical and Literary Introduction*, 2ⁿᵈ Edition with CD Rom, Minneapolis, MN: Fortress, (2005).

Nida, Eugene A. – *Message and Mission: The Communication of the Christian Faith*, Harper & Row, New York, (1960).

Nolan, Albert – *Jesus Before Christianity*, Orbis Books, Mary Knoll, New York, (1978).

Ochs, Carol and Olitzky, Kerry M. – *Jewish Spiritual Guidance: Finding Our Way to God*, Jossey-Bass Publishers, San Francisco, (1997).

Ochser, Schulim and Kohler, Kaufmann – "Nicodemus," *Jewish Encyclopedia*, http://jewishencyclopedia.com/articles/11525-nicodemus .

Oesterly, W. O. E. and Loewe, H. – *Judaism and Christianity*, New York, MacMillan Co., (1937).

Offord, Joseph - "Restrictions of Circumcision under the Romans," *Proc R Soc Med* 1913;6 (Sect Hist Med): pp. 102-107.

O'Neill, J. C. – *Who Did Jesus Think He Was*, E. J. Brill, Leiden, New York, (1995).

Overman, J. Andrew – *Matthew's Gospel and Formative Judaism: The Social World of the Matthew Community*, Minneapolis: Fortress Press, (1990).

Pagels, Elaine – *Adam, Eve, and the Serpent*, Random House, New York, (1988).

————. *The Origin of Satan*, Random House, New York, (1995).

Parsons, John J. – "Hebrew For Christians," https://www.hebrew4christians. com/Grammar/Unit_Six/Pronomial_Suffixes_Plural/pronomial_ suffixes_plural.html .

————. "*Torah sheba'al Peh* – The Oral Torah and Jewish Tradition," www.hebrew4christians.com/articles/Oral_Torah/oral_torah.html .

Patterson, Jeremy James - "Elections: How the Greeks and Romans did them and why lots can be better than votes," *University of St. Andrews, Ancient and Modern Rhetoric*, https://arts.st-andrews.ac.uk/rhetoric/ elections-how-the-greeks-and-romans-did-them-and-why-lots-can-be-better-than-votes/ .

Peppard, Michael – *The Son of God in the Roman World: Divine Sonship in its Social and Political Context*, Oxford University Press, (2011).

Perowne, Stewart – *The Later Herods*, Hodder and Stought Ltd., The Camelot Press Ltd., (1958).

Petrovic, Andej – *Inner Purity and Pollution in Ancient Greek Religion* Vol. I www.academia.edu/3026742/introduction_in_Inner_Purity_and_Purification_in_Ancient_Greek_Religion_Vol_I .

Petuchowski, J. J. and Brocke, Michael – *The Lord's Prayer and Jewish Liturgy*, The Seabury Press, New York, (1978).

Petuchowski, J. J. – *Ever Since Sinai: A Modern View of Torah*, Scribe Publications, New York, (1961).

———. "The *Mumar* – A Study in Rabbinic Psychology," *Hebrew Union College Annual* Volume 30 (1959), pp. 179-190.

Pfeiffer, Charles F. and Harrison, Everett Falconer – *The Wycliffe Bible Commentary*, Chicago, Moody Press, (1962).

Phipps, William E. – *Was Jesus Married: The Distortion of Sexuality in the Christian Tradition*, University Press of America, Lanham, New York, (1986).

———. "Did Jesus or Paul Marry," *Journal of Ecumenical Studies* 5, (1968), pp. 741-744.

Pliskin, Rabbi Zelig – *Love your Neighbor: You and your Fellow Man in the Light of the Torah, A Practical Guide to Man's Relationship with his Fellow Man, Culled from the Full Spectrum of Torah Literature, Divided According to the Weekly Torah Readings*, Yeshivah Aish Ha-Torah Publications, Old City, Jerusalem, (1977).

Poirier, John C. – "Jacob Neusner, the Mishnah and Ventriloquism," *The Jewish Quarterly Review*, 87, Nos. 1-2, July-October 1996, pp. 61-78.

Polkow, Dennis William – *Criteria for Historical Jesus Research*, DePaul University, (1984).

Polzin, Robert M. – *Biblical Structuralism: Method and Subjectivity in the Study of Ancient Texts*, Fortress Press, Philadelphia, (1977).

Pomeranz, Yoni - *Ordinary Jews in the Babylonian Talmud: Rabbinic Representations and Historic Interpretations*, http://www.academia.edu/24432463/Ordinary_Jews_in_the_Babylonian_Talmud_Rabbinic_Representations_and_Historical_Interpretation .

Poulin, Joan – "Loving Kindness towards Gentiles According to the Early Sages," *Theologiques* 11(1-2), (autumn 2003), pp. 89-112.

Pound, Ezra – *ABC of Reading*, London: Routledge & Sons, (1934).

Prager, Dennis and Telushkin, Rabbi Joseph – *The Nine Questions People Ask about Judaism*, New York, Simon and Shuster, (1986).

Proudhon, Pierre Joseph – *The Philosophy of Progress*, LeftLiberty, (2009).

Radin, Max – *The Trial of Jesus of Nazareth*, The University of Chicago Press, (1931).

Ranke-Heinemann, Uta – *Putting Away Childish Things*, Translated by Peter Heinegg, Harper: San Francisco, (1994).

Ratzinger, Joseph and Pope Benedict XVI – *Jesus of Nazareth: From the Baptism in the Jordan to the Transfiguration*, Translated from the German by Adrian J. Walker, Doubleday, New York, (2007).

———. *Jesus of Nazareth: Part Two: Holy Week, from the Entrance into Jerusalem to the Resurrection*, English translation by the Vatican Secretariat of State, Ignatius Press, San Francisco, (2011).

Reckart, Pastor G. – "Passover Crucifixion Dates (26-34AD)," http://jesus-messiah.com/html/passover-dates-26-34ad.html .

Reeves, John C. – "The Essene Hypothesis," *Early Judaism*, https://pages.uncc.edu/john-reeves/course-materials/rels-4107/the-essene-hypothesis/ .

Reich, Aryeh – "The Greek Bible – Light or Darkness?", *Bar-Ilan University's Parashat Hashavua Study Center*, Parashat Va-Yigash 5765/December 16, 2004.

Reiss, Rabbi Moshe – *Christianity: A Jewish Perspective*, http://moshereiss.org/Christianity.htm.

Rhoads, David M. – *Israel in Revolution: 6-74 C.E.: A Political History based on the Writings of Josephus*, Philadelphia, Fortress Press, (1976).

Rich, Tracey R. – *Judaism 101*, (1995-2011), www.jewfaq.org/holidayO.htm#Extra .

Rivkin, Ellis – *A Hidden Revolution*, Abingdon, Nashville, (1978).

Roberts, Paul William – *In Search of the Birth of Jesus: The Real Journey of the Magi*, Riverhead Books, New York, (1996).

Rokeah, David – *Ancient Jewish Proselytism in Theory and in Practice*, Basel: Friedrich Reinhardt, (1996).

Romer, John – *Testament: The Bible and History*, Henry Holt and Company, New York, (1988).

Rordorf, W. – *Sunday, the History of the Day of Rest and Worship in the Earliest Centuries of the Christian Church*, Translated By A. A. K. Graham, Philadelphia: Westminster Press, (1968).

Rosenberg, David and Bloom, Harold – *The Book of J*, Translated by David Rosenberg, Interpretation by Harold Bloom, Grove Weidenfeld, New York, (1990).

Rosenberg, Rabbi Roy A. – *The Concise Guide to Judaism: History, Practice, Faith*, Penguin Books USA Inc., (1990).

Rosenblatt, Naomi H. and Horwitz, Joshua – *Wrestling with Angels*, Delacorte Press, New York, (1995).

Rosenzweig, Franz – *The Star of Redemption*, Notre Dame, In: University of Notre Dame Press, (1985).

Rosovsky, Lorne – "Raise Your Hand if You're a Kohen," *Chabad.org*, https://www.chabad.org/library/article_cdo/aid/762109/jewish/Raise-Your-Hand-If-Youre-A-Kohen.htm .

Rostovtzeff, M. – *Social and Economic History of the Hellenistic World*, 3 Volumes, Oxford University Press, (1986).

Royce, Josiah – *The Problem of Christianity*, Introduction by John E. Smith, The University Press, Chicago, (1968).

Rudd, Steve - "Schools, Education and Literacy of Jews In Synagogues," (2017), http://www.bible.ca/synagogues/Schools-ancient-Synagogue-Literacy-of-Jews-education-reading-writing-first-century-early-Christian-Church-New-Testament-worship-patterned-prototype-liturgy.htm

Rudolph, Kurt – *Gnosis: The Nature and History of Gnosticism*, Translation by Robert McLachlan Wilson, Harper & Row, Publishers, San Francisco, (1983).

Ruether, Rosemary Radford – *Faith and Fratricide: The Theological Roots of Anti-Semitism*, The Seabury Press, Inc., New York, (1974).

Sacks, Rabbi Jonathan – *The Persistence of Faith: Religion, Morality & Society in a Secular Age*, Weidenfeld and Nicolson Ltd., (1991).

Safrai, Shmuel – *The Literature of the Sages: First Part: Oral Torah, Halakha, Mishnah, Tosefta, Talmud, External Tractates*, Philadelphia: Van Gorcum, Fortress Press, (1987).

Safrai, Shmuel and Stern, M. – *The Jewish People in the First Century*, Philadelphia, Fortress Press, (1976).

Saldarim, Anthony J. – *Matthew's Christian-Jewish Community*, Chicago: University of Chicago Press, (1994).

Saldarini, J. – *Pharisees, Scribes, and Sadducees in Palestinian Society: A Sociological Approach*, Wilmington, Delaware: Michael Glazer, (1988).

Salm, Rene – *The Myth of Nazareth: The Invented Town of Jesus*, Edited by Frank Zindler, American Atheist Press, Cranford, New Jersey, (2008), www.nazarethmyth.info .

Sanders, E. P. – *Paul and Palestinian Judaism: A Comparison of Patterns of Religion*, Philadelphia: Fortress Press, (1977).

————. *Jesus and Judaism*, Philadelphia: Fortress Press, (1985).

————. "Common Judaism and the Synagogue in the First Century," *Jews, Christians, and Polytheists*, pp. 1-16.

————. *Jewish Law from Jesus to the Mishnah: Five Studies*, SCM Press, London, Trinity Press International, Philadelphia, (1990).

————. *Jesus, the Gospels, and the Church: Essays in Honor of William R. Farmer*, Macon Ga: Mercer University Press, (1987).

Sandmel, Samuel – *A Jewish Understanding of the New Testament*, KTAV Publishing house, Inc., New York, (1957).

Sanford, John A. – *The Kingdom Within: The Inner Meaning of Jesus' Sayings*, Harper San Francisco, (1987), Originally Published in 1970 by J. B. Lippincott Company.

Sarna, Nahum M. – *Exploring Exodus: The Heritage of Biblical Israel*, Schocken Books, New York, (1986).

Schaff, Philip – *History of the Christian Church*, New York, Scribner's Sons, (1914).

Schecter, Solomon – *Studies in Judaism*, Philadelphia, The Jewish Publication Society of America, (1945).

————. *Aspects of Rabbinic Theology*, Jewish Lights Publishing, Woodstock, Vermont, (1993).

————. "The Quotations form Ecclesiasticus in Rabbinic Literature," *Jewish Quarterly Review*, Volume 3, No. 4, (July 1891), pp. 682-706.

————. "Some Rabbinic Parallels to the New Testament," *The Jewish Quarterly Review*, Volume 12, No. 3 (April 1900), pp. 415-433.

Schecter, Solomon and Bacher, Wilhelm – "Gamliel I," *Jewish Encyclopedia*, http://www.jewishencyclopedia.com/articles/6494-gamaliel-i .

Schecter, Solomon and Eisenstein, Judah David – "Etiquette," *Jewish Encyclopedia*, http://www.jewishencyclopedia,com/articles/5893-etiquette .

Schechter, Solomon and Greenstone, Julius H. – "Leaven," *Jewish Encyclopedia*, http://www.jewishencyclopedia.com/articles/9694-leaven .

————. "Excommunication (Hebrew, 'niddui,' 'herem'), *Jewish Encyclopedia*, http://www.jewishencyclopedia.com/articles/5933-excommunication .

Schecter, Solomon and Levias, Caspar – "Meturgeman ('Interpreter')," *Jewish Encyclopedia*, http://www.jewishencyclopedia.com/articles/10742-meturgeman.

Schecter, Solomon and Mendelsohn, S. – "Haber ('associate'; 'colleague'; 'fellow')" *Jewish Encyclopedia*, http://www.jewishencyclopedia.com/articles/6981-haber .

Schiffman, Lawrence H. and Tzoref, Shani – *The Dead Sea Scrolls at 60: Scholarly Contributions of New York University Faculty and Alumni*, Leiden, Brill, (2010).

Schiller, Mayer – *The Road Back*, Foreword by Norman Lamm, Feldheim Publishers, New York, (1978).

Schofield, Guy – *Crime before Calvary: Herodias, Herod Antipas, and Pontius Pilate: A New Interpretation*, George G. Harrap and Co. Ltd., London, (1960).

Scholem, Gershom – *The Messianic Idea in Judaism*, Schocken Books, New York, (1971).

————. *Sabbatai Zevi: The Mystical Messiah*, Princeton University Press, (1973).

————. *On Kabbalah and its Symbolism*, Translation Ralph Manheim, New York, Schocken, (1965).

————. *Jewish Gnosticism, Merkabah Mysticism, and Talmudic Tradition*, New York, The Jewish Theological Seminary of America, (1960).

Schurer, Emil – *History of the Jewish People in the Time of Jesus Christ*, 5 Volumes, Edinburgh, T. & T. Clark, (1987).

Schwartz, Rabbi Barry L. – *Judaisms Great Debates: Timeless Controversies from Abraham to Herzl*, The Jewish Publication Society, Philadelphia, (2012).

Schweitzer, Albert – *The Quest of the Historical Jesus*, The MacMillan Company, New York, (1948).

Schweizer, Eduard and Madvig, Donald H. - *The Good News According to Mark: A Commentary On the Gospel*, London, SPCK, (1971).

Scobie, Charles H. H. – *John the Baptist*, Philadelphia: Fortress Press, (1964).

Seeley, D. – "Jesus' Temple Act," *Catholic Bible Quarterly* 55, (1993), pp. 263-283.

Sefaria.org – *The William Davidson Talmud, Megillah* 14a, https://www.sefaria.org/Megillah.14a?lang=bi .

Segal, A. F. – "Torah and *nomos* in Recent Scholarly Discussion," *Studies in Religion* 13, (1984), pp. 19-28, reprinted in *Other Judaisms*, pp. 131-145.

Selven, Sebastian - "The Privilege of Taxation: Jewish Identity and the Half-shekel Temple Tax in the Yerushalmi Talmud," *University of Cambridge*, https://www.academia.edu/27866944/The_Privilege_of_Taxation_Jewish_Identity_and_the_Half-shekel_Temple_Tax_in_the_Talmud_Yerushalmi .

Sheehan, Thomas – *The First Coming: How the Kingdom of God Became Christianity*, Random House, New York, (1986).

Sherwin-White, A. N. – *Roman Society and Roman Law in the New Testament*, The Sarum Lectures 1960-1961, Oxford, Clarendon Press, (1963).

Shorter – *Oxford English Dictionary*, 6th Revised Edition, Oxford University Press, (2007).

Shorto, Russell – *Gospel Truth: The New Image of Jesus Emerging from Science and History and Why it Matters*, Riverhead Books, (1997).

Sidgwick, Henry – *Outlines of the History of Ethics for English Readers*, London and New York, MacMillan and Co., (1892).

Siegfried, Carl and Gottheil, Richard – "Hellenism: 'To Speak Greek,' or 'To Make Greek'," *Jewish Encyclopedia*, www.jewishencyclopedia.com/articles/7535-hellenism .

Sigal, Gerald – "Jesus Says, 'I and the Father are One,' Doesn't this show that they are one in essence? *Jews for Judaism.*

Silverstein, Arthur Jay – "The Right of Appeal in Talmudic Law," *Case Western Reserve Journal of International Law*, Volume 6, Issue I, (1973).

Singer, Isidore and Lauterbach, Jacob Zallel – "Megillat Ta`anit ('Scroll of Fasting')," *Jewish Encyclopedia*, http://jewishencyclopedia.com/articles/10555-megillat-ta-anit .

Singer, Isadore, Seligsohn, M., and Bacher, Wilhelm – "Mordecai," *Jewish Encyclopedia*, http://jewishencyclopedia.com/articles/10983-mordecai .

Singer, Isadore, Seligsohn, M., Bacher, Wilhelm, and Eisenstein, Judah David – "Scribes," *Jewish Encyclopedia*, http://jewishencyclopedia.com/articles/13356-scribes .

Sloyan, Gerard S. – *Jesus on Trial: A Study of the Gospels*, Second Edition, Minneapolis, Fortress Press, (2006).

————. *The Crucifixion of Jesus: History, Myth, Faith*, Fortress Press, Minneapolis, (1995).

Smallwood, E. M. – *From Pompey to Diocletian*, Leiden: E. J. Brill, (1976).

Smith, Morton – *Jesus the Magician*, New York: Harper & Row, (1978).

Smith, Payne – *Thesaurus Syriacus*, 2 Volumes, Oxonii, e Typographeo Clarendoniano, (1879 – 1901), p. 596.

Snodgrass, Klyne – *The Parable of the Wicked Tenants: An Inquiry into Parable Interpretation*, Wiff and Stock Publishers, Eugene, Oregon, (1983).

Sowers, Sidney G. – *The Hermeneutics of Philo and Hebrews*, John Knox Press, Richmond, Virginia, (1965).

Sperber, Daniel – "Tax Gatherers," *Encyclopedia Judaica*, The Gale Group, (2008), http://www.jewishvirtuallibrary.org/tax-gatherers .

————. "Money Changers," *Encyclopedia Judaica*, The Gale Group, (2008), http://www.jewishvirtuallibrary.org/money-changers .

Spiegel, Professor Ya'akov S., Department of Talmud – "Rachel's Tombstone: The Reasons for Erecting a Tombstone," *Bar Ilan University*, Translated by Mark Elliott Shapiro, https://www.BIU.AC.IL/JH/Parasha/eng/vayishlach/vayish1 .

Spiro, Solomon J. – "Who was the *Haber*? A New Approach to an Ancient Institution," *Journal for the Study of Judaism*, 2, (1980), pp. 186-216.

Spitzer, Jeffery – "The Birth of the Good Inclination," *My Jewish Learning*, https://www.myjewishlearning.com/article/the-birth-of-the-good-inclination .

Spong, John Shelby – *Born of a Woman*, Harper, San Francisco, (1992).

————. *Resurrection: Myth or Reality?* Harper, San Francisco, (1994).

Spoto, Donald – *The Hidden Jesus: A New Life*, St. Martin's Press, New York, (1998).

Stauffer, Ethelbert – *Jesus, Gestalt und Geschichte*, Bern; Francke, (1957).

Stefani, Piero – "What Does 'Blasphemy' Mean in Judaism?" *Freedom and Democracy*, University of Ferrara, February 21, 2014, at http://www.resetdoc.org/story/00000022351.

Steinsaltz, Adin – *The Thirteen Petalled Rose*, New York, Basic Books, (1980).

————. *Biblical Images*, New York: Basic Books, (1984).

————. *The Talmud: The Steinsaltz Edition* = *Talmud Babli*, New York, N. Y.: Random House, (1989).

————. *Talmudic Images*, N.J.: Jason Aronson Inc., (1997).

Stemberger, Gunter – "Die sogenannte 'Synod von Jabne' und das Fruhe Christentum," *Kairos* 19, (1977), pp. 14-21.

———. *Jewish Contemporaries of Jesus: Pharisees, Sadducees, Essenes*, Minneapolis: Fortress Press, (1995, 1991).

Stendahl, Krister – "Matthew," *Peake's Commentary on the Bible*, eds., Matthew Black and Harold H. Rowley, London, New York, T. Nelson, (1962), p. 796, Section 694b.

———. *The Scrolls and the New Testament*, Harper and Brothers, Publishers, New York, (1957).

———. *The School of St. Matthew: And its Use of the Old Testament*, Uppsala, C. W. K. Gleerup, Lund, (1954).

Stephen, Annelisa – "Voting with the Ancient Greeks: One of the Earliest Artistic Depictions of Voting, 490 B. C." November 6, 2012, https://blogs.getty.edu/iris/voting-with-the-ancient-greeks/ .

Stevenson, Angus and Lindberg, Christine A. – *New Oxford American Dictionary*, Third Edition, Edited by Angus Stevenson and Christine A Lindberg, Oxford University Press, (2010).

Strong, Dr. James – *The Exhaustive Concordance of the Bible*, Riverside Book and Bible House, Iowa Falls, Iowa.

Student, Gil – *The Jesus Narrative in the Talmud: The Real Truth about the Talmud*, http://www.angelfire.com/mt/talmud/jesusnarr.html.

———. "The Oral Law," www.aisdas.org/student/oral.htm .

Suetonius – *History of Twelve Caesars*, Translated into English by Philemon Holland, with Introduction by Charles Whibley, New York, AMS Press, (1967).

Tabor, James D. – *The Jesus Dynasty: The Hidden History of Jesus, His Royal Family, and the Birth of Christianity*, New York, Simon & Schuster, (2006).

———. "Discovering a Lost and Forgotten Early Christian 'Gospel'," *Huffington Post*, September 4, 2014, updated December 6, 2014.

———. "The Signs of the Messiah: 4Q521," *Archaeology and the Dead Sea Scrolls*, https://pages.uncc.edu/james-tabor/archaeology-and-the-dead-sea-scrolls/the-signs-of-the-messiah-4q521/ .

Tabor, James D. and Wise, Michael – "4Q521 'On Resurrection and the Synoptic Gospel Tradition: A Preliminary Study," *Qumran Questions*, Edited by James Charlesworth, Sheffield Academic Press, (1995).

Tacitus – *The Annals; and the Histories*, Chicago: Encyclopedia Britannica, (1952, 1955).

Tchernowitz, Chaim (Rav Zair) – *Toledot ha-Halakah*, 4 Volumes, New York, (1934-1950).

Tejada-Lalinde, Andres A. – "Jesus as the Son of Man in Mark," *Florida International University Electronic Theses and Dissertations*, (3-24-2014).

Telushkin, Rabbi Joseph – *Biblical Literacy*, William Morrow and Company, Inc., New York, (1997).

————. *Hillel: If Not Now, When?*, Schocken Books, New York, (2010).

————. *Jewish Literacy: The Most Important Things to Know about the Jewish Religions its People, and its History*, William Morrow and Company, Inc., (1991, 2001, 2008).

Temkin, Sefton D. – "Cemetery," *Jewish Virtual Library*, www.jewishvirtuallibrary.org/cemetery .

Thaler, Valerie S. – "Jewish Attitudes toward Proselytes: The Second Temple Period," *My Jewish Learning*, www.myjewishlearning.com/article/jewish-attitudes-toward-proselytes .

Thayer, Joseph – *Thayer's Greek-English Lexicon of the New Testament*, Baker Book House, (1994).

Theissen, Gerd – *The Shadow of the Galilean: The Quest of the Historical Jesus in Narrative Form*, Philadelphia: Fortress Press, (1987).

Thiessen, Matthew - "Genealogy, Circumcision and Conversion in Early Judaism and Christianity," *Dissertation submitted in partial fulfillment of the requirements for the degree of Doctor of Philosophy in the Department of Religion in the Graduate School of Duke University*, (2010), https://dukespace.lib.duke.edu/dspace/bitstream/handle/10161/2465/D_Thiessen_Matthew_a_201005.pdf?sequence=1&isAllowed=y .

Theroux, Marcel – "Did Jesus Spend His Missing Years Studying Buddhism in India? Marcel Theroux Visits Ladakh to Find Out," October 9, 2017, www.telegraph.co.uk/travel/destinations/asia/india/articles/ladakh-and-the-unknown-life-of-jesus-christ/ .

Thieleke, Helmut – *The Ethics of Sex*, New York, Harper & Row, (1964).

Thielmann, D. C. – *On Earth As It Is In Heaven*, 2 Volumes, iUniverse, (2016).

Thomas, J. – *Le Movement Baptiste en Palestine et Syrie (150a.v. J. C. – 300a.p. J. C.)*, Gembloux, J. Duculot, (1935).

Toohey, Peter – *Epic: The Genre, Its Characteristics*, Barnard College, Columbia University, (2017), https://firstyear.barnard.edu/epic-genre-its-characteristics .

———. *Reading Epic: An Introduction to the Ancient Narratives*, London, New York, Routledge, (2009).

Torch – "In Search of (the Meaning of) Chametz," *Torch*, https://www.torchweb.org/torah_detail.php?id=49 .

Tov-Lev, Rabbi Asher – "Newly Deciphered Qumran Scroll Revealed to be *Megillat Esther, The Torah: A Historical and Contextual Approach*, Torah.com.

Toy, Crawford Howell and Gottheil, Richard – "Bible Translations: Septuagint," *Jewish Encyclopedia*, http://jewishencyclopedia.com/articles/3269-bible-translations .

Toy, Crawford Howell and Jacobs, Joseph – "Publican," *Jewish Encyclopedia*, http://www.jewishencyclopedia.com/articles/12430-publican .

Toy, Crawford Howell, Barton, George A., Jacobs, Joseph, Abrahams, Israel – "Maccabees, Books of," *Jewish Encyclopedia*, http://jewishencyclopedia.com/articles/10237-maccabees-books-of .

Trocme, Etienne – *Jesus and His Contemporaries*, Translated by R. A. Wilson, SCM Press Ltd., London, (1973).

Tyson, J. B. – "Jesus and Herod Antipas," *Journal of Biblical Literature* 79, pp. 239-246.

Unger, Merrill F. – *Unger's Bible Dictionary*, Chicago: Moody Press, 25th Printing, (1976).

United Church of God – "Does Romans 14 Abolish Laws on Unclean Meats," January 31, 2011, https://www.ucg.org/bible-study-tools/booklets/the-new-covenant-does-it-abolish-gods-law/does-romans-14-abolish-laws-on.

Urbach, E. E. – *The Sages, Their Concepts and Beliefs*, 2 Volumes, Jerusalem: Magnus, (1979).

Vanhoye, Albert – *Let us Confidently Welcome Christ Our High Priest*, Translated by Joel Wallace, Leominster: Gracewing, (2010).

Van Leeuwen, Raymond C. – "Be Fruitful and Multiply," *Christianity Today*, November 12, 2001, pp. 58-61.

Vermes, Geza – *Jesus the Jew: A Historian's Reading of the Gospel's*, MacMillan Publishing Co., Inc., New York, (1973).

————. "Was Crucifixion a Jewish Penalty," (April 2013), standpointmag. co.uk/node/4936/full.

————. *The Changing Faces of Jesus*, Penguin, New York, (2002).

Von Rad, Gerhard – *The Message of the Prophets*, Harper & Row, Publishers, New York, (1965).

Voorsanger, Jacob and Kohler, Kaufmann – "Anathema," *Jewish Encyclopedia*, http://jewishencyclopedia.com/articles/1477-anathema .

Vorster, W. – "Gospel Genre," *Anchor Bible Dictionary* 3, (1992).

Waddell, Glenn G. – "The Meaning of Matthew 18:17B in its Historical and Literary Context and its Application in the Church Today," *A Thesis Submitted to the Faculty in Partial Fulfillment of the Requirements for the Degree of Master of Arts in Religion at Reformed Theological Seminary*, Charlotte, North Carolina, January 2014.

Waite, A. E. – *The Holy Kabbalah*, Introduction by Kenneth Rexroth, University Books, New Hyde Park, New York, (1965).

Walsh, Michael J. – *Commentary on the Catechism of the Catholic Church*, Collegeville, Minn.: Liturgical Press, (1994).

Wayne, Gary – "The Essenes," www.genesis6conspiracy.com/chapter-84-the-essenes/ .

Webster's – *Third New International Dictionary: Unabridged with Seven Language Dictionary*, 3 Volumes, G. & C. Merriam Co., (1966).

Wengst, Klaus – *Pax Romana and the Peace of Jesus Christ*, Philadelphia: Fortress, (1987).

Westerholm, S. – "Torah, Nomos and Law: A Question of Meaning'," *Studies in Religion* 15, (1986), pp. 327-336.

Wikimedia Foundation, Inc. – *Sanhedrin*, https://en.wikipedia.org/wiki/sanhedrin

Wilson, A. N. – *Jesus: A Life*, W. W. Norton & Company, New York, (1992).

Wilson, Barrie – *How Jesus Became Christian*, New York, St. Martin's Press, (2008).

Wink, Walter – *Engaging the Powers: Discernment and Resistance in a World of Domination*, Minneapolis: Fortress Press, (1992).

————. *Jesus and Nonviolence: A Third Way*, Minneapolis, MN: Fortress, (2003).

Winter, P. – *On the Trial of Jesus*, Berlin, De Gruyter, (1961).

————. "The Trial of Jesus," *Trivium*, (1967), p. 109.

Wise, Michael O. – *The First Messiah: Investigating the Savior Before Jesus*, Harper San Francisco, (1999).

Wittig, Susan – "Meaning and Modes of Signification: Toward a Semiotic of the Parable," *Conference on Semiology and Parables*, Vanderbilt University, 15-17 May, (1975).

Wohlgemuth, Rabbi Isaiah – "Hallel," *My Jewish Learning*, https://myjewishlearning.com/articles/hallel/ .

Wolff, Joseph – *Travels and Adventures: Of the Rev. Joseph Wolff*, London, Saunders, Otley and Co., (1860-1861).

Worcester Association (Mass.: 1793 -1820) – *Catechism*, Boston: Isaiah Thomas.

World Book Inc. – *The World Book Encyclopedia*, World Book Inc., (2018).

Wrede, W. – *The Messianic Secret*, J. Clark, Cambridge, (1971).

Wright, N. T. – *Simply Jesus: A New Version of Who He Was, What He Did, and Why He Matters*, Harper One, Harper Collins, (2011).

————. *Judas and the Gospel of Jesus: Have We Missed the Truth About Christianity*, Baker Books, Grand Rapids, Michigan, (2006).

————. *The New Testament and the People of God*, Minneapolis, Fortress Press, (1992).

————. *The Climax of the Covenant: Christ and the Law in Pauline Theology*, Minneapolis: Fortress Press, (1993).

Wroe, Ann – *Pontius Pilate*, Random House, New York, (1999).

Yadin, Yigael – *The Scroll of the Sons of Light against the Sons of Darkness*, Oxford University Press, (1962).

————. *The Temple Scroll*, Random House, New York, (1985).

Yashanet Staff – "Not Subject to the Law of God, Part 7: Historical Reality Concerning What Yeshua and His Followers Believed," http://www.yashanet.com/library/under7.htm .

Yehoshua, Avraham – *Mosaic Sacrifice in the New Testament*, http://SeedofAvraham.net.

Young, F. W. – "Jesus the Prophet: A Re-Examination," *Journal of Biblical Literature* 68, (1949), pp. 285-299.

Zeitlin, Solomon – *Who Crucified Jesus?* New York, London, Harper & Brothers, (1942).

————. "A Life of Yohanan ben Zakkai: A Specimen of Modern Jewish Scholarship," *Jewish Quarterly Review*, 62, 1972, pp. 145-155.

————. "Spurious Interpretations of Rabbinic Sources in the Study of the Pharisees and Pharisaism," *Jewish Quarterly Review*, 62, 1974, pp. 122-135.

Zucker, David J. and Reiss, Rabbi Moshe – "Downplaying the Davidic Dynasty," *Jewish Bible Quarterly* Vol. 42, No. 3, 2014, pp. 185-192.

Zuesse, Evan M. – "The Rabbinic Treatment of 'others' (Criminals, Gentiles) According to Jacob Neusner," *Review of Rabbinic Judaism*, Volume 7, 2004, pp. 191-229.

CPSIA information can be obtained
at www.ICGtesting.com
Printed in the USA
BVHW081322160921
616889BV00001BA/37